JOHN F. TANNER, JR.

Dr. Tanner is the associate dean for the Hankamer School of Business undergraduate programs and the research director of Baylor University's Center for Professional Selling and associate professor of marketing. He earned his PhD from the University of Georgia. Prior to entering academia, Dr. Tanner spent eight years in industry with Rockwell International and Xerox Corporation as both salesperson and marketing manager.

Dr. Tanner has received several awards for teaching effectiveness and research. His sales teaching efforts have been recognized by *Sales & Marketing Management* and the *Dallas Morning News*. Dr. Tanner is also co-author of several other textbooks, including the new *Business Marketing* text with Bob Dwyer, to be published by Irwin. He also wrote the Center for Exhibition Industry Research's *Faculty Guide to Trade Shows*, an instructor's manual for incorporating trade shows into marketing and small business curricula, which is available free to any interested college faculty; just drop him an e-mail with a postal address.

Research grants from the Center for Exhibition Industry Research, the Institute for the Study of Business Markets, the University Research Council, the Wollongong Group, and others have supported Dr. Tanner's research efforts. Dr. Tanner has published over 30 articles in journals such as the *Journal of Marketing, Journal of Business Research, Journal of Personal Selling and Sales Management,* international journals, and others. He serves on the review boards of several journals, including the *Journal of Marketing Education, Journal of Personal Selling and Sales Management,* and *Journal of Marketing Theory and Practice.*

Dr. Tanner writes two monthly columns, one on sales and sales management topics for *Sales and Marketing Strategies & News* and another on trade show issues for *Ideas.* His other trade publications include *Advertising Age's Business Marketing, Decisions, Sales Managers' Bulletin, American Salesman,* and *Potentials in Marketing.* A nationally recognized speaker and author on issues facing the trade show industry, Dr. Tanner has presented seminars at international conventions of several trade organizations, including the International Exhibitor's Association and the Canadian Association of Exposition Managers.

Jeff_Tanner@BAYLOR.EDU

http://hsb.baylor.edu/html/tanner/

Third Edition

SELLING
Building Partnerships

Bart A. Weitz
University of Florida

Stephen B. Castleberry
University of Minnesota, Duluth

John F. Tanner, Jr.
Baylor University

Irwin
McGraw-Hill

Boston, Massachusetts   Burr Ridge, Illinois   Dubuque, Iowa
Madison, Wisconsin   New York, New York   San Francisco, California   St. Louis, Missouri

SELLING: BUILDING PARTNERSHIPS

Irwin/McGraw-Hill

A Division of The **McGraw·Hill** *Companies*

This book is printed on acid-free paper.

2 3 4 5 6 7 8 9 0 VNH/VNH 9 0 9 8 7 (U.S. edition)
1 2 3 4 5 6 7 8 9 0 VNH/VNH 9 0 9 8 7 (International edition)

ISBN 0-256-22826-4

Vice president and editorial director: *Michael W. Junior*
Publisher: *Craig S. Beytien*
Executive editor: *Stephen M. Patterson*
Senior developmental editor: *Nancy Barbour*
Senior marketing manager: *Colleen J. Suljic*
Project manager: *Carrie Sestak*
Production supervisor: *Karen Thigpen*
Senior photo research coordinator: *Keri Johnson*
Cover photo: *Will Panich Photography*
Interior designer: *Ellen Pettengell*
Compositor: *Precision Graphics*
Film house: *H&S Graphics, Inc.*
Typeface: *10/12 Sabon*
Printer: *Von Hoffmann Press, Inc.*

Library of Congress Cataloging in Publication Data
Weitz, Barton A.
    Selling : building partnerships / Barton A. Weitz, Stephen B. Castleberry, John F. Tanner.—3rd ed.
        p.   cm.—(The Irwin series in marketing)
    Includes bibliographical references and indexes.
    ISBN 0-256-22826-4
    I. Selling.   I. Castleberry, Stephen Byron.   II. Tanner, John F.
III. Title.   IV. Series.
    HF5438.25.W2933   1998
    658.85—dc 21   97-21684

When ordering the title, use ISBN 0-07-115626-7.

http://www.mhhe.com

To Edward Weitz, a great father and salesman.

BART WEITZ

To my parents, Katie and Glenn Castleberry, and to the latest little "partner" in my family, Daniel Josiah.

STEVE CASTLEBERRY

To those most precious: My God, my wife, my children, and my parents.

JEFF TANNER

The Irwin/McGraw-Hill Series in Marketing

Alreck & Settle
The Survey Research Handbook, *2/E*

Anderson, Hair & Bush
Professional Sales Management, *2/E*

Arens
Contemporary Advertising, *6/E*

Bearden, Ingram & Laforge
Marketing: Principles & Perspectives, *2/E*

Bearden, Ingram & Laforge
Marketing Interactive, *1/E*

Belch & Belch
Introduction to Advertising and Promotion: An Integrated Marketing Communications Approach, *4/E*

Bernhardt & Kinnear
Cases in Marketing Management, *7/E*

Berkowitz, Kerin, Hartley & Rudelius
Marketing, *5/E*

Bowersox & Closs
Logistical Management, *1/E*

Bowersox & Cooper
Strategic Marketing Channel Management, *1/E*

Boyd, Walker & Larreche
Marketing Management: A Strategic Approach with a Global Orientation, *3/E*

Cateora
International Marketing, *9/E*

Churchill, Ford & Walker
Sales Force Management, *5/E*

Churchill & Peter
Marketing, *2/E*

Cole & Mishler
Consumer and Business Credit Management, *11/E*

Cravens
Strategic Marketing, *5/E*

Cravens, Lamb & Crittenden
Strategic Marketing Management Cases, *5/E*

Crawford
New Products Management, *5/E*

Dillon, Madden & Firtle
Essentials of Marketing Research, *2/E*

Dillon, Madden & Firtle
Marketing Research in a Marketing Environment, *4/E*

Dobler, Burt, & Lee
Purchasing and Materials Management: Text and Cases, *6/E*

Douglas & Craig
Global Marketing Strategy, *1/E*

Etzel, Walker & Stanton
Marketing, *11/E*

Faria, Nulsen & Roussos
Compete, *4/E*

Futrell
ABC's of Relationship Selling, *5/E*

Futrell
Fundamentals of Selling, *5/E*

Gretz, Drozdeck & Weisenhutter
Professional Selling: A Consultative Approach, *1/E*

Guiltinan & Paul
Cases in Marketing Management, *1/E*

Guiltinan, Paul & Madden
Marketing Management Strategies and Programs, *6/E*

Hasty & Reardon
Retail Management, *1/E*

Hawkins, Best & Coney
Consumer Behavior, *7/E*

Hayes, Jenster & Aaby
Business to Business Marketing, *1/E*

Johansson
Global Marketing, *1/E*

Johnson, Kurtz & Scheuing
Sales Management: Concepts, Practices & Cases, *2/E*

Kinnear & Taylor
Marketing Research: An Applied Approach, *5/E*

Lambert & Stock
Strategic Logistics Management, *3/E*

Lambert, Stock, & Ellram
Fundamentals of Logistics Management, *1/E*

Lehmann & Winer
Analysis for Marketing Planning, *4/E*

Lehmann & Winer
Product Management, *2/E*

Levy & Weitz
Retailing Management, *3/E*

Levy & Weitz
Essentials of Retailing, *1/E*

Loudon & Della Bitta
Consumer Behavior: Concepts & Applications, *4/E*

Lovelock & Weinberg
Marketing Challenges: Cases and Exercises, *3/E*

Mason, Mayer & Ezell
Retailing, *5/E*

Mason & Perreault
The Marketing Game!

Mcdonald
Modern Direct Marketing, *1/E*

Meloan & Graham
International and Global Marketing Concepts and Cases, *2/E*

Monroe
Pricing, *2/E*

Moore & Pessemier
Product Planning and Management: Designing and Delivering Value, *1/E*

Oliver
Satisfaction: A Behavioral Perspective on the Consumer, *1/E*

Patton
Sales Force: A Sales Management Simulation Game, 1/E

Pelton, Strutton & Lumpkin
Marketing Channels: A Relationship Management Approach, *1/E*

Perreault & McCarthy
Basic Marketing: A Global Managerial Approach, *12/E*

Perreault & McCarthy
Essentials of Marketing: A Global Managerial Approach, *7/E*

Peter & Donnelly
A Preface to Marketing Management, *7/E*

Peter & Donnelly
Marketing Management: Knowledge and Skills, *5/E*

Peter & Olson
Consumer Behavior and Marketing Strategy, *4/E*

Peter & Olson
Understanding Consumer Behavior, *1/E*

Quelch
Cases in Product Management, *1/E*

Quelch, Dolan & Kosnik
Marketing Management: Text & Cases, *1/E*

Quelch & Farris
Cases in Advertising and Promotion Management, *4/E*

Quelch, Kashani & Vandermerwe
European Cases in Marketing Management, *1/E*

Rangan
Business Marketing Strategy: Cases, Concepts & Applications, *1/E*

Rangan, Shapiro & Moriarty
Business Marketing Strategy: Concepts & Applications, *1/E*

Rossiter & Percy
Advertising and Promotion Management, *2/E*

Stanton, Spiro, & Buskirk
Management of a Sales Force, *10/E*

Sudman & Blair
Marketing Research: A Problem-Solving Approach, *1/E*

Thompson & Stappenbeck
The Marketing Strategy Game, *1/E*

Ulrich & Eppinger
Product Design and Development, *1/E*

Walker, Boyd & Larreche
Marketing Strategy: Planning and Implementation, *2/E*

Weitz, Castleberry & Tanner
Selling: Building Partnerships, *3/E*

Zeithaml & Bitner
Services Marketing, *1/*

Preface

What an amazing time to be alive! At a recent ceremony honoring a professor who is 101 years old, we were discussing the changes that had occurred over her lifetime—how small the world must seem now with air travel, automobiles, and so forth.

The changes in business since the second edition of *Selling: Building Partnerships* seem almost as amazing. In the Preface to the last edition, we mentioned that the information highway is becoming a reality. Now, in this edition, we have incorporated Internet exercises into each chapter. Students are already doing their library work from the computer, citing articles downloaded from the Internet.

Faculty are also becoming more experienced with the Internet. Want to find out the latest in teaching selling? Then check out our home page; we will post teaching ideas if you will send them to us via e-mail. We will also call your attention to current articles and other resources for use in your classes.

In spite of the growth of the Internet, face-to-face meetings and personal relationships between sellers and buyers are more important than ever before. The average cost of a sale has come down, thanks to the new technologies and methods of communicating. Yet research indicates that personal visits and personal contact are still the most effective approach for building committed relationships. And as ISO 9000 and other quality initiatives take root, salespeople face growing responsibilities to manage the entire value chain: within their companies, with suppliers, and with customers. All of these factors make the skills of partnering more important now than ever before.

Our Philosophy

The skills of partnering go well beyond the arena of selling a product. Strategic alliances are important to virtually all businesses and all aspects of business. That is why we are excited to see professional selling continue to grow in the number of schools teaching the course, as a required course for marketing majors at many schools, and as part of the core curriculum for all business majors at a few institutions.

Our assumption, then, is not that all students of sales will become salespeople. Students in this course should learn principles of selling so well that they would have enough self-confidence to begin making calls if provided with no additional training by their employers, even if those calls occurred in a nonselling field (for example, an accountant soliciting new business). At the same time, more students than ever before who have no plans to enter the sales profession are being exposed to selling. One of our objectives in this book is to provide sound partnering and communication skills that will be useful no matter what occupations students may enter.

Another objective is to integrate material from other "theory-driven" courses. While nothing may be more practical than a good theory, students sometimes say that this is the only class in which they learned something they could use. We continue to work on integrating material from other courses and disciplines to illustrate the application of theories in the practice of selling. Several of you have told us you have had the same experience and found this book to be useful in integrating material. We are glad we have been successful and hope you find this edition will do an even better job.

Partnering and Sales Education

The importance of partnering to business and partnering skills to students has changed the way sales has been taught. Several unique features place this book at the cutting edge of sales technology and partnering research:

1. A revision of the traditional selling process—approach, opening, making a presentation, demonstrating benefits, overcoming objections, and closing—into the new partnering process. The new process includes strategically planning each sales call within a larger account strategy, making the sales call, strengthening communications, responding helpfully to objections, obtaining commitment, and building partnerships.

2. A thorough description of the partnering and buying processes used by business firms and the changes occurring in these processes, as well as methods of internal and external partnering to deliver total quality.

3. An emphasis throughout the text on the need for salespeople to be flexible—to adapt their strategies to customer needs and buyer social styles.

4. A complete discussion of how effective selling and career growth are achieved through planning and continual learning.

5. The growing role of salespeople in learning organizations to carry the voice of the customer to all parts of the organization and beyond to suppliers and facilitators.

These unique content features are presented in a highly readable format, supported with examples from current sales programs and salespeople and illustrated with four-color exhibits and photographs. If you have used this book before, you will find that almost all Selling Scenarios (boxed field examples) are new to this edition, and all profiles of salespeople (which open each chapter) have been re-written. With so many changes occurring in selling over the past few years, a new edition must, necessarily, be *new*. Yet you will find the same practicality and theory application of the previous editions.

Partnering: From the Field to the Classroom

We have improved the text based on feedback from users and reviewers. What is different is that *Selling: Building Partnerships* was also reviewed by sales executives and field salespeople who are locked in the daily struggle of adapting to the new realities of selling. They have told us what the field is like now, where it is going, and what students must do to prepare themselves for the challenges they will face in the next century.

Students have also reviewed chapters. They are, after all, the ones who must learn from the book. We asked for their input prior to and during the revision process. And, judging by their comments and suggestions, this book is effectively delivering the content.

As you can see in About the Authors, we have spent considerable time in the field in a variety of sales positions. We continue to spend time in the field, observing and serving professional salespeople. We believe the book has benefited greatly from this never-ending developmental process.

Users of the first two editions will find several improvements in this edition:

- *Exploring the Net.* At the end of each chapter, you will find exercises that call on students to use the Internet in addition to the usual end-of-chapter discussion questions and cases. These exercises are designed to encourage the use of the Internet as an everyday tool for gathering information and communicating with others.

- *A greater focus on small and mid-size companies, with examples.* In addition to Fortune 500 firms, we have included examples of small and mid-size firms. We are finding that more students are taking jobs in regional firms, in part due to corporate downsizing but also due to the opportunities such businesses offer.

- *Expanded coverage of prospecting.* Technology continues to change the nature of the sales position, and Chapter Seven now includes prospecting tools such as CD-ROMs, the Internet, e-mail, and other technological advances. The chapter also focuses on selling deeper to customers, prospecting from current customer lists in keeping with the idea of building long-term relationships.

Text Features and Supplement

All features in this edition of *Selling: Building Partnerships* are designed to help instructors be more effective and to help students develop skills they can use every day and in the field.

Profiles of field salespeople set the stage for each chapter. In each profile, the salesperson discusses his or her experiences and how they relate to the material that follows. This edition includes many new and interesting profiles.

Each chapter begins with a series of questions that will guide the student's reading experience. In each chapter, **Selling Scenarios** present the real-life experiences of professional salespeople. Most Selling Scenarios are new to this edition; many were written specifically for the text. The Selling Scenarios are tied to the material within each chapter, reinforcing the concepts and presenting applications of selling principles.

A feature called **Thinking it Through** will help students internalize key concepts. Thinking it Through is an involving exercise that can be the substance for a lively classroom dialogue or a short-essay exam question. Most important for students, Thinking it Through will allow them to experience the concepts as they read, increasing their comprehension and retention. Based on user feedback, we have increased the number of Thinking it Throughs.

Expanded global references are now marked with a global symbol. Most chapters have at least two global references that apply the material to other cultures or settings. A prime example is the negotiations chapter (Chapter Fourteen). All chapters have expanded international coverage, as well as coverage of the multicultural diversity within the United States.

Key Terms at the end of each chapter are followed by page references so the student can easily look up the definitions. The lists of key terms will help students prepare for exams; the chapter references will improve their retention because they will be more likely to read supporting material rather than just a definition. You will find many new terms, such as *learning organization,* discussed in detail in this new edition.

The **Questions and Problems** at the end of each chapter are also designed to involve the student, but in a slightly different manner. Users of the second edition will find many new questions and problems. The questions are designed to (1) integrate concepts and definitions, (2) require the student to apply a concept to a selling situation, or (3) generate discussion during class. Therefore, students will want to review the questions to study for exams, while the instructor can use them to stimulate classroom discussion. These questions entail more than just looking up a list in the chapter; they require thought and help to develop critical thinking skills. Also, since many are new to this edition, students cannot rely on libraries of stock answers.

New to this edition are internet exercises, **Exploring the Net.** Given the importance of this technology and students' ability to explore the Internet for information, we believe it is important to structure their exploration within the sales area. You'll find a number of exercises that encourage students to apply material from the chapter, integrating it with information found on the Internet. We hope you and your students find these as much fun and as interesting as we have.

Additional References can be found at the end of each chapter. We've used these to guide students for additional research for term papers and other projects. Most of the additional references are academic research articles, but you'll also find practitioner-oriented books and pertinent articles from magazines such as *Sales & Marketing Management* and *Personal Selling Power.*

Cases also appear at the end of each chapter. We have found these cases work well as daily assignments and as frameworks for lectures, discussion, or small-group practices. Some cases are tied to the Videotapes for complete integration. Many of them have been tested in our classes and have been refined based on student feedback. A few user favorites have been revised and updated, but most cases are new.

New **Role Play Cases** are also provided in the text, with various buyer roles in the Instructor's Manual. We have included guidelines for students on how to prepare for role plays. These role plays serve two functions. First, students can practice their partnering skills in a friendly environment that will encourage personal growth. Second, the role plays are written to serve as minicases, which is unique to this text. Student observers will see situations that call for applications of many of the concepts and principles covered in the text. Both vicarious and experiential learning are enhanced for the observers.

We are pleased to include with the text a sample of **GoldMine** software. GoldMine is a contact management software used to create a customer database, which is combined with word-processing, calendaring, and other similar functions. Salespeople can use these to develop strategies, and the calendaring feature helps to set and meet deadlines for their accounts. For salespeople with many customers to keep track of, GoldMine is an excellent tool. Exercises are included in the Instructor's Manual for gaining experience in using this software.

Instructor's manuals are available with every text, but the quality often varies. Because we teach the course every

semester, as well as present and participate in basic sales seminars in industry, we believe we have created an **Instructor's Manual** that can significantly assist the instructor. We have also asked instructors what they would like to see in a manual. In addition to suggested course outlines, chapter outlines, lecture suggestions, answers to questions and cases, and transparencies (many that are not from exhibits in the book), we include helpful suggestions on how to use the videotapes. We also include many of the in-class exercises we have developed over the years. These have been subjected to student critique, and we are confident you will find them useful. You will also find a number of additional role play scenarios.

Students do need to practice their selling skills in a selling environment, and they need to do it in a way that is helpful. Small-group practice exercises, complete with instructions for student evaluations, are provided in the Instructor's Manual. These sessions can be held as part of class but are also designed for out-of-class time for instructors who want to save class time for full-length role plays.

The **Test Bank** has been carefully and completely rewritten. Questions are directly tied to the learning goals presented at the beginning of each chapter and the material covered in the Questions and Problems. In addition, test questions cover the key terms. Application questions are provided so that students can demonstrate their understanding of the key concepts by applying those selling principles.

Instructors and students alike have been enthusiastic about the **Videotapes** that were created especially for this package. Corporate training videos, Learning International's Professional Selling Skills seminar, and customized videos developed expressly for this new edition have been carefully integrated with material from the text.

Each segment is short (generally under 10 minutes), with opportunities for stopping and discussing what has been viewed. Students can also watch the videos outside of class. Video information, including in-class and homework exercises, is incorporated into the Instructor's Manual so that all users can make the most of the videos.

We are also pleased to add a new dimension to the ancillary package—a highly interactive **CD-ROM** entitled *Sell to Needs.* This CD is produced by The Wilson Learning Corporation, a firm that has trained millions of individuals around the world to be effective salespeople. Important sales concepts are taught in a highly engaging format with the use of video and stop-action pauses for you to test what you've learned. You'll receive feedback as you go along, learning from correct and incorrect choices that you make. All video scenes and situations are real-world. Once you've learned the material, you move to the Mastery Simulation, an interactive simulation that lets you apply all the skills in a series of challenging scenarios. Some of the scenarios have a time limit and the buyer may end the meeting if you provide a wrong response. Finally, the Sales Builder component helps you to apply and transfer the concepts you have learned to your own unique selling situation. You can move through the CD in any sequence you desire; you're not forced to follow one path to learning. This encourages the user to come back to the CD again and again, learning form each experience.

We welcome you to visit our website: http://www.cba.ufl.edu/CRER/bweitz/sales

Acknowledgments

Staying current in the rapidly changing field of professional selling is a challenge. Our work has been blessed with the excellent support of reviewers, users, editors, salespeople, and students. People such as Earl Honeycutt at Old Dominion, Don McBane with Clemson, and others have been very helpful. The following reviewers also added important insights:

James S. Boles, *Georgia State University*

Larry Powell Butts, *State Technical Institute at Memphis*

Frances T. DePaul, *Westmoreland Community College*

James I. Gray, *Florida Atlantic University*

Raymond Hagelman, *Nassau Community College*

James A. Healey, *Chabot College*

Katie Kemp, *Middle Tennessee State University*

Linda Reynolds, *Sacramento City College*

Dennis Walter Schneider, *Fresno City College*

Readers will become familiar with many of the salespeople who contributed to the development of the third edition through various selling scenarios or profiles. However, other salespeople and sales executives contributed in less obvious but no less important ways. For providing video material, reviewing chapters, updating cases, providing material for Selling Scenarios, or other support, we'd like to thank the following professionals:

Julie Autry, sales representative, *ConAgra*

Steve Bainbridge, national account manager, *The Wilson Learning Corporation*

Bill Boardman, area sales manager, *ConAgra*

Tracey Brill, senior pharmaceutical consultant, *Smith Kline Beecham Pharmaceuticals*

Jim Bruce, district manager, *Wallace*

Dick Crovisier, sales manager, *Central Transportation Systems*

Danny Cummings, senior account executive, *Wallace*

Debra Dinnocenzo, senior vice president, marketing, *Learning International*

Jeffrey Ducate, account executive, *San Antonio Convention and Visitor's Bureau*

Carroll Fadal, regional vice-president, *Texas Life*

Tia Falcone, account executive, *Time Warner Cable*

Sandra Garrett, branch manager, *Personnel One Temporary and Permanent Personnel*

Todd Graf, president, *Integrated Communications Systems and Solutions, Inc.*

Wade Hallisey, rental agent, *Rollins Truck Leasing*

Karen Johnson, corporate recruiter, *Mantek*

George J. Kebala, account executive, *Direct Marketing Technology Inc.*

Richard Langlotz, branch sales manager, *Minolta Business Systems*

Lori Liles, senior account executive, *AT&T*

Mary Ann Masarech, product manager, *Learning International*

Vince Nall, president, *Ideal Industries*

Bob Newzell, host, *"Sales Talk"*

Kris Rainey, salesperson, *Procter & Gamble*

Jerry Robison, pharmaceutical sales representative, *Hoechst Marion Roussel*

Trent Weaver, account executive, *Mobile Technology Inc.*

Alan Wester, vice-president of sales, *Freeman Exhibit Corporation*

Ron Williams, national account manager, *Champion Apparel*

David Yesford, director of interactive technology, *The Wilson Learning Corporation*

In addition to the support of these individuals, many companies provided us with material. We would like to express our sincere gratitude for their support.

The editorial and staff support from Irwin/McGraw-Hill, was again exceptional. We really appreciate the support provided by Steve Patterson and the wonderful staff assembled for this project. We particularly thank Nancy Barbour, who kept us on time, listened to and encouraged us, and served as a creative sounding board; Mike Hruby, who located and obtained most of the photographs; our project manager, Carrie Sestak; Laurie Sander and Jon Christopher, who coordinated the production of this edition. Nick Childers of Arthur Scott Productions once again delivered an excellent video package.

Several people assisted in manuscript preparation, including: Kathy Brown and Margaret Jones, and we gratefully appreciate their help.

Many students and instructors have made comments that have helped us strengthen the overall package. They deserve our thanks, as do others who prefer to remain anonymous.

Bart Weitz
Steve Castleberry
Jeff Tanner

Contents in Brief

Contents

Prologue

Selling: Building Partnerships is divided into five parts. In Part One, you will learn about the field of selling. This includes topics such as the nature, role, and rewards of selling and what partnering really means, as well as the legal and ethical responsibilities of salespeople.

Part Two describes the fundamental skills needed to be successful as a salesperson. You will learn about the buying process, the principles for communicating effectively, and methods for adapting to the unique styles and needs of each customer.

In Part Three you will explore the activities performed to build partnerships between buyers and sellers. After completing this section, you should have enhanced skills and understanding about prospecting, planning, discovering needs, using visual aids and conducting demonstrations effectively, responding to objections, obtaining commitment, and providing excellent after-sale service.

Special applications are covered in Part Four. You will learn about formal negotiating as well as the exciting and somewhat unique role of selling to resellers.

Part Five discusses how a salesperson can improve his or her effectiveness. This includes managing your time and territory, working with your company, and managing your career.

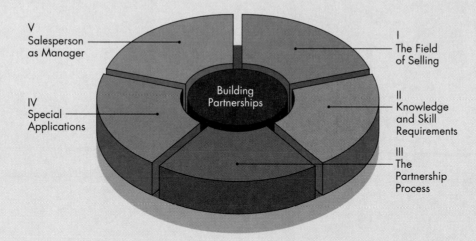

P art One introduces the nature of personal selling. In Chapter One, we define personal selling and illustrate how everyone can use skills associated with effective selling. Then we discuss the importance of selling and salespeople in business. A review of the evolution of personal selling illustrates how modern salespeople focus on developing long-term relationships—partnerships—between their firm and its customers. Finally, we outline the activities performed by salespeople and the skills needed to be a successful salesperson.

Part One

The Field *of* Selling

In Chapter Two, we discuss the nature of the partnering relationships salespeople build with their customers. First, we examine the different types of relationships that arise between firms and their customers. Then we review the evolution of these relationships over time. Finally, we explore the role of the salesperson in this evolutionary process.

In Chapter Three, we focus on ethical and legal responsibilities confronting salespeople. First, we review some of the situations that require salespeople to make ethical choices. The development of a selling partnership is based on mutual trust and respect; both are more likely to exist when salespeople have a strong code of ethics and behave in accordance with these ethical principles. After examining these ethical decisions, we discuss the laws that govern selling activities. Laws define the appropriate behavior in relationships; however they indicate only a minimum acceptable level of conduct.

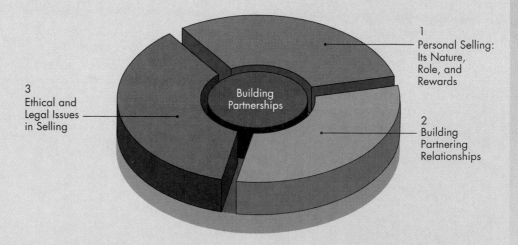

1
Personal Selling:
Its Nature,
Role, and
Rewards

Building
Partnerships

3
Ethical and
Legal Issues
in Selling

2
Building
Partnering
Relationships

Chapter One

Selling *and* Salespeople

The world of commerce has changed dramatically over the last twenty years. Now businesses compete in global markets using sophisticated communication, transportation, and management information systems. These changes in the business environment have expanded the responsibilities of salespeople and

Some Questions Answered in this Chapter Are:

What is selling?

Why should you learn about selling even if you do not plan to be a salesperson?

What is the role of personal selling in a firm?

What are the different types of salespeople?

What are the rewards of a selling career?

increased their importance in the success of their firms.

The days of a salesperson carrying a brief-case of brochures and knocking on doors to drum up interest in his or her own company's products are waning. Today's salespeople coordinate the resources of their companies to help customers solve problems. They use e-mail and faxes to communicate with customers and support staff around the world; download information from their firm's data warehouse into laptop computers so they can know more about their prospects and customers; and develop multimedia presentations to illustrate the benefits of their firms' products and services.

This chapter discusses the importance of personal selling to business firms and how the nature of selling is changing from persuading prospects to buy products to managing the firm's relationships with its customers. The chapter concludes with a description of the activities salespeople perform, the skills needed to be a successful salesperson, and the rewards of a sales career.

PROFILE

While completing a BS degree in marketing at Indiana University, Pamela Kathrens worked part-time at IBM as a marketing support assistant in Fort Wayne, Indiana. Kathrens says, "I wanted to get hands-on experience in marketing in order to better understand what type of career in marketing I would excel in and enjoy the most. After just a short time at IBM, I decided that sales was a great fit for me and, upon graduation, I began my full-time career at IBM."

"The key selling skill in my position is being able to take a strong customer-driven approach to problem solving. I personally feel a sense of commitment to my customers and am always their advocate for IBM."

Since then Kathrens has proceeded rapidly through the ranks in IBM's sales organization and is currently a senior client representative, responsible for coordinating sales initiatives with over a dozen large manufacturing firms in the Fort Wayne area. Her responsibilities include developing and maintaining key executive, information technology, and end-user relationships with her clients.

"I work closely with my clients to identify business problems and areas of opportunity in which IBM can create value-added for the customer. I have to engage appropriate resources and recommend solutions to meet my clients' business needs. The solutions I generate can involve a combination of hardware, software, technical services, and consulting. One of the most important roles I play is to manage customer satisfaction. In order to maintain solid customer relationships, which drive more business opportunities, it is imperative that we provide a superior level of customer service throughout and beyond the sales cycle. We have a large stake in our customers' business, and I must emphasize that we are here to support our clients in the long term.

PAMELA KATHRENS
IBM

"The key selling skill in my position is being able to take a strong customer-driven approach to problem solving. I personally feel a sense of commitment to my customers and am always their advocate for IBM. Other desirable selling characteristics include being tenacious, persistent, self-motivated, and having a strong work ethic. Also, the ability to be creative and dynamic as situations change is very important. Almost all of the opportunities I work on today require creativity and the ability to adapt to change."

These qualities proved indispensable when Kathrens recently led an IBM team on a large selling engagement: "This particular customer is an extremely well-informed buyer, and they operate at a very high level of intensity. They value strong business relationships with their key suppliers and have high expectations with respect to the degree of responsiveness and attentiveness to their needs."

While working with the customer, Kathrens identified an opportunity to replace their current business and manufacturing information systems with superior systems that would better meet their requirements in a cost-effective manner. The IBM solutions package also included the provision of both business and technology consulting throughout the implementation process. Kathrens says, "The selling cycle was long and tough, and this meant that the whole IBM team had to demonstrate perseverance. As the customer's decision criteria evolved, we had to communicate with the customer and each

3

other on a daily basis, constantly reworking strategies and solutions to match their needs. In the end, we prevailed because the customer was able to sense our commitment and dedication to the project and understood that we were so focused on enabling their future success. This project is currently in the implementation phase and, given our sustained performance, I have no doubt that this customer will continue to do business with IBM for a very long time."

Visit Our Website@
http://www.ibm.com/

WHY LEARN ABOUT PERSONAL SELLING?

Personal selling is an *interpersonal communication process during which a seller uncovers and satisfies the needs of a buyer to the mutual, long-term benefit of both parties.* This definition stresses that selling is more than making a sale and getting an order. The objective is to build a relationship—a partnership—by providing long-term benefits to both the seller and the customer. Thus, selling involves helping customers identify problems, offering information about potential solutions, and providing after-the-sale service to ensure long-term satisfaction. Influence and persuasion are only one part of selling.

Everyone Sells

This text discusses personal selling as a business activity undertaken by salespeople. But the principles of selling are useful to everyone, not just those people with the title of salesperson. Influencing people and developing mutually beneficial, long-term relationships are vital to all of us. Thus, the principles of selling are useful even if you do not plan to work as a salesperson.

Thinking *it* Through

Think of an instance during the last month when you tried to influence someone but did not succeed. What was your objective? How did you try to influence the person? Why did you fail? How would you handle the situation differently if you had it to do over again?

As a college student, you might use selling techniques to convince another student to go out on a date or get your professor to let you enroll in a course that was closed out. When you near graduation, you will confront a very important sales job: selling yourself to an employer.

To get a job after graduation, you will go through the same steps used in the sales process (discussed in Part Three, Chapters Seven through Twelve). First, you will identify some potential employers. Based on an analysis of each employer's needs, you will develop a presentation to demonstrate your ability to satisfy those needs. During the interview, you will listen to what the recruiter says, ask and answer questions, and perhaps alter your presentation based on the new information you receive during the interview. At some point, you might negotiate with the employer over starting salary. Eventually you will try to secure a commitment from the employer to hire you. This is selling at a very personal level. (Chapter Eighteen reviews the steps you need to undertake to get a sales job.)

People in business use selling principles all the time. Engineers convince management to support their R&D projects; industrial relations executives use selling approaches when negotiating with unions; and aspiring management trainees sell themselves to associates, superiors, and subordinates to get raises and promotions.

Traditionally, lawyers, accountants, doctors, and architects believed it was unprofessional to engage in selling their services. They waited for customers to come to

SELLING SCENARIO 1.1

Everyone Sells at Kiwi International

In 1992, Bob Iverson formed Kiwi International Airlines by getting pilots and other workers from bankrupt Eastern and American Airlines to contribute $10 million. The airline, named after a small, flightless bird, reminds the employee-owners that they too were once unable to fly.

The company has only 14 marketing and sales representatives to call on the 7,000 travel agents in the United States, so all employees of Kiwi have their job responsibilities—and, in addition, they have their sales responsibilities: "Selling is considered a point of honor here."

Employees are assigned 10 travel agents near their homes. "Our business comes from the little guy on the corner," says Maxine Krill, director of sales administration, "so we want our employees to become friends with their local agents and give them whatever help they can."

Kiwi periodically launches ``sales blitzes'' in its key markets: Newark, Atlanta, Orlando, and Chicago. As many as 15 pairs of Kiwi employees—pilots, flight attendants, executives, and mechanics—fly into a target market and spend two or three days calling on agents. When Kiwi pilots walk into an agency, they really get the customer's attention: ``Most travel agents have never met a pilot and they are really impressed,'' Krill says.

Sources: Allison Lucas, "On a Wing and a Prayer," *Sales & Marketing Management,* May 1996, p. 22; Martin Fojt, "High Flying Employee Ownership," *Journal of Services Marketing,* Fall 1995, pp. 49–51; Joe Brancatelli, "On a Wing and a Sale," *Selling,* November 1993, pp. 43–47.

them. But times are changing. Faced with increased competition and more cost-conscious customers, these professionals are becoming salespeople. A growing number of professional service firms are hiring salespeople to help them develop new business and teach their service providers how to sell. Salespeople in these situations are typically called *business development managers* or *business consultants.*[1]

People in nonbusiness situations also practice the art of selling. Presidents encourage politicians in Congress to support their programs; charities solicit contribu-

Everyone can benefit from learning the principles of selling—from a ninth grader who sold 3,250 boxes of Girl Scout cookies to the former Senate Majority leader running for President of the United States.

Dozier/Wide World Photos

Robert Kusel/Tony Stone

EXHIBIT 1.1				
The 20 Largest U.S. Sales Forces				

Rank	Company	Estimated Number of U.S. Salespeople	U.S. Employees	1995 Sales Revenues ($ millions)
1	General Electric	25,000	222,000	$70,028
2	Sara Lee	21,000	149,100	17,719
3	Prudential	20,000	92,966	42,911
4	AMP	16,000	40,800	5,227
5	State Farm	16,000	71,437	40,810
6	Allstate	14,200	44,349	22,793
7	Merrill Lynch	13,800	46,000	21,513
8	Frito-Lay	12,000	30,000	5,049
9	Travelers	11,225	47,600	16,538
10	Phillip Morris	10,000	151,000	53,139
11	IBM	9,700	252,215	71,940
12	Dun & Bradstreet	9,400	49,500	5,415
13	Microsoft	8,988	19,641	5,937
14	Dean Witter, Discover	8,575	30,779	7,934
15	Alco Standard	8,550	36,500	9,892
16	American Express	7,945	70,347	15,841
17	Equitable	7,800	12,200	7,273
18	Metropolitan	7,500	40,797	27,977
19	Interstate Bakeries	7,500	35,000	1,233
20	SunAmerica	6,500	15,000	1,052

Source: "The Selling Power 200," *Selling Power,* November/December 1996, pp. 52–57.

tions and volunteers to run their organizations; and doctors try to convince their patients to adopt healthier lifestyles. People skilled at influencing others and developing long-term relationships are usually leaders in our society.

Salespeople in Businesses

Importance to Company

Even if you are not interested in becoming a salesperson, you need to know what salespeople do and how they do it, because salespeople play a critical role in linking the firm and its customers. All of the jobs in a company depend on salespeople selling the firm's products and services. Firms exist only when they make sales. Selling Scenario 1.1 describes how everyone sells at Kiwi International Airlines.

Exhibit 1.1 lists the 20 largest sales forces in the United States. Note that Microsoft, a company noted for its technological leadership, has more than one-third of its employees in sales and customer support.

Role in a Learning Organization

In addition to generating revenue for the company, salespeople are the eyes and ears of the company in the marketplace. Salespeople are a critical element in the development of a learning organization. A **learning organization** acquires information about its environment and remembers this information so that it can guide the organizational decisions and actions even if the employees in the organization change.[2]

Two types of organizational learning are adaptive learning and generative learning. Adaptive learning is the most basic form of learning. *Adaptive learning* refers to developing knowledge to do the present activities better. For example, when Bob Meyer, a salesperson at Ballard Medical Products, was demonstrating a medical device, a surgeon commented that he could not tell whether the device was working properly because the tube was opaque. Meyer relayed this information to the vice president of engineering, and the product was redesigned, substituting a clear tube for the opaque tube. Meyer also learns a lot about customer needs when he conducts training sessions for all of the nurses in hospitals using Ballard devices. This information provides a valuable input to distribution, pricing, and advertising decisions for Ballard's present product lines.[3]

Generative learning occurs when firms go beyond their present products, markets, policies, and procedures to develop new insights. Salespeople also provide critical input to this type of learning that affects strategic decision making by their firms. They are often the first to know when their customers' needs are changing. For example, at Flexatard, a manufacturer of fitness bodywear, salespeople provide information on customer reactions to changing fashions, new styles introduced by competitors, and approaches the company is considering to satisfy activewear users' needs. They know what the trends are and what new ideas will capture the imaginations of their customers.[4]

Two critical processes of organization learning are information acquisition and information dissemination. Because salespeople are in constant contact with the marketplace, they play an important role in information acquisition. They are typically the firm's best source of information about what customers want and what competitors are doing and provide a critical input to the firm's strategic intelligence system.[5]

But to be effective members of a learning organization, salespeople need to be skillful at disseminating the knowledge they have acquired to other people in their companies. In Chapter Seventeen, we discuss this issue as an aspect of the relationship between salespeople and their companies.

While salespeople are intimately involved in organizational learning, they also need to continually learn how to do their jobs better. Issues related to self-improvement are discussed in Chapters Five and Eighteen.

Role of Selling in Marketing Communications

A marketing communications program is the firm's effort to provide customers with information about its products and services and where and how they can be bought, and to influence customers to buy them. Exhibit 1.2 classifies the different communication methods retailers use based on whether they're impersonal or personal and paid or unpaid.

Methods for Communicating with Customers

Advertising and promotions are examples of paid impersonal communications. Advertising uses impersonal mass media such as newspapers, TV, radio, direct mail, and the internet to provide information to customers. Sales promotions offer extra value and incentives to customers to purchase products during a specific period of time. For example, Coca Cola offered products at reduced prices to supermarket chains during its 1996 Olympics promotion. (See Chapter Fifteen for more information on promotions to retailers.)

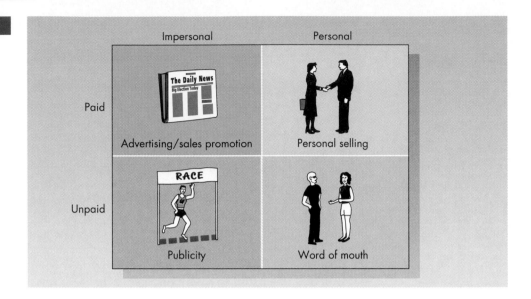

Salespeople are the primary vehicle for providing paid personal communications to customers. Many people think—incorrectly—that advertising is the most important part of the firm's promotion program. However, industrial companies place far more emphasis on personal selling than on advertising.[6] Even in consumer products firms such as Lever Brothers, which spends over $1 billion annually on advertising, personal selling plays a critical role. Although advertising informs customers about Lever Brothers' products, salespeople make sure the products are available and properly displayed in retail stores. All marketing people at Lever Brothers spend considerable time in the field with salespeople, learning about the needs of the retail stores as well as those of the ultimate consumers.

The primary method for generating unpaid impersonal communication is publicity. Publicity is communications through significant unpaid presentations about the firm (usually a news story). An example of publicity is IBM's sponsorship of a chess match between Karpov, the world chess champion, and an IBM computer program.

Finally, firms communicate with their customers at no cost through word of mouth (communication among buyers about a firm). For example, salespeople often ask a customer to recommend their firms' products to another customer (see Chapter Seven).

Strengths and Weaknesses of Communication Methods

Exhibit 1.3 compares communication methods in terms of control, flexibility, credibility, and cost. Firms have more control when using paid versus unpaid methods. When using advertising and sales promotions, companies can determine the message's exact content and the time of its delivery. They have a bit less control over the communications delivered by salespeople and have very little control over the content or timing of publicity and word-of-mouth communications.

Personal selling is the most flexible communication method, because salespeople can talk with each customer, discover the customer's specific needs, and develop unique presentations for that customer. Other communication methods are less flexible. For example, ads deliver the same message to all customers.

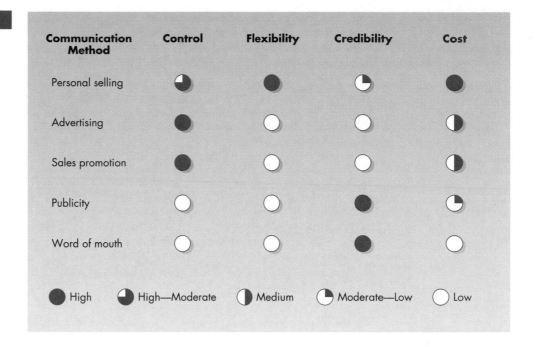

EXHIBIT 1.3

Comparison of
Communication
Methods

Communication Method	Control	Flexibility	Credibility	Cost
Personal selling	High—Moderate	High	Moderate—Low	High
Advertising	High	Low	Low	Medium
Sales promotion	High	Low	Low	Medium
Publicity	Low	Low	High	Moderate—Low
Word of mouth	Low	Low	High	Low

High   High—Moderate   Medium   Moderate—Low   Low

Because publicity and word of mouth are communicated by independent sources, their information is usually more credible than the information in paid communication sources. For example, customers tend to doubt claims made by salespeople and in ads since they know retailers are trying to promote their merchandise, but they may trust information provided by a person from another firm they meet at a trade show.

Personal selling is the most costly method of communication. A presentation by a salesperson costs over $100—almost 10,000 times more than exposing a customer to a newspaper, radio, or TV ad.

Integrated Marketing Communications

Since each of the communication vehicles has strengths and weaknesses, many firms are developing communication programs that coordinate the use of the different vehicles to maximize the impact of the program on customers. These coordinated efforts are called **integrated marketing communications**.[7]

A.B. Dick used an integrated marketing communication program to introduce its Century 3000 two-color printing press. The key benefit of the press is to enable printers to make short-run color printing profitable. To emphasize the cost effectiveness of the press, the firm built the campaign around the theme "The Color of Money," the title of the movie staring Tom Cruise and Paul Newman. A special event built around the theme was used to generate publicity.

The company obtained names of potential customers (leads) by placing ads in trade publications offering readers Color of Money posters that provided information about its printing business. Additional leads were generated with direct mail of an oversized $100 bill accompanied by a letter talking about the opportunity to make big bucks. Customers were asked to send back a card that included some information to qualify them as potential customers.

Qualified customers were sent a six-minute video. When the video was mailed, salespeople were notified. The direct-mail campaign peaked the prospects' interest and helped the salespeople get appointments for a presentation.

One of the most successful parts of the campaign was the development of a newsletter distributed to customers. The newsletter described success stories illustrating how printers had made money using the press. It built relationships with customers by giving them ideas for new applications. The newsletter also served as a method for passing along favorable word of mouth from satisfied printers to prospects.[8]

WHAT DO SALESPEOPLE DO?

The activities of salespeople depend on the type of selling job they choose. The responsibilities of salespeople selling steam turbines for Westinghouse differ greatly from those of salespeople selling pharmaceuticals for Upjohn or paper products for Scott Paper. But certain basic activities are common to all types of selling, regardless of the product or the company. In addition to face-to-face and telephone contact with customers, all salespeople have to undertake servicing, internal selling, and reporting activities.

Selling

Sales jobs involve prospecting for new customers, increasing sales to existing customers, making sales presentations, demonstrating products, negotiating price and delivery terms, and writing orders. But these sales-generating activities (discussed in Chapters Seven through Twelve) are only part of the job. Exhibit 1.4 shows how salespeople spend their time. On average, they work over 46.5 hours a day; many work through lunch. However, only 31 percent of their time is spent in face-to-face contact with existing customers. An additional 25 percent goes to prospecting for new customers and working with existing customers by phone. The rest of their time is spent in meetings, selling internally, traveling, waiting for a sales interview, doing paperwork, and servicing customers.[9]

Face-to-face selling is only one part of a salesperson's job. The Parker Hannifin salesperson (right) is building a partnering relationship by checking the performance of the valves he sold. The Carlson Wagonlit sales rep (left) is working with travel agents in her home to office to make sure that one of her corporate clients is getting billed properly.

Bill O'Connell

Courtesy Parker Hannifin

EXHIBIT 1.4

How Salespeople Spend Their Time Each Week

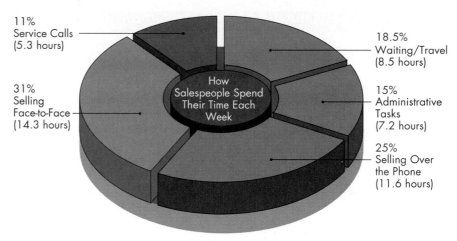

11%
Service Calls
(5.3 hours)

18.5%
Waiting/Travel
(8.5 hours)

31%
Selling
Face-to-Face
(14.3 hours)

How Salespeople Spend Their Time Each Week

15%
Administrative
Tasks
(7.2 hours)

25%
Selling Over
the Phone
(11.6 hours)

Source: Christen Heide, *Dartnell's 29th Sales Force Compensation Survey 1996–97* (Chicago: The Dartnell Corporation, 1996), p. 117.

Servicing Customers

The salesperson's job does not end when the customer places an order. Sales representatives must make sure customers get the benefits they expect from the product. Thus, salespeople work with other company employees to ensure that deliveries are made on time, equipment is properly installed, operators are trained to use the equipment, and questions or complaints are resolved quickly. Providing these services is critical to developing partnerships, the long-term objective of selling. (Chapter Thirteen focuses on developing partnerships through customer services.)

Selling and servicing customers can be very challenging in less developed countries where many customers are difficult to reach. For example, Sabritas, Mexico's largest snack food company, has an extensive distribution system to reach customers in isolated mountain and jungle villages. Salespeople drive specially equipped vans to make weekly calls on these remote villages. They often sleep in their vans or in customers' stores. Salespeople reach villages in the lake region by canoe and ride donkeys into some mountain villages.[10]

Internal Selling

Salespeople also spend time in meetings, coordinating the activities of their firms to solve customer problems. Dick Holder, president of Reynolds Metal Company, spent five years "selling" Campbell Soup Company on using aluminum cans for its tomato juice products. He coordinated a team of graphic designers, marketing people, and engineers to educate Campbell about a packaging material it had never used before.[11] Approaches for improving efficiency in performing these nonselling activities are discussed in Chapter Sixteen.

Providing Information to the Company and Preparing Information for Customers

In their reporting activities, salespeople provide information to their firms about expenses, calls made, future calls scheduled, sales forecasts, competitor activities, business conditions, and unsatisfied customer needs. Much of this information is now transmitted electronically among the company, its salespeople, and its customers. For example, each night Gillette merchandisers plug their laptop computers into telephones, dial a host computer, and transmit information about retail conditions in the supermarkets they visited during the day. Then they receive instructions about what they should do during tomorrow's store visits. The salesperson responsible for the ac-

SELLING SCENARIO 1.2

How a Laptop Computer Saved the Day

Each night, salespeople at Curtin Matheson Scientific, a distributor of clinical and laboratory supplies in Baton Rouge, Louisiana, download all the ordering and shipping information for their customers from the company mainframe to their laptop computers. This information really came in handy when Scott Salling called on one of his accounts and met the buyer. The buyer immediately began criticizing Curtin Matheson for its poor service and delivery. So Salling took out his laptop and showed her the records for all of her company's recent purchases. Only one order had not been delivered on time. Because Salling had the information at his fingertips, he was able to correct the buyer's unfavorable image.

Source: Ginger Trumfio, "For the Love of the Laptop," *Sales & Marketing Management,* Part II, March 1995, pp. 31–32. Reprinted with permission from Bill Communications.

count reviews the information from the merchandisers to plan a presentation for the headquarters buyer for razors and blades. The salesperson also uses the information to provide instructions for merchandisers on future calls.[12]

Over 3.5 million salespeople use laptop computers.[13] Selling Scenario 1.2 illustrates how a salesperson used his laptop to impress a new buyer. The next section describes the basic types of sales positions. These positions differ in terms of the time spent on the various activities outlined above.

TYPES OF SALESPEOPLE

Almost everyone is familiar with people who sell products and services to consumers in retail outlets. Behind these **retail salespeople** is an army of salespeople working for commercial firms. Consider a VCR you might purchase in a store. To make the VCR, the manufacturer bought processed material, such as plastic and electronic components, from various salespeople. In addition, it purchased capital equipment from other salespeople to mold the plastic, assemble the components, and test the VCR. Finally, the VCR manufacturer bought services such as an employment agency to hire people and an accounting firm to audit the company's financial statements. The manufacturer's salespeople then sold the VCRs to a wholesaler. The wholesaler purchased transportation services and warehouse space from other salespeople. Then the wholesaler's salespeople sold the VCRs to a retailer.

Selling and Distribution Channels

As the VCR example shows, salespeople work for different types of firms and call on different types of customers. These differences in sales positions come from the many roles salespeople play in a firm's distribution channel. A **distribution channel** is a set of people and organizations responsible for the flow of products and services from the producer to the ultimate user. Exhibit 1.5 shows the principal types of distribution channels used for business-to-business and consumer products. Looking at the exhibit, you can see the varied roles salespeople play.

Business-to-Business Products Channels

The two main channels for manufacturers of business-to-business, or industrial, products are (1) direct sales to a business customer and (2) sales through distributors. In the direct channel, salespeople working for the manufacturer call directly on other manufacturers. For example, Nucor salespeople sell steel directly to automo-

EXHIBIT 1.5

Sales Jobs and the
Distribution Channel

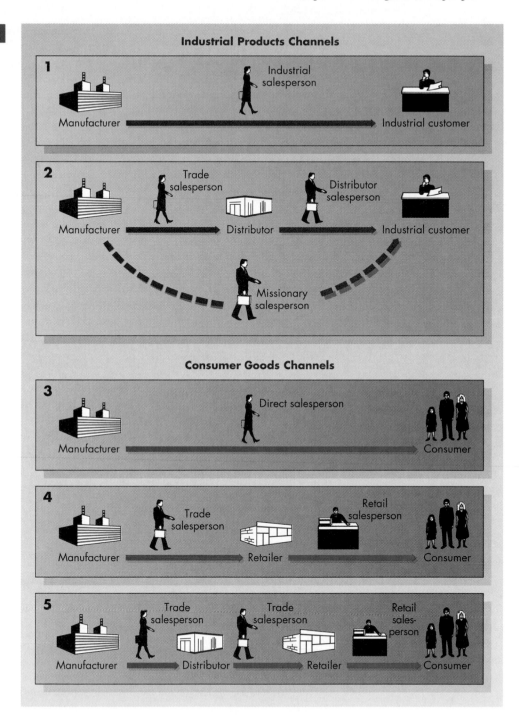

Industrial Products Channels

1 Manufacturer — Industrial salesperson — Industrial customer

2 Manufacturer — Trade salesperson — Distributor — Distributor salesperson — Industrial customer — Missionary salesperson

Consumer Goods Channels

3 Manufacturer — Direct salesperson — Consumer

4 Manufacturer — Trade salesperson — Retailer — Retail salesperson — Consumer

5 Manufacturer — Trade salesperson — Distributor — Trade salesperson — Retailer — Retail salesperson — Consumer

bile manufacturers, and Dow Chemical salespeople sell plastics directly to toy manufacturers.

In the distributor channel, the manufacturer employs salespeople to sell to distributors. These salespeople are referred to as **trade salespeople** because they sell to firms that resell the products rather than using them within the firm. Distributor salespeople sell products made by a number of manufacturers to businesses. For example, some Motorola salespeople sell microprocessors to distributors such as Arrow Electronics, and Arrow salespeople then resell the microprocessors and other electronic components to customers such as Digital Equipment. Chapter Fifteen focuses on the special issues confronting trade salespeople.

Many firms use more than one channel of distribution and thus employ several types of salespeople. For example, Motorola and Dow Chemical have trade salespeople who call on distributors and direct salespeople who call on large companies.

In the second business-to-business channel (see Exhibit 1.5), a missionary salesperson is employed. **Missionary salespeople** work for a manufacturer and promote the manufacturer's products to other firms. However, those firms buy the products from distributors or other manufacturers, *not* directly from the salesperson's firm. For example, sales representatives at Driltech, a manufacturer of mining equipment, call on mine owners to promote their products. The mines, however, place orders for drills with the local Driltech distributor rather than with Driltech directly. Normally, missionary and local distributor salespeople work together to build relationships with customers.

Frequently, missionary salespeople call on people who influence a buying decision but do not actually place the order. For example, Du Pont sales representatives call on clothing designers to encourage them to design garments made with nylon, and Merck sales representatives call on physicians to encourage them to prescribe Merck pharmaceutical products.

Consumer Products Channels

The remaining channels shown in Exhibit 1.5 are used by manufacturers of consumer products. The third channel shows a firm, such as State Farm Insurance, whose salespeople sell insurance directly to consumers. The fourth and fifth channels show manufacturers that employ trade salespeople to sell to either retailers or distributors. For example, Revlon uses the fourth channel when its salespeople sell directly to Wal-Mart. However, Revlon uses the fifth channel to sell to small, owner-operated retailers through distributors.

Some of the salespeople shown in Exhibit 1.5 may be **manufacturers' agents.** Manufacturers' agents are independent businesspeople who are paid a commission by a manufacturer for all products or services sold. Unlike distributors and retailers, agents never own the products. They simply perform the selling activities and then transmit the orders to the manufacturers.

Describing Sales Jobs

Descriptions of sales jobs focus on certain factors:

1. The customer's relationship to the salesperson's firm.
2. The salesperson's duties.
3. The importance of the purchase decision to the customer.
4. Where the salesperson contacts the customer.
5. The products or services sold.
6. The role the salesperson plays in securing a commitment from the customer.

Customer-Firm Relationship: New or Continuing?

Some sales jobs emphasize finding and selling to new customers. Selling to prospects requires different skills than selling to existing customers. To convince prospects to purchase a product they have never used before, salespeople need to be especially self-confident and aggressive. They must be able to deal with the inevitable rejections that occur when making initial contacts with potential customers. On the other hand, salespeople responsible for existing customers place more emphasis on building relationships and servicing customers than on selling to them.

Duties Taking Orders or Creating Alternatives?

Some sales jobs focus primarily on taking orders. For example, most Frito-Lay salespeople go to grocery stores, check the stock, and prepare an order for the store manager to sign.

However, some Frito-Lay salespeople sell only to buyers in the headquarters of supermarket chains. Headquarters selling requires a much higher level of skill and creativity to do the job effectively. These salespeople work with buyers to develop new systems and methods to increase the retailer's sales and profits.

The Buying Decision: How Crucial Is It to the Customer?

Consumers and businesses make many purchase decisions each year. Some decisions are important to them, such as purchasing a home or a telephone system. Others are less crucial, such as buying candy or cleaning supplies.

Sales jobs involving important decisions for customers differ greatly from sales jobs involving minor decisions. Consider the company that needs a computer-controlled drill press. Buying the drill press is a big decision. The drill press sales representative needs to be knowledgeable about the customer's needs and the features of drill presses. The salesperson will have to interact with a number of people involved in the purchase decision.

Intangible benefits are more difficult to demonstrate than tangible benefits. Thus, this AIA life insurance agent in Malaysia has a more challenging job than an automobile salesperson.

Munshi Ahmed

Contact Location: Field or Inside Sales?

Field salespeople spend considerable time in the customer's place of business, communicating with the customer face to face. **Inside salespeople** work at their employer's location and typically communicate with customers by telephone or letter.

Field selling typically is more demanding than inside selling because it entails more intense interactions with customers. Field salespeople are more involved in problem solving with customers, whereas inside salespeople often respond to customer-initiated requests.

Products or Services: Tangible versus Intangible Benefits

The nature of the benefits provided by products and services affects the nature of the sales job. Products such as chemicals and trucks typically have tangible benefits: Customers can objectively measure a chemical's purity and a truck's payload. The benefits of services, such as business insurance or investment opportunities, are more intangible: customers cannot easily see how the insurance company handles claims or objectively measure the riskiness of an investment.[14]

Intangible benefits are harder to sell than tangible benefits, because it is more difficult to demonstrate intangible benefits to customers. It is much easier to show a customer the payload of a truck than the benefits of carrying insurance.

Securing Customer Commitment: The Salesperson's Role.

Sales jobs differ by the types of commitments sought and the manner in which they are obtained. For example, the Du Pont missionary salesperson encouraging clothing designers to use Du Pont synthetic fibers might ask the designer to make a commitment to use the fiber but does not undertake the more difficult task of asking the designer to place an order. If the designer decides to use nylon fabric in a dress, the order for nylon will be secured by the salesperson calling on a company that makes the fabric.

Thinking *it* **Through**	Which of the types of selling jobs just described do you think you would do well? Why do you think you would be effective in those activities and not in others?

The Sales Jobs Continuum

Exhibit 1.6 uses the factors just discussed to illustrate the continuum of sales jobs in terms of creativity. Sales jobs described by the responses in the right-hand column require salespeople to go into the field and call on new customers who make important buying decisions. These selling assignments emphasize selling to new customers rather than building relations with old customers, promoting products or services with intangible benefits, and/or gaining commitments from customers. These types of sales jobs require the most creativity and skill and, consequently, offer the highest pay. Selling Scenario 1.3 describes how a salesperson in a complex selling environment sold over $7 million of computer software. The next section examines the responsibilities of specific types of salespeople in more detail.

SELLING SCENARIO 1.3

Selling $7 Million of Computer Software

After working 19 years in sales for various computer companies, Barry Davis took a position with Lotus to sell its newly developed groupware, Lotus Notes.® In 1991, groupware, a type of program that enables company employees to communicate and collaborate across all departments worldwide, was unknown. Davis had to start from scratch with prospects, making them aware of the program's capabilities and benefits.

In 1991, Davis convinced General Motors and Arthur Andersen to purchase 15,000 and 60,000 copies of the program, respectively—the largest sales of PC software sold in single copies. Davis did not just sell Notes to GM, he built a relationship. "We developed a strategic partnership. We convinced them we'd be with them for the long-term," he says. In making these sales,

he used a new strategy for selling complex software: a sales team composed of a senior salesperson and a technical expert.

After making these big sales, Davis was made the head of a new account group, code named Swarm, that focused on the top 25 prospects. The experience was one of the highlights of his career. Davis says, "It was one of the best groups ever assembled. I couldn't wait to get up in the morning and sell for my company." As the leader of Swarm, Davis made Notes into an international phenomenon—the primary reason IBM paid billions of dollars to acquire the entire company (Lotus) in 1996.

Source: "Sales Challenger," *Selling Power,* November/December 1996, pp. 18–20.

Examples of Sales Jobs

JCPenney Retail Salesperson

JCPenney salespeople sell to customers who come into their stores. In many cases, the customers know what they want; the salesperson just rings up the sale. However, JCPenney, like most department stores, is upgrading its salespeople from order takers to relationship builders. The company is encouraging salespeople to keep customer books, notify customers of new merchandise, and make special appointments with key customers to present merchandise selected to meet their needs.

EXHIBIT 1.6			
Creativity Level of Sales Jobs	**Factors in Sales Jobs**	**Lower Creativity**	**Higher Creativity**
	Nature of Customer. Does the salesperson contact predominantly:	Present customers?	New prospects?
	Nature of salesperson's duties. Is the emphasis of the salesperson's duties on:	Servicing customers?	Persuading customers?
	Importance of buying decision. Do the the salesperson's selling activities take place:	Inside the company?	In the field?
	Nature of salesperson's duties. Do the products or services sold by the salesperson have:	Tangible benefits?	Intangible benefits?
	Closing skills. Is the level of skills required to gain commitment:	Low?	High?

This pharmaceutical salesperson is engaging in missionary selling when he presents the benefits of his products to a doctor. The salesperson understands that the doctor will not place an order, but he is attempting to get the doctor to prescribe the pharmaceutical for her patients so his company will get an order from the patient's drug store.

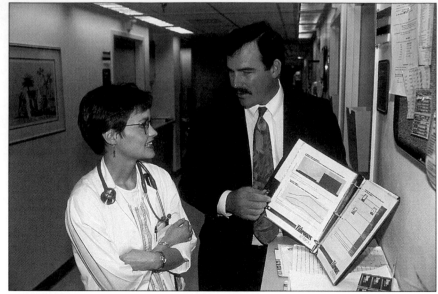

David J. Sams/Tony Stone Images

Kraft/General Foods Packaged Goods Salesperson

Kraft salespeople increase the sales of their firm's products by influencing retailers and distributors to stock their brands and then servicing them. Most Kraft salespeople service existing customers rather than finding new ones. They typically make regularly scheduled calls on customers in an assigned territory. Some of the responsibilities of a Kraft trade salesperson are

1. Convincing the retailer to buy and display all Kraft products in its stores.
2. Making sure the retailer has enough stock displayed on shelves and stored in the back room so that an out-of-stock condition will not arise.
3. Counting stock and preparing orders for the store manager if inventories are low.
4. Checking to see that Kraft products are priced competitively.
5. Trying to get Kraft products displayed on shelves where consumers can see them easily.
6. Encouraging managers to develop special displays for Kraft products and helping them build the displays.
7. Convincing store managers to feature Kraft products in advertising and place in-store ads and signs to promote the sale of Kraft products.

Merck Pharmaceutical Salesperson

Salespeople who represent the classic example of missionary sales work for pharmaceutical companies such as Merck. Merck salespeople provide information on their products to physicians, pharmacists, and other people licensed to provide medical services in their territories. Typically they make four to eight calls on doctors and three to six calls on pharmacists each day, usually without an appointment.

The salespeople spend 10 to 15 minutes with doctors on each call. Their presentations include accurate information about the symptoms for which a pharmaceutical is effective, how effective it is, and what side effects might occur. Doctors consider these presentations an important source of information about new products.

Hewlett-Packard Computer Salesperson

Some of the most challenging sales jobs involve selling capital goods. Hewlett-Packard salespeople sell computers used to control manufacturing processes. Because these capital equipment purchases are made infrequently, Hewlett-Packard salespeople often approach new customers. The selling task requires working with customers who are making a major investment and are involved in an important buying decision. Many people are involved in this sort of purchase decision. Hewlett-Packard salespeople need to demonstrate both immediate, tangible benefits and future, intangible benefits.

The next section reviews the skills required to be effective in the sales positions discussed above.

CHARACTERISTICS OF SUCCESSFUL SALESPEOPLE

For the last 100 years, many people have written books and articles discussing why some people are successful in selling and other are not. After all of this research, no one has identified the profile of the "perfect" salesperson because sales jobs are so different. As the job descriptions in the previous section show, the characteristics and skills needed for success when selling for Kraft differ from those needed for success when selling for Hewlett-Packard.

In addition, all customers are different. Some like to interact with an aggressive salesperson, whereas others are turned off by aggressive behavior. Some are all business and want formal relationships with salespeople, whereas others look forward to chatting with salespeople in an informal way. Thus, the stereotype of the hard-driving, back-slapping sales personality will not succeed with all customers.[15] No magic selling formula works in all sales jobs or with all customers.

Although no one personality profile exists for the ideal salesperson, successful salespeople are hard workers and smart workers. They are highly motivated, dependable, ethical, knowledgeable, good communicators, flexible, and emotionally intelligent.

Motivation

Most salespeople work in the field without direct supervision. Under these conditions, they may be tempted to get up late, take long lunch breaks, and stop work early. But successful salespeople do not succumb to these temptations. They are "self-starters" who do not need the fear inspired by a glaring supervisor to get them going in the morning or keep them working hard all day.

Spending long hours on the job is not enough. Salespeople must use their time efficiently. They need to maximize the time spent in contacting customers and minimize the time spent in traveling and waiting for customers. To do this, salespeople must organize and plan their work (a subject discussed in more detail in Chapter Sixteen).

Finally, successful salespeople are motivated to learn as well as work hard. They must continually work at improving their skills by analyzing their past performance and using their mistakes as learning opportunities.[16]

SELLING SCENARIO 1.4

Bankers Become Salespeople

Linda Pera knew she had made the transformation from banker into salesperson when one of her clients offered her a job on his sales force. She had received offers from clients to become a comptroller or VP of finance, but never a salesperson. Pera had studied finance in college and was an account officer at Fidelity First, the 25th largest bank in the United States.

In the 1980s Fidelity First, like most banks, lost 40 percent of its business to nonfinancial institutions. To regain this lost business, Fidelity changed its corporate culture. Account officers like Linda Pera were renamed "relationship bankers." Sales goals were established. The compensation of the relationship bankers was changed to include incentives for getting business and maintaining customer relationships.

The relationship bankers learn about selling in training sessions that teach them the steps in the sales process from prospecting to making a sale. However, Pera believes the most important training she has gotten is on the job. She spends three days a week prospecting for new customers. Her division manager usually goes with her when she is about to close a deal with a new client.

Fidelity's clients appreciate this new approach. Eric Sambol, executive VP of Sambol Construction Company, says banks often call on him to get his business, but Fidelity's relationship bankers are "able to recognize our needs and are not shy in pursuing them. They've always met our financial goals and that makes it unnecessary to go elsewhere."

Source: Weld Royal, "Take It to the Bank," *Sales & Marketing Management,* October 1995, pp. 6–27. Reprinted with permission from Bill Communications.

Dependability and Trustworthiness	In some types of selling, such as used-car sales, the salesperson rarely deals with the same customer twice. However, this book deals with business-to-business selling situations in which the customer and salesperson have a continuing relationship—a partnership. Such salespeople are interested not just in what the customers will buy this time but also in getting orders in the years to come. Selling Scenario 1.4 illustrates how banks are building strong customer relationships by converting their account managers into salespeople.

Customers develop long-term relationships only with salespeople who are dependable and trustworthy. When salespeople say the equipment will perform in a certain way, they had better make sure the equipment performs that way! If it doesn't, the customer will not rely on them again. (Chapter Two focuses on the development of long-term relationships with customers.)

Ethical Sales Behavior

Honesty and integrity are important components of dependability. Over the long run, customers will find out who can be trusted and who cannot. Good ethics is good business. (Ethical sales behavior is such an important topic that Chapter Three is devoted to it.)

Customer and Product Knowledge

Effective salespeople need to know how businesses make purchase decisions and how individuals evaluate product alternatives. In addition, they need product knowledge—how their products work and how the products' features are related to the benefits customers are seeking. (Chapter Four reviews the buying process, and Chapter Six discusses product knowledge.)

Courtesy Colgate-Palmolive Company   Courtesy Parker Hannifin Corporation

Salespeople need to be flexible, adapting their sales approach to the situation. The Colgate-Palmolive salesperson (left) uses a different approach when selling an open market vendor in Mexico compared to a buyer in a large supermarket chain. The Parker Hannefin (right) salesperson emphasizes easy installation when selling O-rings to one customer in the U.K. and high reliability with another customer.

Communication Skills

The key to building strong long-term relationships is being responsive to a customer's needs. To do that, the salesperson needs to be a good communicator. But talking is not enough; the salesperson must listen to what the customer says, ask questions that uncover problems and needs, and pay attention to the responses.

To compete in world markets, salespeople need to learn how to communicate in international markets. For example, business is conducted differently in Europe than in the United States. In the United States, business transactions generally proceed at a rapid pace, whereas Europeans take more time reaching decisions. European customers place more emphasis on the rapport developed with a salesperson, whereas U.S. firms look more at the size and reputation of the salesperson's company. Because Europeans want to do business with salespeople they like and trust, they spend more time building a close personal relationship.[17] (Chapter Five is devoted to developing communication skills, with considerable emphasis on communicating in other cultures.)

Flexibility

The successful salesperson also realizes that the same sales approach does not work with all customers; it must be adapted to each selling situation. The salesperson must be sensitive to what is happening and flexible enough to make those adaptations during the sales presentation.[18]

Donald Trump, the real estate developer, emphasized the importance of flexibility: "Great salespeople truly understand the people they are dealing with. They know when to take a low-key approach, when to be more assertive, or when to sell with pizzazz. Flexibility is the key. The biggest mistake you make is to sell the same way with all people."[19]

Exhibit 1.3 on page 9 indicates that personal selling is the most costly marketing communication vehicle. Why do companies spend money on personal selling when it is so expensive? The higher cost is justified by its greater effectiveness. Personal selling works better than any other communication vehicle because salespeople are able to develop a unique message for each customer. Salespeople can do "market research" on each customer by asking questions and listening carefully. They then use this information to develop and deliver a sales presentation tailored to the needs and beliefs of each customer. In addition, salespeople can observe verbal and nonverbal behaviors (body language) in their customers and, in response, adjust their presentation. If the customer is uninterested in the contents of the presentation or turned off by the salesperson's style, the salesperson can make changes quickly.

In contrast, advertising messages are tailored to the typical customer in a segment and thus are not ideally suited to many of the customers who may see the ad. Advertisers are also limited in how fast they can make adjustments. Salespeople can adjust on the spot, but it may take months to determine that an advertisement is not working and then develop a new one.

Only personal selling provides the opportunity to be truly adaptive in making presentations. Consequently, selling effectiveness hinges on the salesperson's ability to practice adaptive selling and exploit this unique opportunity. (Adaptive selling is treated in detail in Chapter Six.)

Emotional Intelligence[20]

Salespeople span the boundary between their companies and the companies' customers. At times the objectives of the company can differ from those of the customers. The company wants the salesperson to make profits and the customer wants to buy a product that meets its needs at the lowest price. Dealing with these conflicting objectives can be very stressful for salespeople.

To cope with conflicting company and customer objectives, rude customers, and indifferent support staff, effective selling requires a high degree of emotional intelligence. **Emotional intelligence** is the ability to effectively understand and use one's own emotions and the emotions of people with whom one interacts. Emotional intelligence has four aspects: (1) knowing one's own feelings and emotions as they are experienced, (2) controlling one's emotions to avoid acting impulsively, (3) recognizing customers' emotions (called *empathy*), and (4) using one's emotions to interact effectively with customers. We discuss aspects of emotional intelligence as they relate to adaptive selling and effective verbal and nonverbal intelligence in Chapters Five and Six.

Thinking *it* **Through**	Which of the characteristics listed above are needed to be an effective teacher, engineer, banker, or actor?

Are Salespeople Born or Made?[21]

On the basis of the preceding discussion, you can see that the skills required to be a successful salesperson can be learned. People can learn to work hard, plan their time, and adapt their sales approach to their customers' needs. Research has shown that innate characteristics such as personality traits, gender, and height are largely unrelated to sales performance. In fact, companies show their faith in their ability to teach sales skills by spending over $10 billion each year on training programs. The next section discusses the rewards you can realize if you develop the skills required for sales success.

REWARDS IN
SELLING

Personal selling offers interesting and rewarding career opportunities. Presently more than 7 million people in the United States work in sales positions and the number of sales positions is growing.[22] A recent survey of sales managers reports that 38 percent were hiring more salespeople to increase the size of their sales forces whereas only 15.2 percent were decreasing sales force size.[23] Sales positions are challenging, exciting, and financially rewarding. They can provide the base for promotion to management positions in a firm or for launching a new business.

Independence and
Responsibility

Many people do not want to spend long hours behind a desk, doing the same thing every day. They prefer to be outside, moving around, meeting people, and working on different problems. Selling ideally suits people with these interests. The typical salesperson interacts with dozens of people daily. Most of these contacts involve challenging, new experiences.

Selling also offers unusual freedom and flexibility. It is not a nine-to-five job. Most salespeople decide how to spend their time; they do not have to report in. They have the freedom to determine what they do during a day, to decide which customers to call on and when to do paperwork. Long hours may be required on some days, and other days may bring fewer demands.

Because of this freedom, salespeople are like independent entrepreneurs. They have a territory to manage and few restrictions on how to do it. They are responsible for the sales and profits the territory generates. Thus, their success or failure rests largely on their own skills and efforts.

Financial Rewards

The financial rewards of selling depend on the level of skill and sophistication needed to do the job. For example, salespeople who sell to businesses typically are paid more than are retail salespeople, because the buying process in businesses is more complex and difficult to manage. Exhibit 1.7 shows average 1995 salaries, including base salary, commissions, and bonuses, for salespeople at different levels.

Such salary averages can be very misleading, however. People in sales often make over $100,000 a year; some make over $1 million. Occasionally the top salespeople

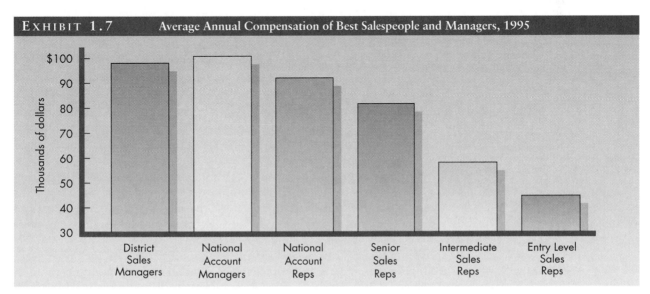

EXHIBIT 1.7   Average Annual Compensation of Best Salespeople and Managers, 1995

Source: Christen Heide, *Dartnell's 29th Sales Force Compensation Survey 1996–97* (Chicago: The Dartnell Corporation, 1996), pp. 66–76.

in a firm will make more than the chief executive officer (CEO). For example, Garry Lauer, Silicon Graphics vice president in charge of the firm's 1,230-person worldwide sales force, made over $1 million in 1995. During the last eight years, his salespeople have boosted Silicon Graphics' annual sales revenues from less than $100 million to over $1 billion. CEO Ed McCrackin recognizes the importance of Lauer and his sales force: "I view Gary as the Steve Young of Silicon Graphics. He's the quarterback for our sales team."[24]

Management Opportunities

Selling jobs provide a firm base for launching a business career. A study of senior managers reported that 28 percent of the presidents of the 1,000 largest U.S. companies had marketing experience.[25] Although selling can launch corporate careers, many entrepreneurs also work in sales before starting their own companies. For example, after a divorce left her on her own, Mary Kay Ash supported herself and her three small children by selling cleaning supplies at in-home demonstrations. She went on to start Mary Kay Cosmetics, now an international cosmetics firm with annual sales of over $5 billion. Ross Perot began his career selling computers for IBM. He started his own computer system management firm, EDS, which he eventually sold to General Motors, and, during his 1992 campaign for the U.S. presidency, received the most votes of any third-party candidate in history. Selling Scenario 1.5 describes how the CEO of Goodyear started in sales and continues to sell every chance he can.

Even though selling offers opportunities for advancement, many salespeople promoted to management positions return to selling later. Ed Nunn sold for Enerpac Group, a Wisconsin tool manufacturer, for six years and was offered the position of national sales manager—at a $10,000 pay cut. Everyone told him, "Oh, Ed, you gotta take it; it's good for your career." At first he liked training salespeople and working in the field with them. But as time passed, the administrative work, the meetings, and being tied to a schedule made him long to return to selling. One morning he realized the managerial life was not for him: "I was standing in an office getting chewed out because I came in at 8:20 instead of 8:00. I looked at my boss and said, 'What difference does it make? Sometimes I'm here till seven or eight at night." And he said,'But Ed, no one sees you then.' I've never been big on details or hanging around the factory [office] for show. I want to be out doing something." So Nunn quit and went to work for another company as a salesperson.[26]

Summary

In summary, you should study personal selling because we all use selling techniques. If you want to work in business, you need to know about selling because salespeople play a vital role in business activities. Finally, you might be interested in taking a job in selling. Selling jobs are inherently interesting because of the variety of people encountered and activities undertaken. In addition, selling offers opportunities for financial rewards and promotions.

Salespeople engage in a wide range of activities, including providing information on products and services to customers and employees within their firms. Most of us are not aware of many of these activities because the salespeople we meet most frequently work in retail stores. However, the most exciting and challenging sales positions are in business-to-business selling.

The specific duties and responsibilities of salespeople depend on the type of selling position. However, most salespeople engage in other tasks in addition to influencing customers. These tasks include managing customer relations, working with other people in their firms, reporting on activities in their territories and traveling.

SELLING SCENARIO 1.5

*CEO of
Goodyear Is
Still Selling*

Stanley Gault, the recently retired CEO and chairperson of Goodyear, started selling at a young age: "When I was 12 years old, I was working for my uncle during the summer. I started out sweeping the floors and doing odd jobs. He would teach me how to sell these appliances, so that I could talk to customers while he was busy. I sold my first refrigerator when I was 12. I even remember the model number, GE NC 8. It sold for $200."

After graduating college, Gault started his business career at GE on the service desk, taking orders from distributors. From there he went into field sales and worked his way up to become the head of GE's major appliance business prior to joining Goodyear as CEO.

Every time Gault addresses an audience, including stockholders' meetings, he urges people to check their tires and replace them with a set of new Goodyear tires. When meeting Ameritech's chairperson, Gault's description of the new Acquatred tire so impressed the pilot of the Ameritech corporate jet that he went out and bought two sets of tires, one for himself and one for his wife. Gault says, "Selling isn't the role of sales and marketing people. I feel that communicating the benefits of our product is everyone's job in the company."

Sources: Robert Waterman, *What America Does Right: Learning from Companies That Put People First.* (New York: W.W. Norton, 1994); "Stanley Gault," *Personal Selling Power,* 15th Anniversary Issue, 1995, pp. 34–38.

Sales jobs can be classified by the roles salespeople and their firms play in the channel of distribution. The nature of the selling job is affected by whom salespeople work for and whether they sell to manufacturers, distributors, or retailers. Other factors affecting the nature of selling jobs are the customer's relationship to the salesperson's firm, the salesperson's duties, the importance of the buying decision to the customer, the place where the selling occurs, the tangibility of the benefits considered by the customer, and the degree to which the salesperson seeks a commitment from customers.

Research on the characteristics of effective salespeople indicates that many different personality types can be successful in sales. However, successful salespeople do share some common characteristics: They are highly motivated, dependable, ethical, knowledgeable, good communicators, flexible, and emotionally intelligent.

KEY TERMS

distribution channel 12
emotional intelligence 22
field salespeople 16
inside salespeople 16
integrated marketing communications 9
learning organization 6

manufacturers' agents 14
missionary salesperson 14
personal selling 4
retail salespeople 12
trade salespeople 13

QUESTIONS AND PROBLEMS

1. What personal benefits can you get from taking a personal selling course?

2. Chris James has been teaching history in high school for two years since graduating college. He is considering taking a job with a pharmaceutical company. The job involves calling on doctors and explaining the benefits of the firm's products. What are the similarities and differences between his teaching job and the selling job he is considering?

3. How do you think the training programs for a sales position differ in a stockbrokerage firm and a capital equipment manufacturer (e.g., General Electric's robotics division)? Consider the programs in terms of length and content.

4. Do you think going to college helps a person become a more effective salesperson? Why or why not?

5. Cal Hernandez worked his way through college by selling in a local department store. He has done well on the job and is one of the top salespeople in the jewelry department. Last week, Cal was offered a job with Revlon in trade selling. After training, he will be responsible for selling Revlon products to small, owner-operated drugstores. Explain to him the differences between selling in a department store and his Revlon sales job.

6. Discuss the following myths about selling:

   a. Salespeople do not serve a useful role in society.

   b. Salespeople are born, not made.

   c. Selling is just a bag of tricks.

   d. A salesperson should never take no for an answer.

   e. A good salesperson can sell anything to anybody.

7. What rewards does a selling career offer?

8. Some outstanding salespeople are poor sales managers. Why? Compare and contrast the skills needed in sales with those needed in sales management.

9. Would society benefit if large insurance companies decided to eliminate all of their salespeople and sell insurance through the mail at a lower price to the customer?

10. Many people have a negative impression of salespeople and careers in selling. Why do you think this negative opinion exists?

11. Assume you are a sales manager and you need to recruit someone for the following sales positions. For each position, list the qualities you would want in the recruit.

    a. Salesperson selling computers to businesses.

    b. College textbook salesperson.

    c. Used-car salesperson.

    d. Salesperson selling laundry detergent to supermarkets.

EXPLORING THE NET

Some organizations and trade publications that focus on personal selling and sales management have sites on the Internet. Visit the following sites and report on what the important current issues in personal selling and sales management are.

Sales & Marketing Management Magazine
http://www.smmmag.com/billcomm.htm

Selling Power Magazine
http://www.sellingpower.com

Marketing Times Magazine
http://www.smei.org/MT/index.html

National Association of Sales Professionals
http://www.nasp.com

Sales and Marketing Executives International
http://www.smei.org

In this chapter, we mentioned that one of the characteristics of effective salespeople is emotional intelligence. You can learn more about emotional intelligence and take short tests to measure your own emotional intelligence at the following sites:

http://www.utne.com/cgi-bin/eq

http://www.swiftsite/isaei/index.html

CASE PROBLEMS

CASE 1.1
Justin Diamond Takes a Course in Selling

Justin Diamond is a sophomore at Piedmont Junior College. He is talking with a group of friends about his selling course.

JUDY JAMISON Why are you taking that selling course?

JUSTIN Well, I've been thinking about what I would like to do when I graduate. I thought I might go into sales. So I took the course to see what it was all about. I really like the course.

ABBIE RODGERS But you've spent two years in college. Some of my friends went to work as salespeople in our local department store after graduation. You don't need a college education to be a salesperson.

JUSTIN I think there are a lot of sales jobs that do require a college degree. Maybe some of the jobs are different than selling in a department store.

JUDY You really have to be pushy to be a good salesperson. I just don't want to have to twist someone's arm to buy something. I am not the sales type. I like people and care about them too much.

ABBIE But you sure wouldn't get bored. You meet new people all the time. Each sales call is different. I can see why Justin likes the course.

JUSTIN But I guess I'm like Judy. I can't keep a poker face. And I blush whenever I try to hide the truth. How can I succeed in sales if I'm so transparent?

ABBIE I don't know. I think you could learn to control your feelings more with experience.

JUDY How about the workload? You'd be on the road all the time, with no time for family life.

ABBIE At least you'd have an exciting job. Who wants a nine-to-five job sitting behind a desk? And think of all those weekday afternoons that you can take off and go sailing!

JUSTIN My parents are really against my going into sales. They say that people don't respect salespeople.

Questions

1. How would you reply to each statement made by Justin and his friends?

2. What could you tell Justin to help him understand his friends' and parents' views on selling?

CASE 1.2
Ray Patel Develops a Marketing Plan for His New Internet Business

Ray Patel has just completed his MBA at the University of Illinois. In the last semester of the program, Ray took a course on entrepreneurship. During the class, Ray worked with a team of other students to develop a plan for a business he wants to start when he graduates. His idea is to provide a service to businesses: the design of home pages (locations in cyberspace on the Internet) for businesses. The sites would have interesting graphics and text describing the product and services offered by the businesses. The price for designing a home page for a business ranges from $1,000 to $50,000 depending on the amount of information and graphics the firm wants.

Ray is very interested in technology. He has an undergraduate degree in computer sciences and has been fascinated by the rapid increase in Internet surfing to search for information. Ray is a creative multimedia computer programmer. He has developed some unique techniques for incorporating three-dimensional diagrams and full-motion videos. His classmates frequently comment that his personal home page, which he designed, is very exciting and attractive.

Based on some market research performed by the group, Ray is confident that the demand for his service is significant and that he can easily generate $500,000 in sales during the first year. His parents are willing to lend him $75,000 to start his business.

Ray's concern is to tell people about his service and his capabilities and then convince them to buy the service from him. Ray is not very confident in his ability to sell the service to businesses himself. He is very good at analyzing business situations, had excellent grades in his MBA program, but is not very aggressive.

He has thought about hiring a salesperson, but the people he thought had the skills needed to sell his service wanted to make $75,000 a year. They were willing to work on a 20 percent commission, but Ray thought that was too much money to pay just to sell his service. Rather than paying for a salesperson, he is considering making up a home page for his business and describing the service on it. He also plans to make up a brochure describing his service and mail the brochure to potential customers. The cost for advertising on his home page and through direct mail is less than $10,000—about a tenth of the cost of hiring a salesperson.

Questions

1. What should Ray do to communicate his new service to prospects?

2. Should he emphasize personal selling, direct mail, or electronic advertising? Why?

ADDITIONAL REFERENCES

Brooksbank, Rodger. "The New Model of Personal Selling: Micromarketing." *Journal of Personal Selling and Sales Management*, Spring 1995, pp. 61–66.

Cespedes, Frank. "Industrial Marketing: Managing New Requirement." *Sloan Management Review*, Spring 1994, pp. 45–60.

Cravens, David. "The Changing Role of the Sales Force." *Marketing Management*, Fall 1995, pp. 49–57.

Dorsey, David. *The Force.* New York: Random House, 1994.

Dubinsky, Alan. "What Marketers Can Learn from the Tin Man." *Journal of Services Marketing*, 2, 1, 1994, pp. 9–20.

Hise, Richard, and Edward Reid. "Improving Performance of the Industrial Salesforce in the 1990's." *Industrial Marketing Management*, October 1994, pp. 273–79.

Kelly, Robert. "Toward a More Diverse Salesforce." *Sales & Marketing Management*, March 1994, p. 34.

Simintras, A. C.; G. A. Lancaster; and J. W. Cadogan. "Perceptions and Attitudes of Salespeople Towards the Overall Sales Job and the Work Itself." *Journal of Managerial Psychology*, 9, 7, 1994, pp. 3–10.

Sujan, Harish; Barton Weitz; and Nirmalya Kumar. "Learning Orientation, Working Smart, and Effective Selling." *Journal of Marketing*, July 1994, pp. 39–52.

Strale, William; Rosann Spiro; and Fran Acito. "Marketing and Sales: Strategic Alignment and Functional Implementation." *Journal of Personal Selling and Sales Management*, Winter 1996, pp. 1–20.

Swenson, Michael; William Swinyard; Fredrick Langrehr; and Scott Smith. "The Appeal of Personal Selling as a Career: A Decade Later." *Journal of Personal Selling and Sales Management,* Winter 1993, pp. 51–64.

"The Top 25 Sales Forces," *Sales & Marketing Management,* November 1996, pp. 38.

Trumfio, Ginger. "The Future Is Now." *Sales & Marketing Management,* November 1994, pp. 74–78.

Visanathan, Madhubalan, and Eric Olson. "The Implementation of Business Strategy: Implications for the Sales Function." *Journal of Personal Selling and Sales Management,* Winter 1993, pp. 34–50.

Chapter Two

Building Partnering Relationships

Paul Baron, vice president of sales and marketing at Quaker Oats, emphasizes the changing nature of the selling environment: "The complexity of the sale has intensified tremendously in the last 5 or 10 years. There's no longer a homogeneous sale. Every single sales event is an event itself. It's no longer just a product and a program. Now it's

Some Questions Answered in this Chapter Are:

How has the nature of personal selling changed over time?

What different types of relationships exist between buyers and sellers?

What are the characteristics of successful partnerships?

What are the benefits and risks in partnering relationships?

How do relationships develop over time?

What are the new responsibilities of salespeople in the partnering era?

starting to be a product, the financial package around it, and how you can deliver."

Buyers are demanding higher levels of service and product quality from fewer suppliers than ever before. To compete in this complex and dynamic environment, companies are looking for partners to help gain an advantage over their competitors. For example, companies involved with the Internet, from Netscape to Microsoft, are partnering with Sun Microsystems to utilize Java in their applications.

In the first chapter, we briefly discussed the activities of salespeople in general. In this chapter, we explore in more depth the role of salespeople in building relationships in the partnering era. We begin by examining the different types of exchange relationships in which salespeople are involved. Then we review the characteristics of successful buyer-seller relationships. We conclude with a review of how relationships develop over time and the activities salespeople perform in relationship development. The specific activities salespeople engage in to develop and maintain good relationships with customers are discussed in more detail in Chapter Thirteen.

PROFILE

"In my opinion, the selling function at General Motors emphasizes the need to build a partnering relationship with the independent businesspeople who comprise our dealer network," says Cecilia Pomes de Fueslein. Pomes de Fueslein has been with GM for the past nine years, having joined the automotive sales leader after completing, with honors, an MBA with a concentration in marketing at Mercer University in Atlanta. Prior to that, Pomes de Fueslein obtained a BA in business from the University of Medellin in Colombia, where she also worked for Scott Paper Company for three years.

". . . the ideal situation is one where we work together as partners, not in a legal sense, but in the sense that we each do our part to attain mutually beneficial outcomes."

CECILIA POMES DE FUESLEIN
General Motors

them as *partners* who help us achieve our mutual objectives. After all, our survival depends on the ability of our dealers to successfully accomplish their own goals. In fact, the ideal situation is one where we work together as partners, not in a legal sense, but in the sense that we each do our part to attain mutually beneficial outcomes.

At GM, Pomes de Fueslein began her career in the marketing and product planning department at the GMC Truck Division, based in Pontiac, Michigan. In that position, she had the complete planning responsibility for the midsize and full-size van lines.

"My experience in the market planning function helped me significantly with my next assignment, as a district sales manager in charge of 50 dealerships in Texas," she says. "I understood the importance of bringing a strategic focus to my job as a sales consultant to our dealers. At GM, we view our distribution system as an area in which we have, and should maintain, a distinctive competency. So we realize the need to carefully nurture the relationship we have with our dealers. It is extremely important that we treat

"In today's environment, we are often in a situation where the demand for our truck products exceeds our available supply. Therefore, it is critical that we have open communication and foster trust with our dealer network. One of the key responsibilities of a district sales manager is to assist dealers in developing business plans to increase sales and profits, while ensuring that GM's divisional goals are met. To help on that end, we provide sales training and dealership management training for the dealership salespeople and business planning personnel. We also support the dealer marketing groups in their advertising and promotional efforts. Finally, we must, on an ongoing basis, facilitate communication between the dealer and division to resolve conflicts and improve dealer and customer satisfaction.

"This is a very challenging job because we are dealing with independent investors and must try to assist them to overcome the many external factors that might present roadblocks to reaching our goals. So we have to be cognizant, for example, of the regulations, laws, and environmental concerns that affect our planning.

"The reward for me is knowing that I am a part of making something happen, that I am helping in the implementation of a vision for tomorrow, and that what I do has a positive impact in terms of affecting our business relationships with the dealers."

Pomes de Fueslein recently joined the newly created Pontiac/GMC dealer development team as a dealer network manager, where she will help spearhead GM's effort to plan, evaluate, and coordinate the strategic relocation of Pontiac/GMC sales and service outlets in a 15-state area.

Visit Our Website@
http://www.gm.com

THE EVOLUTION OF PERSONAL SELLING

The nature of business and the role of salespeople have changed a lot in this century. Bill Gardner, a retired computer salesperson, confesses that "I sold systems that people didn't want, didn't need, and couldn't afford." At one time, Gardner would have been admired for his skill in convincing customers to buy things they did not need. Now Gardner's statement is embarrassing to many professional salespeople.[1] Exhibit 2.1 illustrates how the role of the salesperson has evolved from taking orders through persuading customers to building partnerships.[2]

Production Orientation

Prior to 1930, demand for products exceeded supply. Competition was limited. Manufacturers focused on making products. They had little concern for buyers' needs and developing products to satisfy those needs. For example, Henry Ford made one car, the Model T, in one color, black. The role of **production-oriented salespeople** who dominated this time period was taking orders.

Traditionally, telephone sales reps (left) and automobile salespeople (center) have engaged in market relationships with their customers, while the ARA account managers (right) build partnering relationship with private label buyers from department store chains. However, even telephone reps and automobile salespeople are now placing more emphasis on long-term customer relationships.

Stretch Tuemmler

Christopher Bissell/Tony Stone Images

Courtesy ARA Services

EXHIBIT 2.1		Production	Sales	Marketing	Partnering
The Evolution of Personal Selling	**Time Period**	Before 1930	1930 to 1960	1960 to 1990	After 1990
	Objective	Making sales	Making sales	Satisfying customer needs	Building relationships
	Orientation	Short-term seller needs	Short-term seller needs	Short-term customer needs	Long-term customer and seller needs
	Role of Salesperson	Provider	Persuader	Problem solver	Value creator
	Activities of Salespeople	Taking orders, delivering goods	Aggressively convincing buyers to buy products	Matching available offerings to buyer needs	Creating new alternatives, matching buyer needs with seller capabilities

Sales Orientation

After the stock market crash in 1929, the sellers' market shifted to a buyers' market. There were not enough customers to buy all of the products manufactured. Competition among manufacturers increased significantly.

The role of **sales-oriented salespeople** developed in this time period to create demand for products. To persuade customers that they needed a supplier's products, salespeople relied on aggressive selling techniques. The salesperson's job was to coax customers to buy the company's products even if the customers did not want or need them—the type of selling Bill Gardner did.

Marketing Era

During the **marketing era** in the late 1950s and the 1960s, the marketing concept emerged as a response to increased customer sophistication and competition. The **marketing concept** is a business philosophy emphasizing that the key to business success is satisfying customer needs. According to this philosophy, all employees, not just marketers and salespeople, orient themselves toward satisfying customer needs. Engineers design products customers want, not products that are challenging to design. Production people build products that customers need, not products that are easy to manufacture. **Marketing-oriented salespeople** emerged in this time period as problem solvers. They were responsible for identifying the customer's needs and demonstrating how their products will satisfy those needs.

Selling became much more complex. Salespeople developed greater product knowledge and better communication skills. Firms began to use specialized sales forces. For example, some computer manufacturers had separate sales forces calling on financial services, retailing, manufacturing, and government customers.

Marketing-oriented salespeople often are responsible for employing all of their company's resources to solve a customer's problem. For example, an AT&T account executive manages a team of 80 people, including experts in accounting, finance, engineering, and marketing, to ensure that Merrill Lynch's needs for telecommunication services are being satisfied.

Partnering Era

In the early 1990s, both sellers and buyers recognized that they could develop strategic advantages over their competitors by working together. Rather than treating suppliers as interchangeable parts, manufacturers developed close, long-term relationships with a few suppliers. By freely exchanging sensitive information, the suppliers could develop products specifically tailored to the manufacturers' needs.[3]

Partnering-oriented salespeople are value creators. These salespeople work with their customers and their companies to develop solutions that enhance the profits of both. In this capacity, salespeople have two roles. First, they develop an understanding of each customer's needs and convince the customer that their firm has the capabilities to satisfy those needs. Then they go back to their company and arrange for the firm's employees to create an offering tailored to the customer's needs.

Raymond Catledge, CEO of Union Camp, emphasizes this point: "Good salespeople do much more than talk with customers. One of the toughest jobs salespeople have is to sell their own company. It's their job to articulate their customers' needs in a way their company can satisfy them."[4] (In Chapter Seventeen, we discuss internal selling in more detail.)

The objective of the partnering-oriented salesperson is to develop long-term relationships with customers. These relationships are similar to close friendships. They involve commitments by both parties to work together in a mutually beneficial manner. The parties focus on long-term outcomes and do not quibble about short-term problems.

As Exhibit 2.1 shows, the orientations of salespeople emerged in different time periods. However, all of these selling orientations still exist in business today. For example, inbound telephone salespeople working for direct-mail catalog retailers like Lands End and Spiegel are providers with a production orientation. They answer an 800 number and simply take orders. Many outbound telephone, real estate, and insurance salespeople are persuaders with a sales orientation. They use high pressure selling techniques to get prospects to place orders. However, partnering-oriented selling is becoming more and more common in business today. Selling Scenario 2.1 illustrates how even traditional high-pressure auto salespeople are embracing partnership selling.

Even though many sales jobs do not involve building long-term partnerships, we stress the concept of developing partnering relationships throughout this textbook because the roles of salespeople in many companies are evolving toward a partnering orientation. For example, when Franklin Green became the sales manager for the Fiber Glass Reinforcement Division of PPG Industries, the sales force was "a group of order takers and goodwill ambassadors." He immediately created a stronger selling orientation by developing a plan for scheduling sales calls on customers and teaching salespeople to use time management techniques. Green then started transforming the sales force into problem solvers by training salespeople to recognize how changing technology would create new needs for their customers. Salespeople were required to interview customers and develop work plans outlining those needs. Now PPG is emphasizing a partnering orientation. Sales teams are created to work with each customer. The teams work with each customer's development staff to create and test products designed for the customer's applications. Green sums up the new role of the salesperson as a value creator: "The pivotal function of the sales organization is to exercise leadership with, and on behalf of, the customer. If the overall organization was to be truly customer driven, the sales force had to assume this vital role."[5]

The concept of partnership selling is discussed throughout the book. However, this chapter focuses on the nature and development of partnering relationships,

SELLING   SCENARIO   2 . 1

Automobile Salespeople Change from Pressuring to Partnering

Automobile selling traditionally has been based on the use of high-pressure tactics to "move the metal." Horace Hull and James Dobbs, two Memphis auto dealers, developed the "good guy-bad guy" approach used by most dealerships. The salesperson is on the customer's side, negotiating an initial price; then the sales manager takes over as the "bad guy," bumping the price higher.

This selling-oriented approach moves the metal but does not make customers happy or build long-term relationships. Only 35 percent of the auto buyers surveyed felt they were well treated by the dealer, and 21 percent rated the dealer as having excellent or very good integrity. Customers think they got a good deal until they walk out the door and look inside to see salespeople doing "high fives."

Saturn dealers and used-car superstores like CarMax are changing the way cars are sold. They are emphasizing customer satisfaction as a step toward building repeat business and favorable word of mouth. There is no haggling over price for a Saturn or a used car at CarMax. The price you pay is the price on the sticker. But that's just one part of the change.

Saturn is committed to ensuring that buyers are satisfied customers. When you pick up your new car, representatives from sales, service, and parts gather around to give you the keys and assure you of their support in the future. When you take your car in for service, it is cleaned, vacuumed, and even polished when returned.

And the salespeople have a better frame of mind. Brian Jamison, a Saturn dealer sales manager, says, "I was planning to get out of this business. I couldn't stand all of the games we played with customers. This way feels a lot better."

Sources: Keith Naughton, "The Revolution in the Showroom," *Business Week,* February 19, 1996, pp. 70–76; Jaclyn Fierman, "The Death and Rebirth of the Salesman," *Fortune,* July 25, 1994, pp. 80–91; Jack Falvey, "The Selling of Saturn," *Sales & Marketing Management,* October 1994, pp. 26, 30.

and Chapter Thirteen reviews the activities of salespeople in cultivating these relationships.

TYPES OF RELATIONSHIPS

Each time a transaction occurs between a buyer and a seller, the buyer and the seller have a relationship. Some relationships may involve many transactions and last for years; others may exist only for the few minutes during which the exchange of goods for money is made.

This section describes three basic relationship types and their distinguishing characteristics. These relationships include market exchanges, functional relationships, and strategic partnerships.[6] Exhibit 2.2 summarizes the characteristics of these relationship types.

Market Exchanges

A **market exchange** is a short-term transaction between a buyer and a seller who do not expect to be involved in future transactions with each other. For example, suppose you are driving on a highway to Florida for a spring vacation. The generator light in your car comes on. You stop at the next gas station, and the service attendant says your car needs a new generator. The generator will cost $250, including installation. At this point, you might pay the quoted price, bargain with the service attendant for a lower price, or drive to another service station a block away and get a second opinion. After you select a service station, agree on a price, have the gener-

Characteristics of the Relationship	Type of Relationship		
	Market Exchange	Functional Relationship	Strategic Partnerships
Time horizon	Short term	Long term	Long term
Concern for other party	Low	Medium	High
Trust	Low	High	High
Investment in relationship	Low	Medium	High
Nature of relationship	Conflict, bargaining	Cooperation	Collaboration
Risk in relationship	Low	Medium	High
Potential benefits	Low	Medium	High

ator replaced, and pay for the service, you have completed a market exchange. Neither you nor the service station attendant expects to engage in future transactions.

Because the parties in the transaction do not plan on doing business together again, both the buyer and the seller in a market exchange pursue their own self-interests. In the example above, you try to pay the lowest price for the generator and the service station tries to charge the highest price for it. The service station is not concerned about your welfare, just as you are not concerned about the service station's welfare.

Sometimes firms engage in a series of market exchanges over a long period of time because the buyers find it easier to buy repeatedly from the same supplier rather than search for a new supplier every time they need an item. For example, a NYNEX buyer purchases office supplies—paper, file folders, pens, and pencils—for the company. However, the buyer and the office supply distributor have little interest in working closely together. The relationship between the buyer and the distributor's salesperson is not critical to NYNEX's survival as a corporation. The purchase and sale of office supplies is routine. The buyer can decide to deal with another distributor. However, the buyer probably will switch suppliers only if problems arise. Thus, the salesperson's job in this type of relationship is to make sure these problems do not arise.

Even in these long-term market exchanges, both parties are interested primarily in their own profits and are unconcerned about the welfare of the other party. In market exchanges, price is the critical decision factor. It serves as a rapid means of communicating the bases for the exchange. Basically, the buyer and the salesperson in a market exchange are always negotiating over how to "split up the pie"—who is going to make more in the transaction. Thus, a market exchange is a **win-lose relationship,** because when one party gets a larger portion of the pie, the other party gets a smaller portion.

On the positive side, market exchanges offer buyers and sellers a lot of flexibility. Buyers and sellers are not locked into a continuing relationship, and thus buyers can switch from one supplier to another to make the best possible deal. However, these minimal relationships do not work well when buyers and sellers have an opportunity to increase the size of the pie by developing products and services tailored to their needs. These more complex transactions cannot be conducted solely on the basis of price. A high level of trust and commitment is needed to manage these types of relationships, since buyers and sellers need to share sensitive information.

**Long-Term
Relationships**

Market exchanges represent a small portion of the transactions between buyers and sellers. Most transactions between buyers and sellers involve long-term relationships. These long-term relationships are **win-win relationships.** By working together, both parties benefit because the size of the pie increases. Two types of long-term relationships are functional relationships and strategic partnerships.

Functional Relationships

Functional relationships are long-term business relationships in which the buyer and the salesperson have a close personal relationship that allows them to communicate effectively. These personal relationships create a cooperative climate between the salesperson and the customer. When both partners feel safe and stable in the relationship, open and honest communication takes place. Salesperson and buyer work together to solve important problems. They are not concerned about little details because they trust each other enough to know these will be worked out.

The benefits of a functional relationship go beyond simple increased short-term profits. Although both partners are striving to make money in the relationship, they are also trying to build a working relationship that will last a long time. For example, Bill Stack, manager of the Eastern Communication Region for General Electric's Information Services in Louisville, Kentucky, reports: "We had a client who was a vice president when his company became involved in a leveraged buyout. He was forced out of his job. Our sales rep actually carried the guy's résumé around for months trying to help him connect with another job. Eventually, our client wound up with a small pharmaceutical company that was about to place an order with another vendor. He flew to the home office in London, stopped the order, and gave it to our sales rep strictly on the basis of their relationship and our past performance. That sale wound up being worth close to half a million dollars."[7]

In this chapter we talk about business relationships, but these concepts also apply to personal relationships. A functional relationship is like a close friendship. In a close friendship, you are not concerned with how the "pie is split up" each day because you are confident that, over the long run, each of you will get a fair share. You trust your friend to care about you, and she or he trusts you in return. The founder of the country's largest department store chain, James Cash Penney, once said, "All great businesses are built on friendship."

Functional relationships, like close personal relationships, can be very rewarding. Due to the honest, straightforward communications, the parties can reduce the buying cost and time. However, these relationships carry risks. The buyers and the sellers often must make short-term sacrifices. A buyer may have to wait longer for the delivery of some components because the buyer recognizes that the supplier is having trouble with some new equipment. The buyer accepts the late delivery, trusting that the supplier will return the favor. For example, next year there may be a shortage of the components. The supplier will help the buyer out and make sure the buyer gets all of the components needed.

**Strategic
Partnerships**

Strategic partnerships are long-term business relationships in which the partners make significant investments to improve the profitability of both parties. In these relationships, the partners have gone beyond trusting each other to "putting their money where their mouths are." They take risks to expand the pie, to give the partnership a strategic advantage over other companies.[8]

Starbucks has a partnering relationship with United Airlines. Both parties have invested in the relationship and benefit from it. Starbucks sells more coffee and United Airlines provides better services for it customers.

We're about to give airplane coffee a good name.

United is now serving Starbucks® coffee in every class, on every flight worldwide. An improvement that makes perfect sense, coming from the more than 50,000 employees who own United. After all, we don't just work here. We drink the coffee, too. Come fly our friendly skies.

UNITED AIRLINES

Courtesy United Airlines

For example, Michael DiMartino, national account executive at Starbucks, developed a strategic relationship with United Airlines. United agreed to serve Starbucks coffee exclusively on all of it flights, and Starbucks developed a special blend available only on United flights. Starbucks went the extra mile to make the partnership work. "A lot of companies will roast coffee and ship it to you, but we were interested in training flight attendants and inspecting and modifying the on-board brewing equipment," DiMartino says. Through the partnership, United is able to increase the satisfaction of its customers by giving them an excellent cup of coffee and Starbucks sells more coffee.[9]

Strategic partnerships are created for the purpose of uncovering and exploiting joint opportunities.[10] Members of strategic partnerships have a high level of dependence on and trust in each other, share goals and agree on how to accomplish those goals, and show a willingness to take risks, share confidential information, and make significant investments for the sake of the relationship.

Wollin, a small plastic parts manufacturer, developed a strategic relationship with Whirlpool, a much larger corporation. Whirlpool shared confidential information with Wollin about its design plans for a new, energy-efficient washing machine. With this information, Wollin used its expertise to develop some plastic parts tailored to the design plans. These unique parts were superior to the standard parts that could be purchased from other parts suppliers. Whirlpool took a risk in sharing the information about its new product and eventually buying parts that were available from only one supplier. Wollin took a risk in designing parts without a firm order and producing parts that could be sold to only one customer. However, by taking these risks, the performance and eventual sales of the new washing machine were enhanced and both parties benefited.[11]

Similarly, Levi Strauss teams worked with JCPenney to create a specially designed area in its stores to display Dockers merchandise. Then teams from each company developed sophisticated inventory control systems to make sure the stores were always stocked with the styles and sizes that were selling well. As a result, JCPenney is now Levi Strauss's largest customer worldwide. JCPenney also increased its own profits, because it was able to offer a unique display and in-stock merchandise to its customers that were not available from competitive department stores.[12]

Moving from a functional relationship to a strategic partnership is like moving from steady dating to marriage. When businesses enter into strategic partnerships, they are wedded to their partners for better or worse. For example, if the Dockers merchandise had not sold well, both JCPenney and Levi Strauss would have lost money. Strategic partnerships are risky, and they reduce flexibility. Once JCPenney formed a true strategic partnership with Levi Strauss, it could not "date around" with Levi Strauss's competitors.

 In cultures outside the United States, long-term relationships are very important. In Japan, for example, several organizations may join together to form a *keiretsu,* or family of companies. These families of companies may include a bank, a transportation company, a manufacturing company, and distribution companies that share risks and rewards and jointly develop plans to exploit market opportunities. Keiretsus are thus strategic partnerships among several companies rather than between only two.

Summary

Most salespeople are involved in either market exchanges or functional relationships. Strategic partnerships are rare. Exhibit 2.3 illustrates the differences in the nature of selling in market exchanges and long-term relationships.

Each of these types of relationships has its pluses and minuses.[13] Companies cannot develop a strategic advantage from a market exchange, but they do get the flexibility to buy products from the supplier with the lowest cost when the order is placed. On the other hand, strategic partnerships create a win-win situation, but the companies are committed to each other and flexibility is reduced. In the next section, we talk about the characteristics of successful relationships, relationships that have the potential to develop into strategic partnerships.

Thinking *it* Through

Consider the relationships you have with other people. Which relationships are like market exchanges, functional relationships, and strategic partnerships? Think about a close relationship you have. How did it develop? How do you and the other person act differently in this relationship than you both do in other relationships with passing acquaintances?

CHARACTERISTICS OF SUCCESSFUL RELATIONSHIPS

A good long-term relationship satisfies the goals of both parties. Some companies use the term *partnering* but do not really understand what it means. For example, Allan Weydahl, a regional sales director at Nalco, likes to work with a customer that says, " 'Please quit talking about money, that's not the issue we're talking about. We're talking about product and how you're going to get it here and how

EXHIBIT 2.3	Market Exchange Selling Goal: Making a Sale	Long-Term Relationship Selling Goal: Building Trust
Selling in Market Exchanges and Long-Term Relationships	**Making Contact** • Find someone to listen • Make small talk • Ingratiate and build rapport	**Initiating the Relationship** • Engage in strategic prospecting and qualifying • Gather and study precall information • Identify buying influences • Plan the initial sales call • Demonstrate an understanding of the customer's needs • Identify opportunities to build a relation ship • Illustrate the value of a relationship with the customer

	Closing the Sale
	• Delivering a sales pitch to:
	  • Get the prospect's attention
	  • Create interest
	  • Build desire
	  • Get the prospect to take action
	• Stay alert for closing signals
	• Use trial closes
	• Overcome objections
	• Close early and often
		Developing the Relationship
		• Select an appropriate offering
		• Customize the relationship
		• Link the solution to the customer's needs
		• Discuss customer concerns
		• Summarize the solution to confirm benefits
		• Secure commitment

	Following Through • Reestablish contact • Resell self, company, and products	**Enhancing the Relationship** • Assess customer satisfaction • Take actions to ensure satisfaction • Maintain open, two-way communications • Expand collaborative involvement • Work to add value and enhance mutual opportunities

Source: Adapted from Thomas Ingram, "Relationship Selling: Moving from Rhetoric to Reality," *Mid-American Journal of Business,* 11 (1996), p. 6.

we're going to use it.' That kind of partner is a joy to do business with. On the other hand, you get a company that calls us in and says 'We want a partnership,' and what they really want is to use their purchasing power to get the lowest possible price."[14]

Successful relationships involve cultivating the *mutual* benefits as the partners learn to trust and depend on each other more and more. As trust develops, buyer and salesperson are able to resolve conflicts as they arise, settle differences, and compromise when necessary. The foundations of successful, long-term relationships are (1) mutual trust, (2) open communication, (3) common goals, (4) a commitment to mutual gain, and (5) organizational support (see Exhibit 2.4).

Mutual Trust

The key to the development of successful, long-term customer relationships is trust. Lou Pritchett, former senior vice president of sales at Procter & Gamble, once said, "Cost reduction throughout the total system can be accomplished when trust replaces skepticism. Trusting suppliers, customers, and employees is one of the most effective, yet most underutilized, techniques available to management."[15]

EXHIBIT 2.4

Foundations of Successful Relationships

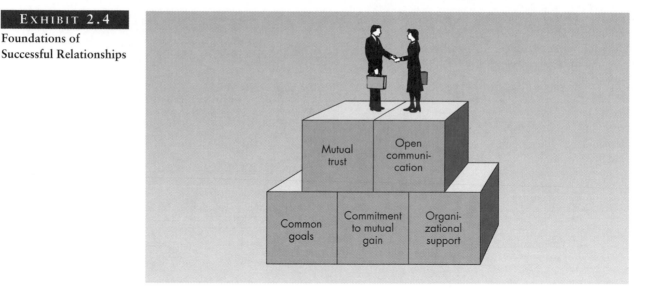

What Is Trust?

Trust is a belief by one party that the other party will fulfill its obligations in a relationship.[16] Three aspects of trust are perceived dependability, capability or expertise, and concern for the other party. Buyers trust salespeople when they are confident that the salespeople will follow through on their promises and commitments. To develop this confidence, the buyers must believe the salespeople and the salespeople's companies have the capability to meet their commitments. Finally, the buyers need to believe that the salespeople are concerned about the buyers' interests. Thus, if special circumstances arise and the initial promises need to be changed, the salespeople will consider the buyers' interests under the new circumstances.

When salespeople and buyers trust each other, they are more willing to share relevant ideas, clarify goals and problems, and communicate more efficiently. Information shared between the parties becomes increasingly comprehensive, accurate, and timely. There is less need for salesperson and buyer to constantly monitor and check up on each other's actions, because both believe the other party would not take advantage of them if given the opportunity.[17]

Without trust, the salesperson and the buyer are unlikely to take the risks associated with working closely together to achieve mutually beneficial outcomes, such as reducing distribution costs or improving product development. For example, an apparel manufacturer wants to deliver new styles to its customers faster. To achieve this goal, it must get cooperation from its suppliers. The manufacturer has a better chance of realizing its goal by approaching a supplier that can see the benefits of working together with the manufacturer and is willing to take a chance and alter its normal routines. If the manufacturer and the supplier trust each other, they will be more willing to try new and different ways of doing business, because each knows that its partner is similarly committed to the relationship. Further, they believe that any gains and losses resulting from their partnership will even out over the long run, so they are not afraid to sustain a short-term loss for the sake of gaining a greater long-term advantage.

Baxter cements its partnership with the Seton Medical Center by committing its employees to delivering medical supplies directly to hospital floors. To provide this service, Baxter trains its employees on the unique supply needs and procedures of the Seton Medical Center.

John Storey

Developing Trust

Buyers develop trust in salespeople when the salespeople consistently take the buyers' needs and interests into account. For example, salespeople who have a track record of consistent deliveries and reliable performance and who cultivate a positive, interpersonal relationship with their customers earn valuable trust.

Today's customers are especially sensitive to signs of unreliable performance. Unreliable performance, lack of smooth coordination, or an inability to communicate in a timely and accurate manner are signals that a long-term relationship may be difficult to successfully implement and manage over time.

Salespeople develop trust by going beyond the buyer's expectations. For example, John Dowling, a commercial real estate agent, negotiated a generous electricity allowance for one of his clients. The credit was to be applied to overtime air-conditioning charges, but when the bill came in, the credit Dowling had expected wasn't there; the electricity usage was much higher than he had expected. To find out why, Dowling flew to New Orleans to check the client's meters. He took a hotel room across from the client's building and observed the building. He found five full floors of lights kept on at night. So the client began turning the lights off in the evenings, but the results still didn't satisfy Dowling. He sent in a team to investigate and ultimately wound up installing motion detectors to help control the utility usage. Dowling's efforts to go the extra mile on a customer's behalf enabled him to create an incredible level of trust with his customers.[18]

Open Communication

Open and honest communication is a key building block for developing successful relationships. Buyers and salespeople in a relationship need to understand what is driving each other's business, their roles in the relationship, each firm's strategies, and any problems that arise over the course of the relationship.

Customer knowledge facilitates communications and builds trust. Ellen Manzo, an award-winning area manager at AT&T Computer Systems in Parsippany, New Jersey, explains, "It's critical to do a lot of account research, especially if you're servicing a small number of accounts. I go to the library, I go through Dun & Bradstreet and news clipping services, and I get the last 18 months of articles on the company. I buy a share of stock in the company so that I receive all the proxy statements and quarterly information. I try to get on the customer's mailing list." Manzo also requires all of her new salespeople to go through an extensive research exercise before they ever call on a customer, and she develops strategies for visits with her reps on major accounts.[19] (Chapter Five focuses on approaches for improving communications.)

Cultural differences in communication style can be easily misunderstood and thus hinder open and honest communications. For example, all cultures have ways to avoid saying *no* when they really mean no. In Japan, maintaining long-lasting, stable relationships is very important. To avoid damaging a relationship, customers rarely say *no* directly. Some phrases used in Japan to say *no* indirectly are "It's very difficult," "We'll think about it," and "I'm not sure," or leaving the room with an apology. In general, when Japanese customers do not say *yes* or *no* directly, it means they want to say *no*.[20]

Shared Goals

Salespeople and customers must have common goals for a successful relationship to develop. Shared goals give both members of the relationship a strong incentive to pool their strengths and abilities. When goals are shared, the partners can focus on exploiting opportunities rather than arguing about who will benefit the most from the relationship. Selling Scenario 2.2 illustrates how a Hewlett-Packard salesperson shares the same goals with her firm's partner, Texas Instruments.

When Johnson & Johnson (J&J) and Kmart commit to reducing out-of-stock occurrences at the store level, they both work toward this goal. J&J cannot fall behind on its shipments, and Kmart cannot be lackadaisical about getting the product on the shelf in a timely manner. A common goal gives both firms an incentive to cooperate, because they know that by doing so both will be able to achieve a higher level of sales than before.

Shared goals also help to sustain the partnership when the expected benefit flows are not realized. If one J&J shipment fails to reach a Kmart store on time due to an uncontrollable event, such as misrouting by a trucking firm, Kmart will not suddenly call off the whole arrangement. Instead, Kmart is likely to view the incident as a simple mistake and will remain in the relationship. Kmart knows J&J is committed to the same goal in the long run.

Clearly defined, measurable goals are also very important. Kmart and J&J might monitor the number of stockouts, late deliveries, order-processing time, and sales every week or month to assess how well they are meeting their goals. Without this information, there is a significant risk that the partners will not agree that anything was actually done.

Effective measuring of performance is particularly critical in the early stages of the partnership. The achievement of explicitly stated goals lays the groundwork for a history of shared success, which serves as a powerful motivation for continuing the relationship and working closely together into the future.

Commitment to Mutual Gain

Members of successful partnerships actively work to create win-win relationships by looking for overlapping areas of opportunity in which both can prosper. For example, Clark Equipment Company manufactures forklift trucks, pallet trucks, and other mobile material-handling equipment. It recently began to integrate its partnering suppliers into its design process by sharing detailed information on costs, cost

Donna Crowell, Global Partner Manager

If you want to reach Donna Crowell, a Texas-based salesperson at Hewlett-Packard (HP), try calling her at Texas Instruments. Texas Instruments (TI) does a lot more than buy products from HP. It also makes software that runs on HP computers. Crowell is the global partner manager for the TI account, and her primary job is to make sure that HP computers are the primary platform for TI software. Since every sale of TI software is also a potential sale for HP computers, Crowell spends most of her time coordinating the efforts of HP and TI salespeople selling to end users. Her performance is measured by the sales generated through the relationship for both firms.

Crowell has to know as much about TI's business as she knows about HP's business. She works with a host of people at TI, from the president of the software division to the account managers and product develop-

ers. In her job, she has to wear multiple hats: "There are multiple people, multiple companies, and multiply products involved."

Cromwell uses all of her sales skills to sell people at HP on taking steps to build the HP-TI relationships. She works to make appointments, keeps in touch, and makes presentations to her internal customers on opportunities for TI and HP to do more business. She also knows the value of internal public relationships. When HP and TI land a big sale together, Crowell reports the deal in a newsletter that goes out to the HP sales force. "Salespeople love a success story," she says.

Source: Francy Blackwood, "Selling With vs. Selling To," *Selling,* December 1995, pp. 28–30. Reprinted with permission from Institutional Investors, Inc.

targets, profitability targets, and business strategies. By working closely with its suppliers, Clark improved its product quality and sales, which increased its orders for the vendors' products, outcomes that were mutually satisfying to both parties.[21]

The most successful relationships involve mutual dependency. One party is not more powerful than the other party. Mutual dependency creates a cooperative spirit. Both parties search for ways to expand the pie and minimize time spent on resolving conflicts over how to split it.

Credible Commitments

As a successful relationship develops, both parties make credible commitments to the relationship. **Credible commitments** are tangible investments in the relationship. They go beyond merely making the hollow statement "I want to be a partner." Credible commitments involve spending money to improve the products and services sold to the other party.[22] For example, a firm may hire or train employees, invest in equipment, and develop computer and communication systems to meet the needs of a specific customer. These investments signal the partner's commitment to the relationship in the long run.

Organizational Support

Another critical element in fostering good relationships is providing boundary-spanning employees—the purchasing agents and salespeople—with the necessary support.[23]

Structure and Culture

The organizational structure and management provide the necessary support for the salespeople and buyers in a partnering relationship. All employees in the firm need to "buy in," in other words, accept the salesperson's and buyer's roles in developing the partnership. Partnerships created at headquarters should be recognized and treated as such by local offices, and vice versa. Without the support of the respective companies, the partnership is destined to fail.

Firms interested in developing long-term customer relationships build a partnering culture throughout the organization. Creating and maintaining this culture can be difficult, however. Joe Durrett, senior vice president of sales at Kraft General Foods, notes that "the biggest difficulty is changing attitudes. You must reengineer what you have because there are no experienced salespeople you can bring into the company who relate to this team approach."[24] Selling Scenario 2.3 describes the resources Baxter Healthcare directs toward building relationships.

Training

Special training is required to sell effectively in a relationship-building environment. Salespeople need to be taught how to identify customer needs and work with the customer to achieve better performance.

Kraft General Foods (KGF) uses a program called Navigator to train its salespeople in partnering. In this program, salespeople pretend to work for a KGF clone, Pathfinder Foods. Pathfinder sells to three hypothetical customers: a traditional supermarket chain, a discounter, and a distributor to independent grocers. Salespeople are asked early on, "Which retailer has a competitive advantage in today's market?" Inevitably, every employee falls into the trap of trying to guess. No one ever gets it right. The right answer is that *all* of the customers have the opportunity to be suc-

To effectively build partnerships, salespeople must make sure that their products offer important benefits to their customers. Armstrong Tile salespeople hold training sessions for retailers to show them how to increase their profits by selling Armstrong tile.

Courtesy Armstrong World Industries, Inc.

Everyone at Baxter Healthcare Supports Partnership Selling

At hospital supply giant Baxter Health-care Corporation, the emphasis on partnering has, paradoxically "enabled us to increase our sales force at the same time that we have decreased it," says Baxter's senior vice president of quality leadership David Auld. Auld estimates that in the past several years, "We have taken about 40 percent out of our sales force staff. Instead of focusing on the use of sales reps, Baxter has formed a joint relationship at every significant level of the two organizations." In essence, every employee has taken on a sales role.

"Our senior people meet with the customer's senior people so that we understand what their mission is, what their strategy is, and what is important to them. Then we can go back and mobilize our resources to address those specifically," Auld explains. "At the other end of the spectrum, Baxter has its warehouse workers team up with those working in the warehouses at the hospitals that are Baxter customers, so that our warehouseman, our picker, now is a salesman. We now have designated pickers, people in our warehouses who are designated to serve specific hospitals as customers, and two or three times a month they will jump on the delivery truck and ride it to that customer." During those visits, the designated pickers study the customer warehouse operations to try to figure out how Baxter can pack its shipments to make it easier for the customers to unload, unpack, and distribute the Baxter deliveries.

"Baxter has found that these close relationships create a formidable competitive barrier," Auld explains. "They bind the customer to us and make it difficult for anyone who might try to take the business away. What we have found is that these nonsales relationships, which are focused on issues that are relevant to the customer, are among the strongest selling features that we have."

Source: B. G. Yovovich, "Partnering at Its Best," *Business Marketing*, March 1992, pp. 36–37. Reprinted with permission from *Business Marketing*.

cessful. Every salesperson should develop a unique sales strategy that will help his or her customer outsell its competition.[25]

Training is critical in helping salespeople identify ways to make it easier for the customer to do business with them. At Alcoa Aluminum, sales representatives are trained to look at what their customers do to a product that Alcoa could make for them. For example, one salesperson noticed that customers stack materials in skids in various-size stacks, sometimes 10 feet tall. When an order is pulled from inventory, a forklift driver must go into the stacks and pull a particular skid. Sometimes the skids are not stacked with a packing ticket on the outside, so the driver has a hard time identifying the right skid. Alcoa began to put a package ticket on both ends of the skid so that the driver can always see the package number, no matter how it is stacked.

Rewards

Reward systems on both sides of the relationship should be coordinated to encourage supportive behaviors. In the market exchanges, buyers are rewarded for wringing out concessions from the salespeople, and salespeople are rewarded on the basis of sales volume. In a partnering relationship, rewarding short-term behaviors can be detrimental. Thus, companies are beginning to reward salespeople and buyers based on the quality of the relationships they develop.[26]

SELLING SCENARIO 2.4

Selling in Japan

Chuck Laughlin, co-author of *Sumurai Selling: The Ancient Art of Service in Sales,* says that in Japan "a salesperson will spend a lot of time in the very early stages of developing a relationship and not even mention a company or product, [whereas] in the United States, the company and the product come out from the first call. We [in the United States] may be into the middle of the sales process within days [or] hours, whereas a Japanese selling person can spend a year building a relationship before beginning to introduce his product."

To make an initial contact with a customer, salespeople in Japan must have a formal introduction. For example, the president of the salesperson's company will make a formal request to the president of a potential customer firm to introduce his or her sales manager. After the sales manager makes the initial contact, she or he will introduce the salesperson.

To encourage salespeople to focus on the relationship and not just sales, Japanese companies pay their salespeople 100 percent salary, with no incentive or commission based on the amount they sell. Salespeople are often referred to as "salarymen."

Source: Paula Champa, "How to Sell in Japan," *Selling,* December 1993, pp. 39–47. Reprinted with permission from Institutional Investors, Inc.

For example, IBM changed its sales compensation to base bonuses and commissions on the profitability of the sales to IBM and the satisfaction of the customers buying IBM products and services. Salespeople are given information about product costs and some authority to adjust prices. Any price reductions salespeople make affect their compensation. In addition, customer satisfaction information is collected periodically, and 40 percent of the salesperson's compensation is based on the results of these surveys.[27]

SELLING IN A PARTNERING ERA

In the partnering era, salespeople are relationship managers. They are responsible for making sure that their companies develop the appropriate types of relationships with each customer. They are using increasingly sophisticated technologies to marshal their firms' resources toward solving customer problems and moving the relationships through the phases described in the previous section.

Many American firms are just entering the partnering era. Selling Scenario 2.4 describes how the concept of relationship building is critical in Japanese selling.

Relationship Managers

As more companies evolve into the partnering era, the terms *personal selling* and *salesperson* no longer represent what people in this position do and are. These employees are becoming **relationship managers** rather than simply salespeople. They are responsible for working with people in their companies to develop problem solutions.

Until recently, Procter & Gamble did not have good relationships with major retailers. Retailers considered P&G salespeople to be very knowledgeable, but often believed they were arrogant, dictated what products to stock and how to display them, and had little regard for the customer's needs. Now P&G salespeople manage employee teams that focus on developing good relationships with retailers. A team might include employees in finance, distribution, and manufacturing. When a major retailer complains about a late shipment, the P&G distribution team member talks to the retailer's transportation person to solve the problem.

Salespeople build partnering relationships using technology to provide answers to customer questions quickly and reliably.

Courtesy Ram Mobil Data

Using Technology to Increase Efficiency

Partnering relationships are built on effective communications. To improve communications with customers, salespeople are making greater use of computers, telecommunications, and videos.

Over 25 percent of the firms contacted in a recent survey used portable computers in their sales forces.[28] Computer use ranges from providing information during a sales call to analyzing a customer's problems. Ryder Truck developed a computer model that salespeople use to help customers compare the costs of leasing and purchasing trucks. The salesperson questions the customer about estimated mileage and the type of trucks needed, enters the answers into a laptop computer, hits a single key, and reviews the printout with the customer.

Companies are developing video presentations to demonstrate complex product benefits. According to Thomas Bird, president of Gould Inc.'s test and measurements division, "One of the problems in technical sales is that some salespeople do not exactly convey what the inventor or manufacturer had in mind when the product was designed." To overcome this problem, Gould spent $200,000 to produce videocassette presentations and $75,000 to equip salespeople with VCRs. The use of new technologies to improve selling effectiveness is discussed throughout the text.

Professionalism in Selling

As the rate of change in technology increases, products become more complex, and customers demand long-term relationships, salespeople need to develop a more professional approach to deal effectively with the business environment in the new millennium. A **professional** is someone who engages in an occupation requiring great skill or knowledge and whose capabilities are respected by co-workers and clients.

Most successful salespeople, like successful doctors and lawyers, possess the qualities of a professional: knowledge, concern for others, dependability, a personal code of ethics, maturity, and image.[29] In Chapter One, we discussed the importance of knowledge and continually learning, concern for others, a personal code of ethics, and dependability and trustworthiness as characteristics of successful salespeople.

Maturity

Mature people recognize that some of their experiences will be negative. Setbacks will occur in their personal lives and their careers. However, mature people do not focus on these disappointments. They use these more negative experiences as a basis for achieving success in the future.

Maturity is critical for salespeople, because they do not make a sale each time they contact a prospect. Failures are inevitable. The best hitters in baseball make an out 6 out of 10 times they come to bat. The professional salesperson, like the Hall of Fame hitter, is not discouraged by these outs.

Image

Self-image is the ideas and feelings that one has about oneself. These thoughts affect the way one processes information and interacts with other people. For example, consider salespeople who feel they are "failures." Instead of learning how to improve their skills and performance, these salespeople look for ways to fail.

On the other hand, professionals have a positive self-image. They have confidence in their abilities. This confidence can be developed over time by focusing on the future and past successes rather than on failures. Professionals treat failures as learning experiences. They analyze the failures to find out what they can do to improve their performance in the future. To develop this confidence, professionals are continually learning about their companies' products, their customers, and the industries. They attend seminars and read extensively. They are more concerned about learning and long-term performance than about making the sale tomorrow.[30]

SUMMARY

As we discussed in Chapter One, many businesses are moving from the marketing era into the partnering era. However, even in the partnering era, most transactions between buyers and sellers will not be strategic partnerships. Many exchanges will continue to be market transactions and functional relationships.

Functional relationships and strategic partnerships are characterized by a mutual concern of each party for the long-run welfare of the other party. Both of these types of long-term relationships are based on mutual trust. However, the strategic partnerships involve the greatest commitment because the parties are willing to make significant investments in the relationship.

Mutual trust, open communications, common goals, a commitment to mutual gain, and organizational support are key ingredients in successful relationships. These five factors form the foundation for win-win relationships between customers and salespeople.

Customers trust salespeople who they think are dependable, capable, and concerned about their welfare. To build trust, salespeople need to be consistent in meeting the commitments they make to customers. They also need to demonstrate their concern for the well-being of customers.

In the partnering era, firms view salespeople as relationship managers. They provide the resources and incentives to motivate salespeople to seek partnering relationships with customers. Salespeople who are successful in partnership selling are professionals just as doctors and lawyers are.

KEY TERMS

credible commitments 44	production-oriented salespeople 32
functional relationship 37	professional 48
market exchange 35	relationship manager 47
marketing concept 33	sales-oriented salespeople 33
marketing era 33	self-image 49
marketing-oriented salespeople 33	strategic partnership 37
maturity 49	trust 41
partnering era 34	win-lose relationship 36
partnering-oriented salespeople 34	win-win relationship 37

QUESTIONS AND PROBLEMS

1. What is the difference between a win-win and a win-lose buyer-seller relationship?

2. Many different titles are now being used for salespeople, including account executives, sales executives, and account managers. Why are companies using these different titles for employees who were formerly called salespeople?

3. Why do companies want to enter into long-term relationships with customers?

4. Read each of the following statements and indicate which describe you (*yes*), which do not describe you (*no*), or which you are not sure describe you (*?*):

   _____ I typically say the right thing.

   _____ I like myself.

   _____ People don't like me.

   _____ I am often discouraged.

   _____ I don't try hard.

   _____ I am involved in a lot of activities.

   Based on your answers, do you have a strong or negative self-image? Why is a positive self-image important for a salesperson?

5. What factors should a salesperson consider when deciding with which customers he or she wants to develop a close relationship?

6. What is the difference between a market exchange and a functional relationship?

7. When a salesperson negotiates price with a buyer, somebody wins and somebody loses. If the seller makes a price concession, the salesperson's company makes less money and the buyer makes more. How is it possible for a buyer and a salesperson to have a win-win relationship?

8. Assume you have a functional relationship with a buyer. You have been informed that the next order placed by the buyer is going to be late. The buyer has told you it is critical for the order to be delivered on time. You contact the factory and cannot do anything to speed up delivery. What should you do next?

9. What are the five foundations for a successful relationship?

10. What can salespeople do to increase the level of trust a buyer has in them?

EXPLORING THE NET

The following sites are used by companies looking for salespeople and people looking for sales jobs. Visit these sites and locate the descriptions of different types of sales positions. Describe how these sales positions differ from one another.

http://www.careerlab.com/15best.html

http://www.espan.com

http://www.jobtrack.com/jobguide

http://www.occ.com/occ

http://www.careermosiac.com

http://www.yahoo.com/business/employment

http://www.careers.org

http://point.lycos.com/reviews/database/buca.html

CASE PROBLEMS

**CASE 2.1
Customer for Life?
Don't Count On It.**

Greg Alba firmly believes in the benefits of developing long-term relationships with customers. He is a salesperson at Stansfield, the oldest manufacturer and distributor of office equipment in the Pacific Northwest. Greg says, "I take care of customers that have been doing business with our company long before I was born. Our competitors are always looking for ways to steal our customers, but we have a 'customer for life philosophy.'"

But Greg is having a problem with a customer: the school district in Bellevue, Washington, which he first started doing business with 10 years ago. Over the years, Greg had developed an excellent relationship with the business manager and several members of the school board, but the district used five suppliers for its office equipment. Greg recalls, "Suddenly I was dealing with new people who felt no loyalty to us. In an effort to streamline their operations, they decided they would only use one supplier for office equipment, and it looks like we are not going to be that supplier."

A committee was formed to make the decision, and several members of the committee were strong supporters of the competition. "They were spreading around a lot of misinformation about our company," Greg says. "In fact, one of the committee members told me we did not have a chance."

The committee decided to hear presentations from three suppliers, including Stansfield. Greg is deciding what he should stress in the presentation. Should he emphasize Stansfield's 100 years of experience in office supply business in the Pacific Northwest or the company's knowledge of the school district's needs and its expertise in the office supply business? Or should he focus on crafting a proposal offering the lowest possible price?

Question

Which strategy should Greg Alba use? Why?

**CASE 2.2
Too Much of a
Good Thing**

Heather Jones has always believed she could never make too many sales. Then came the day she made one sale too many. Jones is the owner and president of Promotions, Inc., a company that manages product sampling and promotional programs targeted toward children, teens, and teachers in elementary and secondary schools. Companies use these programs to get potential customers to try their products and to increase sales.

Most of the programs Promotions, Inc., manages are cooperative. Groups of products and coupons from different manufacturers are assembled and distributed to children in specific age groups. Promotions offers an exclusive guarantee for each cooperative program. Once a firm has decided to participate in a program, competitive products will not be included in the package.

Jones' oldest and largest client, Specialty Products (SP), was "challenged" in the shampoo category for a new promotion package directed toward the teenage female market. A competitor of SPs, Smith & Lynch (a larger firm than SP), wanted to take part in the program with its shampoo sample if SP decided not to participate.

After a week of deliberation, SP said it was not prepared to make a decision about participating in the teen promotion package. The client told Jones, "do what you have to do." And she did. Jones told Smith & Lynch, a new client for her company, that it had the shampoo slot in the promotion. And that was that, until SP phoned a week later, after the contract with Smith & Lynch was signed. SP had changed its plans and wanted to be in the promotion package. Yes, it was late. Yes, there was one shampoo too many. Yes, it was Jones's largest client.

Questions

1. Jones believes she has two options. First, she could ask Smith & Lynch to withdraw. After all, SP was Jones's largest and oldest client. Second, she could tell SP the truth and honor the contract with Smith & Lynch. Jones had given SP the chance, and she was now obligated to stand by her new client. What should Jones do?

2. What other options, if any, might be better than those mentioned in question 1?

ADDITIONAL REFERENCES

Bell, Chip. *Customers as Partners: Building Relationships That Last.* Baltimore: Berrett-Koehler Publishers, 1994.

Berling, Robert. "The Emerging Approach to Business Strategy: Building a Relationship Advantage." *Business Horizons,* July/August 1993, pp. 16–27.

Chapman, Joe, and Stephanie Rauck. "Relationship Selling: A Synopsis of Recent Research." In *Developments in Marketing Science,* vol. 18, ed. Roger Gomes. Coral Gables, FL: Academy of Marketing Science, 1995, p. 163.

Dunn, Dan, and Claude Thomas. "Partnering with Customers." *Journal of Business and Industrial Marketing,* January 1994, pp. 13–24.

Ellram, Lisa. "Partnering Pitfalls and Success Factors." *International Journal of Purchasing and Materials Management,* April 1995, pp. 36–44.

Ingram, Thomas. "Relationship Selling: Moving from Rhetoric to Reality." *Mid-American Journal of Business,* 11, no. 1 (1996), pp. 1–13.

Laneros, Robert; Robert Beck; and Richard Plank. "Maintaining Buyer-Supplier Partnerships." *International Journal of Purchasing and Materials Management,* July 1995, pp. 3–11.

Keenan, William, Jr. "Is Your Sales Force Ready for Partnering?" *Sales & Marketing Management,* August 1994, p. 62.

Mohr, Jakki, and Robert Spekman. "Characteristics of Successful Partnerships: Attributes, Communication Behavior, and Conflict Resolution Techniques." *Strategic Management Journal,* February 1993, pp. 23–45.

Morgan, Robert, and Shelby Hunt. "The Commitment-Trust Theory of Relationship Marketing." *Journal of Marketing,* July 1994, pp. 20–38.

Raymond, Mary Ann, and John F. Tanner, Jr. "Maintaining Customer Relationships in Direct Selling: Stimulating Repeat Purchase Behavior." *Journal of Personal Selling and Sales Management,* Summer 1994, pp. 67–76.

Wilson, David T. "An Integrated Model of Buyer-Seller Relationships." *Journal of Academy of Marketing Science,* Fall 1995, pp. 335–45.

Wilson, Larry. *Stop Selling, Start Partnering.* Essex Junction, VT: Oliver Wright, 1994.

Chapter Three

Ethical *and* Legal Issues *in* Selling

Consider the following situation. A salesperson for a consumer electronics manufacturer is negotiating a $100,000 sale with the buyer for a discount store chain. The buyer says, "I like your new, large-screen TVs. I would really appreciate getting one as a gift." If the salsperson makes the sale, he will get a commission of

Some Questions Answered in this Chapter Are:

Why do salespeople need to develop their own codes of ethics?

What ethical responsibilities do salespeople have toward themselves, their firms, and their customers?

Do ethics get in the way of being a successful salesperson?

What guidelines should salespeople consider when confronting situations involving an ethical issue?

What laws apply to personal selling?

$7,000. It would cost him $2,000 to buy the TV and give it to the buyer. What should he do? Would it be illegal to give the gift to the buyer? Would it be ethical?

Everyone confronts situations that involve making ethical choices. However, ethics are particularly important in personal selling. Salespeople often have to balance their personal needs with the needs of their companies and their customers. This chapter examines the salesperson's personal code of ethics and the laws that should govern the salesperson's personal behavior when conflicts arise.

PROFILE

Jens Wiik Jensen has a master's degree in export engineering from the Copenhagen College of Engineering in Denmark. He recalls, "While I was in college, I combined my formal studies with a one-year internship in waste water and water treatment at Kurita Water Industries Ltd. in Tokyo. I was extremely impressed with the economic growth prospects in Japan and the Asia-Pacific region in general, so when I graduated, I took a position with Dow Chemical in Kuala Lumpur, Malaysia. My placement was in the Liquid Separation Department, which covered the geographic area including Malaysia, Singapore, Brunei, and Thailand. My basic responsibilities included handling existing distributors for ion exchange resins and liquid membranes and providing technical support for these accounts, as well as trying to further develop the market for Dow's products in this region. The ion-exchange resins are used to demineralize the water that is used in boilers to prevent scaling and chemical deposits inside the boilers, turbines, and pipes. Jensen describes one of his more challenging experiences: "One of the customer groups I handled involved petroleum and chemical accounts in Borneo, Sarawak, and Sabah in East Malaysia. These accounts included several paper mills, plywood factories, and plantations located far out in the jungle and reachable only by Jeeps or small speedboats. Apart from the challenges that traveling there posed, I was dealing with people who had very diverse cultural backgrounds, such as Indians, Malays, Chinese, and some of the original people from the jungle. This meant having to cope with language and cultural barriers, as well as ethical commercial barriers that had to be handled with great care."

He continues, "Many businesses there secure their sales through the use of 'kickbacks' to the appropriate decision makers. This posed a difficult problem because it was hard for us to win competitive bids on price or technical superiority alone. In the end, I found a way around this dilemma. Part of the cultural norms there is that they like to do business with friends and on

"It was very important that I was able to build trusting relationships with the key players."

JENS WIIK JENSEN
Pacifico Enviro Sdn. Bhd.

basis of long-term relationships. As in any sales job, I had to work on many different levels of the organizations, but my clear focus was on cultivating friendships with many different people in various key positions in the buying center. This meant that continuous visits and follow-up played a key role in getting the sale. It was very important that I was able to build trusting relationships with the key players."

Jensen recently left Dow to start his own company, Pacifico Enviro Sdn. Bhd., which is also based in Malaysia. His customers are Malaysian and Singaporean waste and water treatment companies doing projects in the region spanning China to Indonesia.

Visit Our Website@
http://www.dow.com

CONFLICTING NEEDS FACED BY SALESPEOPLE

We all have needs and values that guide our daily lives. But once you take a sales job with a firm, you must consider the needs and values of the firm and your customers as well as your own personal needs.

Exhibit 3.1 displays the different objectives and needs of salespeople, their firms, and their customers. Both the salesperson's company and its customers want to make profits. But sometimes these objectives are conflicting. For example, should a salesperson tell a customer about problems his or her firm is having with a new product? Concealing this information might make it easier to make a sale, increase the company's profits, and enhance the salesperson's chances of getting a promotion and a bonus, but it could also decrease the customer's profits when the product does not perform adequately. In the situation described at the beginning of the chapter, the salesperson's moral values concerning bribes may be in conflict with his desire to succeed in his new job and the buyer's personal needs for a large-screen TV.[1]

Such conflicts often are not covered by company policies and procedures, and managers may not be available to provide advice. Thus, salespeople must make decisions on their own, relying on their ethical standards and understanding of the laws governing these situations.

As discussed in Chapter Two, most businesses try to develop long-term, mutually beneficial relationships with their customers. Salespeople are the official representatives of their companies. They are responsible for developing and maintaining these relationships, which are built on trust. Partnerships between buyers and sellers cannot develop when salespeople behave unethically or illegally.[2]

This chapter examines ethical and legal issues in personal selling. *Laws* dictate which activities society has deemed to be clearly wrong, the activities for which salespeople and their companies will be punished. However, most sales situations are not covered by laws. Salespeople must then rely on their own codes of ethics and/or their firms' and industries' codes of ethics to determine the right thing to do.

Exhibit 3.2 illustrates the relative importance of ethical and legal principles in the three types of relationships discussed in Chapter Two. Legal principles guide market exchange relationships. The issues governing buying and selling in these relationships are straight forward. The terms and conditions are well defined and can easily be written into a traditional contract.

Both ethical and legal issues play significant roles in functional relationships. Contracts are used to record the terms and conditions; however, many issues cannot be reduced to contractual terms. For example, a salesperson might make a conces-

E X H I B I T 3 . 1	**Company Objectives**	**Salesperson Objectives**	**Customer Objectives**
Conflicting Objectives	Increase profits	Increase compensation	Increase profits
	Increase sales	Receive recognition, and promotion	Solve problems, satisfy needs
	Reduce sales costs	Satisfy customers	Reduce costs
	Build long-term customer relationships	Build long-term customer relationships	Build relationships with suppliers
		Maintain personal code of ethics	

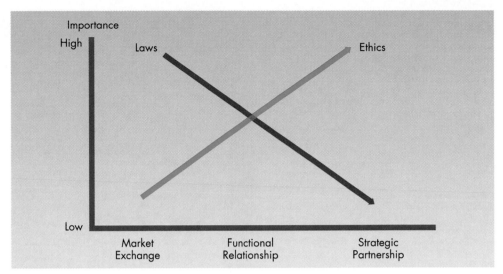

EXHIBIT 3.2

Relative Importance of Ethical and Legal Principles in Relationships

Source: Adapted from Gregory Gundlach and Patrick Murphy, "Ethical and Legal Foundations of Relational Exchanges," *Journal of Marketing,* October 1993, p. 40. Reprinted with permission from American Marketing Association.

sion for a buyer with a special problem, anticipating that the buyer will reciprocate on future orders.

Ethical principles become increasingly important in strategic partnerships. Due to the high levels of investment and uncertainty, the parties in the relationships cannot accurately assess the potential benefits—the size of the pie—accruing from strategic investments in the relationships or the contributions of each party in producing those benefits. Thus, the parties in a strategic partnership have to trust one another to "divide the pie" fairly.[3]

ETHICAL ISSUES

Ethics are the principles governing the behavior of an individual or a group. These principles establish appropriate behavior. Defining the term is easy, but determining what those principles are is difficult. What one person thinks is right another may consider wrong.

What is ethical can vary from country to country and from industry to industry. For example, offering bribes to overcome bureaucratic roadblocks is an accepted practice in Middle Eastern countries but is considered unethical, and even illegal, in the United States.

An ethical principle can change over time. For example, some years ago doctors and lawyers who advertised their services were considered unethical. Today such advertising is accepted as common practice.

Although there are no absolute rules for ethical behavior, each salesperson needs to develop a personal code of ethics. A code of ethics helps salespeople deal with the following difficult situations:

- Should you give an expensive gift to a buyer?
- If a buyer tells you it is common practice to pay off purchasing agents to get orders in his or her country, should you do it?
- Is it acceptable to use a high-pressure sales approach when you know your product is the best for the customer's needs?

Striking workers express their views about the ethics and legality of business decisions made by Archer Daniels Midland's Chairman Dwayne Andreas.

Seth Perlma/World Wide Photos

- Should you attempt to sell a product to a customer if you know a better product exists for that application?
- Is it ethical to tell a customer about the poor performance features of a competing product?
- Should you put the cost of a hotel room on your expense account even though you stayed at a friend's house during the business trip?
- If your supervisor suggests that you pad your expense account to make extra money, should you do it?

Thinking *it* Through	How would you respond to each of the statements listed above? Why? Do you think your friends and your family would respond the same way you did?

Some people hesitate to pursue a sales career because they think selling will force them to compromise their principles. Students often think salespeople and sales managers are unethical. However, some studies (summarized in Exhibit 3.3) suggest that sales managers have a greater concern for ethical standards than college students do.[4] Good ethics are good business! Sales managers and salespeople know that.

To maintain good relationships with their companies and customers, salespeople need to have a clear sense of right and wrong so that their companies and customers can depend on them when questionable situations arise. To provide guidelines in making ethical decisions, many companies have codes of ethics for their salespeople. An outline of Motorola's policy appears in Exhibit 3.4.

EXHIBIT 3.3 **Ethical Standards of Sales Managers and Students**	Students and sales managers were asked to indicate their level of agreement with statements concerning ethics in sales. Their average responses on a 5-point scale, where 1 is strongly disagree and 5 is strongly agree, are shown below:	

Statement	Level of Agreement	
	Managers	Students
Generally salespeople have high ethics.	3.61	3.11
I am unwilling to violate any company policies in order to make a sale.	3.43	2.98
I would always be ethical in sales.	4.23	3.63
Sales managers expect results even if a salesperson has to be a little unethical to get the sale.	1.97	3.16
I would never lie to a buyer.	3.95	4.17
If I had to, I would cheat just a little in order to make a sale.	2.36	2.01
It is more important to be unethical and make the sale than to be ethical and not make the sale.	1.68	2.19
Taking pens home from the office is unethical.	3.04	2.55
Dating one's boss in unethical.	2.95	2.65
Lying to one's boss is unethical.	4.65	3.96
If I knew for sure I couldn't get caught, I would be more willing to be unethical.	1.70	2.26

Source: J. B. DeConninck and D. J. Good, "Perceptual Differences of Sales Practitioners and Students Concerning Ethical Behavior," *Journal of Business Ethics,* Fall 1989, pp. 667–76. Copyright 1989. Reprinted by permission.

In the following sections, we discuss the ethical situations salespeople may confront in their relationships with their customers, competitors, and colleagues (other salespeople).[5] (In Chapter Seventeen, we review the company's ethical and legal obligations to its salespeople and society in general.)

Relationships with Customers

Areas of ethical concern involving customers include using deception; offering gifts, bribes, and entertainment; divulging confidential information; and back-door selling.

Deception

Deliberately presenting inaccurate information, or lying, to a customer is illegal. However, misleading customers by telling half-truths or withholding important information is a matter of ethics. Frequently salespeople believe it is the customer's responsibility to uncover potential product problems. They answer questions but don't offer information that might make a sale more difficult. For example, a salesperson selling satellite communication systems might tell a customer that the system will work in all weather but fail to inform the customer about problems in locations surrounded by tall buildings.

Customers expect salespeople to be enthusiastic about their firm and its products. They recognize that this enthusiasm can result in a certain amount of exaggeration. Customers also expect salespeople to emphasize the positive aspects of their

EXHIBIT 3.4

Ethics Policy for
Motorola Salespeople

Improper Use of Company Funds and Assets

The funds and assets of Motorola may not be used for influential gifts, illegal payments of any kind, or political contributions, whether legal or illegal.

The funds and assets of Motorola must be properly and accurately recorded on the books and records of Motorola.

Motorola shall not enter into, with dealers, distributors, agents, or consultants, any agreements that are not in compliance with U.S. laws and the laws of any other country that may be involved, or that provide for the payment of a commission or fee that is not commensurate with the services to be rendered.

Customer/Supplier/Government Relationships

Motorola will respect the confidence of its customers. Motorola will respect the laws, customs, and traditions of each country in which it operates but, in so doing, will not engage in any act or course of conduct that may violate U.S. laws or its business ethics. Employees of Motorola shall not accept payments, gifts, gratuities, or favors from customers or suppliers.

Conflict of Interest

A Motorola employee shall not be a supplier or a competitor of Motorola or be employed by a competitor, supplier, or customer of Motorola. A Motorola employee shall not engage in any activity where the skill and knowledge developed while in the employment of Motorola is transferred or applied to such activity in a way that results in a negative impact on the present or prospective business interest of Motorola.

A Motorola employee shall not have any relationship with any other business enterprise that might affect the employee's independence of judgment in transactions between Motorola and the other business enterprise.

A Motorola employee may not have any interest in any supplier or customer of Motorola that could compromise the employee's loyalty to Motorola.

Compliance with the Code of Conduct is a condition of employment. We urge you to read the complete code.

Should any questions remain, you are encouraged to consult your Motorola law department. In the world of business, your understanding and cooperation are essential. As in all things, Motorola cannot operate to the highest standards without you.

Source: Company document.

products and spend little time talking about the negative aspects. But practicing **deception** by withholding information or telling "white lies" is clearly unethical. Such salespeople take advantage of the trust customers place in them. When buyers uncover these deceptions, they will be reluctant to trust the salesperson in the future.

When salespeople fail to provide customers with all of the information about their products, they lose an opportunity to develop trust. By revealing both positive and negative information, salespeople can build up their credibility. Selling Scenario 3.1 illustrates how being honest and straightforward pays off in the long run.

Bribes, Gifts, and Entertainment

Bribes and kickbacks may be illegal. **Bribes** are payments made to buyers to influence their purchase decisions, whereas **kickbacks** are payments made to buyers based on the amount of orders placed. A purchasing agent personally benefits from bribes, but bribes typically have negative consequences for the purchasing agent's firm because the product's performance is not considered in buying decisions.

SELLING   SCENARIO   2.1

Good Ethics Is Good Business

The most difficult ethical dilemmas arise when there is a lot of competitive pressure and the stakes are high. In these situations, it's tempting for salespeople to say and do things that achieve short-term results but sacrifice long-term relationships.

Rick Shih-Hsieh is an IBM marketing specialist in Chicago. One of his biggest customers was going to place a half-million-dollar order for PCs, but wanted delivery of 500 units in two months. Rick knew IBM and his competitors would not be able to meet this delivery schedule because there was an industry shortage of a critical microprocessor. Rick told the customer he could not meet the delivery requirements, but one of his competitors made the commitment and got the order.

"One good thing about working for IBM is that the company has a strong ethical code of conduct. I kept management informed about the situation, and they supported me all the way even though we lost the order. The competitors didn't deliver as promised. Now the purchasing agent really respects me and this situation will strengthen our relationship. He knows that I'm going to be straight with him."

Source: Personal communication.

Taking customers to lunch is a commonly accepted business practice. Over 85 percent of salespeople indicated they take customers to lunch occasionally or frequently. However, fewer than half occasionally take customers to dinner or for a drink, and only 25 percent entertain customers with leisure activities such as golf or fishing.[6]

Determining what gifts and entertainment are acceptable and what are not brings up ethical issues. To avoid these issues, more than half of the U.S. companies in a recent survey have set policies that forbid employees to accept gifts (more than pencils or coffee cups) or entertainment from suppliers. These firms require that all

Most salespeople take customers to lunch. However, paying for a lavish meal can make a customer feel uncomfortable and is considered unethical.

Jay Thomas/International Stock

gifts sent to the employee's home or office be returned. Wal-Mart, the largest retailer in the world, goes one step further, allowing contact between buyers and vendors only at business meetings at Wal-Mart's or the vendor's headquarters. On the other hand, many companies have no policy on receiving gifts or entertainment. Some unethical employees will accept and even solicit gifts even though their company has a policy against such practices.

To develop a productive, long-term relationship, salespeople need to avoid embarrassing customers by asking them to engage in activities they might see as unethical. If a salesperson wants to give a gift out of friendship or invite a customer to lunch to develop a better business relationship, she or he should phrase the offer so that the customer can easily refuse it. For example, a salesperson with a large industrial firm might have this conversation with a customer:

SALESPERSON John, we have worked well together over the last five years, and I would like to give you something to show my appreciation. Would that be OK?

BUYER That's very nice of you, but what are you thinking of giving me?

SALESPERSON Well, I want to give you a Mount Blanc pen. I have really enjoyed using my pen over the last few years, and I thought you might like it also. Is that OK?

BUYER I would appreciate that gift. I have seen your pen and admired it.

Buyers typically are sensitive about receiving expensive gifts, according to Debra Sieckman, director of sales at Allied Van Lines. "It's a bit like getting roses after a first date. You appreciate the gesture, but you wonder, 'What is the motive?'"[7] Some guidelines for gift giving are as follows:

- Check your motives for giving the gift. The gift should be given to foster a mutually beneficial, long-term relationship, not to obligate or pay off the customer for placing an order.
- Make sure the customer views the gift as a symbol of your appreciation and respect, with no strings attached. Never give customers the impression that you are attempting to buy their business with a gift.
- Make sure the gift does not violate the customer's or your firm's policies.
- The safest gifts are inexpensive business items imprinted with the salesperson's company's name or logo.

Even when customers encourage and accept gifts, lavish gifts and entertainment are both unethical and bad business. Treating a customer to a three-day fishing trip is no substitute for effective selling. Sales won this way are usually short-lived. Salespeople who offer expensive gifts to get orders may be blackmailed into continually providing these gifts to obtain orders in the future. Customers who can be bribed are likely to switch their business when presented with better offers.

 Giving gifts in other countries requires special attention. Exhibit 3.5 lists some suggestions.

Special Treatment

Some customers try to take advantage of their status to get special treatment from salespeople. For example, a buyer asks a salesperson to make a weekly check on the performance of equipment even after the customer's employees have been thor-

EXHIBIT 3.5 **It's Not the Gift That Counts, But How You Present It**	**Japan** Do not open a gift in front of a Japanese customer unless asked, and do not expect the Japanese customer to open a gift in front of you. Avoid ribbons and bows as part of the gift wrapping. Bows are viewed as unattractive, and different ribbon colors can have different meanings. Do not offer a gift depicting a fox or a badger. The fox is a symbol of fertility and the badger a symbol of cunning. **Europe** Avoid red roses and white flowers, even numbers, and the number 13. Do not wrap flowers in paper. Do not risk the impression of bribery by spending too much on the gift. **Arab World** Do not give a gift when you first meet a customer. It may be misinterpreted as a bribe. Give a gift in front of others when you do not have a personal relationship with the customer. **Latin America** Gifts should be given on social occasions, not in the course of business. Avoid the colors black and purple. Both are associated with the Catholic Lenten season. **China** Never make an issue of a gift presentation, either publicly or privately.

Source: Phillip Catoera, *International Marketing,* 9th ed. (Burr Ridge, IL: Richard D. Irwin), p. 100.

oughly trained in the operation and maintenance of the equipment. Providing this extra service may upset other customers who do not get the special attention. In addition, the special service can reduce the salesperson's productivity. Salespeople should be diplomatic but careful about undertaking requests to provide unusual services.

Confidential Information

During sales calls, salespeople often encounter confidential company information such as new products under development, costs, and production schedules. Offering information about a customer's competitor in exchange for an order is unethical.

Long-term relationships can develop only when customers trust salespeople to maintain confidentiality. By disclosing confidential information, a salesperson will get a reputation for being untrustworthy. Even the customer who solicited the confidential information will not trust the salesperson, who will then be denied access to information needed to make an effective sales presentation.

Back-Door Selling

Sometimes purchasing agents require that all contacts with the prospect's employees be made through them because they want to be fully informed about and control the buying process. The purchasing agent insists that salespeople get their approval before meeting with other people involved in the purchase decision. This policy can

EXHIBIT 3.6	
Buyers' View of Unethical Sales Behaviors	• Exaggerates benefits of product • Lies about product availability • Lies about competition • Sells products that people do not need • Is not interested in customer needs • Answers questions even when he or she does not know the correct answer	• Passes the blame for something he or she did to someone else • Misrepresents guarantees • Makes oral promises that are not legally binding • Sells hazardous products

Source: Adapted from William Bearden, Thomas Ingram, and Raymond LaForge. *Marketing: Principles and Perspectives* (Burr Ridge, IL: Richard D. Irwin, 1995), p. 512.

make it difficult for a new supplier to get business from a customer using a competitor's products.

Salespeople engage in **back-door selling** when they ignore the purchasing agent's policy, go around his or her back, and contact other people directly involved in the purchasing decision. Back-door selling can be very risky and unethical. If the purchasing agent finds out, the salesperson may never be able to get an order. To avoid these potential problems, the salesperson needs to convince the purchasing agent of the benefits to be gained by direct contact with other people in the customer's firm.

Exhibit 3.6 summarizes some research revealing specific sales behaviors that buyers think are unethical. The research suggests that buyers will go out of their way to avoid salespeople who engage in these practices.[8]

Relationships with the Salesperson's Company

Because salespeople's activities in the field cannot be closely monitored, their employers trust them to act in the company's best interests. Professional salespeople do not abuse this trust. They put the interests of their companies above self-interest. Taking this perspective may require them to make short-term sacrifices to achieve long-term benefits for their companies and themselves. Some problem areas in the salesperson-company relationship involve expense accounts, reporting work-time information and activities, and switching jobs.

Expense Accounts

Many companies provide their salespeople with cars and reimburse them for travel and entertainment expenses. Developing a reimbursement policy that prevents salespeople from cheating and still allows them the flexibility they need to cover their territories and entertain customers is almost impossible. Moreover, a lack of tight control can tempt salespeople to use their expense accounts to increase their income.

To do their jobs well, salespeople need to incur expenses. However, using their expense accounts to offset what they consider to be inadequate compensation is unethical. A salesperson who cannot live within the company compensation plan and expense policies has two ethical alternatives: (1) persuade the company to change its compensation plan or expense policy or (2) find another job.

In using the company's expense account, you should act as though you are spending your own money. Eat good food, but don't go to the most expensive restaurant in town. Stay in clean, comfortable, safe lodgings, but not in the best hotel or the best room in a hotel. When traveling, you should maintain the same standards of living and appearance that you do at home.

Reporting Work-Time Information and Activities

Employers expect their salespeople to work full time. Salespeople on salary are stealing from their employers when they waste time on coffee breaks, long lunches, or unauthorized days off. Even salespeople paid by commission cheat their companies if they don't work full time. Their incomes and company profits both decrease when they take time off.

To monitor work activities, many companies ask their salespeople to provide daily call reports. Most salespeople dislike this clerical task. Some provide false information, including calls they never made. Giving inaccurate information or bending the truth is clearly unethical. A failure to get an appointment with a customer is not a sales call. Providing a brief glimpse of a product is not a demonstration.

Switching Jobs

When salespeople decide to change jobs, they have an ethical responsibility to their employers. The company often makes a considerable investment in training salespeople and then provides them with confidential information about new products and programs. Over time, salespeople use this training and information to build strong relationships with their customers.

A salesperson may have good reasons to switch jobs. However, if a salesperson goes to work for a competitor, she or he should not say negative things about the previous employer. Also, disclosing confidential information about the former employer's business is improper. The ethical approach to leaving a job includes the following:[9]

- Give ample notice. If you leave a job during a busy time and with inadequate notice, your employer may suffer significant lost sales opportunities.

- Offer assistance during the transition phase. Help your replacement learn about your customers and territory.

- Don't burn your bridges. Don't say things in anger that may come back to haunt you. Remember that you may want to return to the company or ask the company for a reference in the future.

Relationships with Colleagues

To be effective, salespeople need to work together with other salespeople. Unethical behavior by salespeople toward their co-workers, such as engaging in sexual harassment and taking advantage of colleagues, can weaken company morale and have a negative effect on the company's reputation.

Sexual Harassment

Sexual harassment includes unwelcome sexual advances, requests for sexual favors, jokes or graffiti, and physical conduct. Harassment is not confined to requests for sexual favors in exchange for job considerations such as a raise or promotion; simply creating a hostile work environment can be considered sexual harassment. Some actions that are considered sexual harassment are engaging in suggestive behavior, treating people differently because they are male or female, lewd sexual comments and gestures, joking that has a sexual content, showing obscene photographs, staring at a co-worker in a suggestive manner, alleging that an employee got rewards by engaging in sexual acts, and spreading rumors about a person's sexual conduct.

Unwelcome physical contact is sexual harassment. It is illegal and unethical.

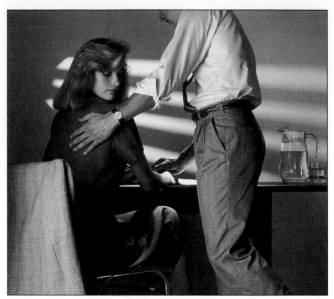

Frank Gardener/The Stock Market

Customers as well as co-workers, can sexually harass salespeople. Salespeople are particularly vulnerable to harassment from important customers who may seek sexual favors in exchange for their business. Following are some suggestions for dealing with sexual harassment from customers:

- Don't become so dependent on one customer that you would consider compromising your principles to retain the customer's business. Develop a large base of customers and prospects to minimize the importance of one customer.
- Tell the harasser or write the harasser a letter stating that the behavior is offensive, is unacceptable, and must be stopped. Clearly indicate that you are in control and will not be passive.
- Utilize the sexual harassment policies of your firm and your customer's firm to resolve problems. These policies typically state the procedure for filing a complaint, the person responsible for investigating the complaint, the time frame for completing the investigation, and how the parties will be informed about the resolution.[10]

Thinking *it* **Through**	Assume you are a female who has recently graduated from college. You accept a sales trainee position and your sales manager is a middle-aged male. After several months on the job, he says to you, "I really think you're doing a good job. I want to develop a special relationship with the saleswomen who work for me. Let's have dinner tonight so we can get started on that special relationship." What would you do?

Taking Advantage of Other Salespeople

Salespeople can behave unethically when they are too aggressive in pursuing their own goals at the expense of their colleagues. For example, it is unethical to fail to

SELLING SCENARIO 3.2

Turning a Competitor's Negative Comments into A Sale

Steve Shilling is director of sales in New York City at Northern Telecom, a major international telecommunications firm. Using his knowledge of his own and competing products, he turned a competitor's attempt to discredit Northern Telecom products into an advantage.

When Shilling called on the communications manager of a large industrial company, he was surprised by the manager's skeptical, almost hostile attitude. He found out the reason for the chilly reception: A competitor had given the manager a long list of supposed drawbacks to Northern Telecom's products.

Instead of bad-mouthing the competitor, Shilling addressed each point on the list and demonstrated that many—although not all—were invalid. By calmly exposing the erroneous points and frankly admitting the valid ones, Shilling gained credibility and undermined the competitor. The customer became interested in talking with Shilling.

After discussing the customer's application, Shilling explained that his product could solve the problem but the competitor's could not, even though the latter's sales brochure indicated that it could. Shilling knew this would provoke the purchasing agent, who favored the competitor, to prove him wrong. Shilling landed a $1 million contract when the purchasing agent found the competitor had made a false claim.

Source: Adapted from Edward Doherty, "How to Steal a Satisfied Customer," *Sales & Marketing Management*, March 1990, p. 42. Reprinted with permission from Bill Communications.

---

relay a customer's phone message to another salesperson or make critical comments about a colleague to one's boss. Colleagues usually discover such unethical behavior and return the lack of support.

Relationships with Competitors

Clearly it is unethical and often illegal to make false claims about competitors' products or sabotage their efforts. For example, a salesperson who rearranges the display of a competitor's products to make it less appealing is being unethical. This type of behavior can backfire. When customers detect these practices, the reputation of the salespeople and their companies may be permanently damaged. Selling Scenario 3.2 recounts one such incident.

Another questionable tactic is criticizing a competitor's products or policies. Although you may be tempted to say negative things about a competitor, this approach usually does not work. Customers will assume you are biased toward your own company and its products and discount negative comments you make about the competition. Some customers may even be offended. If they have bought the competitor's products in the past, they may regard these comments as a criticism of their judgment.

A PERSONAL CODE OF ETHICS

Salespeople develop a sense of what is right and wrong—a standard of conduct—from family and friends long before they go to work. Although they should abide by their own codes of ethics, salespeople may be tempted to avoid difficult ethical choices by developing "logical" reasons for unethical conduct. For example, a salesperson may use the following rationalizations:[11]

- All salespeople behave unethically in this situation.
- No one will be hurt by this behavior.

- This behavior is the lesser of two evils.
- This is the price one has to pay for being in business.

Salespeople use such reasoning to avoid feeling responsible for their behavior and being bound by ethical considerations. Even though the pressure to make sales may tempt salespeople to be unethical and act against their internal standards, maintaining an ethical self-image is important. Compromising ethical standards to achieve short-term gains can have adverse long-term effects. When salespeople violate their own principles, they lose self-respect and confidence in their abilities. They may begin to think that the only way they can make sales is to be dishonest or unethical.

Short-term compromises also make long-term customer relationships more difficult to form. As discussed earlier, customers will be reluctant to deal with the salesperson again. Also, they may relate these experiences to business associates in other companies.

Exhibit 3.7 lists some questions you can ask yourself to determine whether a sales behavior or activity is unethical. The questions emphasize that ethical behavior is determined by widely accepted views of what is right and wrong. Thus, you should engage only in activities about which you would be proud to tell your family, friends, employer, and customers.

Your firm can strongly affect the ethical choices you will have to make. When you view your firm's polices or requests as improper, you have three choices:

1. Ignore your personal values and do what your company asks you to do. Self-respect suffers when you have to compromise principles to please an employer. If you take this path, you will probably feel guilty and be dissatisfied with your job in the long run.

2. Take a stand and tell your employer what you think. Try to influence the decisions and policies of your company and supervisors.

3. Refuse to compromise your principles. Taking this path may mean you will get fired or be forced to quit.

You should not take a job with a company whose products, policies, and conduct conflict with your standards. Before taking a sales job, investigate the com-

Exhibit 3.7 **Checklist for Making Ethical Decisions**	1. Would I be embarrassed if a customer found out about this behavior? 2. Would my supervisor disapprove of this behavior? 3. Would most salespeople feel that this behavior is unusual? 4. Am I about to do this because I think I can get away with it? 5. Would I be upset if a salesperson did this to me? 6. Would my family or friends think less of me if I told them about engaging in this sales activity? 7. Am I concerned about the possible consequences of this behavior? 8. Would I be upset if this behavior or activity were publicized in a newspaper article? 9. Would society be worse off if everyone engaged in this behavior or activity? If the answer to any of these questions is *yes*, the behavior or activity is probably unethical and you should not do it.

pany's procedures and selling approach to see if they conflict with your personal ethical standards. These issues concerning the relationship between salespeople and their compnaies are discussed in more detail in Chapter Seventeen.

LEGAL ISSUES

Laws codify, or classify, many ethical principles. Society has determined that some activities are clearly unethical and has decided to use the legal system to prevent people from engaging in these activities. Salespeople who violate these laws can cause serious problems for themselves and their companies—problems more serious than just being considered unethical by a buyer. By engaging in illegal activities, salespeople expose their firms to costly legal fees and hundreds of millions of dollars in fines.[12]

The activities of salespeople in the United States are affected by three forms of law: statutory, administrative, and common. **Statutory law** is based on legislation passed either by state legislatures or by Congress. The main statutory laws governing salespeople are the Uniform Commercial Code and antitrust laws. **Administrative laws** are established by local, state, or federal regulatory agencies. The Federal Trade Commission is the most active agency in developing administrative laws affecting salespeople. However, the Securities and Exchange Commission regulates stockbrokers, and the Food and Drug Administration regulates pharmaceutical salespeople. Finally, **common law** grows out of court decisions. Precedents set by these decisions fill in the gaps where no laws exist.

This section discusses current laws affecting salespeople, but every year important new laws are developed and court decisions rendered. Thus, you should contact your firm for advice when a potential legal issue arises.

Uniform Commercial Code

The **Uniform Commercial Code (UCC)** is the legal guide to commercial practice in the United States. In its provisions, the code defines a number of terms related to salespeople.

Agency

A person who acts in place of his or her company is an **agent.** Authorized agents of a company have the authority to legally obligate their firm in a business transaction. This authorization to represent the company does not have to be in writing. Thus, as a salesperson, your statements and actions can legally bind your company and have significant financial impact.

Sale

The UCC defines a **sale** as "the transfer of title to goods by the seller to the buyer for a consideration known as price." A sale differs from a **contract to sell.** Any time a salesperson makes an offer and receives an unqualified acceptance, a contract exists. A sale is made when the contract is completed and title passes from the seller to the buyer.

The UCC also distinguishes between an offer and an invitation to negotiate. A sales presentation is usually considered to be an **invitation to negotiate.** An **offer** takes place when the salesperson quotes specific terms. The offer specifically states what the seller promises to deliver and what it expects from the buyer. If the buyer accepts these terms, the parties will have established a binding contract.

Salespeople are agents when they have the authority to make offers. However, most salespeople are not agents because they only have the power to solicit written offers from buyers. These written offers, called **orders,** become contracts when they are signed by an authorized representative in the salesperson's company. Sometimes these orders contain clauses stating that the firm is not obligated by its salesperson's statements. However, the buyer usually can have the contract nullified and may even sue for damages if salespeople make misleading statements, even though they are not official agents.

Title and Risk of Loss

If the terms of the contract specify **FOB (free on board) destination,** the seller has title until the goods are received at the destination. This means that any loss or damage incurred during transportation is the responsibility of the seller. The buyer assumes this responsibility and risk if contract terms call for **FOB factory.** The UCC also defines when titles transfer for goods shipped COD (cash on delivery) and goods sold on consignment. Understanding the terms of the sale and who has title can be useful in resolving complaints about damaged merchandise.

Oral versus Written Agreements

In most cases, oral agreements between a salesperson and a customer are just as binding as written agreements. Normally, written agreements are required for sales over $500. Salespeople must be careful when signing written agreements, because they may be the legal representatives of their firms.

The Super Valu produce buyer on the right is inspecting a shipment of grapes from Chile. Since the produce was shipped FOB destination, Super Valu is not responsible for the merchandise until it is delivered to the Super Valu warehouse.

Courtesy SUPERVALU INC.

Obligations and Performance

When the salesperson and the customer agree on the terms of a contract, both firms must perform according to those terms in "good faith." In addition, both parties must perform according to commonly accepted industry practices. Even if salespeople overstate the performance of their products, their firms have to provide the stated performance and meet the terms of the contract.

Warranties

A **warranty** is an assurance by the seller that the products will perform as represented. Sometimes a warranty is called a *guarantee*. The UCC distinguishes between two types of warranties, expressed and implied. An **expressed warranty** is an oral or a written statement by the seller. An **implied warranty** is not actually stated but is still an obligation defined by law. For example, products sold using an oral or a written description (the buyer never sees the products) carry an implied warranty that the products are of average quality. However, if the buyer inspects the product before placing an order, the implied warranty applies only to any performance aspects that the inspection would not have uncovered. Typically, an implied warranty also guarantees that the product can be used in the manner stated by the seller.

Salespeople can create a warranty for their products through inadvertent comments and actions. For example, a chemical company was liable for a product that did not meet the performance standards the salesperson promised, even though the sales brochure contradicted the salesperson's claims for the product. Salespeople can also create an implied warranty when they are knowledgeable about the customer's specific application and recognize that the customer is relying on their judgment.

Factual statements made by the salesperson about his company's new product are an expressed warranty. They legally bind his company, particularly when the customer has limited knowledge about the product.

David Sams/Tony Stone Images

Salespeople can also offset the effects of warnings provided by a firm. For example, when securities salespeople indicated that legally required warnings in the documents describing the investment were unimportant and could be ignored, the company offering the securities was liable for millions of dollars when customers were disappointed with the financial returns from the securities.

Problems with warranties often arise when the sale is to a reseller (a distributor or retailer). The ultimate user—the reseller's customer—may complain about a product to the reseller. The reseller, in turn, tries to shift the responsibility to the manufacturer. Salespeople often have to investigate and resolve these issues.

Misrepresentation or Sales Puffery

In their enthusiasm, salespeople may exaggerate the performance of products and even make false statements to get an order. Over time, common and administrative laws have defined the difference between illegal misrepresentation and sales puffery. Not all statements salespeople make have legal consequences.[13] However, misrepresentation, even if legal, can destroy a business relationship and may involve salespeople and their firms in lawsuits.

Glowing descriptions such as "Our service can't be beat" are considered to be opinions or sales puffery. Customers cannot reasonably rely on these statements. However, statements about the inherent capabilities of products or services, such as "Our system will reduce your inventory by 40 percent," may be treated as statements of fact and warranties. Here are examples of such statements found to be legally binding:

- This is a safe, dependable helicopter.
- Feel free to prescribe this drug to your patients, doctor. It's nonaddicting.
- This equipment will keep up with any other machine you are using and will work well with your other machines.

Factual statements become particularly strong indicators of an expressed warranty when salespeople sell complex products to unsophisticated buyers. In these situations, buyers rely on the technical expertise and integrity of the salespeople. However, when salespeople deal with knowledgeable buyers, the buyers are obligated to go beyond assertions made by the salespeople and make their own investigation of the product's performance.

 U.S. salespeople need to be aware of both U.S. laws and laws in the host country when selling internationally. All countries have laws regulating marketing and selling activities. In Canada, all claims and statements made in advertisements and sales presentations about comparisons with competitive products must pass the **credulous person standard.** This means the company and the salesperson have to pay damages if a reasonable person could misunderstand the statement. Thus, a statement like "This is the strongest axle in Canada" might be considered puffery in the United States but be viewed as misleading in Canada, unless the firm had absolute evidence that the axle was stronger than any other axle sold in Canada.

To avoid legal and ethical problems with misrepresentation, you should try to educate customers thoroughly before concluding a sale. You should tell the customer as much about the specific performance of the product as possible. Unless your firm has test results concerning the product's performance, you should avoid offering an opinion about the product's specific benefits for the customer's application. If you don't have the answer to a customer's question, don't make a guess. Say that you don't know the answer and will get back to the customer with the information.

Illegal Business Practices

The Sherman Antitrust Act of 1890, the Clayton Act of 1914, the Federal Trade Commission Act of 1914, and the Robinson-Patman Act of 1934 prohibit unfair business practices that may lessen competition. These laws are used by the courts to create common law that defines the illegal business practices discussed in this section.

Business Defamation

Business defamation occurs when a salesperson makes unfair or untrue statements to customers about a competitor, its products, or its salespeople. These statements are illegal when they damage the competitor's reputation or the reputation of its salespeople.

Following are some examples of false statements that have been found to be illegal:

- Company X broke the law when it offered you a free case of toilet paper with every 12 cases you buy.
- Company X is going bankrupt.
- You shouldn't do business with Company X. Mr. Jones, the CEO, is really incompetent and dishonest.

You should avoid making negative comments about a competitor, its salespeople, or its products unless you have proof to support the statements.

Reciprocity

Reciprocity is a special relationship in which two companies agree to buy products from each other. For example, a manufacturer of computers agrees to use microprocessors from a component manufacturer if the component manufacturer agrees to buy its computers. Such interrelationships can lead to greater trust and cooperation between the firms. However, reciprocity agreements are illegal if one company forces another company to join in the agreement. Reciprocity is legal only when both parties consent to the agreement willingly.

Tying Agreements

In a **tying agreement,** a buyer is required to purchase one product in order to get another product. For example, a customer who wants to buy a copy machine is required to buy paper from the same company, or a distributor that wants to stock one product must stock the manufacturer's entire product line. Because they reduce competition, tying agreements typically are illegal. They are legal only when the seller can show that the products must be used together, that is, that one product will not function properly unless the other product is used with it.

Tying agreements are also legal when a company's reputation depends on the proper functioning of equipment. Thus, a firm can be required to buy a service contract for equipment it purchases although it need not buy the contract from the manufacturer.

Conspiracy and Collusion

An agreement between competitors before customers are contacted is a **conspiracy,** whereas **collusion** refers to competitors working together while the customer is making a purchase decision. For example, competitors are conspiring when they get together and divide up a territory so that only one competitor will call on each prospect. Collusion occurs when competitors agree to charge the same price for equipment that a prospect is considering. These examples of collusion and conspiracy are illegal because they reduce competition.

Interference with Competitors

Salespeople may illegally interfere with competitors by:

- Trying to get a customer to break a contract with a competitor.
- Tampering with a competitor's product.
- Confusing a competitor's market research by buying merchandise from stores.

Restrictions on Resellers

Numerous laws govern the relationship between manufacturers and resellers—wholesalers and retailers. At one time, it was illegal for companies to establish a minimum price below which their distributors or retailers could not resell their products. Today this practice, called **resale price maintenance,** is legal in some situations.

Manufacturers do not have to sell their products to any reseller that wants to buy them. Sellers can use their judgment to select resellers as long as they announce their selection criteria in advance.

One sales practice considered unfair is providing special incentives to get a reseller's salespeople to push products. For example, salespeople for a cosmetics company may give a department store's cosmetics salespeople prizes based on the sales of their product. These special incentives, called **spiffs** (or **push money**), are legal only if the reseller knows and approves of the incentive and it is offered to all of the reseller's salespeople.

Price Discrimination

The Robinson-Patman Act became law because independent wholesalers and retailers wanted additional protection from the aggressive marketing tactics of large chain stores. Principally, the act forbids price discrimination in interstate commerce. While Robinson-Patman applies only to interstate commerce, most states have passed similar laws to govern sales transactions between buyers and sellers within the same state.

Court decisions related to the Robinson-Patman Act define **price discrimination** as a seller giving unjustified special prices, discounts, or services to some customers and not to others. To justify a special price or discount, the seller must prove that it results from (1) differences in the cost of manufacture, sale, or delivery; (2) differences in the quality or nature of the product delivered; or (3) an attempt to meet prices offered by competitors in a market. Thus, a seller must treat all customers equally. If a seller offers a price discount or special service to one customer, it must offer it to all customers. Different prices can be charged, however, if the cost of doing business is different. For example, a customer who buys in large volume can be charged a lower price if the manufacturing and shipping charges for higher-volume orders are lower.

Firms also may not offer special allowances to one reseller unless those allowances are made available to competing resellers. Because most resellers compete in limited geographic areas, firms frequently offer allowances in specific regions of the country.

Rick Marley/West Stock   Courtesy SUPERVALU INC.; Photo by James Schnepf

The Robinson Patman act requires salespeople to offer the same prices and services to the corner grocery store on the left and the supermarket chain on the right. Different prices can only be offered when the cost of doing business with the two customers differs.

Legal Guidelines

To reduce the chances of violating laws governing sales practices, you should adopt the following guidelines:[14]

- Be sure that all specific statements about your product's performance, such as technical characteristics and useful life, are accurate.
- Be sure that all specific positive statements about performance can be supported by evidence. If you make strong positive statements that cannot be supported, use very general wording, such as "high quality" and "great value."
- If your customers do not pay attention to warnings and operating instructions, remind them to read this information. Never suggest that this information can be ignored.
- If customers contemplate using your product incorrectly or in an inappropriate application, caution them specifically about how the product should be used.
- Assess your customer's experience and knowledge. Your legal obligations are greater with unsophisticated customers.
- Don't make negative statements about a competitor's product, financial condition, or business practices. Never pass along rumors about competitors.

ETHICAL AND LEGAL ISSUES IN INTERNATIONAL SELLING

Ethical and legal issues are very complex when selling in international markets. Value judgments and laws vary widely across cultures and countries. What is commonly accepted as right in one country can be completely unacceptable in another country. For example, a small payment to expedite the loading of a truck is considered a cost of doing business in some Middle Eastern countries but may be viewed as a bribe in the United States.

In many countries, there is a clear distinction between payments for lubrication and payments for subordination. **Lubrication** involves small sums of money or gifts,

will be more successful than salespeople who compromise their own and society's ethics for short-term gain.

Statutory laws (such as the Uniform Commercial Code) and administrative law (such as Federal Trade Commission rulings) guide the activities of salespeople in the United States. Selling in international markets is quite complex, because salespeople need to be aware of differences in ethical judgments and laws, both those of the United States and those of the host country, related to sales activities.

KEY TERMS

administrative law 69
agent 69
back-door selling 64
bribes 60
business defamation 73
collusion 73
common law 69
conspiracy 73
contract to sell 69
credulous person standard 72
cultural relativism 76
deception 70
ethical imperialism 76
ethics 57
expressed warranty 71
FOB (free on board) destination 70
FOB factory 70
Foreign Corrupt Practices Act 77

implied warranty 71
invitation to negotiate 69
kickbacks 60
lubrication 75
offer 69
order 70
price discrimination 74
reciprocity 73
resale price maintenance 74
sale 69
sexual harassment 65
spiffs (push money) 74
statutory law 69
subordination 76
tying agreement 73
Uniform Commercial Code (UCC) 69
warranty 71

QUESTIONS AND PROBLEMS

1. What is a definition of ethics?

2. What is the Uniform Commercial Code?

3. Why are salespeople more likely to confront ethical situations than people in other occupations?

4. For centuries, the guideline for business transactions was the Latin term *caveat emptor* (let the buyer beware). This principle suggests that the seller is not responsible for the buyer's welfare. Is this principle still appropriate in modern business transactions? Why or why not?

5. Consider each of the following situations and indicate whether the salesperson behaved illegally, unethically, or inappropriately or whether the behavior was appropriate.

   a. The buyer's secretary asks you out as you are leaving the plant after making a sales call, and you accept.

   b. You have a customer who is about to place an order. You know the product's price will be reduced in two weeks, and if the buyer knew about the price reduction, she would wait two weeks to place the order. Therefore, you don't inform the buyer about the impending price reduction.

   c. You accept an invitation from a buyer to take you out to dinner in appreciation for all the support you have provided over the last three months.

   d. You ask a buyer about the experiences he has had with a competitor's products.

   e. You go directly to see the head of the engineering department because the buyer will not see you.

   f. You take the afternoon off after making a big sale.

6. What should a salesperson do if he or she believes a competitor is making unethical statements about his or her product?

7. Why are laws enacted to regulate the behavior of salespeople and firms?

8. Consider this statement: "Sales managers, not salespeople, have to be concerned with the legal implications of selling activities." Do you agree with this statement? Why or why not?

9. For each of the following situations, evaluate the salesperson's action and indicate what you think the appropriate action would be.

    a. A business major is being considered for a sales job. During the interview, the sales manager indicates that company officials want to meet the student's husband before offering her a job. Such a meeting is necessary, the company believes, because a salesperson's spouse can be helpful in influencing customers during social events.

    b. A cosmetics manufacturer begins a program of providing extra incentives to retail clerks in cosmetics departments. The salespeople for the cosmetics company are instructed to contact retail clerks and offer them $1 for each item they sell from the manufacturer's product line. The company instructs the salespeople not to mention this program to the management of the retail stores.

    c. In some Latin American countries, a cash payoff to customers who do a favor for a salesperson is considered normal. A young, inexperienced salesperson is given the responsibility for sales in such a Latin American country. When a buyer confronts the salesperson with a demand for a cash payoff in return for a larger order, the salesperson complies.

    d. A salesperson selling small business computers is asked by a customer if the computer has software for an inventory control system. The salesperson replies that an inventory control software package is available as part of the standard software system that comes with each unit. The salesperson has answered the question truthfully but has failed to mention that the inventory control software is useful only in a few special situations and probably will not meet the customer's needs.

    e. A salesperson picks up an order at a customer's plant but forgets to turn it in to the order-processing department. After a few weeks, the customer calls to complain about the slow delivery. The salesperson realizes the order has not been turned in and immediately submits it. Then the salesperson tells the customer that the slow delivery is due to a mistake by the order-processing department because the truth may jeopardize her future relations with the customer.

    f. The custom of the trade is that competitive firms submit bids based on specifications provided by the buyer; then the buyer places an order with the firm offering the lowest bid. After a salesperson submits a bid, the purchasing agent calls him and indicates that the bid is $100,000 too high. The buyer asks the salesperson to submit another bid at a price $100,000 lower.

    g. A customer gives a salesperson a suggestion. The salesperson does not turn in the idea to her company, even though the company's policy manual states that all customer ideas should be submitted with the monthly expense report. Instead, the salesperson quits her job and starts her own business using the customer's suggestion.

    h. A student interviews for a job. The job is attractive, but the salary is about $2,000 lower than those for other sales jobs. When the student tells the interviewer about the low salary, the interviewer says, "You can pick up about $50 a week by padding your expense account."

    i. Jim Hanson is a sales representative for a plastics manufacturer. His company has always had a policy of uniform pricing for all customers. One of his largest customers, Hoffman Container, always tries to bargain for special prices. The buyer is now threatening to use another supplier unless Jim agrees to a special price concession.

Jim's sales manager has agreed to the concession. Jim has just gotten a similar-size order from one of Hoffman's competitors at a price 10 percent higher than Hoffman is demanding. What should Jim do? Does Jim have any responsibility to Hoffman's competitor?

EXPLORING THE NET

Visit the following Internet sites, which provide information about general business ethics and selling ethics. Write a report on the insights you gain from this information.

http://www.condar.depaul.edu/ethics/ethb11.htm

http://www.ethics.ubc.ca/papers/business.html

http://www.acusd.edu/ethics/resources.html

The National Association of Sales Professionals has a code of conduct for salespeople and a discussion and test of sales ethics at its site (http://www.nasp.com). Visit the site and evaluate the code of conduct according to the sales ethics test.

CASE PROBLEMS

CASE 3.1
Confronting an Ethical Dilemma in a New Territory

Tracey Lewis received his BA in June 1996 and joined Baby Works, Inc., as a sales trainee. He expected to work for six to nine months as a trainee and then be assigned to a sales territory. Baby Works is a large manufacturer of children's wear, with annual sales in excess of $20 million. It employs 25 salespeople, who are paid a straight commission of 6 percent. They all report to the national sales manager, Susan Hoyt.

In November 1996, Larry Kennedy, the sales representative covering the Atlanta territory, died suddenly. Larry had been a longtime employee of Baby Works and was highly regarded for his selling abilities. When news of the sales rep's death reached headquarters, Susan Hoyt asked Tracey Lewis to take over the territory. She went on to explain that she was going on a four-week business trip to Europe and would be unable to introduce Tracey to customers in the territory.

During his first two weeks in the territory, Tracey visited most of its key customers. He made several sales and opened some new accounts. After this success, he felt confident enough to meet with the buyer for his largest account, Tom White of the Kiddie World chain. The previous year, Kiddie World had ordered $80,000 in merchandise. Tracey, anxious to present the new spring line and to establish rapport with this key customer, arranged a dinner date with Tom.

The dinner meeting went well. After some social conversation, Tracey presented the new line and asked Tom what he thought of it. Tom said he was impressed, but he was also considering two competitive lines. After Tracey explained how Baby Works' line was superior, Tom told him that Larry Kennedy had given him a $500 bonus before each season. Tom said, "I hope we can work together the way Larry and I did. There are a lot of good lines and a lot of good salespeople, but Larry was something special."

Question

1. What would you do if you were in Tracey Lewis's position?

CASE 3.2
Selling in Latin America

California Tool Company has a one-person sales office in a large Latin American country. Danny Wheeler has been in that country for 10 years and is retiring this year. His replacement is Bob Green, a top sales rep covering Texas and New Mexico.

Danny has been very successful in spite of his unique style and his refusal to conform to company policies. Some senior executives complained about Danny to the former CEO, who responded, "If he's making money—and he is—then leave the guy alone." However, the new CEO is reorganizing California Tool to be a global firm in which a loner like Danny would probably not fit in. In fact, the CEO specifically chose Bob to replace Danny because Bob is an organization person.

When Bob arrived at the Latin American California Tool office, Danny was on his way to inspect some California Tool machines. Some adjustments had to be made in the machines before they would be acceptable to the government agency buying them. After inspecting the machines, Bob and Danny had lunch.

DANNY Bob, did you see any problems with the S-27s we just looked at?

BOB No, they looked fine to me.

DANNY I suspect this is one of the most sophisticated instances of bribe taking I've come across in my 10 years here. Most of the time they're more honest about their *mordidas* than this.

BOB What is *mordidas*?

DANNY *Mordidas* is a little grease to expedite the action. It's a local word for a slight offering. You might call it a bribe.

BOB Do we pay bribes to get an order?

DANNY Oh, it depends on the situation, but it's something you have to deal with. Here's the story. When the S-27s arrived, we began uncrating them and right away the local engineer for the agency told me there is a vital defect with the machines. I agreed to have our staff engineer check all the machines and make the necessary adjustments, but he said there wasn't enough time for an engineer to come from the States. He said the machines could be adjusted locally. We could pay him and he would make the arrangements. What could I do? I paid him $1,200 for each machine.

BOB I don't like it. We've got good products, and they are priced right. We give good service and keep plenty of spare parts in Latin America. Why should we have to pay bribes? In addition, paying bribes to a government official is illegal.

DANNY Look, you're not back in the States any longer. If you stop these payoffs your sales are going to go down because our competitors from Germany, Italy, and Japan will pay them.

BOB I know. But wrong is wrong, and we want to operate differently now. We want to expand our operation here and make a long-term commitment. One of the first things we must avoid is unethical behavior.

DANNY But *is* it unethical? Everyone does it, and the people here even pay *mordidas* to each other. Remember, "When in Rome do as the Romans do."

BOB I can't buy that. We have to differentiate ourselves from the rest of our competition. Graft and unethical behavior have to be cut out to build lasting relationships. By taking the high road, we will strengthen our position.

DANNY I know it's hard to accept. Probably the most disturbing problem in these developing countries is graft. And frankly, we really don't know how to deal with it. It bothered me at first. But now I think it makes its own economic contribution because it's as much a part of the economic process as a payroll. Are we developers of wealth, helping to push the country to greater economic growth, or are we missionaries? Or should we be both?

Questions

1. Danny seems to imply that there is a difference between business activities in Latin America and those in the United States. Do you think there is a difference? Is what Danny did ethical?

2. If Danny should not have paid the bribe, what should he have done, and what might have been the consequences?

3. What are California Tool's interests in this situation, and should they be considered?

ADDITIONAL REFERENCES

Boedecker, Karl; Fred Morgan; and Jeffery Stoltman. "Legal Dimensions of Salespersons' Statements: A Review and Managerial Suggestions."*Journal of Marketing*, January 1991, pp. 70–80.

Chonko, Lawrence; John Tanner; and William Weeks. "Ethics in Salesperson Decision Making: A Synthesis of Research Approaches and an Extension of the Scenario Method." *Journal of Personal Selling & Sales Management*, Winter 1996, pp. 35–52.

Donaldson, Thomas, and Thomas Dunfee. *Business Ethics as Social Contracts*. Cambridge, MA: Harvard Business School Press, 1997.

Gundlach, Gregory. "The Role of Legal and Nonlegal Approaches Across the Exchange Process Exchange Governance." *Journal of Public Policy & Marketing*, Fall 1994, pp. 246–53.

Jackson, Donald; Stephan Tax; and John Barnes. "Examining the Salesforce Culture: Managerial Applications and Research Propositions." *Journal of Personal Selling & Sales Management*, Fall 1994, pp. 1–14

Lazniak, Gene, and Patrick Murphy. *Ethical Marketing Decisions: The Higher Road*. Boston: Allyn & Bacon, 1993.

McCracken, Gail, and Thomas Callahan. "Is There Such a Thing as a Free Lunch?" *International Journal of Purchasing & Materials Management*, Winter 1996, pp. 44–50.

Peterson, Robin. "Selling and Sales Management in Action : An Examination of Industrial Sales Representative Accuracy in Discriminating Selected Legal and Illegal Actions." *Journal of Personal Selling & Sales Management*, Spring 1994, pp. 67–72.

Smith, N. C., and J. A. Quelch. *Ethics in Marketing*. Burr Ridge, IL: Richard D. Irwin, 1993.

Tansey, Richard; Gene Brown; Michael Hyman; and Lyndon Dawson. "Personal Moral Philosophies and the Moral Judgments of Salespeople." *Journal of Personal Selling & Sales Management*, Winter 1994, pp. 59–75.

Turner, Gregory; Stephens Taylor; and Mark Hartley. "Ethics, Gratuities, and Professionalism of the Purchasing Function." *Journal of Business Ethics*, September 1995, pp. 761–70.

Wotruba, Thomas. "A Comprehensive Framework for the Analysis of Ethical Behavior, with a Focus on Sales Organizations." *Journal of Personal Selling & Sales Management*, Spring 1990, pp. 29–42.

The basis of effective personal selling is understanding the customer's needs and communicating how your product or service satisfies those needs. Part Two provides information about the knowledge and skills needed to be an effective salesperson.

Chapter Four focuses on customers—the process they go through in making purchase decisions and the factors they consider in evaluating alternatives. The chapter also outlines changes occurring in the way businesses buy products and services, and shows how these changes will affect what salespeople do.

Part Two

Knowledge *and* Skill Requirements

Chapter Five reviews communication principles. It explains how salespeople can collect information about their customers by listening, asking questions, and observing nonverbal behaviors. Methods for using verbal and nonverbal communication to influence customers are also discussed.

Effective selling requires salespeople to adopt both the style and content of their sales presentations to satisfy the needs of a customer. Chapter Six discusses why flexibility is important and how salespeople can develop the knowledge to effectively practice adaptive selling.

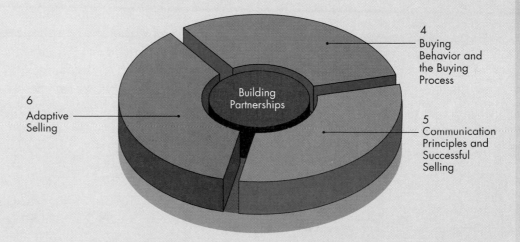

6
Adaptive Selling

Building Partnerships

4
Buying Behavior and the Buying Process

5
Communication Principles and Successful Selling

Chapter Four

Buying Behavior *and* *the* Buying Process

Superior customer knowledge enabled Bill Meyer, vice president of sales at Chemineer Corporation, to snatch a million-dollar contract from a complacent competitor. Chemineer makes mixing equipment for chemical plants. When Meyer received an inquiry from a major chemical company, he assumed the inquiry was

Some Questions Answered in this Chapter Are:

What are the different types of customers?

How do organizations make purchase decisions?

What factors do organizations consider when evaluating products and services?

Who is involved in the buying decision?

What should salespeople do in the different types of buying situations?

What changes are occurring in organizational buying, and how will these changes affect salespeople?

a mere formality because the company bought all of its mixing equipment from a competitor. The key decision maker was concerned about mechanical problems of mounting and supporting an unusually large mixing tank. Meyer found out who the other decision makers were and arranged for them to talk with customers using similar-size tanks made by Chemineer.

Meanwhile, Chemineer's competitor was unaware of the customer's concerns. As the established supplier, it didn't keep on top of the customer's new needs. Chemineer won the contract, despite a slightly higher price, because Meyer knew more about the customer.

To be effective, salespeople must know what their customers need, who will be involved in the purchase decision, and how the purchase decision will be made. The more salespeople know about their customers, the more effective they will be in satisfying those customers' needs.

PROFILE

Seymour Barker is director of the buying group for the Kitchenaid and Major Appliance Division Whirlpool Corporation in Benton

Harbor, Michigan. He has a BS in business administration from Central State University in Ohio and an MBA with a concentration in marketing from Indiana University in Bloomington, Indiana.

Barker explains, "My responsibilities at Whirlpool are multifaceted. I am in charge of developing, negotiating, and implementing our national group sales programs through our major appliance committees as well as overseeing our promotional budget and organizing national group trade shows. I joined Whirlpool 23 years ago and have worked all over the country in various sales positions. I began as a sales manager trainee in Minneapolis, and then worked in a variety of selling capacities in Florida and Georgia before becoming director of product marketing at our branch office in Dallas.

"You need to be able to analyze and determine the buying behavior patterns of your customers and then adapt your selling strategy to conform to the requirements of those processes."

SEYMOUR BARKER
Whirlpool

"Selling is an extremely challenging field and requires that you master skills in a number of critical areas. You need to be able to analyze and determine the buying behavior patterns of your customers and then adapt your selling strategy to conform to the requirements of those processes. My objective is always to try to develop win-win situations for our clients and Whirlpool, even when those positions initially appear to be polar opposites. At Whirlpool, we are always looking to sell our best products at good prices with volume commitments from those who buy from us. Conversely, our customers are looking for the best product quality at the lowest prices and without a volume commitment.

"I was recently involved in a challenging situation where I was trying to develop a merchandising program in a difficult area. In the appliance industry, there is a phenomenon taking place where the smaller outfits are being driven out of business by larger, national chains. This was the group of buyers with whom I was trying to develop a merchandising program that had all the right elements for Whirlpool and them. One element of our strategy at Whirlpool involves a requirement for our business partners to commit to a volume increase from one year to the next. Since the businesses in this particular group were actually losing share, I knew that would pose a stumbling block to negotiating a volume increase for us. If you push too hard, you run the risk of losing the customer because they feel they cannot commit to the terms of the program that you want them to sign up for. In the end, I had to discuss the issue with our VP and get him to realize that we were dealing with shrinking opportunities in that channel.

"The deal I finally concluded the negotiation process with was one where we agreed that this customer group could receive the benefits of the merchandising program if they maintained their market share, which satisfied both the customers and my management.

"I really enjoy selling and love the opportunity it gives me to develop creative solutions to problems while working with a finite set of resources."

Visit Our Website@
http://www.whirlpool.com

TYPES OF
CUSTOMERS

Salespeople interact with a wide of variety of customers, including producers, resellers, government agencies, institutions, and consumers. Each of these customer types has different needs and uses a different process to buy products and services. Thus, salespeople need to use different approaches when selling to each type of customer.

Producers

Producers buy goods and services to manufacture and sell other goods and services to their customers. Buyers working for producers are involved in two types of buying situations: They make buying decisions as original equipment manufacturers (OEMs) or as end users and resellers.

Original Equipment Manufacturers

When buyers purchase goods (components, subassemblies, raw and processed materials) to use in making their products, they are acting as **original equipment manufacturers (OEMs).** For example, General Motors buys glass windshields from PPG and uses the windshields in the automobiles it sells to consumers. The windshields directly affect the performance and cost of GM's cars. Thus, quality and cost are important concerns for GM's OEM purchases. Companies like General Motors buy more than $60 billion annually—over $170 million each day—for products such as steel, upholstery, and tires.

Salespeople sell products and services to an OEM such as Boeing on the left. Boeing salespeople sell planes to end users such as American Airlines on the right. American Airlines then sells services (air transportation) to consumers and businesses.

Paul Chesley/Tony Stone Images

David Joel/Tony Stone Images

Some components develop such a good reputation for quality that they help sell the producers' products. For example, personal computer manufacturers advertise that Intel microprocessors are inside their computers. Thus, customers who believe Intel microprocessors offer superior performance are more inclined to purchase a personal computer with the label "Intel Inside."

Most OEM purchases are for standardized products and services bought in large quantities on an annual contract. The purchasing department negotiates the contract with the supplier; however, engineering and production departments evaluate the products and can affect the choice of suppliers. When sellers custom design OEM products to buyers' specifications, the buyers' engineering and production areas have much more influence in the choice of vendor.

End Users

When producers buy goods and services to support their own production and operations, they are acting as **end users.** End-user buying situations include the purchase of capital equipment; maintenance, repair, and operating (MRO) supplies; and services. **Capital equipment** items are major purchases, such as mainframe computers and machine tools, that the producer uses for a number of years. **MRO supplies** are minor purchases, such as paper towels and pencils, that have a short useful life. Services include telephone connections, employment agencies, consultants, and shipping.

Since capital equipment purchases typically require major financial commitments, many people, including high-level corporate executives, are involved in the purchase decision. Reliability, service, and support are often important considerations, because an equipment failure can shut down the producer's operation. Capital equipment buying often focuses on operating cost rather than the initial purchase price, because the equipment is used over a long period of time.

MRO supplies and services are typically a minor expense and therefore are usually less important to businesses. Purchasing agents typically oversee these buying decisions. Because they often do not want to spend the time to evaluate all suppliers, they tend to purchase from vendors who have performed well in the past. Some professional services, such as accounting, advertising, and consulting, are more important to the company and may be treated as capital equipment purchases.

Resellers

Resellers buy finished products or services with the intention to resell them to businesses and consumers. For example, Barnes & Noble buys large quantities of books from publishers and resells them to consumers visiting their stores. McKesson Corporation is a wholesaler that buys heath care products from manufacturers and resells them to drugstores.

Because resellers do not use the products, they are interested primarily in the attractiveness of the products to their customers. For example, Du Pont promotes the benefits of Stainmaster™ carpets to stimulate consumer demand and thus encourage carpet distributors and retailers to stock and sell the carpets. Resellers are also interested in services provided by suppliers that make the resale of the product more profitable.[1] Selling Scenario 4.1 describes how a salesperson sells Nike shoes to a major reseller. (The special needs of resellers and approaches for selling to them are discussed in Chapter Fifteen.)

Note that the same customer can act as an OEM manufacturer, an end user, and a reseller. For example, Dell Computer makes OEM buying decisions when it pur-

SELLING SCENARIO 4.1

Selling Nike Shoes to the Troops

Dan Fleshman is responsible for selling Nike footwear to the 700 worldwide base exchanges operated by five branches of the U.S. armed forces (Army, Navy, Air Force, Coast Guard, and Veterans). When he took over the accounts 10 years ago, Nike was selling only $10 million a year to the military. Now sales are over $70 million annually.

"We don't just make deals. We try to get involved in all aspects of the business . . . ," Fleshman says. Fleshman addressed two fundamental problems in building military sales. First, all of the bases were ordering the same 20 units each year. "We had to convince them to carry more styles and to tailor assortments to individual bases. If it's a training base, you need more men's and women's running shoes. If it's a

regular base, you need to merchandise for families." Second, the distribution system was very inefficient. Orders would sit in government warehouses for more than a month before they were sent to Nike. Fleshman developed a system to bypass the government warehouses, and bases now receive shoes directly from Nike in less than 10 days after an order is placed.

"We have to be partners and help customers plan their business," Fleshman says. "Instead of just identifying problems, we have to propose solutions and make sure the solutions get implemented."

Source: Robert Sharoff, "For Service, Send in the Troops," *Selling,* November 1994, pp. 70–71. Reprinted with permission from Institutional Investors, Inc.

chases microprocessors for its computers, acts as an end user when it buys a machine to bend sheet metal for the cases that house the computers, and functions as a reseller when it buys software to resell to its computer customers when they place orders.

Government

The largest customers for goods and services in the United States are federal, state, and local governments, which purchase over $1 trillion of goods and services annually. More than half of these purchases are made by the federal government, making it the largest customer in the world.[2]

Government buyers typically develop detailed specifications for a product and then invite qualified suppliers to submit bids. A contract is awarded to the lowest bidder. However, government agencies are beginning to purchase more commercial products using less red tape.[3]

Effective selling to government agencies requires a thorough knowledge of their unique procurement procedures and rules. Salespeople also need to know about projected needs so they can influence the development of the buying specifications. For example, Harris Corporation worked for six years with the Federal Aviation Administration and finally won a $1.7 billion contract to modernize air traffic communication systems.

Some resources available to salespeople working with the federal government are

- Guidelines for selling to the government published by U.S. Government Printing Office.
- The *Commerce Business Daily,* which contains all invitations for bids issued by the federal government.
- The *Procurement Automated Source System (PASS),* the Small Business Administration database with information on over 900 federal purchasing agents and prime contractors working on federal contracts.[4]

Selling this attack helicopter to the government requires a thorough knowledge of government procedures and regulations.

Courtesy Parker Hannifin Corporation

 Many international salespeople are selling to government agencies, even though private companies may be their biggest customers in the United States. For example, Northern Telecom, a Canadian company that manufactures telephone equipment, sells to private companies such as Bell South and IBM in the United States but to the post, telephone, and telegraph (PTT) government agency in many countries in Europe, Asia, and Africa. Selling to foreign governments is very challenging. The percentage of domestic product (countries may require that a certain percentage of the product be manufactured or assembled locally) and exchange rates (the value of local currency in U.S. dollars) are as important as the characteristics of the product. Different economic and political systems, cultures, and languages also can make international selling difficult.

Institutions

Another important customer group consists of public and private institutions such as churches, hospitals, and colleges. Often these institutions have purchasing rules and procedures that are as complex and rigid as those used by government agencies.

Packaged goods manufacturers, such as Heinz, sell to both resellers (supermarkets) and institutional customers (restaurants and hospitals). These customers have different needs and buying processes. Thus, Heinz has one sales force calling on supermarkets and another sales force selling different products to restaurants.

Consumers

Consumers purchase products and services for use by themselves or by their families. A lot of salespeople sell insurance, automobiles, clothing, and real estate to consumers. However, college graduates often take sales jobs that involve selling to business enterprises, government agencies, or institutions. Thus, the examples in this text focus on these selling situations, and this chapter discusses organizational rather than consumer buying behavior.

In the next section, we contrast the buying processes of consumers and organizations. Then we describe the buying process organizations use in more detail, including the steps in the process, who influences the decisions, and how salespeople can influence the decisions.

SELLING SCENARIO 4.2

Some Sales Take Forever

Forget the fast break and slam dunk. For Chuck Smith, a salesperson at Walker Interactive Systems, selling is a slow, deliberate, half-court game. It took Walker three years to sell a $1 million general ledger system to an aircraft manufacturing division of a large corporation. The process began when the customer issued a request for information (RFI). Since each sale requires so much time, Smith had to determine immediately whether it was worth spending the time to respond to the RFI.

Based on Smith's response to the RFI, the customer selected Walker as a potential supplier. Smith assembled an account team of product specialists and technical experts to develop a proposal. He says, "We got the people on our team bonding with the people on their team. You have to meet all of the functional and technical requirements, but I believe that people buy from people they like and trust."

A year after the initial RFI, Smith's team had developed strong relationships with the division's contact people, but Smith discovered they did not have authority to sign off on the order. Despite previous assurances, the parent company had final approval and decided the corporation was no longer going to buy mainframe systems. Smith had to forge ahead with a new round of presentations to the corporation. He "trained" the division personnel to sell the concept to their corporate counterparts and finally closed the sale, three years after the RFI.

Smith typically makes five sales a year. He has 4 or 5 deals going with a high probability of success and another 10 in the initial stages. Here are tips for success in long-cycle sales:

- Stay in touch. Call the customer, check on the status, and mail information so the customer will keep you on the top of its mind.
- Stay energized. Keep things moving on your side. Bring the team up to date. Ask for suggestions on how to move things along.
- Stay busy. Always have several sales going.

Source: Francy Blackwood, "Close, Yet So Far Away," *Selling,* September 1994, pp. 24–26. Reprinted with permission from Institutional Investors, Inc.

ORGANIZATIONAL BUYING AND SELLING

The salespeople you encounter most frequently sell to consumers. They have a very different job than do the salespeople who call on organizations. Since the organizational buying process typically is more complex than the consumer buying process, selling to organizations often requires more skills and is more challenging.[5]

Complexity of the Organizational Buying Process

The typical organizational purchase is much larger and more complex than the typical consumer purchase. Organizations use highly trained, knowledgeable purchasing agents to make these decisions. Many other people in organizations are involved in purchase decisions, including engineers, production managers, business analysts, and senior executives.

Organizational buying decisions often involve extensive evaluations and negotiations over a period of time. The average time required to complete a purchase is five months, and during that time salespeople need to make many calls to gather and provide information. Selling Scenario 4.2 describes the time and effort required to make a major sale.

The complexity of organizational purchase decisions means that salespeople must be able to work effectively with a wide range of people. For example, when selling a new additive to a food processor such as Nabisco, an International Flavors and Fragrances salesperson may interact with advertising, product development, legal, production, quality control, and customer service people at Nabisco. The salesperson needs to know the technical and economic benefits of the additive to Nabisco and the benefits to consumers.

In addition, the salesperson coordinates all areas of his or her own firm to assist in making the sale. The salesperson works with research and development to provide data on consumer taste tests, with production to meet the customer's delivery requirements, and with finance to set the purchasing terms. (Working effectively within the salesperson's organization is discussed in more detail in Chapter Seventeen.)

The complexity of organizational selling is increasing as more customers become global businesses. For example, Deere and Company has a special unit to coordinate worldwide purchases. The unit evaluates potential suppliers across the globe for each of its product lines and manufacturing facilities.[6] Thus, a salesperson selling fan belts to Deere must work with the special corporate buying unit as well as with the employees at each manufacturing location around the world.

Derived versus Direct Demand

Salespeople selling to consumers typically can focus on the individual consumer or family needs. Organizational selling often requires salespeople to know about the customer's customers. Sales to OEMs and resellers are based on derived demand rather than direct demand. **Derived demand** means that purchases made by these customers ultimately depend on the demand for their products—either other organizations or consumers. For example, J.R. Simplot sells 1.5 billion pounds of potatoes to McDonald's restaurants. Its sales depend on how many french fries McDonald's sells.[7] When demand is derived, salespeople must understand the needs of the ultimate user as well as those of the immediate customer.

Sometimes salespeople can stimulate the demand for their products by directing their efforts toward the ultimate customer. For example, Procter & Gamble salespeo-

DuPont encourages retailers to buy its Stainmaster© carpet by promoting the benefits of the carpet to the retailer's customers, creating a derived demand.

Courtesy E. I. du Pont de Nemours and Company

ple set up in-store displays so consumers will buy more of their products. When the consumers do buy more, the supermarkets place more orders with Procter & Gamble.

THE ORGANIZATIONAL BUYING PROCESS

To effectively sell to organizations, salespeople need to understand how organizations make purchase decisions. This section discusses the steps in the organizational buying process, the different types of buying decisions, and the people involved in making the decisions.[8]

Steps in the Buying Process

Exhibit 4.1 shows the eight steps in an organizational buying process.

Recognizing a Need or a Problem (Step 1)

The buying process starts when someone realizes that a problem exists. Employees in the customer's firm or outside salespeople can trigger this recognition. For example, a supermarket cashier might discover that the optical scanner is making mistakes in reading the bar code labels. Salespeople often trigger the buying process by demonstrating how their products can improve the efficiency of the customer's operation.

EXHIBIT 4.1

Steps in the Organizational Buying Process

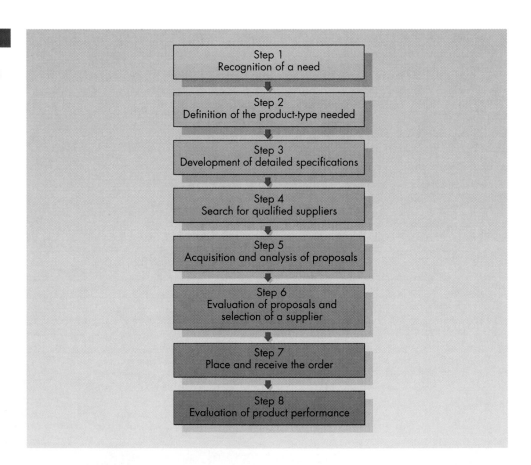

Step 1
Recognition of a need

Step 2
Definition of the product-type needed

Step 3
Development of detailed specifications

Step 4
Search for qualified suppliers

Step 5
Acquisition and analysis of proposals

Step 6
Evaluation of proposals and selection of a supplier

Step 7
Place and receive the order

Step 8
Evaluation of product performance

Defining the Product Needed (Step 2)

After identifying a problem, organization members develop a general approach to solving it. For example, a production manager who concludes that the factory is not running efficiently recognizes a problem, but this may not lead to a purchase decision. The manager may think the inefficiency is caused by poor supervision or unskilled workers.

However, a production equipment salesperson might work with the manager to analyze the situation and show how efficiency could be improved by purchasing some automated assembly equipment. When this occurs, the problem solution is defined in terms of purchasing a product or service—the automated assembly equipment needed—and the buying process moves to step 3.

Development of Specifications (Step 3)

In step 3, the specifications for the product needed to solve the problem are prepared. Potential suppliers will use these specifications to develop proposals. The buyers will use them to objectively evaluate the proposals.

Steps 2 and 3 offer great opportunities for salespeople to influence the outcome of the buying process. Using their knowledge of their firm's products and the customer's needs, salespeople can help develop specifications that favor their particular product. For example, a Hyster forklift might have superior performance in terms of a small turning radius. Knowing this advantage and the customer's small, tightly packed warehouse, the Hyster salesperson might influence the customer to specify a very small turning radius for forklifts, a turning radius that only Hyster forklifts can provide. Competing salespeople, who first become aware of this procurement after the specifications were written, will be at a severe disadvantage.

Searching for Qualified Suppliers (Step 4)

After the specifications have been written, the customer looks for potential suppliers. The customer may simply contact previous suppliers or go through an extensive search procedure: calling salespeople, asking for a list of customers, and checking with the customers on each supplier's financial stability and performance.

Acquiring and Analyzing Proposals (Step 5)

In step 5, qualified suppliers are asked to submit proposals. Salespeople work with people in their company to develop their proposal.

Evaluation of Proposals and Selection of a Supplier (Step 6)

Next, the customer evaluates the proposals. After selecting a preferred supplier, further negotiations may take place concerning price, delivery, or specific performance features.

Placement of an Order and Receipt of Product (Step 7)

In step 7, an order is placed with the selected supplier. The order goes to the supplier, who acknowledges receipt and commits to a delivery date. Eventually the product is shipped to the buying firm, which inspects the received goods and then pays the supplier for the product. During this step, salespeople need to make sure the paperwork is correct and their firm knows what has to be done to satisfy the customer's requirements.

Evaluation of Product Performance (Step 8)

In the final step of the purchasing process, the product's performance is evaluated. The evaluation may be a formal or an informal assessment made by people involved in the buying process.[9]

Salespeople play an important role in this step. They need to work with the users to make sure the product performs well. In addition, salespeople need to work with purchasing agents to ensure that they are satisfied with the communications and delivery.

This after-sale support ensures that the salesperson's product will get a positive evaluation and he or she will be considered a qualified supplier in future procurement.[10] This step is critical to establishing the successful long-term relationships discussed in Chapter Two. (Building relationships through after-sale support is discussed in more detail in Chapter Thirteen.)

Creeping Commitment

Creeping commitment means that a customer becomes increasingly committed to a particular course of action while going through the steps in the buying process. As decisions are made at each step, the range of alternatives narrows; the customer becomes more and more committed to a specific course of action and even to a specific vendor. Thus, it is critical that salespeople be very involved in the initial steps so they will have an opportunity to participate in the final steps, as illustrated by the Chemineer sales situation introducing this chapter.

Thinking *it* Through	Think of a major decision you have made, such as buying a car or a computer or finding an apartment and signing a lease. What steps did you go through in making this decision? How can you relate your decision-making process to the eight steps in the organizational buying process? Did any decisions you made early in the process affect decisions you made later in the process?

TYPES OF ORGANIZATIONAL BUYING DECISIONS

Many purchase decisions are made without going through all of the eight steps described above. For example, a Frito-Lay salesperson may check the supply of his or her products in a supermarket, write out a purchase order to restock the shelves, and present it to the store manager. After recognizing the problem of low stock, the manager simply signs the order (step 6) without going through any of the other steps. However, if the Frito-Lay salesperson wanted the manager to devote more shelf space to Frito-Lay snacks, the manager might go through all eight steps in making and evaluating this decision.

Exhibit 4.2 describes three types of buying decisions—new tasks, straight rebuys, and modified rebuys—along with the strategies salespeople need to use in each situation. In this exhibit, the "in" company is the seller that has provided the product or service to the company in the past, and the "out" company is the seller that is not or has not been a supplier to the customer.[11]

New Tasks

When a customer purchases a product or service for the first time, a **new-task** situation occurs. Most purchase decisions involving capital equipment or the initial purchase of OEM products are new tasks.

EXHIBIT 4.2	New Task	Modified Rebuy	Straight Rebuy
Types of Organizational Buying Decisions			
Customer Needs			
Information and risk reduction	Information about causes and solutions for a new problem Reduce high risk in making a decision with limited knowledge.	Information and solutions to increase efficiency and/or reduce costs.	Generally needs are satisfied.
Nature of Buying Process			
Number of people involved in process	Many	Few	One
Time to make a decision	Months or years	Month	Day
Key steps in the buying process	1, 2, 3, 8	3, 4, 5, 6, 8	5, 6, 7, 8
Key decision makers	Executives and engineers	Production and purchasing managers	Purchasing agent
Selling Strategy			
For in supplier	Monitor changes in customer needs; respond quickly when problems and new needs arise; provide technical information	Act immediately when problems arise	Reinforce relationship with customers; make sure all of customer's needs are satisfied
For out supplier	Suggest new approach for solving problems; provide technical advice	Respond more quickly than present supplier when problem arises; encourage customer to consider an alternative; present information on how new alternative will increase efficiency	Convince customer of potential benefits from reexamining choice of supplier; secure recognition and approval as an alternative supplier

Since the customer has not made the purchase decision recently, the company's knowledge is limited and it goes through all eight steps of the buying process. In these situations, customers face considerable risk. Thus, they typically seek information from salespeople and welcome their knowledge. For example, when NBC decided to upgrade the technology of its studio equipment, it assembled a nationwide team of engineers, production supervisors, and buyers. It asked seven major electronics manufacturers from around the world to submit proposals.[12]

From the salesperson's perspective, the initial buying process steps are critical in new-task situations. During these steps, the alert salesperson can help the customer define the characteristics of the needed product and develop the purchase specifications. By working with the customer in these initial steps, the salesperson can take advantage of creeping commitment and gain a significant advantage over the competition.

A Frito-Lay salesperson takes inventory of snacks to prepare a refill order for the store manager to sign. In this situation, the manager will make a straight rebuy decision and not go through the eight steps in the buying process.

©Jay Brousseau

The final step, postpurchase evaluation, is also critical. Buyers making a new purchase decision are especially interested in evaluating results. They will use this information in making similar purchase decisions in the future.

Straight Rebuys

In a **straight rebuy** situation, the customer buys the same product from the same source it used when the need arose previously. Since customers have purchased the product or service a number of times, they have considerable knowledge about their requirements and the potential vendors. MRO supplies and services and reorders of OEM components often are straight rebuy situations.

Typically, a straight rebuy is triggered by an internal event, such as a low inventory level. Since needs are easily recognized, specifications have been developed, and potential suppliers have been identified, the latter steps of the buying process assume greater importance.

Some straight rebuys are computerized. For example, many hospitals use an automatic reorder system developed by Baxter, a manufacturer and distributor of medical supplies. When the inventory control system recognizes that levels of supplies such as tape, surgical sponges, or IV kits have dropped to prespecified levels, a purchase order is automatically generated and transmitted electronically to the nearest Baxter distribution center.

When a company is satisfied and has developed a long-term supplier relationship, it continues to order from the same company it has used in the past. Salespeople at "in" companies want to maintain the strong relationship; they do not want the customer to consider new suppliers. Thus, they must make sure orders are delivered on time and the products continue to get favorable evaluations.

Salespeople trying to break into a straight rebuy situation—those representing an "out" supplier—face a tough sales problem. Often they need to persuade a customer to change suppliers even though the present supplier is performing satisfactorily. In such situations, the salesperson hopes the present supplier will make a critical mistake, causing the customer to reevaluate suppliers. To break into a straight rebuy situation, salespeople need to provide very compelling information to motivate the customer to treat the purchase as a modified rebuy.

Modified Rebuys

In a **modified rebuy** situation, the customer has purchased the product or a similar product in the past but is interested in obtaining new information. This situation typically occurs when the "in" supplier performs unsatisfactorily, a new product becomes available, or the buying needs change. In such situations, sales representatives of the "in" suppliers need to convince customers to maintain the relationship and continue their present buying pattern. When "in" suppliers have strong customer relationships, they are the first to find out when the requirements have changed and provide the supplier's salespeople with information to assist them in responding to the new requirements.

Salespeople with "out" suppliers want customers to reevaluate the situation and actively consider switching vendors. The successful sales rep will need to influence all the people taking part in the buying decision. The types of employees involved are discussed in the next section.

WHO MAKES THE BUYING DECISION?

As we discussed previously, a number of people are involved in making new-task and modified rebuy organizational decisions. This group of people is called the **buying center,** an informal, cross-department group of people involved in a purchase decision. People in the customer's organization become involved in a buying center because they have formal responsibilities for purchasing or they are important sources of information. In some cases, the buying center includes experts who are not full-time employees. For example, consultants usually specify the air conditioning equipment that will be used in a factory undergoing remodeling. Thus, the buying center defines the set of people who make or influence the purchase decision.[13]

Salespeople need to know the names and responsibilities of all people in the buying center for a purchase decision. For example, Gus Maikish heads a 21-person sales team responsible for IBM's business with a major New York City bank. He says, "There are many people involved in a major sale, and each one has a specific stake in the outcome. One will be concerned with reliability, another with processing speed, someone else with obsolescence."

The buying center for an MRI scanner in a hospital may include the three types of people shown below: the technician operating the equipment (end user), radiologists (gate keepers), and the hospital administrator (decider).

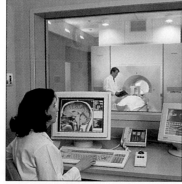

Pete Saloutos/The Stock Market   Mug Shots/The Stock Market   Jose L. Pelaez/The Stock Market

To coordinate a major sale, Maikish uses a matrix. Each vertical column is labeled with the name of key influencers in a specific area of the bank, such as investment banking, securities trading, or data processing. Along the side of the matrix, he lists all of the factors that might be considered in evaluating the proposal (e.g., software availability, ease of user interface). Then, in the matrix squares, he checks off the factors important to each influencer.[14]

The composition of the buying center may change for each purchase decision, particularly for new tasks. Thus, salespeople frequently build detailed files for each customer, including organization charts and the responsibilities of each person. Even this information may need to be supplemented for specific buying situations.

Users

Users, such as the manufacturing-area personnel for OEM products and capital equipment, typically do not make the ultimate purchase decision. However, they often have considerable influence in the early and late steps of the buying process—need recognition, product definition, and postpurchase evaluation. Thus, users are particularly important in new-task and modified rebuy situations. Salespeople often attempt to convert a straight rebuy to a modified rebuy by demonstrating superior product performance or a new benefit to users.

Influencers

People inside or outside the organization who directly or indirectly provide information during the buying process are **influencers.** These members of the buying center may provide details on product specifications, criteria for evaluating proposals, or information about potential suppliers. For example, the marketing department can influence a purchase decision by indicating that the company's products would sell better if they included a particular supplier's components. Architects can play the critical role in the purchase of construction material by specifying suppliers, even though the ultimate purchase orders will be placed by the contractor responsible for constructing the building.

Gatekeepers

Gatekeepers control the flow of information and may limit the alternatives considered. For example, the quality control and service departments may determine which potential suppliers are qualified sources.

Purchasing agents often play a gatekeeping role by determining which potential suppliers are to be notified about the purchase situation and are to have access to relevant information. In some companies, all contacts must be made through purchasing agents. They arrange meetings with other gatekeepers, influencers, and users. When dealing with such companies, salespeople often are not allowed to contact these members of the buying center directly. When salespeople find purchasing agents restricting their access to important information, they are tempted to bypass the purchasing agents and make direct contact. This back-door approach can upset purchasing agents so much that they may disqualify the salesperson's company from the purchase situation.[15]

Deciders

In any buying center, one or more members of the group, **deciders,** make the final choice. Determining who actually makes the purchase decision for an organization is often difficult. For straight rebuys, the purchasing agent usually selects the vendor and places the order. However, for new tasks, many people influence the decision and several people must approve the decision and sign the purchase order.

In general, senior executives get more involved in important purchase decisions, those that have a greater effect on the performance of the organization. For example, the chief executive officer (CEO) and chief financial officer (CFO) would play

EXHIBIT 4.3	Importance of Hospital Buying Center Members in the Buying Process for Intensive-Care Monitoring Equipment				
Step in Buying Process	Physicians	Nurses	Hospital Administrators	Engineers	Purchasing Agents
Need recognition (step 1)	High	Moderate	Low	Low	Low
Specification of product (step 3)	High	High	Moderate	Moderate	Low
Analysis of proposal (step 5)	High	Moderate	Moderate	High	Low
Selecting a supplier (step 6)	High	Low	High	Low	Moderate

an important role in purchasing a telephone system, because this network would have a significant impact on the firm's day-to-day operations.

To sell effectively to organizations, salespeople need to know the people in the buying center and their involvement at different steps of the buying process. Consider the following situation. Salespeople selling expensive intensive-care monitoring equipment know that a hospital buying center for the type of equipment they sell typically consists of physicians, nurses, hospital administrators, engineers, and purchasing agents. Through experience, they also know the relative importance of these buying center members in various stages of the purchasing process (see Exhibit 4.3). With this information, the intensive-care equipment salespeople know to concentrate on physicians throughout the process, nurses and engineers in the middle of the process, and hospital administrators and purchasing agents at the end of the process.

In some countries, it is difficult to determine who the members of the buying center are. For example, in China, Craig McLaughlin of Texaco reports that salespeople frequently negotiate with representatives of the customer who do not have the authority to make a decision. In some cases, the delegation of authority is not clearly defined within the company. To identify the decision makers in the buying center, McLaughlin emphasizes that there is no point in discussing the situation unless the customer is willing to reveal its chain of command. "They may not necessarily give you a straight answer, and sometimes they may not even know themselves, but it's a step in the right direction."[16]

SUPPLIER EVALUATION AND CHOICE

At several steps in the buying process, members of the buying center evaluate alternative methods for solving a problem (step 2), the qualifications of potential suppliers (step 4), proposals submitted by potential suppliers (step 5), and the performance of products purchased (step 8). Based on these evaluations, they select potential suppliers and eventually choose a specific vendor.

The evaluation and selection of products and suppliers are affected by the needs of both the organization and the individuals making the decisions (see Exhibit 4.4). Often these organizational and personal needs are classified into two categories: rational needs and emotional needs. **Rational needs** are directly related to the performance of the product. Thus, the organizational needs discussed in the next section are examples of rational needs. **Emotional needs** are associated with the personal rewards and gratification of the person buying the product. Thus, the personal needs of buying center members often are considered emotional needs. In this section, we first focus on the organizational needs, then we examine how the personal needs of buying center members affect the buying process.

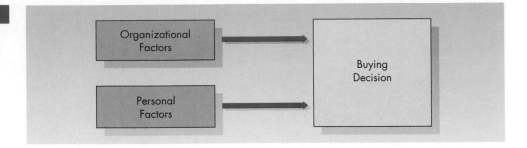

EXHIBIT 4.4
Factors Influencing Organizational Buying Decisions

Organizational Needs and Criteria

Organizations consider a number of factors when they make buying decisions, including economic factors such as price, product quality, and supplier service.

Economic Criteria

The objective of businesses is to make a profit. Thus, businesses are very concerned about buying products and services at the lowest cost. For example, the Appliance Division of General Electric held a meeting with over 300 suppliers to announce its Target 10 program. The goal of the program is to cut supplier costs by 10 percent. If suppliers want to continue to sell to GE, they will need to cut their prices.[17]

Organizational buyers are now taking a more sophisticated approach to evaluating the cost of equipment. Rather than simply focusing on the purchase price, they consider installation costs, the costs of needed accessories, freight charges, estimated maintenance costs, and operating costs, including forecasts of energy costs.

This buyer needs a high volume office copier. The copier's speed and reliability are very important to him. However, you would probably place the highest importance on cost if you were buying a copier for your personal use.

Courtesy Canon U.S.A. Inc.

Life-cycle costing, also referred to as the *total cost of ownership,* is a method for determining the cost of equipment or supplies over their useful lives. Using this approach, salespeople can demonstrate that a product with a higher initial cost will have a lower overall cost. An example of life-cycle costing appears in Exhibit 4.5. (Approaches salespeople can use to demonstrate the value of their products to customers are discussed in more detail in Chapter Ten.)

Quality Criteria

Many firms now recognize that the quality and reliability of their products are as important to their customers as the prices of their products.[18] To improve the quality of the products they sell, firms are adopting a **total quality management (TQM)** approach to managing their business. TQM is a set of programs and policies designed to meet customer needs by delivering defect-free products when customers want them 100 percent of the time. Management provides the resources and atmosphere to enable and encourage employees to meet the firm's quality goals. Each employee is given the appropriate tools and trained in how to achieve total quality in his or her job.[19]

Firms that have adopted TQM programs expect their suppliers to provide support for their efforts to provide quality products. Salespeople often need to describe how their firms will support the customer's TQM objectives.

To satisfy customer quality needs, salespeople need to know what organizational buyers are looking for. For example, when farmers are buying seeds, they want seeds that will produce uniform vegetables and fruits that grow at the same rate so they can be efficiently harvested at the same time.

International customers frequently are very demanding about product quality. Giddings & Lewis Measurement Systems made a technological breakthrough that enabled it to provide superior precision measuring devices at lower prices. However, the firm could not sell its systems to European automobile manufacturers. When visiting the Mercedes Benz plant in Stuttgart, Germany, salespeople found out why. They were told the unattractive casing for the equipment demonstrated a lack of concern for product quality and customer needs. Giddings & Lewis hired an industrial design firm to develop a new package, and its sales increased dramatically.[20]

Service Criteria

Organizational buyers want more than products that are low cost, perform reliably, and are aesthetically pleasing. They also want suppliers that will work with them to solve their problems. One primary reason firms are interested in developing long-

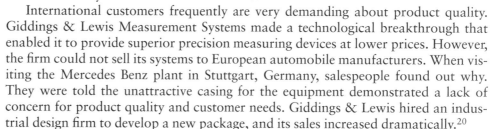

EXHIBIT 4.5		Product A	Product B
Life-Cycle Costing	Initial cost	$ 35,000	$ 30,000
	Life of machine	10 years	10 years
	Power consumption per year	150 Mwh*	180 Mwh
	Power cost at $30/Mwh	$ 45,000	$ 54,000
	Estimated operating and maintenance cost over 10 years	$ 25,000	$ 30,000
	Life-cycle cost	$105,000	$114,000

Note: A more thorough analysis would calculate the net present value of the cash flow associated with each product's purchase and use.

*Mwh = megawatt-hour

term relationships with suppliers is so they can learn about each other's needs and capabilities and use this information to enhance their products' performance. **Value analysis** is an example of a program in which suppliers and customers work together to reduce costs and still provide the required level of performance.[21]

Representatives from the supplier and the purchasing department and technical experts from engineering, production, or quality control usually form a team to undertake the analysis. The team begins by examining the product's function. Then members brainstorm to see if changes can be made in the design, materials, construction, or production process to reduce the product's costs but keep its performance high. Some questions addressed in this phase are the following:

- Can the part be eliminated?
- If the part is not standard, can a standard (and presumably less expensive) part be used?
- Does the part have greater performance than this application needs?
- Are unnecessary machining or fine finishes specified?

Salespeople can use value analysis to get customers to consider a new product. This approach is particularly useful for the out supplier in a straight rebuy situation. Scott Paper Company's salespeople use value analysis to sell hand towels and toilet paper. Because Scott products are of high quality and sell at a premium price, Scott sales representatives have to prove that the products are worth the extra money. Using value analysis, they help purchasing agents determine how much it costs to use the product rather than how much the product costs. They focus on the price per use, such as the number of dries per case of paper towels, rather than the price per case. Scott even designed a paper towel dispenser to reduce the number of refills needed and thus reduce maintenance labor cost.

Each year, *Purchasing* Magazine asks its 100,000 readers to nominate an outstanding salesperson with whom they work. The top 10 salespeople all help buyers increase the profits of their companies (see Exhibit 4.6).

Individual Needs of Buying Center Members

In the previous section, we discussed criteria used to determine whether or not a product satisfies the needs of the organization. However, buying center members are people. Their evaluations and choices are affected by their personal needs as well as the organization's needs.

Types of Needs

Buying center members, like all people, have personal goals and aspirations. They want to get a raise, be promoted to a high-level position, have their managers recognize their accomplishments, and feel they have done something for their company or demonstrated their skills as a buyer or engineer.

Salespeople can influence members of the buying center by developing strategies to satisfy individual needs. For example, demonstrating how a new product will reduce costs and increase the purchasing agents' bonus would satisfy the purchasing agents' economic safety needs. Encouraging an engineer to recommend a product employing the latest technology might satisfy the engineer's need for self-esteem and recognition by his or her engineering peers.

Risk Reduction

Members of the buying center tend to be more concerned about losing benefits they have now than about increasing their benefits. They place a lot of emphasis on

EXHIBIT 4.6

Top Salespeople Add
Value

Mark Mennen, sales rep, Copper & Brass Sales:
"[Mennen] studied our product line and determined [a new material] might cut tool use, speed production, and provide consistency. He then went to bat with his company to aggressively compete on price based on his calculation of our potential."

David Beck, purchasing manager, E.R.L.

John Cady, account manager, Revere Electric Supply Company
"Continually monitors orders we place to show price/cost improvement by suggesting alternative products or technologies . . . . He has recommended new technology that was both lower priced and more efficient . . . estimated cost savings from Cady's suggestions in 1995, $122,000."

Lori Theine, purchasing agent, Abbott Labortories

Steve Altheide, B. F. Welch (independent manufacturer's agent):
"[Altheide] is always suggesting a better part that sells for less over what our engineers have come up with . . . and works with distributors we actually buy through to help them on pricing so they can pass it along to us."

Connie Smithers, buyer, Automated Controls Corporation

John Wells, salesperson, Industrial Seal:
"[Wells was instrumental in] implementing a repair program that his company puts together and ships to us ready to go . . . intelligent outsourcing that benefits his company and cuts our costs by 40 percent."

Robert Goss, purchasing agent, Korelco America Inc.

Skip Wagonseller, strategic account manager, Sunoco Products Company:
"We had been using stainless steel overlay on the top chime of our fiber drums to prevent corrosion. Skip proposed the use of another material . . . that prevents corrosion, eliminates the safety hazard of a metal overlay, and reduces our costs for an annual savings of $24,000."

Fred Stemmer, manager for packaging services, Air Products & Chemicals

Source: Jim Morgan, "The Best Sales Reps Will Take on Their Bosses for You," *Purchasing*, November 7, 1996, pp. 50–52.

avoiding taking risks that may result in poor decisions, decisions that can adversely affect their personal reputations and rewards as well as their organization's performance. To reduce risk, buying center members may collect additional information, develop a loyalty to present suppliers, and/or spread the risk by placing orders with several vendors.[22]

Since they know that suppliers try to promote their own products, customers tend to question information received from vendors. They usually view information from trade publications, colleagues, and outside consultants as more credible than information provided by salespeople and company advertising and sales literature because it comes from independent sources.

Advertising and sales literature tends to be used more in the early steps of the buying process. Word-of-mouth information from friends and colleagues is very important in the proposal evaluation and supplier selection steps. Word-of-mouth information is especially important for risky decisions, decisions that will have a significant impact on the organization and/or the buying center member.[23]

Another way to reduce uncertainty and risk is to display **vendor loyalty** to suppliers, that is, continue buying from suppliers that have proven satisfactory in the past.

By converting buying decisions into straight rebuys, the decisions become routine, minimizing the chances of a poor decision. Organizations tend to develop vendor loyalty for unimportant purchase decisions. In these situations, the potential benefits from new suppliers do not compensate for the costs of evaluating these suppliers.[24]

The consequences of choosing a poor supplier can be reduced by using more than one vendor. Rather than placing all orders for an OEM component with one supplier, for example, a firm might elect to purchase 75 percent of its needs from one supplier and 25 percent from another. Thus, if a problem occurs with one supplier, another will be available to fill the firm's needs. If the product is proprietary— available from only one supplier—the buyer might insist that the supplier develop a second source for the component.

These risk reduction approaches present a major problem for salespeople working for "out" suppliers. To break this loyalty barrier, these salespeople need to develop trusting relationships with customers. They can build trust by offering performance guarantees or consistently meeting personal commitments. Another approach would be to encourage buyers to place a small trial order so that the salesperson's company can demonstrate the product's capabilities. On the other hand, the salesperson for the "in" supplier wants to discourage buyers from considering new sources, even on a trial basis.

Vendor Analysis

Organizational buyers frequently use a formal method, called *vendor analysis,* to summarize the benefits and needs satisfied by a supplier. When using this procedure, the buyer rates the supplier and its products on a number of criteria such as price, quality, performance, and on-time delivery.[25] Note that the ratings of suppliers can be affected by the perceptions and personal needs of the buyers. Then the ratings are weighted by the importance of the characteristics and an overall score or evaluation of the vender is developed. Exhibit 4.7 shows a vendor evaluation form used by Chrysler Corporation.

The appendix to this chapter describes the multi-attribute model. This model is useful in analyzing how members of the buying center evaluate and select products. The model also suggests strategies salespeople can use to influence their evaluations.

Thinking
it
Through

Perform a vendor analysis of the alternatives you considered for a recent large purchase such as a bicycle, stereo, or piece of furniture. Make a chart with the headings *price, performance, reliability,* and *ease of purchase.* Under each heading, comment on how well the product you bought satisfied your needs and how well the other product you were considering may have satisfied your needs. Did the product you bought offer superior performance on all characteristics? Were some characteristics more important than others?

TRENDS IN ORGANIZATIONAL BUYING

The business environment is changing dramatically as firms approach the new millennium. Major changes include the increasing cost of raw materials, the development of new technologies, and increased competition from international firms and in deregulated industries. These changes put organizations under pressure to improve product quality, control the cost of purchased material, and minimize inventories.[26] Some changes in organizational buying stimulated by these changes are discussed next.

Increasing Importance of Purchasing Agents

Most major firms have elevated their directors of purchasing to the level of senior vice president to reflect the increasing importance of this function. Purchasing managers provide a critical function in the learning organization. They collect informa-

EXHIBIT 4.7

Sample Vendor Analysis Form

Supplier Name: _____   Type of Product: _____
Shipping Location: _____   Annual Sales Dollars: _____

	5 Excellent	4 Good	3 Satisfactory	2 Fair	1 Poor	0 N/A
Quality (45%)						
Defect rates	——	——	——	——	——	——
Quality of sample	——	——	——	——	——	——
Conformance with quality program	——	——	——	——	——	——
Responsiveness to quality problems	——	——	——	——	——	——
Overall quality	——	——	——	——	——	——
Delivery (25%)						
Avoidance of late shipments	——	——	——	——	——	——
Ability to expand production capacity	——	——	——	——	——	——
Performance in sample delivery	——	——	——	——	——	——
Response to changes in order size	——	——	——	——	——	——
Overall delivery	——	——	——	——	——	——
Price (20%)						
Price competitiveness	——	——	——	——	——	——
Payment terms	——	——	——	——	——	——
Absorption of costs	——	——	——	——	——	——
Submission of cost savings plans	——	——	——	——	——	——
Overall price	——	——	——	——	——	——
Technology (10%)						
State-of-the-art components	——	——	——	——	——	——
Sharing research & development capability	——	——	——	——	——	——
Ability and willingness to help with design	——	——	——	——	——	——
Responsiveness to engineering problems	——	——	——	——	——	——
Overall technology	——	——	——	——	——	——

Buyer: _____   Date: _____
Comments: _____

Source: Chrysler Corporation

tion about new developments in the marketplace that will enable their firms to increase quality and reduce costs. In addition, to improve efficiency and coordination of logistical activities, firms are combining purchasing, transportation, inventory control, and warehouse activities into an all-encompassing materials management department.[27]

To meet these new responsibilities, purchasing managers are upgrading their skills and placing more emphasis on the use of computer information and control systems. The National Association of Purchasing Management (NAPM) has a rigorous certification program requiring a minimum of three years of experience and formal coursework in quantitative techniques. To achieve certification, candidates must pass four examinations.

For example, Al Mulvey, vice president of purchasing and administration at J. I. Case (located in Racine, Wisconsin), is one of a new breed of purchasing managers. He has a degree in engineering and an MBA and has taught courses in negotiating skills, international business, and value analysis. Mulvey emphasizes that in the past, purchasing agents and salespeople focused on "beating each other up over the amount of profit." Now he is more interested in discovering ways to reduce Case's manufacturing costs: "The ability to negotiate manufacturing costs requires an even stronger relationship with suppliers than it has in the past."

Mulvey wants salespeople to make a "technical infusion" into J. I. Case. A salesperson who spoke with him about Case's involvement in financial leases illustrates the concept. The salesperson had done his homework. He could talk knowledgeably about Case's customers and current suppliers, how prices were set, how leases were structured, and the tax advantages. The salesperson presented an opportunity for Case to carve a niche in the truck-leasing business. According to Mulvey, "His work amounts to a technical infusion on the management side. His company is making a contribution to our business mission instead of coming to me and simply saying, 'Give me your business.'"[28]

Exhibit 4.8 shows the salesperson characteristics that impress and annoy buyers.

Centralized Purchasing

Purchasing is becoming more centralized. Rather than having each manufacturing facility contract for supplies to meet its own production needs, more purchasing is done at a central location, such as corporate headquarters. Through centralization, purchasing agents can become specialists, concentrating on particular items and developing extensive knowledge about the uses, specifications, and suppliers for those items.

For example, each airline program at Boeing—737, 747, and 757—had its own purchasing department. To control costs, Boeing formed a materials division to coordinate the company's relationships with its vendors. The new division encourages standardization of parts across the existing and new airline designs. It promotes the development of long-term relationships with suppliers, involving them as early as possible in the design of new planes.

To effectively sell to a centralized purchasing department, many firms use a national account management organization concept. In this type of sales organization, a **national account manager (NAM)** is responsibile for coordinating the firm's efforts to satisfy the needs of a major customer.[29] The NAM works directly with the centralized purchasing department and coordinates the activities of salespeople calling on decentralized locations. When strong relationships exist, customers may actually determine who will call on their accounts. For example, Sherwin-Williams, a large paint supplier, lets Sears select the sales team that will service the Sears account.

Supply Chain Management

A major concern of producers and resellers is to reduce the amount of inventory they have in stock. For example, a study of the supermarket inventory found that if packaged goods manufacturers and supermarket chains coordinated their production, shipping, transportation, and receiving activities, the amount of inventory in

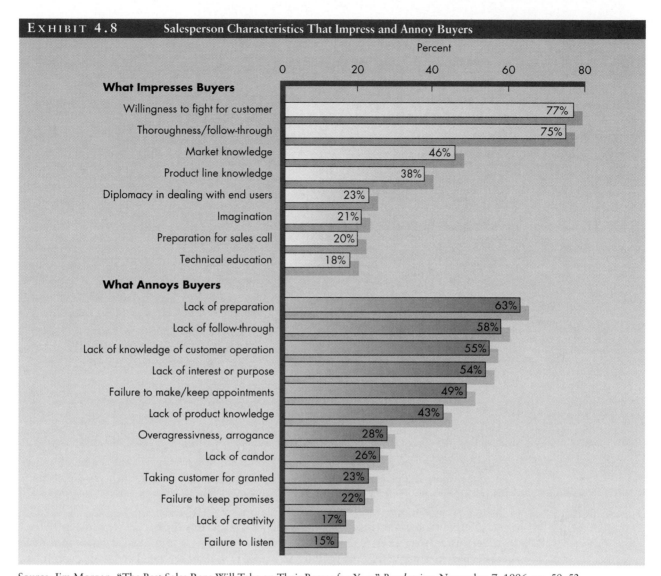

EXHIBIT 4.8   Salesperson Characteristics That Impress and Annoy Buyers

Source: Jim Morgan, "The Best Sales Reps Will Take on Their Bosses for You," *Purchasing*, November 7, 1996, pp. 50–52.

the stores and warehouses could be reduced by $40 billion.[30] **Supply chain management** is a set of programs undertaken to increase the efficiency of the distribution that moves products from the producer's facilities to the end user.

The **just-in-time (JIT) inventory control** system is an example of a supply chain management system used by a producer to minimize its inventory by having frequent deliveries, sometimes daily, just in time for assembly into the final product.[31] In theory, each product delivered by a supplier must conform to the manufacturer's specifications every time. It must be delivered when needed, not earlier or later, and it must arrive in the exact quantity needed, not more or less. The ultimate goal is to eventually eliminate all inventory except products in production and transit.

To develop the close coordination needed for JIT systems, manufacturers tend to rely on one supplier. The selection criterion is not the lowest cost but the ability of the supplier to be flexible. As these relationships develop, employees of the supplier have offices at the customer's site and participate in value analysis meetings with the

Companies are interested in using just-in-time inventory control systems to reduce their inventory carrying costs. Providing deliveries when the customers need the products is an important benefit.

Courtesy Rockwell International

supplier. The salesperson becomes a facilitator, coordinator, and even marriage counselor in developing a selling team that works effectively with the customer's buying center. (The manufacturer and supplier develop a strategic partnership, which we discussed in Chapter Two.)

Resellers are also interested in managing their inventories more efficiently. Retailers and distributors work closely with their suppliers to make sure they minimize their inventory investments and are still able to satisfy the needs of their customers. These JIT inventory systems are referred to as **quick-response** or **efficient consumer response (ECR) systems** in a distribution channel context.[32] (Partnering relationships involving these systems are discussed in more detail in Chapter Fifteen.)

Material requirements planning (MRP) systems are an important element in JIT programs. These systems are used to forecast sales, develop a production schedule, and then order parts and raw materials with delivery dates that minimize the amount of inventory needed, thereby reducing costs. Effective JIT requires that customers inform suppliers well in advance about their production schedules and needs.

Many firms use elaborate computer systems to keep track of inventories, orders, and deliveries. These systems help firms uncover and eliminate suppliers whose late deliveries and defective products cause scheduling problems. Many customers and suppliers link computer systems, sharing information about sales, production, and shipment and receipt of products. These computer-to-computer linkages between suppliers and buyers are referred to as **Electronic Data Interchange (EDI).**[33]

Global Sourcing

Corporations no longer focus on buying from suppliers in their own countries. Purchasing agents consider potential suppliers around the globe. For example, the $10,000 paid for General Motors' LeMans in 1991 consisted of

- $3,000 for labor and assembly in South Korea.
- $1,850 for engines, transaxles, and electronics made in Japan.
- $700 for styling and design engineering in Germany.
- $400 for small components from Japan, Singapore, and Taiwan.
- $250 for advertising done in Britain.
- $50 for data processing in Barbados and Ireland.

Not all these suppliers are independent companies. Some are General Motors subsidiaries and joint ventures. But the global sourcing for the LeMans illustrates the growing need for salespeople to recognize the global nature of competition and the importance of understanding the network of relationships a customer has.[34]

Outsourcing

Another major trend in business is outsourcing. **Outsourcing** is the purchasing of goods and services that were previously made by the firm. In an effort to reduce costs, firms are buying more and more goods and services from more efficient suppliers. Some common activities that are being outsourced are computer systems operation and maintenance, trucking and transportation services, and jobs that can be completed in a specific time frame.[35]

Long-Term Customer-Supplier Relationships

As we discussed in Chapters One and Two, organizational customers and suppliers are developing mutually dependent partnering relationships. The supplier needs the customer's orders to meet financial objectives; the customer needs the supplier and its salespeople to make sure products are delivered when needed, products perform to specifications and are reliable, and spare parts and service are provided. This interdependency makes obtaining a specific purchase order only one point in a long-term relationship between the organizational buyer and the seller.

All of the trends we have discussed in this chapter can be implemented only when buyers and sellers have strong relationships. For example, effective supply chain management can be realized only when companies share sensitive information about their long-term plans and short-term production and sales. The general trend in organizational buying is to reduce the number of suppliers and develop strategic partnerships with the remaining suppliers.[36]

SUMMARY

Salespeople sell to many different types of customers, including consumers, business enterprises, government agencies, and institutions. This text focuses on selling to businesses rather than to consumers. Selling to organizations differs from selling to consumers because organizations are more concentrated, demand is derived, and the buying process is more complex.

The organizational buying process consists of eight steps, beginning with the recognition of a need and ending with the evaluation of the product's performance. Each step involves a number of decisions. As organizations progress through these steps, decisions made at previous steps affect subsequent steps, leading to a creeping commitment. Thus, salespeople need to be involved in the buying process as early as possible.

The length of the buying process and the role of different participants depend on the customer's past experiences. When customers have had considerable experience in buying a product, the decision becomes routine—a straight rebuy. Few people are involved, and the process is short. However, when customers have little experience in buying a product—a new task—many people are involved and the process is quite lengthy.

The people involved in the buying process are referred to as the *buying center.* The buying center is composed of people who are users, influencers, gatekeepers, and deciders. Salespeople need to understand the roles buying center members play to effectively influence their decisions.

Individuals in the buying center are concerned about satisfying the economic, quality, and service needs of their organization. However, they are people and thus have personal needs they want to satisfy.

Organizations in the 1990s are facing an increasingly dynamic and competitive environment. Organizational buying practices are changing to help firms cope with the greater environmental uncertainties. Some of these changes are the increasing importance of purchasing agents, the longer-term orientation in evaluating costs and vendors, the use of computer systems for planning and inventory control, and the development of long-term relationships with selected vendors.

KEY TERMS

buying center 97
capital equipment 87
creeping commitment 94
deciders 98
derived demand 91
efficient consumer response (ECR) system 108
electronic data interchange (EDI) 108
emotional needs 99
end users 87
gatekeepers 98
influencers 98
just-in-time (JIT) inventory control 107
life-cycle costing 101
material requirements planning (MRP) 108
modified rebuy 97

MRO supplies 87
national account manager (NAM) 106
new task 94
original equipment manufacturer (OEM) 86
outsourcing 109
producer 86
quick-response system 108
rational needs 99
resellers 87
straight rebuy 96
supply chain management 107
total quality management (TQM) 101
users 98
value analysis 102
vendor loyalty 104

QUESTIONS AND PROBLEMS

1. What is the difference between a new task and a straight rebuy?

2. Sam Bowie, a purchasing agent, views his decision to buy chemicals used to clean the plant floors as a routine purchase decision. Assume you are a salesperson working for a chemical distributor from which Bowie does not currently order. How would you try to make a sale to Bowie?

3. A chain of fast-food restaurants wants to buy new electronic cash registers. What differences in criteria for evaluating supplier proposals might be used by (a) the purchasing agent, (b) the engineering department, (c) the sales manager, and (d) the head of the legal department?

4. Assume you are calling on a customer for the first time. You have just found out the customer needs a product such as the one you are selling. What questions would you ask to learn how to sell your product to this customer?

5. Buying centers are often made up of people from different areas in the organization (such as purchasing and engineering) who have different criteria for selecting products. How do these people with different needs ever reach a decision? What can a salesperson do to minimize any conflict among members of the buying center?

6. Assume you work for a manufacturer that sells office equipment to dealers (resellers). In the opinion of your company, would you be more successful if you sold as much equipment to a dealer as possible or if you helped the dealer sell equipment to its customers? Would there be any difference between the long- and short-term effects of these two approaches? Why or why not? How could you, as a salesperson, help the dealer sell its inventory of your products?

7. What are the different types of people in a buying center?

8. Why might management place pressure on purchasing agents to buy from the lowest bidder? Why might a purchasing agent ignore this pressure and buy from a higher-priced bidder?

9. Under what conditions might loyalty to a supplier be economically efficient? When might it be inefficient or wasteful?

10. Assume you are selling a health care plan to a company. You attend a meeting of people in the company who will participate in the buying decision. Based on the following conversation, which type of buying center person do you think each individual is?

   "We need a health plan for our employees. The plan must have doctors who are close to where our employees work, not close to the plant," says Fred, the plant manager.

   "I'll work with you to develop the specifications for the plan," offers Mark, the human resource director.

   "I want to make sure that my doctor is covered under the plan," notes Rachael, a production supervisor.

   "I will review the plan and let you know what my final decision is," says Shirley, the CEO.

   Based on your classification of these people, at what stages in the buying process will each have the most influence?

EXPLORING THE NET

- Assume you work for a company that sells products to universities. The following university purchasing departments have sites on the Internet:

  University of Texas–Austin
  http;//www.utexas.edu/admin/purchasing

  New York University
  http://www.nyu.edu/pages/purchasing

  University of British Columbia
  http://www.purchasing.ubc.ca

  Cornell University
  http://www.univco.cornell.edu/purchasing/purchasinghome.html

  Southern University Purchasing Consortium for Bath, Bristol, Brunel, and Exeter Universities in the United Kingdom
  http://www.soton.ac.uk/"infoserv/supplies/consort/supc.html

  Visit these sites. What information does each site provide that would help you, as a salesperson, learn about the buying process and buying center members in these universities?

- The National Association of Purchasing Managers (NAPM) provides information to assist purchasing managers and sponsors research on industrial buying behavior. Visit the headquarters site (http://napm.org/napm.html) and the site for the Silicon Valley chapter in Northern California (http://catalog.com/napmsv/welcome.htm). What information do these sites provide that would help you develop a better understanding of the needs of purchasing managers and the organizational buying process?

CASE PROBLEMS

CASE 4.1
General Electric Streamlines Its Purchasing Practices

General Electric (GE), along with Whirlpool, Frigidaire, Maytag, and Raytheon, dominates the white-goods market. GE spends in excess of $20 billion annually on products and services bought from over 45,000 suppliers worldwide. It spends over $7 billion on OEM components alone. Like many companies, GE is developing stronger relationships with key suppliers and reducing the number of suppliers.

GE's purchasing is both centralized and decentralized. Each of the company's 12 divisions does its own buying, except when products are used by several divisions. The company has a single computer supplier and a single travel agency. Purchase decisions for these types of products and services are made by a "council of users," a group consisting of a representative from each division.

The manager of purchasing activities emphasizes to potential suppliers that if they cannot provide GE with the best, GE cannot provide the best products to its customers.

Questions

1. What criteria are most important to GE representatives when they make decisions to buy OEM parts for GE appliances?

2. Who are likely to be the members of the buying center when GE buys aluminum for one of its appliances?

Source: William Bearden, Thomas Ingram, and Raymond LaForge, *Marketing: Principles and Perspectives* (Burr Ridge, IL: Richard D. Irwin, 1995), p. 150.

CASE 4.2
Advanced Surgical Systems

On January 13, 1998, Steve Slaughter, a sales engineer at Advanced Surgical Systems, learned that Shands Medical Center had placed an order with Gamma Technology for a gamma knife. Slaughter was very disappointed by the decision; he had been working on the sale for eight months. He reviewed his call reports to try to understand why Advanced Surgical Systems did not get the order.

Background

The gamma knife is a state-of-the art, computer-controlled, medical instrument enabling neurosurgeons to noninvasively shrink different types of brain tumors. The typical gamma knife system costs about $3 million. Advanced Surgical Systems and Gamma Technology are the leaders in developing the gamma knife technology and sell these systems internationally.

Gamma Knife Customers   The customers for gamma knives are large public or privately owned hospitals. Hospitals tend to use formal procedures to make purchase decisions, including developing specifications and then requiring firms to provide bids based on those specs.

Buying Center   Typically, four groups of people take part in the buying decision: the neurosurgeons affiliated with the hospital, engineers, administrators, and people in supporting government agencies, which frequently provide funding. The neurosurgeons are the doctors who actually use the equipment in surgical procedures. Hospital engineers write technical specifications for the equipment. They have a good understanding of the state of the art in technology. Their principal concern is patient safety. Administrators, who are responsible for the financial well-being of the hospital, consider both potential revenues and the cost of the scanner. Administrators are typically wary about buying an expensive technological "toy" that may become obsolete in a few years. In some hospitals, administrators are the top decision makers; in others, they are simply buyers. People in supporting agencies are usually not directly involved with the purchase decision, but they must approve the expenditure. They have the greatest influence over hospital administrators.

Shands Medical Center   The Shands Medical Center is a large hospital associated with the University of Florida, servicing the Gainesville, Florida, community. The hospital is a leading teaching center and has an excellent neurosurgery department.

Sales Calls on Shands Medical Center

June 5, 1997 Office received a call from Dr. Swait, the head of the neurosurgery department at Shands, regarding a gamma knife. I was assigned to make the call on the doctor. Looked through the files to see if we had sold anything to the hospital before. We hadn't. Made an appointment to see Dr. Swait on June 9.

June 10, 1997 Called on Dr. Swait, who informed me of a recent decision by hospital directors to set aside funds next year for the purchase of a gamma knife. Swait wanted to know what we had to offer. Told him the general features of our gamma knife system. Gave him some brochures. He asked a few questions that led me to believe that Gamma Technology had already come to see him. Told me to check with Dr. Roche, the hospital's chief engineer, regarding the specs. Made an appointment to see him again in 10 days. Called on Dr. Roche, who was not there. His secretary gave me a lengthy document, the gamma knife specs.

June 12, 1997 Read the specs last night. Looked like they had been copied straight from Gamma Technology's technical manual. Showed them to our product specialist, who confirmed my hunch that our system exceeded the specs. Made an appointment to see Dr. Roche next week.

June 16, 1997 Called on Dr. Roche. Told him about our system's features and the fact that we met all the specs set down on the document. He looked somewhat unimpressed. Left technical documents on our system with him.

June 19, 1997 Called on Dr. Swait. He had read the material I had left with him. Looked sort of pleased with the features. Asked about our upgrading scheme. I told him we would upgrade the system as new features became available. Unlike the Gamma Technology system, ours can be made to accommodate the latest technology. There will be no risk of obsolescence for a long time. He was quite impressed. Also answered his questions regarding precision of the focusing system and our service capability. Just before I left, he inquired about our price. Told him I would have a quote for him at our next meeting. Made an appointment to see him on July 23, after he returned from his vacation. He told me to get in touch with Carl Hartmann, the hospital's top administrator, in the interim.

July 2, 1997 Called on Hartmann. It was difficult to get an appointment with him. Told him about our interest in supplying his hospital with our gamma knife, which met all the specs as defined by Dr. Roche. Also informed him of our excellent service capability. He wanted to know which other hospitals in the country had purchased our system. Told him I would drop him a list of buyers in a few days' time. He asked about the price. Gave him an informal quote of $3.1 million—a price my boss and I had arrived at since my visit to Dr. Swait. He shook his head, saying, "Other gamma knives are cheaper by a wide margin." I explained that our price reflected the latest technology, which was incorporated into it. Also mentioned that the price differential was an investment that could pay for itself several times over because our automated alignment system reduces the time to complete a surgery. He was noncommittal. Before I left his office, he instructed me not to talk to anybody else about the price. Asked him if I could tell Dr. Swait. He said I should not. Left him with a lot of material on our system.

July 3, 1997 Took Hartmann a list of three other hospitals that had bought our system. He was out. Left it with his secretary, who recognized me. Learned from her that Gamma Technology was competing for the order. She also volunteered the information that "prices are so different, Mr. Hartmann is confused." She added that the final decision will be made by a committee made up of Hartmann, Professor Swait, and one other person whom she could not recall.

July 18, 1997 Called on Dr. Roche. Asked him if he had read the material on our system. He had, but did not have much to say. Repeated some of the key operational advantages our product has compared to Gamma Technology's system. Left him some more technical documents. On the way out, stopped by Hartmann's office. His secretary told me that we had received favorable comments from the hospitals using our system.

July 23, 1997 Professor Swait was flabbergasted to hear that I could not discuss our price with him. Told him of the hospital administrator's instructions to that effect. He was not convinced, especially when Gamma Technology had already told him their quote of $2.7 million. When he had calmed down, he wanted to know if we were going to be at least competitive. Told him our system was more advanced than Gamma Technology's. Promised him we would do our best to come up with an attractive offer. Then we talked about his vacation and sailing experience in the Florida Keys. He said he loved key lime pie.

August 18, 1997 Called to see if Hartmann had returned from his vacation. He had. While checking his calendar, his secretary told me that our system seemed to be the "nuerosurgeon's choice" but that Hartmann had not yet made up his mind.

August 29, 1997 Visited Hartmann, accompanied by the regional manager. Hartmann seemed bent on the price. He said, "All companies claim they have the latest technology." So he could not understand why our offer was "so much above the rest." He concluded that only a "very attractive price" could tip the balance in our favor. After repeating the operational advantages that our system enjoyed over Gamma Technology, my boss indicated that we were willing to lower our price to $2.9 million if the equipment was ordered before the end of the current year. Hartmann said he would consider the offer and seek "objective" expert opinion. He also said a decision would be made before Christmas.

September 16, 1997 Called on Professor Swait, who was too busy to see me for more than 10 minutes. He wanted to know if we had lowered our price since the last meeting with him. I said we had. He shook his head, saying laughingly, "Maybe that was not your best offer." He then wanted to know how fast we could make deliveries. Told him within six months. He did not respond.

October 2, 1997 Discussed with our regional manager the desirability of inviting one or more people from Shands to visit Advanced Surgical Systems' headquarters near Chicago. The three-day trip would have given the participants a chance to see the scope of the facilities and become better acquainted with gamma knife applications. The idea was finally rejected as inappropriate.

October 3, 1997 Dropped in to see Hartmann. He was busy, but had the time to ask for a formal "final offer" from us by November 1. On my way out, his secretary told me of "a lot of heated discussions" concerning which scanner seemed best suited for the hospital. She would not say more.

October 24, 1997 The question of price was raised in a meeting between the regional manager and the managing director. I had recommended a sizable cut in our price to win the order. The national sales manager seemed to agree with me. But the managing director was reluctant. His concern was that too much of a drop in price looked "unhealthy." He finally agreed to a final offer of $2.95 million. Made an appointment to see Hartmann later that week.

October 29, 1997 Took our offer of $2.95 million in a sealed envelope to Hartmann. He did not open it but commented that he hoped the scanner question would be resolved soon to the "satisfaction of all concerned." Asked him how the decision was going to be made. He evaded the question but said he would notify us as soon as a decision was reached. Left his office feeling that our price had a good chance of being accepted.

November 20, 1997 Called on Professor Swait. He had nothing to tell me but that "the gamma knife is the last thing I like to talk about." Felt he was unhappy with the way things were going. Tried to make an appointment with Hartmann in November, but he was too busy.

December 5, 1997 Called on Hartmann, who told me that a decision would probably not be reached before January. He indicated that our price was "within the range" but that all the competing systems were being evaluated to see which seemed most appropriate for the hospital. He repeated that he would call us when a decision was reached.

January 17, 1998 Received a brief letter from Hartmann thanking Advanced Surgical Systems for participating in the bid for the MR scanner and informing it of the decision to place the order with Gamma Technology.

Questions

1. Who were the members of the buying center for the MR scanner? What important benefits were these buying center members seeking?
2. Why did Slaughter lose the sale? What should he have done differently?

**APPENDIX:
Multi-Attribute
Model of Product
Evaluation and
Choice**

The multi-attribute model is a useful approach for understanding the factors individual members of a buying center consider to evaluate products and make choices. The vendor analysis form used by Chrysler (see Exhibit 4–7) illustrates the use of this model in selecting vendors. The model also provides a framework for developing sales strategies.

The **multi-attribute model** is based on the idea that people view a product as a collection of characteristics, or attributes. They evaluate a product by considering how each characteristic satisfies the firm's needs and perhaps their individual needs. The following example examines a firm's decision to buy laptop computers for its sales force. The computers will be used by salespeople to keep track of information about customers and provide call reports to sales managers. At the end of each day, salespeople will call headquarters and transmit their call reports through a modem.

**Performance
Evaluation of
Characteristics**

Assume the company narrows its choice to three hypothetical brands: Apex, Bell, and Deltos. Exhibit A.1 gives information the company collected about each of these brands. Note that the information goes beyond the physical characteristics of the product to include services provided by the potential suppliers.

Each buying center member, or the group as a whole in a meeting, might process this objective information and evaluate the laptop computers on each characteristic. These evaluations appear in Exhibit A.2 as ratings on a 10-point scale, with 10 being the highest rating and 1 the lowest.

How do members of the buying center use this set of evaluations to select a laptop computer? The final decision depends on the relationship between the performance evaluations and the company's needs. The buying center members need to consider the degree to which they are willing to sacrifice poor performance on one attribute for superior performance on another. The members of the buying center must make some trade-offs.

EXHIBIT A.1

Information about
Laptop Computers

| | Brand | | |
Characteristic	Apex	Bell	Deltos
Reliability rating	Very good	Very good	Excellent
Weight (pounds)	2.0	4.5	7.5
Size (cubic inches)	168	305	551
Speed (clock rate in megahertz)	20	35	30
Internal memory (in megabytes)	80	100	120
Display visibility	Good	Very good	Excellent
Number of service centers in United States	70	30	10

EXHIBIT A.2

Performance Evaluation
of Laptop Computers

Characteristic	Brand Ratings		
	Apex	Bell	Deltos
Reliability	5	5	⑧
Weight	⑧	5	2
Size	⑧	6	4
Speed	3	⑧	6
Internal memory	3	5	⑧
Display visibility	2	4	6
Service availability	⑦	5	3

No one product will perform best on all characteristics. For example, Apex excels on size, weight, and availability of convenient service; Bell has superior speed; and Deltos provides better reliability and internal memory.

Importance Weights

In making an overall evaluation, the buying center member needs to consider the importance of each characteristic. These importance weights may differ from member to member. Consider two members of the buying center: the national sales manager and the director of management information systems (MIS). The national sales manager is particularly concerned about motivating his salespeople to use the laptop computers. He believes the laptops must be small and lightweight and have good screen visibility. On the other hand, the MIS director foresees using the laptop computers to transmit orders and customer inventory information to corporation headquarters. She believes expanded memory and processing speed will be critical for these future applications.

Exhibit A.3 shows the importance these two buying center members place on each characteristic using a 10-point scale, with 10 representing very important and 1 representing very unimportant. In this illustration, the national sales manager and the MIS director differ in the importance they place on characteristics; however, both have the same evaluations of the brands' performance on the characteristics. In some cases, people may differ on both importance weights and performance ratings.

EXHIBIT A.3   Information Used to Form an Overall Evaluation

Computer Characteristic	Importance Weights		Brand Performance Ratings		
	Sales Manager	MIS Director	Apex	Bell	Deltos
Reliability	4	4	5	5	8
Weight	6	2	8	5	2
Size	7	3	8	6	4
Speed	1	7	3	8	6
Internal memory	1	6	3	5	8
Display visibility	8	5	2	4	6
Service availability	3	3	7	5	3
Overall evaluation					
Sales manager's			167	152	143
MIS director's			130	169	177

Overall Evaluation

A person's overall evaluation of a product can be quantified by calculating the sum of the performance ratings multiplied by the importance weights. Thus, the sales manager's overall evaluation of Alpha would be as follows:

$$4 \times 5 = 20$$
$$6 \times 8 = 48$$
$$7 \times 8 = 56$$
$$1 \times 8 = 3$$
$$1 \times 3 = 3$$
$$8 \times 2 = 16$$
$$3 \times 7 = \underline{21}$$
$$167$$

Using the national sales manager's and MIS director's importance weights, the overall evaluations, or scores, for the three laptop computer brands appear at the bottom of Exhibit A.3. These scores indicate the level of benefits the brands provide as seen by these two buying center members.

Value Offered

The cost of the computers also needs to be considered in making the purchase decision. One approach for incorporating cost calculates the value—the benefits divided by the cost—for each laptop. The prices for the computers and their values are shown in Exhibit A.4. The sales manager believes Apex provides more value. He would probably buy this brand if he were the only person involved in the buying decision. On the other hand, the MIS director believes that Bell and Deltos offer the best value.

Supplier Selection

In this situation, the sales manager might be the key decision maker and the MIS director might be a gatekeeper. Rather than using the MIS director's overall evaluation, the buying center might simply ask her to serve as a gatekeeper and determine if these computers meet her minimum acceptable performance standards on speed and memory. Both laptops pass the minimum levels she established of a 20-megahertz clock rate and an 80-megabyte internal memory. Thus, the company would rely on the sales manager's evaluation and purchase Apex laptops for the sales force.

Even if a buying center or individual members do not go through the calculations described above, the multi-attribute model is a good representation of their

---

EXHIBIT A.4

Value Offered by Each Brand

Computer Brand	Overall Evaluation (Benefit Points)	÷	Cost of Computer	=	Assigned Value (Benefit Points per Dollar Spent)
Sales manager					
Apex	167		$1,050		0.16
Bell	152		1,100		0.14
Deltos	143		1,150		0.12
MIS manager					
Apex	130		$1,050		0.12
Bell	169		1,100		0.15
Deltos	177		1,150		0.15

product evaluations and can be used to predict product choices. Purchase decisions are made as though a formal multi-attribute model were used.

If you were selling the Bell computer to the national sales manager and MIS director depicted in the text and in Exhibits A.3 and A.4, how would you try to get them to believe that your computer provides more value than Apex or Deltos does? What numbers would you try to change?

Implications for Salespeople

How can salespeople use the multi-attribute model to influence their customers' purchase decisions? First, the model indicates what information customers use in making their evaluations and purchase decisions. Thus, salespeople need to know the following information to develop a sales strategy:

1. The suppliers or brands the customer is considering.
2. The product characteristics being used in the evaluation.
3. The customer's rating of each product's performance on each dimension.
4. The weights the customer attaches to each dimension.

With this knowledge, salespeople can use several strategies to influence purchase decisions. First, salespeople must be sure their product is among the brands being considered. Then they can try to change the customer's perception of their product's value. Some approaches for changing perceived value are

Approach 1: Increase the performance rating for your product.

Approach 2: Decrease the rating for a competitive product.

Approach 3: Increase or decrease an importance weight.

Approach 4: Add a new dimension.

Approach 5: Decrease the price of your product.

Assume you are selling the Bell computer and you want to influence the sales manager so that he believes your computer provides more value than does the Apex computer. Approach 1 involves altering the sales manager's belief about your product's performance. To raise his evaluation, you would try to have the sales manager perceive your computer as small and lightweight. You might show him how easy it is to carry—how it better satisfies his need for portability. The objective of this demonstration would be to increase your rating on weight from 5 to 7 and your rating on size from 6 to 8.

You should focus on these two characteristics, because they are the most important to the sales manager. A small change in a performance evaluation on these characteristics will have a large impact on the overall evaluation. You would *not* want to spend much time influencing his performance evaluations on speed or internal memory, because these characteristics are not important to him. Of course, your objectives when selling to the MIS director would be different, because she places more importance on speed and internal memory.

This example illustrates a key principle in selling. In general, salespeople should focus primarily on product characteristics that are important to the customer— characteristics that satisfy the customer's needs. They should not focus on the areas of superior performance (such as speed in this example) that are not important to the customer.

Approach 2 involves decreasing the performance rating of Apex. This can be dangerous. Customers prefer dealing with salespeople who say good things about their products, not bad things about competitive products.

In Approach 3, you change the sales manager's importance weights. You want to increase the importance he places on a characteristic on which your product excels, such as speed, or decrease the importance of a characteristic on which your product performs poorly, such as display visibility. For example, you might try to convince the sales manager that a fast computer will decrease the time salespeople need to spend developing and transmitting reports.

Approach 4 encourages the sales manager to consider a new characteristic, one on which your product has superior performance. For example, suppose the sales manager and MIS director have not considered the availability of software. To add a new dimension, you might demonstrate a program specially developed for sales call reports and usable only with your computer.

Approach 5 is the simplest to implement: Simply drop your price. Typically, firms use this strategy as a last resort, because cutting prices decreases profits.

Each of these strategies illustrates the concept that salespeople need to adapt their selling approach to the needs of each customer. Using the multi-attribute model, salespeople decide how to alter the content of their presentation—the benefits to be discussed—based on customer beliefs and needs. (Chapter Six describes adaptive selling in more detail and illustrates it in terms of the form of the presentation—the communication style the salesperson uses.)

ADDITIONAL REFERENCES

Dean, J. W., Jr., and J. R. Evans. *Total Quality: Management, Organization and Strategy.* St. Paul, MN: West, 1994.

Deeter-Schmelz, Dawn R., and Rosemary Ramsey. "A Conceptualization of the Functions and Roles of Formalized Selling and Buying Teams." *Journal of Personal Selling and Sales Management,* Spring 1995, pp. 47–60.

Drumwright, Minette. "Socially Responsible Organizational Buying: Environmental Concerns as Noneconomic Buying Criteria." *Journal of Marketing,* July 1994, pp. 1–19.

Germain, Richard; Cornelia Droge; and Patrica Daugherty. "The Effect of Just-in-Time Selling on Organizational Structure: An Empirical Investigation." *Journal of Marketing Research,* Fall 1994, pp. 471–80.

Hill, Ned, and Michael Swenson. "The Impact of Electronic Data Interchange on the Sales Function." *Journal of Personal Selling and Sales Management,* Summer 1994, pp. 79–87.

Hutt, Michael, and Thomas Speh. *Business Marketing Management,* 5th ed. Fort Worth, TX: Dryden Press, 1995.

Kauffman, Ralph G. "Influences on Industrial Buyers' Choice of Products: Effects of Product Application, Product Type, and Buying Environment." *International Journal of Purchasing and Materials Management,* March 22, 1994, pp. 29–33.

Reed, Richard; David Lemak; and Joseph Montgomery. "Beyond Process: TQM Content and Firm Performance." *Academy of Management Review,* January 1996, pp. 173–202.

Sharma, Arun, and Rajnandini Pillai. "Customers' Decision-Making Styles and Their Preference for Sales Strategies: Conceptual Examination and an Empirical Study." *Journal of Personal Selling and Sales Management,* Winter 1996, pp. 21–33.

Skipworth, Mark. "The View from the Other Side—What Buyers Think of Sales Pitches." *American Salesman,* October 1994, pp. 12–15.

Venkatesh, R.; Ajay Kohli; and Gerald Zaltman. "Influence Strategies in Buying Centers." *Journal of Marketing,* October 1995, pp. 71–82.

A stockbroker is telling a client about the benefits of buying stock in JCPenney. She says, "JCPenney is an excellent buy. Its price-earnings ratio is depressed because of uncertainties in GDP growth. But NAFTA offers great opportunities for expansion into Mexico." The stockbroker wants to communicate the bene-

Chapter Five

Using Communication Principles *to* Build Relationships

Some Questions Answered in this Chapter Are:

What are the basic elements in the communication process?

Why are listening and questioning skills important?

How can salespeople develop listening skills to collect information about customers?

How do people communicate without using words?

What are the barriers to effective communication?

fits of buying stock in JCPenney, but the client may not interpret this message correctly because he is not familiar with the terms *NAFTA, GDP,* and *depressed price-earnings ratio.* The stockbroker may recognize the lack of understanding by observing the client's facial expression and then say, "Let me explain my reasoning in more detail." Or the client might try to understand the stockbroker's message by asking, "What does depressed price-earnings ratio mean?" But the client may be embarrassed by his lack of understanding and respond, "I don't think I am interested in buying stocks now."

Effective communication is a key element in building close personal and business relationships. To adapt your sales presentation to customers, you need to learn about their needs as well as communicate product benefits to them. The communication principles discussed in this chapter can help everyone, including salespeople, avoid misunderstandings and improve relationships.

PROFILE

Kevin Irvin is an IBM client representative based in South Bend, Indiana. He has been with IBM for seven years and presently has responsibility for sales to industrial and manufacturing businesses in the Midwest. Irvin has a BS in marketing from Indiana University and has been awarded six marketing excellence and three general manager's awards for his sustained, high level of accomplishment at IBM.

". . . both listening and questioning skills are crucial in determining exactly what the client's real problem is."

KEVIN IRVIN
IBM

"My major responsibility is to find cost-effective solutions to a variety of client problems," Irving says. "To be successful in this position, it is very important to have effective communication skills. After all, communication processes play a critical role in all phases of the work I do—from the problem identification stage to developing, proposing, and implementing successful solutions. First, both listening and questioning skills are crucial in determining exactly what the client's *real* problem is. I attempt to speak with as many people as possible on the customer side, because each individual sometimes provides information concerning only a particular facet of the overall problem. I also try to identify people in the client organization who have a 'bigger picture' perspective. That allows me to develop a more complete and integrative representation of the client's problem.

"By identifying the true nature of the problem up front, I am able to ensure not only that the problem is of sufficient priority but also that our recommended solution is both comprehensive and cost effective. In addition, at this stage I have to learn as much as possible about the client's business and the industry in which the client operates, and so listening and questioning skills also have relevance here.

"At IBM, we use a team approach to designing and implementing solutions. So communication skills are important as I describe the nature of the problem to the team of specialists we have at IBM and then communicate our proposed solution back to the client. Typically, I have to act as a liaison between the client organization and representatives from several specialist areas at IBM, which might include hardware, software, service, and systems personnel.

"Effective communication in selling also involves more than just listening, questioning, and then generating solutions. There is a dynamic aspect to communication that is characterized by an active, two-way exchange of ideas. This approach leads to greater participation and interest on the part of the client and allows the client to feel a sense of involvement with respect to the process, as well as some ownership in terms of the recommended solution. As a result, the selling and implementation aspects of my job become much easier."

Irvin really enjoys his work. "I travel quite a bit and have the opportunity to meet many interesting people and learn about a variety of industries. I also enjoy being able to identify and solve customers' problems and, when they are satisfied with our work, I feel a sense of accomplishment from being able to help them improve their business."

Visit Our Website@
http://www.ibm.com

BUILDING RELATIONSHIPS THROUGH TWO-WAY COMMUNICATION

As we discussed in Chapter Two, open and honest communications are a key to building trust and developing successful relationships. To build successful relationships, buyers and sellers need to have a good understanding of each other's needs. Two-way communications are necessary for this understanding to occur.

As Exhibit 5.1 shows, the parties in **two-way communication** both send and receive information. Salespeople send messages to customers and receive feedback from them. Customers provide feedback by sending messages to salespeople and receiving responses in turn.

Consider a salesperson who is demonstrating a complicated product to a customer. At some point in the presentation, a perplexed look flits across the customer's face. The salesperson receives this nonverbal message and then asks the customer what part of the presentation needs further explanation. The feedback the customer's expression provides tells the salesperson his message is not being received. The customer then sends verbal messages to the salesperson in the form of questions concerning the operation and benefits of the product.

Two-way communication is essential for tailoring the presentation to satisfy customer needs. Without it, salespeople cannot determine what the customer's needs are. In addition, feedback from customers enables the salesperson to make adjustments, to determine if messages about product benefits are being received accurately and correct inaccuracies.

Two-way communication also provides the customer with greater satisfaction. People learn more when they participate. For example, when a professor lectures to you, you may lose interest. But you will pay much closer attention in class when the

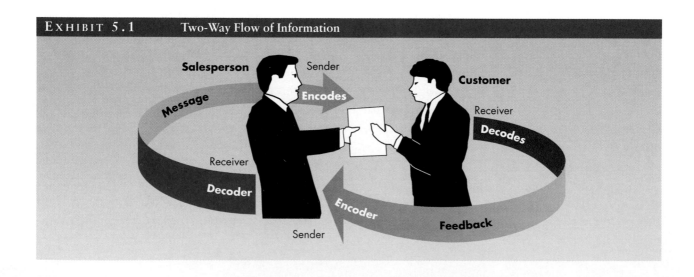

EXHIBIT 5.1   Two-Way Flow of Information

Salesperson   Sender
Message   Encodes
Customer
Receiver
Decodes
Receiver
Decoder
Encoder
Sender   Feedback

professor calls on you to be part of class discussion. Participation also leads to more enjoyment. People do not like being talked to without being able to ask questions or respond.

The Communication Process

Developing communication skills begins with understanding the communication process. The process has three basic elements: the sender, the message, and the receiver. Exhibit 5.2 shows how these elements are related.

The process begins with the sender, the message source. In personal selling, this is a salesperson. However, in more general terms, the sender can be anyone who wishes to communicate an idea, such as a political candidate, a college professor, or a minister. The sender wants to communicate some thoughts and ideas to the receiver. Since the receiver cannot read the sender's mind, the sender must translate these ideas into words. The translation of thoughts into a message is called **encoding.**

The sender's message is transmitted to the receiver by voice in a face-to-face interaction or over the telephone, or in a written form such as a letter or proposal. Then the receiver must decode the message and try to understand what the sender intended to communicate. **Decoding** involves interpreting the meaning of the received message.

Communication Breakdowns

Communication breakdowns can be caused by encoding and decoding problems and the environment in which the communications occur. The following sales interaction between a copier salesperson and a prospect illustrates problems that can arise in encoding and decoding messages:

What the salesperson wants to say: We have an entire line of copiers. But I think the Model 900 is ideally suited for your needs, because it provides the basic copying functions at a low price. It's our basic model.

What the salesperson says (encodes): The Model 900 is our best-selling copier. It is designed to economically meet the copying needs of small businesses like yours.

What the customer hears: The Model 900 is a low-price copier for small businesses.

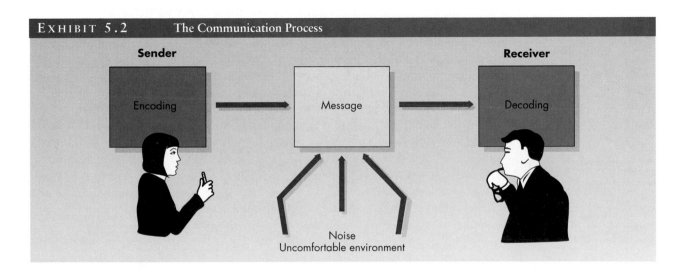

EXHIBIT 5.2   The Communication Process

Background noise on an airfield can hinder effective communications. This salesperson should attempt to move the discussion to a quieter location so the customer will not be distracted by the noise.

Walter Bibikow/The Image Bank

What the customer thinks (decodes): This company makes low-price copiers with limited features. They are designed for businesses that don't have much money to spend for a copier. We need a copier with more features. We should invest in a better copier that will meet our future needs.

What the customer says: I don't think I'm interested in buying a copier now.

In this situation, the salesperson assumed that price was very important to the prospect, and the prospect misinterpreted the salesperson's message to indicate that the company made only low-price, low-performance copiers.

Communications can also be inhibited by the environment in which the communication process occurs. For example, noises can distract the salesperson and the customer. **Noises** are sounds unrelated to messages being exchanged by the salesperson and the customer, such as ringing telephones or other conversations nearby. To improve communication, the salesperson should attempt to minimize the noises in the environment by closing a door to the room or suggesting that the meeting move to another, quieter place.

Finally, people communicate most effectively when they are physically comfortable. If the room is too hot or too cold, the salesperson should suggest changing the temperature controls, opening or closing a window, or moving to another room. Neither salesperson nor prospect should be thinking about the room temperature instead of listening to each other.

Thinking *it* Through	Think of a recent face-to-face interaction you had with another person when a communication problem occurred. What caused the miscommunication? Was it a two-way communication with feedback? Did noises affect the interaction?

MODES OF COMMUNICATION

Exhibit 5.3 shows four modes for communicating with customers. To build partnering relationships, salespeople need to master each of these modes. The four modes are based on whether the salesperson is sending messages to or receiving messages from the customer and what channel is being used to communicate, verbal or nonverbal. **Verbal communication** involves the transmission of words either in face-to-face communication, over a telephone, or through written messages. But messages are often communicated without words through nonverbal means such as facial expressions and body movements. In the next sections, we discuss these four communication modes.

SENDING VERBAL MESSAGES

Messages communicated verbally are encoded into symbols called *words*. Words, however, are just symbols; they have different meanings to different people. Consider a presentation by a salesperson working for a fabric manufacturer. During the presentation, the salesperson indicates that the fabrics the company makes are of high quality, are durable, and their colors are *fast*. But will the prospect know what *fast* means? The dictionary lists over 30 definitions of *fast*. Some of them have to do with very different things, including eating habits, running, or behavior on a date. In this case, of course, the salesperson is pointing out that the colors will not fade despite frequent washing or dry cleaning.

Effective Use of Words

Each industry has its own trade jargon. A college textbook sales representative, for example, must know the meaning of technical expressions such as *test bank, transparency, quarters,* and *instructor's manual.* But salespeople cannot assume all of their customers will be familiar with this trade jargon. They need to check with their customers continually to determine whether their sales messages are being interpreted properly.

Words have different meanings in different cultures and even in different regions of the United States. In England, the hood of a car is called the *bonnet* and the trunk is called the *boot*. In Boston, a *milkshake* is simply syrup mixed with milk, while a *frappe* is ice cream, syrup, and milk mixed together. Similarly, the words *ship* and *boat* have very different meaning to sailors.

Characteristics of Words

Words can be either abstract or concrete as well as emotional or neutral. Concrete, fact-oriented words and expressions usually convey more information and are less likely to be misinterpreted than are abstract, conceptual words. The purity of water

EXHIBIT 5.3 Modes of Communication	Communication Channel	Sending Messages to Customer	Receiving Messages from Customer
	Verbal	Asking questions Presenting information	Listening
	Nonverbal	Using body language, voice characteristics, spacing, and appearance to send messages	Reading body language, voice characteristics

is communicated more effectively by saying, "The mineral content of this water is under one part per million" than by saying, "This water is pure."

Many words related to politics, gender, and race elicit strong emotional responses that inhibit effective communication. Politicians are particularly adept at using words that typically involve a positive emotional response. Who could be against programs such as Truth in Lending, the Fair Deal, or the Right to Work?

Using Effective Words

Words are tools. Word artists have the power to be soft and appealing or strong and powerful. They can use short words and phrases to demonstrate strength and force or to provide charm and grace (e.g., "clean, crisp copies," "library quiet"). With practice, words may be used, like the notes of a musical scale, to create the proper mood.

In making sales presentations, you should choose words that have strength and descriptive quality. Avoid words such as *nice, pretty, good,* and *swell* and phrases that make you sound like an overeager salesperson such as "a great deal," "I guarantee you will . . . ," and "No problem!"

Every salesperson should be able to draw on a set of words to help present the features of a product or service. The words might form a simile, such as "This battery backup is like a spare tire"; a metaphor, such as "This machine is a real workhorse"; or a phrase drawing on sensory appeal, such as "smooth as silk" and "strong as steel."

Tom Hopkins, a lecturer and author on selling techniques, advises against using words that trigger fear and slow down the positive buying impulse. Exhibit 5.4 illustrates how more positive, pacifying words can be used in place of negative words.

Painting Word Pictures

Salespeople can use word pictures to help customers understand the benefits of a product or a feature of the product. A **word picture** is a story designed to help the

EXHIBIT 5.4		
Using Positive Rather Than Negative Words	**Don't Say**	**Do Say**
	Cost or price	Investment
	Down payment	Initial investment
	Contract	Agreement or paperwork
	Buy	Own
	Sell	Get involved
	Sign	Okay, approve, or authorize
	Deal	Opportunity
	Problem	Challenge
	Objection	Area of concern
	Customer	People, companies we serve
	Cheaper	More economical
	Appointment	Visit
	Prospect	Future client
	Commission	Fee for service

Source: Francy Blackwood, "Back to Basics," *Selling,* April 1996, p. 39. Reprinted with permission from Institutional Investors, Inc.

EXHIBIT 5.5

Example of a Word
Picture

Situation

A Jeep Cherokee salesperson is calling on Jill, the owner of a commercial real estate firm. The goal of the word picture is to demonstrate the value of the four-wheel drive option.

Word Picture

Jill, picture for a moment the following situation. You've got this really hot prospect—let's call him Steve—for a remote resort development. You're in your current car, a Cadillac DeVille. You've been trying to get Steve up to the property for months, and this is his only free day for several weeks. The property, up in the northern Georgia mountains, is accessible only by an old logging road. The day is bright and sunny, and Steve is in a good mood. When you reach the foot of the mountains, it turns cloudy and windy. As you wind up the old, bumpy road, a light rain begins. You've just crossed a small bridge when a downpour starts; rain comes down like cats and dogs. Steve looks a little worried. Suddenly your car's tires start spinning. You're stuck in the mud.

Now let's replay the story, assuming you buy this Jeep Wagoneer we've been talking about. [Salesperson quickly repeats the first two paragraphs of this story, substituting Jeep Cherokee for Cadillac DeVille] Suddenly your car tires start spinning. You're stuck in the mud. Calmly you reach down and shift into four-wheel drive. The Jeep pulls out easily, and you reach the destination in about five minutes. Although it's raining, the prospect looks at the land and sees great potential. On the way back down the mountain, you discuss how Steve should go about making an offer on the property. Jill, I hope I've made a point. Can you see why the four-wheel drive option is important for you, even though it does add to the base price of the car?

buyer visualize a point. For example, Exhibit 5.5 provides a word picture that a Jeep Cherokee salesperson might use when calling on a commercial real estate owner.

To use a word picture effectively, the salesperson needs to paint as accurate and reliable a picture as possible. No attempt at puffery should be made. Word pictures should be honest attempts to help the buyer accurately visualize the situation.

Tailoring Words to the Customer

Customers can have different styles of communicating. Some may be very visual; others may prefer an auditory communication mode; and still others communicate in a feeling mode. Salespeople need to adapt their word choices to the customer's preferred communication style. For example, customers with a visual orientation prefer words like *see, observe, demonstrate,* and *clarity;* customers with an auditory orientation prefer words like *announce, hear,* and *mention;* and customers who communicate in a feeling mode like words such as *touch, sensitive,* and *grasp.*[1]

Voice
Characteristics

A salesperson's delivery of words affects how the customer will understand and evaluate his or her presentations. Poor voice and speech habits make it difficult for customers to understand the salesperson's message. **Voice characteristics** include rate of speech, loudness, pitch, quality, and articulation.

Speech Rate

We normally speak at 120 to 160 words per minute. Customers have a tendency to question the expertise of salespeople who talk slower than the normal rate. A salesperson who talks faster than this rate should consciously try to slow down when first meeting a customer and then gradually build up to his or her normal rate.

Salespeople should also vary their rate of speech, depending on the nature of the message and the environment in which the communication occurs. Simple messages can be delivered at faster rates, while more difficult concepts should be presented at slower rates. Salespeople should speak more slowly in a noisy area. Telephone calls should be conducted at a lower speech rate, because the listener lacks visual information to help interpret the words. In general, varying the rate of speech helps to maintain attention.[2]

Loudness

Loudness should be altered based on the nature of the communication situation, in a similar manner to that for speech rate. To avoid monotony, salespeople should learn to vary the loudness of their speech. Loudness can also be used to emphasize certain parts of the sales presentation, indicating to the customer that these parts are more important.

Salespeople should use customer reactions to determine the appropriate loudness. For example, if a customer backs away, the salesperson is talking too loudly; if a customer leans closer, the salesperson is talking too softly.

Inflection

Inflection is the tone of speech. At the end of a sentence, the tone should decrease, indicating the completion of a thought. When the tone goes up at the end of a sentence, listeners often sense uncertainty in the speaker.

Articulation

Articulation refers to the production of recognizable sounds. Poor articulation has three common causes: (1) locked jaw, (2) lazy lips, and (3) lazy tongue. Articulation is best when the speaker opens his or her mouth properly; then the movements of the lips and tongue are unimpeded. When the lips are too close together, the enunciation of certain vowels and consonants suffers.

Asking Questions

Asking questions is a critical element in effective verbal communications.[3] Questioning gets customers to participate in the sales interview. They have a chance to actively engage in conversation rather than just listen to a presentation. This holds the attention of the customer, who ends up learning and remembering more about the product. Questioning also shows the salesperson's interest in the customer and his or her problems. Finally, by asking questions, salespeople are able to collect information about customers and test their assumptions during all phases of the sales interaction, from prospecting to closing. A salesperson may have a lot of information about the customer before the sales call, but there is no guarantee that this precall information is accurate. Salespeople can use questions to either confirm or disprove the precall analysis. Some guidelines for asking good questions follow.

Encourage Longer Responses

Closed-ended questions can be answered with a word or short phrase. Such questions draw little information from the customer. **Open-ended questions,** questions for which there are no simple answers, encourage greater communication.

For example, the closed-ended question "Have you heard of our company?" will probably result in a simple *yes* or *no* answer. Then the salesperson will need to ask a follow-up, open-ended question, such as "Why haven't you heard of our company?" or "What have you heard about our company?" Here are some examples of closed- and open-ended questions:

Closed-Ended Questions	Open-Ended Questions
Are you interested in buying laptop computers for your sales force?	Why haven't you bought laptop computers for your sales force?
Are you satisfied with your present supplier of aluminum cans?	What problems are you having with your present supplier of aluminum cans?

Space Out Questions

When salespeople ask several questions, one right after another, customers may feel threatened. They may think they are being interrogated rather than participating in a conversation. Some customers react by disclosing less rather than more information. For this reason, questions should be spaced out so the customer has time to answer each question in a relaxed atmosphere. One method for spacing out questions is to encourage prospects to elaborate on their responses. In this way, customers believe they are volunteering information rather than being forced to divulge it.

If a number of questions are really necessary, the salesperson might ask a permission question first, such as "Do you mind if I ask you some questions about your operations so we can see if our products might be of use to you?"

Ask Short, Simple Questions

Questions that have two or more parts should be avoided. The customer may not know which part to answer, and the salesperson may not know which part has been answered. For example:

SALESPERSON How much time do you spend making your annual budget and your sales forecasts?

CUSTOMER Oh, about three weeks.

Does this mean the customer spends three weeks on both tasks or only on one?

Long questions are hard to remember and to answer. For example: "With so many complicated reports to prepare and review, is it difficult for you to determine your direct material and labor costs and determine how much shelf space to allocate to laundry detergent in the 20,000- and 40,000-square-foot stores?" Long questions can lose the customer's attention. Some customers may be annoyed by questions that force them to ask the salesperson for clarification.

Avoid Leading Questions

Questions should not suggest an appropriate answer. Such questions may put words into the customer's mouth rather than drawing out what the customer actually thinks. For example:

SALESPERSON Why do you think this is a good product?

CUSTOMER Well, you said it has a low price and is very reliable.

The salesperson's question encouraged a positive response and discouraged a negative one. Even though such questions may get the responses the salesperson wants to hear, they may mask the customer's true feelings.

Some questions salespeople can use to collect and maintain the flow of information from the customer are discussed next.

Thinking *it* **Through**	What are some good questions you can ask your instructor to find out what he or she is looking for on your next class assignment, that is, questions that will help you get a better grade on the assignment?

Questions to Collect Information

Questions used to collect information usually start with the word *who, what, where, how,* or *why.* Responses to these questions give the salesperson a better understanding of the prospect, the prospect's business, and the present competition. It is best to start by asking for publicly available information; such questions are the easiest to answer. Some examples of these questions are:

> Who uses the copier?
>
> What is your policy concerning returns?
>
> Why is the Edgewood plant relocating to Oregon?
>
> How much are you paying for the resistors now?

The above questions are used to uncover specific facts.

Questions can also be used to discover the customer's feelings on a subject. Some examples of these questions are:

> How do you feel about leasing versus buying trucks?
>
> What's your reaction to the new government safety regulations?
>
> How do you feel about increasing your hardware inventory level?

At times, customers may be reluctant to express their feelings on a subject. In these situations, indirect questions can be used to get customer reactions. Such questions ask customers to respond to the known views of a third party:

> *Electronic News* had a recent article on the increased use of microswitches. Do you find this to be the case?
>
> The Apex air conditioner got a good rating in *Consumer Reports.* Do you think it will sell well to your customers?

Questions can also be used to get a customer to articulate a specific problem. For example, a salesperson selling a fax machine with an advantage in paper quality might use the following series of questions:

SALESPERSON Your fax machine uses treated paper, doesn't it?

CUSTOMER Yes, it does.

SALESPERSON Some of my other customers have told me that faxes on treated paper are difficult to copy because of the gray cast of the fax. Have you experienced that as well?

CUSTOMER Well, yes. The paper this machine uses isn't the best. It doesn't look very good.

Compare the previous conversation with one using a closed-ended question:

SALESPERSON The quality of the faxes from your machine isn't very good. Right?

CUSTOMER It's OK.

When customers realize the disadvantage of their present product, the salesperson can illustrate the consequences of the disadvantage by asking additional questions:

SALESPERSON How does the high energy cost of running our equipment affect you?

CUSTOMER Well, we don't like it.

SALESPERSON How does the faster speed of our equipment decrease your production costs?

CUSTOMER The speed really helps us. That's why we bought your equipment.

SALESPERSON Does the speed justify the higher energy cost?"

CUSTOMER I think it does.

Questions to Maintain the Flow of Information

A good way to maintain the flow of information is to offer verbal and nonverbal encouragement, such as saying, "Really?," "Uh-huh," "That's interesting," and "Is that so?" and nodding your head. Let's look at the effect of a sequence of these encouragement signals:

CUSTOMER Then this salesperson asked me if I was interested in getting lower costs than I was getting from Delta.

SALESPERSON That's interesting. Tell me more about that.

CUSTOMER Well, he said that at my current usage level he could save me about $25 a month.

SALESPERSON Is that right?

CUSTOMER Then came the kicker.

SALESPERSON Uh-huh?

CUSTOMER When I asked about service, the whole picture changed.

SALESPERSON I see.

CUSTOMER In short, they were going to give me a lower cost, all right. But they weren't going to give me much in the way of service.

Another approach for maintaining the flow of information is to make positive requests for additional information, such as

Can you give me an example of what you mean?

Please, tell me more about that.

The third type of approach for maintaining the flow of information is to make neutral statements that reaffirm or repeat a customer's comment or emotion. They allow the salesperson to dig deeper, and they stimulate customers to continue their thoughts in a logical manner. By reaffirming a customer's statement, the saleperson can respond to the customer without agreeing or disagreeing with him or her. Some examples of these questions are:

You said you were dissatisfied with your present service?

So you need the self-correcting feature?

Reaffirming a customer's statement is particularly effective with customers who are angry, upset, or in some other highly emotional state. Often these emotions persist until the customer recognizes that the emotions are being acknowledged. For example:

CUSTOMER Look, I've just about had it with you, your company, and your pumps!

SALESPERSON It's pretty obvious you're upset, Ms. Roberts.

CUSTOMER Of course I am. That's the third time this week the pump has gone on the fritz!

By acknowledging customers' emotional states, salespeople let them know they are being heard, which usually reduces the level of negative feelings. This allows salespeople to focus on the problem causing the emotion.

Purchasing agents develop impressions of salespeople based on the quality of their questions. Exhibit 5.6 reports some of the best and worst questions salespeople can ask.

EXHIBIT 5.6 The Best and Worst Questions Salespeople Can Ask	**Worst Questions** *What does your company do?* "The worst thing a salesperson can ask is information they should know. I don't have time to educate them about our products." (Dee Johnson, vice president, purchasing, O'Sullivan Company, Winchester, Virginia) *What will it take to get your business?* "This question makes it sound like the customer will do whatever it takes to buy into your business—which is definitely not a long-term solution." (John Semanik, contracts manager, Sun Microsystems, Sunnyvale, California) *Are you the person who is going to make the buying decision?* "Why are you there and why is the salesperson there if you are not going to make the buying decision?" (Beverly Miller, president and director of purchasing, Miller/Bevco, Kansas City, Missouri) *Can we do something for you?"* "Salespeople should never hint at gifts or perks they can offer in exchange for closing a deal. Ethics is very important to me, so it is paramount they treat me professionally." (Thomas Catalano, buyer, Climax Manufacturing Company, Lowville, New York) **Best Questions** *What kind of value-added are you looking for?* "To me added value—such as just-in-time delivery or promising a full-time specialist—is more important than price." (Dee Johnson) *What can I do to make your job easier?* "You hope the salesperson is trying to come up with a solution to your problem, not just focusing on price." (John Semanik) *If your interested in my product, how do you plan to use it?* "Salespeople should be interested in how their products and services fit into your business." (Beverly Miller) *How can we help improve your product or process?* "I want to know that a salesperson is interested in how his company can add value to my company . . . . It's important to know what both sides of the desk can bring to the equation." (Thomas Catalano)

Source: Brian Tracey, "Stop Talking . . . and Start Listening," *Sales & Marketing Management,* February 1995, pp. 84–88. Reprinted with permission from Bill Communications.

SELLING SCENARIO 5.1

Keeping Cool When the Customer Boils Over

Simply listening can calm down an irate customer and build a long-term relationship. Greg Gondeck, a regional sales manager at Gestner Corporation, a distributor of copiers and office equipment, first met the school superintendent when he received a call telling him to bring over a truck and haul his copiers away. He went to see the customer immediately. The superintendent's secretary said, "Oh, no, you're really in for it," grabbed her coat, and left. Gondeck then listened to the customer vent his rage for an hour and a half.

Gondeck paid attention to every detail of the story, and in the end agreed with the customer. "I didn't try to deny it, minimize it, or put it aside. I faced the mistake we made head on, gave him my personal guarantee that things would be different from that point forward, and worked out a copier solution that really met his requirements."

That afternoon Gondek left the customer with a $17,000 order and the start of a long-term relationship. By listening to the customer, Gondeck showed his respect and learned about the customer's needs.

Source: Nancy McCann, "Keep Cool When the Client Boils Over," *Selling,* December 1995, p. 21. Reprinted with permission from Institutional Investors, Inc.

Listening to Verbal Communications from Customers

Many people believe effective communication is achieved by talking a lot. Inexperienced salespeople often go into a selling situation thinking they have to outtalk the prospect. They are enthusiastic about their product and company, and they want to tell the prospect all they know. However, salespeople who monopolize conversations cannot find out what customers need. Actually, listening is probably the most critical aspect of effective communication. Selling Scenario 5.1 illustrates the importance of being a good listener.

To be an effective listener, the salesperson on the left demonstrates an interest in what the customer is saying and actively thinks about questions for drawing out more information.

©Tony Stone Worldwide/Andy Sacks

For example, Richard Greene, the top producer at Merrill Lynch, establishes relationships with clients by listening: "I don't go to a meeting with something to sell. I want information about the customer's risk profile so I can do the right job for him." Greene understands that listening can win over customers. All customers like to have a chance to express their views. Greene says, "His kids don't listen to him. His wife doesn't listen to him—and he doesn't listen to her . . . . Then all of a sudden he goes to breakfast with me. He starts to answer a question. And he doesn't get interrupted. Before his eggs cool, I have another client."[4]

People can speak at a rate of only 120 to 160 words per minute, but they can listen to over 800 words per minute. This difference is referred to as the **speaking-listening differential**. Because of this differential, people often become lazy listeners. They do not pay attention and often remember only 50 percent of what is said immediately after they hear it.

Active Listening

Effective listening is not a passive activity. More than just hearing what the speaker is saying, good listeners project themselves into the mind of the speaker and attempt to feel the way the speaker feels. If a customer says she needs a small microphone, the salesperson needs to listen carefully to find out what the term *small* means to this particular customer, how small the microphone has to be, why she needs a small microphone, and what she will be willing to sacrifice to get a small microphone. Through effective listening, the salesperson can consider the customer's specific needs in recommending a type of microphone.

Effective listeners actively think while they listen. They think about the conclusions toward which the speaker is building, evaluate the evidence being presented, and sort out important facts from irrelevant ones. **Active listening** also means the listener attempts to draw out as much information as possible. Gestures can motivate a person to continue talking. Head nodding, eye contact, and an occasional "I see," "Tell me more," and "That's interesting" demonstrate an interest in and understanding of what is being said.

Suggestions for active listening include (1) repeating information, (2) restating or rephrasing information, (3) clarifying information, (4) summarizing the conversation, (5) tolerating silences, and (6) concentrating on the ideas being communicated.[5]

Repeating Information

During a sales interaction, the salesperson should verify the information she or he is collecting from the customer. A useful way to verify information is to repeat, word for word, what has been said. This technique minimizes the chance of misunderstandings. For example:

CUSTOMER I'll take 15 cases of personal-size Ivory soap and 12 cases of family-size.

SALESPERSON Sure, Mr. Johnson. That will be 15 cases of personal-size and 12 cases of family-size.

CUSTOMER Wait a minute. I got that backward. I want 12 cases of personal-size and 15 cases of family-size.

SALESPERSON Fine. 12 personal and 15 family. Is that right?

CUSTOMER Yes. That's what I want.

Salespeople need to be careful when using this technique, however. Customers can get irritated with salespeople who echo everything they say.

Restating or Rephrasing Information

To verify a customer's intent, salespeople should restate the customer's comment in their own words. This ensures that the salesperson and customer understand each other. For example:

CUSTOMER The service isn't quite what I had expected.

SALESPERSON I see, you're a little bit dissatisfied with the service we've been giving you.

CUSTOMER Oh, no. As a matter of fact, I've been getting better service than I thought I would.

Clarifying Information

Another way to verify a customer's meaning is to ask questions designed to obtain additional information. These can give a more complete understanding of the customer's concerns. For example:

CUSTOMER Listen, I've tried everything. I just can't get this drill press to work properly.

SALESPERSON Just what is it that the drill press doesn't do?"

CUSTOMER Well, the rivets keep jamming inside the machine. Sometimes one rivet is inserted on top of the other.

SALESPERSON Would you describe for me the way you load the rivets onto the tray?

CUSTOMER Well, first I push down the release lever and take the tray out. Then I push that little button and put the rivets in. Next, I push the bottom again, put the tray in the machine, and push the lever.

SALESPERSON When you put the tray in, which side is up?

CUSTOMER Does that make a difference?

This exchange shows how a sequence of questions can give a clearer definition of the problem and help the salesperson determine its cause.

Summarizing the Conversation

An important element of active listening is mentally summarizing points that have been made. At critical spots in the sales presentation, the salesperson should present his or her mentally prepared summary. Summarizing provides both salesperson and customer with a quick overview of what has taken place and lets them focus on the issues that have been discussed. Summarizing also lets the salesperson change the direction of the conversation. For example:

CUSTOMER . . . So I told him I wasn't interested.

SALESPERSON Let me see if I have this straight. A salesperson called on you today and asked if you were interested in reducing your costs. He also said he could save you about $25 a month. But when you pursued the matter, you found out the dollar savings in costs were offset by reduced service.

CUSTOMER That's right.

SALESPERSON Well, I have your account records right here. Assuming you're interested in getting more for your dollar with regard to copy costs, I think there's a way we can help you—without having to worry about any decrease in the quality of service.

CUSTOMER Tell me more.

Tolerating Silences

This technique could more appropriately be titled "Bite your tongue." At times during a sales presentation, a customer needs time to think. This need can be triggered by a tough question or an issue the customer wants to avoid.

While the customer is thinking, periods of silence occur. Salespeople may be uncomfortable during these silences and feel they need to say something. However, the customer cannot think when the salesperson is talking. By tolerating silences, salespeople give customers a chance to sell themselves. The following conversation about setting an appointment demonstrates the benefits of tolerating silence:

SALESPERSON What day would you like me to call on you?

CUSTOMER Just a minute. Let me think about that.

SALESPERSON [silence]

CUSTOMER Okay, let's make it on Monday, the 22nd.

SALESPERSON Fine, Ms. Quinn. What time would be most convenient?

CUSTOMER Hmmm . . .

SALESPERSON [silence]

CUSTOMER Ten o'clock would be best for me.

Concentrating on the Ideas Being Communicated

Frequently what customers say and how they say it can distract salespeople from the ideas the customers are actually trying to communicate. For example, salespeople may react emotionally when customers use emotion-laden phrases such as "bad service" or "lousy product." Rather than getting angry, the saleperson should try to find out what upset the customer so much. Salespeople should listen to the words from the customer's viewpoint instead of reacting from their own viewpoint.

READING CUSTOMERS' NONVERBAL MESSAGES

When two people communicate with each other, spoken words play a surprisingly small part in the communication process. Words are responsible for only 40 percent of the information people acquire in face-to-face communication. The voice characteristics account for 10 percent of the message received, and the remaining 50 percent comes from nonverbal communications.[6] **Nonverbal communications** are forms of expression—body language, space, and appearance—that communicate thoughts and emotions without using words.

Nonverbal communications provide a lot of information to the receiver, because the sender has difficulty controlling it. Since senders have less control over nonverbal communications, receivers tend to trust these communications more than verbal statements. For example, a customer claims to be happy about a salesperson's pro-

SELLING SCENARIO 5.2

Sherlock Holmes and Selling Skills

In an episode from *The Memoirs of Sherlock Holmes,* Holmes and Watson return to their Baker Street lodgings to learn from the pageboy that a man had called during their absence, waited impatiently for awhile, and finally departed in a state of agitation, leaving his pipe behind on the table. Holmes picks up the pipe, examines it briefly, and makes the following observations to Watson:

Now it has, you see, been twice mended: once in the wooden stem and once in the amber. Each of those mends—done, as you observe, with silver bands—must have cost more than the pipe did originally. The man must value the pipe highly when he prefers to patch it up rather than buy a new one with the same money. . . . The owner is obviously a muscular man, left-handed, with an excellent set of teeth, careless in his habits, and with no need to practice economy.

So what has this to do with selling? Surely the answer to that question is elementary. If Sherlock Holmes had not given up his paper route early in life to become a detective, he might well have gone on to become a superlative salesperson. His keen powers of observation would have provided him with so many clues about his prospects' needs, desires, attitudes, and emotions that he would have been able to make effective presentations.

At the beginning of the sales interview, the prospect is always a mystery: So much about him or her is unknown. The difference between the successful and unsuccessful salesperson is the ability to extract clues from the prospect. Observing and listening are the two best ways to do this. Salespeople should emulate the keen eyes and ears and the analytical approach for which Sherlock Holmes was renowned.

Source: Craig Bridgman, "The Power of Observation," *Personal Selling Power,* October 1986, p. 10.

---

posal and indicates her happiness by smiling. However, people can detect fake smiles very accurately. The salesperson who feels the smile is not genuine will discount the customer's words and think the customer really is not pleased by the proposal.[7] Selling Scenario 5.2 compares the observational powers of Sherlock Holmes to those of successful salespeople.

Some nonverbal communications have more universal meaning than do verbal communications. The same facial muscles are used to communicate emotions such as happiness, anger, surprise, and fear in many different cultures. The cultural differences in nonverbal communications arise not from the meanings of the expressions but from when to appropriately display the expressions.[8]

Body Language

Customers provide a lot of information through their body language. The elements of **body language** are body angle, facial expressions, arms, hands, and legs.[9] Each of these channels is important in face-to-face communication; however, combinations of elements are needed to accurately interpret body language.

Body Angle

Back-and-forth motions indicate a positive outlook, while side-to-side movements suggest insecurity and doubt. Body movements directed toward a person indicate a positive regard, while leaning back or away suggests boredom, apprehension, or possibly anger. Changes in position may indicate a customer wants to end the interview, strongly agrees or disagrees with what has been said, or wants to place an order.

©Michael Abramson   John Feingersh/The Stock Market

Customers communicate through body language. The customer on the left is giving a negative signal by rais-ing his hands with the palm turned away from him and sitting further back in his seat. The doctor on the right is giving positive signals indicating interest in what the salesperson is saying.

Face

The face has many small muscles capable of communicating innumerable messages. Customers can use these muscles to indicate interest, expectation, concern, disap-proval, or approval.

The eyes are the most important area of the face. The pupils of interested or ex-cited people tend to enlarge. Thus, by looking at a customer's eyes, salespeople can often determine when their presentations have made an impression. For this reason, many Chinese jade buyers wear dark glasses so they can conceal their interest in spe-cific items and bargain more effectively.

Eye position can indicate a customer's thought process.[10] Eyes focused straight ahead mean a customer is passively receiving information but devoting little effort to analyzing the meaning and not really concentrating on the presentation. Intense eye contact for more than three seconds generally indicates customer displeasure. Staring indicates coldness, anger, or dislike.

Customers look away from the salesperson while they actively consider informa-tion in the sales presentation. When the customer's eyes are positioned to the left or right, the salesperson has succeeded in getting the customer involved in the presenta-tion. A gaze to the right suggests the customer is considering the logic and facts in the presentation, while gazing to the left suggests more intense concentration based on an emotional consideration. Eyes cast down offer the strongest signal of concen-tration. However, when customers cast their eyes down, they may be thinking, "How can I get my boss to buy this product?" or "How can I get out of this conver-sation?" When customers look away for an extended period, they probably want to end the meeting.

Significant cultural differences exit concerning eye contact between individuals. In the United States, salespeople look customers directly in the eyes when speaking or listening to them. Direct eye contact is a sign of interest in what the customer is saying. In other cultures, looking someone in the eyes may be a sign of disrespect. For example,

- In Japan, looking a subordinate directly in the eyes indicates that the subordinate has done something wrong. When a subordinate looks a supervisor directly in the eyes, the subordinate is displaying hostility.
- Arabs dislike eye contact, and Americans often feel that their eyes dart around. This, unfortunately, gives some Americans the impression that Arabs are shifty.
- Brazilians look at people directly even more than Americans do. Americans tend to find this direct eye contact, when held over a long period of time, to be disconcerting.[11]

Skin color and skin tautness are other facial cues. A customer whose face reddens is signaling that something is wrong. That blush can indicate either anger or embarrassment. Tension and anger show in a tightness around the cheeks, jawline, or neck.

Arms

A key factor in interpreting arm movements is intensity. Customers will use more arm movement when they are conveying an opinion. Broader and more vigorous movement indicates the customer is more emphatic about the point being communicated verbally.

Hands

Hand gestures are very expressive. For example, open and relaxed hands are a positive signal, especially with palms facing up. Self-touching gestures typically indicate tension.

Involuntary gestures, such as tightening of a fist, are good indicators of true feelings. The meanings of hand gestures differ from one culture to another. For

The open hands on the left are a positive buying signal for a salesperson. The intertwined fingers in the middle indicate the customer needs to express his power and authority. On the right, the customer is playing with his hands indicating underlying tension.

All photos by Michael Hruby

example, in the United States the thumbs-up expression means everything is all right, but in the Middle East it is an obscene gesture. In Japan the OK sign made by holding the thumb and forefinger in a circle symbolizes money, but in France it indicates that something is worthless.[12]

Legs

When customers have uncrossed legs in an open position, they send a message of cooperation, confidence, and friendly interest. Legs crossed away from a salesperson suggest that the sales call is not going well.

Thinking *it* **Through**	Turn on a television set, but keep the sound off. Look at the actors. Can you determine their emotions by looking at their body language? Look closely to see if you can detect the patterns of body language we have discussed.

Body Language Patterns

No single gesture or position defines a specific emotion or attitude. To interpret a customer's feelings, salespeople need to consider the pattern of the signals via a number of channels. Exhibit 5.7 explains eight patterns of nonverbal expression.

Detecting Customers' Hidden Emotions and Feelings

In business and social situations, people treat one another politely and are considerate of one another's feelings. Thus, salespeople often have difficulty knowing what a customer is really thinking. For example, smiling is the most common way to conceal a strong emotion.

During a product demonstration, it is important to know what benefits and features are attractive to the customer. Thus, salespeople need to know whether a customer's smile is real or just a polite mask. The muscles around the eyes reveal whether a smile is real or polite. When a customer is truly impressed, the muscles around the eyes contract, the skin above the eyes comes down a little, and the eyelids are slightly closed.

Some signals that customers may be hiding their true feelings are as follows:

- Contradictions and verbal mistakes. People often forget what they said previously. They may leak their true feelings through a slip of the tongue or a lapse in memory.

- Differences in two parts of a conversation. In the first part of a conversation, a customer may display some nervousness when asked about the performance of a competitor's product and give a flawless response outlining the product's benefits. Later in the conversation, the evaluation of the competitor's product may be much more convoluted.

- Contradictions between verbal and nonverbal messages. For example, facial expression may not match the enthusiasm indicated by verbal comments. Also, a decrease in nonverbal signals may indicate the customer is making a cautious response.

- Nonverbal signals such as voice tone going up at the end of a sentence, hesitation in the voice, small shrugs, increased self-touching, and stiffer body posture, suggest that the customer has concerns.

EXHIBIT 5.7	Patterns of Nonverbal Expression				
	Cues from the Five Channels				
Pattern	**Body Angle**	**Face**	**Arms**	**Hands**	**Legs**
Power, dominance, superiority	Sitting astride chair Exaggerated leaning over Standing while others sit	Piercing eye contact	Hands on hips	Hands behind neck Hands behind back Steepling (fingertips touching)	Legs over chair Feet on desk
Nervousness, submission, apprehension	Fidgeting Shifting from side to side	Head down Minimal eye contact Constant blinking	Hands to face, hair Rubbing back of neck	Wringing hands Fingers clasped	
Disagreement, anger, skepticism	Turning body away	Negative shake of head Lips pursing Eyes squinting Chin thrust out Frown	Arms crossed Finger under collar	Fist Finger pointing Hands grasping edge of desk	Legs crossed
Boredom, disinterest	Head in palm of hands	Lack of eye contact Looking at door, at watch, out window Blank stare		Playing with object on table Shuffling papers Drumming on table	Tapping feet
Suspicion, secretiveness, dishonesty	Moving body away Sideways glance Cross arms or legs with body forward	Avoiding eye contact Squinting eyes Smirking	Touching nose while speaking Pulling ear while speaking	Fingers crossed	Feet pointing toward exits
Uncertainty, indecision	Pacing back and forth	Head down or tilted Biting lip Shifting eyes left and right	Pinching bridge of nose Tugging at pants Scratching head	Pulling neck	Look of concentration while tapping feet
Evaluation	Head tilted slightly Ear turned toward speaker	Slight blinking of eyes Eye squinting Eyebrows raised Nodding	Hands gripping chin Putting glasses in mouth	Putting index finger to lips	Kicking foot slightly
Cooperation, confidence, honesty	Leaning forward in seat Sitting far up in chair Back and forth movement of body	Good eye contact Slight blinking Smile	Putting hands to chest Free movement of arms and hands	Open hands Palms toward other person	Legs uncrossed Feet flat on floor

When customers disguise their true feelings, they are often trying to be polite, not deceptive. To uncover the customer's true feelings and build a relationship, the salesperson needs to encourage the customer to be frank by emphasizing that she or he will benefit from an open exchange of information. Here are some comments a salesperson can make to encourage forthright discussion:

Perhaps there is some reason you cannot share the information with me.

Are you worried about how I might react to what you are telling me?

I have a sense there is really more to the story than what you are telling me. Let's put the cards on the table so we can put this issue to rest.[13]

Selling Scenario 5.3 illustrates how Japanese businesspeople build relationships by avoiding the word *no* but avoiding the *no* can create misunderstandings and prevent relationships from developing.

SENDING MESSAGES WITH NONVERBAL COMMUNICATIONS

The previous section discussed how salespeople can observe body language to develop a better understanding of their customers. Salespeople use body language, voice characteristics, spacing, and appearance to send messages to their customers.

Using Body Language

Body language can be used to communicate more effectively with customers. For example, salespeople should strive to use the cooperative cues shown in Exhibit 5.7. Cooperative cues indicate to customers that the salesperson sincerely wants to help them satisfy their needs. On the other hand, salespeople should avoid using power cues. These cues will intimidate customers and make them uncomfortable.

Face

Nonverbal communications are very difficult to manage. Facial reactions are often involuntary, especially during stressful situations. Lips tense, foreheads wrinkle, and eyes glare without salespeople realizing they are disclosing their feelings to a customer. Salespeople will be able to control their facial reactions only with practice.

As with muscles anywhere else in the body, the coordination of facial muscles requires exercise. Actors realize this need and attend facial exercise classes to control their reactions. Salespeople are also performers to some extent and need to learn how to use their faces to communicate emotions.

Nothing creates rapport like a smile. The smile should appear natural and comfortable, not a smirk or an exaggerated, clownlike grin. To achieve the right smile, stand before a mirror or a video camera and place your lips in various smiling positions until you find a position that feels natural and comfortable. Then practice the smile until it becomes almost second nature.

Eye Contact

Appropriate eye contact varies from situation to situation. People should use direct eye contact when talking in front of a group to indicate sincerity, credibility, and trustworthiness. Glancing from face to face or staring at a wall has the opposite effect. However, staring can overpower customers and make them uncomfortable.

Hand Movements

Hand movements can have a dramatic impact. For example, by exposing the palm of the hand, a salesperson indicates openness and receptivity. Slicing hand movements and pointing a finger are very strong signals and should be used to reinforce only the most important points. In most cases, pointing a finger should be avoided. It will remind customers of a parent scolding a child.

SELLING SCENARIO 5.3

No "No's" Builds Relationships in Japan

All cultures have ways to avoid saying *no* when they really mean *no*. *No* can be rude, offensive, and disrupt harmony. In Japan, maintaining long-term relationships is of utmost importance and saying *no* is avoided at all costs.

The Japanese have developed a number of interesting techniques to avoid saying *no*. Some terms used to indicate *no* are "It's very difficult," "We'll think about it," "I'm not sure," and "We'll give it some thought." An American salesperson can also misunderstand a Japanese customer who listens politely and then says *hai* when the salesperson is finished. *Hai* can mean *yes*, but typically it means "I hear you. Unknowing American salespeople who have been trained not to take *no* for an answer can misinterpret the lack of *no* as a signal that there is hope of making a sale.

American customers generally respond with a *yes* or *no* and then give you their reasons why. Japanese customers tend to give long explanations first and then leave the conclusion ambiguous. Etiquette dictates that a Japanese customer may tell the salesperson what he or she wants to hear, not respond to the question at all, or be evasive. This ambiguity often leads to misunderstandings.

Source: Phillip Caterora, *International Marketing,* 9th ed. (Burr Ridge, IL: Richard D. Irwin, 1996), p. 127.

When salespeople make presentations to a group, they often use too few hand gestures. Gestures should be used to drive home a point. But if a salesperson uses too many gestures, acting like an orchestra conductor, people will begin to watch the hands and miss the words.

Posture and Body Movements

Shuffling one's feet and slumping both give an impression of a lack of self-confidence and self-discipline. On the other hand, an overly erect posture, such as that of a military cadet, suggests rigidity. Salespeople should let comfort be their guide when searching for the right posture.

To get an idea of what looks good and feels good, stand in front of a mirror and shift your weight until tension in your back and neck is at a minimum. Then gently pull your shoulders up and back, and elevate your head. Practice walking by taking a few steps. Keep the pace deliberate, not halting; deliberate movements indicate confidence and control.

Thinking it Through

Pay close attention to your instructor's next lecture. How does he or she use body language and voice characteristics to emphasize important points?

Matching the Customer's Communication Style

Salespeople develop better rapport when they match the verbal and nonverbal behavior of their customers. Consider a salesperson from New York selling to a customer in Texas. Communication in this sales interaction will be effective only if the salesperson slows his or her rate of speech and avoids using expressions only another New Yorker would understand.

Evangeline Caridas, a Xerox Rep of the Year, says that if "you speak loud and fast and go in and talk to a prospect [who is] soft-spoken and slow, you're in for a real mismatch. You've got to slow to match the tone and speed of your client. You're communicating 'I'm not like you', maybe even that 'I don't like you.' We all like people who are like us."[14]

This matching process also extends to body language. Michael McCasky, writing in the Harvard Business Review, noted that "In moments of great rapport, a remarkable pattern of nonverbal communication can develop. Two people will mirror each other's movements—dropping a hand, shifting their body at exactly the same time."[15] The more customers and salespeople share language, speech patterns, and nonverbal behavior, the greater the sense of rapport and mutual understanding they will have.

COMMUNICATING IN A HIGH-TECHNOLOGY ENVIRONMENT

Salespeople can now use technology (e-mail, fax, and voice mail) to communicate with their customers. You call the customer and get his or her voice mail. You call again and the secretary says to fax the information. You call again. The secretary says the prospect is out of town and suggests you e-mail him or her. Technology makes the transfer of information fast and easy. But it also holds the salesperson at arm's length and makes it difficult to develop rapport. High tech doesn't replace face-to-face interactions, it supplements and enhances it. Following are some suggestions for putting high touch into high tech:[16]

1. Accept the need to communicate through electronic media, but don't be lulled into thinking immediacy means the same thing as intimacy in communications.

2. Learn the customer's preferences and find out what tools the customer uses and how she or he likes to communicate. Adapt the content to the customer's preferred communication style.

Developments in technology enable salespeople to improve their communications with customers by using a number of different modes.

Courtesy Motorola Corporation

3. Avoid "techno-overkill"—use electronic communications when speed is critical, but written communication may be better when the customer wants to study the information at his or her leisure.

4. Make the communication meaningful. Customers are drowning in information. Use visual graphs to reduce data. Don't send junk faxes, and don't talk to your customer's voice mail until the time runs out. Busy customers like some chit-chat, but don't get carried away.

5. Customize your messages. Replace a general reference with a "meaningful specific," such as customer name, company name, and other details important to the customer. Develop a personal hallmark, such as a unique cover for a fax. Use a fresh message on voice mail each day. Tell callers in the message if a time limit exists for your voice mail. Offer options to talk to someone immediately.

6. Sometimes impress customers with speed. Speed is invaluable for damage control. Use technology to exceed a customer's expectations, such as responding immediately to urgent calls via fax or e-mail.

7. Don't deliver bad news via e-mail; rather, use e-mail to arrange a meeting to discuss the issue.

SPACE AND PHYSICAL CONTACT

Distance during Interactions

The physical space between a customer and a salesperson can affect the customer's reaction to a sales presentation. Exhibit 5.8 shows the four distance zones people use when interacting in business and social situations. The intimate zone is reserved primarily for a person's closest relationships, the personal zone for close friends and those who share special interests, the social zone for business transactions and other impersonal relationships, and the public zone for speeches, teachers in classrooms, and passersby.[17] The exact sizes of the intimate and personal zones depend on age, gender, culture, and race. For example, the social zone for Latin Americans is much closer than that for North Americans. Latin Americans tend to conduct business transactions so close together that North Americans feel uncomfortable.

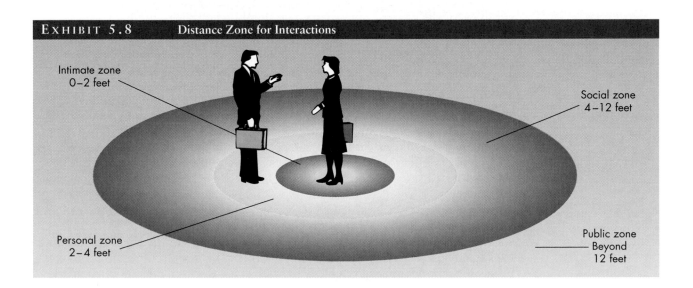

EXHIBIT 5.8   Distance Zone for Interactions

Intimate zone
0–2 feet

Social zone
4–12 feet

Personal zone
2–4 feet

Public zone
Beyond
12 feet

Customers may react negatively when salespeople invade their intimate or personal space. To show the negative reaction, they may assume a defensive posture by moving back or folding their arms. While approaching too close can generate a negative reaction, standing too far away can create an image of aloofness, conceit, or unsociability.

In general, salespeople should begin customer interactions at the far end of the social zone and not move closer until an initial rapport has been established. If the buyer indicates that a friendlier relationship has developed, the salesperson should move closer.

Touching

People fall into two touching groups: contact and noncontact. Contact people usually see noncontact people as cold and unfriendly. On the other hand, noncontact people view contact people as overly friendly and obtrusive.

Although some customers may accept a hand on their backs or a touch on their shoulders, salespeople should limit touching to a handshake. Touching clearly enters a customer's intimate space and may be considered rude and threatening—an invasion.

APPEARANCE

Physical appearance, specifically dress style, is an aspect of nonverbal communication that affects the customer's evaluation of the salesperson. Two priorities in dressing for business are (1) getting customers to notice you in a positive way and (2) getting customers to feel comfortable trusting you. If salespeople overdress, their clothing may distract from their sales presentation. Proper attire and grooming, however, can give salespeople additional poise and confidence.

At one time, dressing for work was simple: You just reached in the closet and picked from your wardrobe of blue, gray, and pinstripe suits. Today things are not that simple. With casual days and dress-down Fridays, styles and dress codes vary considerably across offices. During a given day, a salesperson may have to visit his or her company's and customers' offices, each of which may have a different dress code. Some suggestions for proper dress follow.[18]

Business clothes project an image of the salesperson, the salesperson's company, and the product. Salespeople will feel most comfortable using their own natural style plus some common sense. Standards of acceptable business dress vary in different areas of the country, and salespeople should adapt their clothing styles accordingly. Consider corporate culture, too. How do the executives of the company dress? What image do they project? Finally, remember the customer: The salesperson's business dress should make both of them comfortable.

Dress Like the Customer

The appropriate style of dress varies depending on the person's occupation, social status, age, physical size, and geographic location. Salespeople can get some useful clues about appropriate styles by observing their customers. They should attempt to match the styles of their customers and avoid dressing more stylishly or expensively. Dressing better than your customers may create an impression of greater authority, but also may make customers feel uncomfortable and defensive. Before visiting a new prospect, a salesperson should find out what the dress code is, particularly if visiting a branch office or a manufacturing site, places other than the corporate headquarters where formal standards typically prevail.

Salespeople should wear classic dresses, suits, and accessories. High-fashion clothing should be avoided; it costs too much, goes out of style too soon, and may look unprofessional or unbusinesslike unless the salesperson works in the fashion industry.

Casual Dress Codes

Many companies are adopting more casual dress codes or instituting dress-down days. Norm Pifer, national sales manager at Alco Chemical, believes dressing down is good for sales, particularly for salespeople working in heavy industry. "Dressing down gives the appearance of a willingness to get one's hands dirty. And successful salespeople often get their hands dirty." On the other hand, Sean Ciemiewicz argues, "When a rep wears a suit, he blends in with all of the other people a buyer is going to meet in the day."[19]

If you elect to dress casually, you need to pay greater attention to your clothes because the clothes will be more revealing than a business suit. You must remember that you are going to work, not shuffling around the house. Wearing shorts and sport shirts suggests that you are confusing the boundaries between work and play, your career and your social life. Polo shirts and khaki pants are the basics, but you might want to show more imagination and personal flair. Men can show more flair by wearing a dressier pair of pants and a long- or short-sleeve shirt made from a fabric with more color and texture. Women can show a sense of fun and self-confidence by adding more color and wearing skirts, blouses, and accessories.[20]

Hints for Men

The suit is the focal garment in business dress, particularly when you are interacting with upper-middle-class decision makers. Choose color, material, fit, and accompanying garments and accessories carefully. In general, darker suits give a more authoritative image; lighter colors create a friendlier one. Pinstripes convey the most authority, followed in descending order by solids, chalk stripes, and plaids (which must be very subtle). Natural fibers such as wool (or wool-polyester blends that look and feel like wool) are preferable. They look better and wear better than most synthetics. Cottons and linens, while comfortable, wrinkle too easily.

White-on-white patterns and solid white shirts are the most effective, adding credibility; blues and other pale pastels are also popular. Shirts, as a rule, should be lighter than the suit and the tie darker than the shirt. Shirt stripes should always be close together, clearly defined, and of one coordinating color on a white background.

Ties are important indicators of the salesperson's status, credibility, and personality. A good rule is to wear suits and shirts in basic colors and let the tie provide the accent color. For example, the accent color for a navy suit and white shirt can be provided by a striped red-and-navy tie. The tie tip should come just to the belt buckle, and its width should harmonize with the width of the suit lapels. Bow ties give off negative signals, and tie pins and clasps are currently out of style. Silk is the best choice for tie material; it looks elegant and wears well.

As for accessories, the less, the better. Stay away from bracelets and pins, and wear simple, small cuff links. Shoes should be black, brown, or cordovan, in lace-up, wingtip, Gucci-type buckle, or all-leather, slip-on styles. Never wear shoes with multiple colors, platforms, or high heels with business dress. Most belts are acceptable. Buckles should be small, clean, and traditional. Attaché cases are positive symbols of success.

Hints for Women

In 1977, when John Molloy wrote his book, *Dress for Success*, businesswomen were advised to wear only very conservative navy or gray suits, tailored blouses, and string ties. They were entering professions dominated by men (such as selling), and they needed to give clear signals that they were serious about their jobs and were members of the company team. In those days, the more women in these "uniforms" looked like men, the more easily they were accepted in the business world.

Today, thanks to those pioneers, women just beginning their careers have the luxury of dressing with more flair and style while still maintaining a dignified, professional look. Women in business can now signal that they are good at, and relaxed about, their jobs and that they know the difference between business and private life. A good business wardrobe still starts with navy, black, and gray suits worn with light-colored blouses. But you can also add suits in more cheerful shades, wool or silk dresses with jackets, and blazers with coordinated skirts. As with menswear, women's suits look and wear best in natural fibers or blends that look and feel like natural fibers. Women should choose a suit whose jacket and skirt lengths complement their figure shape and height. It should be stylish without being so trendy that it will look dated in a short time.

Women's blouses have little more variety than men's shirts in color, style, and fabric. Cotton and silk are the best fabric choices; they are much more professional looking than sheer polyester or slithery silk imitations. Keep blouses businesslike, feminine but tailored, soft but not see-through, plain or with small prints.

Choose shoes and hose to complement the outfit. Black, brown, navy, or cordovan are always acceptable shoe colors. Tailored, classic pumps should have heels no higher than 1 or $1^1/_2$ inches (especially if the job requires walking), and should be combined with neutral or color-coordinated hose to look both professional and feminine. Fishnet or patterned hose, ankle straps, chunky loafers, and trendy boots are best left for after-hours wear.

Accessories such as ties, scarves, simple pins, gold chains, and plain watches can make even a plain, dark suit look dressy and businesslike. Chunky jewelry and clanking bracelets are out. Silk scarves can add flair and a touch of color if tied or draped attractively. Scarves are becoming more popular and acceptable today than the so-called ties that were formerly a required part of the uniform.

The businesswoman's hairstyle should share many of the same characteristics her clothes do: subtle, formal, comfortable, and easy to care for. Hair length is not an issue, but it must be managed effectively.

ADJUSTING FOR CULTURAL DIFFERENCES

In international selling situations, salespeople need to recognize that business practices differ around the world.[21] For example, Americans tend to think that agreements require formal, written contracts. However, many other cultures have strong moral principles in which verbal agreements are just as binding as written agreements. People in these cultures may find an insistence on written contracts insulting because they feel their honor is being questioned.

Americans assume that all the terms in a contract, such as price and delivery, remain constant throughout the contract. However, Greek businesspeople view a contractual agreement as the initial step in the negotiation. After the agreement is signed, Greek customers will continue to negotiate, and will keep negotiating until the products or services are delivered. In Korea, the common practice is to adjust the terms of a contract if changes occur in the economy or in the price of raw materials. Selling Scenario 5.4 illustrates how selling approaches differ in high-context and low-context cultures.

Use of Language

Communication in international selling often takes place in English, because English is likely to be the only language salespeople and customers have in common. To communicate effectively with customers whose native language is not English,

Selling in High-Context and Low-Context Cultures

Customers in different cultures process verbal and nonverbal information differently. In **low-context cultures** such as the United States and Germany, words carry most of the information in communications. In **high-context cultures** such as Japan and Arab countries, more information is contained in factors surrounding the communications such as the background, associations, and basic values of the salesperson and customer.

For example, in a high-context culture, who the salesperson is has as much or more importance than a formal analysis of the product benefits. The following table shows some other differences.

Sources: Edward Hall and Mildred Hall, *Understanding Cultural Differences* (Yarmough, MA: Intercultural Press, 1990), Syed Akhter, *Global Marketing* (Cincinati: South-Western, 1995).

Issue	High Context	Low Context
Person's word	Is his or her bond	Not to be relied on "Get it in writing"
Lawyers	Not very important	Very important
Space	People share common space and stand close to each other	People have a private space around themselves and resent intrusions into their space
Time	Everything is dealt with eventually	Wasting time is to be avoided
Negations	Lengthy so that the parties can get a chance to know one another	Accomplished quickly
Competitive bidding	Not very common	Very common

salespeople need to be careful about the words and expressions they use. People who use English in international selling should:[22]

1. Use common English words that a customer would learn during the first two years of studying the language. For example, use *expense* rather than *expenditure,* or *stop* instead of *cease.*

2. Use words that do not have alternative meanings. For example, *right* has many alternative meanings, while *accurate* has fewer. When you use words that have several meanings, recognize that nonnative speakers will usually use the most common meaning to interpret what you are saying.

3. Avoid slang expressions peculiar to American culture, such as "slice of life," "struck out," "wade through the figures," and "run that by me again."

4. Use rules of grammar more strictly than you would in everyday speech. Make sure you express your thoughts in complete sentences, with a noun and a verb.

5. Use action-specific verbs, as in "*start* the motor," rather than action-general verbs, as in "*get* the motor going."

6. Never use vulgar expressions, tell off-color jokes, or make religious references.

Even if you are careful about the words you use, misunderstandings can still arise because terms have different meanings, even among people from different Eng-

The US salesperson needs to recognize the differences in communicating in high-context Arab cultures versus the low-context American culture.

Dick Berwin/The Image Bank

lish-speaking countries. For example, in the United States "tabling a proposal" means delaying a decision, while in England it means that immediate action is to be taken. In England, promising to do something by the end of the day means doing it when you have finished what you are working on now, not within 24 hours. In England, *bombed* means the negotiations were successful, while in the United States is has the opposite meaning.

Time and Scheduling

International salespeople need to understand the varying perceptions of time in general and the time it takes for business activities to occur in different countries. For example, in Latin American and Arab countries, people are not strict about keeping appointments at the designated times. If you show up for an appointment on time in these cultures, you may have to wait several hours for the meeting to start.

Lunch is at 3:00 PM in Spain, 12:00 noon in Germany, 1:00 PM in England, and 11:00 AM in Norway. In Greece, no one makes telephone calls between 2:00 PM and 5:00 PM. The British arrive at their desks at 9:30 AM, but like to do paperwork and have a cup of tea before getting any calls. The French, like the Germans, like to start early in the day, frequently having working breakfasts. Restaurants close at 9:00 PM in Norway, just when dinner is starting in Spain. The best time to reach high-level Western European executives is after 7:00 PM, when daily activities have slowed down and they are continuing to work for a few more hours. However, Germans start going home at 4:00 PM.[23]

Body Language

Gestures and body language can have different meanings across the globe. For example, the "thumbs-up" gesture is considered offensive in the Middle East, rude in Australia, and a sign of "OK" in France. It's rude to cross your arms in

Turkey. Crossing your feet and showing the bottoms of your shoe soles is insulting in Japan.[24]

SUMMARY

This chapter discussed the principles of communication and how they can be used to build trust in relationships, improve selling effectiveness, and reduce misunderstandings. The communication process consists of a sender, who encodes information and transmits messages, to a receiver, who decodes the messages. A communication breakdown can occur when the sender does a poor encoding job, when the receiver has difficulty decoding, and when noise interferes with the transmission of the message.

Effective communication requires a two-way flow of information. At different times in the interaction, both parties will act as sender and receiver. This two-way process enables salespeople to adapt their sales approach to the customer's needs and communication style.

Four communication modes discussed in this chapter are interpreting verbal and nonverbal communications from customers and sending verbal and nonverbal communications to customers. Listening is a valuable communication skill that enables salespeople to adapt effectively. To listen effectively, salespeople need to be actively thinking about what the customer is saying and how to draw out more information. Some suggestions for actively collecting more information from customers are: repeat, restate, clarify, summarize the customer's comments, and demonstrate an interest in what the customer is saying.

More than 50 percent of communication is nonverbal. Nonverbal messages sent by customers are conveyed by body language. The five channels of body language communication are body angle, face, arms, hands, and legs. No single channel can be used to determine the feelings or attitudes of customers. Salespeople need to analyze the body language pattern composed of all five channels to determine when a customer is nervous, bored, or suspicious.

When communicating verbally with customers, salespeople must be careful to use words and expressions their customers will understand. Effective communication is facilitated through the use of concrete, neutral words rather than abstract, emotional words.

Asking questions gets the customer involved in the interaction and provides additional information that can be used to develop and adapt the sales presentation. Open-ended questions encourage longer responses. In addition, questions should be spaced out, short and simple, and not suggest an appropriate answer.

Salespeople can use nonverbal communication to convey information to customers. In addition to using the five channels of body language, salespeople need to know the appropriate distances between themselves and their customers for different types of communications and relationships.

Salespeople also communicate to their customers through their appearance. Physical appearance and dress can be used to create a favorable impression. In general, salespeople should try to dress like the customers they are calling on.

Finally, two-way communication increases when salespeople adjust their communication styles to the styles of their customers. In making such adjustments, salespeople need to be sensitive to cultural differences when selling internationally.

KEY TERMS

active listening 134
articulation 128
body language 137
closed-ended questions 128
decoding 123
encoding 123
high-context culture 149
inflection 128
low-context culture 149

noises 124
nonverbal communication 136
open-ended questions 128
speaking-listening differential 134
two-way communication 122
verbal communication 125
voice characteristics 127
word picture 126

QUESTIONS AND PROBLEMS

1. Why is two-way communication preferable to one-way communication?

2. Make a chart with three columns: item of clothing, what I want my clothing to communicate to others, and what others will think my clothing is communicating. In the first column, list the clothing you are wearing now. In the second column, describe the message you want to communicate. Have someone else fill in the third column describing what the clothing communicates to him or her.

3. Identify what the following body language cues indicate:

   a. Tapping a finger or pencil on a desk.

   b. Stroking the chin and leaning forward.

   c. Leaning back in a chair with arms folded across the chest.

   d. Sitting in the middle of a bench or sofa.

   e. Assuming the same posture as the person with whom you are communicating.

4. Assume you are selling breakfast cereal to a supermarket buyer. Make up three questions designed to initiate two-way communication with the prospect.

5. "Understanding nonverbal communication is more important to salespeople than understanding verbal communication." Do you agree? Why or why not?

6. Many people do not like to hear the words *sell* or *sold*. Why would you be unlikely to say the following to a friend: "Look at the new personal computer I was sold yesterday"?

7. Give two examples each of open-ended and closed-ended questions. Why do open-ended questions generally improve communications?

8. What is the difference between the communication styles in high-context and low-context cultures?

9. Ross Thomas is a 25-year-old computer salesperson who calls on insurance companies, banks, and department stores. He views himself as a "free thinker" and wears the latest apparel and hair styles. At the present time his hair is quite long, giving him an "in" look. He buys casual clothing because he can wear it at work and for leisure activities. What advice would you give Ross about his appearance? Why? Should he dress differently when calling on banks versus department stores?

EXPLORING THE NET

Several of the career planning and job opportunity sites on the Internet offer advice on how to interview for a job and dress for the job interview. Visit the site:

http//www.careercity.com/edge/getjob/getjob.htm

Relate the material on how to communicate with a potential employer to the material on buyer-seller communications in this chapter. How do the listening and questioning skills, nonverbal communications, and dress suggestions in the chapter relate to performance in a job interview.

CASE PROBLEMS

CASE 5.1
Celestial Seasoning Teas

Cheryl Wright, a sales representative for Celestial Seasoning Teas, calls on Danny Taylor, the beverage buyer for Giant Markets, a chain of 12 supermarkets headquartered in Omaha, Nebraska. Wright is trying to persuade Taylor to carry a new line of decaffeinated, flavored teas.

WRIGHT How's business?

TAYLOR Well, now that you ask, sales have slowed down. I was just looking over our sales analysis and . . .

WRIGHT Danny, maybe our new line of decaffeinated flavors will add some excitement to the beverage section. They are really attracting a lot of attention. Did you see our ad in *Progressive Grocer*?

TAYLOR I saw the ad last week. I don't see how I can . . .

WRIGHT Good! Then you know all about the test market results for the six new decaffeinated flavors. Our research shows that a lot of elderly consumers like having flavored coffee after dinner but are afraid that the caffeine will keep them up. The new line has done particularly well with the elderly segment.

TAYLOR Well, I can understand the concern about caffeine, but . . .

WRIGHT Everyone is more health conscious now. Customers really want more health foods—low fat, low cholesterol, no additives. We really think these decaffeinated teas fit right into this trend. We have developed an exciting marketing program to get you to carry the new line. If you agree to stock four out of the six decaffeinated flavors and feature the line in your weekly ad, we'll give you a 20 percent discount on your first order and pay for the space in your weekly ad.

TAYLOR I have to stock four flavors?

WRIGHT I knew you'd be excited. We also can set a special in-store tasting for your customers.

TAYLOR That sounds interesting. You know our target market is younger, blue-collar workers. Do you have any data on which flavor sells best to that segment?

WRIGHT They like all the flavors. Pick the ones you like, and I'm sure they will sell well. The Red Zinger and Apple Spice are excellent. Can I take your order?

TAYLOR I've got an appointment coming in soon. Could you leave some material that I can look through? I'll get back to you.

WRIGHT Sure. I've got some brochures in my briefcase. Can we set up an appointment?

TAYLOR Well, business has been really hectic. Let me give you a call. Thanks for stopping by.

Questions

1. Is Cheryl Wright a good listener? Why or why not?

2. What indicates that Wright has something to learn about communications skills?

3. Rewrite this dialogue to show how Wright should have handled this sales call.

CASE 5.2
Ocala Office Supply

Chris McCallum is a sales representative for Ocala Office Supply Company. He has just walked into the office of Jim Sanchez, the office manager at Bear Archery. McCallum is 25 years old and has been working for Ocala Office Supply for six months. He is dressed in a blue pinstripe suit. Sanchez is a large man, about 50 years old, and is wearing a plaid flannel shirt and slacks. He is sitting behind his desk, leaning back in his chair with his arms crossed.

McCALLUM [*walking around the desk to shake hands with Sanchez*] Good morning, Mr. Sanchez. It's a pleasure to meet you. How are you today?

SANCHEZ I'm fine. I was expecting you 15 minutes ago. I have an appointment soon, so I don't have much time.

McCALLUM I'm only five minutes late. I got held up in the traffic around the mall.

SANCHEZ [*moving around in his chair and crossing his arms again*] Okay. Maybe it wasn't 15 minutes. What can I do for you?

McCALLUM I would like to talk to you about our new program for providing office supplies more economically to our partners. The program . . .

SANCHEZ Before you waste a lot of time, we just placed a large office supply order with Chestnut's. We really don't need supplies at this point.

McCALLUM [*crossing his arms, speech rate increasing*] That's too bad. Our program could have reduced your office supply costs by 30 percent.

SANCHEZ [*uncrossing arms, leaning forward*] Really?

McCALLUM [*starting to rise and putting on his coat*] Well, I guess I'm too late.

Questions

1. How could McCallum have communicated better with Sanchez using nonverbal methods?

2. How did McCallum make a mistake in reading the nonverbal messages sent by Sanchez?

ADDITIONAL REFERENCES

Caldini, Robert. *Influence: Science and Practice,* 3rd ed., New York: HarperCollins, 1993.

Castleberry, Stephen, and C. David Sheppard. "Effective Listening and Personal Selling." *Journal of Personal Selling and Sales Management,* Winter 1993, pp. 35–49.

Dawson, Lyndon; Barlow Soper; and Charles Pettijohn. "The Effects of Empathy on Salesperson Effectiveness." *Psychology & Marketing,* July/August 1992, pp. 297–310.

Dion, Paul, and Elaine Notarantonio. "Salesperson Communication Style: The Neglected Dimension in Sales Performance." *Journal of Business Communication,* Winter 1992, pp. 63–77.

Doyle, Stephen, and George Roth. "The Use of Insight Coaching to Improve Relationship Selling." *Journal of Personal Selling and Sales Management,* Winter 1992, pp. 59–64.

Knapp, Mark, and Judith Hall. *Non-Verbal Communications in Human Interactions,* 4th ed. Fort Worth, TX: Holt, Rinehart and Winston, 1996.

Marchetti, Michele. "Memo to Men: Shut up!" *Sales & Marketing Management,* February 1996, p. 28.

Molloy, John. *New Dress for Success.* New York: Warner, 1988.

Pettijohn, Charles; Linda Pettijohn; and Albert Taylor. "The Relationship Between Effective Selling and Effective Counseling." *Journal of Consumer Marketing,* 12, no. 1 (1995), pp. 5–15.

Reingen, Peter, and Jerome Kernan. "Social Perception and Interpersonal Influence: Some Consequences of Physical Attractiveness Stereotype in a Personal Selling Setting." *Journal of Consumer Psychology,* 2, no 1 (1993), pp. 25–38.

Strutton, David; Lou Pelton; and John Tanner, Jr. "Shall We Gather in the Garden: The Effect of Ingratiatory Behaviors on Buyer Trust in Salespeople." *Industrial Marketing Management,* March 1996, pp. 151–62.

Personal selling is the most effective marketing communication medium because it allows salespeople to tailor their presentations to each customer. They can ask questions to determine the customer's needs and make a presentation to show how their products will satisfy those specific needs. By listening and observing nonver-

Chapter Six

Adaptive Selling *for* Relationship Building

Some Questions Answered in this Chapter Are:

What is adaptive selling?

Why is it important for salespeople to practice adaptive selling?

What kind of knowledge do salespeople need to practice adaptive selling?

How can salespeople acquire this knowledge?

What different approaches can salespeople use to adapt their sales strategies, presentations, and social styles?

bal behaviors, they can tell when the presentation is not working and change their approach on the spot.

By comparison, advertising managers are restricted to delivering the same advertising campaign to all customers. The message in the campaign may work for the "typical" customer, but a lot of customers will have different needs and will not be influenced by the message. It may take months for an advertising manager to recognize and change a campaign that is not effective.

Effective salespeople take advantage of this unique opportunity. They use their knowledge of the customer's buying process (Chapter Four) and communication skills (Chapter Five) to learn about their customers and select effective sales strategies. They adapt their selling strategies and approaches to the selling situation. This chapter examines how salespeople can communicate effectively with their customers by practicing adaptive selling.

PROFILE

Dave Mazuchowski is a sales supervisor at Keystone Automotive Warehouse, based in Perrysburg, Ohio. Keystone, owned by five-time

NHRA top fuel dragster world champion Joe Amato, is the world's largest automotive parts warehouse. It markets a full line of traditional and high-performance automotive products to retail outlets across the globe. Mazuchowski, who reports directly to the general manager, has responsibility for the Midwest region of the United States and presently assists in managing a team of 12 sales representatives.

"The key to being successful in this business is to develop a thorough understanding of each customer's needs and then adapt your selling strategy to match that specific situation."

"The key to being successful in this business is to develop a thorough understanding of each customer's needs and then adapt your selling strategy to match that specific situation," he says. "The majority of sales in my region go to truck accessory stores, high-performance/speed shops, and standard automotive parts outlets, as well as to some businesses that are hybrids of these three categories.

"Many of these shops actually compete in rather dissimilar markets. So I have to take the time to learn the nature of each customer's business and then act as though *I* am the store owner. In order to build long-term selling relationships with these stores, my overall strategy is to take responsibility for the profitability of each of my customer's businesses.

"Adaptive selling techniques also play a role in dealing with the very different personalities of the store owners. Building trust is absolutely critical, and so you have to be able to give customers the feeling that you are actually on

DAVE MAZUCHOWSKI
Keystone Automotive Warehouse

their payroll. Of course, you are sometimes walking a fine line in that you want to give your customers the best prices, payment terms, and delivery schedules, but without overstepping the bounds of your employer. I also find that my own participation in drag racing gives me more credibility with my customers because I can speak their 'language' and am often able to provide appropriate technical support. In this job, problem-solving skills are very important. You have to be a quick thinker and be able to settle a variety of issues on the spot, such as delivery, warranty, and billing problems."

Mazuchowski did not always know he was going to embark on a career in sales. "While I was going to Owens Technical College in Perrysburg, Ohio, I worked in retail sales for Ramchargers Performance Center, a speed shop in Toledo. I really enjoyed my job, did extremely well, and was promoted to store manager after two years. My move to Keystone gave me the opportunity to further challenge myself in this exciting business.

"I work long hours, but the rewards are definitely there. At the end of a good day, I have the satisfaction of knowing that I not only helped Keystone's profits but also helped my customers put more money in their pockets. Sometimes customers will call me up and tell me that I made a big difference and that they are now moving into a bigger building or hiring additional salespeople."

Mazuchowski's outstanding performance earned him his current position after only three years with Keystone, and the company rewarded him with an all-expenses-paid Caribbean cruise last year and a trip to Las Vegas the year before.

TYPES OF
PRESENTATIONS

Three types of presentations salespeople use are: (1) the standard memorized presentation, (2) the outlined presentation, and (3) the customized presentation. These presentations illustrate the differences between adaptive and nonadaptive selling.[1]

Standard
Memorized
Presentation

The **standard memorized presentation,** also called a *canned presentation,* is a completely memorized sales presentation. The salesperson presents the same selling points in the same order to all customers. Some companies insist that their salespeople memorize the entire presentation and deliver it word for word. Others believe that salespeople should be free to make some adjustments to suit their own personalities.

The standard memorized presentation ensures that the salesperson will provide complete and accurate information about the firm's products and policies. Because it includes the best techniques and methods, the standard memorized presentation brings new salespeople up to speed quickly and gives them confidence. Many pharmaceutical salespeople use a standard memorized presentation because they need to accurately communicate technical information to doctors in a short period of time. This type of presentation is also used in telemarketing and direct selling. However, the standard memorized presentation offers no opportunity for the salesperson to tailor the presentation to the needs of the specific customer.

Outlined
Presentation

The **outlined presentation** is a prearranged presentation that outlines the most important sales points to be discussed when calling on a customer. Outlined presentations often have a standard introduction, standard answers to common objections raised by customers, and a standard method for getting the customer to place an order. An example of an outlined presentation appears in Exhibit 6.1.

An outlined presentation can be very effective because it is well organized. Two senior sales executives emphasize that salespeople should "prepare an outline of points in the order in which you want to cover them and stick to it at all costs."[2] This type of sales presentation is more informal and natural than the standard memorized presentation, and it provides more opportunity for the customer to participate in the sales interaction.

Customized
Presentation

The **customized presentation** is a written and/or oral presentation based on a detailed analysis of the customer's needs. To develop the presentation, the sales representative gets the customer to agree to a needs analysis. The salesperson may bring in specialists, such as engineers or systems designers, to conduct the study. Then this information is analyzed and used to make the presentation.

This type of presentation offers an opportunity to use the communication principles discussed in the last chapter to discover the customer's needs and problems and propose the most effective solution for satisfying those needs. The customized presentation builds the customer's respect for the salesperson and his or her company.

EXHIBIT 6.1	Scenario: A Proctor & Gamble Salesperson Calling on a Grocery Store Manager	
Example of an Outlined Presentation	**Step in Sales Presentation**	**Say Something Like This**
	1. Introduction and reinforcement of past success.	"Good morning, Mr. Babcock. I was talking with one of your stockers, and he said our Crest end-of-aisle display was very popular with customers last weekend. He said he had to restock it about three times. Looks like you made a wise decision to go with that program."
	2. Reiterate customer's needs.	"I know that profits and fast turns are what you are always looking for."
	3. Introduce new Sure antiperspirant campaign.	"We have a new campaign coming up for our Sure line."
	4. Explain ad campaign and coupon drops.	"We will be running a new set of commercials on all three network news programs . . . also, we'll be adding an insert in the Sunday coupon section with a 35-cents-off coupon."
	5. Explain case allowances.	"We are going to give you a $1.20 case allowance for every case of Sure you buy today."
	6. Ask for end-of-aisle display and order of cases	"I would propose that you erect an end-of-aisle display on aisle 7 . . . and that you order 20 cases."
	7. Thank manager for the order.	"Thank you, and I know the results will be just as good as they were for our Crest promotion."

The customer recognizes the sales representative as a professional who is helping to solve problems, not just sell products. Cultivating this view is an important step in developing a partnering relationship.

Each of the presentation types just discussed involves a different level of skill, cost, and flexibility. Standard memorized presentations can be delivered at a low cost by unskilled salespeople with little training. On the other hand, the customized presentation can be very costly, requiring highly skilled people to analyze the customer's needs. Salespeople have the greatest opportunity to adapt their presentations to customer needs when using the customized presentation and the least opportunity when using the standard memorized presentation. The next section discusses the importance of this opportunity to adapt sales presentations.

ADAPTIVE SELLING AND SALES SUCCESS

Salespeople practice **adaptive selling** when they use different sales presentations for different customers and alter their sales presentation during a sales call based on the nature of the sales situation.[3] An extreme example of nonadaptive selling is using the standard memorized presentation, since the same presentation is used for all customers. The customized presentation illustrates adaptive selling because the presentation is tailored to the specific needs of the customer.

Adaptive selling is featured in this textbook because it forces the salesperson to practice the marketing concept. It emphasizes the importance of satisfying customer needs and building long-term partnerships. Selling Scenario 6.1 illustrates how international salespeople need to adapt their sales approaches.

The communication principles described in Chapter Five are required to practice adaptive selling successfully. For example, a Briggs & Stratton sales representative may believe a customer is interested in buying an economical, low-horsepower

SELLING SCENARIO 6.1

The American Approach Does Not Always Work

Sylvia Acevedo, director of Latin American sales at Autodesk, lives by the principle that you have to adapt your selling style to the manners and mindsets of your customers. This prinicple is particularly important in international sales, where culture clashes are common.

Americans are driven by a sense of urgency that is not important to many of Acevedo's customers. "Latin Americans know Americans want to rush, to close the deal, and they use it against Americans," she explains. Acevedo was working on a big sale in Brazil. Two financial executives from the United States flew to Brazil to finalize the financial terms with the customer's VP of finance. The Brazilians kept postponing the meeting, and by Thursday the Americans were getting really antsy. They wanted to close the deal and go home for the weekend. When the meeting was postponed again until Monday, the Americans decided to agree to all of the Brazilian VP's terms so they could go home.

Acevedo's customer was simply doing business based on its values and experience. "You have to realize that in the United States, the most prized things are time and money. In other countries relationships are prized the most," she says. In the United States relationship develops after the sale. In Latin America, it has to develop before a sale is made. Acevedo typically makes three calls on Latin American customers before talking about the product and five calls before she can get down to serious business.

Source: Fancy Blackwood, "Not-So-Foreign Concepts," *Selling,* October 1995, pp. 26–28. Reprinted with permission from Institutional Investors, Inc.

motor. While presenting the benefits of a low-cost motor, the sales rep discovers, by observing nonverbal behaviors, that the customer is not interested in the discussion of overall operating costs. At this point, the rep asks some questions to find out if the customer would pay a higher price for a more efficient motor with lower operating costs. Based on the customer's response, the rep may adopt a new sales strategy, presenting a more efficient motor and demonstrating its low operating costs.

Effective salespeople adapt their presentation to the sales situation. This seed salesperson is using a different approach selling to these small farmers than he uses selling to large corporate farmers.

Steve Leonard/Tony Stone Images

Selecting the appropriate sales strategy for a sales situation and making adjustments during the interaction are crucial to successful selling. When questioned about the best advice on selling they had ever received, successful salespeople emphasized the importance of being flexible and adaptive. For example, Don Perreault, vice president of sales and marketing at Transistor Electronics, recalls this advice:

> *Be a chameleon. Change colors to fit the terrain. As salespeople, we must be able to change our characters to satisfy the present needs of selling—in other words, you have to be able to wear many hats.*[4]

Thomas Glickman, director of sales and marketing at Diamedix, emphasizes that adaptive selling requires creativity:

> *You have to be creative when you're looking for your customer's hot button, because each customer is different. Then you have to activate the hot button by being innovative in your sales approach.*[5]

Practicing adaptive selling does not mean salespeople should be dishonest with customers about their products or their personal feelings, or be someone they are not. Adaptive selling means they should alter the content and form of their sales presentation so that customers will be able to absorb the information easily and find it relevant to their situation.

Thinking *it* **Through**	Do you act differently when living on campus compared to living at home? How do you change your behavior when you go home over school breaks? How do you behave when you go to a restaurant with a date? With some friends? With your parents? Why do you behave this way in each situation?

The advantages and disadvantages of the three types of sales presentations illustrate the benefits and drawbacks of adaptive selling. Adaptive selling gives salespeople the opportunity to use the most effective sales presentation for each customer. However, uncovering needs, designing and delivering different presentations, and making adjustments require a high level of skills. The objective of this textbook is to help you develop the skills and knowledge required to practice adaptive selling.

KNOWLEDGE AND ADAPTIVE SELLING

A key ingredient in effective selling is knowledge.[6] Salespeople need to know about the products they are selling, the company they work for, and the customers they will be selling to. Interviews with purchasing agents reveal the importance they place on a salesperson's knowledge: "Do your homework. Am I the one you want to see? I buy axles for our trucks. Don't call on me with your line of office supplies." "Read our annual report. Read anything you can about us. Follow the trades. Know ahead of time what we're up against in the market, what we're trying to do. If I offer to show you around, jump at the chance. Or better yet, ask me yourself."[7] Selling Scenario 6.2 describes how a salesperson built partnering relationships on her customer knowledge.

Knowledge enables the salesperson to build self-confidence, gain the buyer's trust, satisfy customer needs, and practice adaptive selling. Customers today demand information about the products they buy. They seek the advice of salespeople. When salespeople have a thorough knowledge about their products and customers,

SELLING SCENARIO 6.2

Knowing Your Customer

Before making a sales presentation, Maria Bayne, a senior consultant at Johnson & Higgens, a risk management consulting firm, learns all she can about the customers' business. She goes beyond their insurance needs to find out about their culture and management style. "If they're involved in TQM, I read up on it; if they follow Stephen Covey's recommendation, I brush up on his writings. Then I use key words and expressions in my presentations."

Bayne's ability to communicate her knowledge won her a customer who was not even the target of her presentation. Several executives from other firms were in the room when Bayne made a presentation to a retailer.

"We didn't get the prospect, but one of the other people in the room was impressed enough to give us his business."

Bayne emphasizes that her use of her customer's term is only icing on the cake. Her assessment of the customer's insurance needs and knowledge of the industry are critical. As a woman, she says, "I usually have to work harder to make sure I'm perceived as credible," and using the right words earns the respect of her customers.

Source: Nancy Arnott, "It's a Woman's World," *Sales & Marketing Management,* March 1995, p. 57. Reprinted with permission from Bill Communications.

they know they can provide a service to their customers. By becoming a reliable source of information, a salesperson wins the buyers' respect and trust.

Product and Company Knowledge

Salespeople need to have a lot of information about their company and its products. For example, a buyer might say, "I'm satisfied with our present supplier. I see no reason to change." The informed salesperson might respond, "Company X is a fine company. But last year our firm sold three times as many units. IBM, Xerox, and Apple gave us an outstanding vendor award. A *Purchasing* magazine survey of buy-

The salesperson selling filters has to have extensive knowledge about the operation of water purification systems and benefits provided by different types of filters.

Courtesy Parker Hannifin Corporation

ers reported that we were number one in on-time deliveries. Let me explain what this can mean for you."

Purchasing agents rate product knowledge as one of the most important attributes of good salespeople. Effective salespeople need to know how products are made, what services are provided with the products, how the products relate to other products, and how the products can satisfy customers' needs. For example, a buyer for men's suits might want specific information to judge the quality of a suit. The salesperson may need to tell the buyer about the fabric used in making the suit and the method used to sew the garment to support his or her claims about the quality of the suit.

In many situations, the service provided is more important than the performance of the product. Efficient servicing of capital equipment assures the manufacturer that costly shutdowns will be minimized. Delays in providing service when equipment fails can result in substantial financial losses.

Customers often want salespeople to explain how their products will work with other products. For example, a salesperson selling a laser printer needs to know with which computers it can interface. The Kodak salesperson introducing a new film should know with which Kodak and Canon cameras it can and cannot be used.

But the most important knowledge is how the product will satisfy the customer's needs, not the technical details about the product. Customers are not interested in just the facts about a product; they are interested in what the product will do for them. The salesperson's job is to provide information about the features of a product and tell the customer how those features translate into benefits. For example, a wider hitting area (feature) in a golf club results in straighter and longer shots even when the ball is not hit perfectly (benefit).

Salespeople also need to know about their competitors' products as well as their own, since they are frequently asked to compare their products to competitors'. A buyer for a meat-packing plant might say, "The Model 41Z made by Company X is one of the most energy-efficient refrigeration units in its size class," to which the salesperson might respond, "The Model 41Z certainly was a leader in energy efficiency when it was introduced in 1995. But our 800 series was designed using a new heat transfer technique that was not available in 1995. Tests show that our units have 10 to 15 percent greater energy efficiency than units using the older technology."

Finally, international salespeople must recognize that customers in different cultures can seek different benefits for the same product. For example, Levi jeans are sold in over 70 countries. However, unique advertising themes are developed to appeal to customer needs in each country. Consumers in Brazil are strongly influenced by fashion trends in Europe, and thus advertisements shown in Brazil are filmed in Paris. In the United Kingdom, the advertising emphasizes that Levis are an American brand worn by cowboys in the Wild West. Australian ads focus strictly on the product benefits: the tight fit and durability.[8]

Organizing Knowledge of Sales Situations and Customers into Categories

Even more important than product and company knowledge is detailed information about the different types of sales situations and customers salespeople may encounter and which sales presentation works best in each situation. Theoretically, salespeople can treat each sales situation differently. In practice, however, they typically do not have time to develop unique strategies for each sales situation. Hence, effective salespeople tend to categorize sales situations. Each category contains a description of the customer and the most effective presentation for that customer type.

By developing categories, salespeople reduce the complexity of selling and free up their mental capacity to think more creatively; they also use knowledge gained

Outstanding performers in sales and sports organize their knowledge into categories. Brett Favre success is due to his ability to recognize different patterns of defenses and develop a strategy for responding to each pattern. In a similar manner, successful salespeople are able to recognize different sales situation and use appropriate sales approaches in the situations.

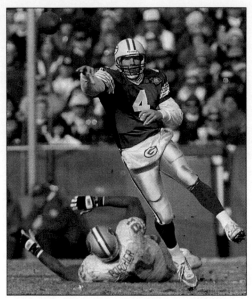

Robert Borea/World Wide Photos

through past experiences. When they encounter a customer with needs different than those they have dealt with previously—a customer who does not fit into an existing category—they add a new category to their repertoire. Salespeople with more categories, or customer types, have more selling approaches to use and thus have a greater opportunity to practice adaptive selling—to adjust their sales presentation to specific customer needs.[9]

The ability to organize knowledge into categories leads to better performance in many areas, not just personal selling. For example, sports stars such as Troy Aikman and Shaquille O'Neal organize their extensive knowledge into categories and have more categories than less skilled players. These categories describe types of defenses rather than types of sales situations. Aikman and O'Neal use cues, such as the positioning of the strong safety or the center, to recognize these defensive categories. For each pattern they have a strategy, such as passing to the receiver with single coverage or posting up on the left side of the lane.[10]

The categories salespeople use can focus on the benefits the customer seeks, the person's role in the buying center, the stage in the buying process, or the type of buying situation. For example, Orvel Ray Wilson, author of *Guerrilla Selling,* uses the customer's desk as a cue for organizing knowledge. A cluttered desk suggests that "This customer needs lots of choices. He has ten projects going on simultaneously, and two calls on hold while you are making your presentation. He sees the world as a series of choices and alternatives, and he needs to be given options—otherwise he can't make a decision." On the other hand, the customer with a neat desk makes buying decisions by going through a series of logical steps and will be bothered if you do not go through the presentation in logical order.[11] Selling Scenario 6.3 describes a scheme for categorizing retail customers that a student developed during her summer internship selling in a retail store.

Categories can help salespeople organize knowledge, but international salespeople need to avoid stereotyping buyers on the basis of their national origin. For ex-

SELLING SCENARIO 6.3

Customers Come in 31 Flavors

Cynthia Carter, a University of Florida undergraduate, spent 12 weeks as a paid summer intern in a JCPenney store. Working part of that time as a sales associate, she developed insights into how to effectively sell to different customer types. "Experienced sales associates recognize that customers come in all shapes, sizes, and flavors. Some are more pleasant to deal with, but the true skill of the successful sales associate lies in the ability to assist every type of customer, all 31 flavors." Carter describes some of the "customer flavors" that she encountered during her internship:

- The *vanilla customer* answers, "I'm just looking" to every question you ask or suggestion you offer. They're rather faceless and uninteresting, but they often actually need your assistance. It's most important that you don't threaten them by being overbearing, but simply let them know you are available when they realize they need your assistance.
- The *I'll take four cones—chocolate, strawberry, bubble gum, and peanut butter and jelly— customer* has three screaming children with her, terrorizing the racks and dressing rooms. She doesn't have much time to shop. Ask her what she needs and she responds, "Anything that doesn't need ironing." She really needs your help. Give a "hanger gun" to her kids, sit her in a dressing room, find out her size, and bring her clothes to try on. She'll be very grateful for your help and will be back to spend money dressing her children.
- The *"Why don't you have banana marshmallow swirl?" customer* gets very upset when she can't find what she wants. She freely criticizes the store

for not having merchandise that *everyone* has. This customer needs to be handled with kid gloves. The key is to be *very* humble, *very* helpful, and *very* ready to point out similar items that the customer may find appealing. Use the JCPenney catalog as a backup, since items in the catalog can be delivered in two days. Remember, never lose your cool and never tell the customer she is wrong.

- The *rum raisin customer* wants high quality and will pay high prices. Avoid the polyester/cotton blends and focus on the silks, suedes, and linens. Give a lot of personal attention and fashion-conscious advice. Stress add-on sales. If you can win her fashion trust, you can make a big sale.
- The *tofu, granola sorbet customer* needs sturdy fabrics with lots of big pockets for rock collecting in Montana. Durability and practicality are much more important than fashion. Forget the 24-inch, triple-strand pearls and go for the Durango khaki outfit. She'll pay the price for the right clothes.
- The *birthday cake customer* is a frantic husband, boyfriend, or father who realized over lunch that today is the big day and he forgot. He usually doesn't know her size or even her weight and height. You can try to guess, but the best bet is suggesting a non-form-fitting sweater or coordinating earrings and necklace. You need to take control of the occasion and offer concrete advice—and tell him that returns are handled most smoothly if he saves the receipt.

Source: Adapted from Michael Levy and Barton Weitz, *Retailing Management,* 3rd ed. (Burr Ridge, IL: Irwin/McGraw-Hill, 1998).

ample, Americans are often viewed as cold and unfriendly by people from other countries. Yet, as we will see later in the section on social styles, some Americans are amiables, some are drivers, some are expressives, and some are analyticals. The same holds true for buyers from other countries; when we see them as all being the same, we lose precious information that enables us to adapt. Categories are useful when organizing knowledge, but not when the categories become stereotypes.

**Approaches for
Developing
Knowledge**

Salespeople acquire most knowledge about company products and policies, customer needs, and selling situations through company training programs, analyses of company reports and trade publications, discussions with supervisors and other salespeople, and learning on the job.

Tap the Knowledge from Sales Experts

Companies frequently tap the knowledge of their best salespeople and use this knowledge to train new salespeople. For example, a telecommunications company conducted in-depth interviews with its top performers. Through these interviews, it learned about the types of situations these salespeople encountered and what strategies they used in each situation.

The company developed role plays for each sales situation and used them when training new salespeople. Such role playing enabled the new salespeople to experience the variety of situations they would actually encounter on the job. The strategies recommended by the top salespeople served as a starting point for the trainees to develop their own sales methods for handling these situations.

If your company does not tap the knowledge of sales experts, you can do it. When you meet senior salespeople at a meeting, you should ask them how they handle difficult situations you have encountered. For example, have they had any success selling product X? What types of customers are they selling it to? What do they emphasize in their presentations?

Read Manuals and Trade Publications

Information about the salesperson's company, its products, and its competitors is available from many sources, including company sales manuals and newsletters, sales meetings, plant visits, and business and trade publications. In many large corporations, information is provided to salespeople during periodic training classes and sales meetings. But salespeople cannot rely on these formal programs as their only source of information; learning new information is a process that never ends.

Knowledgeable salespeople read sales bulletins and announcements from their companies and articles in the trade publications about their customers and their industries. They ask company employees questions about new programs and products. They collect information about competitors from customers and by looking in on customer displays in trade shows.

Ask for Feedback on What You Are Doing

Frequently the feedback salespeople get from their supervisors focuses on their performance (for example, "Did you achieve your performance goals?"). However, diagnostic feedback is much more useful than performance feedback for improving performance over the long run. **Diagnostic feedback** provides information about what one is doing right and what one is doing wrong. The following example illustrates the difference between performance and diagnostic feedback:

SALES MANAGER You didn't do a good job of selling that customer. You will need to improve if you want to sell him in the future.

SALESPERSON Why do you think I didn't make the sale?

SALES MANAGER You stressed the low maintenance cost, but he wasn't interested in maintenance cost. Did you see how he kept looking around while you were talking about how cheap it is to maintain the product?

SALESPERSON What do you think I should do next time?

SALES MANAGER You might try spending more time finding his hot button. Maintenance cost isn't it.

The sales manager initially provided performance feedback, but the salesperson asked for diagnostic feedback. Such feedback provides reasons for sales successes and failures. With this information, salespeople can build their knowledge of sales situations and improve their performance. They should ask their supervisors to analyze their performance, not simply evaluate it. Rick Conrad, chief operating officer of Bell Atlantic Mobile, emphasizes that a salesperson can also get feedback directly from customers: "If you win, always ask the vendor why you won. And if you lose, ask why. Customers often surprise you."[12]

Analyze Successes and Failures

Salespeople encounter many different types of selling situations; thus, they have an opportunity to use different sales presentations. Sometimes they will use the wrong presentation and lose an order. Effective salespeople learn from their mistakes, using them to build a greater knowledge base. If salespeople disregard failures or blame the failures on someone else, they lose a valuable opportunity for learning. Salespeople should also try to learn from their successes. After making a sale, they should analyze what they did to achieve the outcome. Chapter Eighteen provides more information on how salespeople improve their skills throughout their careers.

When analyzing their performance, salespeople need to assign the right reasons for the outcomes. Salespeople have a natural tendency to take personal credit for successes and blame their company or competitors for failures. A salesperson might say, "I made that sale because I am great, a super salesperson," or "I lost that sale because my company's delivery was poor." Such reasoning does not help salespeople learn. It doesn't show them what to do in the future to make sales or avoid failures. The performance analysis should focus on the sales strategies used, identifying the specific strategies causing the performance and determining if and how they should be changed in the future.

The key question when analyzing a sales situation is "Why?" If you first offer some reason over which you have no control, such as the competition was too tough or your products don't work well, think deeper and come up with reasons to which you can respond. Formulate strategies you can use to overcome competition or limitations in product performance.

Develop an Intrinsic Orientation toward Your Work

People can have two types of orientation toward their jobs: intrinsic or extrinsic. People with an **intrinsic orientation** get rewards from doing the job itself. They enjoy their work; they find it challenging and fun. People with an **extrinsic orientation** view their jobs as something that has to be done, either to get extrinsic rewards (e.g., more pay) or to avoid punishments (e.g., getting fired). For these people, their jobs provide extrinsic rewards, but doing the job itself is not rewarding. Most people get both types of rewards from their jobs, but they tend to emphasize one type over the other.

Selling frequently emphasizes extrinsic rewards: If you do well, you will make more money, get promoted, or win awards. This emphasis encourages you to work hard, but it can distract you from learning how to do your job better. You may begin to think you are just working for the money and your job is not fun.

When salespeople find their jobs challenging and fun, they want to learn how to do them better. They view their jobs as a challenge, like a video game. They want to try new sales methods and learn from their successes and failures, so they can improve their scores. Effective salespeople enjoy the challenge of selling. They like to try new selling methods, find new customers, sell new products, and figure out how to make a tough sale. If they find they do not enjoy their selling jobs, they probably will not learn from their experiences and improve their performance.

THE SOCIAL STYLE MATRIX: A TRAINING PROGRAM FOR BUILDING ADAPTIVE SELLING SKILLS

To be effective, salespeople need to use their knowledge about products and customers to adapt both the content of their sales presentations—the benefits they emphasize to customers and the needs they attempt to satisfy—and the style they use to communicate with customers. The **social style matrix** is a popular training program that companies use to assist salespeople in adapting their communication styles.

David Merrill and Roger Reid discovered patterns of communication behaviors, or social styles, that people use when interacting with one another.[13] They found that people who recognize and adjust to these behavior patterns have better relationships with other people. A sales training program based on this research begins by helping trainees understand their own social styles and identify their customers' styles. Then the trainees learn how to make appropriate adjustments in their sales behaviors to become more effective.

Dimensions of Social Styles

This training program uses two critical dimensions to understand social behavior: assertiveness and responsiveness.

Assertiveness

The degree to which people have opinions about issues and make their positions clear to others publicly is called **assertiveness.** Having strong convictions does not make a person assertive; assertive people express their convictions publicly and attempt to influence others to accept their beliefs.

Assertive people speak out, make strong statements, and have a take-charge attitude. When under tension, they tend to confront the situation. Unassertive people rarely dominate a social situation, and they often keep their opinions to themselves. Exhibit 6.2 shows some verbal and nonverbal behavioral indicators of assertiveness.

Responsiveness

The second dimension, **responsiveness,** is based on how emotional people tend to get in social situations. Responsive people readily express joy, anger, and sorrow. They appear to be more concerned with others and are informal and casual in social situations. Less responsive people devote more effort toward controlling their emotions. They are described as cautious, intellectual, serious, formal, and businesslike. Exhibit 6.3 lists some indicators of responsiveness.

EXHIBIT 6.2	Less Assertive	More Assertive
Indicators of Assertiveness	"Ask" oriented	"Tell" oriented
	Go-along attitude	Take-charge attitude
	Cooperative	Competitive
	Supportive	Directive
	Risk avoider	Risk taker
	Makes decisions slowly	Makes decisions quickly
	Lets others take initiative	Takes initiative
	Leans backward	Leans forward
	Indirect eye contact	Direct eye contact
	Speaks slowly, softly	Speaks quickly, intensely
	Moves deliberately	Moves rapidly
	Makes few statements	Makes many statements
	Expresses moderate opinions	Expresses strong opinions

Categories of Social Styles

The two dimensions of social style, assertiveness and responsiveness, form the social style matrix shown in Exhibit 6.4. Each quadrant of the matrix defines a social style type, discussed in more detail shortly. *Drivers* are high in assertiveness and low in responsiveness. *Expressives* are high in assertiveness and high in responsiveness. *Amiables* are high in responsiveness and low in assertiveness. Finally, *analyticals* are low in both assertiveness and responsiveness.

Some well-known people illustrate these social styles. President Carter, TV commentator Ted Koppel, Spock in *Star Trek,* and Data in *Star Trek: The Next Generation* are in full control of their emotions and are very thoughtful. They are examples of analyticals. In contrast, Muhammad Ali, Liza Minelli, Carl Martin, and Jesse Jackson are expressives.

Former president Ronald Reagan and media mogul Ted Turner illustrate the difference between amiables and drivers. Reagan's warm personality and unassuming manner demonstrated an amiable social style. In contrast, Turner's nonresponsive, high-control approach, coupled with an aggressive posture, is consistent with a driver social style. Other examples of drivers are Lucy in the "Peanuts" comic strip,

EXHIBIT 6.3	Less Responsive	More Responsive
Indicators of Responsiveness	Controls emotions	Shows emotions
	Cool, aloof	Warm, approachable
	Talk oriented	People oriented
	Uses facts	Uses opinions
	Serious	Playful
	Impersonal, businesslike	Personable, friendly
	Moves stiffly	Moves freely
	Seldom gestures	Gestures frequently
	Formal dress	Informal dress
	Disciplined about time	Undisciplined about time
	Controlled facial expressions	Animated facial expressions
	Monotone voice	Many vocal inflections

EXHIBIT 6.4   Social Style Matrix

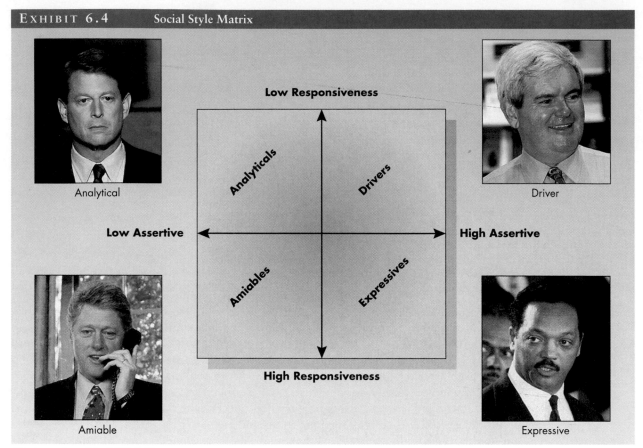

Analytical

Driver

Amiable

Expressive

All photos from World Wide Photos

Roseanne, and Bart Simpson, whereas Jay Leno, Jerry Seinfeld, and Christine in "Coach" are famous amiables.

Thinking *it* Through	What do you think your social style is? Why do you think so? Can you think of times when you have been very assertive, very unassertive, very responsive, and very unresponsive?

Drivers

Drivers are high on assertiveness and low on responsiveness. The slogan of drivers, who are task-oriented people, might be "Let's get it done now, and get it done my way." Drivers have learned to work with others only because they must do so to get the job done, not because they enjoy people. They have a great desire to get ahead in their companies and careers.

Drivers are swift, efficient decision makers. They focus on the present and appear to have little concern with the past or future. They generally base their decisions on facts, take risks, and want to look at several alternatives before making a decision. Analyticals also like facts and data, but drivers want know how the facts affect results—the bottom line. They are not interested simply in technical information.

To influence a driver, salespeople need to use a direct, businesslike, organized presentation with quick action and follow-up. Proposals should emphasize the effects of a purchase decision on profits.

Expressives

Expressives are high on assertiveness and high on responsiveness. Warm, approachable, intuitive, and competitive, expressives view power and politics as important factors in their quest for personal rewards and recognition. While expressives are interested in personal relationships, their relationships are primarily with supporters and followers recruited to assist them in achieving their personal goals.

People with an expressive style focus on the future, directing their time and effort toward achieving their vision. They have little concern for practical details in present situations. Expressives base their decisions on their personal opinions and the opinions of others. They act quickly, take risks, but tend to be impatient and change their minds easily.

When selling to expressives, salespeople need to demonstrate how their products will help the customer achieve personal status and recognition. Expressives prefer sales presentations with product demonstrations and creative graphics rather than factual statements and technical details. Also, testimonials from well-known firms and people appeal to expressives' need for status and recognition. Expressives respond to sales presentations that put them in the role of innovator, the first person to use a new product.

Amiables

Amiables are low on assertiveness and high on responsiveness. Close relationships and cooperation are important to amiables. They achieve their objectives by working with people, developing an atmosphere of mutual respect rather than using

The body language of the buyer on the left suggests he is a driver. He is engaging in direct eye contact with the salesperson and stating his views forcefully. (left) The doctor is an analytical. If he decides to prescribe Floxin, the pharmaceutical that the salesperson is detailing, it will be because he has carefully considered all of the facts and made a reasoned decision. (right)

Courtesy Ceridan Corporation

Courtesy Johnson & Johnson; photo by Ted Kawalerski

power and authority. Amiables tend to make decisions slowly, building a consensus among people involved in the decision. They avoid risks and change their opinions reluctantly.

Salespeople may have difficulty detecting an amiable's true feelings. Because amiables avoid conflict, they often say things to please others even though their personal thoughts differ. Therefore, salespeople need to build personal relationships with amiables. Amiables are particularly interested in receiving guarantees about a product's performance. They do not like salespeople who agree to undertake activities and then do not follow through on commitments. Salespeople selling to amiables should stress the product's benefits in terms of its effects on the satisfaction of employees.

Analyticals

Analyticals are low on assertiveness and low on responsiveness. They like facts, principles, and logic. Suspicious of power and personal relationships, they strive to find a way to carry out a task without resorting to these influence methods.

Because they are strongly motivated to make the right decision, analyticals make decisions slowly, in a deliberate and disciplined manner. They systematically analyze the facts, using the past as an indication of future events.

Salespeople need to use solid, tangible evidence when making presentations to analyticals. Analyticals are also influenced by sales presentations that recognize their technical expertise and emphasize long-term benefits. They tend to disregard personal opinions. Both analyticals and amiables tend to develop loyalty toward suppliers. For amiables, the loyalty is based on personal relationships; analyticals' loyalty is based on their feeling that well-reasoned decisions do not need to be reexamined.

Thinking *it* Through	If you were hiring salespeople, what social style would you look for? Why?

Identifying Customers' Social Styles

Exhibit 6.5 lists some cues for identifying the social styles of customers or prospects. Salespeople can use their communication skills to observe the customer's behavior, listen to the customer, and ask questions to classify the customer.

Merrill and Reid caution that identifying social style is difficult and requires close and careful observation. Salespeople should not jump to quick conclusions based on limited information. Some suggestions for making more accurate assessments are as follows:

- Concentrate on the customer's behavior and disregard how you feel about the behavior. Don't let your judgment be clouded by your feelings about the customer or by thoughts about the customer's motives.

- Avoid assuming that specific jobs or functions are associated with a social style, such as "He must be an analytical because he is an engineer."

- Attempt to get customers to reveal their styles rather than react to your style. Ask questions rather than making statements. For example, you might say, "I

	Social Style	Cues
EXHIBIT 6.5 Cues for Recognizing Social Styles	Analytical	Technical background Achievement awards on wall Office is work oriented, showing much activity Conservative dress Likes solitary activities (e.g., reading, individual sports)
	Driver	Technical background Achievement awards on wall No posters or slogans on office walls Calendar prominently displayed Furniture placed so contact with people is across desk Conservative dress Likes group activities (e.g., politics, team sports)
	Amiable	Liberal arts background Office has friendly, open atmosphere Pictures of family displayed Personal mementos on wall Desk placed for open contact with people Casual or flamboyant dress Likes solitary activities (e.g., reading, individual sports)
	Expressive	Liberal arts background Motivational slogan on wall Office has friendly, open atmosphere Cluttered, unorganized desk Desk placed for open contact with people Casual or flamboyant dress Likes group activities (e.g., politics, team sports)

understand you are involved with setting industry standards for new plastic connectors. Can you tell me something about it?"

- Test your assessments. Look for clues and information that may suggest you have made an incorrect assessment of a customer's social style. If you look only for confirming cues, you will filter out a lot of important information.

Social Styles and Sales Presentations

In addition to teaching trainees in the above-mentioned program how to assess social style, the trainees' social styles are assessed. Each is asked to have a group of his or her customers complete a questionnaire and mail it to the director of the training program. These responses are used to determine the trainee's style. Trainees frequently are surprised by the difference between their self-perceptions and the perceptions of their customers.

Interpreting self-ratings requires great caution. Self-assessments can be very misleading because we usually do not see ourselves the same way others see us. When you rate yourself you know your own feelings, but others can only observe your behaviors. They don't know your thoughts or your intentions. We also vary our behavior from situation to situation. The indicators listed in Exhibits 6.2 and 6.3 merely show a tendency to be assertive or responsive.

Is there one best social style for a salesperson? No. None is "best" for all situations; each style has its strong points and weak points. Driver salespeople are efficient, determined, and decisive, but customers may also find them pushy and dominating. Expressives have enthusiasm, dramatic flair, and creativity but can also seem opinionated, undisciplined, and unstable. Analyticals are orderly, serious, and thorough, but customers may view them as cold, calculating, and stuffy. Finally, amiables are dependable, supportive, and personable but may also be percieved as undisciplined and inflexible.

The sales training program based on the social style matrix emphasizes that effective selling involves more than communicating a product's benefits. Salespeople must also recognize the customer's needs and expectations. In the sales interaction, they should conduct themselves in a manner consistent with customer expectations. Exhibit 6.6 indicates the expectations of customers with different social styles.

Although each customer type requires a different sales presentation, the salesperson's personal social style tends to determine the sales technique he or she typically uses. For example, drivers tend to use a driver technique with all customer types. When interacting with an amiable customer, they will be efficient and businesslike even though the amiable customer would prefer to deal with a more relationship-oriented and friendlier salesperson.

This sales training program emphasizes that to be effective with a variety of customer types, *salespeople must adapt their selling presentation to the customer's social style.* Versatility is the key to effective adaptive selling.

Versatility

The effort people make to increase the productivity of a relationship by adjusting to the needs of the other party is known as **versatility**. Versatile salespeople—those able to adapt their social styles—are much more effective than salespeople who do not adjust their sales presentations. Exhibit 6.7 compares behaviors of more versatile and less versatile people.

As stated above, sales training programs based on the social style matrix suggest that effective salespeople adjust their social styles to match their customers' styles. For example, salespeople with a driver orientation need to become more emotional and less aggressive when selling to amiable customers. Analytical salespeople must

EXHIBIT 6.6	Customer Expectations Based on Social Styles			
Area of Expectation	**Customer's Social Style**			
	Driver	**Expressive**	**Amiable**	**Analytical**
Atmosphere in sales interview	Businesslike	Open, friendly	Open, honest	Businesslike
Salesperson's use of time	Effective, efficient	Leisurely, to develop relationship	Leisurely, to develop relationship	Thorough, accurate
Pace of interview	Quick	Quick	Deliberate	Deliberate
Information provided by salesperson	Salesperson's qualifications; value of products	What salesperson thinks; whom he/she knows	Evidence that salesperson is trustworthy, friendly	Evidence of salesperson's expertise in solving problem
Salesperson's actions to win customer acceptance	Documented evidence, stress results	Recognition and approval	Personal attention and interest	Evidence that salesperson has analyzed the situation
Presentation of benefits	*What* product can do	*Who* has used the product	*Why* product is best to solve problem	*How* product can solve the problem
Assistance to aid decision making	Explanation of options and probabilities	Testimonials	Guarantees and assurances	Evidence and offers of service

EXHIBIT 6.7	Less Versatile	More Versatile
Indicators of Versatility	Limited adaptability to others' needs	Able to adapt to others' needs
	Specialist	Generalist
	Well-defined interests	Broad interests
	Firm on principles	Negotiates issues
	Predictable	Unpredictable
	Single-minded	Looks at many sides of an issue

increase their assertiveness and responsiveness when selling to expressive customers. Exhibit 6.8 shows some techniques for adjusting sales behaviors in terms of assertiveness and responsiveness.

The Role of Knowledge

The social style matrix illustrates the importance of knowledge, organized into categories, in determining selling effectiveness through adaptive selling. Sales training based on the social style matrix teaches salespeople the four customer categories, or types (driver, expressive, amiable, and analytical). Salespeople learn the cues for identifying them. Salespeople also learn what adjustments they need to make in their communication styles to be effective with each customer type.

AN ALTERNATIVE TRAINING SYSTEM FOR DEVELOPING ADAPTIVE SELLING SKILLS

The social style matrix developed by Merrill and Reid is one of several sales training methods based on customer classification schemes. Rather than using assertiveness and responsiveness, V. R. Buzzotta and R. E. Lefton use the dimensions of warm-hostile and dominant-submissive,[14] and Gerald Manning and Barry Reece use dominance and sociability dimensions to classify customers.[15] The Chailly Group classifies buyers into four categories—experts or gate swingers (nonusers), new users, experienced users, and routine users—based on their role in the purchase decision and the type of purchase decision.[16] Selling Scenario 6.4 illustrates how Berlitz trains salespeople for cross-cultural selling.

EXHIBIT 6.8	Adjusting Social Styles	
	Adjustment	
Dimension	**Reduce**	**Increase**
Assertiveness	Ask for customer's opinion	Get to the point
	Acknowledge merits of customer's viewpoint	Don't be vague or ambiguous
	Listen without interruption	Volunteer information
	Be more deliberate; don't rush	Be willing to disagree
	Let customer direct flow of conversation	Take a stand
		Initiate conversation
Responsiveness	Become businesslike	Verbalize feelings
	Talk less	Express enthusiasm
	Restrain enthusiasm	Pay personal compliments
	Make decision based on facts	Spend time on relationships rather than business
	Stop and think	Socialize; engage in small talk
		Use nonverbal communication

SELLING SCENARIO 6.4

Training for International Sales

Many of the sales skills taught in the United States can be used when selling in other countries. However, Dean Foster of Berlitz Cross Cultural emphasizes that "Sales training needs to be tailored to different cultures. Salespeople should be allowed to learn in an environment they are used to." For example, Americans tend to focus on end results, what they learned in training, whereas the French feel more comfortable focusing on the process of learning.

ADD Latin America, a subsidiary of Abbott Laboratories, concentrates its training efforts on building relationships between the customer and the salesperson and spends less time on product knowledge. In Latin American countries, nobody buys anything until they are comfortable with and trust the salesperson. Foster says, "People aren't as emotional in the United States as they are in Latin America. Here we have to focus our training on searching for feelings, finding the hidden motivators that determine a buying decision."

Source: "Training for International Sales," *Sales & Marketing Management,* June 1996, p. 72. Reprinted with permission from Bill Communications.

Expert Systems

Expert systems have been developed to assist salespeople in understanding their customers and developing effective sales strategies.[17] An **expert system** is a computer program that mimics a human expert. The program contains the knowledge, rules, and decision processes employed by experts and then uses these elements to solve problems, suggest strategies, and provide advice similar to that of an expert.

Some expert selling systems incorporate a model similar to the social style matrix described earlier. For example, one system first asks salespeople to respond to a set of agree-disagree statements to assess their own personalities. Here are some of these statements:

I like to take charge of situations.

I want social recognition at work.

I take more risks than most salespeople.

I desire feedback on my performance.

Then the computer program asks salespeople to describe a specific customer in terms of a set of adjectives, such as *talkative, apprehensive, achieving, social,* and *independent.* Using the self-assessment and the customer assessment, the computer program produces a sales strategy report containing six sections:

What to Expect from Your Customer

How to Succeed with Your Customer

Customer-Specific Preparation Strategy

Customer-Specific Opening Strategy

Customer-Specific Presentation Strategy

Customer-Specific Closing Strategy

Portions of a sales strategy report provided by an expert system appear in Exhibit 6.9. Most expert systems store the information salespeople provide about their customers. As salespeople collect more information, assessments can be modified and updated and revised sales strategy recommendations can be generated.

EXHIBIT 6.9	Excerpts from the Sales Edge© Sales Strategy Report

What to Expect

In dealing with Mr. J. B., you may feel he comes on heavy-handed, cocky, and with too much energy. Rather than feeling overwhelmed or stressed by him, you can turn his attributes to your advantage by letting him take the lead. This will give him the power he wants and allow you to collect information that you need . . .

How to Succeed

You Both Like to Work Quickly Both you and Mr. J. B. are spontaneous and act with abruptness. Further, neither of you is particularly interested in all the details involved in the sale. Mr. J. B. is the type of buyer who will purchase based on a general, superficial product description. If possible, take some time to determine the fit of your product to Mr. J. B.'s needs and expectations. Remember that although Mr. J. B. may purchase impulsively, he may be dissatisfied later if the product does not perform to his satisfaction . . .

Mr. J. B. Will Want to Dominate . . .
Focus on Business . . .
Find Out What His Business Needs Are . . .
Plan to Answer Objections in an Expert Manner . . .
Expect Mr. J. B. to Take Risks . . .
Expect Mr. J. B. to Bargain Hard . . .
Business Facts Are What Counts . . .
Success and Achievement Are the Keys . . .
Apply Your Powers of Persuasion . . .

Customer-Specific Opening Strategies

1. Establish a Balance of Social and Business Interests Since Mr. J. B. finds business exciting and is attracted to innovations and creative ideas, emphasize new and exciting ideas in your opening. Mr. J. B. is very social and will feel most comfortable if you are friendlier than you would normally be. Make an effort to be extra pleasant. Take an active interest in Mr. J. B. Show genuine, sincere interest in him and his business. Use compliments when you can.

2. Needs Analysis: Mr. J. B. Knows What He Wants . . .

Customer-Specific Presentation Strategies

1. Innovations, Major Benefits, and Excitement It is essential for you to present your product to fulfill Mr. J. B.'s stated needs and to enhance his views and positions. Highlight areas of innovation; make your presentation exciting. Do not give extra details. Stick to the major features. Be persuasive. Do not hesitate to try to sell your product to Mr. J. B.; make him think he sold it himself. Move your presentation along at a quick pace.

2. Deal with Stated Objections . . .

Source: Robert Collins, "Artificial Intelligence in Personal Selling," *Journal of Personal Selling and Sales Management*, May 1994, pp.58–66.

Limitations of Training Methods

The training methods such as the social style matrix and expert systems described in the previous sections are simply a first step in developing knowledge for practicing adaptive selling. They emphasize the need to practice adaptive selling—to use different presentations with different customers—and stimulate salespeople to base their sales presentations on an analysis of the customer. But these methods are limited; they present only a few types of customers, and classification is based on the form of communication (the social style), not on the content of the communication (the specific features and benefits stressed in the presentation).

In addition, accurately fitting customers into the suggested categories is often very difficult. Customers act differently and have different needs in different sales encounters: A buyer may be very amiable when engaging in a new-task buying situation and be analytical when dealing with an "out" salesperson in a straight rebuy.

Amiable buyers in a bad mood may act like drivers. By rigidly applying the classification rules, salespeople may actually limit their flexibility, reducing the adaptive selling behavior these training methods emphasize.

Finally, the knowledge these training programs provide is very general. It is not related to the specific types of customers to whom you will be selling or the specific products you will be selling. To be an effective salesperson, you need to develop knowledge about the specific sales situations you will encounter.

SUMMARY

By practicing adaptive selling, salespeople exploit the unique properties of personal selling as a marketing communication tool: the ability to tailor messages to individual customers and make on-the-spot adjustments. Extensive knowledge of customer and sales situation types is a key ingredient in effective adaptive selling.

To be effective, salespeople need to have considerable knowledge about the products they sell, the companies for which they work, and the customers to whom they sell. In addition to knowing the facts, they need to understand how those facts relate to benefits their customers are seeking.

Experienced salespeople organize customer knowledge into categories. Each category has cues for classifying customers or sales situations and an effective sales presentation for customers in the category.

To develop more extensive knowledge of customers, salespeople need to use information from their firms' market research studies, ask for feedback, analyze their successes and failures, and develop an intrinsic orientation toward their work.

The social style matrix, developed by Merrill and Reid, illustrates the concept of developing categorical knowledge to facilitate adaptive selling. The matrix defines four customer categories based on a customer's responsiveness and assertiveness in sales interactions. To effectively interact with a customer, a salesperson needs to identify the customer's social style and adapt his or her style to match the customer's. The sales training program based on the social style matrix provides cues for identifying social style and presentations salespeople can use to make adjustments.

The social style matrix is one example of a categorical scheme salespeople can use to improve their knowledge and adaptability. However, other schemes are used, and some have been incorporated into expert system computer programs.

KEY TERMS

adaptive selling 159
amiable 171
analytical 172
assertiveness 168
customized presentation 158
diagnostic feedback 166
driver 170
expert system 176

expressive 171
extrinsic orientation 167
intrinsic orientation 167
outlined presentation 158
responsiveness 168
standard memorized sales presentation 158
social style matrix 168
versatility 174

QUESTIONS AND
PROBLEMS

1. Would a person with an amiable social style be better at selling than a person with an analytical style? Why or why not?

2. "A good salesperson can sell any customer." Do you agree? Why or why not?

3. What do you think about the following statement? "Good salespeople need to be aggressive. They need to have powerful voices and a winning smile."

4. What social styles would you assign to the following people?

    a. Zonker in "Doonesbury."

    b. Clint Eastwood.

    c. Mike Wallace on "60 Minutes."

    d. Jessica Fletcher (Angela Lansbury) in "Murder, She Wrote."

    e. Roseanne.

    f. Seinfeld.

5. What are the strengths and weaknesses of each of the four social styles in terms of effective selling?

6. If you were an expressive, what adjustments would you make in selling to an amiable?

7. A salesperson who is a driver is preparing to deliver a presentation. What suggestions can you make to improve the salesperson's performance?

8. Sarah Jones sells footballs, basketballs, volleyballs, and other rubber sporting goods products to sporting goods retailers. What facts about her company would a sporting goods retailer be interested in? Why would the retailer be interested in knowing these facts?

9. Suppose that during a sales call, a customer says, "Your computer software could never do everything you say it will." How would you respond if this were an analytical customer? An amiable?

10. The market research undertaken by a hospital supply company identified three types of hospitals. Traditional hospitals believe patient satisfaction is based on the quality of medical staff and hospital supplies are unimportant. Private hospitals believe supplies are important because they affect the staff's efficiency. Marketing-oriented hospitals view supplies as an important element in creating a comfortable, customer service–oriented image. What type of sales presentation would you use if you were selling bedsheets and pillowcases to each of these hospital types? What products and benefits would you emphasize in each case?

EXPLORING THE
NET

The social style matrix is one of many methods of classifying customers. Another popular method used in marketing, based on the lifestyles of consumers, is called VALS2© (. Go to

http://www. future.sri.com/aboutvals.html

and read about the set of VALS2 categories. Take the test to see which category you fall into. How does these scheme compare in usefulness to the social style matrix described in the chapter?

CASE PROBLEMS

CASE 6.1
Using the Social Style Matrix to Develop Sales Presentations

Sergio Remo

His office is relatively neat. Some nicely framed diplomas and achievement certificates decorate the walls. Two reference posters with helpful business data are pinned to the wall nearest the desk. The desk holds several in-out baskets, all clearly labeled. Two chairs are set up so that Remo faces visitors directly across the desk.

Chris James

Lots of things cover his walls: framed, autographed photos of sports notables; a Chamber of Commerce citizenship citation; children's colorful crayon drawings; and a large newspaper ad with a clever headline. Propped against a cabinet full of trophies stands a tennis bag with a racquet. You count at least eight stacks of papers and magazines. The visitors' chairs are pulled close to the desk.

Judy Zachery

Her office walls contain one oil painting and some nicely framed prints. A large stack of business periodicals rests on the credenza behind the desk. The pen and pencil set on the desk has an achievement plaque with Zachery's name on it. Although current work clutters the desk, the rest of the office is well organized. You notice a to-do list with today's date on it next to the telephone. The desk divides the room in two and separates you from the occupant.

Emmit Saunders

His office is pleasant and really looks "worked in." You notice a couple of file folders on the floor behind the desk. Two attractive nonbusiness posters (not framed) hang on the walls, along with four small, framed group photos. You notice a number of souvenirs on the desk. Chairs are comfortable and casually arranged. An assortment of snapshots is tucked in the frame of a family portrait on the desk.

Questions

1. Identify each customer's social style.
2. Outline the technique you would employ to sell to each customer.

CASE 6.2
Intercable

Heather Little is a salesperson at Intercable, the company with the cable TV rights for the city of Detroit and its surrounding suburbs. After Little graduated from Wayne State University with a BA in history, she went to work for the city in the community services department. When the economy slowed down, she was laid off and went to work for Intercable, where she has been working in sales for two years. Little is married, has two children, and is an active volunteer in programs for homeless persons.

Little is making her first call on Carl Perkins, the new director of advertising at Detroit National Bank. As Little enters Perkins's office, she notices several graphs on the wall indicating the number of new accounts opened, total deposits, and market share over time. A plaque signifying Perkins's selection as Midwest Advertising Executive of the Year is prominently displayed.

LITTLE [*extends her hand warmly, then takes a seat*] Good Morning, Mr. Perkins. This is really a beautiful day. How are you?

PERKINS [*hesitates at first, then extends his hand*] I have just a few minutes to talk with you. My schedule is really tight today. Now tell me what you have to offer. [*Sits down without demonstrating an emotional response*]

LITTLE Let me take a second to tell you why I made an appointment to see you. I was talking with Joan Waters at Fidelity Mutual Life Insurance. She said she met you at a recent Midwest Advertising Executives luncheon. She has been using Intercable in her media plan and mentioned you might be interested in advertising on cable TV.

PERKINS I really can't remember Ms. Waters. You meet so many people at these luncheons.

LITTLE She really is an interesting person. We worked together as volunteers in the Homeless in America program last fall. Are you involved in many community activities?

PERKINS Not really. [*Looks at his watch*]

LITTLE Well, Ms. Waters told me you were developing a new advertising campaign for the bank. I hear the campaign will stress customer service. I really think that is a great idea. Banks should be more concerned about providing good service.

PERKINS We did a lot of market research to develop this new campaign. Our research shows that customer service is particularly important to people in the eastern suburbs. We hope to increase our share of new deposits by 3 percent over the next six months. Tell me something about what you can do for us.

LITTLE I think we are the ideal media for your new campaign. Fidelity Mutual has been very pleased with the response to their commercials for homeowner insurance policies.

PERKINS That's interesting. What is its target market?

LITTLE They have been targeting their campaign toward lower-income families in the western suburbs. Their homeowner policy sales doubled six months after they placed the first ads on cable TV.

PERKINS Doubled?

LITTLE At least doubled, I think.

PERKINS Could you be more specific about your reach in the eastern suburbs? How many families subscribe to your cable TV service? How often do they watch the cable channels?

LITTLE I don't have the specific information with me, but I know that our coverage is very good. More and more people are watching cable channels. You know . . .

PERKINS Excuse me, but I have to go to another meeting. When you get some more specific information, why don't you leave it with my assistant?

Questions

1. What are Little's and Perkins's communication styles? On what do you base your assessments?

2. How effective do you think Little was on this sales call?

3. What adjustments should Little have made in her sales presentation to increase her effectiveness?

ADDITIONAL REFERENCES

Bowers, Michael, and D. Layne Rich. "The Effect of Product and Market Factors on the Communication Styles of Salespeople." *Developments in Marketing Science,* vol. 14, ed. Robert King. Richmond, VA: Academy of Marketing Science, 1993, pp. 232–37.

Brown, Gene; Unal Boya; Neil Humphreys; and Robert Wilding. "Attributes and Behaviors of Salespeople Preferred by Buyers: High Socializing vs. Low Socializing Industrial Buyers." *Journal of Personal Selling and Sales Management,* Winter 1993, pp. 26–31.

Creyer, Elizabeth, and William Ross. "Salesperson Impression and Strategy Formulation." *Marketing Letters,* July 1994, pp. 225–34.

Gelman, Jan. "There's a Lot to Be Gained from Losing Business. So Live and Learn." *Selling,* June 1995, pp. 58–61.

Hwan, Dong Lee, and Richard Olshavsky. "Adapting to What? A Contingency Approach to Sales Interactions Based on a Comprehensive Model of Consumer Choice." In *Marketing Theory and Applications,* ed. Chris Allen et al., Chicago: American Marketing Association, 1992, p. 224.

Plank, Richard E. "The Impact of Adaptive Selling on Sales Effectiveness within the Pharmaceutical Industry." *Journal of Marketing Theory and Practice,* Summer 1994, pp. 106–25.

Sharma, Arun, and Rajnandini Pillai. "Customers' Decision-Making Styles and Their Preference for Sales Strategies: Conceptual Examination and Empirical Study." *Journal of Personal Selling and Sales Management,* Winter 1996, pp. 21–31.

Thomas Stafford. "Conscious and Unconscious Processing of Priming Cues in Selling Encounters." *Journal of Personal Selling and Sales Management,* Spring 1996, pp. 37–44.

Vink, Jaap, and Wilem Verbeke. "Adaptive Selling and Organizational Characteristics: Suggestions for Future Research." *Journal of Personal Selling and Sales Management,* Winter 1993, pp. 16–23.

Whittler, Tommy. "Eliciting Consumer Choice Heuristics: Sales Representatives' Persuasion Strategies." *Journal of Personal Selling and Sales Management,* Fall 1994, pp. 41–53.

Part Three

P art One of this book provided a general introduction to the nature of selling jobs. In Part Two we reviewed concepts of buyer behavior, communication principles, and the adaptive selling framework. In Part Three we explore the activities required to build long-term relationships and partnerships. As the circular figure illustrates, these activities do not necessarily follow a step-by-step sequence; instead they occur throughout the partnership-building process.

The Partnership Process

Chapter Seven covers material on identifying prospects. Chapter Eight outlines how to gain precall information, plan each call, and make appointments effectively.

In Chapter Nine you will learn how to make a good impression. You will also discover techniques to effectively uncover the prospect's needs and then relate your solution to those needs.

Chapter Ten covers the use of communication tools such as visual aids, samples, and demonstrations. Chapter Eleven will help you learn how to respond helpfully to concerns raised by the buyer, while Chapter Twelve provides guidance in obtaining commitment. Finally, Chapter Thirteen summarizes methods and activities used to develop and enrich meaningful partnerships.

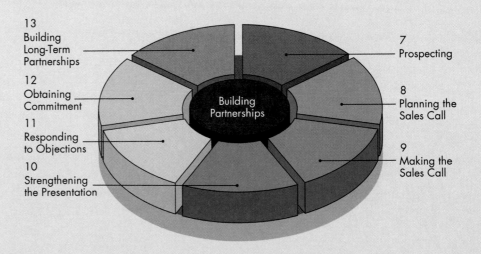

13
Building
Long-Term
Partnerships

12
Obtaining
Commitment

11
Responding
to Objections

10
Strengthening
the Presentation

Building
Partnerships

7
Prospecting

8
Planning the
Sales Call

9
Making the
Sales Call

Chapter Seven

Prospecting

One of the most important activities for most salespeople is locating qualified prospects. In fact, the selling process generally begins with prospecting. You can be the best salesperson in the world in terms of listening, asking questions, discovering needs, giving presentations, helpfully responding to objections, and obtain-

Some Questions Answered in this Chapter Are:

Why is prospecting important for effective selling?

Are all sales leads good prospects? What are the characteristics of a qualified prospect?

How can prospects be identified?

How can the organization's promotional program be used in prospecting?

What elements comprise an effective prospecting plan, and how should the plan be developed?

How can a salesperson overcome a reluctance to prospect?

ing commitment, but if you are calling on the wrong person or organization, none of this does you any good! This chapter provides resources to help you prospect effectively and efficiently.

PROFILE

After graduating from the University of Minnesota, Duluth, in 1995 with a major in marketing, Todd Graf started his own business called Integrated Communication Systems and Solutions, Inc. (ICSS). ICSS is a high-tech firm specializing in Macintosh/Unix/ Windows NT installation and consulting; Internet consulting; Web site creation and management; and LAN/-WAN design, configuration, and implementation. Graf is president and chief salesperson at ICSS and has achieved phenomenal success in the first year of the firm's existence in the greater Chicago marketplace. Graf isn't new to selling. In fact, he owned and managed several businesses while still in college!

When speaking of his business, Graf is the first to recognize the importance of prospecting. "You have to keep getting out there, talking to people, and finding out what their needs are. Prospecting is critical to survive in this environment." Fortunately, in less than one year, satisfied customers have already become Graf's primary source of new leads. "If you treat people right and do exactly what you promise (plus a little more!), the referrals will come. I'm happy about the way I have met customers' needs and made a big difference in their firms. I'm also happy about the long-term benefits of maintaining a win-win perspective with my clients.

"You have to keep getting out there, talking to people, and finding out what their needs are. Prospecting is critical to survive in this environment."

"You must learn *very, very* fast in order to survive in today's business world. Things are changing in our industry daily, and it's important to keep up. Only by doing so can you meet your customers' needs in the best way possible."

"Motivation and energy are the keys to success today. Don't give up, and don't let any setbacks stop you from continuing forward.

"Always treat your customers the way you would want to be treated. I sell some pretty technically oriented services and products and could usually talk way over my customers' heads. I don't. I explain things in the easiest, most layman terms as possible. I pay particular attention to the customer's comfort level. Are they comfortable with the way I am explaining something? Are we moving too fast? Is this what they want to be hearing? You have to be aware of this or you will lose a lot of clients."

With regard to operating a new business right out of college, Graf has some advice: "You must learn to find a proper balance in everything: relationships with your customers, pros-

TODD GRAF
Integrated Communication Systems and Solutions, Inc.

pecting for new clients, generating proposals and quotes, your personal life, installing systems that you've sold, billing and account collection, maintaining an office, and yes, tons of *paperwork!* There is no end to the paperwork in a business! It could get overwhelming if you didn't manage it well and keep on top of it."

What advice does Graf have for college students? "Get used to working hard. When I was in college, I heard other students complain about having to give a presentation and study for an exam in the same week. That's nothing! I work long days, usually from 7:00 AM to 12:30 AM, and make many presentations in a week. In one fairly typical week, I gave four presentations in four days for proposals that added up to over $300,000. Add on top of that my meetings with current customers, prospecting for new clients, working up extensive proposals, and everything else I did and you'll realize that work is work."

One person who knows Graf well provides her perspective. She says, "Todd Graf has a dynamic ability to relate, connect, and create winning scenarios. This is seen historically as related in family photos, personal challenges and outcomes, but most subtly in the smiles and human extension with which Todd is received by those in the present, that he has interacted with in the past. Observing Todd in the present, his drive for working 20-hour days is clearly fueled by his underlying belief in who he is, what he's doing, and his commitment toward creating win-win situations. Watching Todd work, it becomes clear that he has a refined, 'survival of the fittest' philosophy. This personal philosophy is the fuel that keeps Todd charged, engaged, and able to motivate himself and those around him."

Of course given ICSS's business, Graf is on the Net. The next time you're cruising, feel free to stop by his Web site or drop him an e-mail message (tgraf@icss.com). "Selling is fun; I can't imagine doing anything else!" says Graf. "Where else can you see the results of your hard work in such a clear way? Good luck to you!"

Visit Our Website@
http://www.icss.com

THE IMPORTANCE OF PROSPECTING

The process of locating potential customers for a product or service is called **prospecting**. A list of prospects is critical to the success of both experienced and new salespeople. In fact, many experts note that prospecting is the *most* important activity a salesperson does.

Today extensive changes are taking place in population movements, the creation of new businesses and products, the shifting of businesses to new lines and expansion of old-line companies, and methods of distribution. These changes are resulting in an estimated 15 to 20 percent annual turnover of customers. In addition, salespeople must find new customers to replace those that switch to competitors, go bankrupt, move out of the territory, merge with noncustomers, or decide to do without the product or service. A salesperson may need to prospect even in existing accounts due to mergers, downsizing by firms, and job changes or retirements of buyers. Thus, salespeople need to develop effective prospecting skills.

Prospecting is more important in some selling fields than in others. For example, the stockbroker or real estate sales representative with no effective prospecting plan usually doesn't last long in the business. In these sales positions, as a general rule, it takes 100 contacts to get 10 prospects who will listen to presentations, out of which 1 will buy. Each sale, then, represents a great deal of prospecting. It is also important in these fields to prospect continually. Some sales trainers relate this to your car's gas tank: You don't wait until you are on empty before you fill up!

Some sales positions require less emphasis on locating new leads. For example, a Procter & Gamble sales representative in a certain geographic area would know all the potential prospects for Crest toothpaste (all the grocery stores, drugstores, convenience stores, etc.) because they are easy to identify. For the same reason, a Du Pont sales rep selling a new line of automobile finishes to auto manufacturers can easily identify all of the automakers worldwide. A Lockheed salesperson assigned exclusively to sell the F16 fighter jet to Taiwan, South Korea, Greece, and Singapore would not spend any time trying to locate new governments to call on. For these types of sales positions, prospecting as we normally think of it (i.e., looking for new leads) is not an important part of the sales process. This does *not* mean salespeople can ignore these leads, however, as the next section discusses. They still have to assess whether or not they are good prospects.

CHARACTERISTICS OF A GOOD PROSPECT

Some salespeople mistakenly consider everyone a prospect without first finding out whether these people really provide an opportunity to make a sale. Prospecting actually begins with locating leads. A **lead** is a potential prospect, a person or an organization that may or may not have what it takes to be a true prospect.

Next, the salesperson qualifies the lead. If the salesperson determines that the lead is a good candidate for making a sale (has a need, ability to pay, etc.), that person or organization becomes a **prospect.** Many leads will not become prospects. The process of determining whether a lead is in fact a prospect is called **qualifying a lead.** Exhibit 7.1 displays the relationship between the steps in the selling process and the terminology we use to refer to the "buyer."

Naturally, the amount of time spent trying to determine who is a prospect varies in different types of selling. It depends on such factors as the type of product or service, the value of the salesperson's time, and the profit per sale. The following five questions will help to qualify leads and pinpoint the good prospects:

1. Does the lead have a want or a need that the purchase of my products or services can satisfy?
2. Does the lead have the ability to pay?
3. Does the lead have the authority to buy?
4. Can the lead be approached favorably?
5. Is the lead eligible to buy?

These questions can be asked about the person who is a lead, the lead's firm, or both. Chapter Eight discusses how to begin gathering the information needed to answer these questions, and Chapter Nine provides further instruction on how to gather the remaining needed information during actual sales calls. For now, let's look at each question a little more closely.

Does a Want or Need Exist?

Research has supplied no infallible answers to why customers buy, but it has found many reasons. As we pointed out in Chapter Four, customers buy to satisfy practical needs as well as intangible needs, such as prestige or aesthetics.

Determining whether leads need a salesperson's products or services is not always simple. Many firms use the telephone to assess needs. Sometimes an exploratory interview is conducted to determine whether a lead has needs the seller's

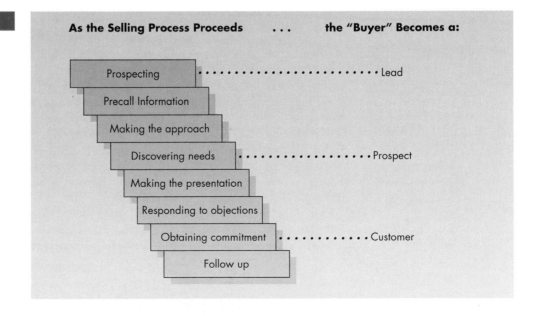

EXHIBIT 7.1

Relationship between the Steps in the Selling Process and the Designation of the "Buyer"

As the Selling Process Proceeds   . . .   the "Buyer" Becomes a:

Prospecting · · · · · · · · · · · · · · · · · · · Lead
Precall Information
Making the approach
Discovering needs · · · · · · · · · · · · · · · Prospect
Making the presentation
Responding to objections
Obtaining commitment · · · · · · · · · · Customer
Follow up

Progressive firms use
telemarketers to qualify
leads before sending a
salesperson on a call.

Courtesy United Stationers

products can satisfy. Also, almost everyone has a need for some product lines; for example, practically every organization needs paper, desks, telephones, and fire insurance.

By using high-pressure tactics, sales may be made to those who do not need or really want a product. Such sales benefit no one. The buyer will resent making the purchase, and a potential long-term customer will be lost. The lead must want to solve his or her need to be considered a qualified prospect.

Does the Lead Have the Ability to Pay?

The ability to pay for the products or services helps to separate leads from prospects. For example, the commercial real estate agent usually checks the financial status of each client to determine the price range of office buildings to show. A client with annual profits of $100,000 and cash resources of $75,000 may be a genuine prospect for an office building selling in the $200,000 to $250,000 bracket. An agent would be wasting time, however, by showing this client an office building listed at $1 million. The client may have a real desire and need for the more expensive setting, but the client is still not a real prospect for the higher-priced office building if he or she doesn't have the resources to pay for it.

Ability to pay includes both cash and credit. Many companies subscribe to a credit rating service offered by such firms as Dun & Bradstreet, Moody's, ValueLine, and Standard & Poor's. Like many things, this information is also now available on CD-ROM (see Exhibit 7.2). Salespeople can use information from these sources to determine the financial status and credit rating of a lead. They can also qualify leads with information obtained from local credit agencies, consumer credit agencies such as TRW, noncompetitive salespeople, and the Better Business Bureau.

Salespeople are sometimes surprised at their leads' credit ratings. Some big-name firms have poor ratings. Even the federal government does not always pay its bills on time. For example, one study found that the Justice Department makes over 16 percent of its payments late, while the State Department isn't far behind at 15 percent.[1]

EXHIBIT 7.2

Business America
CD-ROM: A Source
of Information about
Companies

Source: A Service of American Business Information, Inc.

Does the Lead Have the Authority to Buy?

A lead may have a real need for a product and the ability to pay for it but lack the authority to make the purchase. Knowing who has this authority saves the salesperson time and effort and results in a higher percentage of closed sales. As discussed in Chapter Four, many people are typically involved in a purchase decision and frequently it is unclear who has the most influence. For example, Dalcon Tool and Die, a machine tool company, planned its sales efforts assuming its machines were being purchased by production managers. Careful analysis, however, showed that only 10 percent of the sales came from production executives. The rest came from engineers (44 percent), purchasing agents (29 percent), and others (17 percent), because they had the authority to make the purchase decision. Based on this survey, the company redirected its sales efforts toward engineers and purchasing agents, and profits increased by 22 percent over the next two-year period.

A good way to find out if the lead has the authority to buy is to simply ask that person. One top sales trainer suggests that salespeople ask the buyer this question: "Do we need to invite anyone else to our meeting whose presence you believe is required for a decision to be made, either at this time or in the future?"[2]

More and more firms are delegating their purchasing tasks to outside vendors.[3] These vendors, often called **systems integrators,** have the authority to buy products and services from others. Systems integrators usually assume complete responsibility for a project, from its beginning to follow-up servicing. An example would be

Andersen Consulting, a division of Arthur Andersen & Company, acting as a systems integrator for the complete robotics system of a new Chrysler plant. In that scenario, every potential vendor would actually be selling to Andersen Consulting, not to Chrysler. When systems integrators are involved, salespeople need to delineate clearly who has the authority to purchase. Sometimes the overall buyer (Chrysler in our example) will retain veto power over potential vendors.

Can the Lead be Approached Favorably?

Some people may have a need, the ability to pay, and the authority to buy but still not qualify as prospects because they are not accessible to the salesperson. For example, the president of a large bank, a major executive of a large manufacturing company, or the senior partner in a well-established law firm normally would not be accessible to a young college graduate starting out as a sales representative for an investment trust organization. Getting an interview with these people may be so difficult and the chances of making a sale so small that the sales representative eliminates them as possible prospects.

Is the Lead Eligible to Buy?

Eligibility is an equally important factor in finding a genuine prospect. For example, a salesperson who works for a firm that requires a rather large minimum order should not call on leads that could never order in such volume. Likewise, a representative who sells exclusively to wholesalers should be certain the individuals he or she calls on are actually wholesalers, not retailers.

Another factor that may determine eligibility for a particular salesperson is the geographic location of the prospect. Most companies operate on the basis of **exclusive sales territories,** meaning that a particular salesperson can sell only to certain prospects (e.g., only doctors in a three-county area) and not to other prospects. A salesperson working for such a company must consider whether the prospect is eligible, based on location, to buy from him or her.

Salespeople should also avoid targeting leads already covered by their corporate headquarters. Large customers or potential customers that are handled exclusively by corporate executives are often called **house accounts.** For example, if Hilton Hotels considers PepsiCo a house account, a local Hilton Hotel salesperson (who sets up events and conventions at the hotel) located in New York City should not try to solicit business from one of PepsiCo's divisions located in New York City. Instead, all PepsiCo business would be handled by a Hilton executive at Hilton corporate headquarters.

Other Criteria

Leads that meet the five criteria are generally considered excellent prospects. Some sellers, however, add other criteria. For example, DEI Management Group instructs its salespeople to classify leads by their likelihood of buying. Salespeople may have a long list of people they believe need their product, can pay for it, have authority to buy it, and are approachable and eligible. If, however, these companies have absolutely no interest in buying, the salesperson should look elsewhere. Otherwise the salesperson will just waste additional time on this lead and fail to prospect for better leads.

Criteria can include many things. Some firms look at the timing of purchase to determine whether a lead is really a good prospect. Relevant questions to consider include "How soon before the prospect's contract with our competitor expires?" and "Is a purchase decision really pending? How do we know?" Still other firms look at the long-term potential of developing a partnering relationship with a lead. Some questions to ponder include "What is the climate at their organization—are they looking to develop partnering relationships with suppliers? Do any of our competitors already have a partnering relationship with them?" Answers to these and other questions help a firm determine whether a prospect is worth pursuing at this time.

HOW AND WHERE TO OBTAIN LEADS

Prospecting sources and methods vary for different types of selling. A sales representative for Tenneco selling corrugated containers, for example, may use a different system than banking or office products salespeople would use. Exhibit 7.3 presents an overview of some of the most common lead-generating methods, which will now be described.

Satisfied Customers

Satisfied customers are the most effective sources for leads. Customers, particularly those who are truly partners with the seller, often refer the seller to other prospects. Referrals of leads in the same industry are particularly useful, because the salesperson already has a better understanding of the unique needs of this type of organization (e.g., "If I have sold to a bank already, I have a better understanding of banks' needs").

To maximize the usefulness of satisfied customers, salespeople should follow several logical steps.[4] First, they should make a list of potential references (i.e., customers who might provide leads) from among their most satisfied customers. This will be much easier if they have maintained an accurate and detailed database of customers. Next, they should decide what they would like each customer to do (e.g., have the customer write a personal letter of introduction, see if the customer would be willing to take phone inquiries, have the customer directly contact prospects for them, or have the customer provide a generic letter of reference). Finally, salespeople should ask the customer for the names of leads and for the specific type of help she or he can provide. And they should give the customer time to think of names. Often people have trouble coming up with a list of good leads off the tops of their heads.[5]

Why aren't more customers willing to offer referrals? Probably because they know that if the salesperson somehow doesn't do a good job, they will be blamed. For this method of prospecting to work, the salesperson must continually keep the referring customer and the prospect fully satisfied. Also, asking for referrals when a new customer signs the order may be too soon. It would probably be best to wait until the new customer has had a chance to use the product and experience both the product's benefits and the level of salesperson service.[6]

EXHIBIT 7.3		
Overview of Common Sources of Leads	**Source**	**How Used**
	Satisfied customers	Current and previous customers are contacted for additional business and leads.
	Endless chain	Salesperson attempts to secure at least one additional lead from each person he or she interviews.
	Center of influence	Salesperson cultivates well-known, influential people in the territory who are willing to supply lead information.
	Networking	Salesperson uses personal relationships with those who are connected and cooperative to secure leads
	Promotional activities	Salesperson ties into the company's direct mail, telemarketing, and shows to secure and qualify leads.
	Lists and directories	Salesperson uses secondary data sources, which can be free or fee based.
	Canvassing	Salesperson tries to generate leads by calling on totally unfamiliar organizations.
	Spotters	Salesperson pays someone for lead information.
	Telemarketing	Salesperson uses phone and/or telemarketing staff to generate leads.
	Sales letters	Salesperson writes personal letters to potential leads.
	Other sources	Salesperson uses noncompeting salespeople, people in his or her own firm, friends, etc. to secure information.

Satisfied customers not only provide leads, they are usually prospects themselves for additional sales. This situation is sometimes referred to as **selling deeper** to a current customer. Salespeople should never overlook this profitable opportunity. In fact, one research study found that increasing sales 5 percent with current customers resulted in a 10 percent increase in net income.[7]

Endless-Chain Method

In the **endless-chain method,** sales representatives attempt to get at least one additional lead from each person they interview. This method works best when the source is a satisfied customer and partner; however, it may also be used even when a prospect does not buy.

For example, at the conclusion of a meeting, the following conversation might ensue:

SELLER Jim, you told me that you belong to several professional trade associations. Since you said you liked what I'm offering you, maybe you know of some other members who could use my services?

BUYER Well, you know, maybe Sarah Harkins, and even Josh Smyth, could use this service too.

SELLER You know a lot more about these people than I do. If you were me, whom would you call first?

BUYER Harkins, I would guess.

SELLER When I call Ms. Harkins, may I mention that we are doing some work with you?

Some people object to having their names used as a means of opening the door to friends or business acquaintances. Others, particularly those who trust the salesperson and/or are enthusiastic about the products or services, will not hesitate to provide the names of additional prospects. They may even write a letter or card of introduction for the sales representative. The name of a lead provided by either a customer or a prospect, known as a **referred lead,** is generally considered to be the most successful type of lead. Exhibit 7.4 illustrates how a sales representative used the endless-chain method to produce $25,690 in business (selling fax machines) within a 30-day period. All the sales resulted directly or indirectly from the first referral from an engineer to whom the sales rep had sold a mere $1,250 of equipment.

Center-of-Influence Method

In the **center-of-influence method,** the salesperson cultivates a relationship with well-known, influential people in the territory who are willing to supply lead information. Exhibit 7.5 illustrates the concept visually. Ross Perot understands the importance of centers of influence and prefers to call them "eagles." "You don't capture eagles by the flock," he says, "you catch them one at a time. When you catch one, you treasure it like a jewel."[8] A friend of one of the authors likes to call centers of influence "bell cows," because the rest of the "herd" follow their lead.

This method, like the endless-chain method, works best if the center of influence is already a satisfied customer of the salesperson. Here is the way an industrial cleaning service salesperson used the center-of-influence method when meeting with a well-known and respected maintenance engineer:

Now I've had the chance to explain my service, and you've had the opportunity to meet my cleaning crew. I wonder if you will do me a favor? You mentioned that it was probably the best-designed package you've ever seen. Can you think of any of your business associates who could benefit from such a plan? Does one come to your mind right away?

EXHIBIT 7.4   Example of the Endless-Chain Method of Prospecting

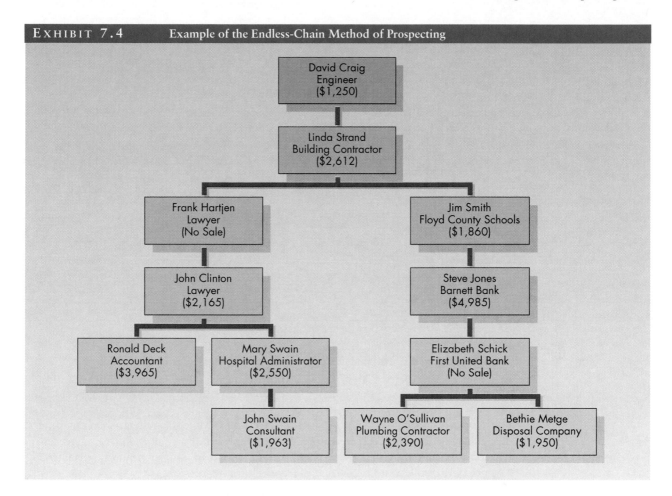

In industrial sales situations, the centers of influence are frequently people in important departments not directly involved in the purchase decision, such as quality control, equipment maintenance, and receiving. The salesperson keeps in close touch with these people over an extended period, solicits their help in a straightforward manner, and keeps them informed about sales that result from their aid.

One true story illustrates the method's use. A Xerox representative found that decision makers from several companies would get together and visit on occasion. These accounts formed a **buying community,** a small, informal group of people in similar positions, often from several companies, who communicate regularly, both socially and professionally. The rep also found that one particular decision maker in that group, or community, would share the results of any sales call with the other members of the community. Thus, a call on that account had the power of seven calls. By working carefully with this center of influence, the rep closed nine orders among the seven accounts, with sales that totaled over $450,000!

Centers of influence may never buy. One church furnishings representative told of a pastor who suggested that the rep call on two other churches, both of which were in the market for pews. The pastor who made the referral has not purchased pews in over 10 years and probably will not for many more. But the rep continues to spend time with that pastor, who is an important center of influence in the pastoral community.

Illustration of the
Center-of-Influence
Method

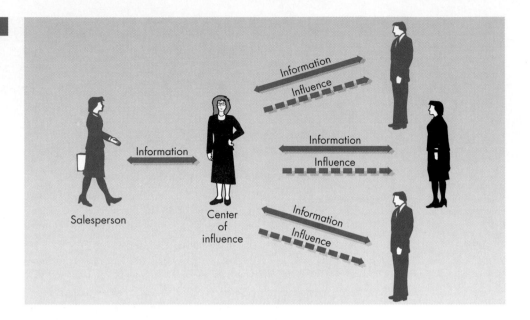

Networking

Networking is the utilization of personal relationships by connected and cooperating individuals for the purpose of achieving goals. In selling, networking simply means establishing connections (i.e., networks) to other people and then using those networks to generate leads, gather information, generate sales, and so on. Note that networking can, and often does, include centers of influence and satisfied customers.

Networking is crucial in many selling situations. For example, trying to sell in China without successful networking (called *guanxi* in China) would be disastrous.[9] Almost everyone could benefit by networking more actively.

Successful networkers offer a number of practical suggestions.[10] First, you must make a special effort to move outside your own "comfort zone" when in a social setting. Learn to mingle with people you don't already know. One expert calls this acting like a host instead of like a guest. Second, spend most of your initial conversation with a new contact talking about his or her business, not yours, and don't forget to learn about the person's nonbusiness interests. Third, follow up with your new contact on a regular basis with cards, notes of congratulations about awards or promotions, gifts, and articles and information that might help her or him. Whenever you receive a lead from your contact, send a handwritten, personal note thanking the person for the information, regardless of whether the lead buys from you. Whenever possible, send your new contact lead information as well.

Promotional Activities

Most companies elicit a steady supply of sales leads from advertising, catalogs, publicity, direct mail, trade shows, and seminars. Successful salespeople develop an effective system for utilizing and managing such leads.[11]

Inquiries

Firms have developed sophisticated systems to generate inquiries from leads. For example, Hewlett-Packard (HP) sends out direct mail to potential prospects for its color copiers.[12] The firm also places advertisements in trade publications, such as *Presentations*. A reader of the ad can request additional information by using the 800 number in the ad or by using the reader service card at the back of the magazine.

HP also participates in postcard packs. A **postcard pack** is a group of postcards (usually between 15 and 50 different cards) that provide information from a number of firms. Each firm has one card, usually describing one product or service. One side of HP's postcard contains information about a specific product or service (e.g., the HP CopyJet). The other side, which is prestamped, carries HP's address. A company interested in learning more about HP's product simply fills in its name and address and drops the card in the mail.

Anyone who inquires about HP's products receives a cover letter, information about the advertised product, and a follow-up inquiry card. A copy of the inquiry goes to the appropriate salesperson. Based on knowledge of the territory, the salesperson decides whether a personal follow-up is appropriate. If the inquirer returns the second inquiry card (frequently called a **bounceback card**), HP again notifies the salesperson. Then the salesperson can follow up on the lead with a visit or a phone call.

A growing trend is to tie the marketing promotion to an 800 number and the inquirer's fax machine. The prospect calls the 800 number, talks to a salesperson (or a voice-activated system, such as voice mail), and is then asked to supply his or her fax number. The requested information is sent within seconds, often while the salesperson is still on the phone with the prospect.[13]

A rapidly growing method of generating inquiries is through the use of expanding computer networks on the Internet, including MCI Mail, CompuServe, America Online, AT&T WorldNet Services, Microsoft Network, and so forth. Successful salespeople are using aspects of these networks such as the World Wide Web, e-mail, listservers, bulletin boards, forums, roundtables, and talk groups to connect to individuals and companies that may be interested in their products or services. For example, Joe Davis receives and answers about 100 e-mail messages a day in connection with his consulting business.[14] New technologies, which are unfolding at a dizzying pace, allow a selling firm to provide information to prospects using a variety of methods, including audio, videos (e.g., showing product demonstrations or plant tours), and text (e.g., letters of reference, product specifications, specials, lists of contacts).

Shows

Many companies display or demonstrate their products at trade shows, conventions, and fairs. They have sales representatives present to demonstrate their products to inquiring visitors, many of whom salespeople have not called on before.

Often the primary function of salespeople at shows is to qualify leads for future follow-up. Typically having only 5 to 10 minutes with a prospect, they need to get down to business and qualify the visitor quickly.[15] At other trade shows (e.g., furniture shows), salespeople actually sell and therefore generally spend more time with the buyer. Chapter Fifteen provides more information on how to close sales at shows.

Successful salespeople practice adaptive selling when interacting with prospects who stop by their booths.[16] Thus, instead of mechanically asking, "Are you enjoying the show?" or "Can I help you with something today?", sharp salespeople try to discover if the lead has a need or a want that they can meet. The seller then provides the lead with helpful information and gathers information that will be used later in further qualifying the lead and preparing for a sales call.

Seminars

Today, many firms use seminars to generate leads and provide information to prospective customers. For example, a local pharmaceutical representative for

©Oscar and Associates, Inc.   Courtesy In Focus Systems

Trade shows and seminars are two effective activities that help salespeople discover and qualify leads.

Bristol-Myers Squibb will set up a seminar for 8 to 10 oncologists, and invite a nationally known research oncologist to give a presentation to this group. The research specialist usually discusses some new technique or treatment being developed. During or after the presentation, the pharmaceutical representative for Bristol-Myers Squibb will describe how Squibb's drug Taxol® will help in the prevention of heart disease. Selling Scenario 7.1 explains how an industrial marketer successfully uses seminars to generate prospects.[17]

Lists and Directories

Individual sales representatives can develop prospect lists from such sources as public records, telephone directories, chamber of commerce directories, newspapers, club membership lists, and professional or trade membership lists. Secondary sources of information from public libraries also can be useful. For example, industrial trade directories are available for all states (see Exhibit 7.6 on page 198). Exhibit 7.7, page 199, lists some particularly useful secondary sources.

Salespeople can purchase a number of prospecting directories and lead-generating publications. In fact, it has been estimated that "there are no fewer than *four* lists available of virtually every business phone number in America."[18] You can purchase, by geographical area, mailing lists for all gerontologists (specialists in geriatrics), Lions Clubs, T-shirt retailers, yacht owners, antique dealers, Catholic high schools, motel supply houses, nudists, multimillionaires, pump wholesalers, and thousands of other classifications. Many of these directories now come on computer disks and CD-ROMs for easy access.

Salespeople should keep in mind that purchased lists can have several drawbacks. The lists may not be current. They may contain some inaccurate information regardless of the guarantee of accuracy. People who are on lists may be targeted by many, many firms and thus be less open to hearing from another salesperson. Finally, because lists are easy to obtain and use, some salespeople tend to rely on them exclusively when other methods of prospecting might result in better leads.

Using Seminars as a Selling Tool

Andrew Corporation, an Orland Park, Illinois, manufacturer of electronic communication equipment, may be one of the most savvy practitioners of business-to-business seminars, according to Allen J. Konopacki, a noted seminar consultant. Before it launched its first seminar series in early 1988, the company carefully orchestrated and pretested every facet of the program.

To target the right crowd, the company relied mainly on its own database, consisting largely of inquiries. Experts in the seminar field regard this core group as the most fruitful source of new business. For this year's series, Andrew Corporation also rented three trade magazine mailing lists and matched them with its own list to come up with a final registry of 43,000 names. The company likes to mix current customers with new prospects in a 1:2 ratio, figuring that satisfied clients not only may buy more but may also pass along word-of-mouth testimony about the company's products.

To reach its audience, the sales and marketing department prepared and sent out a four-page invitation to its free, daylong seminar. It detailed the topics to be covered, suggested who should attend, and asked for two names to be listed on a reply card or by way of an 800 number.

During the lunch break, sitting at each lunch table of 10 participants is a sales, marketing, or telemarketing rep, who acts as a facilitator and sounding board. The reps' job, apart from presenting a company face to the group, is to gather reactions to the morning sessions, provide the names of contacts at Andrew Corporation (if asked), and request each attendee to fill out a one-page evaluation form.

The questionnaire, which takes about 10 minutes to complete, is the company's key vehicle for feedback. It asks such relevant questions as each person's reason for attending, his or her upcoming product requirements, and the status of any project, including installation date, value of total project, budgeting phase, and the name of the key decision maker. "We never try to close a sale at our seminars," says one manager. "That comes later, after we evaluate the responses to the questionnaires."

A preliminary review starts right after lunch. The sales team separates the responses into three categories: (1) qualified leads—companies with projects and budgets approved and ready for implementation in less than one year; (2) companies with plans for a project and perhaps a tentative installation date; and (3) those that have no set plans but may be seeking information on the market and available products. The evaluations then travel to corporate headquarters, where the sales manger takes immediate action on those in the top-priority category.

Source: Adapted from Tom Murray, "Seminar Selling," *Sales & Marketing Management,* September 1990, pp. 54–58. Used by permission.

Most lists are simply names and telephone numbers. However, prospecting systems can be much more elaborate. For example, construction firms in some large cities can, for a fee, have access to computerized databases of planned construction projects that meet the user's criteria (type of work to be performed, amount budgeted for the project, method of payment, etc.). Such lists obviously include much more than just names and phone numbers of leads.

In international selling situations, procuring lists can be much more difficult. One of the biggest problems in selling in Mexico under NAFTA is that mailing lists and databases simply do not exist.[19] Nor is this phenomenon unique to Mexico; many firms dealing in international selling environments face similar problems.[20]

Canvassing

Before learning about other prospecting methods, college students often assume salespeople spend most of their time making cold calls. In using the **cold canvass method,** or **cold calls** (by *call* we mean a personal visit, not a telemarketing call), a

Source: Manufacturers' News. Inc.

sales representative tries to generate leads for new business by calling on totally unfamiliar organizations. Historically, this method was used extensively. However, cold canvassing can waste a salesperson's time, since many companies have neither a need for the product nor the ability to pay for it. This fact stresses the importance of qualifying the lead quickly in a cold call so as not to waste time. Also, today cold canvassing is considered rude by many purchasing agents and other professionals.

In a survey, salespeople rated making cold calls as the part of the job they liked least.[21] Thus, as mentioned earlier, most firms now encourage their salespeople to qualify leads instead of relying on the cold call. In fact, American Express Financial Advisors (Amex) banned cold calling for its 8,000 salespeople nationwide in late 1995.[22] This has forced the reps to use other methods, such as networking and referrals.

Some companies use a selective type of cold canvass they refer to as a *blitz*. In a **blitz,** a large group of salespeople attempt to make calls on all of the prospective businesses in a given geographical territory on a specified day. For example, an office

EXHIBIT 7.7

Partial List of Secondary Sources of Lead Information

Middle Market Directory (Dun & Bradstreet). Lists 14,000 firms worth between $500, 000 and $1 million.

Million Dollar Directory (Dun & Bradstreet). Lists names, addresses, and business lines of firms worth more than $1 million.

Thomas Register of American Manufacturers (Thomas). Annual that lists manufacturers by product classifications, company profits, and specific product information.

Encyclopedia of Associations (Gale). Lists 21,500 national associations, more than 4,000 international organizations, and more than 50,000 regional, state, and local organizations.

Standard & Poor's Register of Corporations, Directors, and Executives (Standard & Poor's). Annual publication listing names, titles, and addresses for over 50,000 firms.

Directory of Corporate Affiliations (Macmillan Directory Division). Lists 4,000 U.S. firms as well as their more than 40,000 divisions, subsidiaries, and so on.

Moody's Industrial Directory (Moody's). Annual that lists names, type of business, and a brief financial statement for over 10,000 publicly held corporations.

U.S. Industrial Directory (Time). Annual that lists sales, employees, and financial statistics for the 500 largest industrial firms and 50 largest diversified service firms.

Trade Shows and Professional Exhibits Directory (Gale). Lists more than 3,200 trade shows, including location, timing, attendance expected, and so on.

World Scope: Industrial Company Profiles (Wright Investor's Service). Extensive coverage of 5,000 companies from 25 countries within 27 major industry groupings.

National Trade and Professional Associations (Columbia Books). Lists over 6,200 trade and professional associations, along with pertinent information about each.

The International Corporate 1000 (Graham & Trotman). Profiles of the 1,000 largest companies in the world—650 from Europe, South America, the Middle East, and the Pacific Basin and 350 from the United States and Canada.

Dun's Direct Access (Dun & Bradstreet). Information on 9 million U.S. companies that can be accessed by dialing directly from a PC.

Business Lists-On-Disc (American Business Information). Complete database on 9.2 million U.S. businesses on CD-ROM.

Hoover's Handbook of American Business (The Reference Press). Profiles of 500 major U.S. companies available in hard copy or CD-ROM.

TrackAmerica. A database management company that offers information on 10 million U.S. businesses and 90 million consumers available online from a PC.

machine firm may target a specific four-block area in the city of Detroit, bring in all of the salespeople from the surrounding areas, and then have them go out and, in a period of one day, call on every business located in that four-block area. The purpose is to generate leads for the local sales representative as well as build camaraderie and a sense of unity among the salespeople.

Thinking it Through

Assume your sales manager instructs you to make five cold canvass calls a day, even though you simply do not have the time. Also, for the service you are selling, this method has proven to be a poor technique. When you question your manager, he says, "It worked for me. It'll work for you, too!" What would you say in response? If he refused to change his mind what would you do?

Spotters

Some salespeople use **spotters,** also called **bird dogs.** These individuals will, for a fee, provide leads for the salesperson. The sales rep sometimes pays the fee simply for the name of the lead, but more often pays only if the lead ends up buying the product or service. Spotters are usually in a position to find out when someone is ready to make a purchase decision. For example, a janitorial service firm employee who notices that the heating system for a client is antiquated and hears people complaining about it can turn this information over to a heating contractor.[23]

A more recent development is the use of outside paid consultants to locate and qualify leads. This happens more often when small firms attempt to secure business with very large organizations. For example, Synesis Corporation, a small firm specializing in computerized training, used the services of a consultant to identify and develop a lead. The result of one lead was a major contract with AT&T.[24]

Telemarketing

Increasingly, firms are relying on telemarketing to perform many functions sales representatives used to perform. *Telemarketing* is a systematic and continuous program of communicating with customers and prospects via telephone and/or other person-to-person electronic media. Telemarketing is not limited to consumer sales; as you will see, all of the examples used in this section involve business-to-business companies. Telemarketing is now used to sell everything from 25-cent supplies to $10 million airplanes.

In **outbound telemarketing,** telephones are used to generate and then qualify leads. **Inbound telemarketing** uses a telephone number (usually an 800 number) that leads and/or customers can call for additional information. For example, Motorola Corporation's Land Mobile Products Sector, which sells mobile communication systems to such diverse entities as contractors, hotels, and police stations, uses outbound telemarketing to generate and then qualify leads for its sales force. Qualified leads are turned over to field sales representatives if the order is large enough to warrant an outside sales rep. If the prospect needs a smaller system, a separate telemarketing salesperson will handle the account. Motorola also uses inbound telemarketing by providing an 800 number for people who want more information about a product or service Motorola offers. Because of this excellent telemarketing organization, Motorola's field reps have more time to spend with qualified prospects and more time to develop long-term customer relations.

Limitations of Telephone Prospecting

While a wonderful tool that can enhance productivity for many salespeople, the telephone has some limitations. First, customers may find telephone calls an annoying inconvenience. In fact, new rules adopted by the Federal Trade Commission (FTC) require significant disclosures before a telemarketer can even begin selling to consumers (although this rule does not apply specifically in business-to-business selling, salespeople need to be aware of its provisions).[25] Unexpected calls may interrupt customers involved in meetings or concentrating on their work. When telephoning customers—in fact, at all times—salespeople need to respect the customers' privacy and not abuse the privilege.

Second, telephones limit communications to verbal messages. For this reason, the telephone may be a poor choice when salespeople need to show the product to determine whether someone is a prospect. Also, salespeople cannot read customers' nonverbal cues in a telephone conversation and thus may miss or misunderstand a customer's message.

Third, attracting and maintaining the customer's attention and interest is harder over the telephone. During face-to-face encounters, people are generally more polite and will concentrate on the person with whom they are talking. But customers talking on the telephone can engage in other activities; they may even continue to work or read a report or magazine.

Fourth, outbound telemarketers sometimes call firms without knowing anything about them. This can lead to embarrassing mistakes, as Beth Cocchiarella found when she made a telemarketing call to the competition. "I was mortified," she said.[26] Can you imagine asking your competitor if they would like to see your new product? Since then her firm has invested in a system that provides the telemarketer with more information about the company he or she is calling, hopefully avoiding similar embarrassing situations.

Finally, saying *no* is much easier over the phone than in person. Because they cannot see the salesperson, customers may even be rude during telephone conversations. To end a phone conversation by hanging up is easy; to walk away from a face-to-face conversation with a salesperson is harder.

Tie-in with Other Tools

Firms are learning to use direct mail tied to inbound and outbound telemarketing to reach potential prospects effectively. For example, one firm offers a catalog to interested parties. After receiving a request, the firm sends out a catalog and has a salesperson follow up with a phone call about a week after the mailing. This phone call allows the salesperson to gauge the strength of the lead as a prospect.[27]

Prospecting via Sales Letters

Prospecting sales letters should be integrated into an overall prospecting plan. For example, Xerox salespeople who handle smaller businesses send prospecting sales letters every day. They follow up three days later with a telephone prospecting call and ask for an appointment for a personal visit. The telephone call begins with a question about the letter.

Like the telephone, sales letters have limitations. Once the message is sent, it cannot be modified to fit the prospect's style. The sender also has no chance to alter the message on the basis of feedback. Blanket mailings, then, can seem impersonal.

Because people in business receive so much mail, sales letters should be written with care.[28] Think about the amount of junk mail you receive and how much you throw away without a second glance. Sales letters must stand out to be successful.

One way to make sales letters stand out is to include a promotional item with the mailer. First National Bank of Shreveport, Louisiana, targeted certified public accountants for one mailer. The bank timed the mailers to arrive on April 16, the day after the federal income tax filing deadline. Included in each mailer was a small bottle of wine, a glass, and cheese and crackers—a party kit designed to celebrate the end of tax time. The bank followed up with telephone calls two days later and ultimately gained 21 percent of the CPAs as new customers.

The salesperson must first consider the objective of the letter and the audience. What action does the salesperson desire from the reader? Why would the reader want to undertake that action? Why would the reader not want to undertake the action? These questions help guide the salesperson in writing the letter.

Gain Attention

The opening paragraph must grab the reader's attention, just as a salesperson's approach must get a prospect's attention in a cold call. Two approaches that can work well in sales letters are the benefit opener and the curiosity opener. Exhibit 7.8

EXHIBIT 7.8

Sales Letter Approaches

A. Curiosity Opener

August 29, 1997

Barbara Boeding, Editor
The American Salesman
424 N. Third St.
Burlington, IA 52601

Dear Ms. Boeding:

On the first day a new product was available for order taking, one sales rep had seven customers order for a total in sales of $450,000. Even more amazing, he only made one sales call on one prospect! How did he do it? By identifying and managing a "buying community."

B. Benefit Opener

September 29, 1997

Ms. Paulette S. Withers, Editor
Sales Manager's Bulletin
Bureau of Business Practice
24 Rope Ferry Rd.
Waterford, CT 06386

Dear Ms. Withers:

Field sales managers everywhere complain about a lack of support from their own organization. To get that support, though, they require better skills in working with other functional areas, such as manufacturing and administration. The proposed article, "Internal Marketing," will show your readers how to use their sales skills to develop stronger relationships with people in their own organization.

contains examples of both. They come from letters actually used to sell articles to magazines. Each opening gives the readers a reason to continue reading, drawing them into the rest of the letter. Another way to gain attention is to have a loyal client whom the prospect respects write the introduction (or even the entire letter) for the salesperson.[29]

Present Benefits

The next paragraph or two, the body of the letter, will reflect the answers to the questions of why the reader would and would not want to take the desired action. Benefits of taking the action should be presented clearly, without jargon, and briefly. The best-presented benefits are tailored to the specific individual, especially when the salesperson can refer to a recent conversation with the reader. A reference such as the following example can truly personalize the letter:[30]

As you said during my phone call to set up this appointment, Ms. Powers, the most important factor is speed. The RX-4000 is the fastest lift available in its class, meaning that your dock personnel can handle the increases you are forecasting.

If the salesperson and the buyer do not know each other, part of the body of the letter should be used to increase credibility. References to satisfied customers, market research data, and other independent sources can be used to improve credibility. For example,

> *Inventory Management and Control magazine rated the RX-4000 as not only the fastest but also the most trouble-free lift on the market.*

Seek Action

The final paragraph should seek commitment to the desired course of action. Whatever the action desired, the letter must specifically ask that it take place. The writer should leave no doubt in the prospect's mind as to what he or she is supposed to do. Exhibit 7.9 details how the ending paragraph should tell the reader what to do, make it sound easy, and why it should be done now, and end with a positive picture.

A postscript (PS) can also be effective. Postscripts stand out because of their location and should be used to make an important selling point. Alternatively, they can be used to emphasize the requested action, such as pointing out a deadline.

Thinking *it* Through	What do you hate most of all about junk mail? Can you see any patterns in the way junk mailings present their sales messages? Could a field salesperson adapt some of their ideas to an industrial or trade selling situation?

Other Sources of Leads	Many salespeople find leads through personal observation. For example, by reading trade journals carefully, salespeople can learn the names of the most important leaders (and hence decision makers) in the industry.[31] Sellers also read general business

EXHIBIT 7.9 **Action Close (Hook)**	The action close in the letter must do four things: 1. Tell the reader what to do: **Respond.** Avoid *if* (if you'd like to try . . .") and *why not* ("Why not send in a check?"). They lack positive emphasis and encourage your reader to say *no*. 2. Make the action sound easy. Tell them to fill in the information on the reply card, sign the card (for credit sales), put the card and check (if payment is to accompany the order) in the envelope, and mail the envelope. If you provide an envelope and pay postage, stress those facts. 3. Offer a reason for acting promptly. Reasons for acting promptly are easy to identify when a product is seasonal or there is a genuine limit on the offer—time limit, scheduled price rise, limited supply, etc. Sometimes you may be able to offer a premium or a discount if the reader acts quickly. When these conditions do not exist, remind readers that the sooner they get the product, the sooner they can benefit from it; the sooner they contribute funds, the sooner their dollars can go to work to solve the problem. 4. End with a positive picture. Depict the reader enjoying the product (in a sales letter) or the reader's money working to solve the problem (in a fund-raising letter). The last sentence should never be a selfish request for money. The action close can also remind readers of the central selling point, stress the guarantee, and mention when the customer will get the product.

Source: Kitty Locker. *Business and Administrative Communication* (Burr Ridge, IL: Richard D. Irwin, 1989), p. 306.

Page from the
Clark Reports

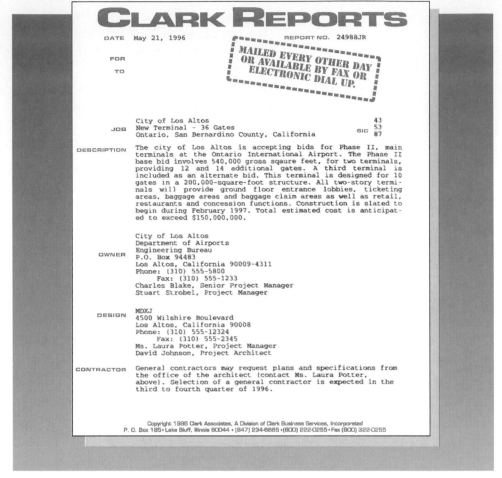

Source: ©1996 Clark Associates, a Division of Clark Business Services, Incorporated

publications (such as *Business Week* and *The Wall Street Journal*) and the local newspapers and just keep their eyes open when they drive through their territories. Also, a number of fee-based publications provide the same current information (Exhibit 7.10 gives an example for the publication *Clark Reports*). The information they provide allows the salesperson to spend more time actually selling.

Nonsales employees within the salesperson's firm can also provide leads. Some companies strongly encourage this practice. For example, Computer Specialists Inc., a computer service firm, pays its nonsales employees a bonus of up to $1,000 for any names of prospective customers they pass along. In one year, the program resulted in 75 leads and nine new accounts.[32]

Government agencies can supply lead information. For example, the Commerce Department has identified some of the hottest prospects in the new Economic Union searching for aircraft and aircraft parts, construction materials, computers and home electronics, and so forth.[33]

Leads can be found in many other places. Salespeople for noncompeting but related products can often provide leads, as can members of trade associations. Good friends can also provide leads. Mark McCormack offers this advice when dealing with friends: Maintain a posture that you would rather have your friends as friends than as customers.[34] Of course, one of the best ways to learn about where new busi-

Courtesy Hunt Wesson, Inc.

ness opportunities may present themselves is to keep up with regional, national, and world trends from such sources as *American Demographics* and *World Watch* magazines and industry surveys (*Manufacturing USA, Service USA, Standard & Poor's Industry Surveys, U.S. Industrial Outlook,* etc.).

GETTING THE MOST OUT OF PROSPECTING

After salespeople separate leads from prospects, they carefully analyze the relative value of each prospect. This grading of prospects, or establishing a priority list, results in increased sales and the most efficient use of time and energy.

Learn to Effectively Qualify and Evaluate Prospects

Many companies conduct extensive research to determine what distinguishes a good prospect. For example, Metier Management Systems, a division of Lockheed Corporation, identified 17 key criteria for assessing leads. In a monthly sales prospect review meeting (which often lasted four to six hours per salesperson), salespeople had to demonstrate that their leads were in fact qualified prospects.[35]

Keep Good Records

The information and the type of prospect file needed vary by type of business. Many industrial salespeople keep a file card for each customer and each prospect. They may also complete a formal call report after each meeting.

Many salespeople now use PC laptop–based software packages to keep track of prospects. Salespeople at CONAM Inspection (a firm that sells lab services to industrial firms, water plants, and power plants) use the ACT package. A sample screen from such a package appears in Exhibit 7.11. Notice that the salesperson can store and quickly retrieve all sorts of information, including call objectives, notes about prior calls, "to-do" information, and reminders. A number of sources are available to help salespeople learn about the latest software programs developed to keep good track of prospects and leads.[36]

Salespeople are becoming increasingly technologically advanced. Their use of software and hardware to track prospects is often tied into a large, complete system for managing their time and territories (Chapter Sixteen will discuss this issue more fully). For example, Jeffrey Epstein tracks his prospects with a software package

Source: Used by permission of Conductor Software, Inc.

called GoldMine by GoldMine Software Corporation.[37] His leads come on CD-ROMs from American Business Information, Inc. (including information on 10 million U.S. companies), which are tied into his system. The GoldMine software also documents the results of his phone calls and personal visits. He stays connected to his customers and leads via a digital pager from Skytel Corporation. All phone and e-mail messages are instantly routed into Epstein's database.

Set Quotas

Most effective prospecting plans include weekly and monthly quotas for obtaining new prospects. In the long run, prospecting goals can be as important as sales goals, and quotas remind the salesperson to keep a constant lookout for new names to fill the prospect pipeline.

Evaluate Results

Salespeople need to evaluate the profitability of any sales resulting from various lead-generating activities instead of just counting the number of names a particular method yields.[38] They should study the methods used by the most successful salespeople in their firm, because salespeople differ greatly in their ability to judge the strength of leads.[39]

Analysis may show that the present system does not produce enough prospects or the right kinds of prospects. Sales reps may, for example, depend entirely on referred names from company advertising or from the service department. If these two sources do not supply enough names to produce the sales volume desired, other prospecting methods should be considered.

A salesperson should not hesitate to scrap time-honored prospecting systems even if they have been used for years in the firm or industry or even used by the salesperson's own sales manager. One of the key tenets of the learning organization (see Chapter One) is to actively "unlearn" traditional but detrimental practices.[40] If a prospecting method that used to be excellent is no longer producing solid, profitable leads, it should be discarded for a more appropriate method.

SELLING SCENARIO 7.2

Prospect Even When Your Competitors Stop

John Paul Jones, senior territory manager for Monsanto, describes an unusual prospecting circumstance that led to a major sale.

"It was 1967 and I had been in sales for about three years. I was servicing western New York State. I was driving down the road in the middle of a terrible snowstorm on my way to a prospective client. I'm a native Floridian, so I was not prepared for that climate, and I was almost forced off the road. In desperation, I pulled into the parking lot of the Alliance Tool & Die Company to wait out the storm. While I was sitting there, I decided to go inside and see what local business conditions were like. I wasn't trying so much to make a sale as to maybe pick up a few leads.

"I went in and introduced myself to the manager and told him I'd been in Rochester six months and that the weather here stinks. I asked him if he needed a lot of plastic materials. He said no, but asked me what product I was pushing. I told him nylon and he told me that the chemical products division office of General Motors across the street was looking for nylon for about 18 different applications. He gave me the name of a person to speak to.

"To get there, I had to walk because of the weather. It was about 4 PM, and the person's receptionist told me he had a lot of appointments that day, but many of them canceled because of the snow, and he might see me. He did.

"Before I even took a seat, he asked me if we had the capacity to make 2 to 3 million pounds of nylon a year. Without blinking an eye, I said yes, even though I wasn't sure. He then told me that GM had to develop a special grade of the material and that we were just about six months behind our competitors. So I had to go back to our R&D people while our competitors were making inroads.

"Six months later, one of them pulled out of the competition because they didn't have the capability to take this on for the long term, and in the next 12 to 14 months another also dropped out.

"It took us a year to develop the product in the lab. But with two rivals dropping out, we eventually became the second source of supply for this material (DuPont became the first), which was used for the automobile emission control devices that were mandated by the Environmental Protection Agency.

"So a situation that I was forced into by a snowstorm turned out to be one of Monsanto's major products in the late 60s and early 70s."

Source: Reprinted from "Strange Tales of Sales," *Sales & Marketing Management*, June 3, 1985, p. 46. Used by permission.

Overcome Reluctance to Prospecting

People often stereotype salespeople as bold, adventurous, and somewhat abrasive. This view that salespeople are fearless is more fiction than fact. Salespeople often struggle with a reluctance to prospect that persists no matter how well they have been trained and how much they believe in the products they sell. Many people are uncomfortable when they initially contact other people, but for salespeople reluctance to call can be a career-threatening condition.

Research shows a number of reasons for reluctance to call.[41] Reasons include worrying about worst-case scenarios, spending too much time preparing, being overly concerned with looking successful, fear of making group presentations, guilt at having a career in selling, fear of appearing too pushy, feeling intimidated by people with prestige or power, fear of losing friends or family approval, fear of using the phone for prospecting, and having a compulsive need to argue, make excuses, or blame others.

Reluctance to call can and must be overcome to sell successfully. Several activities can help. For example, listen to the excuses other salespeople give to justify their call-reluctant behavior and identify the excuses you use to avoid making calls. Then evaluate the validity of those excuses. Also, recount your own successes, or those of others, that resulted from prospecting effectively. Selling Scenario 7.2 tells how a prospecting situation turned out to be extremely profitable.

Finally, it may help to know that discipline and persistence pay off. Consider these facts: Only 50 percent of all sales leads are ever followed up by the selling firm; this means that a full 50 percent are never followed up at all! For business advertising inquiries specifically, only 15 percent ever result in a salesperson's call.[42] This doesn't make sense, because many leads do end up buying from someone. One estimate is that 45 percent of all leads actually end up buying.[43]

SUMMARY

Locating prospective customers is the first step in the sales process. New prospects are needed to replace old customers lost for a variety of reasons and to replace lost contacts in existing customers due to plant relocations, turnover, mergers, downsizing, and other factors.

Not all sales leads qualify as good prospects. A qualified prospect has a need that can be satisfied by the salesperson's product, has the ability and authority to buy the product, can be approached by the salesperson, and is eligible to buy.

Many methods can be used to locate prospects. The best source is a satisfied customer. Salespeople sometimes obtain leads through their customers by using the endless-chain and center-of-influence methods. Companies provide leads to salespeople through promotional activities such as advertising, inquiries, telemarketing, trade shows, and seminars. Salespeople can also use networking, lists and directories, cold canvassing (including blitzes), spotters, and other helpful contacts.

Effective prospecting requires development of a plan. The plan hinges on keeping good records, setting quotas, evaluating the results of the prospecting effort, experimenting with new methods, following through, and overcoming reluctance to prospect.

KEY TERMS

bird dog 199
blitz 198
bounceback card 195
buying community 194
center-of-influence method 192
cold call 197
cold canvass method 197
endless-chain method 192
exclusive sales territories 190
house accounts 190
inbound telemarketing 200

lead 186
networking 194
outbound telemarketing 200
postcard pack 194
prospect 187
prospecting 186
qualifying a lead 187
referred lead 192
selling deeper 192
spotter 199
systems integrator 189

QUESTIONS AND PROBLEMS

1. If you were a salesperson for the following companies, how would you develop a prospect list?
   a. A manufacturer of relatively small-size farm equipment.
   b. A travel agency specializing in Austrian adventures.
   c. A manufacturer of an antitheft alarm device for bicycles.
2. How would you develop a prospect list under the following situations?
   a. You belong to a social organization on campus that needs to recruit new members.
   b. You are a marketing student about to graduate from college, and you want to find a full-time sales position.

c. You are a veteran salesperson for Dell computers and are being transferred to Dell's new office in Leverkusen, Germany.

3. What information do you need to qualify the leads generated in each part of question 2?

4. What information should a salesperson collect to qualify leads for the following?

    a. A commercial printer that specializes in printing elaborate four-color books.

    b. Sponsorship of the local community theater.

    c. Hospital gowns.

5. "Salespeople should focus their energy on leads that are small firms, firms that may not yet qualify as prospects for our larger competitors. We'll let our competitors go after the larger prospects." Comment on this statement.

6. Assume you are starting a career as a stockbroker. Develop a system for rating prospects. The system should contain several important factors for qualifying prospects and scales with which to rate the prospects on these factors. Use the system to rate five of your friends.

7. In industrial sales situations, several people influence the purchase decision. Suppose you have just completed an interview with an industrial prospect and believe you should contact other people in the company. How will you raise the subject with the prospect?

8. Salespeople are often reluctant to prospect for new customers. What advice would you give to a new salesperson to help him or her overcome reluctance to prospecting?

9. What are some ways you can engage in networking now to increase your odds of landing a good job after you graduate?

EXPLORING THE NET

• Familiarize yourself with the characteristics of a good prospect described in this chapter. Then, hop on the Web and look at home pages for firms that solicit inquiries from prospective buyers. Some possible hits include:

    http://www.wallace.com

    http://www.symantec.com

    http://www.hilton.com

    http://www.fortune-group.com

    http://www.bnet.att.com

    http://www.portercase.com

    http://www.westinghouse.com

    http://www.fedex.com

    http://www.perrent.com

    1. To what extent does the home page request information to ascertain whether or not the respondent is a good prospect? In other words, if you contacted one of these sites, would they know if you have the ability to pay, the authority to buy, a need that they can satisfy, and so on?

    2. In general, how effective is the home page in generating your interest as a potential prospect? What things could you change to make it more effective?

• One way to prospect is to engage in cold calls using the cold canvass method. Some people use the Internet's listservers or talk groups to try to discover prospects. This is usually done indirectly by subscribing to the group and then posting a message that includes some information about the seller's product and how he or she can be contacted.

Assume you are a salesperson in one of the three situations in question 1 in the Questions and Problems section.

1. Can you identify talk groups or listservers that would reach a sizable group of leads?

2. Write a message that you could post to generate interest in your product or service. Note: You are not being asked to actually subscribe and post the message.

CASE PROBLEMS

CASE 7.1 Makrolon® Returnable Milk Bottles*

Bayer is a diversified, international chemical and pharmaceutical company with world headquarters in Germany. Bayer offers customers a wide range of products and services from engineering materials to graphic systems.

The firm has developed a new product consisting of Bayer's Makrolon polycarbonate resin. Recently the Meierei-Zentrale dairy in Berlin decided to replace its conventional glass bottles with the new Makrolon ones. Other dairies in Austria and Switzerland have also decided to switch to this new material. The new plastic bottles have also been increasing in usage in the Netherlands.

Bottles made from the new resin have a number of attractive features. They are five times lighter than glass, are highly resistant to breaking, and take up 30 percent less space in crates and on shelves than conventional round bottles. The lighter weight and improved stowage density also benefit the environment by reducing fuel consumption during transportation. The new plastic bottles are good for up to 100 return trips. Even when they are no longer able to be reused, the recycled polycarbonate can be used as a raw material to produce computer housings and automotive components.

Tests show that Makrolon is a superior material for the packaging of both dairy products and other foodstuffs. It is tasteless and can easily be colored to protect the vitamins in foods and drinks.

Consumers have readily accepted the new bottles. A large study conducted in Berlin found that most consumers favored the lightweight, break-resistant, returnable bottles.

Bayer believes the timing is right to introduce the bottles and technology to Spain. You have been assigned to prospect for new accounts in that country.

*Information for this case was derived from the 1995 Bayer annual report.

Questions

1. What prospecting methods would you use?
2. How will you qualify the leads you find? What qualifying factors will be most important?
3. How will you organize your prospecting activities? How will you keep good records?

CASE 7.2 Identifying Actual Leads

This exercise is designed to improve your skill at identifying actual leads. Consider the following list of products and services:

A new herbicide for soybeans.

Transport services (you are a trucking company) for transporting milk.

A software package for accountants that has been on the market two years.

A newly designed walking shoe.

For *each* product and service listed, answer the following questions.

Questions

1. Provide a list of company names and addresses for five leads. Make any assumptions necessary. You don't have to find out whether or not they already use the product or service. Explain where you got the list of names.

2. Briefly describe how you could qualify each lead (as to whether or not it is a prospect).

3. What other sources of leads could you use for each product and service listed? Which sources would probably be the best?

ADDITIONAL REFERENCES

Brock, Richard T. "How to Get Quality Sales from Qualified Leads." *Sales & Marketing Management*, August 1990, pp. 94–95.

Campanelli, Melissa. "On the Right Track." *Sales & Marketing Management*, August 1995, pp. 47–51.

Dubin, Burt. "Referral Magic!" *Managers Magazine*, April 1990, pp. 8–15.

Emerick, Tracy. "The Trouble with Leads." *Sales & Marketing Management*, December 1992, pp. 57–79.

Farber, Barry J., and Joyce Wycoff. "Relationships: Six Steps to Success," *Sales & Marketing Management*, April 1992, pp. 50–58.

Jolson, Marvin A., and Thomas R. Wotruba. "Prospecting: A New Look at This Old Challenge." *Journal of Personal Selling and Sales Management,* Fall 1992, pp. 59–66.

Messer, Carla, and James Alexander. "Classifying Your Customers." *Sales & Marketing Management*, July 1993, pp. 42–43.

Murray, Tom. "Seminar Selling." *Sales & Marketing Management*, September 1990, pp. 54–58.

"Prospecting Is Where the Gold Is." *Institutional Distribution*, May 15, 1990, p. 70.

Rosenfield, James R. "Generating Leads Scientifically." *Sales & Marketing Management*, December 1994, pp. 30–31.

Szymanski, David M., and Gilbert A. Churchill, Jr. "Client Evaluation Cues: A Comparison of Successful and Unsuccessful Salespeople." *Journal of Marketing Research*, May 1990, pp. 163–74.

Tanner, John F. "Tapping into Your Buyer's Community." *American Salesman*, April 1990, pp. 3–6.

Van Doren, Doris C., and Thomas A. Stickney. "How to Develop a Database for Sales Leads." *Industrial Marketing Management*, August 1990, pp. 201–8.

Wilson, Larry. *Stop Selling, Start Partnering* (Essex Junction, VT: Oliver Wright Publications, 1994).

Chapter Eight

Planning *the* Sales Call

Salespeople are vulnerable to the great temptation to call on a prospect or customer without planning what to say and how to say it. Depending on spur-of-the-moment thinking is easy. However, all salespeople benefit from planning their calls in advance. This chapter discusses the kind of precall information you

Some Questions Answered in this Chapter Are:

Why should salespeople plan their sales calls?

What precall information is needed about the individual prospect and the prospect's organization? How can this information be obtained?

What is involved in setting call objectives?

Should more than one objective be set for each call?

How can appointments be made effectively and efficiently?

will need to gather and suggests where you can gather it, how to plan the sales call, and how to make appointments.

PROFILE

After graduating with a BBA degree in 1992, Tracey Brill started selling for one of the largest firms in the grocery products industry. She felt lucky to get an offer from this firm because it seemed everyone wanted to work for them. After a few months, she found it wasn't the right job for her.

Now she is right where she wants to be, a senior pharmaceutical consultant for Smith Kline Beecham Pharmaceuticals. And awards and honors have followed Brill with every position she has held. She was recently named the top salesperson in her region and even won the Kytril Challenge award for the largest increase in market share in the region. At an upcoming awards meeting, she will receive three top awards. What's her secret?

"If I were asked what the key to my success is, I would have to say the way I plan," Brill says. I don't get nervous when I hear objections because I know how to handle them. I'm not afraid of any questions because I know I am an expert for each product I promote. I really feel I bring a valuable service to the offices I call on. I feel this way because of the way I prepare before my calls.

"I make sure I keep up to date on what is going on in each product market and the industry as a whole. I read journals, review my training materials, and know my competitors. I also know my customer's business. I ask questions to find out what is impacting his or her business. I want to know about new managed care changes that can affect my customer's business, so I joined a grassroots program to learn more.

"I also want to know about the physician's interests. As one doctor told me, 'I am an individual, a person, then there is my profession.' In other words, no matter how much I plan for a call, that day maybe he or she doesn't want to talk about business; instead maybe he or she wants to talk about stocks or boating. I am fortunate that I am able to call on my customers every two weeks or every month. If for some reason he or she would rather talk about stocks, it's okay, because I know that maybe this is a 'bad day.' The doctors appreciate when I respect their 'bad day.' This doesn't happen often, but it is good for a representative to recognize it. It has really helped me build rapport.

"I was given a new territory and started calling on some different specialties. I found that several physicians were really involved in the stock market. I began reading *The Wall Street Journal* and following some of the same stocks

> *"I make sure I know my objectives for each call and really plan questions in a way that a physician would not feel on guard."*

TRACEY BRILL
*Smith Kline Beecham
Pharmaceuticals*

that they did, and found I enjoyed it too. This really helped me to relate to their interests and the business sense many of these physicians had. I was able to communicate about a topic he or she was interested in. Then I was able to talk about a topic of my interest: my medications.

"I make sure I know my objectives for each call and really plan questions in a way that a physician would not feel on guard. Have you ever had someone ask you several questions and you didn't want to answer because you didn't know why they were asking? Well, I have. Ironically enough, I was asked several questions from a physician the first time I had met her. She was asking me who our product managers were, what their phone numbers were, if they bought computer programs, and what they were looking to do in the future. I didn't answer her questions because I didn't know her purpose and felt offended that she would ask me these questions without even knowing me. To me, that was a good example of how I would not want to plan a sales call. That is why planning objectives and questions in advance is beneficial. I then know the purpose of my visit, can explain it to the physician, and ask questions without it seeming like I am trying to find out some secret. Also, by setting objectives you have something set to accomplish. I do not get immediate sales data. I actually get my sales data three months later. For example, I get December data in March of next year. So setting objectives gives me an immediate sense of accomplishment.

"I have a one-month rotation schedule, but because schedules fluctuate and appointments tend to rule an itinerary, I am not always able to follow a routing in that way. Every month I print out my physician base listed in my computer and check off the physicians I have seen. I keep notes on each call in my computer and review this information before my next call so I remember what we discussed and what I needed to follow up on for the next call.

"To me planning includes routing, planning questions, planning what I would like to discuss on a call, and preparing all my materials I need for the day. However, planning is so much more than that. The most important thing to me is to know my business better than anyone else, and that includes my products, my competitors, the market, managed care, my customers' business, and my customers' interests."

Visit Our Website@
http://occ.com.sbpharm/

WHY PLAN THE SALES CALL?

Successful salespeople believe advance planning of the sales interview is essential to achieving success in selling. The salesperson should remember that the buyer's time is valuable. Without planning the sales call, a salesperson quite easily may cover material in which the buyer has no interest, try to obtain an order even though that is an unrealistic expectation for this sales call, or strike off into areas that veer from what the buyer actually needs to hear. The result is wasted time and an annoyed prospect. However, by having a clear plan for the call, the salesperson more likely will not only obtain commitment but also win the buyer's respect and confidence.

Salespeople should also remember the value of their own time. Proper planning helps them meet their call objectives efficiently as well as effectively. They then have more time to make additional calls, conduct research on the target customer or other customers, fill out company reports, and complete other necessary tasks. The result is better territory management. (See Chapter Sixteen for more discussion about time and territory management.)

Of course, planning must fit into the salesperson's goals for the account. Some accounts will have greater strategic importance and thus will require more planning. (See Chapter Sixteen for a discussion about classifying accounts and prospects.) Those accounts with which a firm is partnering will obviously need the most planning, whereas smaller accounts may warrant less planning. Also, salespeople must not make planning an end unto itself and a way to avoid actually making calls. Exhibit 8.1 provides a flow diagram that shows how the concepts in this chapter are related.

OBTAINING PRECALL INFORMATION

Often the difference between making and not making a sale depends on the amount of homework the salesperson does before making a call. The more information the salesperson has about the prospect, the higher the probability of meeting the prospect's needs and developing a long-term relationship. However, the salesperson must be

---

EXHIBIT 8.1

A Flow Diagram of the Planning Process

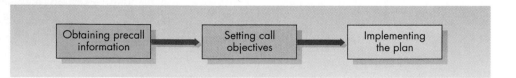

aware of the costs involved in collecting information. At some point, the time and effort put into collecting information become greater than the benefits obtained.

The following dialogue shows what can happen in a sales call made with inadequate precall information:

SALESPERSON Good morning, Mr. White. I'm Bob Thompson, the new sales rep for McNeil Clothing.

CUSTOMER My name is Wasits, not White.

SALESPERSON Oh! I'm sorry. I should have asked your secretary to spell your name when I called to make an appointment. I want to show you our new fall line. It is ideally suited for the growing teenage market.

CUSTOMER Most of our customers are middle-aged. I don't want to attract teenagers to my store. They make a lot of noise, and they bother the older customers.

SALESPERSON Well, we also have a line for the middle-aged market. Here's some photographs of the items in the line. [*Reaches into his pocket for a package of cigarettes and puts one in his mouth.*] Would you like a cigarette?

CUSTOMER I don't smoke, and smoking really bothers me. The smell gets into the clothing in our store. Please don't smoke.

By not obtaining precall information, this salesperson immediately encountered several embarrassing situations. With such a poor start, the salesperson is unlikely to attain his call objective.

Gathering information from individuals in the prospect's firm before making the call on the prospect is often a wise investment of time.

Courtesy ARA Services Inc.

Clearly a salesperson who has been calling regularly on a prospect or customer may have less need to collect a lot of additional information; records and notes from prior calls may be adequate to prepare for the sales call. The same holds true for a new salesperson if the previous one kept good records. But beware! In this fast-paced world of the late 1990s, things are changing every day. Don't assume your knowledge about the account is automatically up to date. Consider the following dialogue:

SALESPERSON [*walking up to the receptionist of one of his best customers*] Hello, Jim. I'm here to see Toby. I have some information I promised to share with her about our new manufacturing process. She was pretty excited about seeing it!

RECEPTIONIST [*looking tired*] Sorry, Jeff. Toby was transferred last week to our Michigan plant. Haven't you heard about our latest reorganization? Just went into effect two weeks ago. I'm still trying to figure it out. It seems that all of our engineering people are moving to the Michigan plant . . .

SALESPERSON [*looking confused and worried*] No, I hadn't heard! Well, who took Toby's job? He or she really needs to see this information.

RECEPTIONIST [*picking up the phone for an incoming call*] No one took her place. It's not going to be the same around here anymore.

Of course, before you make an initial call on a prospect, you will often expend considerable effort on collecting precall information about both the individual prospect and the prospect's company. Don't expect this information gathering to be quick, easy, or cheap. For example, Tom Carnes, owner of a printing firm in Las Vegas, wanted to increase his sales in the legal market. He learned that paralegals usually control the flow of paper in law offices and that a professional association of paralegals existed. He decided to meet with the leader of that organization for two hours twice a month for two or three months to learn about the legal market, paying her $500 for each meeting. The efforts in gaining precall information paid off with sales of $600,000 in the first year alone.[1]

It is important to learn and maintain current knowledge about both the prospect as an individual and his or her firm. The sections that follow examine each of these areas more closely.

The Prospect/Customer as an Individual

To obtain useful information about a prospect or a customer (we will refer to both as prospects for the sake of simplicity), salespeople should attempt to find answers to the following questions:

What is the prospect's name? How does he or she pronounce it?

What is the prospect's attitude toward salespeople in general and toward the salesperson's company?

What does the prospect view as important characteristics of the product or service? How does the prospect evaluate the salesperson's product and the competitor's product on these factors? (See the appendix to Chapter 4 for a review of the multi-attribute model.)

What are the prospect's job aspirations, attitudes toward risk, and level of self-confidence in decision making?

What are the prospect's reference groups (clubs, professional organizations, family, etc.), and what are the norms of each group?

What are the prospect's interests (hobbies, sports, reading, etc.), and what does the prospect not enjoy?

What are some aspects of the prospect's background (education, family status, successes, failures)?

What is the prospect's personality style (driver, amiable, analytical, expressive—see Chapter Six)?

What is the prospect's decision-making style[2] (entrepreneurial, planning, bureaucratic)?

To whom does the prospect report? Does the prospect need to justify the purchase decision to this person?

If this list seems long, consider the fact that Harvey Mackay, one of the leading business writers of our century, actually lists 66 questions (the "Mackay 66") that a seller should ask about a customer.[3] Most firms have developed their own unique lists of questions that salespeople need to consider to call on a prospect successfully.

The Prospect's/Customer's Organization

Information about the prospect's/customer's company (again, for simplicity, we will just refer to both as prospects) obviously helps the salesperson to better understand the environment in which he or she will work.[4] It allows the salesperson to more quickly identify problem areas and respond accordingly. For example, in a modified rebuy situation, it would not be necessary to educate the prospect about general features common to the product class as a whole. Using up the prospect's valuable time by covering material he or she already knows is minimized. Answers to the following questions provide useful information about the prospect's organization:

Is this a manufacturing, wholesaling, or retailing organization? How large is it? What products or services does it provide?

What types of customers does the organization sell to?[5] What benefits does the organization's target market seek?

Who are the organization's primary competitors? How do the competitors differ in their business approaches?

What type of buying process is this situation—new task, straight rebuy, or modified rebuy? (See Chapter Four for a review.)

How much does the organization purchase in the product category? Does the organization buy from several suppliers or only one? Why?

Why does the organization buy from its present suppliers?[6] Is it satisfied with them? Why or why not?

Who are the other potential competitors? What are their strengths and weaknesses?

Who are the people involved in the purchase decision for the product category? How do they fit into the formal organizational structure? Into the informal organizational structure? Into this specific buying process (gatekeeper, influencer, etc.)? Who is most influential? Which of them carry great influence but are opposed to us (often called **influential adversaries**)?

What current problems does the organization face?

What policies does the organization have regarding salespeople, sales visits, purchasing, and pricing?

What is the organization's financial position and its future?

In what stage in the buying cycle is the organization?

What other firms might the organization be considering (i.e., who are the seller's potential competitors)?

<table>
<tr><td>

Thinking
it
Through

</td><td>

It's your first day on the job as a new salesperson. You were handed a stack of blank prospecting forms and told to fill them out completely for each new prospect. Most of the information you are requested to secure seems to make a lot of sense. However, you notice that you are asked to find out each prospect's attitude toward military service and the names of each prospect's children. You don't feel comfortable asking for this kind of personal information. What are you going to do?

</td></tr>
</table>

Sources of Information

To gather all of the information listed above for every prospect and organization is initially impossible. The goal is to gather what is both possible and profitable. Remember, your time is also valuable! Also, realize that some salespeople prefer to spend all of their time finding out information instead of making sales calls. There must be a proper balance between time spent in acquiring information and time spent making calls.

Much information will be in the lists and directories from which the prospect's name came.[7] Some information may have been gleaned at a trade show the prospect attended. Libraries also provide a wealth of information about publicly traded firms. Databases (e.g., NEXIS[8]) to which the salesperson can subscribe are available and can provide a great deal of information.

As we mentioned in Chapter Seven, much information can be found online from such sources as AT&T WorldNet Service. According to one expert, "Fifteen years ago, when 'consultative selling' became the buzzword for successful sales, it took a great deal of time researching and discovering the needs of a client. Now, a salesperson can learn as much as there is to know about prospects and customers in practically no time at all."[9]

Secretaries and receptionists in the prospect's firm usually are a source of the richest information. Use caution, however, because these important people are accustomed to having salespeople pry for all sorts of free information. Prioritize your questions and provide justification for asking them. Above all, treat secretaries and receptionists with genuine respect.

Also, talk to noncompeting salespeople. In fact, one of the best sources of information is the prospect's own salespeople. Sales trainer Lee Boyan notes, "They are easy to reach because they return phone calls, they understand your situation, and are usually empathetic."[10]

Traditional secondary data sources can also be helpful (we described many of them in Chapter Seven, when we discussed sources of prospects). Firms such as Standard & Poor's, Hoover's, Wards, and Moody's publish a number of manuals and directories that are available in many public libraries. These sources can help answer questions about brand names, key contacts, historical information, the current situation and outlook for the firm and the industry, location of plants and distribution centers, market shares, and so on.[11]

You can even use a service that, for a fee, will scan information and provide you with periodic updates that can assist your selling and planning efforts. For example, IBM infoSage is an online information service that will tailor information to your needs.[12] How does it work? First, the seller creates a personal profile outlining his or her interests, industry, competitors, and so on. Then infoSage continually monitors over 2,200 information sources and sends the salesperson only information directly related to his or her needs via the Internet, e-mail, or the Web.

Many other sources can provide information. Check your company's files to see if the prospect has ever done business with the firm before. Review any direct inquiries made by the prospect (from direct-mail inquiries, through the telemarketing division of your firm, etc.). A center of influence will often be able to provide some information. Occasionally a prospect will be important enough to warrant hiring an outside consultant to gather some of this information.

Don't expect companies to sit down and give you all of this information. According to Phil Farris, president of a leading training organization, gone are the days when salespeople would familiarize themselves with a company by dropping by the office and interviewing some managers. Farris notes, "Now because of time demands, customers no longer have time to educate salespeople. They say, 'If you don't know this stuff, I don't want to deal with you.'"[13]

To demonstrate the creativity possible in gathering information, Harvey Mackay relates how his first boss taught him to learn about competitor activity. MacKay and his boss

drove to our arch competitor's plant. We parked about 50 yards away from the shipping department and waited until the trucks began to exit to make the day's deliveries. The rest of the day, we followed those trucks. By the end of the day, we had a good idea of our competition's local customer base, obtained in record time and at no cost.[14]

SETTING CALL OBJECTIVES

The most important step in planning is to set objectives for the call. Merely stating the objective "I want to make a sale" will not suffice. The customer's decision-making process (see Chapter Four) involves many steps, and salespeople need to undertake many activities as they guide customers through the process.

Yet, as Neil Rackham, an internationally respected sales researcher, notes, "It's astonishing how rarely salespeople set themselves call objectives of any kind—let alone effective ones. Although most books on selling emphasize the importance of clear call objectives, it's rare to see these exhortations turned into practice."[15] Why is this true? Probably because many salespeople want to start *doing something* instead of "wasting time" *planning*. But without a plan, they actually increase their chances of wasting time.

As a first step in setting objectives, the salesperson should review what has been learned from precall information gathering. Any call objectives should be based on the results of this review. Also, the seller must keep in mind the relationship the firm wishes to have with the prospect. Not all prospects will or should become partners with the seller's firm.[16]

Criteria for Effective Objectives

All objectives should be specific, realistic, and measurable. A call objective that meets only one or two of these criteria will be an ineffective guide for the salesperson. We will now examine each criterion in more detail.

An objective must be specific to be effective. It should state exactly what the salesperson hopes to accomplish, who the objective targets are, and any other details (suggested order quantity, suggested dates for future meetings, length of time needed for a follow-up survey, etc.). Specific objectives help the salesperson avoid "shooting

Even if the salesperson fails to achieve his primary call objective, he will be encouraged if he at least achieves his minimum call objective.

Courtesy Hunt Wesson, Inc.

from the hip" during the presentation and perhaps moving the prospect along too rapidly or too slowly.

Objectives must also be realistic. Often inexperienced salespeople have unrealistic expectations about the prospect's or customer's response in the sales call. For example, if Ford Motor Company currently uses Firestone tires on all of its models, a B.F. Goodrich salesperson who expects Ford to change over to B.F. Goodrich tires in the first few sales calls has an unrealistic objective. For objectives to be realistic, the salesperson needs to consider factors such as cultural influences. For example, some firms have a corporate culture of being extremely conservative. Creating change in such a culture is very time consuming and often frustrating for the seller. The national culture also becomes very important in selling to international prospects. When selling to Arab or Japanese businesses, salespeople should plan to spend at least several meetings getting to know the other party. Selling in Russia continues to be often slowed down due to bureaucracy and incredible amounts of red tape. As these examples illustrate, culture is an important consideration in attempts to set realistic call objectives.

Finally, call objectives must be measurable (which suggests they should normally be in writing) so that salespeople can evaluate each sales call at its conclusion and determine if the objectives were met. For example, if a salesperson's stated objective was to "get acquainted with the prospect" or "establish rapport," how would the salesperson assess whether this goal was achieved? How can someone measure "getting acquainted"? To what extent would the salesperson have to be acquainted with the prospect to know that he or she achieved the sales call objective? A more measurable sales call objective (as well as a more specific and realistic one) would be something like the following: "To get acquainted with the prospect by learning what clubs or organizations she or he belongs to, what sports the prospect follows, what his or her professional background is, and how long the prospect has held the current position." With this revised call objective, a salesperson could very simply determine whether the objective was reached.

An easy way to help ensure that objectives are measurable is to set objectives that require a buyer's response. For example, achieving the objective of "make a follow-up appointment with the buyer" is easy to measure.

Successful salespeople in almost every industry have learned the importance of setting proper call objectives. For example, Dr Pepper's salespeople are required to set objectives for each call that are specific, measurable, and achievable, as well as compatible with the company's objectives (e.g., to have the grocer set up an end-of-aisle display that holds 50 cases of Dr Pepper during the follwing week's promotional campaign).[17] Pharmaceutical salespeople for CIBA-Geigy also set very clear objectives for each sales call they make on a physician. Then they lay out a series of objectives for subsequent calls so that they know exactly what they hope to accomplish over the next several visits. Some experts recommend that salespeople write down their call objectives on a piece of paper and keep them in view while they are on the sales call. Having the objectives in sight helps the salesperson focus on the true goals of the sales call.[18] All of these examples have a common theme: The salesperson realizes the importance of setting specific, realistic, measurable call objectives. Exhibit 8.2 lists examples of call objectives that meet the above criteria.

Setting More Than One Call Objective

Some salespeople have learned the importance of setting multiple objectives for a sales call. For example, I. Martin Jacknis, president of Results Marketing, Inc., not only sets a **primary call objective** (the actual goal he hopes to achieve) before each sales call but also sets a **minimum call objective** (the minimum he hopes to achieve). He realizes that at times the call does not go exactly as planned because the

EXHIBIT 8.2

Examples of Call Objectives

- To have the prospect sign an order for 100 pair of Levi's jeans.
- To have the prospect agree to come to the Atlanta branch office sometime during the next two weeks for a hands-on demonstration of the copier.
- To set up another appointment for one week from now, at which time the buyer will allow me to do a complete survey of her printing needs.
- To learn the names of all other key players in this decision that the prospect can identify.
- To inform the doctor of the revolutionary anticlogging mechanism that has been incorporated into our new drug and have her agree to read the pamphlet I will leave.
- To have the buyer agree to pass my information along to the buying committee with his endorsement of my proposal.
- To have the prospect agree to call several references that I will provide to develop further confidence and trust in my office cleaning business.
- To schedule a coop newspaper advertising program to be implemented in the next month.
- To have the prospect agree to use our brand of computer paper for a trial period of one month.
- To have the prospect agree on the first point (of our four-point program) and schedule another meeting in two days with an agenda of discussing the second point.
- To have the retailer agree to allow us space for an end-of-aisle display for the summer presentation of Raid insect repellent.
- To have the prospect initiate the necessary paperwork to allow us to be considered as a future vendor.
- To have me fully understand and appreciate the principal risks that adopting my product would pose to the buyer.

prospect is called away, the salesperson does not have all the necessary facts, and so forth. Although rarely met within the upcoming call, a **visionary call objective,** the most optimistic objective that could occur, is also set. The visionary call objective should relate to what the salesperson hopes to accomplish for the account over the long term (i.e., the account objectives; see Chapter Sixteen). For example, the primary call objective of a Nestlé Foods rep might be to secure an order from a grocer for 10 cases of Nestlé Morsels for an upcoming coupon promotion. A minimum call objective would be to sell at least 5 cases, whereas a visionary call objective would be to sell 20 cases, set up an end-of-aisle display, and secure a retail price of $2.19.

It is possible to have more than one primary call objective for a single call. For example, several primary objectives a salesperson might hope to accomplish in a single meeting are to sell one unit, determine the buying center members for another product, and have the prospect agree to send along a packet of information to an executive. In this example, if the salesperson genuinely hopes and expects to achieve all three objectives in the next meeting, they will all be considered primary call objectives. To aid in planning the call, some trainers would suggest that the rep in this example further prioritize these primary objectives into two groups: The most important primary objective would still be called the primary objective, while the remaining ones would be called **secondary call objectives.** So, in this example, if selling the product were the most important thing to accomplish in the next meeting, the objectives would be as follows:

Primary call objective	Sell one unit
Secondary call objectives	Determine the buying center members for another product
	Have the prospect agree to send along a packet of information to an executive

Jacknis notes several benefits of multiple call objectives. First, they help take away the salesperson's fear of failure; most salespeople can achieve at least their stated minimum objective. Second, multiple objectives tend to be self-correcting. Salespeople who always reach their visionary objective realize they are probably setting their sights too low. On the other hand, if they rarely meet even their minimum objective, they probably are setting their goals too high.[19]

Setting Objectives for Several Calls

By developing a series of very specific objectives for future calls, the salesperson can develop a comprehensive strategy for the prospect or customer. This is especially important for those with a partnering relationship. As an example of setting multicall objectives, Exhibit 8.3 gives a set of call objectives for several visits over a period of time. The left side of the exhibit contains the long-term plan and each call objective that the Panasonic salesperson developed for Johnson Electronics. Note the logical strategy for introducing the new product, the V500. The right side of Exhibit 8.3 gives the actual call results.

The salesperson was not always 100 percent successful in achieving the call objectives; several subsequent ones needed to be modified. For example, because the meeting on October 10 resulted in the buyer dropping K555 tape decks, the call objectives on November 10 and November 17 needed to reflect that K555 was no longer a product carried by Johnson Electronics. The seller may also want to add a call objective for October 17: to discuss more about the situation with K555 (because of the outcome of the October 10 meeting) and perhaps try to reintroduce it. This example

EXHIBIT 8.3	Multiple-Call Objectives of a Panasonic Salesperson Selling to Johnson Electronics		
Overall Plan Developed on Oct. 1		**Actual Call Results**	
Expected Date of the Call	**Call Objective**	**Date of Call**	**Call Results**
Oct 10	Secure normal repeat orders on K33 and K555 tape decks. Increase normal repeat order of K431 CD player from three to five units. Provide product information for new video-disk product V500.	Oct. 10	Obtained normal order of K33. Steve decided to drop K555 (refused to give a good reason). Only purchased four K431 players. Seemed responsive to V500 but needs a point-of-purchase (POP) display.
Oct. 17	Erect a front-counter POP display for V500 and secure a trial order of two units.	Oct. 18	Steve was out. His assistant didn't like the POP (thought it was too large!). Refused to use POP. Did order one V500. Told me about several complaints with K431.
Nov. 10	Secure normal repeat orders for K33, K555, and K431. Schedule one co-op newspaper ad for the next 30 days featuring V500. Secure an order for 10 V500s.	Nov. 8	Obtained normal orders. Steve agreed to co-op ad but bought only 5 V500s. Thinks the margins are too low.
Nov. 17	Secure normal repeat orders of K33, K555, and K431. Secure an order for 20 V500s.	Nov. 18	Obtained normal order on K33, but Steve refused to reorder K431. Claimed the competitor product (Sony) is selling much better. Obtained an order of 15 units of V500.

illustrates the importance of keeping good records, making any necessary adjustments in the long-term call objectives, and then preparing for the next sales call.

John Kirwan, a consultant specializing in major account selling, recommends that a salesperson include the following considerations when developing multicall objectives and strategies:[20]

> Have you made contact with all the key players? (If not, what will you say and how will you say it?)
>
> Do you understand all the business, technical, political, and personal issues involved? (If not, how can you discover them?)
>
> Do you know what your competitor's strengths, weaknesses, and strategies are? (If not, how will you learn?)

The key is to include consideration of these and related informational issues when setting multicall objectives.

One sales vice president for a large sales force has some specific advice about setting objectives:

The primary objective of the first session is to have another chance to visit. What this allows you to do is have your standards relatively low because you are trying to build a long-term relationship. You should be very sensitive to an opportunity to establish a second visit. What you want to do is identify aspects of the business conversation that require follow up and make note of them. . . . The key is not the first visit . . . it is the second, the third, the twenty-second visit.[21]

Appointments increase the chances of seeing the right person and having uninterrupted time with the prospect.

Ron Chapple/FPG

MAKING AN APPOINTMENT

After collecting information about the prospect and the prospect's firm and setting objectives, the next step is generally to make an appointment. Many sales managers insist that their salespeople make appointments before calling on prospects or customers. They have found from experience that working by appointment saves valuable selling time. One large sales organization has estimated that advance appointments increase the effectiveness of their sales force by at least one-third.

Appointments dignify the salesperson. Appointments get the sales process off to a good start by putting the salesperson and the prospect on the same level—equal participants in a legitimate sales interview. Appointments also increase the chances of seeing the right person and having uninterrupted time with the prospect. This section describes how to see the right person at the right time and the right place, how to work through barriers, and how to phone for an appointment.

How to Make Appointments

Experienced sales representatives use different contact methods for different customers. They have found through trial and error that a certain method of making an appointment works well with a regular customer but may be entirely ineffective with a new prospect. (Keep in mind that in multicall situations, an appointment for the next call is usually made at the conclusion of the visit.) They have also found that knowledge of many different methods and techniques for making appointments is extremely helpful in obtaining sales interviews. Some of the basic principles and techniques are discussed next.

The Right Person

Some experts emphasize the importance of going right to the top. When *Sales & Marketing Management* asked its executive advisory panel, "Should salespeople go over the heads of purchasing agents?", the majority responded with a conditional *yes*.[22] Terry Booten, a seasoned salesperson and sales training consultant, agrees: "After years of selling there's a rule I always stick to: When I'm making my initial sales call, I go right to the top executive."[23] Why this advice? Booten notes several reasons: The president is most likely the one signing, or at least okaying, the check; it's the president's job to cultivate the business—only the president knows what the president really wants; the president knows the company's buying and investment criteria; and the president is usually the nicest person.

After carefully studying over 35,000 sales calls, Neil Rackham offers a radically different view from those just mentioned.[24] His research suggests that a salesperson should initially try to call on the **focus of receptivity,** the person who will listen receptively and provide the seller with needed valuable information. Note that this person may not be the decision maker or the one who understands all of the firm's problems. The focus of receptivity, according to the research, will then lead the salesperson to the **focus of dissatisfaction,** the person who is most likely to perceive problems and dissatisfactions. Finally, the focus of dissatisfaction leads to the **focus of power,** the person who can approve action, prevent action, and/or influence action. Getting to the focus of power too quickly can lead to disaster, because the seller has not built a relationship and really learned the buyer's needs. In summary, Rackham notes, "There's a superstition in selling that the sooner you can get to the decision maker the better. Effective selling, so it's said, is going straight to the focus of power. That's a questionable belief."[25]

Of course, nothing is more frustrating than thinking you are making a final presentation only to realize you are not talking to the decision maker. To illustrate, for years a Nekoosa paper salesperson called mainly on printers. After a careful analysis of sales records and the sales potential, the salesperson concluded that the territory was not producing maximum sales volume. Many sales were lost because the printers lacked the authority to specify the brand of paper their clients used. The sales representative solved this problem by contacting the printers' sales reps and finding out from them which clients normally specified a certain brand of paper when placing printing orders. The paper sales rep then contacted those printers' clients directly and explained the merits of the company's products to them.

Buying companies frequently want to manage all interactions between their firms and the salesperson and have set up policies, procedures, and channels to accomplish this. Is it acceptable to bypass these "normal channels" and use a backdoor approach (see Chapter Four) when making calls? In other words, do firms frown on salespeople who bypass the traditional routine? The answer depends on many factors. Cultural norms always play a part. When asked if it is generally acceptable to bypass hierarchical lines, 75 percent of the Italian respondents said *no,* whereas only 22 percent of the Swedish respondents said *no* (in the United States, 32 percent said *no*).[26]

Whether to actually go over the buyer's head depends on many factors. How important is the account? What are the chances of securing the business? What will the company's reaction be? What damage will be done to the long-term relationship? Salesperson Joe Cousineau had to ask himself these very questions after being rudely brushed off by the purchasing agent of one of his biggest potential clients.[27] Cousineau's response was to call the company president, figuring he really had nothing to lose. The president asked if anyone else had witnessed the purchasing agent's rude behavior. Fortunately, the receptionist had seen it all. After verifying Cosinueau's story with the receptionist, the president not only offered Cosinueau an appointment to see him but he also ended up buying Cosinueau's full-blown program. What happened to the rude purchasing agent? His company forced him to take a position as a salesperson, perhaps to have him experience firsthand the rejection he had been doling out to salespeople who called on him.

Frequently in industrial selling situations, no one person has the sole authority to buy a product. The salesperson may first be required to obtain the approval of a line organization representative or of an operating committee. For example, a forklift sales representative for Clarke found that he had to see the safety engineer, the methods engineer, the materials-handling engineer, and the general superintendent before he could sell the product to a certain manufacturing company. In this case, the salesperson should try to arrange a meeting with the entire group as well as with each individual.

The Right Time

Much has been written about the best time of day for sales interviews. Certain salespeople claim the best time to see prospects is right after lunch, when they are likely to be in a pleasant mood. Others try to get as many appointments as they can during the early morning hours because they believe the prospects or customers will be in a better frame of mind then. There is little agreement on this subject, for obviously the most opportune time to call will vary by customer and type of selling. The salesperson who calls on wholesale grocers, for example, may find from experience that the best time to call is from 9 AM to 11 AM and from 1:30 PM to 3:30 PM. A hospital rep, on the other hand, may discover that the most productive calls on surgeons are made between 8:30 AM and 10 AM and after 4 PM.

For most types of selling, the best hours of the day are from approximately 9 AM to 11:30 AM and from 1:30 PM to 4 PM. This is particularly true for business executives, who like to have the first part of the day free to read their mail and answer correspondence and the latter part of the day free to read and sign their letters. (Chapter Sixteen provides more information about the proper time to make calls.)

Although the above hours may be the most favorable, salespeople need not restrict appointments to these times. Each salesperson soon learns the most favorable hours and days for each customer. Certainly for those customers with which the firm is partnering, extra care should be taken to make calls at times that are favorable for both buyer and seller.

The Right Place

The sales call must take place in an environment conducive to doing business. Often the salesperson has no say in where the call will take place. When possible, however, the salesperson should choose a place free of distraction for all parties. Selling Scenario 8.1, pages 228–229, describes the use of topless bars, a setting that is hardly free of distractions but is still used by many salespeople today. In addition to distractions, topless bars present a number of additional problems for the salesperson who uses them to achieve sales. For example, is it ethical to gain business using such exploitative tactics? Also, once a buyer has purchased on the basis of this entertainment, chances are the seller will have to keep it up or lose the customer.

Cultivating Relationships with Subordinates

Busy executives usually have one or more subordinates who plan and schedule interviews for them. These **barriers** (or **screens,** as salespeople sometimes call them) often make seeing the boss rather difficult. For example, a secretary, who usually feels responsible for conserving his or her superior's time, tries to discover the true purpose of each salesperson's visit before granting an interview with the boss.

Salespeople should go out of their way to treat all subordinates with respect and courtesy. First, it is the right thing to do. Second, subordinates can be the true key to the salesperson's success or failure with their organization. They may not be able to buy the salesperson's product, but they can often kill his or her chances for a sale.

Salespeople should work toward achieving a friendly relationship with the prospect's subordinates.

Courtesy Citibank

Sales strategists have identified three basic ways to interact with the screen. The salesperson can go "over the screen." This occurs when the seller, while talking to the screen, drops names of people higher up in the organization. As a result, the screen may allow the seller in to see the boss right away for fear of getting into trouble. Or the salesperson can go "under the screen" by trying to make contact with the prospect before or after the screen gets to work (or while the screen is taking a coffee break). Finally, the salesperson can work "through the screen" by simply involving the screen in the process.

Thinking *it* Through	Do you see problems in working "over the screen"? How about working "under the screen"? What might this do to long-term relationship development?

Telephoning for Appointments

There are several ways to make an appointment, including in person, by mail, or by phone. Making an initial appointment in person would be desirable (the salesperson could gather more precall information) but is usually too time consuming for the salesperson. Using the mail requires a lot of lead time and may also result in the letter getting misplaced or unread in the "junk mail" clutter. Therefore, the phone is most often used to make the initial appointment. Salespeople can save many hours by phoning to make appointments.

Salespeople need to use the phone correctly and effectively.[28] All of us have used telephones since childhood; many of us have developed bad habits that reduce our effectiveness when talking over the phone. Perfect your phone style by practicing alone before making any calls. Make sure you know what you want to say before placing the call. It is a polite gesture to start by asking, "Is this a good time to talk?"

"I'm Sorry, Where Did You Say You Would Like to Go?"

Meetings with clients and prospects should occur in places free of distractions. Right? Then how does this measure up?

Upon entering the bar, the salesperson waves a big stack of money and shouts "Where are the girls?" A young woman walks over and ". . . wishes him happy birthday. Then she straddles his lap and removes her bikini top. The woman yanks at his shirt, baring his chest, and begins grinding against [him] in time to a Van Halen song. . . . Her attire, at this moment consists of a G-string and high heels . . . the woman lowers to her knees . . . licking her way delicately down to [his] stomach . . ."

Sounds like something from the old, old days of selling? Actually, this real scene occurred in the mid-1990s and continues to occur daily. As one writer put it, "Even in an era when social conservatism is ascendant, when corporate America is wising up to the legal hazards of sexual harassment and discrimination, and when TQM mantras dictate that sales decisions be governed by cost and merit, the valet parking lots at strip bars are packed full." The number of topless bars is increasing, not decreasing, with some states even allowing nude dancers to make full contact with customers.

One observer of a Fortune 500 firm's Cleveland office found that ". . . taking customers to topless bars was not only commonplace but often required." The firm had an official policy of not allowing this sort of business expense. However, reps and sales managers generally found ways to get reimbursed for these expenses.

In a survey of male salespeople, a whopping 49 percent admitted they had been to a topless bar with a customer and 50 percent said it didn't bother them. Only 25 percent said they would rather lose a customer than go to a topless bar. Also, 35 percent said their company doesn't allow it, although 49 percent said their company just "looks the other way." Who suggested these

Don't be too rushed to be nice; it is *never* acceptable to be rude. And don't forget to smile as you talk. Even though the prospect won't see it, she or he will hear it in your enthusiastic tone of voice.

Active listening (see Chapter Five) is as important when conversing over the phone as when conversing in person. Take notes and restate the message or any action you have agreed to undertake. In addition, you will need to encourage two-way communication. If you have ever talked with two-year-olds over the phone, you know that if you ask them a *yes* or *no* question, they tend to shake their heads "yes" or "no" rather than verbalize a response. Similarly, you cannot nod your head to encourage someone to continue talking on the phone. Instead, you must encourage conversations with verbal cues such as "Uh-huh," "I see," or "That's interesting." Finally, just as in face-to-face conversation, you must be able to tolerate silences so that customers have an opportunity to ask questions, agree or disagree, or relate a point to their circumstances.

What if in trying to reach the prospect you reach his or her voice mail instead? Here are some tips from experts.[29] If you are making a cold call to set up an appointment, it is usually best not to leave a message. Instead, go to the operator and try to reach the prospect's secretary and find a good time to call back. If you have a referral or have talked to the person before, leave a clear, concise message that includes a suggested time for the person to call you back (so you will know when to expect the call and can be prepared yourself). When leaving a message, don't just talk and talk until the tape runs out. A little casual conversation is fine, but remem-

SELLING SCENARIO 8.1 *(concluded)*

trips? In 72 percent of the cases, it was the customer who suggested visiting the topless bar. Oh, and in case you're wondering, 73 percent of the married salesmen did tell their spouses of their visit to the topless bar.

What about saleswomen? In the same survey, only 5 percent said they had ever been to a topless bar with a customer and 57 percent felt it gave male salespeople an unfair advantage over female salespeople. Eight-five percent of the female salespeople said they would rather lose a customer than go to a topless bar; only 8 percent said it didn't bother them. Mary MacKinnon, a sales rep for hospital equipment in Atlanta, summed up the view many women might have: "Simply put: business entertainment at topless bars is inappropriate. The establishments degrade women. They discriminate against female reps. And they don't necessarily work as a sales tool."

She has a point about discrimination. Although no lawsuits have yet been filed with the EEOC citing topless bars as a cause of sexual harassment, they could be. "If you had been asked to go or made to go you could have clearly filed for sexual harassment," says Verna Barksdale, director of the Atlanta chapter of 9 to 5, a national association of working women.

David Dorsey sums up the situation well: "There's nothing wrong with entertaining a customer. Yet, when a customer cares less about the quality of your product than your readiness to treat him to an evening of simulated sex, it probably doesn't bode well for business in the long run. The problem is, how do you avoid it when the practice has become commonplace? . . . When a sales rep starts paying more attention to a buyer's fantasy life than his business needs, both parties will ultimately pay the price."

Sources: Rob Zeiger, "Sex, Sales & Stereotypes," *Sales & Marketing Management,* July 1995, pp. 48, 51; Andy Cohen, "Topless Bars Dress Up Their Act," *Sales & Marketing Management,* July 1995, p. 54; Rob Zeiger, "Dancers: They're Not Here to Fall in Love," *Sales & Marketing Management,* July 1995, p. 56; David Dorsey, "Risky Business," *Sales & Marketing Management,* July 1995, p. 128; Mary MacKinnon, "How Topless Bars Shut Me Out," *Sales & Marketing Management,* July 1995, p. 53.

ber that the prospect's time is important. Also, make your message compelling, for example, "Alan, I just fell into a terrific opportunity, but it's an offer I can only pass along to a few customers. It's a now-or-never thing. Timing is tight. If you want to hear the details, call me at (phone number) before the close of business Thursday."[30] *Slowly* repeat your name and phone number at the end of your message. And remember, *never* leave bad news on voice mail.

Exhibit 8.4 presents a scenario for using the phone to make an appointment. A salesperson should use what feels comfortable for him or her and discard any techniques that do not feel natural.[31]

A potential customer may have objections, reasons for not granting an interview. The goal of the telephone call, however, is to make an appointment, not to sell the product or service. Exhibit 8.5 shows appropriate responses to common objections Xerox copier salespeople encounter when making appointments.

When salespeople call for appointments, prospects frequently ask questions about the product or service. But the salesperson should not be drawn into giving a sales presentation over the telephone. Again, the purpose of the call is to obtain an appointment, not to make a sale. In fact, some firms use their telemarketing staff to set appointments for salespeople to avoid being drawn into a complete sales presentation.

Some salespeople have their secretaries make telephone appointments for them. This often gives them greater prestige in the mind of the prospect or customer. If the secretary cannot obtain an appointment, the salesperson may make a second call, using a different approach.

EXHIBIT 8.4		
Using the Telephone to Gain an Appointment	1. State customer's name.	"Hello, Mr. Walker?" *(pause)*
	2. State your name.	"This is Glen Scott, with Gamma Industries."
	3. Check time.	"Did I call at a convenient time, or should I call later?" *(pause)*
	4. State purpose and make presentation.	"I'm calling to let you know about our new office copier. It has more features than the present copiers and could be a real money saver."
	5. Close.	"Could you put me on your calendar for 30 minutes next Monday or Tuesday?"
	6. Show appreciation, restate time, or keep door open.	"Thank you, Mr. Walker. I'll be at your office at 9AM on Tuesday."
		[or]
		"I appreciate your frankness, Mr. Walker. I'd like to get back to you in a couple of months. Would that be all right?"

At times, salespeople may have to use determination, persistence, and ingenuity to obtain interviews, but they should never resort to deceitful or dishonest tactics. The use of subterfuge to obtain appointments has no place in modern selling. Salespeople who select prospects carefully in terms of product needs should not have to conceal the purpose of the visit.

EXHIBIT 8.5		
Responses to Objections Concerning Appointments	**Objection from a Secretary**	**Response**
	"I'm sorry, but Mr. Wilkes is busy now."	"What I have to say will only take a few minutes. Should I call back in a half-hour, or would you suggest I set up an appointment?"
	"We already have a copier."	"That's fine. I want to talk to Mr. Wilkes about our new paper-flow system design for companies like yours."
	"I take care of all the copying."	"That's fine, but I'm here to present what Xerox has to offer for a complete paper-flow system that integrates data transmission, report generation, and copiers. I'd like to speak to Mr. Wilkes about this total service."
	Objection from the Prospect	**Response**
	"Can't you mail the information to me?"	"Yes, I could. But everyone's situation is different, Mr. Wilkes, and our systems are individually tailored to meet the needs of each customer. Now . . . *[benefit statement and repeat request for appointment]*."
	"Well, what is it you want to talk about?"	"It's difficult to explain the system over the telephone. In 15 minutes, I can demonstrate the savings you get from the system."
	"You'd just be wasting your time. I'm not interested."	The general objection is hiding a specific objection. The salesperson needs to probe for the specific objection: "Do you say that because you don't copy many documents?"
	"We had a Xerox copier once and didn't like it."	Probe for the specific reason of dissatisfaction and have a reply, but don't go too far. The objective is to get an appointment, not sell a copier.

Source: Courtesy of Xerox Corporation. Used by permission.

SELLING SCENARIO 8.2

Plan for the Objections You Might Hear, ... But Be Careful!

This was my first call on this female physician. I introduced myself and the firm I represent and she immediately knew the product that pertained to her practice. Without hesitation she blurted out, "You have to tell your company that this drug does not work! They need to come out with a new dosage schedule or something. It does not work and I have never had a problem with your competitor's product."

Immediately, one would think that this is an efficacy objection [efficacy simply means is the drug effective at doing what it's supposed to do]. A planned way to handle this objection would be to show a comparative study between the two drugs. This should be helpful, right? I'll admit this was tempting. Instead, I asked her: "What information can I provide you that you feel would be most beneficial to prove my drug's efficacy—head-to-head comparisons, medical query, hospital formularies [which drugs hospitals allow to be used in them], FDA approval information, or what?"

Her response was interesting. "I follow [one] hospital's protocol in my practice and that's all that matters to me."

Lucky for me I knew that hospital's protocol and I knew that they had changed their protocol to using my drug exclusively. Asking the physician what proof source she was interested in made all the difference. It saved a lot of time, too.

Sometimes if you overplan how you will respond to objections, you may come up with one "best" answer that you plan to give for a specific objection. However, that may not be what your customer wants to hear. Be careful. Plan several ways in which you might be able to answer an objection. Then, after the objection is raised, probe first, then use the most appropriate response. Your customer will thank you for it!

Source: Tracey Brill, personal correspondence; used with permission.

FURTHER PLANNING NEEDED

In addition to the activities described in this chapter, a successful salesperson thinks ahead to the meeting that will occur and plans accordingly. For example, salespeople should plan how they intend to make a good first impression and build credibility during the call. It is also important to plan how to further uncover the customer's needs and strengthen the presentation. Salespeople should anticipate the questions and concerns the prospect may raise and plan to answer them helpfully; Selling Scenario 8.2 offers some tips for this activity. All of these issues will be discussed in detail in the next several chapters. For now, be aware that these activities should be planned *before* the meeting begins.

SUMMARY

This chapter stressed the importance of planning the sales call. Developing a clear plan saves time for both salespeople and customers. In addition, it helps salespeople increase their confidence and reduce strain.

As part of the planning process, salespeople need to gather as much information about the prospect as possible before the first call. They need information both about the individual prospect and about the prospect's organization. Sources of this information include lists and directories, secretaries and receptionists, noncompeting salespeople, direct inquiries made by the prospect, and other sources.

To be effective, a call objective should be specific, realistic, and measurable. In situations requiring several calls, the salesperson should develop a plan with call objectives for each future call. Also, many salespeople benefit from setting multiple levels of objectives—primary, minimum, and visionary—for each call.

As a general rule, salespeople should make appointments before calling on customers. In this way, they can be sure they will talk to the right person.

A number of methods can be used to make appointments. Perhaps the most effective is the straightforward telephone approach. This includes stating the salesperson's name, establishing a link with the prospect or customer, stating the purpose of the call, and asking for an appointment.

KEY TERMS

barriers 226	minimum call objective 221
focus of dissatisfaction 225	primary call objective 221
focus of power 225	screens 226
focus of receptivity 225	secondary call objectives 222
influential adversaries 217	visionary call objective 222

QUESTIONS AND PROBLEMS

1. Suppose you belong to Friends of the Library, an organization that plans to hold a dinner to raise funds for new book acquisitions. To be a success, the event will need a great deal of community support, especially from local businesses.

   a. What sources will you use to identify potential sponsors?

   b. What information do you need to qualify them properly?

2. Setting call objectives takes time and effort on the part of the salesperson. Are there any situations in which it would not make sense for a salesperson to set a call objective? If so, what are they?

3. "Setting call objectives reduces my ability to be adaptable during the call." Respond to this salesperson's statement.

4. Evaluate the following objectives for a sales call:

   a. Show and demonstrate the entire line of 10 color inkjet printers.

   b. Find out more about competitors' services under consideration.

   c. Increase the buyer's trust in my company.

   d. Determine which service the prospect is currently using and how much it costs.

   e. Have the buyer agree to hold our next meeting at some third location (other than either party's office).

   f. Get an order for 15 AV-8B Harrier II Plus combat jets.

   g. Make the buyer more comfortable with the fact that our firm has been in business only three months.

5. Think for a moment about trying to secure a job. Assume you are going to have your second job interview next week with Kimberly Clark for a sales position. Most candidates go through a set of four interviews. List your primary objective, minimum objective, and visionary objective.

6. Why is making appointments before visiting a customer desirable? Under what circumstances might the salesperson not need to make appointments?

7. Assume you are trying to sell several new styles of couches to a furniture store. Your boss listed three possible objectives for your next call: sell 2 new styles, sell 10 new styles, and have the prospect watch a demonstration that shows the couches' wearability. Which is probably the primary objective, the minimum objective, and the visionary objective?

8. Evaluate the following approach for getting an appointment: "Ms. Thompson, I'm going to be working in your area next week. When can I come by to tell you about our new product?"

9. Much attention is given to the best time of day for sales interviews. List the best time of day to call on the following individuals:

    a. A college professor (to sell textbooks).

    b. A lawyer (to sell investigative services).

    c. A product manager (to sell magazine ad space).

    d. A janitor (to sell janitorial supplies).

    e. A senior buyer at a grocery store's corporate headquarters (to sell a new food product).

    f. A computer operations supervisor (to sell repair services).

    g. An accountant (to sell fax machines).

10. Review the list of prospects in question 9 and identify:

    a. The worst time of day to call on each individual.

    b. The worst time of year to call on each individual.

EXPLORING THE NET

One of the most important aspects of planning for a sales call is obtaining information about the prospect's organization. Sometimes this information can be obtained from the prospect's home page. Visit at least two of the Web sites listed here and answer the questions that follow.

    http://www.ibm.com

    http://www.ge.com

    http://www.media.com

    http://www.eaton.com

    http://www.viewsonic.com

    http://www.pg.com

    http://www.pepsico.com

    http://www.motorola.com

1. Look at the list of questions enumerated in this chapter that provide useful information about the prospect's organization (Is this a manufacturing, wholesaling, or retailing organization? How large is it? What products or services does it provide?, etc.). Which questions can be answered simply by studying the company's home page?

2. Why would it always be wise to view a prospect's home page before making a first visit?

CASE PROBLEMS

**CASE 8.1
Johnson's Office Products**

Johnson's distributes business forms for almost every office and business need. The company's corporate headquarters are located in Pittsburgh. Johnson's sells products through regional and district offices in the United States. Sales representatives are usually assigned to specific geographic areas. However, in some larger cities, they are assigned certain key customers.

Joseph Newman, who sells in the Minneapolis area, has been with the company 20 years and is planning to retire in six months. In general, he has done a fairly good job in his territory. Minnesota Power, however, has never given any business to Johnson's. Newman has called on the purchasing agent regularly but has never been able to obtain an order for Johnson's business forms. The purchasing agent has told Newman on several occasions that it is impossible to give Johnson's any business because Minnesota Power has entered into an exclusive agreement for all printing work with a local concern, Twin Cities Printing. Newman has heard indirectly that the Twin Cities Printing sales representative is a close friend of the purchasing agent.

Cindy Beaudin has been a sales representative for Johnson's for eight years. She worked three years in the Chicago area and during the last five years has been in the San Francisco area. Beaudin, an excellent sales rep, has a solid background in office systems and methods work. The eastern regional sales executive has told Beaudin she will take over Newman's territory in Minneapolis when Newman retires. Plans call for Beaudin to work with Newman in the Minneapolis area during the last month of his service. Telling Beaudin of her new assignment, the sales manager said she wanted Newman to introduce Beaudin to the regular customers in the new territory. In addition, she said, "Cindy, I want you to concentrate on getting some business from Minnesota Power. There is no reason why we shouldn't be getting some of that business. I told Newman that I wanted you to spend whatever time was necessary to break that account open for us."

Questions

1. Assume you are Cindy Beaudin. List your call objectives for your first call with Minnesota Power. Develop a three-call follow-up schedule, and list the objectives for each call.

2. What kind of information would you like to have about Minnesota Power? How could you obtain that information?

3. Assume the purchasing agent suggests that you call directly on Minnesota Power's vice president of purchasing. Also assume the purchasing agent refuses to help set up this meeting. Describe in detail how you would go about making such an appointment.

CASE 8.2
Komatsu
Off-Highway
Trucks*

Komatsu Ltd., headquartered in Japan, is an international leader of manufacturing construction equipment and industrial machinery. The firm also is involved in civil engineering, construction, electronics, and other ventures. With over $10 billion in annual sales, Komatsu has established itself as a reliable partner for its customers.

In April 1995, Komatsu Singapore Pt., Ltd., the firm's regional headquarters in South Asia-Pacific, established Komatsu Saigon Company, Ltd., to provide better product support and manufacture additional products in the region.

Among other products, Komatsu manufactures the world's largest off-highway haul truck, the Haulpak 930E, with an unmatched capacity of 310 tons per load. It is used primarily by mining operators to move large amounts of ore, coal, and other substances from pits to the processing areas.

Ryoichi Suga has just been named the principal salesperson for the Haulpak 930E in Western Australia, a very strong iron ore–producing area. Suga has learned that one large mine, Carnarvon Mining Company, is already in the process of negotiating with Caterpillar for new mining trucks. The mine currently operates 42 Caterpillar mining trucks, many of which are getting old. The chief negotiator for Carnarvon is William Spaulding. Spaulding has agreed to have a short meeting with Suga in three weeks.

* Information for this case was developed using the Komatsu 1995 annual report and other sources.

Questions

1. What kind of information should Suga gather about Spaulding before meeting with him?

2. What kind of information should Suga gather about Carnarvon Mining Company before meeting with Spaulding?

3. What sources can Suga use to gather the needed information?

ADDITIONAL REFERENCES

Dion, Paul; Debbie Easterling; and Shirley Jo Miller. "What Is Really Necessary in Successful Buyer/Seller Relationships?" *Industrial Marketing Management,* 24 (1995), pp. 1–9.

Grewal, Dhruv, and Arun Sharma. "The Effect of Salesforce Behavior on Customer Satisfaction: An Interactive Framework." *Journal of Personal Selling and Sales Management,* Summer 1991, pp. 13–24.

Henry, Porter. *Secrets of the Master Sellers.* New York: AMACOM, 1987.

Ingram, Thomas N.; Charles H. Schwepker, Jr.; and Don Hutson. "Why Salespeople Fail." *Industrial Marketing Management,* 1992, pp. 225–30.

Mayo, Edward, and Lance P. Jarvis. "The Power of Persuasion: Lessons in Personal Selling from the White House." *Journal of Personal Selling and Sales Management,* Fall 1992, pp. 1–8.

McGarvey, Robert. "Best Sellers: The Nation's Top Sales Pros Share Their Secrets." *Entrepreneur,* August 1996, pp. 100–10.

O'Hara, Bradley S.; James S. Boles; and Mark W. Johnston. "The Influence of Personal Variables on Salesperson Selling Orientation." *Journal of Personal Selling and Sales Management,* Winter 1991, pp. 61–68.

Wilson, Harrell. "Over There: On Being a Stranger in a Strange Land." *Success,* May 1993, p. 8.

Wotruba, Thomas R. "The Evolution of Personal Selling." *Journal of Personal Selling and Sales Management,* Summer 1991, pp. 1–12.

Wotruba, Thomas R., and Stephen B. Castleberry. "Job Analysis and Hiring Practices for National Account Marketing Positions." *Journal of Personal Selling and Sales Management,* Summer 1993, pp. 49–65.

Chapter Nine

Making *the* Sales Call

At this point in the sales process, we assume an appointment has been made, sufficient information about the prospect and his or her organization has been gathered, and the salesperson has developed strong objectives for the call. In this chapter, we will discuss how to make the actual sales call. Exhibit 9.1 on page 238 provides an organizing framework for our discussion.

Some Questions Answered in this Chapter Are:

How should the salesperson make the initial approach to make a good impression and gain the prospect's attention?

How can the salesperson develop rapport and increase source credibility?

Why is discovering the prospect's needs important, and how can a salesperson accomplish this?

How can the salesperson most effectively relate the product or service features to the prospect's needs?

Why is it important for the salesperson to make adjustments during the call?

How does the salesperson recognize that adjustments are needed?

How can a salesperson effectively sell to groups?

We will consider how to make a good impression and begin developing a long-term relationship. We will also examine the initial needs assessment phase of a relationship and how to relate solutions to those needs. Finally, we will discuss the salesperson's need to be adaptable to make the sales call effectively.

PROFILE

Jerry Robison has been a pharmaceutical sales representative with Hoechst Marion Roussel since graduating from the University of Georgia in 1987 with a BBA in marketing. He has won six sales awards in his eight years with the company. During the last five years, he has been a hospital representative calling on teaching institutions in the New Orleans area. Basically, his job entails calling on doctors, administrators, and other health care professionals at several big teaching hospitals. Robison describes his success as follows.

"Because each July new residents and fellows start at the medical institutions, I have an opportunity to meet many different people. I have found that it is very important to make a good first impression. The way you handle yourself in the first couple of minutes will leave a lasting impression in the minds of your new clients. After introducing myself, I try to learn what I can about the person, including hometown, medical school, and family. Then I let the person know what pharmaceuticals I sell. I know that I will have plenty of time in the future to discuss my products with the person in more detail.

"To succeed in sales, you must be the expert on both your company's and your competitor's products. I spend several hours a week reading the literature so that I can talk at the same level as the physicians I am calling on. Even with the preparation, I still get asked questions that I do not know the answers to. Instead of making an educated guess, I tend to say, 'I do not know the answer, but I will find out.' I now have a good reason for calling on the doctor the next time. Following up with the doctor with the correct answer helps strengthen your relationship with your clients. Another way to set yourself apart from your competition is to discuss with the clients the limitations of your products. Doctors need to know both when your products should and should not be used.

"Selling to physicians is a long-term process where each sales call builds upon itself. It is very important for me to keep detailed notes of

JERRY ROBISON
Hoeschst Marion Roussel

> *"Selling to physicians is a long-term process where each sales call builds upon itself. It is very important for me to keep detailed notes of all my discussions with doctors. Before I go into a sales call, I review my notes and develop my sales strategy."*

all my discussions with doctors. Before I go into a sales call, I review my notes and develop my sales strategy. The strategy for the call can be anything from telling the doctor that your product has been added to a managed care formulary to comparing your drug to a competitive product.

"Before you can have a successful sales presentation, you have to get your client's attention. I usually start off by talking about some of the things that are important to the doctor, such as family, sports, or growth of a certain managed care plan. Humor is also a good way to gain attention with the right physicians. Without the doctor's attention, you are just wasting both of your time.

"Good selling skills are very important for successful selling. Asking questions to uncover needs and buying motives is very important. Many representatives tell the doctors what they want to tell them as opposed to what the doctor wants to hear. You will be much more successful if you first uncover the doctor's needs and then show how your product meets those needs. Telling the doctor the features of your products is nice, but you will be much more effective if you transfer the features to benefits. Telling a doctor that your drug has a low side effect profile is helpful. Telling a doctor that he or she will probably get fewer complaints from the patients will mean more to the physician.

"Because of the changes in medicine, it is getting harder to get quality time in front of physicians. Good rapport with the office staff will increase your chances of seeing the doctor. Just calling the staff members by name and showing an interest in them will help you in the office. If a secretary tells you the doctor has only a minute and you spend a half-hour with the client, you may never get back to see the person again. Also, during the sales call it is important to read the doctor's body language to determine how the doctor is reacting to your discussion. The worst thing you can do is to make the doctor wonder if you are ever going to leave the office.

"Pharmaceutical sales is a very challenging yet rewarding career. It is nice to know that the products I sell help people live longer, more productive lives."

An actual sales call can be quite varied, depending on the specific situation the salesperson encounters as well as the extent of the relationship the salesperson has already established with the other party. In this chapter, we will discuss the important elements of sales calls in general. However, keep in mind that some activities, such as making a good first impression, are not as important for partnering customers as they are for leads on whom you are making a first call.

MAKING A GOOD IMPRESSION

Successful salespeople have learned the importance of making a good impression. When salespeople fail to arrive on time, make a poor entrance, fail to gain the buyer's interest, or lack rapport-building skills, it is difficult for them to secure commitment and build partnerships.[1] This section discusses how salespeople can manage the buyer's impression of them, a process often called **impression management.**

One of the most important ways to ensure a good first impression is to be well prepared (as we discussed in Chapter Eight). Some salespeople prepare a checklist of things to take to the presentation so they won't forget anything.

Waiting for the Prospect

Being on time for a planned sales call is critical to avoid giving the buyer a negative impression. Because of this, salespeople often arrive a few minutes early and have to

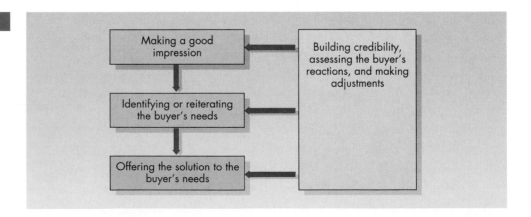

EXHIBIT 9.1

Essential Elements of the Sales Call

Making a good impression → Identifying or reiterating the buyer's needs → Offering the solution to the buyer's needs

Building credibility, assessing the buyer's reactions, and making adjustments

Courtesy 3M

Courtesy Hunt Wesson, Inc.

Courtesy Johnson & Johnson;
photo by Ted Kawalerski

Sales calls can occur in practically every location.

wait to see the prospect. Further, the prospect occasionally is running behind and lets the salesperson wait beyond the appointment time. Either scenario can result in salespeople sitting and waiting, sometimes for long periods, for their prospects to see them.

Every salesperson must expect to spend a certain portion of each working day waiting for sales interviews. Successful salespeople make the best possible use of this time by working on reports, studying new-product information, planning and preparing for their next calls, and obtaining additional information about the prospect. (Chapter Sixteen covers time management more fully.)

Some sales managers instruct their sales representatives not to wait for any prospect, under normal circumstances, more than 15 minutes after the appointment time. Exceptions are necessary, of course, depending on the importance of the customer and the distance the salesperson has traveled. In all cases, salespeople should keep the sales call in perspective, realizing that their time is also valuable. (Chapter Sixteen discusses just how valuable that time really is!)

When the salesperson arrives, the receptionist may merely say, "I'll tell Mr. Jones that you are here." After the receptionist has spoken with Mr. Jones, the salesperson should ask approximately how long the wait will be. When the wait will be excessive and/or the salesperson has another appointment, it may be advisable to explain this tactfully and to ask for another appointment. Usually the secretary either will try to get the salesperson in to see the prospect more quickly or will make arrangements for a later appointment.

The Entrance

In the first meeting between a salesperson and a prospect or customer, the first two minutes can be very important. Making a favorable first impression usually results in a prospect who is willing to listen. A negative first impression, on the other hand, sets up a barrier that may never be hurdled. (Note that one advantage in partnering relationships is that the salesperson has already established a bond and has built a reputation based on his or her prior actions.)

The entrance, like the presentation itself, can occur anywhere. For someone selling portable cellular telephones, for example, it can occur in a traditional office setting, while a farmer is sitting on his or her combine or tractor, or in the yard of a tow truck operator. The key is for the salesperson to be adaptable to the situation and make an effective entrance for that particular scenario.

Very First Impressions

Many salespeople make a poor impression without realizing it. They may know their customer's needs and their own product, but overlook seemingly insignificant things that can create negative impressions. To avoid this, Ann Sabath suggests that salespeople use the business etiquette called "Rules of Twelve":[2]

- The salesperson's first 12 words should include a form of "thank you" (e.g., "Thank you for seeing me").
- The 12 inches from the shoulders up should suggest high-quality grooming (e.g., hair, collar, etc. are neat).
- The first 12 footsteps should reflect confidence by using erect posture, a lengthy stride, and a brisk pace.

Also, the salesperson should not forget to smile! Watch what happens when you look at someone and smile. In 99 out of 100 times, you will receive a smile in return.[3]

It is also important to remember prospects' names and how to pronounce them. There are many ways to try to remember names (e.g., associating the name with someone else you know with the same name). The key is to pronounce the prospect's name correctly.

Thinking *it* **Through**	Assume you walk into a prospect's office very confidently, using erect posture and walking at a brisk pace. When you offer your hand, you suddenly notice the prospect has no right arm. What should you do and/or say?

Handshaking

Salespeople should not automatically extend their hand to a prospect, particularly if the prospect is seated.[4] Shaking hands should be the prospect's choice. If the prospect offers a hand, the salesperson should respond with a firm but not overpowering

Women should shake hands in the same manner as men.

Ron Chapple/FPG

handshake while maintaining good eye contact. Chances are that you have experienced both a limpid handshake—a hand with little or no grip—and a bone-crunching grip. Either impression is often lasting and negative. Also, if you tend to have sweaty hands, carry a handkerchief.

Women should shake hands in the same manner men do. They should avoid offering their hand for a social handshake (palm facing down and level with the ground, with fingers drooping and pointing to the ground). Likewise, a man should not force a social handshake from a woman in a business setting.

The salesperson selling in an international context needs to carefully consider cultural norms regarding the appropriateness of handshaking, bowing, and other forms of greeting. For example, the Chinese prefer no more than a slight bow in their greeting, while an Arab businessperson may not only shake hands vigorously but also keep holding your hand for several seconds. A hug in Mexico communicates a trusting relationship, while in Germany such a gesture would be offensive because it suggests an inappropriate level of intimacy. In some cultures, it is important to offer a business card at both the beginning and the end of a meeting.[5]

The Appropriate Stance

When salespeople stand in front of their prospects, they must not appear to be either insecure or overly aggressive. A confident appearance can be achieved by

- Keeping feet about 12 inches apart to improve stability.
- Standing at a 45-to-90-degree angle to the customer. Standing straight across from the customer can seem threatening.
- Keeping the shoulders relaxed and the arms off of the hips.
- Standing two to four feet from the customer. Standing too close can be seen as threatening, while standing too far away gives an impersonal feeling. (See Chapter Five for a discussion of space and physical contact guidelines.)

As with handshaking, these guidelines need to be modified for regional and cultural differences. In some rural areas, hands on the hips indicate a relaxed posture and suggest a certain degree of informality and friendship. Arabs would probably interpret hands on the hips as a threat or a challenge. In Latin America, culture dictates that business conversations occur much closer than two to four feet.

Selecting a Seat

Many calls will not involve sitting down at all (e.g., talking to a store manager in a grocery store aisle, conversing with a supervisor in a warehouse, asking questions of a surgeon in a post-op ward). When the parties will be seated, the best arrangement is around a small table or with the salesperson at the side of the customer's desk. When salespeople are seated, they can more easily observe all five channels of nonverbal communication—body angle, face, arms, hands, and legs (see Chapter Five)—and show brochures and other visual aids from a comfortable position.

When selecting a seat, it is a good idea to look around and start to identify the prospect's social style and status (see Chapter Six). For example, in the United States, important decision makers usually have large, well-appointed, private offices. But be careful. In Kuwait, a high-ranking businessperson may have a small office and lots of interruptions. Don't take that to mean he or she is a low-ranking employee or is not interested.

Asking permission to sit down is usually unnecessary. The salesperson should read the prospect's nonverbal cues to determine the right time to be seated.

**Getting
the Customer's
Attention**

Recall from Chapter Six that there are several types of sales presentations, including standard memorized, outlined, and customized. In this chapter, we will assume the salesperson has chosen a customized presentation.

Getting the customer's attention is not a new concept. It is also the goal of many other activities you are familiar with (e.g., advertising, making new friends, writing an English composition, giving a speech, writing a letter to a friend).

Time is very valuable to prospects, and prospects concentrate their attention on the first few minutes with a salesperson to determine whether they will benefit from the interaction. The first few words the salesperson says often set the tone of the entire sales call. The **halo effect** (how and what you do in one thing changes a person's perceptions about other things you do) seems to operate in many sales calls. If the salesperson is perceived by the prospect as effective at the beginning of the call, she or he will be perceived as effective during the rest of the call, and vice versa.

Some experts argue that the customer's name should be used in the opening statement. Dale Carnegie, a master at developing relationships, said a person's name is "the sweetest and most important sound" to that person. Using a person's name indicates respect and a recognition of the person's unique qualities. Others disagree with this logic, claiming that using the person's name, especially more than once in any length of time, sounds phony and insincere. Perhaps the best approach is to use the prospect's name in the opening, then use it sparingly during the rest of the call.

Some approaches to opening a sales call are described next. An **approach** is a method designed to get the prospect's attention and interest quickly and to make a smooth transition into the next part of the presentation (which is usually to more fully discover the prospect's needs). Because each prospect and sales situation differs, salespeople should be adaptable and be able to use any or a combination of openings. Also, keep in mind that approaches are usually less important with partnering customers whom the salesperson has already met.

Introduction Approach

In the **introduction approach,** salespeople state their names and the names of their companies, and they may hand the prospect their business cards. Handing the prospect a business card helps the prospect remember the salesperson's name and firm. Prospects may not hear the name because they are busy sizing up the salesperson. Some salespeople think a business card can be distracting and find that giving their card at the end of the interview is more effective.

The introduction approach is the simplest way to open a sales call. However, it is perhaps the least effective way because it is unlikely to generate much interest. It is used most often in conjunction with other methods.

Here is a basic introduction approach:

Ms. Fontaine, thank you for seeing me today. My name is John Locklear, and I'm with Best Foods.

Referral Approach

Using the name of a satisfied customer or a friend of the prospect can begin a sales call effectively. Salespeople frequently present letters of introduction or testimonials. The **referral approach** is often effective with amiables and expressives (see Chapter Six) because they like to focus on relationships.

Sharing letters from satisfied customers helps this salesperson introduce a new product to a pig farmer in Ireland.

Courtesy Merck & Co., Inc.

Because prospects often will contact these references, salespeople should use only the names of individuals and companies to whom they would like the prospect to talk. Successful salespeople always gain permission from references prior to using them. Dropping names and stretching the truth concerning third parties will almost always backfire. Also, remember that "The right contact may get you in the door, but it's knowledge that gets and keeps the business."[6]

Here are some examples of referral approaches:

Mr. Lewis, I appreciate your seeing me today. I'm here at the suggestion of Ms. McQueen of Brock Control Systems, Inc. She thought you would be interested in our new marketing and sales productivity system.

Mr. Braden, several of the other CPAs in town are now using our database management software package. Here are some letters they have written about what our service has meant to them.

Benefit Approach

Perhaps the most widely used sales call opening is the **benefit approach,** which focuses the prospect's attention on a product benefit. For this approach to be effective, the benefit must be of real interest to the prospect. Unless the salesperson knows the prospect's needs (either from good precall information gathering or from other visits), this approach cannot succeed. In addition, it should be specific, something the prospect can actually realize and something that can be substantiated during the presentation. The benefit approach is effective for drivers and analyticals (who like to get down to business rather quickly), because it gets right to the point. For example,

Mr. Scofield, I would like to tell you about a copier that can reduce your copying costs by 15 percent.

Your secretary can save one hour per day using the spelling checker and auto-merge features of this new version of WordPerfect's word processing package.

Ms. Twombly, AT&T can save your firm at least $100,000 by transmitting voice, data, and images all at the same time, over one line, using our new ISDN network.

Product Approach

The **product approach** involves actually demonstrating a product feature and benefit as soon as the salesperson walks up to the prospect. Its advantage is that it appeals to the prospect visually as well as verbally; handing the product to prospects for their examination adds even more involvement. This approach can be very effective for expressives. Here are several examples:

[*Carrying a portable fax, 2 $\frac{1}{2}$″ × 6″ × 12″, into an office*] Ms. Joyner, you spend a lot of time on the road as an investigative lawyer. Let me show you how this little fax machine can transform your car's cellular phone into an efficient, effective 'office.'

[*Handing the buyer a scarf made out of a new synthetic material*] Is it silk or something else?

[*Handing a photograph of a computer-controlled milling machine to a production manager*] How would you like to have this machine in your shop?

One salesperson uses an interesting approach for her doctors that resembles a product approach for the service features of her product, a prescription drug:

[*Playing a recording of a telephone ringing*] That call could be one of your patients calling to complain about her estrogen replacement therapy. But not if she is on *our* drug.

Compliment Approach

Most people enjoy being praised or complimented, but such an approach poses a danger. Insincere flattery is often obvious and offensive to prospects. In using the **compliment approach,** the compliment must be both sincere and specific. Sincerity relates directly to specificity. For example, the compliment "Mr. Smith, congratulations on the cost savings you achieved through the recent reorganization" is far more effective than "Mr. Smith, you are a really good businessperson."

Also, complimenting the obvious will not be effective. Chances are that others have already complimented the prospect about obviously noteworthy things (e.g., a golf tournament trophy in the office, a much publicized and unusual fourth-quarter profit for the prospect's firm).

The compliment approach can also backfire. One salesperson, when calling on a 55-year-old man, noticed a picture of a beautiful 25-year-old woman on the buyer's desk. The seller said, "You certainly have a beautiful daughter," to which the buyer replied, "That's my wife!" It is generally best to stick to neutral topics unless you are sure of your information.

The compliment approach can be effective for all personality types. Here are two examples:

I noticed as I walked in that you are carrying the new INX15 machines. They are going to set a new standard of excellence in your industry. You're the first dealer I've called on who is displaying them. It's perfect evidence of your innovativeness and quest for quality!

I was calling on one of your customers, Jackson Street Books, last week, and the owner just couldn't say enough good things about your service. It sure says a lot about your operation to have a customer just start praising you out of the blue.

Question Approach

Beginning the conversation with a question or by stating an interesting fact in the form of a question is the **question approach**. It gets the customer's attention, motivates a response, and initiates two-way communication. The following questions illustrate this approach:

Ms. Garnett, what is your reaction to the brochure I sent you on our new telemarketing service?

Mr. Ledford, if I can show you a way to reduce your turnover, would you be interested?

Ms. Stiles, have you heard of the new free delivery service our firm is offering to doctors' offices such as yours?

One variation of the question approach is called the **Socratic approach**.[7] In this approach, the customer is queried as to his or her opinion of a crucial topic. The topic is usually related to the seller's product and the buyer's need. Apparently this approach is successful because it focuses on the customer's needs and does so in a way that lets the customer be in charge of the meeting. For example, a salesperson might start off a presentation by asking,

Ms. Johnson, I'm prepared today to talk about the new cargo dividers we briefly discussed on the phone. If you could give me your perspectives on that issue, we can focus this meeting on exactly what interests you.

Developing Rapport

Rapport in selling is a close, harmonious relationship founded on mutual trust. Ultimately the goal of every salesperson should be to establish rapport with each customer. Often salespeople can accomplish this with some friendly conversation early in the call. Part of this process involves identifying the prospect's social style and making necessary adjustments (see Chapter Six).

The talk about current news, hobbies, mutual friends and the like that usually breaks the ice for the actual presentation is often referred to as **small talk**. Examples include the following:

I understand you went to OSU? I graduated from there too, with a BBA, in 1990!

Did you happen to see the Cowboys game on TV last night?

I was just talking to Jane Wester, the controller, downstairs. She and I are on the same softball team, and wow, can she ever pitch a fastball!

Customers are more receptive to salespeople with whom they can identify, that is, with whom they have something in common. Thus, salespeople will be more effective with customers with whom they establish such links as mutual friends, common hobbies, or attendance at the same schools. Successful salespeople engage in small talk more effectively by first performing **office scanning,** looking around the prospect's environment for relevant topics to talk about.

Be careful, however, when engaging in small talk, or it can be to your detriment. Jeannette Scollard tells of a client who asked her opinion of the economic outlook. "I foolishly told him my view of the economy, which was that it was going up. He was so put out that I would disagree with him. It took me years to repair our relationship."[8] It is generally best to avoid controversial topics.

Of course, salespeople should consider cultural and personality differences and adapt the extent of their nonbusiness conversation accordingly. For example, an AT&T rep would probably spend considerably less time in friendly conversation with a New York City office manager than with, say, a manager in a rural Texas town. Businesspeople in Africa place such high value on establishing friendships that the norm calls for a great deal of friendly conversation before getting down to business. Amiables and expressives tend to enjoy such conversations, whereas drivers and analyticals may be less receptive to spending much time in nonbusiness conversation. Also, there would not be a need for small talk if the salesperson had utilized the question or product approach when getting the customer's attention.

It is important to maintain rapport with all contacts within the buyer's organization. Selling Scenario 9.1 describes what can happen when a salesperson forgets to do this.

When Things Go Wrong

Making and maintaining a good impression is important. How nice it would be if the beginning of every call went as smoothly as we have described here. Actually, things do go wrong sometimes. (Question 3 in the Questions and Problems section at the end of this chapter allows you to think about what you would do in some rather awkward situations. You should read them even if your professor doesn't assign them!)

The best line of defense when something goes wrong is to maintain the proper perspective and a sense of humor. It's probably not the first thing you have done wrong and probably will not be your last. A good example of a call going downhill fast is the following experience, related by a salesperson:

> *I pulled my right hand out of the pocket and stuck it forward enthusiastically to shake. Unfortunately, a ball of lint, about the size of a pea, had stuck to the tip of my fingers and was now drifting slowly down onto the document he had been reading. We both watched it descend, as compelling as the ball on New Year's Eve. We shook hands, anyway. I said, "Excuse me," and bent forward to blow the ball of lint off the document. As I did so, I put a dent in the front edge of his desk with my briefcase.*[9]

The worst response by this salesperson would be to faint, scream, or totally lose control. A better response would include a sincere apology for the dent and an offer to pay for any repairs. Further, proper planning might have prevented this situation in the first place. If the salesperson had walked into the room with his hands out of his pockets, he would not have picked up the lint.

Of course, you can get into trouble without even saying a word. Be careful when using gestures in other cultures because they often take on different meanings. For example, the OK sign (touching your thumb to your index finger) actually means "worthless" in France, "can I have small change?" in Japan, and "the bird" in Brazil.[10] Imagine the reactions you would get by giving the OK sign at the conclusion of signing a contract in each of these cultures!

Don't Forget Anyone

Don't ever underestimate or downplay anyone in the prospect's or client's organization. One salesperson in our company had done an excellent job of selling to a major account, her largest. In meetings, the vice president of marketing was her main contact and there were numerous other people in attendance at most meetings. One of the circulation directors, who appeared to be fairly new, was also in most meetings, but the salesperson, who had a great relationship with the vice president of marketing, paid little attention to this circulation director. She essentially ignored the relationship with this lower-level manager.

Sure enough, when the vice president of marketing got promoted, and the circulation director became the new vice president of marketing, there was a problem.

In spite of the great relationship the salesperson had with the previous vice president of marketing, and despite the fact that the salesperson had otherwise been doing a good job, the new vice president of marketing asked for a new salesperson.

Although this type of situation rarely happens (in fact, it has only happened twice in our company's history), the price paid by the salesperson can be enormous. It's the stuff of which ruined careers are made. The strategy is to treat *all* contacts at a prospect or client organization exactly as if they were your *main* contact.

Source: George J. Kiebala, Account Executive, Direct Marketing Technology, Inc., personal correspondence, May 5, 1993, used by permission.

IDENTIFYING THE PROSPECT'S NEEDS

Once the salesperson has entered and captured the buyer's attention, it is time to find out what the buyer's needs are. To do this, a salesperson might use transition sentences like the following (assuming a product approach was used to gain attention): "Well, I'm glad you find this little model interesting. And I want to tell you all about it. But first, I need to ask you a few questions to make sure I understand what your specific needs are. Is that okay?" If the buyer gives permission, the salesperson then begins to ask questions about the buyer's needs.

It's important for this salesperson to discover the farmer's problems before describing his new fertilizer product.

Andy Sacks/Tony Stone Images

Occasionally a salesperson makes the mistake of starting with product information rather than with a discussion of the prospect's needs.[11] The experienced salesperson, however, attempts to find out the prospect's needs and problems at the *start* of the relationship. In reality, discovering needs is still a part of qualifying the prospect.

Research continually demonstrates the importance of needs discovery. An analysis by Huthwaite, Inc., of more than 35,000 sales calls in 23 countries over a 12-year period revealed that what distinguished successful salespeople was their ability to discover the prospect's needs.[12] Discovering needs was more important than opening the call strategically, handling objections, or using closing techniques effectively.

There is an underlying reason for every customer need. It is important that the salesperson continue probing until he or she uncovers the root problem or need. This has been termed "finding the need behind the need"[13] and is graphically illustrated in Exhibit 9.2.

Given the importance of needs discovery, it is not surprising that most sales training programs now teach salespeople how to discover the prospect's needs. How successful are these programs? According to one study, 87 percent of 432 buyers at firms of all sizes said that salespeople do not know how to ask the right questions about their companies' needs.[14] Almost half said the biggest problem with salespeople is that they talk too much. Another study found that salespeople's perceptions of their customers' needs were less accurate than perceptions formed by sales mangers or customer service personnel.[15] This information reinforces the importance of salespeople learning how to discover needs and letting the prospect talk.

As you discover needs, keep in mind that this process can be very uncomfortable for the prospect. The prospect may resent your suggesting that there could be a problem or a better way to do things. When faced with direct evidence that things could be better, the prospect may express fear (fear of losing his or her job if things are not corrected, or of things changing and the situation getting worse than it is now). Also, remember that the amount of time and effort needed to discuss needs varies greatly depending on the type of industry, the nature of the product, the

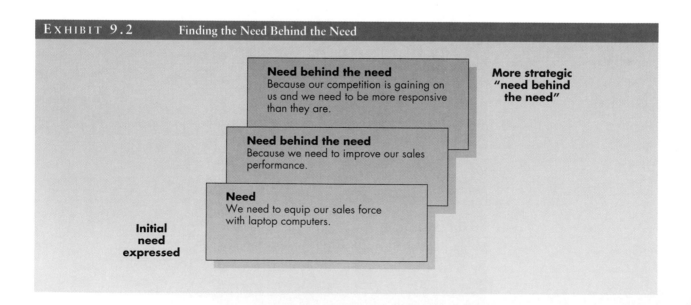

EXHIBIT 9.2   Finding the Need Behind the Need

Need behind the need
Because our competition is gaining on us and we need to be more responsive than they are.

More strategic "need behind the need"

Need behind the need
Because we need to improve our sales performance.

Need
We need to equip our sales force with laptop computers.

Initial need expressed

length of the relationship with the buyer, and so forth. We will come back to this issue after we examine methods of identifying needs.

Remember to Communicate Effectively

Chapter Five covered most of the important communication principles regarding how to effectively ask questions of the prospect and be a better listener. Remember to speak naturally while asking questions. You don't want to sound like a computer asking a set of rote questions. Nor do you want to appear to be following a strict word-for-word outline that you learned in your sales training classes.[16]

Remember, it is a good idea to gain permission before beginning to ask questions. For example, you might say something like, "Do you mind if I ask you a few questions so I can learn more about ways to serve your needs?"

We will now briefly describe two of the most widely used systems of needs identification taught to salespeople today.

Asking Open and Closed Questions

In the first method of needs discovery, salespeople are taught to distinguish between open and closed questions and then encouraged to utilize more open questions. Many highly respected sales training organizations, like Wilson Learning Corporation and Learning International, utilize this type of approach. **Open questions** require the prospect to go beyond a simple *yes/no* response. They encourage the prospect to open up and share a great deal of useful information. For example:

> What kinds of problems have the new federal guidelines caused for your division?
>
> What do you know about our firm?
>
> When you think of a quality sound system, what comes to mind?

Closed questions require the prospect to simply answer *yes* or *no* or to offer a short, fill-in-the-blank type of response. Examples include:

> Have you ever experienced computer downtime as a result of an electrical storm?
>
> Is fast delivery important for your firm?
>
> Customers have expressed a desire to have many features, including four channels, AC/DC power, a four-year warranty, and easily upgradable equipment. Which of these are important to you?

In most cases, salespeople need to ask both open and closed questions. Open questions help to paint the broad strokes of the situation, whereas closed questions help to zero in on very specific problems and attitudes. Some trainers believe simple, closed questions are best at first. Prospects become accustomed to talking and start to open up. After a few closed questions, the salesperson moves to a series of open questions. At some point, he or she may revert back to closed questions.

What are some good (and bad) questions that salespeople ask? A group of certified purchasing managers gave their perspectives and examples of good questions, which include:

> What kind of value-added are you looking for?
>
> How can we help improve your product or process?
>
> If you're interested in my product, how do you plan to use it?
>
> What can I do to make your job easier?

Examples of bad questions, according to this panel, include:

What does your company do?

Can we do something for you?

Are you the person who is going to make the buying decision?

Who are you buying from now?

What will it take to get your business?[17]

Exhibit 9.3 contains an illustrative dialogue of a bank selling a commercial checking account to a business. In this sales presentation, the salesperson's questions follow a logical flow. Note that follow-up probes are often necessary to clarify the

EXHIBIT 9.3	Salesperson's Probe	Prospect's Response
Using Open and Closed Questions to Discover Needs	Have you ever done business with our bank before? [closed]	No, our firm has always used First of America Bank
	I assume, then, that your checking account is currently with First of America? [closed]	Yes.
	If you could design an ideal checking account for your business, what would it look like? [open]	Well, it would pay interest on all idle money, have no service charges, and supply a good statement.
	When you say "good statement" what exactly do you mean? [open]	It should come to us once a month, be easy to follow, and help us reconcile our books quickly.
	Uh-huh. Anything else in an ideal checking account? [open]	No, I guess that's about it.
	What things, if any, about your checking account have dissatisfied you in the past? [open]	Having to pay so much for our checks! Also, sometimes when we have a question, the bank can't answer it quickly because the computers are down. That's frustrating!
	Sure! Anything else dissatisfy you? [open]	Well, I really don't like the layout of the monthly statement we get now. It doesn't list checks in order; it has them listed by the date they cleared the bank.
	Normally, what balance do you have on hand in your account? What minimum balance can you maintain? [closed]	About $8,500 now. We could keep a minimum of around $5,000, I guess.
	Are you earning interest in your account now? [closed]	Yes, 3 percent of the average monthly balance if we maintain at least a $5,000 balance.
	What kind of service charges are you paying now? [closed]	$25 per month, 25 cents per check, 10 cents per deposit.
	[more questions]	
	Is there anything else that I need to know before I begin telling you about our account? [open]	No, I think that just about covers it all.

prospect's responses. At the conclusion of asking open and closed questions, the salesperson should have a good feel for the needs and wants of the prospect.

One final suggestion is to summarize the prospect's needs. For example,

> So, let me see if I have this right. You are looking for a checking account that pays interest on your unused balance and has a monthly statement . . . Is that correct?

This helps to solidify the needs in the prospect's mind and ensure that the prospect has no other hidden needs or wants.

SPIN Technique

The SPIN method of discovering needs was developed by Huthwaite, Inc., after analyzing thousands of actual sales calls.[18] The results indicated that successful salespeople go through a logical needs identification sequence, which Huthwaite labeled **SPIN:** Situation questions, Problem questions, Implication questions, and Need payoff questions. SPIN works for those salespeople involved in a **major sale,** one that involves a long selling cycle, a large customer commitment, an ongoing relationship, and large risks for the prospect if a bad decision is made. Major sales can occur anywhere but often involve large, major, or national accounts. For example, both Johnson Wax and Firestone use SPIN for their major accounts but use other techniques for smaller accounts.

SPIN actually helps the prospect identify unrecognized problem areas. Often, when a salesperson simply asks an open question such as "What problems are you having?" the prospect replies, "None!" The prospect isn't lying; he or she just may not realize that a problem exists. SPIN excels at helping prospects test their current opinions or perceptions of the situation. Also, SPIN questions may be asked over the course of several sales call, especially for large or important buyers.

Situation Questions

Early in the sales call, salespeople ask **situation questions,** general data-gathering questions about background and current facts. Because these questions are very broad in nature, successful salespeople learn to limit them; prospects quickly become bored or impatient if they hear too many of them. Inexperienced and unsuccessful salespeople tend to ask too many situation questions. In fact, many situation-type questions can be answered through precall information gathering and planning. If a salesperson asks too many situation questions, the prospect will think the salesperson is unprepared. Examples of situation questions include:

> What's your position? How long have you been here?

> How many people do you employ? Is the number growing or shrinking?

> What kind of handling equipment are you using at present?

> How long have you had it? Did you buy or lease it?

Problem Questions

When salespeople ask about specific difficulties, problems, or dissatisfactions the prospect has, they are asking **problem questions.** Experienced salespeople tend to ask many such questions. In smaller sales, the use of problem questions is strongly related to success. In major sales, however, the salesperson must ask additional kinds of questions to discover needs and obtain commitment. Here are some examples of problem questions:

Do you find your current machine difficult to repair?

Have you experienced any problems with the overall quality of your forklifts?

Do your operators ever complain that the noise level is too high?

Implication Questions

Questions that logically follow one or more problem questions and are designed to help the prospect recognize the true ramifications of the problem are **implication questions.** Implication questions cannot be asked until some problem area has been identified (through problem questions). They attempt to motivate the prospect to search for a solution to the problem. Ultimately implication questions set the stage so that the seriousness of the problem outweighs the cost of the solution (which the salesperson will offer later). Successful salespeople in major sales tend to ask lots of implication questions, such as:

What happens if you ship your customer a product that doesn't meet specs?

Does paying overtime for your operators increase your costs?

What does that do to your price as compared to your competitors'?

Does the slowness of your present system create any bottlenecks in other parts of the process?

Need Payoff Questions

When salespeople ask questions about the usefulness of solving a problem, they are asking **need payoff questions.** They want the prospect to focus on solving the problem rather than continually thinking about the problem itself. In contrast to implication questions, which are problem centered, need payoff questions are solution centered:

If I can show you a way to eliminate paying overtime for your operators and therefore reduce your cost, would you be interested?

So, would you like to see a reduction in the number of products that don't meet quality specifications?

Would an increase in the speed of your present system by 5 percent resolve the bottlenecks you currently experience?

If the prospect responds negatively to a need payoff question, the salesperson has not identified a problem serious enough for the prospect to take action. The salesperson should probe further by asking additional problem questions, implication questions, and then a new need payoff question.

Conclusions about SPIN

One critical advantage of SPIN is that it encourages the prospect to define the need. At no time during the questioning phase does the salesperson ever talk about his or her product. As a result, the prospect views the salesperson more as a consultant trying to help than as someone trying to push a product.

SPIN selling has been taught to thousands of salespeople in Fortune 500 firms. Many salespeople quickly learn to master the technique, whereas others have more difficulty. The best advice is to practice each component and to plan implication and need payoff questions before each sales call. An abbreviated needs identification dialogue appears in Exhibit 9.4; it demonstrates all components of SPIN for a salesperson selling desktop publishing programs.

Reiterating Needs You Have Identified Before the Meeting

The extent to which one has to identify needs during any call depends on the extent and success of precall information gathering. The salesperson may fully identify the needs of the prospect before making the sales call. In that case, reiterating the needs early in the sales call is advisable so that both parties agree about what problem they are trying to solve. For example:

> Mr. Jonesboro, based on our several phone conversations, it appears that you are looking for an advertising campaign that will position your product for the rapidly growing senior citizen market, at a cost under $100,000, using humor and a well-known older personality, and delivered in less than one month. Is that an accurate summary of your needs? Has anything changed since we talked last?

Likewise, in multicall situations, going through a complete needs identification at every call is unnecessary. But it is still best to briefly reiterate the needs identified to that point:

> In my last call, we pretty much agreed that your number one concern is customer satisfaction with your inventory system. Is that correct? Has anything changed since we met last time, or is there anything else I need to know?

Additional Considerations

How many questions can a salesperson ask to discover needs? It depends on the situation. Generally, as the risk of making the wrong decision goes up, so does the amount of time the salesperson can spend asking the prospect questions. For example, a Boeing salesperson could address an almost unlimited number of questions to

---

EXHIBIT 9.4

Using the SPIN Technique to Sell Desktop Publishing

Salesperson Do you ever send work out for typesetting? [situation question]

Prospect Yes, about once a month we have to send work out because we are swamped.

Salesperson Is the cost of sending work out a burden? [problem question]

Prospect Not really. It only costs about 5 percent more, and we just add that to the customer's bill.

Salesperson Do you get fast turnaround? [problem question]

Prospect Well, now that you mention it, at times the turnaround is kind of slow. You see, we aren't given very high priority since we aren't big customers for the printer. We only use them when we have to, you know.

Salesperson What happens if you miss a deadline for your customer because the turnaround is slow? [implication question]

Prospect That only happened once, but it was disastrous. John, the customer, really chewed me out, and we lost a lot of our credibility. Like I say, it only happened once, and I sure wouldn't like it to happen again to John—or any of our customers, for that matter!

Salesperson If I can show you a way to eliminate outside typesetting without having to increase your staff, would you be interested? [need payoff question]

Prospect Sure. The more I think about it, the more I realize I have something of a time bomb here. Sooner or later, it's going to go off!

United Air Lines, because the airline realizes the importance of having Boeing propose the right configuration of airplane. A salesperson for Johnson Wax calling on a local grocery store, on the other hand, has very little time to probe about needs before discussing an upcoming promotion and requesting an end-of-aisle display. Regardless of the situation, the salesperson should carefully prepare a set of questions to ask to maximize the use of available time.

Occasionally the prospect will refuse to provide answers to important questions on the ground that the information is confidential or proprietary. The salesperson can do little except emphasize the reason for asking the questions. Ultimately, the prospect needs to trust the salesperson enough to divulge sensitive data. (Chapters Two and Thirteen discuss trust-building strategies.)

At times, buyers do not answer questions because they honestly don't know the answer. The salesperson should then ask if the prospect could get the information in some way. If not, the salesperson can often ask the buyer's permission to probe further within the prospect's firm for the information.

On the other hand, some buyers not only will answer questions but will appear to want to talk indefinitely. In general, the advice is to let them talk. This is particularly true for many cultures. For example, people in French-speaking countries love rhetoric (the act and art of speaking); attempts to cut them off will only frustrate and anger them.[19]

Thinking *it* **Through**	When prospects reveal facts about their situations and needs, they often provide some very sensitive and confidential information. Assume a prospect at firm A reveals to you her firm's long-term strategy of securing business away from her competitor, firm B. Also assume you are close friends with the buyer at firm B, which is one of your biggest customers. Further assume firm B is beginning to lose market share and you sense that this will result in your commissions falling off. You have at best a 50–50 chance of landing firm A's business. Will you share the confidential information with firm B's buyer? What are the long term consequences of your proposed behavior.

Developing a Strategy for the Presentation

Based on the needs identified, the salesperson should develop a strategy for how best to proceed to meet those needs. This includes sorting through the various options available to the seller to see what is best for this prospect. To do this, the salesperson usually must sort out the needs of the buyer and prioritize them. Decisions have to be made about the exact product or service to recommend, the optimal payment terms to present for consideration, service levels to suggest, product or service features to stress during the presentation, and so on.

Products have many, many features, and one product may possess a large number of features that are unique and exciting when compared to competitive offerings. Rather than overload the customer with all of the great features, successful salespeople discuss only those that specifically address the needs of the prospect. For example, suppose a Panasonic salesperson calls on a prospect who he learns (from SPIN questioning) is looking for a VCR to use only as a playback device for training tapes.[20] In this situation, the Panasonic representative should not discuss, or even mention, that one feature of the VCR is that it is ready to hook up to cable systems with no tuning needed. The buyer has absolutely no need for this feature. To talk about features of little interest to the customer is a waste of time.

OFFERING THE SOLUTION TO THE BUYER'S NEEDS

Once the salesperson had discovered the buyer's needs and has developed a strategy to effectively communicate a solution to those needs, it is time to make a presentation that shows how those needs can be addressed. This includes relating product or service features that are meaningful to the buyer, assessing the buyer's reaction to what is being said, resolving objections (covered in Chapter Eleven), and obtaining commitment (the topic of Chapter Twelve).

The salesperson usually begins offering the solution by making a transition sentence, something like the following: "Now that I know what your needs are, I would like to talk to you about how our product can meet those needs." It is important that the seller translate product features into benefits for solving the buyer's needs.[21]

Relating Features to Benefits

A **feature** is a quality or characteristic of the product or service. Every product has many features designed to help potential customers. A **benefit** is the way in which a specific feature will help a particular buyer and is tied directly to the buying motives of the prospect. A benefit helps the prospect more fully answer the question "What's in it for me?" (Exhibit 9.5 lists examples of features and sample benefits for a tractor.) The salesperson usually includes a word or a phrase to make a smooth transition from features to benefits:

> This china is fired at 2,600° F, and what that means to you is that it will last longer. Since it is so sturdy, you will be able to hand it down to your children as an heirloom, which was one of your biggest concerns.

> This set of golf clubs has shallow-faced fairway woods, which means that you'll be able to get the ball into the air easier. That will certainly help give you the distance you said you were looking for.

> Our service hot line is open 24 hours a day, which means that even your third-shift operators can call if they have any questions. That should be a real help to you, since you said your third-shift supervisor was very inexperienced in dealing with problems.

Buyers are not interested in facts about the product or the company unless those facts help solve their wants or needs. The salesperson's job is to supply the facts and then point out what those features mean to the buyer in terms of benefits. In fact, given that the buyer is helped by identifying his or her needs, the salesperson's responsibility is then to prove how those needs can be satisfied. (Chapter Ten will more fully discuss how to offer proof of assertions.)

Buyers typically consider two or more competitive products when making a purchase decision. Thus, salespeople need to know more than just the benefits their products provide. They need to know how the benefits of their products are superior or inferior to the benefits of competitive products.

Sometimes, when selling certain commodities, it is important to sell the features and benefits of the seller's firm instead of the product. For example, Ray Hanson sells fasteners such as bolts and nuts. He states, "In the fastener industry I have found that a generic product, such as a nut or bolt, doesn't have too many features and benefits. We talk to our potential customers about the features our company has, and how these could benefit them as our customers."[22]

When selling to resellers, salespeople have two sets of benefits to discuss with the prospect: what the features of the product will do for the reseller and what the product features will do for the ultimate consumer of the product. Covering both sets of features and benefits is important. Exhibit 9.6 illustrates the two sets of features.

EXHIBIT 9.5   An Example of Features and Benefits

Introducing the Grand L Series.

Features	Benefits
The transmission allows you to shift-on-the-go between the four main gears and forward to reverse.	You can work more quickly and efficiently.
A larger-diameter clutch disc improves operating efficiency and has a longer life.	You won't spend as much on maintenance costs.
The independent PTO can be switched on and off without stopping.	You can work without being interrupted.
The low-noise, low-emission, E-TVCS diesel engine delivers more power with higher torque rise.	You can get more work done in less time.
A full-floating ISO-mounted flat deck provides ample legroom and minimal vibration.	You'll be more comfortable.
The quick-attach front loader has high lift height and powerful lift capacity.	You can move larger loads with less effort.

Now all you have left to complain about is the weather.

KUBOTA TRACTOR CORPORATION

For more information, write to: Kubota Tractor Corporation, P.O. Box 2992-GCM, Torrance, CA 90509-2992. Financing available through Kubota Credit Corporation.

© 1996 Kubota Tractor Corporation

Source: ©Kubota Tractor Corporation.

EXHIBIT 9.6

Features and Benefits of Jello Fruit & Cream Bars, as Presented to a Grocery Store

Features	Benefits
Of importance to the Final Consumer	
Trusted name brand	Since you trust the Jello brand name, you know that this is a high-quality product.
Only 60 calories per bar	You can enjoy a treat without worrying about it's effect on your weight.
Real fruit in every bite	You are getting needed nutrition from a snack.
Only fruit and cream brand that comes in a variety pack	You will be able to meet the different flavor preferences of your family members.
Each pack has 12 bars	You get a better value by purchasing in this family-size pack. Also, you won't run out of snacks as quickly and have to make a trip back to the grocery store.
Of Importance to the Grocery Store	
Test marketed for 3 years	Because of this research, you are assured of a successful product and effective promotion; thus your risk is greatly reduced.
$10 million in consumer advertising will be spent in the next 18 months	Your customers will come to your store looking for the product.
40-cent coupon with front positioning in the national Sunday insert section	Your customers will want to take advantage of the coupon and will be looking in your freezer for the product.
At the suggested retail price of $3.39, your profit margin will be 20 percent	This has a 5 percent higher profit margin than other fruit and cream bars you sell, so you'll make more profit each time you sell a box.
All advertising will feature Bill Cosby	Both parents and children trust and enjoy Bill Cosby. This will increase their desire to purchase the product. As a result, they will come to the store looking for the product.
Trusted, name brand, 60 calories per bar, real fruit filling, comes in a variety pack, 12 bars in each pack (list of features important to final consumers)	Your customers will like the product and continue to purchase it. This will create fast turnover of the product and result in higher overall sales and profits.

Assessing Reactions

While making a presentation, salespeople need to continually assess the reactions of their prospects.[23] It is important that the prospect agree that the benefits described would actually help him or her. By listening to what buyers say and observing their body language, salespeople can determine whether prospects are interested in the product. If buyers react favorably to the presentation and seem able to grasp the benefits of the proposed solution, the salespeson will have less need to make alterations or adjustments. But if a prospect does not develop enthusiasm for the product, the salesperson will need to make some changes in the presentation.

Using Nonverbal Cues

An important aspect of making adjustments is interpreting a prospect's reactions to the sales presentation. By observing the prospect's five channels of nonverbal communication, salespeople can determine how to proceed with their presentations.

Nonverbal cues are important indicators to help salespeople know when to make adjustments. In this picture, even though all members of the buying team are looking at the salesperson, they seem to be giving off different nonverbal cues. Can you interpret them?

Frank Herholdt/Tony Stone Images

Exhibit 9.7 lists signals, or nonverbal cues, that salespeople who are sensitive to a prospect's body language can read. (Chapter Five provides more detailed information about nonverbal cues.)

Positive nonverbal cues are encouraging for the salesperson, and she or he should send the same cues to the prospect.[24] If the prospect gives mixed signals, the salesperson needs to ask open-ended questions to draw out the prospect's reasons for caution. Negative nonverbal signals indicate a serious problem, and the salesperson should refocus the discussion completely after probing for concerns. The best way to avoid negative signals is to deal effectively with mixed signals when they appear. One of the biggest causes of negative signals is the use of an overly aggressive sales pitch.[25]

Verbal Probing

As salespeople proceed through a presentation, they must take the pulse of the situation. This process is often called a **trial close.** For example, after discussing a particularly important feature that helps to meet the prospect's needs, the salesperson should say something like the following:

How does that sound to you?

Can you see how that feature helps solve the problem you have?

Have I clearly explained this feature to you?

You now know a little more about the service offering. Do you foresee any initial limitations to the service?

The use of such probing questions helps to achieve several things. First, it allows the salesperson to stop talking and encourages two-way conversations. Without

EXHIBIT 9.7	Nonverbal Cues That Signal Prospects' Reactions		
Channel	Positive	Mixed	Negative
Body angle	Upright, direct to salesperson	Leaning away from salesperson	Leaning far back or thrusting toward salesperson
Face	Friendly, smiling, enthusiastic	Tense, displeased, superior	Angry, determined, shaking head
Arms	Relaxed, open	Closed, tense	Tightly crossed or thrusting out
Hands	Relaxed, open	Clasped, fidgeting with objects	Fist, pointed finger
Legs	Uncrossed, crossed toward salesperson	Crossed away from salesperson	Tightly crossed away from salesperson

such probing, a salesperson can turn into a rambling talker while the buyer becomes a passive listener. Second, probing lets the salesperson see whether the buyer is listening and understanding what is being said. Third, the probe may show that the prospect is uninterested in what the salesperson is talking about. This allows the salesperson to redirect the conversation to areas of interest to the buyer. This kind of adjustment is necessary in almost every presentation and underscores the fact that the salesperson should not simply memorize a canned presentation that unfolds in a particular sequence.

Salespeople must *listen*. Often we hear what we want to hear (this is called **selective perception**). Everyone is guilty of this at times. For example, read the following sentence:[26]

Finished files are the result of years of scientific study combined with the experience of years.

Now go back and quickly count the number of *F*s in that sentence. Most non–native English speakers see all six *F*s, whereas native English speakers see only three (they don't count the *F*s in *of* because it is not considered an important word). The point is that once salespeople stop actively listening, they miss many things the buyer is trying to communicate.

Making Adjustments

Salespeople can alter their presentations in many ways to obtain a favorable reaction. For example, salespeople may discover during the sales presentation that the prospect simply does not believe they have the appropriate product knowledge. Rather than continue with the presentation, they should redirect their efforts toward establishing credibility in the eyes of the prospect. Salespeople need to continually adapt to the situation at hand.[27]

Other adjustments might require collecting additional information about the prospect, developing a new sales strategy, or altering the style of presentation. For example, a salesperson may believe a prospect is interested in buying an economical, low-cost motor. While presenting the benefits of the lowest-cost motor, the salesperson discovers the prospect is interested in the motor's operating costs. At this point, the salesperson should ask some questions to find out if the prospect would be interested in paying a higher price for a more efficient motor with lower operating costs. On the basis of the prospect's response, the salesperson can adopt a new sales strategy, one that emphasizes operating efficiency rather than the motor's initial price. In this way, the sales presentation is shifted from features and benefits based on a low initial cost to features and benefits related to low operating costs.

BUILDING CREDIBILITY DURING THE CALL

To develop a close and harmonious relationship, the salesperson must be perceived as having **credibility;** that is he or she must be believable and reliable.[28] A salesperson can take many actions during a sales call to develop such a perception.[29]

To establish credibility early in the sales call, the salesperson should clearly delineate the time she or he thinks the call will take and then stop when the time is up. How many times has a salesperson told you, "This will only take five minutes!" and 30 minutes later you still can't get rid of him or her? No doubt you would have perceived the salesperson as more credible if, after five minutes, he or she stated, "Well, I promised to take no more than five minutes, and I see our time is up. How would you like to proceed from here?" One very successful salesperson likes to ask for half an hour and only take 25 minutes.[30] Salespeople who learn how to accurately calculate the time needed for a call and then stand by their promises will be much more successful in establishing credibility.

Another way to establish credibility is to offer concrete evidence to back up verbal statements. If a salesperson states, "It is estimated that over 80 percent of the

SELLING SCENARIO 9.2 (concluded)

I visited the professor on my next trip and again he thanked me for my recommendation of the competitive microscope. He said it worked perfectly.

Two years later I bumped into that same professor in a corridor, and he asked me to stop by his office to discuss a specialized microscope. When I arrived, the told me the specifications of the scope he needed and it turned out that we had a perfect fit. What he needed was a very expensive industry standard microscope for his application. This was a type of microscope that could be supplied by all my competitors.

"When will you need the scope delivered?" It was a good thing I was sitting down when he replied, "I have the budget approved and we will need all of them when the remodeling of the classroom is completed." I don't remember exactly what I said, but I think I stuttered out something like, "Them?" "Yes," he replied, "We will need 25 scopes to equip the entire classroom." This was the largest order the company had ever received for this model. It was sold without a demonstration, or a sample, or a competitive bid. When I offered to send him a

sample to look over, his reply made my day; no, no—it made my year: "I don't need to see it, I know you would only recommend what I really need, only the best."

That experience taught me a lot, it gave me an understanding of the selling process that has served me well over many years, in many different industries, with all sorts of customers and products. What I am always selling is myself. What I mean is, I'm always selling my relationship with the customer, my credibility, my honesty, my expertise, my concern for my customer. Once I sell me . . . the rest is just a logical process of understanding my customers' needs, their goals, and what will create a true win-win relationship. If you can't create a win-win sale with your customer, never, never accept anything else . . . since the ultimate loser will only be you.

Source: Bob Newzell is host and moderator of "Sales Talk," a one-hour talk/interview show on the Business Radio Network, which is heard on 85 stations around the United States. He is a speaker and sales trainer, and designs special sales training programs for companies across the country.

households in America will own videocassette recorders by 2000," she or he should be prepared to offer proof of this assertion (e.g., hand the prospect a letter or an article from a credible source). This topic will be discussed in greater detail in Chapter Ten.

Many salespeople have found that the most effective way to establish credibility is to present a **balanced presentation** showing all sides of the situation—that is, to be totally honest. Thus, a salesperson might mention some things about the product that make it less than perfect or may speak positively about some exclusive feature of a competitor's product. Will this totally defeat the seller's chances of a sale? No. In fact, it may increase the chances of building long-term commitment and rapport.[31] Selling Scenario 9.2 provides an example of using a balanced presentation. Salespeople can keep customers happy and dedicated by helping them form correct, realistic expectations about the product or service.[32]

Salespeople can build credibility by recognizing subcultural differences, not only in foreign markets but in the United States as well. One expert states, "Business people who don't learn the culture of the African American, Hispanic, or Asian markets won't prosper in the nineties and into the year 2000."[33] Credibility can be established by demonstrating sensitivity to the needs and wants of specific subcultures and avoiding biased or racist language.

In selling complex products, sales representatives often must demonstrate product expertise at the beginning of the sales process. Salespeople can accomplish this by telling the customer, without bragging, about their special training or education.

They can also strengthen credibility with well-conceived insightful questions or comments.

When selling complicated technical products and services, Todd Graf notes, "You have to keep it simple. Teach as you go. Keep it simple. Make transitions slow and smooth and always ask if they understand (half the time they don't). This is key because they may have to go back and explain some of your features to the decision maker who isn't present in this meeting."[34]

Salespeople who establish their expertise will have more credibility when they make their presentations. This is especially true for young-looking and inexperienced salespeople. Tracey Brill, a young salesperson, notes that sellers should never use a word if he or she doesn't know the exact definition. Some buyers may even test the salesperson on this. She relates an example of a call on one doctor:[35]

> BRILL Because "Product X" acts as an agonist at the Kappa receptor, miosis will occur.
>
> DOCTOR What does *miosis* mean?
>
> BRILL It means the stage of disease during which intensity of signs and symptoms diminishes.
>
> DOCTOR No! Miosis means contraction of the pupils.
>
> BRILL I did look it up in the 1989 edition of *Taber's Encyclopedic Medical Dictionary.* I would be happy to bring it in next time I come in because I wouldn't want you to think I would use a phrase without knowing what it meant.

At this point the doctor walked out of the room, and Brill thought she had lost all credibility. Actually, he had just gone out and grabbed a dictionary. The first definition was the contraction of the pupils, and the second was Brill's definition. Brill's definition, not the doctor's, fit the use of the term for this medication. The doctor then shook Brill's hand and thanked her for teaching him a new word! The salesperson's credibility certainly increased.

SELLING TO GROUPS[36]

Selling to groups can be both rewarding and very frustrating. On the plus side, if you make an effective presentation, every member of the prospect group becomes your ally. On the down side, groups behave like groups, with group standards and norms and issues of status and group leadership.

When selling to groups, it is important that the salesperson gather information about the needs and concerns of each individual who will attend. This should include a discovery for *each prospect group member:* his or her status within the group, authority, perceptions about the urgency of the problem, receptivity to ideas, knowledge of the subject matter, attitude toward the salesperson, major areas of interest and concern, key benefits for this person, likely resistance, and ways to handle this resistance.

The salesperson should also discover the ego involvement and issue involvement of each group member.[37] An audience member who is **ego involved** perceives the subject matter to be important to his or her own well-being. For example, a person whose job might be eliminated by the introduction of a new computer system would be highly ego involved with regard to the computer system. An **issue-involved** person considers the subject important even though it may not affect him or her personally. For example, an accountant might be interested in what type of new production equipment will be purchased even though the use of that equipment will not affect the accountant in any direct way. Learning the ego involvement and issue involvement of each member in the audience allows the salesperson to adapt portions of the presentation to the specific needs of particular people.

It is important to develop not only objectives for the meeting but also objectives for what the seller hopes to accomplish with each prospect present at the meeting. Planning may include the development of special visual aids for specific individuals present. The seller must expect many more objections and interruptions in a group setting compared to selling to an individual.

During the presentation, it is usually best to create an informal atmosphere in which group members are encouraged to speak freely and the salesperson feels free to join the group's discussion. Thus, an informal location (e.g., a corner of a large room as opposed to a formal conference room) is preferred. Formal presentation methods, such as speeches, that separate buyers and sellers into *them* versus *us* should be avoided. If the group members decide that the meeting is over, the salesperson should not try to hold them.

Of course, most things you have learned about selling to individuals apply equally to groups. You should learn the names of group members and use them when appropriate. You should listen carefully and observe all nonverbal cues. When one member of the buying team is talking, it is especially important to observe the cues being transmitted by the other members of the buying team who are not currently talking to see if they are, in effect, agreeing or disagreeing with the speaker.

It is quite possible that the selling firm will utilize a selling team when meeting with a group of buyers. In fact, the use of teams is becoming more widespread in learning organizations (see Chapter One for a discussion of learning organizations).[38] Because of the importance of selling teams, this issue will be more fully discussed in Chapter Seventeen.

If the group meeting is actually a negotiation session, many more things must be considered. As a result, we have devoted an entire chapter (Chapter Fourteen) to the topic of formal negotiations.

SUMMARY

Salespeople need to make every possible effort to create a good impression during a sales call. The first few minutes with the prospect are important, and care should be taken to make an effective entrance by giving a good first impression, expressing confidence while standing and shaking hands, and selecting an appropriate seat.

The salesperson can use any of several methods to gain the prospect's attention. Salespeople should adopt the approach that is most effective for the prospect's personality style. Also critical is the development of rapport with the prospect. This can often be enhanced by engaging in friendly conversation.

Before beginning any discussion of product information, the salesperson must first establish the prospect's needs. This can be accomplished by the effective use of open and closed questions. The SPIN technique is very effective for discovering needs in the major sale. In subsequent calls, the salesperson should reiterate the prospect's needs.

When moving into a discussion of the proposed solution or alternatives, the salesperson translates features into benefits for the buyer. He or she also makes any necessary adjustments in the presentation based on feedback provided by nonverbal cues and verbal probing.

A close, harmonious relationship will enhance the whole selling process. The salesperson can build credibility by adhering to stated appointment lengths, backing up statements with proof, offering a balanced presentation, and establishing his or her credentials.

KEY TERMS

approach 242	need payoff questions 252
balanced presentation 260	office scanning 246
benefit 255	open questions 249
benefit approach 243	problem questions 251
closed questions 249	product approach 244
compliment approach 244	question approach 245
credibility 260	rapport 245
ego-involved 262	referral approach 242
feature 255	selective perception 259
halo effect 242	situation questions 251
implication questions 252	small talk 245
impression management 238	Socratic approach 245
introduction approach 242	SPIN 251
issue-involved 263	trial close 258
major sale 251	

QUESTIONS AND PROBLEMS

1. Assume you are selling computer software packages to CPAs (certified public accountants). How long beyond the agreed-on appointment time would you be willing to wait in each of the following situations? Why?

   a. This is your first call on a very important CPA. She is the president of the local CPA organization. You have never met her, nor have you found out anything about her.

   b. This is your first call on one CPA partner of a two-partner firm. The other partner has already heard your presentation and was somewhat impressed.

   c. This is your first call on a small, sole-proprietorship CPA in a small town. You just started selling two weeks ago and have not yet closed any sales. The CPA is an expressive.

   d. You have achieved great success in your territory. This is your fifth call on one of the big CPAs in your city. You have a lot of software installation work to do this afternoon for other clients. This CPA is a driver and rarely has more than five minutes of time to talk to you on a visit.

2. What approach method would you use for each prospect listed in question 1 to get his or her attention? Explain the reasons for your choices.

3. Occasionally things don't go the way you plan them to go. Describe what you would do in each of the following situations.

   a. You offer your hand for a handshake, and the prospect just looks at you.

   b. The seat your prospect offers you is uncomfortable, too low, or in direct sunlight.

   c. You use the referral approach, and the prospect says, "I've never trusted that man anyway."

   d. You use the product approach, and the prospect just keeps playing with the product. You are afraid to move on to your presentation without her attention.

e. You state, "This will take only 15 minutes"; then the prospect rambles and uses up most of your time in trivial chitchat. At the end of 15 minutes, you haven't accomplished your call objectives.

f. In the middle of your presentation, the secretary rings in to inform your prospect that her next appointment has arrived at the front desk.

g. Your hands start to tremble just before you go into the prospect's office.

h. You are presenting your product. As you lean over to get something out of your briefcase, your pants/skirt splits open in the back, with a loud tearing sound.

i. You are at dinner with a prospect, and you accidently spill soup on your tie/scarf.

4. Think for a moment about trying to secure a sales job. Assume you are going to have an interview with a district manager at Wallace, Inc., next week for a sales position. What can you do to develop rapport and build credibility with her?

5. "I don't need to discover my prospect's needs. I sell toothpaste to grocery stores. I know what their needs are: a high profit margin and fast turnover of products!" Comment.

6. Assume you are selling automobile tires to a customer. Develop a series of open and closed questions to discover the prospect's needs.

7. Assume you represent your school's placement service. You are calling on a large business nearby that never hires college graduates from your school. Generate a list of SPIN questions, making any additional assumptions necessary.

8. Prepare a list of features and benefits that could be used in a presentation to other students at your college. The objective of the presentation is to encourage the students to enroll in your selling course.

9. In a selling situation between a salesperson and a prospect, much of what is said is really never heard, and part of what is heard is often misinterpreted by one or both of the parties. What techniques might a salesperson use to improve communication with a prospect?

10. "I always shake hands with anyone I call on. If I didn't shake hands, people would not trust me. Besides, it's common knowledge that you're supposed to shake hands in business settings. It makes you seem more friendly." Comment.

11. In what situations should a salesperson use the prospect's first name? When should a more formal salutation be used?

12. How long should a salesperson wait for the prospect? What factors influence your answer?

EXPLORING THE NET

Many Web sites include massive amounts of information about product and service features. However, as this chapter related, it is most important to list benefits, not just features. Visit two of the sites listed here and answer the questions that follow.

http://www.epson.com

http://www.jvc.com

http://www.usa.canon.com

http://www.micron.com

http://www.motorola.com

http://www.caterpillar.com

http://www.deere.com

1. Does the site include features and benefits of the company's products or services?

2. If the descriptions include mostly features (and not explicitly benefits), why do you think the organization chose to offer the information in this way?

CASE PROBLEMS

CASE 9.1
Sony Computer Displays

John Goins is a salesperson for Sony. Today he called on the corporate headquarters of Best-Buy to introduce a new line of flat panel computer displays. Here is the dialogue that occurred between John and Betsy Miller, a senior buyer at BestBuy:

JOHN [*walking up to Betsy, handing her a flat panel computer display*] Have you ever seen anything like that?

BETSY [*quickly putting the display on her desk and sitting down*] I don't even know what it is! Weren't you going to tell me about a new inkjet printer?

JOHN No, I don't sell inkjet printers. You must have me mixed up with someone else. I'm John Goins from Sony.

BETSY Oh. Well, what can I do for you?

JOHN I'm trying to sell you a new product that's hot on the market today. A low-temperature, polysilicon TFT liquid crystal flat panel display.

BETSY [*looking confused*] What?

JOHN Let me ask you a few questions. What do you look for when trying to decide on a new product?

BETSY I look for a product that has broad appeal to a wide range of customer types. Also, one that will supply BestBuy with a good profit margin. Finally, the product should complement what we already sell and result in cross-selling opportunities.

JOHN What is your buying budget for computer display screen products this year?

BETSY That's pretty confidential information. I'm not sure I want to reveal that to you.

JOHN That's okay. It won't make much difference in my presentation anyway. These new display screens are so neat I know you'll want them regardless of how much you have budgeted to spend.

BETSY You sound awfully sure of yourself!

JOHN I am! These displays use nothing but the best polysilicon thin-film transistors. They are compact and offer outstanding resolutions. Our screens come in sizes ranging from 0.5 inches to the 20-inch class. The result is lower-priced displays with the highest technology available today!

BETSY [*interrupting*] You're listing a lot of features! But how are these things selling?

JOHN Great! Say, did I tell you that we have a money-back guarantee and that the displays are selling like hotcakes?

BETSY I really don't know if you told me or not. What is our cost?

JOHN $435 if you buy over 1,000 units, which shouldn't be too much to buy given the number of stores you have.

BETSY I wonder what our profit margin would be. What do you suggest for a retail price?

JOHN That's up to you. These are a must buy this year, Betsy. Can I sign you up for 1,000 units?"

BETSY I don't know. I don't know how they would fit in with our current products. I'm also worried about our profit margin."

JOHN If you buy today, we could have them delivered in four weeks. Okay?"

BETSY I need to think about it. Maybe you can come back in a few months if you're in the area.

JOHN Well, I think you should . . .

BETSY [*interrupting*] I'm sorry, but I have a meeting upstairs in five minutes. Have a nice day.

Questions

1. Identify the attention-getting approach John used. Discuss its effectiveness and describe any ways in which it could be improved.

2. Did John develop rapport and build credibility? If so, how? If not, what could he have done in this area?

3. Evaluate John's attempt at discovering needs. Provide recommendations for improvement.

4. How well did John relate product features to Betsy's needs? How could he have improved?

5. Was John sensitive enough to recognize when adjustments were necessary in his presentation? If not, suggest ways to improve.

**CASE 9.2
Discovering Needs:
A Prevideo Exercise**

Lexington Medical Supply Company has been in the medical equipment and supplies industry for over 20 years. Until recently, the staple of its business has been laboratory chemicals and glassware.

Lexington has just introduced its first piece of automated equipment: a slide processor. The slide processor is a fully automated device that dramatically increases the speed at which slides for microscopic analysis can be prepared. As a result of carefully dispensing expensive processing chemicals, the unit can save laboratories considerable money on the use of these chemicals; the unit also saves on the labor overtime that is often incurred where a high volume of processing is required or when laboratories are understaffed.

In the video segment you will watch Fred Hernandez, a rep for Lexington Medical Supply Company, calling on Dr. Charlotte Walters, chief of pathology at Memorial Medical Center, the city's largest and most comprehensive health care facility. Fred has been speaking regularly with the laboratory supervisor, Curtis Mathews, and, with Curtis's support, they have arranged for Dr. Walters to see a demonstration of the slide processor.

Fred knows that both Curtis and Dr. Walters would like to modernize the operation of the laboratory, and Fred thinks the purchase of the processor is a good place to start. Fred also knows Dr. Walters will probably need the hospital administrator's approval for a purchase of this size.

Following are important features and benefits of the new slide processor:

Features	Benefits
1. Fully automated	Reduces need for human contact during processing procedures
	Frees technologists to do more challenging and interesting work, reducing boredom and turnover
	Ensures consistent and easily readable slides, which speeds slide analysis
2. High-speed operation	Completes an average day's workload in half the time it takes to process manually, thus reducing overtime expenses
	Eases processing backlogs
3. Precision chemical dispensing	Reduces significantly the use of expensive chemicals, thus cutting lab costs (savings on chemicals typically provide a payback on equipment in two years)

Questions

To help you think through how Fred *could* discover Dr. Walters' needs, answer the following questions:

1. Develop a set of open and closed questions to fully discover Dr. Walters' needs.

2. Develop a set of SPIN questions to discover Dr. Walters' needs.

3. Reread the above material and be prepared to watch the videotape in class. Watch how Fred *actually* discovered Dr. Walters' needs.

ADDITIONAL REFERENCES

Baum, Neil. "The Indispensable Salesperson: Ten Steps to Becoming the Salesperson They Can't Live Without." *Personal Selling Power,* March 1993, p. 54.

Brown, Gene; Unal O. Boya; Neil Humphreys; and Robert E. Widing II. "Attributes and Behaviors of Salespeople Preferred by Buyers: High Socializing vs. Low Socializing Industrial Buyers." *Journal of Personal Selling and Sales Management,* Winter 1993, pp. 25–34.

Brown, Stanley. "This Is No Psych Job: Understanding Your Customers' Hierarchy of Needs Can Help to Ensure Their Satisfaction." *Sales & Marketing Management,* March 1995, pp. 32–33.

Campanelli, Melissa. "Sound the Alarm!" *Sales & Marketing Management,* December 1994, pp. 20–25.

Castleberry, Stephen B., and C. David Shepherd. "Effective Interpersonal Listening and Personal Selling." *Journal of Personal Selling and Sales Management,* Winter 1993, pp. 35–50.

Clayton, Carl K. "Making Productive Interest Calls: Identifying and Meeting a Prospect's Needs Are the Major Goals." *Agri Marketing,* May 1990, pp. 99–101.

Conley, Claire. "Socratic Method of Selling: The Question Is the Answer." *American Salesman,* June 1990, pp. 3–7.

Gabriel, Gail. "Dialogue Selling." *Success,* May 1993, pp. 34–35.

Goolsby, Jerry R.; Rosemary R. Lagace; and Michael L. Boorom. "Psychological Adaptiveness and Sales Performance." *Journal of Personal Selling and Sales Management,* Spring 1992, pp. 51–66.

Gschwandtner, Gerhard, and Pat Garnett. *Non-Verbal Selling Power.* Englewood Cliffs, NJ: Prentice Hall, 1985.

Hanan, Mack. *Consultative Selling: The Hanan Formula for High-Margin Sales at High Levels.* New York: AMACOM, 1990.

Henthorne, Tony L.; Michael S. LaTour; and Alvin J. Williams. "Initial Impressions in the Organizational Buyer-Seller Dyad: Sales Management Implications." *Journal of Personal Selling and Sales Management,* Summer 1992, pp. 57–66.

Keenan, William, Jr., "What's Sales Got to Do with It?" *Sales & Marketing Management,* March 1994, pp. 66–69.

Mackintosh, Gerrard; Kenneth A. Anglin; David M. Szymanski; and James W. Gentry. "Relationship Development in Selling: A Cognitive Analysis." *Journal of Personal Selling and Sales Management,* Fall 1992, pp. 23–34.

McElroy, James C.; Paula C. Morrow; and Sevo Eroglu. "The Atmospherics of Personal Selling." *Journal of Personal Selling and Sales Management,* Fall 1990, pp. 31–41.

Miller, Robert B., and Stephen E. Heiman. *Strategic Selling: The Unique Sales System Proven Successful by America's Best Companies.* New York: Morrow, 1985.

Patton, W. E., III, "Use of Human Judgment Models in Industrial Buyers' Vendor Selection Decisions." *Industrial Marketing Management,* 25 (1996), pp. 135–49.

Peterson, Robert A.; Michael P. Cannito; and Steven P. Brown. "An Exploratory Investigation of Voice Characteristics and Selling Effectiveness." *Journal of Personal Selling and Sales Management,* Winter 1995, pp. 1–15.

Schlossberg, Howard. "Dawning of the Era of Emotion: Companies That Survive Will Go Beyond Satisfying Customers." *Marketing News,* February 15, 1993, pp. 2+.

Strutton, David; Lou E. Pelton; and John F. Tanner, Jr. "Shall We Gather in the Garden: The Effect of Ingratiatory Behaviors on Buyer Trust in Salespeople." *Industrial Marketing Management,* 25 (19), pp. 151–62.

Tsalikis, John; Oscar W. DeShields, Jr.; and Michael S. LaTour. "The Role of Accent on the Credibility and Effectiveness of the Salesperson." *Journal of Personal Selling and Sales Management,* Winter 1991, pp. 31–42.

Tullous, Raydel, and J. Michael Munson. "Organizational Purchasing Analysis for Sales Management." *Journal of Personal Selling and Sales Management,* Spring 1992, pp. 15–26.

Whittler, Tommy E. "Eliciting Consumer Choice Heuristics: Sales Representatives' Persuasion Strategies." *Journal of Personal Selling and Sales Management,* Fall 1994, pp. 41–53.

Zurier, Steve. "Consultative Selling Is Here! Distributors Emphasize Account Service over Order Taking." *Industrial Distribution,* July 1990, p. 49.

While Chapter Nine outlined the mechanics of *what* to present (that is, features and benefits), this chapter teaches *how* to present the material effectively. After studying this chapter, you should be able to bring your presentations "alive," keeping your prospects awake and interested as well as helping them remember what you said.

Chapter Ten

Strengthening *the* Presentation

Some Questions Answered in this Chapter Are:

Why do salespeople need to strengthen their oral communication through the use of other tools such as visual aids, samples, testimonials, and demonstrations?

What methods are available to strengthen the presentation?

How can salespeople utilize visual aids most effectively?

What are the ingredients of a good demonstration?

PROFILE

Tia Falcone graduated from Northern Illinois University with a BS in marketing. One of her classes was in selling. She enjoyed the class but told her professor she did not want a job in sales. Nevertheless, she ended up accepting a sales position with Time Warner Cable.

Time Warner Cable has cable TV systems located throughout the United States. Falcone works for the system that services the western suburbs of Chicago. She is employed in the advertising department as an account executive and sells air time on 16 major cable networks, including ESPN, USA, TNT, CNN, and Lifetime. The local businesses she contacts are restaurants, auto dealerships, furniture stores, grocery stores, banks, and dentists to inquire about advertising their business on cable television.

"I have been working for Time Warner Cable for more than five years." Falcone says. "I love what I do, and I enjoy being in sales. Working for a cable TV system has a great advantage in that if a client wants to advertise in a certain area, they have to buy airtime on the cable TV system in that area. That sounds as if there is no competition, but in reality I compete with other forms of advertising such as direct mail, newspaper, radio, and the yellow pages.

"When I meet with a client for the first time, before trying to sell them, I learn as much as I can about their business. I need to know what they do, who their customers are, where they come from—basically all aspects of their business, including current advertising that they are utilizing. By acquiring this information, I can become their marketing planner and explain to them how advertising on cable TV would benefit their business. Next, I can put together an advertising schedule on networks that will target their customers and I develop an advertising campaign. For example, if a client knows their direct mail is working due to the number of coupons they receive, I can put together a commercial and schedule that will help them increase their redemption rate.

"After I sell the client airtime, a commercial spot needs to be made. The client and I will dis-

> *"The client and I will discuss ideas concerning how to present their business on television. I also show them demo tapes of commercials we have produced for other clients. I present these demo tapes to them on a portable TV/VCR, which is an excellent way of showing them the quality of our commercials and the different ways of producing them."*

TIA FALCONE
Time Warner Cable

cuss ideas concerning how to present their business on television. We will discuss things that make them different from the competition or slogans they use with other types of advertising. I also show them demo tapes of commercials we have produced for other clients. I present these demo tapes to them on a portable TV/VCR, which is an excellent way of showing them the quality of our commercials and the different ways of producing them. The producers, at Time Warner's in-house production department, and I will meet with the client to further discuss the content of their commercial. Once the producer has enough information, he or she writes a few scripts. When the client agrees to a script, a "shoot date" is set and the commercial is filmed. After the commercial is approved by the client, it begins running on the schedule I developed.

"My job does not stop when the commercial runs. I must now service the client: I need to know how things are going. Are they getting a response, have sales picked up, and are they noticing new customers? I stay in touch with them on a continual basis to make sure we are achieving the goals we set. If things aren't going as well as they would like, we may need to change the schedule or make some changes in the commercial. Having a good schedule with a poor commercial can be the reason the client is not seeing results. Servicing a client is just as important as selling the airtime. The goal is to keep that client for a long time.

"One of the benefits of this position is developing long-lasting relationships with these clients, some of which have become friends. I never know when I wake up in the morning how my day is going to go. Being responsible for 40 to 50 different clients makes this job un-predictable every day. In any sales position you will have good days and bad days. But overall, taking a position in sales was one of the best decisions I've made."

Visit Our Website@
http://pathfinder.com/@@KDlv*gQApmiR10St/Corp/divisions/cablehome.html

---

THE IMPORTANCE OF A STRONG PRESENTATION

Communication tools such as visual aids, portfolios, samples, models, testimonials, and demonstrations are an important ingredient in many sales calls. Use of such tools focuses the buyer's attention, improves the buyer's understanding, helps the buyer remember what the salesperson said, offers concrete proof of the salesperson's statements, and contributes to a sense of value.

Keeping the Buyer's Attention

Naturally you want to keep the prospect's attention. If you do nothing but talk about your solution, buyers will easily get bored and stop paying attention. How many times has your mind wandered during classroom lectures while the instructor earnestly discussed some topic? What happened? The instructor lost your attention. In contrast, your attention probably stays high in a class in which the instructor uses visuals effectively, brings in guest speakers, and finds ways to get you actively involved in the discussion.

The same is true of buyer-seller interactions. Unless the salesperson can get the buyer actively involved in the communication process and doing more than just passively hearing the salesperson talk, the buyer's attention will probably turn to other topics.

The buyer's personality can also affect his or her attention span. For example, one would expect an amiable to listen more attentively to a long presentation than, say, a driver would. Thus, an effective salesperson should consider the personality of the prospect and adapt the use of communication aids accordingly.

One way a salesperson can help keep the buyer's attention is through the use of humor.[1] The wonderful effects of laughter will put everyone more at ease, including the salesperson. But beware of off-the-wall humor; it can backfire.

Improving the Buyer's Understanding

Many buyers have difficulty forming clear images from the written or spoken word. Salespeople need to utilize all available communication tools to help such people understand the solution to their problem or the opportunity being presented. An old Chinese proverb says, "Tell me—I'll forget. Show me—I may remember. But involve me, and I'll understand."

Many product benefits cannot be explained adequately in nontechnical language. In such cases, only buyers with a technical background may understand a verbal explanation. But a simple demonstration may show other buyers exactly what benefits they can expect.

To help the prospect better understand, five basic channels may be used: the senses of hearing, sight, touch, taste, and smell. Appeals should be made to as many of these senses as possible. Studies show that appealing to more than one sense, called **multiple-sense appeals,** increases understanding dramatically, as the graph illustrates.

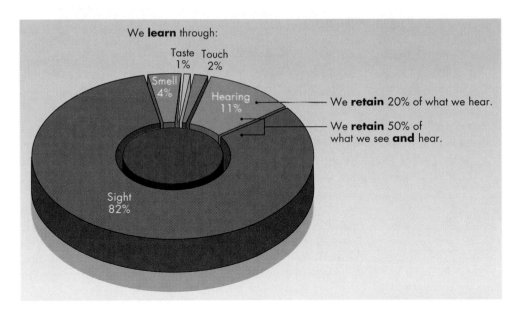

We **learn** through:

Taste 1% Touch 2%

Smell 4%

Hearing 11% — We **retain** 20% of what we hear.

— We **retain** 50% of what we see **and** hear.

Sight 82%

Sellers of some products use appeals to all five senses; others appeal to a maximum of two or three. In selling Ben & Jerry's ice cream novelties to a grocery store manager, the salesperson may describe the product's merits—an appeal to the sense of hearing—or show the product and invite the merchant to taste it—appeals to sight, touch, and taste. Appeals to the merchant's fifth sense, smell, are also possible. On the other hand, salespeople who sell machinery are limited to appeals that will affect the buyers' senses of hearing, sight, and touch.

Helping the Buyer Remember What Was Said

A salesperson may be such an effective orator that the buyer's attention is retained and the buyer fully understands what the seller is saying. This is not enough, however. A truly successful call must achieve one other element: The buyer must remember what was said. Recall that, on average, people immediately forget 50 percent of what they hear; after 48 hours, they have forgotten 75 percent of the message!

Securing an order often requires a number of visits, and in many situations, the prospect must relay to other people information learned in a sales call.[2] In these circumstances, it becomes even more critical that the seller help the buyer remember what was said.

Even selling situations involving one call or one decision maker will be more profitable if the buyer remembers what was said. Vividly communicated features create such a strong impression that the buyer remembers the claims longer and is more likely to tell others about them.

Lasting impressions can be created in many ways. One salesperson swallows some of the industrial cleanser to show that it is nontoxic; another kicks the protective glass in the control panel of a piece of machinery to show that it is virtually unbreakable under even the roughest conditions; still another invites prospects to make an error when using a word processor and then shows how the program spots the error and corrects automatically. A salesperson may demonstrate a weight-sensored alarm system by using the pressure of a feather to activate it. Whatever the method used, the prospect is more likely to remember a sales feature if it is presented skillfully in a well-timed demonstration.

Offering Proof of Salesperson's Assertions

Let's face it: Most people just won't believe everything a salesperson tells them. The communication tools we will discuss in this chapter provide solid proof to back up what the salesperson claims. For example, it is easy for a salesperson to claim that a liquid is nontoxic, but the claim is much more convincing if the salesperson drinks some in front of the prospect.

Creating a Sense of Value

The manner in which a product is handled suggests value. Careful handling gives the impression of value even if no words are spoken. Careless handling implies the product has little value. A rare painting, an expensive piece of jewelry, or a delicate piece of china will be perceived as more valuable if the salesperson uses appropriate props, words, and care in handling it.

The use of communication tools can also make a statement about the importance of the buyer. The prospect should rightfully reflect, "If the seller went to all of this trouble to help me understand, I must be important. I must be worth the attention."

Thinking *it* Through	One of the authors was trained never to use the phrase "Hit this key" when demonstrating how to use a computer to a prospect. Instead, he was trained to say, "Depress this key." Isn't that just being picky? Can simple phrasing changes like that really make a difference to a prospect?

HOW TO STRENGTHEN THE PRESENTATION

Salespeople should ask themselves the following questions: How can I use my imagination and creativity to make a vivid impression on my prospect or customer? How can I make my presentation a little different and a little stronger? With this frame of mind, salespeople will always try to do a better and more effective job of meeting their customers' needs. This section describes many of the communication tools available to such a salesperson. We will explore the use of sales portfolios, models, samples, and gifts; the best way to utilize testimonials; how to effectively use electronic media; how to give powerful demonstrations; how to write effective proposals; and how to quantify the solution. Exhibit 10.1 summarizes the strengths and weaknesses of a variety of visual aids.

EXHIBIT 10.1   Visual Aids: A Comparison

Type of Visual	Relative Cost	Difficulty in Transporting	Complexity in Operating	Effective with Large Groups?
Portfolio	Low	No	Easy	No, unless you use an easel
Models/samples/gifts	Varies	No	Easy	Yes, if you all have one
Testimonials	Low	No	Easy	Yes, if all have a copy
Slides	Medium	Little	Medium	Yes, with large screen
Regular TV/VCR	High	High	Medium	Yes
Compact TV/VCR	High	Little	Easy	No
Laptop computers	High	Medium	Hard	No, unless hooked up to projector
Overhead projectors	Medium	Medium	Easy	Yes
Color video projector	High	High	Medium	Yes
Product demonstrations	Varies	Varies	Varies	Maybe; need hand-on contact

How much is each of the different tools used in real-world sales presentations? A study of 69,000 sales managers provides the following usages:[3]

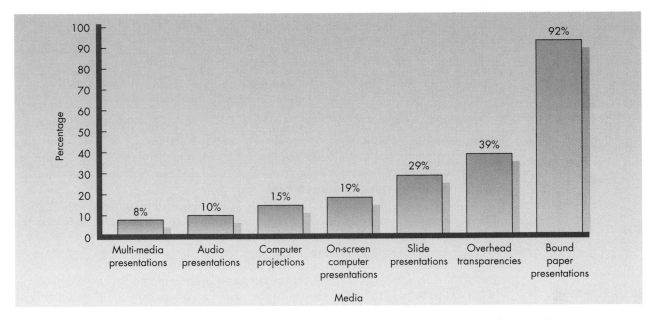

Sales Portfolios

Most salespeople have developed a **portfolio,** which is simply a collection of visual aids that can be used to enhance communication during a sales call. They do not intend to use everything in the portfolio in a single call; rather, the portfolio should contain a broad spectrum of visual aids the salesperson can find quickly should the need arise. In international selling situations where the buyer does not speak the seller's language, visuals are even more important.

Contents of the Portfolio

Tools the salesperson might keep in the portfolio include charts, catalogs, brochures, pictures, advertisements, and testimonials.

Charts   Charts help particularly with illustrating relationships and clearly communicating large amounts of information. Charts may show, for example, advertising schedules, a breakdown of typical customer profiles, details of product manufacture, or profit margins at various pricing points.

Charts can easily be customized by including the name of the prospect's company in one corner or by some other form of personalization. This helps to project the impression that the presentation is fresh and tailor-made for this prospect.[4]

Salespeople also use charts to illustrate the investment nature of purchasing a product. This will be discussed, and an example provided, later in this chapter.

Following are several important hints for developing charts and related visuals:[5]

1. Don't place too much information on a visual; on a textual visual, don't use more than seven words per line or more than seven lines per visual. Don't use complete sentences; the speaker should verbally provide the missing details.

2. Use bullets (dots or symbols before each line to more easily differentiate issues) to emphasize key points.

3. Don't overload the buyer with numbers. Use no more than five or six columns, and drop all unnecessary zeros.

4. Clearly label each visual with a title. Label all columns and rows.

5. If possible, use graphics (e.g., diagrams, pie charts, bar charts) instead of tables. Tables are often needed if actual raw numbers are important; graphics are better for displaying trends and relationships.

6. Use consistent art styles, layouts, and scales for your collection of charts and figures. This will make it easier for the buyer to follow along.

7. Check your visuals closely for typographical errors, misspelled words, and other errors.

Catalogs and Brochures　Catalogs and brochures can help salespeople communicate information to the buyer effectively. The salesperson can not only use them during presentations but can also leave them with the buyer; they will help the buyers remember the issues covered. Brochures often summarize key points and contain answers to the usual questions buyers pose.

Firms often spend a great deal of money developing visually attractive brochures for salespeople. Creatively designed brochures usually unfold in such a way that the salesperson creates and maintains great interest while showing them. Exhibit 10.2 contains a good example of such a brochure.

Pictures, Ads, and Illustrations　Pictures are easy to prepare and relatively inexpensive, and permit a realistic portrayal of the product and its benefits. Photographs of people may be particularly effective. For example, leisure made possible through sav-

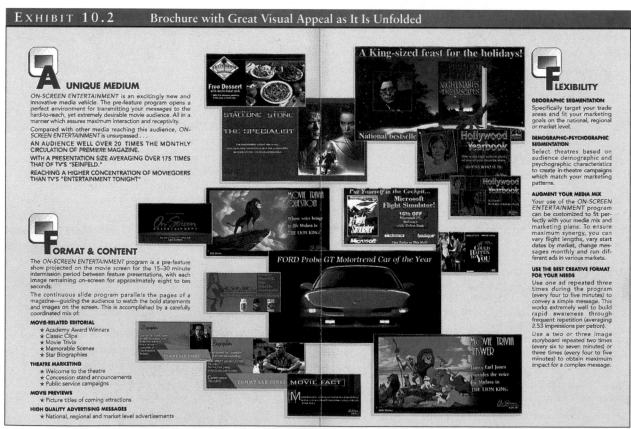

EXHIBIT 10.2　Brochure with Great Visual Appeal as It Is Unfolded

Courtesy the In-Theatre Marketing Company

ings can be communicated via photographs of retired people at a ranch, a mountain resort, or the seashore. Illustrations drawn, painted, or prepared in other ways also help to dramatize needs or benefits. Copies of recent ads may contribute visual appeal. With new technology, even detailed maps can be easily developed, for example, to show how a magazine's circulation matches the needs of potential advertisers.[6]

Testimonials   **Testimonials** are statements, usually letters, written by satisfied users of a product or service. These letters commend the product or service and attest that the writer believes it to be a good buy. For example, company representatives who sell air travel for major airlines have found case histories helpful in communicating sales points. American Airlines recounts actual experiences of business firms, showing the variety of problems that air travel can solve.

The effectiveness of a testimonial hinges on the skill with which it is used and a careful matching of satisfied user and prospect. In some situations, the testimony of a rival or a competitor of the prospective buyer would end all chance of closing the sale; in other cases, this type of testimony may be a strong factor in obtaining commitment. As much as possible, the person who writes the testimonial should be above reproach, well respected by his or her peers, and perhaps a center of influence. For example, when selling to certified public accountants (CPAs), a good source for a testimonial would be the president of the state's CPA association.

Before using a testimonial, the salesperson needs to check with the person who wrote it and frequently reaffirm that he or she is still a happy, satisfied customer. One salesperson for UNISYS Computers routinely handed all prospects a testimonial from a satisfied customer of a new software package. But, unknown to the salesperson, the "satisfied customer" became an unsatisfied one and actually returned the software to UNISYS. (This happens to every vendor of software.) The salesperson kept handing out the letter until one of his prospects alerted him to the situation. He will never know how many other prospects lost interest after contacting that "satisfied customer."

Salespeople should not just hand out a testimonial to every prospect; such letters should be used only if they help to address the buyer's needs or concerns. For example, with a buyer concerned about service, the salesperson could use a testimonial that specifically mentions service. Also, be aware that prospects often discount testimonials, thinking, "I'll bet you used your only satisfied customer, probably a relative, to write this letter. Besides, it talks about things only in very general terms." This kind of thinking highlights the importance of using testimonials strategically rather than routinely.

Displaying the Items

A portfolio can be a collection of loose items. More often, however, the items are placed in some sort of binder or container.

The easel type of portfolio can stand by itself on the prospect's desk or counter. Some larger easel types, those placed on the floor, are used in making presentations to a group. All such easel portfolios are arranged to aid in the anticipated flow of the conversation; the salesperson turns each page after it has been read or used for illustration.

Portfolios also come in binder-type layouts. The contents may be labeled by tabs and punched to fit rings in a binder. This makes the material easy to find and convenient to carry and use. For example, Toledo Scale Company sales representatives use binder portfolios that contain detailed illustrative material indexed and tabbed for all the items Toledo sells.

A large commercial building contractor improved selling efforts by preparing a visual presentation of important facts concerning the business. The spiral-bound portfolio contained such information as thumbnail sketches of the company's key employees, a financial statement, a list of special equipment, copies of letters from satisfied owners of various types of buildings, and pictures of completed industrial plants, apartment houses, stores, supermarkets, and shopping centers. This appeal to the prospect's eye tells a story many words and many minutes cannot equal.

When showing visuals in your portfolio, make sure the portfolio is turned so the buyer can see it easily. Also, don't let the visual interfere with your interaction. It should not be placed, like a wall, between you and the buyer. Remember to look at the buyer, not just at your visual; maintaining eye contact is always important.

Maintain proper control of the visuals during the presentation. Without control, buyers often thumb through catalogs or look ahead at visuals before the salesperson has adequately covered the current visual. One way to do this is to remove the visual after it has been used. This also cuts down on desk clutter and helps you to be more organized. But be careful about removing visuals too quickly. Remember, you are there to meet the buyer's needs. It helps if you can decide which visuals you will leave with the buyer and have copies already made.

Models, Samples, and Gifts

Visual selling aids such as models, samples, and gifts may be a good answer to the problem of getting and keeping buyer interest. Miniature models go to the interview as substitutes for products too large or bulky to transport easily. For example, Brink Locking Systems salespeople carry along a miniature working model of the company's electronic door locks when calling on prison security systems buyers. The model allows them to show how the various components work together to form a fail-safe security network.

Getting samples into the buyer's hands is one of the best ways of helping the buyer evaluate a product.

Courtesy Ace Hardware Corporation

Other salespeople use cross-sectional models to communicate more effectively with the buyer. For example, salespeople for Dixie Bearings use a cutaway model of a power transmission friction reduction product. This helps the buyer, usually an industrial engineer, to clearly see how the product is constructed, resulting in greater confidence that the product will perform as described.

Some sales representatives even carry samples of large and bulky products. Fax machine salespeople for Ambassador Office Equipment have found it pays to bring along the types of machines they plan to sell. When the prospect wants a demonstration, the fax machine is available immediately. Experience has shown that anything can happen if the salesperson gets the interest of the prospect and then must return to the office to get a sample fax machine. Several more calls may be needed to secure an appointment for a demonstration.

Depending on the service or product, samples can make excellent sales aids. Food, office supplies, paper products, and long-distance services exemplify the many products or services that may be sold through the use of samples. Eli Lilly pharmaceutical salespeople almost always leave drug samples for doctors to distribute to their patients. If the drugs perform effectively, the doctors will begin prescribing them for other patients.

Samples and gifts frequently help to maintain the prospect's interest after the call and serve as a reminder for prospects or customers who either buy or do not buy during the presentation. In a Johnson Wax sales campaign, salespeople called on buyers of major chains to describe the promotion. Salespeople walked into each buyer's office with a solid oak briefcase containing cans of aerosol Pledge, the product to be highlighted during the promotion. During the call, the sales representative demonstrated the Pledge furniture polish on the oak briefcase. At the conclusion of the visit, the rep gave the buyer not only the cans of Pledge but also the briefcase. Of course, gift giving must be done with care (see Chapter Three for a discussion of the ethics of gift giving).[7]

Electronic Media

Slides, VCRs, computers, and projectors have become common equipment for the salesperson. Today's more sophisticated buyers are accustomed to watching cable TV and movies that include outstanding graphics, sound, and production. Effective salespeople respond to this trend by using electronic media.

Slides

Slides have been effective selling aids for years. One structural timber firm used slides to convince buyers that laminated wood treated with waterproof glue was a good substitute for steel. Pictures of construction jobs that were actually using laminated arches were converted into a powerful slide show to communicate to architects and builders exactly how and where the company's product was used.

An advantage of slides has always been the relatively low cost of producing them. Also, salespeople can easily tailor the show to any buyer simply by removing and/or reordering the slides. The most effective slide shows utilize multiple projectors and multiple screens along with a stereo sound track. Computers can also be used to give slide presentations.

VCRs

Videocassette recorders (VCRs) are becoming an increasingly more important media tool for salespeople. VCRs improve on slides in that they portray action. Salespeople use VCRs to help the buyer see how quality is manufactured into the product (e.g., a tape showing the production process at the manufacturing plant), how others use the product or service (e.g., a tape showing a group of seniors enjoying the golf course at a retirement resort), promotional support offered with the product (e.g., a tape of the actual upcoming TV commercial for the product), and even testimonials from satisfied users. VCRs are not only used by salespeople in one-on-one and group presentations; they are also used at trade shows and for training the buyer's employees after the sale.

When using VCRs, make sure the video is fast-paced and relatively short. Don't show more than four minutes of a video at one time.

In the past, one of the greatest complaints against VCRs was that they were bulky and impossible to use in office settings. Technology, however, has alleviated these concerns.

Computers

More and more salespeople have adopted laptop computers for use in sales calls in recent years. Computers not only offer excellent visuals and graphics but also allow the salesperson to perform what-if analyses much more easily and graphically. For example, a Procter & Gamble (P&G) key account salesperson was using the computer to demonstrate how a new P&G product would deliver more profit than would a competitor's product in the same shelf space. When the buyer asked what would happen if the P&G product sold for $1.69 instead of the $1.75 suggested price, the salesperson was able to easily change this number in the spreadsheet program. Instantly all charts and graphs were corrected to illustrate the new pricing point, and comparisons with the competitor's product were generated.

Other salespeople use laptop computers to store large amounts of easily retrievable information. For example, Merck pharmaceutical salespeople carry laptops with a database of technical information, as well as complete copies of articles from medical journals. This allows them the flexibility to create completely unique presentations for each physician based on the doctor's need for specific kinds of information. Mike Kling, a salesperson for Becton, has also found benefits from storing lots of information in the computer and then calling up what he needs in a presentation. He states, "My time in front of customers is so much more effective now. I used to have to thumb through a ton of paperwork, but now I just punch a button to give customers prices or product information. It makes me look more professional."[8]

Progressive firms are beginning to explore methods of utilizing high technology to its fullest. Computers can be connected to overhead projectors for group presentations (see Exhibit 10.3). M.D. Buyline, a firm that provides hospitals with information about negotiating for diagnostic medical equipment, equips each of its 20 field account executives with a laptop, a small, 8mm VCR, a speaker, a remote time control unit, and a projection panel.[9] During presentations, salespeople can switch from a 6' × 6' video presentation that includes video testimonials to sales data. One advantage of this particular setup is that the prospect need not have a TV/VCR already in place.

Here are some tips for effectively using multimedia.[10] First, be prepared. Have backup batteries, adapters, and copies of disks. Some experts even suggest that traveling presenters call several rental companies in cities in which they will be presenting to learn about the kinds of equipment they can secure in case of a catastrophe.[11] Second, to avoid embarrassing downtime, get to really know your hardware and software so you can recover if the system crashes. Third, make sure both you and your customer can comfortably view the screens. There should be no glare. Also, the image should be bright enough to view easily (a notorious problem when displaying

EXHIBIT 10.3

Computer Images Can Be Easily Transferred to an Overhead Projector

Courtesy In Focus Systems

computer-generated slide shows using overhead projectors). Fourth, don't let the multimedia presentation replace you, the salesperson, in the meeting. Keep yourself involved in the presentation, and make sure your audience has ample opportunity to ask questions. Fifth, after every presentation, ask yourself what worked well and what did not. Make adjustments accordingly.

Unfortunately, the high cost of technology prevents many salespeople from fully incorporating such tools in their presentations. Presentations with full-motion video can be very costly to produce.[12] Also, high-tech equipment can be difficult to operate and prone to malfunction at the most inopportune times.[13]

Projectors

Overhead projectors are another effective visual medium. The image projected on a wall can be up to 25 times larger than that on a written page, drawing more attention and creating greater impact. Such projectors are noiseless and simple to operate. Overhead transparencies can be made quickly and inexpensively on either a plain paper copier or an infrared transparency maker. One model of projector weighs about 17 pounds, fits under an airplane seat, and looks like a briefcase. This medium can be used for presentations to individuals or to groups.

Other types of projectors are available, some capable of displaying action. For example, Exhibit 10.4 displays a color video projector that is connectable to a VCR or computer.

Product Demonstrations

One of the most effective methods of appealing to the buyer's senses is through product demonstrations, or performance tests. Customers and prospects have a natural desire to prove the product's claims for themselves. Obviously, the proof is much more satisfying and convincing to anyone who is a party to it. However, as Selling Scenario 10.1 discusses, the seller should be aware that some prospects will test the product for reasons other than purchasing it. The following examples

EXHIBIT 10.4

Color Video Projector

Courtesy In Focus Systems

illustrate effective methods of demonstration for each specific situation encountered.

Paper sales representatives use demonstrations to sell quality. Having prospects hold two sheets of paper to the light, the reps point out that in a good grade of paper the fibers are evenly distributed, whereas in a poor grade of paper uneven distribution produces a mottled effect. To show opacity, they have the customer place a material with black lines on it under the sheet and check for show-through.

One enterprising sales representative was having trouble convincing the buyer for a national retailer that his company could provide service at all of the retailer's scattered outlets. On the next trip to the buyer, the sales representative brought along a bag of darts and a map marked with the chain's hundreds of stores and service locations. The buyer was invited to throw darts at the map and then find the nearest stores. The test pointed out that the nearest location for service was always within 50 miles. This "service demonstration" helped win the representative's company a multimillion-dollar order.

Some products can be sold most successfully by getting the prospect into the showroom for a hands-on product demonstration. Showrooms can be quite elaborate and effective. For example, Hewlett-Packard (HP) operates a medical marketing center in Germany. Prospects from across Europe can try all of HP's medical products. Patient responses are electronically simulated, which allows medical personnel to test the equipment in mock-emergency situations.

SELLING SCENARIO 10.1

Beware of Prospects That Are Too Interested

If a prospect is too focused on testing [your product or service] before giving you a try, or is putting an unusual amount of time and effort into the "mechanics" of a test, he or she may not be cognizant of the service aspect (i.e., the personal aspect of the buyer-seller relationship). Often a prospect such as this is, in fact, not interested in making a purchase decision, but rather wants to gather information for other reasons. These reasons might include providing competitive information to a friend or simply gathering information to present to management, or perhaps the prospect is looking to validate his or her current vendor's level of service—but with no intention of switching to a new vendor.

It's best to put selling efforts toward prospects who are committed to the idea of changing vendors and whose actions indicate a desire to learn more about the people, the product, the service, and the relationship that your company would provide. While this clearly does not hold true for all types of selling nor for all situations, when I look back and analyze what percentage of my business came from testing, almost none of our significant accounts tested us before deciding to move their business.

In two specific examples, our company, Direct Tech, expended a tremendous amount of effort, energy, and expense to compete against other "unknown" vendors for a large piece of business which, when the testing was done (and in both cases we had outperformed the other vendors), the decision was nonetheless to stay in-house.

Basically, forget testing, build a good solid relationship, use testimonials, use documentation and proof, then demonstrate superior follow-up and responsiveness—and the sale will be yours.

Source: George J. Kiebala, account executive, Direct Marketing Technology, Inc., personal correspondence, May 5, 1993; used by permission.

Thinking it Through

Many firms provide the salesperson with careful, detailed directions about how to conduct a sales demonstration successfully. One sales manager gave her salesperson these instructions:

"As you reach down to turn the machine on, try to distract the buyer's attention. While our literature claims the machine will start in 10 seconds, it is more like 45 seconds due to the microchips that we had to install under our cost-savings program. As you begin to print the daily activity log, have the buyer look at the log itself, not the screen. The screen will include an error message every time, and our engineers can't seem to find out how to correct it."

What is your reaction to these instructions? Assuming you are the salesperson, what would you say to your manager, and what would you do during the actual sales presentation?

Here are a number of helpful hints for developing and engaging in effective demonstrations:[14]

1. Be prepared. Practice the demonstration until you become an expert. Plan for everything that could possibly go wrong.

2. Secure a proper place for the demonstration, one free of distractions for both you and the buyer. If the demonstration is at the buyer's office, make sure you have everything you need (e.g., power supply, lighting).

Getting the buyer actively involved is critical for effective product demonstrations.

Courtesy Johnson & Johnson; photo by Ted Kawalerski

3. Check the equipment again to make sure it is in good working order prior to beginning the presentation. Have necessary backup parts and supplies (e.g., paper, bulbs).

4. Get the prospect involved in a meaningful way. For example, if selling a tractor to a farmer, don't just drive it for him or her; let the farmer drive the tractor.[15] If a group situation, plan which group members need to participate.

5. Always relate product features to the buyer's unique needs.

6. Make the demonstration an integral part of the overall presentation, not a separate, unrelated activity.

7. The demonstration should be simple, concise, and easily understood. Long, complicated demonstrations add to the possibility that the buyer will miss the point. Avoid any technical jargon except with technically advanced buyers who you know will understand technical terms.

8. If your demonstration includes dead time—that is, time in which the machine is processing on its own—plan what you will do during this period. This is usually a great time to ask the buyer questions and have the buyer ask you questions.

9. Find out whether the prospect has already seen a competitor's product demonstration. If so, strategically include a demonstration of features the buyer liked about the competitor's product. Also, plan to show how your product can meet the prospect's desires and do what the competitor's product will not do.

10. Find out if any buyers present at your demonstration have ever used your product before. Having them assist in the demonstration may be advantageous if they view your product favorably.

11. Probe during and after the demonstration. Make sure buyers understand the features and see how the product can help them. Also, probe to see whether buyers are interested in securing the product.

SELLING SCENARIO 10.2

Demonstrations Can Backfire

Every salesperson has a favorite story to tell in answer to the question "Have you ever had anything go wrong during a demonstration?" Here are a few favorite stories.

Steve was demonstrating the ease of entering information into a computer program designed to generate monthly bills for electric utilities automatically. The buyer calmly sat there as Steve keyed in information for about 15 minutes. Then Steve said, "now, all you have to do to generate those statements is to push this key, right here." The buyer, however, had his eye on a panel and a little switch near the back of the computer. "What's this red key for?" he said, as he opened the panel and pushed the switch. Unfortunately the little red key was a "kill button," which caused the computer to shut itself down, completely wiping out all of the data that Steve had put in. As the screen went blank, the buyer looked at Steve and said, "Oops!" To this day, Steve swears the buyer's act was premeditated.

Dave was demonstrating the ease of using a new copier. Suddenly, as often happens with copiers, the machine jammed. Dave calmly stated, "I'm really glad that happened. It gives me the chance to show you how easy it is to clear a jam in this machine." However, it wasn't that easy. As Dave opened the front panel to remove the offending piece of paper, a column of smoke rose from the machine. The paper was on fire! Dave not only got to show the prospect how to clear a jam, he also had to show the correct procedure for extinguishing fires. The buyer did not place an order for the copier but probably did buy a fire extinguisher for his office on the way back.

Demonstration failures aren't the exclusive territory of high-tech products. Sharon, as she demonstrated a plastic squeeze bottle to a group of potential buyers, asked, "Don't you just hate it when you shake and shake a bottle and the lotion just doesn't come out? Wouldn't it be nice if someone designed a bottle so the lotion would come out in nice, even increments?" At this, Sharon gave the bottle a rather substantial squeeze. Not only did the cap fly off, the lotion spewed all over the buyers at the front. Needless to say, Sharon took no orders that day.

Source: Personal information and Kathleen Hughes, "If You Show It Off and It Won't Work You Have a Problem," *The Wall Street Journal,* June 4, 1987, p. 1.

Remember Murphy's law: What can go wrong will go wrong! And occasionally things do go wrong during a demonstration. Selling Scenario 10.2 provides several examples. If a demonstration "blows up" for any reason, your best strategy usually is to appeal to fate with a humorous tone of voice: "Wow, have you ever seen anything get so messed up? I'll bet Congress couldn't have messed this up better than I have!" Don't let it embarrass or frustrate you. Life is not perfect, and sometimes things just don't work out the way you plan them. If it will help, remember that prospects also are not perfect and sometimes they mess things up as well. Maintaining a cool and level head will probably impress the prospect with your ability to deal with a difficult situation. It may even increase your chances of a sale, since you are demonstrating your ability to handle stress (something that often occurs during the after-sale servicing of an account).

Written Proposals

In some industries, written proposals are an important part of the selling process. As the ConAgra Banquet Foods example in Chapter Fifteen illustrates, some proposals are simple adaptations of brochures developed by a corporate marketing department. But in industries that sell customized products, are involved in a large amount of needs-satisfaction selling, or require competitive bidding (such as many state and local governments do), a written proposal may be necessary for the buyer to organize and compare various offerings.

Proposals are also useful when the salesperson cannot see the decision maker. If, for example, the salesperson is calling on the Tempe, Arizona, office and the final decision will be made in the corporate office in Seattle, a proposal can be used to sell that home office decision maker.

The RFP Process

A document issued by a prospective buyer asking for a proposal may be called a **request for proposal (RFP)**, *request for quote (RFQ)*, or *request for bid (RFB)*. For brevity's sake, we will refer to all of these as RFPs.

The RFP should contain the customer's specifications for the desired product, including delivery schedules. RFPs are used when the customer has a firm idea of the product needed. From the salesperson's perspective, being a part of the specifying process makes sense. Using the needs identification process, the salesperson can assist the customer in identifying needs and specifying product characteristics. The result may be that the only product that can meet the specs is the one sold by that salesperson; when the resulting product truly meets the needs of the customer, that is only fair.

According to purchasers who issue RFPs, proposals that respond to an RFP should include the following:[16]

1. An executive summary containing pricing, time frames, and some product information.
2. Concise responses to questions, with direct references to the original RFP.

What buyers do not want are stacks of material that make them search for their answers; bids priced low in the expectation that the vendor can make it up later in add-ons, changes, and upgrades; and glossy marketing hype.

Writing Proposals

Proposals do the selling job when the salesperson cannot be present. A key issue is keeping the customer's needs in mind. Always write down what the customer needs during the initial meeting. If not, two days later the salesperson will have forgotten some details she or he wanted to cover in the proposal.

Proposals, then, have three parts: an executive summary, a description of the current situation in relation to the proposed solution, and a budget (which details costs). When preparing proposals, salespeople can use the checklist that appears in Exhibit 10.5 to ensure that the proposal proves how the product will satisfy the buyer's needs. Some firms have even developed computer programs to automatically generate sales proposals in response to a set of questions the salesperson answers about a particular customer.[17]

The **executive summary** provides, in one page or less, the total cost minus the total savings (including soft savings), a brief description of the problem to be solved, and a brief description of the proposed solution. It is designed to satisfy the concerns of an executive who is too busy or unwilling to read the entire proposal. The executive summary also serves to pique the interest of all readers by allowing a quick glance at the benefits of the purchase.

Many salespeople actually compare the current situation with the proposed solution on the same sheet. This is accomplished by listing problems with the current product or service in one column and describing how the proposed solution resolves those problems in a second column. The format resembles the Ben Franklin ap-

EXHIBIT 10.5

A Proposal Checklist

A proposal must answer the following questions convincingly:
- *What Problem Are You Going to Solve?*

Show that you understand the problem and the organization's needs. Define the problem as the audience sees it, even if you believe that the presented problem is part of a larger problem that must first be solved.
- *How Are You Going to Solve It?*

Prove that your methods are feasible. Show that a solution can be found in the time available. Specify the topics you'll investigate. Explain how you'll gather data.
- *What Exactly Will You Provide for Us?*

Specify the tangible products you'll produce; explain how you'll evaluate them.
- *Can You Deliver on What You Promise?*

Show that you have the knowledge, the staff, and the facilities to do what you say you will. Describe your previous work in this area, your other qualifications, and the qualifications of any people who will be helping you.
- *What Benefits Can You Offer?*

In a sales proposal, several vendors may be able to supply the equipment needed. Show why the company should hire you. Discuss the benefits—direct and indirect—that your firm can provide.
- *When Will You Complete the Work?*

Provide a detailed schedule showing when each phase of the work will be completed.
- *How Much Will You Charge?*

Provide a detailed budget that includes costs for materials, salaries, and overhead costs.

Source: Kitty Locker, Business and Administrative Communication (Burr Ridge, IL: Irwin, 1989), pp. 401–2.

proach to gaining commitment, described in Chapter Twelve. Such an approach has several advantages: It reminds the customer of the needs actually described in an earlier conversation or an RFP, and it can directly link the benefits of the proposed solution to satisfying those needs. Exhibit 10.6 provides a short example of such a format. If this proposal will be sent to the home office, the salesperson should make it clear that the present situation was identified by the customer's local personnel.

Some proposals are too complicated for such a simple approach. Discussion of the current situation and a description of the proposed solution may each require a

EXHIBIT 10.6

An Example of the Ben Franklin Format

Your Current Vendor (Quick Print)	Our Proposed Solution (Quickie Printers)
No delivery: You must bring it in, using 30 minutes per round trip	Free pickup and delivery: No time is lost driving to or from the copying store; receptionist can stay and do her job, with no more overtime.
Open 8 AM to 6 PM	Open 24 hours per day: Overnight turnaround, which you need for most proposals and bids, now possible on all jobs at no extra cost; gives your marketing staff more time to prepare proposals and bids, resulting in more professional and more profitable bids.
No special discounts	Preferred customer plan: Saves you 5 percent on every order, 10 percent on certain types of jobs; you get more productive workers and copying for less!

separate chapter. Still, readers must be able to quickly relate characteristics of the proposed solution to the needs being met. In fact, don't just assume that a bigger proposal is a better one. One study found that shorter proposals (those with fewer graphics, etc.) actually resulted in more sales.[18]

Presenting the Proposal

Prospects use proposals in many different ways. Proposals can be used to convince the home office that the local office needs the product, or proposals may be used to compare the product and terms of sale with those of competitors. As we mentioned earlier, the intended use will influence the design of the proposal; it will also influence how the salesperson presents the proposal.

When the proposal is going to be sent to the home office, it is wise to secure the support of the local decision maker. While that person is not the ultimate decision maker, the decision may rest on how much effort that person puts into getting the proposal accepted. Salespeople often use a "team effort" approach by asking the local recommending person how to assist in getting the proposal accepted. The salesperson may want to ask for permission to follow up with a phone call directly to the home office, offer to help write a recommendation letter, or ask for permission to have a national account representative or senior executive call on the prospect's home office.

Proposals are often used by buying centers to compare competitive offerings. The salesperson is asked to present the proposal to the buying committee. The challenge is that, as you learned in Chapter Four, buying center members play different roles and have different needs. Therefore, some parts of the presentation and the proposal will be of greater interest to each individual than others. Larry Boyd, sales representative for Quantum Medical, a manufacturer of sonogram equipment, solves this challenge by preparing a separate proposal for each member of the buying committee. Financial information, for example, is usually in the copy the hospital administrator receives.

Quantifying the Solution[19]

As mentioned in Chapter Two, one of the trends in buying is more sophisticated analyses by buyers. This section will explore methods available to help the buyer conduct these types of analyses.

Salespeople can strengthen the presentation by showing the prospect that the cost of the proposal is offset by added value; this process is often called **quantifying the solution.** There are many methods to achieve this goal, and we will examine some of the most common ones here, including simple cost-benefit comparison, return on investment, payback period, net present value, and opportunity cost.

Quantifying the solution is more important in some situations than in others. Some products or services (e.g., replacement parts or repairs) pose very little risk for the prospect. These products are so necessary for the continuation of the prospect's business that very little quantifying of the solution is usually needed. Other products pose moderate risk (e.g., expanding the production capacity of a plant for an existing successful product) or high risk (e.g., programs designed to reduce costs or increase sales; these present higher risk because it is hard to calculate the exact magnitude of the potential savings or sales). For moderate- and high-risk situations, quantifying the solution becomes increasingly important. Finally, certain products pose super-high risk (e.g., brand-new products or services, which are riskier because *no one* can calculate costs or revenues with certainty). Attempts at quantifying the solution are imperative in super-high-risk situations. In summary, the higher the risk to the prospect, the more attention the salesperson should pay to quantifying the solution.

Simple Cost-Benefit Analysis

Perhaps the simplest method of quantifying the solution is to list the costs to the buyer and the savings the buyer can expect from the investment, often called the **simple cost-benefit analysis.** To be realistic and meaningful, information needed to calculate savings must be supplied by the buyer. Exhibit 10.7 shows how one salesperson used a chart to compare the costs and benefits of purchasing a two-way radio system.

Comparative Cost-Benefit Analysis

In many situations, the salesperson also provides a comparison of the present situation's costs with the value of the proposed solution. Or the salesperson compares his or her product with a competitor's product. For example, a company with a premium-priced product may justify the higher price on the basis of offsetting costs in other areas. Or, if productivity is enhanced, the increased productivity has economic value. In the example in Exhibit 10.8, the current washer must be changed three times as often as the new washer, while the new washer costs much more. If a prospect heard that you want $150 for a washer and he has been paying $25, he may say *no* immediately. Even if told it lasts longer, it appears that the new washer is twice as expensive ($15,000 per year versus $7,500). But if you were able to identify

EXHIBIT 10.7			
Cost-Benefit Analysis for a Mobile Radio	**Monthly Cost**		
	Monthly equipment payment (five-year lease/purchase)*		$ 1,352.18
	Monthly service agreement		295.00
	Monthly broadcast fee		464.00
	Total monthly cost for entire fleet		$ 2,111.18
	Monthly Savings		
	Cost savings (per truck) by eliminating backtracking, unnecessary trips (based on $.21/mile × 20 miles × 22 days/month)		$ 92.40
	Labor cost savings (per driver) by eliminating wasted time in backtracking, etc. ($6.50/hour × 25 minutes/day × 22 days/month)		59.58
	Total cost savings per vehicle		151.98
	Times number of vehicles		× 32
	Total monthly cost savings for entire fleet		$ 4,863.36

	Years 1–5	**Year 6+**
Monthly savings	$ 4,863.36	$ 4,863.36
Less: Monthly cost	2,111.18	759.00*
Monthly benefit	2,752.18	4,104.36
Times months per year	× 12	× 12
Annual benefit	$33,026.16	$49,252.32

*Payment reflects ongoing cost of service agreement and broadcast fees.

EXHIBIT 10.8	Your Current Washer			Our Proposal (The Maxi-Seal Washer)		
An Example of a Comparative Cost-Benefit Analysis	Quantity	Cost	Total	Quantity	Cost	Total
Initial cost	300	$ 25	$ 7,500	100	$150	$15,000
Changing cost*	300	120	36,000	100	120	12,000
Total costs per year			$43,500			$27,000
	Proposed savings		$16,500			

*Changing cost per unit = 8 hours × $15 labor = $120.

other costs associated with changing the washer, such as overtime or lost production time, and you could quantify those costs (as Exhibit 10.8 shows), you may be able to prove that the more expensive washer actually saves money. When quantifying costs, it is important to get the prospect to determine how much is lost dollarwise in production time or how much that overtime costs. Prospects will have greater faith in the numbers they provide.

When we examine the proposal in Exhibit 10.8, we see that because the proposed washer is changed less often, the total costs per year are only $27,000 compared to current costs of $43,500. This leads to a proposed savings of $16,500 per year!

Return on Investment

The **return on investment** (ROI) is simply the net profits (or savings) expected from a given investment, expressed as a percentage of the investment:

ROI = Net profits (or savings) ÷ Investment

Thus, if a new product costs $4,000 but saves the firm $5,000, the ROI is 25 percent ($5,000 ÷ $4,000 = 1.25). Many firms set a minimum ROI for any new products, services, or cost-saving programs. Salespeople need to discover the firm's

For large capital outlays, it is usually important to help the prospect see the return on investment, payback period, and/or net present value.

Courtesy Caterpillar Inc.

minimum ROI or ROI expectations and then show that the proposal's ROI meets or exceeds those requirements. In the washer example, ROI would be calculated by taking the savings in labor hours ($36,000 − $12,000 = $24,000) and dividing by the investment. In this case, you would use the incremental cost of $7,500 and ROI equals 320 percent.

Payback Period

The **payback period** is the length of time it takes for the investment cash outflow to be returned in the form of cash inflows or savings. To calculate the payback period, you simply add up estimated future cash inflows and divide into the investment cost. If expressed in years, the formula is

Payback period = Investment ÷ Savings (or profits) per year

Of course, the payback period could be expressed in days, weeks, months, or any other time period.

As an example, suppose a new machine costs $865,000 but will save the firm $120,000 per year in labor costs. The payback period is 7.2 years ($865,000 ÷ $120,000 per year = 7.2 years).

In the washer example (Exhibit 10.8), payback would be calculated by dividing $7,500 (incremental cost of the new washers per year) by $24,000 (savings in labor hours per year), which is .31 years. So in less than four months, the extra cost of the new washers is covered by the savings.

Thus, for the buyer the payback period indicates how quickly the investment money will come back to him or her. It can be a good measure of personal risk for a buyer. When a buyer makes a decision, his or her neck is "on the line," so to speak, until the investment money is at least recovered. Hence it's not surprising that buyers like to see short payback periods.

We have kept the discussion simple to help you understand the concept. In reality, the payback period would be calculated taking into account many other factors, such as investment tax credits and depreciation.

Net Present Value

As you may have learned in finance courses, money left idle loses value over time (i.e., a dollar today is worth more than a dollar next week) due to inflation and the firm's cost of capital. Thus, firms recalculate the value of future cash inflows into today's dollars (this process is called *discounting the cash flows*). One tool to assess the validity of an opportunity is to calculate the **net present value (NPV),** which is simply the net value today of future cash inflows (i.e., discounted back to their present value today at the firm's cost of capital) minus the investment: The actual method of calculating NPV is beyond the scope of this book, but many computer programs and calculators can calculate NPV quickly and easily.

$$\text{Net present value } = \frac{\textit{Future cash inflows discounted}}{\textit{into today's dollars}} - \textit{Investment}$$

As an example of the above formula, let's assume that a $50 million investment will provide annual cash inflows over the next five years of $15 million per year. The cash inflows are discounted (at the firm's cost of capital), and the result is that they are actually worth $59 million in today's dollars. The NPV is thus $9 million ($59 million − $50 million).

As with ROI and payback period, many firms set a minimum NPV. In no case should the NPV be less than $0. Again, we have kept this discussion quite simple to help you understand the basic concept.

Opportunity Cost

The **opportunity cost** is the return a buyer would have earned from a different use of the same investment capital. Thus, a buyer could spend $100 million buying a new computer system, a new $100 million production machine, a $100 million controlling interest in another firm, and so forth.

Successful salespeople identify other realistic investment opportunities and then help the prospect compare the returns of the various options. These comparisons can be made using any of the techniques we have already discussed (simple cost-benefit analysis, ROI, payback period, NPV). For example, a salesperson might help the buyer determine the following information about the options identified:

	NPV	Payback Period
Buying a new telecommunications system	$1.6 million	3.6 years
Upgrading the current telecommunications system	$0.4 million	4.0 years

The key is that salespeople not forget that prospects have a multitude of ways to invest their money.

Other Methods

There are many ways to quantify the solution beyond those discussed here (e.g., turnover, contribution margin, accounting rate of return, after-tax cash flows). Salespeople should use those methods that are understandable to the prospect and reflect the prospect's unique needs and concerns.

When selling to resellers, there are additional ways to quantify the solution. We will discuss these methods fully in Chapter Fifteen.

SUMMARY

Strengthening communication with the buyer is important. It helps to focus the buyer's attention, improves the buyer's understanding, helps the buyer remember what was said, and can create a sense of value.

Many methods of strengthening communication are available. Most salespeople have developed some form of portfolio that includes charts, catalogs, brochures, pictures, and advertisements. Salespeople can also use models, samples, gifts, testimonials, and electronic media such as slides, VCRs, computers, and projectors.

A backbone of many sales presentations is the product demonstration. It allows the buyer to get hands-on experience with the product, something most other communication methods do not offer.

It is often important to quantify the solution so the buyer can evaluate the costs in relation to the benefits he or she can derive from the proposal. Some of the more common methods of quantifying the solution include simple cost-benefit analysis, return on investment, payback period, net present value, and a calculation of opportunity cost.

All communication tools require skill and practice to be used effectively. Outstanding salespeople follow a number of guidelines to improve their use of visuals and demonstrate their products more effectively.

KEY TERMS

executive summary 286
multiple-sense appeals 272
net present value (NPV) 291
opportunity cost 292
payback period 291
portfolio 275

quantifying the solution 288
request for proposal (RFP) 285
return on investment (ROI) 290
simple cost-benefit analysis 289
testimonial 277

QUESTIONS AND
PROBLEMS

1. J. H. Patterson of National Cash Register fame trained sales representatives to "talk with their pencils." What advantages does the use of this type of sales aid offer?

2. A Herman Miller salesperson has planned a sales call to sell the Aeron office chair to a large insurance firm's corporate headquarters. She has developed a presentation around visual illustrations in a desktop easel portfolio. After placing the easel in front of her prospect, she seats herself on the right side and begins her presentation. As she gets to the second page of the portfolio, the prospect picks it up and starts thumbing through it, looking at the pictures and illustrations. The prospect says, "Go ahead with your presentation. I can hear you while I glance through your portfolio."

   a. What should the salesperson do? Explain the reasons for the action you recommend.

   b. How can she effectively communicate product features of office chairs in a portfolio?

3. When it comes to making substantial outlays for hospital surgical equipment, hospital administrators understandably like to be shown the machines. Obviously, however, even the most enterprising sales representative cannot bring an oxygenator (which performs the work of lungs during open heart surgery) to the hospital. The conventional sales rep relies on the power of words to convince administrators to visit the demonstration center or another hospital that is currently using this product. Can you think of a better way to make a presentation to the prospect?

4. Assume you plan a flight demonstration to prove some of the claims you have made for a new-model Piper, Cessna, or Beechcraft airplane. Would the demonstration be the same for each of these three individuals: a nervous person, an economy-minded person, and a performance-minded person? Explain.

5. How could you demonstrate the following products?

   a. A stereo speaker in a showroom.

   b. A word processor in an office.

   c. Shatterproof plate glass in a factory.

   d. Air conditioning in an industrial warehouse.

   e. A water purifier to a potential reseller.

6. What communication tools would you use to provide solid proof for the following concerns expressed by prospects?

   a. "No one has asked me to carry the product."

   b. "I think the costs are higher than my benefit from it."

   c. "I don't believe I could ever learn how to use that product feature."

   d. "I don't have time to go see your plant in New York. Further, I don't think your plant has the most modern equipment, which you'd need to order to produce a product of the quality we are looking for."

   e. "You look too young to service my account."

   f. "I'm not sure how your product compares to the competitor's product."

7. This chapter generally described visual aids as positive, useful tools for salespeople. When should they not be used? Are there any times when they could actually be detrimental to communication effectiveness? Explain.

8. Sometimes things don't go the way you plan them. What would you do in each of the following situations?

   a. The power goes off in the middle of a computer demonstration. As a result, you lose all of the data you have been inputting for the last eight minutes.

   b. The buyer says, "Look, I don't want to see a bunch of pictures and charts! Just tell me how you'll save me money."

   c. You involve the prospect by having her help you calculate the savings she will enjoy with your machine. While putting the last number in the calculator, she apparently hit the wrong key. As a result, she calculates the time needed to recoup her investment as 258 years instead of the actual 14 years.

   d. You hand the prospect a page from your price book. He takes it, looks at it, then opens his desk drawer and tosses it in. Because your industry has severe price competition, your company's policy forbids you to hand out your price sheet to anyone.

   e. You are showing your buyer some items in the portfolio, and you accidently knock it off the desk. The rings open up, and the pages scatter all over the floor.

   f. You offer the prospect a sample of your new food product. He tastes it, makes a face, and says, "That's really pretty awful tasting!"

   g. You are in the middle of using a computer to demonstrate returns on investment at various pricing points. Suddenly you forget how to call up the next screen. No matter how hard you try, you just can't remember what to do next!

   h. You are in the middle of painting a word picture when the buyer is interrupted by a phone call. The call lasts about five minutes. The buyer turns back to you and says, "Now, where were we?"

   i. You turn the lights down for a PowerPoint® presentation. The prospects start nodding and falling asleep, and your *entire* presentation is on the PowerPoint slides. What do you do?

9. What communication tools would you use to communicate the following facts?

   a. "We have been in business for over 100 years."

   b. "I am dependable."

   c. "Even though I've been selling this product for only two months, I do possess the necessary product knowledge."

   d. "I know our last product was a flop, but this product was developed with extensive test marketing."

   e. "Unlike our competitors, our company has never been sued by a customer."

10. Assume you are selling a new sound system to a movie theater in your town. The system will cost $350,000. It is estimated that the new system will improve sound quality so much that more patrons will watch movies. You expect revenues to increase by $39,000 each year over the next 20 years. At the movie theater's cost of capital, the discounted cash inflows have a value today of $400,000. Based on this information,

   a. Calculate the return on investment.

   b. Calculate the payback period.

   c. Calculate the net present value.

EXPLORING THE NET

This chapter emphasized the importance of strengthening the presentation to keep the buyer's attention, among other things. Visit at least two of the Web sites listed here and write a short report on how the company tried to keep your attention. For example, to what extent does the firm include video, sound, slide shows, and the like in its home page? How effective was the device in keeping your attention?

http://www.ford.com

http://www.philips.com

http://www.dupont.com

http://www.goodyear.com

http://www.bayer.com

http://www.baxter.com

http://www.wmx.com

http://www.hitachi.com

http://www.eclipse.mitsucars.com

http://www.altecmm.com

http://www.sharp-usa.com

http://www.agriculture.com

http://www.kodak.com

CASE PROBLEMS

**CASE 10.1
McDonnel
Douglas***

McDonnel Douglas is the world's leading producer of military aircraft and the third-largest commercial aircraft manufacturer. The firm is the 13th largest U.S. exporter and the 69th largest firm in the United States, with annual revenues of $15 billion.

The MD-95 commercial airplane was launched in 1995 to serve the growing market for aircraft that accommodates about 100 passengers. The MD-95 is designed to operate super economically on high-frequency, short-to-medium-range routes. Its basic configuration consists of five-across coach-class seating. All-new interiors include illuminated handrails and larger overhead baggage racks. The MD-95 is environmentally sensitive with reduced fuel consumption, reduced exhaust emissions, and significantly lower sound levels compared to competing aircraft now in service.

Two BMW/Rolls-Royce engines deliver an estimated 18,500 to 21,000 pounds of thrust each. The plane is 124 feet long, 29.3 feet high, and has a total wingspan of 93.3 feet. The MD-95 has a range of 1,781 statute miles in the basic configuration. With optional auxiliary fuel tanks, the plane can travel 2,304 statute miles. The first delivery is scheduled for 1999.

*Information for this case came from the 1995 annual report of McDonnel Douglas.

Questions

1. Describe how you would use the communication tools described in this chapter to sell the MD-95 to one of the major U.S. airlines (e.g. Delta, United, American).

2. Quantifying the solution would be an important part of any presentation to an airline. Describe how you would use the tools noted in this chapter (i.e., simple cost-benefit analysis, comparative cost-benefit analysis, ROI, payback period, NPV, opportunity cost).

**CASE 10.2
Strengthening the
Presentation: A
Prevideo Exercise**

Consolidated Employee Benefits is a national provider of medical and hospital insurance programs to large- and medium-size corporations. Consolidated has set the industry standard for progressive benefits administration. A sophisticated, computerized communications system links all 64 of its regional branch offices. Consolidated is proud of its record of offering its policyholders fast and accurate claims processing and customized benefits programs.

In the video segment you will watch, Dennis Savage, an account executive for Consolidated, is meeting with Tom Hong, vice president of personnel for Arrow Computers, and the benefits administrator, Pat Olsen. Savage has had several meetings with Olsen and has learned that Arrow intends to change its insurance carrier. He also knows that two other companies are vying for the account.

Savage knows that the final decision on a new carrier will be made by Tom Hong and the company treasurer, Jordon Gates. Savage's objective is to get Hong to arrange for him to present a proposal to Gates.

The package Savage is selling has four main features:

Features	Benefits
Fully automated claims processing provides a standard turnaround of seven to ten days and, by special arrangement, a three-to-five-day turnaround	Accelerates claims payments
Highly trained claims administrators who review all claims rejected by system	Ensures reliable claims settlement
	Reduces employee complaints about settlements
Sixty-four regional claims offices located throughout the country	Meets growing company's need for conveniently located offices to ensure efficient service
	Maintains local focus on available medical services
	Provides quick, informed aid to employees from offices that are located nearby
Computerized communications system linking all regional offices with computer terminals in client offices	Minimizes settlement problems by providing online reports

Questions

To help you think about how Savage could strengthen the presentation to Hong and Olsen, answer the following questions:

1. For each of the four features, list several ways Savage can strengthen the presentation (e.g., charts, samples, letters, demonstrations). Make sure your suggestions will provide concrete proof of each asserted feature and benefit.

2. Describe any special tactics you would utilize with regard to strengthening the presentation under the following scenarios:

   a. Hong is a driver, Olsen is an analytical.

   b. Hong is an expressive, Olsen is an expressive.

3. Reread the case and be prepared to watch the videotape in class. Watch how Savage actually strengthened the presentation. Make notes about what Savage had to do before the meeting to prepare to use the tools he employed.

ADDITIONAL REFERENCES

Andersen, Jeff. "Mastering Multimedia." *Sales & Marketing Management,* January 1993, pp. 55–58.

Arch, David. "How to Gracefully Handle Those Pesky Hecklers." *Presentations,* October 1996, p. 28.

"A Selection of Recent Presentation Products." *Business Marketing,* June 1992, p. 36.

Boylan, Bob. "Overheads: Why They're Still No. 1." *Business Marketing,* January 1993, p. 57.

Brown, Priscilla C. "Color Helps the Sell." *Business Marketing,* January 1993, pp. 58–59.

Deeter-Schmelz, Dawn R., and Rosemary Ramsey. "A Conceptualization of the Functions and Roles of Formalized Selling and Buying Teams." *Journal of Personal Selling and Sales Management,* Spring 1995, pp. 47–60.

"Demonstrating with Flair." *Institutional Distribution,* May 15, 1990, p. 106.

Falvey, Jack. "Does Your Company Need First Aid for Its Visuals?" *Sales & Marketing Management,* July 1990, pp. 97–99.

Geco, Susan. "Making Company Tours Pay Off." *Inc.,* February 1993, p. 26.

"Giving Great Presentations." *Success,* May 1990, p. 30.

Jennings, Richard G., and Richard E. Plank. "When the Purchasing Agent Is a Committee." *Industrial Marketing Management,* 24 (1995), pp. 411–19.

Kalish, Karen. *How to Give a Terrific Presentation,* New York: AMACOM, 1997.

Kushner, Malcolm. *Successful Presentations for Dummies,* Foster City, California: IDG Books Worldwide, 1996.

Marchetti, Michele. "Talking 'bout My Generation." *Sales & Marketing Management,* December 1995, pp. 65–68.

Mayfield, Lee A. "Presentations: How to Do It Wrong." *Sales & Marketing Management,* July 1990, pp. 79–81.

Mullich, Joe. "Polishing Your 'Image.'" *Business Marketing,* January 1993, p. 49.

Rehfeld, Barry. "How Large Companies Buy." *Personal Selling Power,* September 1993, pp. 26–33.

Rosenthal, Alan. "How to Improve Presentations: The Race Doesn't Always Go to the Slickest." *Business Marketing,* June 1992, pp. 40–41.

Tartarella, Ron. "Picture This!" *Personal Selling Power,* September 1993, pp. 64–65.

Taylor, Thayer C. "Show and Tell That Sells." *Sales & Marketing Management,* April 1990, pp. 78–85.

Venkatesh, R.; Ajay K. Kohli; and Gerald Zaltman. "Influence Strategies in Buying Centers." *Journal of Marketing,* October 1995, pp. 71–82.

"Wake Me When the Presentation Is Over." *Training,* January 1993, p. 65.

Wilder, Claudyne. "Sales Presentations Require a More Focused Approach." *Presentations,* January 1997, p. 26.

Chapter Eleven

Responding *to* Objections

All salespeople encounter objections during the selling process. All buyers, at some time or other, voice an objection to something the salesperson says or does. In fact, some customers may raise irrational or irrelevant objections that have nothing to do with the product, the company, or the salesperson. Of course, buyers also raise valid concerns and questions.

Some Questions Answered in this Chapter Are:

When do buyers object?

What objections can be expected?

What preparation is necessary to respond to objections?

What methods and techniques are effective when responding to objections?

Skill in responding to objections is just as necessary as skill in making appointments, conducting interviews, demonstrating products, and obtaining commitment. When new salespeople realize buyers' objections are a normal and natural part of the sales process, they can treat such objections as sales opportunities.

PROFILE

After receiving her BBA in marketing at the University of Minnesota–Duluth, Kris Rainey accepted a position with Procter & Gamble, with which she had an opportunity through IN-ROADS to have an internship for two summers. INROADS is an organization that develops and places talented minority youth in business and industry and prepares them for corporate and community leadership. It matches local corporations, many of them Fortune 500 companies, with students majoring in business or engineering for summer internships. It is "dedicated to developing leaders for the 21st century."

Proctor & Gamble (P&G) is a Fortune 500 company that manufactures and distributes consumer goods such as Tide, Charmin, Bounty, Ivory, Folgers, Crest, Cover Girl, Pantene, and Sunny Delight. Its philosophy is to improve the quality of life for its customers as well as its employees. P&G is well known for its commitment to diversity, technology, consultative relationship with customers, and environmental issues. For example after an oil spill in the ocean, Dawn dish soap was used by rescuers to help remove the oil from the feathers of birds and other animals without removing the natural oil off animals' bodies.

"In order to reduce objections, I make sure I have clear objectives for the call. It is extremely important to state your idea, explain the implementation plan, and provide key benefits clearly and concisely."

Kris Rainey has been with Procter & Gamble for two years, in which time she has had three different assignments. Her initial assignment was as an account manager calling on headquarters accounts for the paper sector (Pampers, Luvs, Charmin, Bounty, etc.) Nine months later she had the opportunity to call on retail stores selling to multiple sectors (paper, soap, food and beverage products). Currently she is a regional account manager focusing on shelf technology, which involves reviewing customer data on certain categories and providing customers with the best possible shelving arrangements for the retail stores.

Rainey believes four areas are very important in sales: utilizing technology, thorough preparation, anticipating and handling objections and follow-through. "In sales it is very important that you are computer literate," she says. "I use my computer every day to ana-

KRIS RAINEY
Procter & Gamble

lyze and prepare data for category reviews, sales presentations, expense reports, building planograms, and for everyday communication within the company. And in the future, access to the Internet will allow companies to learn more about their competition and allow them to compete in the global economy.

"My first step for a successful sale is preparation. Each month the first thing I do is develop my agenda for each week. I've found that you first need to make sure you understand the customer's business, their needs, and their key competitors. Not only do I know my customer's business but I research the different personality styles of the key decision makers. I then tailor my presentations to their personalities, i.e., driver, analytical, expressive, or amiable. I make sure to review all my account information and previous call notes before preparing my sales routes and presentations. This allows me to plan my weekly calls and objectives. My main objectives for my calls are the four Ps (product, price, placement, and promotion). Quarterly presentations take the longest (approximately 30 minutes) for my buyers. This is their chance to purchase enough products for ads and displays three months in advance. Within this presentation we discuss new and missing distribution, pricing, promotions, and shelf placement. In order to reduce objections, I make sure I have clear objectives for the call. It is extremely important to state your idea, explain the implementation plan, and provide key benefits clearly and concisely. Time is of the essence for these grocery buyers, so it is important for me to be organized and prepared to stay on time.

Handling objections is just as important as account preparation. Procter & Gamble has provided Rainey with excellent training in selling and objection-handling skills. She explains, "The most common objection that I hear from my buyers when I sell them the quarter is that they do not know how much product they will need in three months. I handle this objection by reviewing with the buyers the ad and price points for the products in the ad. I also show my buyer a chart that shows what they previously ordered during a similar ad and how much product they went through. I help them make their decisions by using product knowledge and data. This makes me more credible with my buyers because I know their business and how much product they can move through during certain ads. By using charts and graphs, I also explain what their profit margin will be if they display and reduce the price on these prod-

ucts. This has been very successful for me because my buyers look to me to be the expert on my products, the quantity they should order for ads, and for keeping them competitive in the market with pricing and promotions."

"In order to obtain commitment from my buyers, I make sure to have them sign off on the quantities ordered, the ship dates, and ad dates. My buyers like the quarterly sale because they are done ordering for the next three months. However, the sale is not done; it is concluded with effective follow-up. I make sure to go into the stores once every two weeks to sell new items, to take care of any questions or issues that might come up within those two weeks, and to make sure we deliver what was promised. I am continuously seeking opportunities for improvement by comparing what was projected with what actually sold. This provides me with materials for the next quarterly presentation as the sell cycle begins again. I believe follow-through and honesty are the keys for building long-term relationships with my buyers."

Visit Our Website@
http://www.pg.com

An **objection** is a concern or a question raised by the buyer. Salespeople should do everything they can to encourage buyers to voice concerns or questions. The worst type of objection is the one the buyer refuses to disclose, because a hidden objection cannot be dealt with.

When Do Buyers Raise Objections?

Salespeople can expect to hear objections at any time during the buyer-seller relationship. Objections are raised when the salesperson attempts to secure an appointment or during the approach, during the presentation, when the salesperson attempts to obtain commitment, and during the after-sale follow-up.

Setting Up an Initial Appointment

Prospects may object to setting the appointment times or dates that salespeople request to introduce the product. This happens especially when products, services, or concepts are unfamiliar to the buyer. For example, a commercial benefits salesperson for Prudential might hear the buyer make the following statement when asked to meet and learn more about a cafeteria-style benefits package: "No, I don't need to

see you. I've not heard much about what you're selling, so it must not be too good."
The same types of objections can also occur during the approach.

The Presentation

Objections often come up to points made in the presentation. For example, a computer disaster recovery salesperson for XL DATACOMP might hear the objection "We've never had a flood before! Why should I pay so much money for a service I may never use?"

Such objections usually show the prospect's interest; thus, they can actually be desirable. Compared to a prospect who just says "No thanks" and never raises his or her concerns, selling is easier when buyers voice their concerns because the salesperson knows where the buyers stand and that they are paying attention.

Buyers sometimes let the salesperson deliver the entire presentation without showing any reaction. Judging the effectiveness of the presentation is difficult in such circumstances.

Attempting to Obtain Commitment

Objections may be voiced when the salesperson attempts to obtain commitment. For example, a Ryerson Steel salesperson who has just asked the buyer permission to talk to the buyer's chief engineer may hear "No, I don't want you talking to our engineers. My job is to keep vendors from bugging our employees."

Skill in uncovering and responding to objections is very important at this stage of the sales call. Also, knowing the objections that are likely to occur helps the salesperson prepare supporting documentation (letters of reference, copies of studies, etc.).

Salespeople who hear a large number of objections at this point in the sales call probably need to further develop their skills. An excessive number of objections may indicate a poor job at needs identification and the omission of significant selling points in the presentation. It may also reveal ineffective probing during the presentation to see if the buyer understands or has any questions about what is being discussed.

After the Sale

Even buyers who have agreed to purchase the product or service can still raise objections. During the installation, for example, the buyer may raise concerns about the time it is taking to install the equipment, the quality of the product or service, the customer service department's lack of friendliness, or the credit department's refusal to grant the terms the salesperson promised. To develop long-term relationships and partnerships with buyers, salespeople must carefully respond to these objections. After-sale service is more fully discussed in Chapter Thirteen.

COMMON OBJECTIONS

Prospects raise many types of objections. While it would be impossible to list every single objection, this section will attempt to outline the most common ones buyers voice. As a backdrop, Exhibit 11.1 lists the major underlying reasons buyers object, and Exhibit 11.2 categorizes the five major types of objections. We will now examine some of the most common objections.

I Do Not Need the Product or Service

A prospect may validly state that the company has no need for what the salesperson is selling. A manufacturer that operates on a small scale, for example, may have no use for expensive machinery designed to handle large volumes of work. Similarly, a salesperson who is selling an accounts receivable collection service will find that a retailer that sells for cash does not require a collection service.

EXHIBIT 11.1

Underlying Reasons Buyers Raise Objections

- For the challenge—seasoned buyers like to make the salesperson work hard for an order.
- Because of a lack of interest—the salesperson has not qualified the prospect or has failed to help the prospect identify a need.
- Buyer does not need or want it right now.
- For the time being—some buyers just tend to procrastinate.
- For no good reason—buyers may not be taking the presentation seriously.
- For misunderstanding—buyers may not fully understand what the salesperson is describing or may need more information.
- Risk is too great—the salesperson has not sufficiently sold value.
- Lack of trust in the seller or the seller's firm.

Source: Part of this exhibit was derived from Richard Kern, "The Art of Overcoming Resistance," *Sales & Marketing Management*, March 1990, pp. 101–4.

Salespeople may encounter objections such as "My business is different" or "I have no use for your service." These objections, when made by an accurately qualified buyer, show that the buyer is not convinced that a need exists. This problem could have been prevented with strong implication and need payoff questions (see Chapter Nine).

If the salesperson cannot establish a need in the buyer's mind, that buyer can logically be expected to object. In **pioneer selling**—selling a new and different product, service, or idea—the salesperson has more difficulty establishing a need in the buyer's mind. For example, salespeople for Alpine Paper Company often hear "I don't think we need it" when the buyer is asked to carry a line of recycled paper products.

I Need More Information

Some buyers offer objections in an attempt to get more information. They may have already decided they want the product or service but wish to fortify themselves with logical reasons they can use to justify the purchase to others. Also, the salesperson may not have provided enough proof about a particular benefit.

Conflict may also exist in the buyer's mind. One conflict could be a struggle taking place between the dictates of emotion and reason. The buyer may be trying to decide between two competitive products or between buying and not buying. What-

Some buyers need more information before committing themselves because they have to justify their decision to others.

Richard Pharaoh/International Stock

EXHIBIT 11.2	*Need*	*Source*
Five Major Types of Objections	"I do not need the product or service."	"I don't like your company."
	"I need more information."	"I don't like you."
	"I've never done it that way before."	
	"I'm just not interested."	*Price*
		"I have no money."
		"The value does not exceed the cost."
	Product	
	"I don't understand."	*Time*
	"I don't like the product or service features."	"I need time to think about it."

ever the struggle, buyers who object to get more information are usually interested, and the possibility of obtaining commitment is good.

I've Never Done It That Way Before

Most human beings are creatures of habit. Once they develop a routine or establish a custom, they tend to resist change. Fear or ignorance may be the basis for not wanting to try anything new or different. The buyer's natural tendency to resist buying a new product or changing from a satisfactory brand to a new one can be found behind many objections.

Some buyers like to raise many objections just to watch salespeople squirm uncomfortably. (Fortunately there aren't many buyers like that!) For example, Peggy, a manufacturer's salesperson for Walker Muffler, used to call on a large auto parts store in an attempt to have the store carry her line of mufflers. Jackie, the store's buyer, gave Peggy a tough time on her first two calls. At the end of her second call, Peggy was so frustrated with the way she was being treated that she decided never to call there again. However, as she was walking out of the store, she ran into a Goodyear rep who also called on Jackie to sell belts and hoses. Since they were on somewhat friendly terms, Peggy admitted her frustrations to the Goodyear rep. He replied, "Oh, that's just the way Jackie operates. On the third call he is always a nice guy. Just wait and see." Sure enough, Peggy's next call on Jackie was not only pleasant, it was also productive! Buyers like Jackie usually just want to see the sales rep work hard for the order.

Habits and customs also help to insulate the prospect from certain risks to some degree. For example, suppose you are selling a new line of office chairs to Harry, a newly promoted assistant buyer. If Jane, the previous assistant buyer and now the senior buyer, bought your competitor's product, Harry would appear to take less risk by continuing to buy from your competitor. If Harry buys from you, Jane may think, "I've been doing business with the other firm for 15 years. Now, Harry, you come in and tell me I've been doing it wrong all these years? I'm not sure you're going to be a good assistant buyer."

I'm Just Not Interested

Some prospects voice objections simply to dismiss the salesperson. The prospect may not have enough time to devote to the interview, may not be interested in the product or service offered, may not be in the mood to listen, or may have decided because of some unhappy experiences not to face further unpleasant interviews.

These objections occur when salespeople make a cold canvass or try to make an appointment. Particularly overaggressive, rude, impolite, or pesky salespeople can expect prospects to use numerous excuses to keep them from making a presentation.

Sometimes buyers won't admit that they do not understand or are just not interested in what the seller is talking about.

©Uniphoto, Inc.

I Don't Understand

Sometimes objections arise because customers do not understand the salesperson's presentation. Since these objections may never be verbalized, the seller must carefully observe the buyer's nonverbal cues. (See Chapter Five for a discussion of nonverbal communication.) Misunderstandings frequently occur with customers who are unfamiliar with technical terms, unaware of the unique capabilities of a product, or uncertain about benefits arising from services provided with the product, such as warranties. Unfortunately, buyers often will not admit they do not understand something.

For example, when desktop publishing programs were first made available for personal computers, a salesperson for an IBM distributor gave a presentation to a very busy plant manager of a consumer products firm. The new software would allow the manager to create and produce the plant's monthly newsletter to plant employees in-house instead of sending the work out to be typeset and run off. The manager, however, did not understand the new product's concept. He thought the software would create the newsletter but the firm would still have to send the work out to be typeset and run off. However, he did not want to appear ignorant and simply told the salesperson he was not interested. The rep never knew that the manager simply had not understood until later, when the manager bought a competitor's desktop publishing program.

I Don't Like the Product or Service Features

Often the product or service has features that do not satisfy the buyer. At other times, the prospect will request features currently not available. Customers may say,

I don't like the design.

It doesn't taste good to me!

I wish you included free maintenance.

We prefer printed circuits.

I was looking for a lighter shade of red.

I can't get my machines repaired quickly by your service technicians.

It took a month for us to receive our last order.

I Don't Like Your Company

Most buyers, especially industrial buyers, are highly interested in the sales representative's company because the buyer is put at risk if the seller's firm is not financially sound, cannot continually produce the product, and so forth. They need to be satisfied with the company's financial standing, personnel, and business policies. Buyers may ask questions such as these:

Isn't your company a new one in the field?

Is it true your company lost money last year?

How do I know you'll be in business next year?

Isn't your firm the one that was indicted by a federal grand jury for price fixing?

Your company isn't very well known, is it?

Who does your designing?

Can your company give us the credit we have been receiving from other companies?

How do I know you can deliver on time?

Your company has a bad image in the industry.

Of course, buyers may not actually voice these concerns due to a desire to avoid appearing rude. But unvoiced questions about the sales rep's company may affect their decisions and the long-term partnerships the sales rep is trying to establish.

I Don't Like You

Sometimes a salesperson's personality clashes with a prospect's. Effective salespeople know they must do everything possible to adjust their manner to please the prospect. At times, however, doing business with some people appears impossible.

Prospects may object to a presentation or an appointment because they have taken a dislike to the salesperson or because they feel they cannot trust the salesperson. Candid prospects may say,

You seem too young to be selling these.

You've never worked in my industry. How can you be trained to know what I need?

I don't like to do business with you.

You're a pest! I don't have any time for you.

You and I will never be able to do business.

More commonly, the prospect shields the real reason and says something like

We don't need any.

Sorry, we're stocked up.

I haven't any time today to discuss your proposition.

In some situations, the buyer may honestly have difficulty dealing with a particular salesperson. If the concern is real (i.e., not just an excuse), the seller's firm sometimes institutes a **turnover (TO),** which simply means the account is given to a different salesperson. Unfortunately, this occasionally occurs because the buyer has gender, racial, or other prejudices, or because the salesperson is failing to practice adaptive selling behaviors.

<table>
<tr>
<td>

Thinking
it
Through

</td>
<td>

Assume you have worked as a salesperson for an industrial chemical firm for six months. You attend a two-week "basic selling skill" course but have not yet attended any product knowledge training classes. You are making a sales call with your sales manager. The buyer says, "Gee, you look too young to be selling chemicals. Do you have a chemistry degree?" Before you get a chance to respond, your manager says, "Oh, he [meaning you] has already completed our one-month intensive product knowledge course. I guarantee he knows it all!" What would you say or do? What would you do if the buyer later asked you a technical question?

</td>
</tr>
</table>

I Have No Money

Companies that lack the resources to buy the product may have been classified as prospects. As indicated in Chapter Seven, the ability to pay is an important factor in lead qualification. An incomplete or poor job of qualifying may cause this objection to arise.

When leads say they cannot afford a product, they may have a valid objection. If so, the salesperson should not waste time; new prospects should be contacted. Selling Scenario 11.1 describes how one seller responded to this objection.

The Value Does Not Exceed the Cost

Most buyers must sacrifice something else to buy a product. The money spent for the product is not available for other things. When we buy as individuals, the choice may be between the down payment on a new car and a vacation trip; for businesses, it may be between expanding the plant and distributing a dividend.

Usually buyers object until they are sure the sacrifice is more than offset by the value of the product or service being acquired. Exhibit 11.3 shows this concept graphically. The question of value received often underlies customers' objections.

Whatever the price of a product or service, somebody will object that it is too high or out of line with the competition. Other common price objections are:

I can't afford it.

I can't afford to spend that much right now.

I never accept the first price quoted by a salesperson.

I was looking for a cheaper model.

I don't care to invest that much; I'll use it only a short while.

I can beat your price on these items.

We can't make a reasonable profit if we have to pay that much for the merchandise.

We always get a special discount.

I'm going to wait for prices to come down.

Although objections about price occur more often than any other kind, they may be just masks to hide the real reason for the buyer's reluctance. (A more complete discussion of dealing with price objections appears in the last section of this chapter.) Implicit in many price objections is the notion of product or service quality. Thus, the buyer who states that "your price is too high" may actually be thinking, "The quality is too low for such a high price."

SELLING SCENARIO   11.1

How to Handle the "I Have No Money" Objection

With regards to the "I have no money" objection, one of the key responsibilities of a salesperson is to focus on the success of your product line. While calling on a Hallmark store last year, we noted that one of our key product lines, the Precious Moments figurines, occupied 20 feet of selling space. While attempting to place a reorder on this product line, the buyer suggested that they had no money or "open to buy" dollars.

From that point we calculated the square footage of our product line in relation to the entire store and then calculated the total dollars purchased and sold over the past 12 months. After our calculations, we determined that this particular Hallmark account was generating $260 per square foot of our product line, which is phenomenal for this industry.

After that calculation and explaining to the owner how we arrived at that amount, we then said, "Now, can you tell us that you don't have any money? What other product lines generate [that kind of profit] for you? May we possibly suggest you reduce your purchases in those other lines and transfer some of your dollars to this product category [Precious Moments figurines]?"

Needless to say, such an analysis of profits per square foot proved worthwhile and not only generated increased sales but also gave the store owner more confidence in the sales representative.

Source: Terry Michaels, personal correspondence; used with permission.

I Need Time to Think About It

Buyers often object to making a decision "now." Many, in fact, believe that postponing an action is an effective way to say *no*. Salespeople can expect to hear objections such as the following, especially from analyticals and amiables (see Chapter Six):

> I haven't made up my mind.
>
> I want to think it over.
>
> I'd like to talk it over with my partner.

This buyer is providing nonverbal cues that say "I need more time to think about it."

Paul Barton/The Stock Market

EXHIBIT 11.3

Value: The Relationship
Between Costs
and Benefits

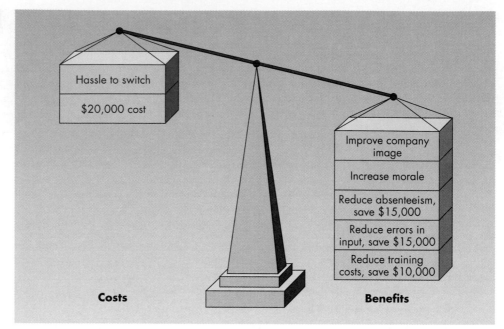

Note: If costs outweigh benefits, the decision will be not to buy. If benefits outweigh costs, the decision
will be to buy.

See me on your next trip.

I'm not ready to buy.

I don't want to commit myself.

I think I'll wait awhile.

I want to look around.

I'm waiting until my inventory goes down.

I want to turn in the old unit at the end of the season.

Just leave me your literature. I'll study it and then let you know what we decide.

Other Objections

Listing every possible objection that could occur under any situation would be impossible. However, following are a number of additional examples of objections salespeople often hear:

I'm not interested.

I'm satisfied with the company we use now.

We have a reciprocity agreement with your competitor.

We are all stocked up.

We have no room for your line.

There is no demand for your product.

You'll have to see Mr. X.

Sorry, but I just don't do business with blacks or women.

My brother-in-law is in the business.

Your competitor just came out with a brand-new product that seems superior to
     yours.

SELLING SCENARIO 11.2

Sexual Harassment on the Job

Probably the most frustrating situation occurs when the buyer sexually harasses the salesperson or requests some form of sexual favor before the "deal can be closed." Consider the following true situations and ask yourself what you would do in each case.

Susan Jayne sells oil products to industrial firms in the Midwest. Once, during the middle of the day, she parked her car in a multilevel car park. As she approached the elevator, one of her customers, Mark, a businessman from a major firm, walked up. Riding up in the otherwise empty elevator with her, he suddenly grabbed Jayne and kissed her.

Paul Jarman works for a mortgage banker in the Southeast as a salesperson. He regularly calls on real estate agents and attempts to develop partnerships between his banks and the agencies. Recently he was faced with this dilemma. Three young, attractive female agents agreed to use Paul's bank exclusively—but only if he would agree to become each agent's sexual partner. Since the agents are very successful, if Paul agreed to their demands he would have earned an estimated $30,000 in commissions each year! Paul was convinced, however, that his wife would not be pleased with the arrangement.

Jeannette Holcomb is a drug detailer for Marion/Merrell-Dow Pharmaceuticals. She has regularly called on Dr. Howard Beane, a very respected and successful cardiologist, for the past three years. Today, as she was describing a new study that was just published, Dr. Beane placed his hand on her leg and said, "Jeannette, why haven't we ever gotten together?" Jeannette was shocked, especially since Dr. Bean's wife was one of his nurses and the office door was wide open!

Sexual harassment occurs in almost every industry. It has been a problem for females for years and now is a growing problem for males. Salespeople need to be prepared. How should you react? It depends on the situation. Linda Lynton offers several suggested responses: directly say "No," use humor, or walk away from the business.

What did our real-world salespeople do in each situation? Susan looked Mark directly in the eye and said, "Mark, don't ever do that again!" He never did.

Paul decided to walk away from the business. He never explained to the agents his reason for not calling on them again.

Jeannette, in a somewhat disappointed tone of voice, softly told Dr. Beane, "We've done business for over three years. Let's not spoil it now." Dr. Beane never mentioned the topic again and continued to prescribe Jeannette's drug.

The situations are true. All names were changed to protect the victims.

Source: Linda Lynton, "The Dilemma of Sexual Harassment," *Sales & Marketing Management*, October 1989, pp. 67–71.

I've heard complaints from my friends who use your product.

I prefer to do business only with Islamic-owned firms.

Sure, we can do business. But I need a little kickback to make it worth my time and trouble.

I believe we might be able to do business if you are willing to start seeing me socially. (Selling Scenario 11.2 delves into this issue more fully.)

It's a lot of hassle in paperwork and time to switch suppliers.

PREPARING TO RESPOND

Develop a Positive Attitude

Responding to objections in a helpful manner requires careful thought and preparation. Exhibit 11.4 overviews the activities of successful salespeople in this regard. To respond to objections effectively, nothing can substitute for having a positive attitude. It is important that sales representatives not only know how to successfully respond to objections but also "how to recognize problems for what they are—a

EXHIBIT 11.4	
Responding to Objections: Traits and Behaviors of Successful Salespeople	• They develop and maintain a positive attitude about objections. • They relax and listen, never interrupting the buyer. • They anticipate objections and prepare helpful responses. • They forestall known concerns before they arise. • They make sure the objection is not just an excuse. • They are sincerely empathetic to the buyer's objections.

logical extension of the selling process rather than a personal affront to their own abilities."[1] Proper attitude is shown by answering sincerely, refraining from arguing or contradicting, and welcoming—even inviting—objections. Objections should be expected and never taken personally.

Simply pretending to be empathetic is useless; buyers can easily see through such pretense. Also, once the buyer gets the idea that the salesperson is talking for effect, regaining that buyer's confidence and respect will be almost impossible. Empathy shows as much in the tone of voice and facial expressions as in the actual words spoken.

The greatest evidence of sincerity, however, comes from the salesperson's actions. One successful advertising agency owner states, "I have always tried to sit on the same side of the table as my clients, to see problems through their eyes." Buyers want valid objections to be treated seriously; they want their ideas respected, not belittled. They look for empathetic understanding of their problems. Real objections are logical to the prospect, regardless of how irrational they may appear to the salesperson. Salespeople must assume the attitude of a helper, a counselor, and an adviser and act accordingly. To do this, they must treat the prospect as a friend, not a foe. In fact, buyers will feel more comfortable about raising objections and will be much more honest the more they trust the salesperson, the better the rapport, and the stronger the partnering relationship.

The temptation to prove the prospect wrong, to say "I told you so" or "I'm right and you're wrong," is always strong. This kind of attitude invites debate, encouraging—perhaps even forcing—the prospect to defend a position regardless of its merits. Egos get involved when prospects find their positions bluntly challenged. Most will try to defend their own opinions under these circumstances because they do not want to lose face. The sales presentation may then degenerate into a personal duel that the salesperson cannot possibly win. Arguing with, contradicting, and showing belligerence toward a prospect are negative, unwise actions.

The reality is that "a typical seller runs into more rejection in the course of a day than most of us have to absorb in weeks, if not months. From an emotional perspective, selling is a rough way to make a living. Your self-respect is on the line every time you walk through a customer's door."[2] However, salespeople must remember that objections present sales opportunities.[3] People who object have at least some level of interest in what the salesperson is saying. Further, objections provide feedback as to what is really on the prospect's mind. Only when this openness exists can a trust partnering relationship form. To capitalize on these opportunities, salespeople must show that they welcome any and all objections. They have to make the prospect believe they are sincerely glad the objection has been raised. This attitude shows in remarks such as the following:

I can see just what you mean. I'd probably feel the same way.

I'm glad you mentioned that, Mr. Atkinson.

That certainly is a wise comment, Ms. Smith, and I can see your problem.

If I were purchasing this product, I'd want an answer to that same question.

Tell me about it.

In dealing with prospects and customers, truthfulness is an absolute necessity for dignity, confidence, and continued relations. Maintaining a positive attitude toward objections will go a long way toward building goodwill.

Anticipate Objections

Salespeople must know that at some time, objections will be made to almost everything concerning their products, their companies, or themselves. Common sense dictates that they prepare answers to objections that are certain to be raised (probably 80 percent or more can be anticipated), because few salespeople can answer objections effectively on the spur of the moment.

Many companies draw up lists of common objections and effective answers and encourage salespeople to become familiar with these lists. Some firms also videotape practice role plays to help salespeople become more proficient in anticipating objections and responding effectively in each situation.

Successful sales representatives may keep a notebook and record new objections they encounter, along with any new ideas for responses; they also pick up helpful suggestions at sales meetings. Successful reps recognize that different personality types may require different types of responses or proof and plan accordingly.

When salespeople know an objection will be raised, they should have good answers ready. This helps to build confidence. Unanticipated or unanswerable objections can easily cause embarrassment and lost sales.

Relax and Listen— Do Not Interrupt

When responding to an objection, listen first, then answer the objection. Allow the prospect to state a position completely. Do not interrupt with an answer, even if the objection to be stated is already apparent to you. Listen as though you have never heard that objection before. Unfortunately, too many salespeople conduct conversations somewhat like the following:

SALESPERSON Mr. Clark, from a survey of your operations, I'm convinced you're now spending more money repairing your own motors than you would by having us do the job for you—and really do it right!

CUSTOMER I wonder if we are not doing it right ourselves. Your repair service may be good. But after all, you don't have to be exactly an electrical genius to be able to . . .

SALESPERSON Just a minute now! Pardon me for interrupting, but there's a point I'd like to make right there! It isn't a matter of anyone being a genius. It's a matter of having a heavy investment in special motor repair equipment and supplies like vacuum impregnating tanks and lathes for banding armatures, boring bearings, and turning new shafts.

CUSTOMER Yeah, but you don't understand my point. What I'm driving at . . .

SALESPERSON I know what you're driving at. And I assure you you're wrong! You forget that even if your own workers are smart cookies, they just can't do high-quality work without a lot of special equipment.

CUSTOMER But you still don't get my point! The idea I'm trying to get across—if I can make myself clear on this *third* attempt—is this: The maintenance workers that we now have doing motor repair work . . .

SALESPERSON Could more profitably spend their time on plant troubleshooting! Right?

CUSTOMER That isn't what I was going to say! I was trying to say that between their troubleshooting jobs, instead of just sitting around and shooting the bull . . .

SALESPERSON Now wait a minute, Mr. Clark. Wait jus-s-t a minute! Let me get a word in here! If you've got any notion that a good motor rewinding job can be done with some-body's left hand on an odd-moment basis, you've got another thing coming. And my survey here will prove it! Listen![4]

Obviously, this type of attitude and interruptions will likely bring the interview to a quick end.

Forestall Known Concerns

Good salespeople, after a period of experience and training, know that certain features of their products or services are vulnerable, are likely to be misunderstood, or are materially different from competitors' products. The salesperson may have products with limited features, may have to quote a price that seems high, may be unable to offer cash discounts, may have no service representatives in the immediate area, or may represent a new company in the field.

In these situations, salespeople often forestall the objection. To **forestall** is to prevent by doing something ahead of time. In selling, this means salespeople raise objections before buyers have a chance to raise them. For example, one salesperson forestalled a concern about the different "feel" of a split computer keyboard (the ones that are split down the middle to relieve stress and strain on the hands):

> I know you'll find the feel to be different from your old keyboard. You're going to like that, though, because your hands won't get as tired. In almost every split keyboard I've sold, typists have taken only one day to get accustomed to the new feel, and then they swear that they would never go back to their old-fashioned keyboard again!

A salesperson might bring up a potential price problem by saying, "You know, other buyers have been concerned that this product is expensive. Well, let me show you how little it will really cost you to get the best."

Some salespeople do such a good job of forestalling that buyers change their minds without ever going on record as objecting to the feature and then having to reverse themselves. Buyers are more willing to change their thinking when they do not feel constrained to defend a position they have already stated.

While not all objections can be preempted, the major ones can be spotted and forestalled during the presentation. Buyers have no need to raise an objection already stated—and answered—by the salesperson.

Forestalling can be even more important in written proposals, since immediate feedback between buyer and seller is not possible. Such forestalled objections can be addressed throughout the proposal. For example, on the page describing delivery terms, the seller could insert a paragraph that begins, "You may be wondering how we can promise an eight-day delivery even though we have such a small production capacity. Actually, we are able to . . . because . . ."

Another option for forestalling objections in written proposals is to have a separate page or section entitled something like "Concerns You May Have with this Proposal." The section could then list the potential concerns and provide responses to them.

Evaluate Objections

Objections may be classified as unsatisfied needs (i.e., real objections) or excuses. **Excuses** are concerns expressed by the buyer that mask the buyer's true objections. Thus, the comment "I can't afford it now" would simply be an excuse if the buyer honestly could afford it now but did not want to buy for some other reason.

An objection to buying is seldom stated as "I don't have any reason. I just don't want to buy." More commonly, the buyer gives a reason that appears at first to be a real objection: "I don't have the money"; or "I can't use your product" may be an excuse. The tone of voice or the nature of the reason may provide evidence that the prospect is not offering a sincere objection.

Salespeople need to develop skill in evaluating objections. No exact formula has been devised to separate excuses from real objections. The circumstances will usually be a clue to the answer. In a cold canvass, when the prospect says, "I'm sorry, I don't have any money," the salesperson may conclude that the prospect does not want to hear the presentation. However, the same reason offered after a complete presentation has been made and data on the prospect have been gathered through observation and questioning may be valid. Salespeople must rely on observation, questioning, knowledge of why people buy, and experience to determine the validity of reasons offered for objections.

EFFECTIVE RESPONSE METHODS

Any discussion of specific methods and techniques for responding to objections needs to emphasize that no one perfect method or technique exists for answering all objections completely. Some prospects, no matter what you do, will never believe their objections have been adequately addressed.

In some instances, spending a lot of time trying to convince the prospect may not be wise. For example, when an industrial recycling salesperson contacts a prospect who says, "I don't believe in recycling," the salesperson may better spend available time calling on some of the vast number of people who do.

Salespeople should develop a procedure for responding to objections. The following steps can be applied and adapted to most selling situations:

1. *Listen carefully; don't interrupt.* Let the prospect talk, and don't get angry! (Remember, we stated earlier that the salesperson should *plan* on not interrupting. Now, in the heat of the presentation it is important to follow through on that promise and *actually* not interrupt.)

2. *Repeat the prospect's objection.* Make sure you understand the objection. Ask questions to permit the prospect to clarify objections. Acknowledge the apparent soundness of the prospect's opinion. In other words, agree as far as possible with the prospect's thinking before providing an answer.

3. *Evaluate the objection.* Determine whether the stated objection is real or just an excuse.

4. *Decide on the method(s) to use in answering the objection.* Some factors to be considered are the phase of the sales process in which the prospect raises the objection; the mood, or frame of mind, evidenced by the prospect; the

reason for the objection; the personality type of the prospect; and the number of times the reason is advanced. Flexibility is critical.

5. *Get a commitment from the prospect.* The answer to any objection must satisfy the prospect if a sale is to result. Get the prospect to agree that the objection has been answered.

This section will describe seven common methods for responding to objections. As Exhibit 11.5 indicates, the first two, direct denial and indirect denial, are used only when the prospect makes an untrue statement. The next five methods—compensation, feel-felt-found, boomerang, pass-up, and postpone—are useful when the buyer raises a valid point or offers an opinion.

Before using any of the methods described in this section, salespeople almost always first need to probe to help the prospect clarify the concerns and to make sure they understand the objection.[5] This is often called the **probing method.** If the prospect says, "Your service is not too good," the salesperson can probe by asking a question. For example,

Not too good?

What do you mean by not too good? Exactly what service are you referring to?

Is service very important to you?

Can you explain what you mean?

I'm not sure I understand.

Many serious blunders have occurred because the salesperson did not understand the question, answered the wrong question, or failed to answer the objection fully.

For example, a sales training manager was listening to a representative for a consulting firm talk about her services. At one point in the conversation, the manager asked, "Has anyone in our industry, the electrical products industry specifically, ever used this training package before?" The consultant answered, "Sure, we have sold this package to several consumer products firms. Why, just last week I received a nice letter from Gillette that had nothing but good things to say . . ." The manager did not buy the training package; he figured if the consultant did not even know how to listen, the sales training package she was selling could not be very good ei-

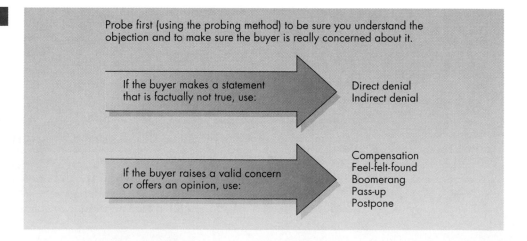

EXHIBIT 11.5

Common Methods
for Responding to
Objections

Probe first (using the probing method) to be sure you understand the objection and to make sure the buyer is really concerned about it.

If the buyer makes a statement that is factually not true, use: →   Direct denial
Indirect denial

If the buyer raises a valid concern or offers an opinion, use: →   Compensation
Feel-felt-found
Boomerang
Pass-up
Postpone

ther. (Chapter Five provided many helpful suggestions regarding the art of questioning and probing.)

Direct Denial

At times salespeople face objections based on incomplete or inaccurate information. They should respond by providing information or correcting facts. When using **direct denial** the salesperson makes a relatively strong statement indicating the error the prospect has made. For example:

> BUYER I am not interested in hearing about your guidance systems. Your firm was one of the companies recently indicted for fraud, conspiracy, and price fixing by a federal grand jury. I don't want to do business with such a firm.

> SALESPERSON I'm not sure where you heard that, but it simply is not true. Our firm has never been involved in such activity, and our record is clean. If you would care to tell me the source of your information, I'm sure we can clear this up. Maybe you're confusing us with another firm.

No one likes to be told that he or she is wrong, so the direct denial must be used with caution. It is appropriate only when the objection is blatantly inaccurate and potentially devastating to the presentation. The salesperson must also possess facts to back up such a denial.

The direct denial should never be used if the prospect is merely stating an opinion or if the objection is true. For example, the direct denial would be inappropriate if the buyer stated the objection that "I don't like the feel of simulated leather products." Direct denial should be avoided even for a false statement if the objection is of little importance to the buyer. An indirect denial or pass-up method would be more appropriate in that case.

Indirect Denial

In the **indirect denial** method, the salesperson denies the objection but attempts to soften the response. The salesperson takes the edge off the response by agreeing with the prospect that the objection is an important one. Prospects expect salespeople to disagree; instead, a salesperson who recognizes the sincerity of the objection will carefully respect the prospect's view. This avoids a direct contradiction and confrontation. To begin an answer, a salesperson would do well to agree with the prospect, but only to the extent that the agreement does not weaken the validity of the salesperson's later denial. For example:

> BUYER Your machines break down more often than most of your major competitors'.

> SALESPERSON I can see why you would feel that way. Just 10 years ago, that statement would have been right on target. However, things have changed with our new quality assurance program. In fact, just last year, Syncos Ratings, a well-respected independent rater of quality in our industry, rated us as number one in the industry for fewest breakdowns.

The important features of indirect denial are that salespeople recognize the position of the customer who makes the objection and then continue by introducing substantial evidence. The beginning statement should always be true and assure the prospect that the question was a good one. Examples of opening statements are:

There is some truth to what you are saying.

With the market the way it is today, I can certainly see why you're concerned about that.

I'll bet 90 percent of the people I call on voice the same concern.

That's really an excellent question, and it allows me the chance to clear up a misconception that perhaps I've given you.

Indirect denial should never be used if the prospect has raised a valid point or is merely expressing an opinion. It can be used for all personality types and would be especially effective for amiables and analyticals, because they like less assertive salespeople.

Compensation Method

Every product has some advantages and some disadvantages compared to competing products. Also, an absolutely perfect product or service has never been developed; the firm always has to make cost-benefit decisions about what features to include.

Buyers note these trade-offs and often object because the salesperson's product is less than perfect. The wise salesperson will admit that such objections are valid and then proceed to show any compensating advantages. This is called the **compensation method** of responding to objections. Here is an example:

PROSPECT This machine has only four filling nozzles. Your competitor's has six nozzles.

SALESPERSON "You're absolutely right. It has only four nozzles, but it costs $4,000 less than the competitor's models, and you said you needed a model that is priced in the lower range. Also, our nozzles are designed for easy maintenance. You only have to remove four screws to get to the filter screens. Most other models have at least 10 screws. That means downtime will be reduced considerably, which is something else you said you were very concerned about.

The compensation method is an explicit use of the multi-attribute model discussed in Chapter Four. A low score on one attribute can be compensated for by a high score on another attribute. In fact, the compensation method is often referred to as the **superior benefit method** because the benefit of one attribute overcomes a concern about a less important attribute. The method can be very effective for many objections and concerns. It seems most appropriate for analyticals, who are accustomed to conducting trade-off analyses. However, it is useful for all other personality types as well.

Of course, the buyer may not value the compensating advantages or may really need the features at issue (e.g., the prospect *must* have six nozzles in order to work with another piece of equipment already owned). In such cases, salespeople can recommend a different product (from their own line, if available, or from a competitor) or search for other prospects.

Feel-Felt-Found Method

When buyers' objections reflect their own attitudes or opinions, the salesperson can show how others held similar views before trying the product or service. In this method, called the **feel-felt-found method**, the salesperson goes on to relate that others actually found their initial opinions to be unfounded after they tried the product:

PROSPECT I don't think my customers will want to buy a CD player with all of these fancy features.

SALESPERSON I can certainly see how you feel. Bob Scott, down the road in Houston, felt the same way when I first proposed that he sell these. However, he found that after he

An older buyer may question the credibility and knowledge of a much younger salesperson. In this situation the salesperson can use the feel-felt-found method to help resolve those concerns.

Time Systems, Inc.; photo by Al Payne

agreed to display them next to his current CD line, customers were very interested. In fact, he called me up four days later to order more.

The sequence of the feel-felt-found method is important, as is the person or persons identified in each stage. It should be "I can see how you feel . . . others felt the same way . . . *yet* they found . . ." Inexperienced salespeople often mix up the order or the parties identified (e.g., "yet you will find").

While the feel-felt-found technique is sound in principle, it should probably be used sparingly. Anyone with knowledge about selling (i.e., buyers) can easily spot this method, and it may appear to be phony or canned.

Proof of the salesperson's assertion in the form of a testimonial letter strengthens the method; in fact, some trainers refer to this as the **third-party testimony method.** If a letter is not available, the salesperson might be able to supply the name and phone number of the third party. The salesperson should always secure the third party's permission first, however. (See Chapter Ten for suggestions for references.)

Although the feel-felt-found method can be used for all personality types, it seems most appropriate for expressives and amiables. Both types tend to care more about what other people think and are doing.

Boomerang Method

When using the **boomerang method** of responding to objections, the salesperson turns the objection into a reason for acting now. It can be used in many situations (e.g., when making an appointment, during the presentation, when attempting to secure commitment, and in postsale situations):

PROSPECT I'm too busy to see you right now.

SALESPERSON I know you are busy, and that's the reason I would like to take 30 minutes of your time. I operate a service designed to save busy executives like yourself up to two hours out of every day.

The boomerang method requires care. It can appear very pushy and "salesy." It sounds like a high-pressure sales tactic you would have heard from someone selling patent medicine in the 1800s ("You can't afford not to buy this amazing little bottle of Dr. Bob's Elixir!").

This method does have useful applications, however. Often the product or service is actually designed to save the buyer substantial amounts of time or money. If the buyer objects to spending either the time to listen or the money, the boomerang method may be a powerful tool to help the buyer see the benefit of investing these resources.

This method works with most personality types. Drivers may require the boomerang technique more often, since they tend to erect time constraints and other barriers and are less willing to listen to just any salesperson's presentation.

Pass-Up Method

At times the buyer voices opinions or concerns more to vent frustration than anything else. When this occurs, the best strategy is often the **pass-up method:** Simply let the buyer talk, acknowledge that you heard the concern, pause, and then move on to another topic.

> BUYER Hey, you use Madonna in your commercials, don't you? Sure you do. Now I want to tell you that I don't like her style or what she stands for! Kids today need a role model they can look up to. What happened to the kind of role models we used to have? It just frustrates me the way rock stars get such a strong following these days!

> SALESPERSON I certainly understand your concern. I remember my dad talking about some of his role models and the respect he had for them. [*Pause*] What were we talking about? Oh yes. I was telling you about the coupon drop we are planning.

In this example, the salesperson used the pass-up method because the buyer apparently was just blowing off steam. If the buyer really wanted some response from the salesperson, this would have become evident during the salesperson's pause; the buyer would have asked a direct question (e.g., "Can't you change your commercials?") or made a statement (e.g., "I refuse to do business with companies that use rock stars in their commercials!").

In reality, a salesperson often can do very little about some of a prospect's opinions. What are the chances that this salesperson's firm will pull a $5 million ad campaign just because one buyer objects? It is very doubtful that a firm would ever take such action unless the buyer had tremendous power in the relationship.

Sometimes the salesperson can use the pass-up method by simply agreeing with the prospect and then moving on, which suggests to the buyer that the concern really should not be much of an issue. For example:

> BUYER You want $25 for this little plastic bottle?!

> SELLER Uh-huh. Now do you see this switch on this side? It's used if you ever need to . . .

The pass-up method should not be used if the objection raised is factually false. Also, it should not be used if the salesperson, through probing, could help clarify the buyer's thinking on the topic. Experience is the key to making such a determination. The pass-up method, due to its nature, should be used very sparingly.

Thinking *it* Through	**H**ow would you feel if someone used the pass-up method on you? Are there times it wouldn't bother you? Are there times it would really bother you?

Postpone Method

In the early part of a sales interview, the prospect may raise objections that the salesperson would prefer to answer later in the presentation, after an opportunity has arisen to discover the prospect's needs. Using the **postpone method,** the salesperson would ask permission to answer the question at a later time:

BUYER [*very early in the call*] How much does the air compressor cost?

SALESPERSON If you don't mind, I would prefer to answer that question in a few minutes. I really can't tell you how much it will cost until I learn more about your air compressor needs and know what kind of features you are looking for.

The prospect will seldom refuse the request if the sales representative appears to be acting in good faith. The sales representative then proceeds with the presentation until the point at which the objection can best be answered.

Some objections are best answered when they occur; others can be responded to most effectively by delaying the answer. Experience should guide the sales representative. The salesperson should take care not to treat an objection lightly or let it appear that he or she does not want to answer the question. Another danger in postponing is that the buyer will be unable to focus on what the salesperson is saying until his or her concern is addressed. On the other hand, the salesperson is responsible for helping the buyer to critically evaluate the solution offered, and often the buyer can process information effectively only after learning preliminary facts.

Salespeople make the most use of the postponement technique when a price objection occurs early in the presentation. However, it can be utilized for almost any type of objection or question. For example, postponing discussions about guarantees, delivery schedules, implementation time frames, and certain unique product features until later in the presentation is often preferable.

What if the buyer is convinced that he or she deserves the answer right now? Then the salesperson should answer the objection now. Salespeople usually have more to lose by demanding that the buyer wait for information than by simply providing the answer when the buyer strongly requests it. For example:

PROSPECT What are the delivery schedules for this new product?

SALESPERSON I would really prefer to discuss that after we talk about our unique production process and extensive quality control measures.

PROSPECT No, I want to know now!

SALESPERSON Well, keep in mind that my later discussion about the production process will shed new light on the topic. We anticipate a four-to-five-month delivery time after the contract reaches our corporate headquarters.

Using the Methods

The seven methods just discussed appear in sales training courses across all industries and geographic boundaries. To help you more easily distinguish the differences among the various techniques, Exhibit 11.6 provides an example of the use of each method for the objection "Your product's quality is too low."

Salespeople often combine methods when answering an objection. For example, a price objection may initially be postponed, then be discussed later using the compensation method. At other times, several methods can be used in one answer. Here is an example:

> BUYER I don't think this product will last as long as some of the other, more expensive competitive products.
>
> SALESPERSON That's probably the very reason you should buy it. [*boomerang method*] It may not last quite as long, but it is less than half the cost of competitive products. [*compensation method*] I can certainly understand your concern, though. You know, Mark Hancock felt the way you do. He was concerned about the product's life. But after he used our product for one year, he found that its life expectancy didn't create any problems for his production staff. [*feel-felt-found method*]

Before moving on with the presentation, the salesperson needs to make sure the buyer agrees that all objections have been completely answered. Without this commitment, the salesperson does not know whether the buyer has understood the answer or whether the buyer's concerns have been fully addressed. To achieve this commitment, the salesperson can use one or more of the following types of phrases:

Did I answer your question?

Does that make sense?

EXHIBIT 11.6	Objection: Your product's quality is too low.
Responding to Objections: Using Each Method	**Responses***

Direct denial: That simply is not true. Our product has been rated as the highest in the industry for the last three years.

Indirect denial: I can certainly see why you would be concerned about quality. Actually, though, our product has been rated as the highest in the industry for the last three years.

Compensation: I agree that our quality is not as high as some of our competitors'. However, it was designed that way for consumers who are looking for a lower-priced alternative, perhaps just to use in a weekend cottage. So you see, our somewhat lower quality is actually offset by our much lower price.

Feel-felt-found: I can certainly understand how you feel. Mortimer Jiggs felt the same way before he bought the product. But after using it, he found that the quality was actually equal to that of other products.

Boomerang: The fact that the quality is lower than in other products is probably the very reason you should buy it. You said that some of your customers are looking for a low-priced product to buy for their grandchildren. This product fills that need.

Pass-up: I understand your concern. You know one of the things I always look for is how a product's quality stacks up against its cost. *[Pause]* Now, we were talking about . . .

Postpone: That's an interesting point. Before discussing it fully, I would like to cover just two things that I think will help you better understand the product from a different perspective. Okay?

*These are not necessarily good answers to the stated objection. Also, the choice of method would depend on whether the objection is factual or not. Thus, the replies given in this table are designed simply to differentiate the various methods.

Before moving on with the presentation, the salesperson needs to make sure the buyer agrees that all objections have been completely answered.

David Joel/Tony Stone Images

Do you see why that is not as important as you originally thought?

I hope I haven't confused you.

Do you have any more questions?

THE PRICE OBJECTION

Sales managers continually hear from salespeople that price is the most frequently mentioned obstacle to obtaining commitment. In fact, about 20 percent of buyers are thought to buy purely on the basis of price (which means that a full 80 percent buy for reasons other than price). As a result, all salespeople need to prepare for price objections. This section will relate the concepts covered in this chapter in the context of this most common objection.

Price is still an issue even between partnering firms. In fact, it appears that price haggling is on the increase.[6] One observer noted, "Industry pundits have noted a trend within distribution toward partnerships in which price plays a limited role. But a simultaneous reality is that many customers continue to buy on price."[7] One leading firm in its industry has estimated that only 3 percent of its orders are sold at list price; the rest are price discounted.[8]

The product's value must be established before spending time discussing price. The value expected determines the price a prospect is willing to pay. The salesperson should build value to a point at which it is greater than the price asked, or there will be no sale. This cannot, as a rule, be accomplished during the early stages of the presentation.

Price objections are best handled with a two-step approach. First, the salesperson should try to look at the objection from the customer's viewpoint, asking questions she or he can use to better understand the customer's perspective:

Too high in what respect, Mr. Jones?

Would you mind telling me why you think my price is too high?

Could you tell me how much we are out of line?

We are usually quite competitive on this model, so I am surprised you find our price high. Are the quotes you have for the same size engine?

What do you feel would be a fair price for this service?

After learning more about the customer's perspective, the next step is to sell value and quality rather than price.[9] All customers prefer to buy less expensive products if they believe they will receive the same benefits. However, many customers will pay more for higher quality when the quality benefits and features are pointed out to them. Many high-quality products appear similar to lower-quality products; thus, salespeople need to emphasize the features that justify a price difference.

For example, a Premier Industrial salesperson who sells industrial fasteners and supplies may hear the objection "That bolt costs $750! I could buy it elsewhere for $75" The salesperson would reply, "Yes, but that bolt is inside the inner workings of your most important piece of production equipment. Let's say you buy that $75 bolt. How much employee time and production downtime would it take to disassemble the machine again and replace that one bolt?" The salesperson would then engage in a complete cost-benefit analysis (see Chapter Ten) to further solidify his or her point.

One pharmaceutical salesperson often hears that her company's drug for migraines is too expensive. Her response is to paint a word picture:[10]

DOCTOR How much does this product cost?

SALESPERSON It costs about $45. . . . There are 15 doses per bottle, so it ends up about $3 per dose.

DOCTOR That's too much money!

SALESPERSON Consider your patients who have to lie in the dark because their heads hurt so badly they can't see straight, can't think straight, and are nauseous from this migraine pain. A price of $3 is really inexpensive to relieve these patients' pain, wouldn't you agree?

Just telling customers about quality and value is not enough; they must be shown. Top salespeople use the communication tools discussed in Chapter Ten to describe more clearly the quality and value of the products. This includes such activities as demonstrating the product, showing test results and quality control procedures, using case histories, and offering testimonials.

Intangible features can also provide value that offsets price. Some of these features are as follows:

1. *Services.* Good service in the form of faster deliveries, technical advice, and field assistance is but one of the many intangibles that can spell value, savings, and profits to a customer.

2. *Company reputation.* For a customer tempted to buy on price alone, salespeople can emphasize the importance of having a thoroughly reliable source of supply: the salesperson's company. It has been demonstrated time and again that quality is measured by the reputation of the company behind it.

3. *The salesperson.* Customers value sales representatives who go out of their way to help with problems and promotions—salespeople who keep their word and follow through when they start something. These services are very valuable to customers.

Unfortunately, the first response of many salespeople to a price objection is to lower the price. Inexperienced salespeople, desiring to gain business, often quote the lowest possible price as quickly as possible. They forget that for a mutually beneficial long-term relationship to exist, their firm must make a fair profit. Also, by cutting prices, the salesperson has to sell more to maintain profit margins, as Exhibit 11.7 clearly illustrates.

EXHIBIT 11.7

Look before You Cut Prices! You Must Sell More to Break Even

There is a business truism that says you can cut, cut, cut until you cut yourself out of business. This can certainly apply to cutting prices in an effort to increase profits. The two don't necessarily go together. For example: Select the gross profit presently being earned from those presented at the top of the chart. Follow the left column down until you line up with the proposed price cut. The intersected figure represents the percentage of increase in unit sales required in order to earn the same gross profit realized before the price cut. Obviously, it helps to know this figure so you don't end up with a lot of work for nothing.

See for yourself: Assume your present gross margin is 25 percent, and you cut your selling price 10 percent. Locate the 25 percent column under Present Gross Profit. Now follow the column down until you line up with the 10 percent cut in selling price in the left-hand column. You will find you will need to sell 66.7 percent more units to earn the same margin dollars as at the previous price.

	Present Gross Profit					
Cut Price	**5.0%**	**10.0%**	**15.0%**	**20.0%**	**25.0%**	**30.0%**
1%	25.0	11.1	7.1	5.3	4.2	3.4
2	66.6	25.0	15.4	11.1	8.7	7.1
3	150.0	42.8	25.0	17.6	13.6	11.1
4	400.0	66.6	36.4	25.0	19.0	15.4
5	—	100.0	50.0	33.3	25.0	20.0
6	—	150.0	66.7	42.9	31.6	25.0
7	—	233.3	87.5	53.8	38.9	30.4
8	—	400.0	114.3	66.7	47.1	36.4
9	—	1000.0	150.0	81.8	56.3	42.9
10	—	—	200.0	100.0	**66.7**	50.0
11	—	—	275.0	122.2	78.6	57.9
12	—	—	400.0	150.0	92.3	66.7
13	—	—	650.0	185.7	108.3	76.5
14	—	—	1400.0	233.3	127.3	87.5
15	—	—	—	300.0	150.0	100.0
16	—	—	—	400.0	177.8	114.3
17	—	—	—	566.7	212.5	130.8
18	—	—	—	900.0	257.1	150.0
19	—	—	—	1900.0	316.7	172.7
20	—	—	—	—	400.0	200.0
21	—	—	—	—	525.0	233.3
22	—	—	—	—	733.3	275.0
23	—	—	—	—	1115.0	328.6
24	—	—	—	—	2400.0	400.0
25	—	—	—	—	—	500.0

Keep in mind that buyers will respond to a seller in different ways, depending on their culture. For example, Germans are known as being thorough, systematic, and well prepared; but they are also rather dogmatic and thus lack flexibility and the desire to compromise.[11] As a result, it could be difficult to deal with a German prospect who raises a price objection.

SUMMARY

Responding to objections is a vital part of a salesperson's responsibility. Objections may be offered at any time during the relationship between buyer and salesperson. They are to be expected, even welcomed, and they must be handled with skill and empathy.

Buyers object for many reasons. They may have no money or they may not need the product. They may need more information or misunderstand some information already offered. They may be accustomed to another product, may not think the value exceeds the cost, or may not like the product's features. They may want to get rid of the salesperson or may not trust the salesperson or his or her company. They may want time to think or may object for many other reasons.

Successful salespeople carefully prepare effective responses to buyers' concerns. They need to develop a positive attitude, refrain from interrupting, anticipate and forestall known objections, and learn how to evaluate objections.

Effective methods of responding to objections are available, and their success has been proven. Methods exist both for concerns that are not true and for objections that either are true or are only the buyer's opinion. Sensitivity in choosing the right method is vital. Nothing will substitute for developing skill in using these methods.

KEY TERMS

boomerang method 317
compensation method 316
direct denial 315
excuses 313
feel-felt-found method 316
forestall 312
indirect denial 315
objection 300

pass-up method 318
pioneer selling 302
postpone method 319
probing method 314
superior benefit method 316
third-party testimony method 317
turnover (TO) 305

QUESTIONS AND PROBLEMS

1. When making cold canvass calls, sales representatives often need to get through a "screen," such as a receptionist, secretary, or assistant, to reach the decision maker. How would you answer the following objections from a screen?

   a. I'm sorry, but Mr. Harris is too busy right now.

   b. We're cutting back on expenditures.

   c. Could you just leave some literature?

   d. A representative of your company was here recently.

   e. I really don't think we can afford your equipment.

2. Categorize each of the following into the five basic types of objections. Then illustrate one way to handle each.

   a. During a demonstration, the customer says, "You know, I really like your competitor's model."

   b. After a sales presentation, the doctor says, "You have a good drug there. Thanks for your time, and if I decide to prescribe it, I'm sure you'll find out."

   c. After the salesperson answers an objection, the prospect remarks, "I guess your product is all right, but—well, I don't think I need one just now. Thanks a lot."

    d. After a thorough presentation, the prospect answers, "No, I'm sorry, we just can't afford it."

    e. After the customer says, "Oh, no! That's really too much money. I've been looking at the same product in an industrial catalog, and I can buy the exact same product at a much lower price."

3. Mary Betando spent considerable time working with a prospective buyer. She thought a good order would be forthcoming on her next call. A portion of her conversation with the buyer went as follows:

> BUYER You know, I like your terms and the styling of your product. But how can I be sure the small parts will hold up and be available?
>
> MARY We've never had any complaints on the parts, and I'm sure they will be easily available.
>
> BUYER You are sure of that?
>
> MARY Well, I've never heard of any problems.
>
> BUYER [*appearing unconvinced and looking at some papers on his desk without glancing up*] I'll let you know later what I plan to do. Thanks for dropping by.

    How can you improve on Mary's answer to the buyer's concern.

4. Discuss the differences between postponing an objection and forestalling an objection.

5. Occasionally, a buyer will offer several objections at one time. How would you respond if a buyer made the following comments without pausing? "Say, does this machine use 110 or 220 volts? What kind of service will you provide monthly? What is the estimated life of this equipment, and have you sold it to anyone else in the area?"

6. Indicate the appropriate action for the sales representative who encounters the following customer attitudes:

    a. I like the things this copier can do—if it really does them. It's kind of hard to believe it'll give me reliable service, though, with all these features that could go wrong.

    b. Let me be plain. Your company's reputation precedes you in this office. I've had more trouble with your company than you would care to hear.

    c. That sounds fine. But there's really no reason to get rid of the copier I've got. It works well enough for anything I use it for.

    d. I see what you're saying. This machine you're talking about could end up saving us some time and money.

7. You are planning on making calls to local high school students with your college admissions staff. Your objective is to help the students see the benefits of attending your college and then have them apply.

    a. Make a list of objections you may expect to encounter.

    b. What can you do to meet these objections effectively? List the answer you would propose and label the method used.

8. How would you attempt to answer the objection "Your new product will have more service problems than your competitor's product" in each of the following situations?

    a. You are calling on an amiable with whom you have been doing business for four years.

    b. You are calling on an expressive for the first time.

    c. You are calling on an analytical who bought one of your products three years ago but has bought nothing since.

    d. You are calling on a driver who currently uses your competitor's product.

9. You have been describing to a secretary and her boss a new office chair that your firm just introduced. The chair is designed to relieve back strain while the sitter uses a personal

computer. The secretary seems very interested and says, "I would really like that!" The boss says, "Well, if it's what you want, OK. How much does it cost?" At your reply, "This one is $498," the boss exclaims, "For that little thing?" What should you say or do?

10. Determining the real reason some customers or prospects habitually refuse to buy can be difficult. They may offer many excuses that disguise the true reason. Before a sale can be closed, the exact reason for not buying must be determined; then the true objection must be answered to the prospect's satisfaction. Answering excuses satisfactorily does little good, because they are not the real hurdles to obtaining commitment. If a customer gives you several reasons for not buying your product, how can you determine whether she or he has stated the real reason? What technique would help to uncover the real objection?

11. For each of the following objections, provide answers that clearly demonstrate the direct denial and indirect denial methods. Assume each objection is not true.

   a. Fishers don't need a boat that goes this fast!

   b. The cost of replacing the air bag in the car will be too high.

   c. I've heard that your firm is a pyramid organization. Products sold in that manner are usually a scam!

   d. Land is inexpensive in this rural area. It would be much easier and more cost effective to just develop a new landfill than to build this recycling operation you are discussing.

   e. I heard your particle board is manufactured using resins that can cause cancer.

   f. The scent of this L'Essence fragrance is not identical to the fragrance you say you are imitating.

12. For each of the following objections, provide answers that clearly demonstrate the compensation method, boomerang method, feel-felt-found method, postpone method, and pass-up method. Assume all the objections are either true or are the prospect's opinion.

   a. Midwest Express does not fly to all the destinations to which our team needs to fly.

   b. I don't think our customers will like the lighter tint of the lenses of your Revo sunglasses.

   c. Your water purification units are not approved by the Environmental Protection Agency.

   d. My customers have never asked for this new L'Oreal hair color product.

   e. Your prices are the absolute highest in the plumbing tool industry.

   f. I don't like the way you use female models in your Coors promotions at bars.

EXPLORING THE NET

This chapter described how many successful salespeople forestall known or suspected objections. now, head to the Web and look at home pages for firms that solicit sales directly on the Web. Some possible hits include:

http://www.mmm.com/office

http://www.hp. com

http://www.astound.com

http://www.nec.com

http://www.da-lite.com

http://www.minnwest.com

http://www.ctxopto.com

1. Has this firm forestalled objections to its products or services? If so, how?

2. Rate the firm's attempts at forestalling objections. In other words, have they done a good job at forestalling the concerns that a potential buyer might have? How might the firm improve in this area?

CASE PROBLEMS

CASE 11.1
Classic Racer Sled

In 1889, Samuel Leeds Allen revolutionized the sport and fun of snow sledding. At that time, all snow sleds were made with wooden runners. Allen replaced the slow wooden runners with steel ones. The result was a lighter, faster, steerable sled that he named the "Flexible Flyer." The new product turned sledding into racing.

Today there are many snow sleds on the market with steel runners. However, very few retailers carry the four-foot "Classic Racer" that Allen created. This sled, still made in America, has outstanding features, including a patented floating crossbar for precise steering, straight-grain hardwood seat and frame, high-strength grooved steel runners, and curved protective bumpers.

Most retailers that cater to snow sports today carry an assortment of plastic snow sleds and snow disks. These items are usually in the $5 to $19 price range. Some retailers carry a less expensive version of the Flexible Flyer or a competitor's brand.

You are a salesperson for the Classic Racer Sled and will soon be calling on Kmart's corporate headquarters. You goal is to introduce these sleds into all Kmarts located in areas that receive significant snowfall each year. You hope to convince the senior buyer at Kmart that there is a latent demand for the product. Many baby boomers who are just now having their children played with Classic Racer Sleds when they were growing up. You hope to explain that people of this generation often buy toys for their children based on nostalgia. The sled has a suggested retail price of $57.

Kmart stores in areas that receive heavy snowfall each year carry about six different plastic snow sleds and snow disks ranging in price from $7 to $15. Kmart doesn't sell any brand of metal sled at this time, but did sell a very inexpensive brand about five years ago. Sales have remained fairly steady over the past few years.

It is May 1, and you have never called on this buyer before.

Questions

1. What objections could the buyer raise?

2. Provide a response to each objection you listed in question 1. Include the name of the method you recommend for each one.

CASE 11.2
Responding to
Objections: A
Prevideo Exercise

Commercial Furniture Systems (CFS) is a manufacturer and importer of modular office furniture and accessories. CFS offers its clients traditional office furniture as well as its designer-influenced Lugano Line. The Lugano Line was created specifically to meet the requirements of ultramodern design applications and unusual office layout situations.

CFS has recently brought to market several new products, including System-Tech office workstations and a line of replaceable modular wall panels that are available in a number of different materials.

CFS is very proud of its newly developed computerized inventory and truck-tracking system, an innovation it believes will place the firm way ahead of the competition.

In the office furniture industry, it is not unusual for interior designers and furniture manufacturers (like CFS) to develop strong professional relationships. When these relationships exist, it is difficult for a competing manufacturer to gain recognition from a designer.

In this video segment, Catherine Craig, an account executive for CFS, is meeting with Joyce Lee, vice president of special projects for Clinton Associates, a large architectural design firm. Craig was referred to Lee by one of Clinton's clients. Craig knows that Clinton designed the interiors of several buildings for the Miller & Huntsman organization and that in each case it specified furniture from Harrison Company. She also knows Lee is very happy with Harrison Company.

Craig's objective is to convince Lee to review a proposal for the use of CFS products on a Miller & Huntsman project.

Questions

To help you think about the objections Joyce Lee might raise in this meeting and how you think Catherine Craig should respond, answer the following questions.

1. List objections you think might occur during this first meeting between Lee and Craig.

2. Describe how you would respond to each objection listed in question 1. Be sure to label the method you recommend.

3. Reread the case and be prepared to watch the videotape in class. Watch for Lee's *actual* objections and how Craig responded. Evaluate Craig's responses.

ADDITIONAL REFERENCES

Bahls, Steven C., and Jane Easter Bahls. "The Price Is Wrong: Matching Your Competitors' Prices Could Be Illegal." *Entrepreneur,* May 1996, pp. 74–76.

Falvey, Jack. "Dealing with Difficult Customers." *Sales & Marketing Management,* April 1995, pp. 20–21.

Fine, Leslie M.; C. David Shepherd; and Susan L. Josephs. "Sexual Harassment in the Sales Force: The Customer Is NOT Always Right." *Journal of Personal Selling and Sales Management,* Fall 1994, pp. 15–29.

"How I Overcame Tough Objections." *Builder,* May 1991, p. 74.

Kennedy, Danielle. "Objection! Customers' Objections Offer a Window of Opportunity for Closing the Sale." *Entrepreneur,* February 1996, p. 99.

Kern, Richard. "The Art of Overcoming Resistance." *Sales & Marketing Management,* March 1990, pp. 101–4.

Chapter Twelve

Obtaining Commitment

Obtaining commitment occurs throughout the sales process, beginning with such actions as asking for an appointment and concluding with asking for the sale. In a partnership, sales result only when the buyer is convinced that the decision to purchase is wise. Once needs are identified and satisfied, attempting to gain commitment is a logical part of the selling

Some Questions Answered in this Chapter Are:

How much emphasis should be placed on closing the sale?

Why is obtaining commitment important?

When is the best time to obtain commitment?

What methods of securing commitment are appropriate for developing partnerships?

How should pricing be presented?

What should a salesperson do when the prospect says *yes*? When the prospect says *no*?

What causes difficulties in obtaining commitment, and how can they be overcome?

process. This chapter will describe how to obtain commitment in an honest, straightforward way.

PROFILE

Trent Weaver currently holds two positions with Mobile Technology, Inc. (MTI), a national shared service imaging firm that provides magnetic resonance imaging scans (MRIs) and other medical services. Originally hired as manager of managed care programs, Weaver has taken on additional responsibilities as the sales representative for the Texas, Oklahoma, and New Mexico regions. Both positions require him to utilize his sales experience and, most important, obtain commitment from prospects.

A managed care organization is a form of insurance company that works with hospitals, physicians, and companies such as Weaver's to provide health care for large groups of people, such as a large company's employees and their families. Weaver says, "When tackling the managed care side of my job, I must convince my customers to contract with MTI-owned and operated imaging centers." This can be a tough sale for Weaver because managed care organizations are reducing the number of vendors while submitting all vendors to tough quality review processes. At the same time, they are driving down price. As Weaver notes, "Most organizations like MTI must double patient volumes in order to maintain same-center revenues from the previous year. Obtaining commitment to increase market share becomes all the more important."

"Because the dollar value is high and there can be significant amounts of risk, most buyers are very cautious, and thus closing the prospect becomes all the more difficult."

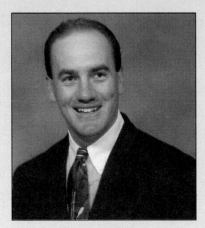

TRENT WEAVER
Mobile Technology, Inc.

"As a sales rep, I am attempting to sell hospitals and group practice organizations shared imaging services. These organizations are making a financial commitment many times in excess of $1 million over a three-year period. Because the dollar value is high and there can be significant amounts of risk, most buyers are very cautious, and thus closing the prospect becomes all the more difficult." Weaver has to get all the buyers to give their stamp of approval or run the risk of losing the deal. "Four people can be in favor, but if one key buyer is not, chances are I will not get the deal. I must therefore understand each buyer and their needs or reasons for being involved in the decision. Then I can communicate precisely how my product can and will meet their department/organization's goals."

Selling medical services is no quick sale. Weaver says, "I am selling for the long term. Quick sales that end up short of win-win will affect both organizations negatively." Weaver recognizes that if he wins at the expense of his client, he loses credibility and future business: "If the prospect wins and I lose, I've lost my company's profit."

Weaver believes organizations buy because of the trust they have in the salesperson. "When buying a service, the quality and consistency of that service become more important than price," he explains. Often belief in quality and consistency comes down to a belief in the word of the salesperson. "Because the sales process is somewhat long for shared services, typically four months to one year, it is during that process that I begin to build trust and I am able to slowly and methodically handle any objections and problems that may arise during that period. If I promise to phone, fax, send material, I make sure it gets done. All these things combine to get me to the end result, which is a signature and a handshake."

Weaver also believes that "Buyers are smarter and more thorough these days." He has to know his own service inside and out, as well as those of his competitors. Then, and only then, can he develop the trust and credibility it takes to close the sale.

OBTAINING COMMITMENT TODAY

Asking for the buyer's business, often called **closing,** has always received a great deal of emphasis in sales training. Hundreds of books, audiocassettes, videocassettes, and seminar speakers have touted the importance of closing. According to conventional wisdom, the key to success in any sale is to find a method or methods of closing that will make the decision maker say *yes.*

However, a more effective perspective on this topic has emerged. Tony Alessandra, a well-respected sales trainer, sums it up this way:

Forget 150 ways to handle objections or 50 ways to close the sale. These are commando selling techniques or gimmicks that make up for not being good. . . . The only way to develop a long-term relationship with a customer is to use a nonmanipulative, consultative selling technique. The key to nonmanipulative selling is trust. A good salesperson establishes trust by being candid, honest, forthright, and most of all a good listener.[1]

Other trainers also believe the traditional emphasis on the close damages trust, insults the buyer's intelligence, and raises the possibility of losing commitment altogether.[2] Tim Conner, president of an international sales training organization, states:

The emphasis in sales for decades has been on the "close" of the sale. I believe that this selling strategy is no longer appropriate given present consumers' attitudes, intelligence, and their need for practical solutions and increased information about products and services available to them today from a wide variety of organizations.[3]

Solid research has provided strong evidence that questions heavy reliance on closing techniques. The research, based on more than 35,000 sales calls over 12 years, has found that in a major sale, reliance on closing techniques actually *reduces* the chances of making a sale.[4] Further, salespeople who were specifically trained in closing actually closed *fewer* sales. For very-low-priced products (as in door-to-door magazine sales), however, closing techniques may increase the chances of a sale.

So why even cover closing at all? Because there are nonmanipulative and trustworthy ways to gain commitment, and because obtaining commitment is critical for the success of salespeople and their firms. Without a buyer's commitment, no sale takes place. Also, buyers will rarely volunteer to make the purchase, even when that decision is obviously the right thing to do. One company looks at a sale as "just another way of reaffirming the relationship," meaning that commitment to the relationship is more important than any single sale.[5] This chapter will cover the topic of obtaining commitment in a manner that is consistent with the theme of the book: developing and building long-term partnerships.

The process of obtaining commitment occurs throughout the natural, logical progression of any sales call. Recall from Chapter Four that creeping commitment occurs when a customer becomes committed to a particular course of action throughout the buying process. Salespeople actually gain commitment repeatedly: when asking for an appointment, checking to see if all of the customer's needs have been identified, and when asking if the prospect would like to see a demonstration or receive a proposal. Commitment, of course, is more than just securing an order. As Exhibit 12.1 illustrates, salespeople will attempt to obtain a commitment that is consistent with the objectives of the particular sales call.

The Importance of Securing Commitment

Overall, gaining commitment tells the salesperson what to do next and defines the status of the client. For example, gaining a needs identification appointment may mean that you have a "suspect"; at the end of that call, gaining commitment for a demon-

EXHIBIT 12.1 Examples of Commitments Salespeople May Attempt to Obtain*	To have the prospect *sign an order* for 100 pairs of Levi's jeans. To have the prospect *agree* to come to the Atlanta branch office sometime during the next two weeks for a hands-on demonstration of the copier. To *set up another appointment* for one week from now, at which time the buyer will allow a complete survey of her printing needs. To *learn the names* of all other key players in this decision that the prospect can identify. To inform the doctor of the revolutionary anticlogging mechanism that has been incorporated in our new drug and *have her agree* to read the pamphlet I will leave. To have the buyer agree to *pass my information along* to the buying committee with his endorsement of my proposal. To have *the prospect agree to call several references* that I will provide in order to develop further confidence and trust in my office cleaning business. To *schedule a co-op newspaper advertising program* to be implemented in the next month. To have the prospect agree to use our brand of computer paper for a *trial period* of one month. To have the prospect agree *on the first point* (of our four-point program) and schedule another meeting in two days with an agenda for discussing the second point. To have the retailer *agree to allow us space* for an end-of-aisle display for the summer promotion of Raid. To have the *prospect initiate the paperwork* that would allow us to be considered as a future vendor.

*Note the similarity between this table and Exhibit 8.2, which provides examples of call objectives. Actually, a perfect positive relationship should exist between call objectives and closing attempts.

stration means you have a prospect. Gain an order and you gain a customer. Without gaining commitment, the salesperson may waste time doing the wrong things.

Salespeople need to become proficient in obtaining commitment for several other good reasons. First, if they fail to obtain commitment, it will take longer (more sales calls) to obtain a sale, if at all. Taking more time means fewer sales because time for prospecting and other important activities is lost. Second, assuming the product truly satisfies the prospect's needs, the sooner the prospect buys, the sooner she or he can realize the benefits of the product or service. Third, the company's future success depends on goodwill and earning a profit. Finally, not only does securing commitment result in financial rewards for the salesperson; meeting needs is also intrinsically rewarding for the seller.

Thinking *it* **Through**	Think for a moment about a major purchase that you made, such as a stereo or a car. During the shopping process, what were some of the worst closes you experienced? What really angers you when you try to shop for major purchases? What made the difference between those experiences and the ones you found satisfying?

SETTING THE PRICE

Often, price is the last element of the deal to be presented and discussed. Yet it is often one of the most important factors when the buyer makes the decision. The final price is really a function of the terms and conditions of the sale and depends on several factors. For example, Paula Shelton, a salesperson for Cort Furniture in Washington, DC, encountered a buyer who demanded a 15 percent price cut and several extra benefits or he would cancel a large order. She almost gave in to close the sale, but then realized that getting the sale at that price and with the extra services meant that Cort would lose money. So she set up payment terms that were more favorable to the buyer but maintained the original price—and kept the customer.

Factors that affect price are the use of quantity and other discounts, as well as credit and shipping terms. Figuring out the final actual price can be difficult, especially in situations with many options and packages rather than standardized products. Companies such as Norand Corporation (a manufacturer of pen-input computers and wireless networks) are providing their salespeople with laptops and software to configure products and calculate pricing options.[6]

Discounts

Discounts are given for many reasons, such as based on the type of customer (e.g., wholesaler or retailer, senior citizen or younger adult), quantity purchased, or some other factor. (Discounts used in selling to resellers are discussed in Chapter Fifteen.) The most common type of discount is the quantity discount.

Quantity discounts encourage large purchases by passing along savings resulting from reduced processing costs. Businesses offer two types of quantity discounts: (1) the single-order discount and (2) a cumulative discount. An office equipment company offering a 10 percent discount on a single order for five or more facsimile machines is an example of a single-order discount. When offering a **cumulative discount,** that same company might offer the 10 percent discount on all purchases over a one-year period, provided the customer purchases more than five fax machines. The customer may sign an agreement at the beginning of the year promising to buy five or more machines, in which case the customer will be billed for each order at the discounted price (10 percent off). If the customer fails to purchase five fax machines, a single bill will be sent at the end of the year for the amount of the discount (10 percent of the single-unit price times the number of fax machines actually purchased). Another method would be to bill the customer at the full price, then rebate the discount at the end of the year based on the actual number of fax machines purchased.

Credit Terms

Most U.S. sales are made on a credit basis, with **cash discounts** allowed for early payment. These cash discounts are the last discount taken, meaning that if a quantity discount was also offered, the cash discount would be calculated after the quantity discount was taken off. A common discount is 2/10, n/30, which means the buyer can deduct 2 percent from the bill if paid in 10 days from the date of invoice. Otherwise, the full amount must be paid in 30 days. Another common discount is 2/10, EOM, which means the 10-day period begins at the end of the month. For example, if the customer received $1,000 worth of supplies on February 15 with terms of 2/10, EOM, and paid the bill on March 5, the customer would pay $980 (that is, $1,000 \times 2\% = \$20$ discount for paying cash; $1,000 - \$20 = \$980$). But if the customer paid on March 11, the bill would be the full $1,000.

Shipping Costs

The terms and conditions of sale include shipping costs. The seller who quotes an **FOB (free on board)** price agrees to load the goods on board a truck, freight car, or other means of transportation.

A great many variations exist in the use of FOB, but the term is used to specify the point at which the buyer assumes responsibility for both the goods and the costs of shipping them. Thus, FOB destination would mean the buyer will take responsibility for the goods once they reach the buyer's location, and the seller will pay the freight.

If Thompson and Sons receives a shipment "FOB Origin," it means that Thompson and Sons was responsible for shipping; if the shipment was "FOB Destination," it means that the company Thompson bought from took care of shipping.

Jim Erickson/The Stock Market

Suppose Johnson Wax quotes an FOB origin. It will load the truck at its Racine, Wisconsin, plant, but the buyer bears the responsibility for paying for shipping. If Johnson Wax sold a truckload of Raid to Tom Thumb (a grocery chain headquartered in Dallas) under terms of FOB destination, Johnson Wax would pay for shipping and would have the Raid delivered to Tom Thumb's Dallas warehouse, where warehouse personnel would unload the truck.

The terms and conditions of a sale, including but not limited to price, can often play as important a role as the product itself in determining what is purchased. Creative salespeople understand the terms and conditions they have to work with so that they can meet the needs of their buyers while also meeting the profit objectives of their own companies.

Presenting Price

Price is often discussed at the end of the presentation simply because the salesperson may not know what that price will be until the final solution is agreed on. Because price is so important to the buyer, it is worth considering how price should be presented.

Most firms set prices after careful study of the competitors' offerings, the value delivered by the product or service, and the cost of providing the product or service. For these reasons, the price should represent a reasonable and fair picture of the product's or service's value. Therefore, never apologize for a price or present the price apologetically; rather, present it with confidence.

Russ Berry, known as Father Troll because his company made the troll dolls popular, relates this story about when he began his business. He needed a warehouse because he worked out of his apartment in Manhattan and there was no room to store inventory. So he knocked on the door of a house that had a sign in the window reading "Garage for rent." He expected to pay $75 a month for the garage, but when the owner of the house said the rent was $50, Berry's response was "$50!" The owner thought Berry was objecting to the price, so he responded, "Okay, $35." Berry, as have many other astute businesspeople, learned to always respond with skepticism to the first price offered. Yet in his story, he believed the value of the garage was more than twice what he actually paid for it.[7]

In addition to presenting the price with confidence, remember that price is not the focus of your presentation. The real issue is satisfying the needs of the buyer, of which budget is only one. True, a budget limitation can halt progress toward a sale. The real issue, though, is the total cost of ownership, which means the buyer should also factor in the value of the benefits delivered.

WHEN TO ATTEMPT TO OBTAIN COMMITMENT

Novice salespeople frequently ask themselves these questions: Is there a right time to obtain commitment? How will customers let me know they are ready to buy? Should I make more than one attempt? What should I do if my first attempt fails?

The "right" time to attempt to gain commitment is when the buyer appears ready, as evidenced by buying signals. Some salespeople say that one psychological moment in each sales presentation affords the best opportunity for this and, if this opportunity is bypassed, securing commitment will be difficult or impossible. This is not true, however. Seldom does one psychological moment govern the complete success or failure of a sales presentation.

Most buyers will commit themselves only when they clearly understand the benefits and costs of such a decision. At times this point occurs early in the call. A commitment to purchase a large system, however, usually will not occur until a complete presentation and several calls have been made and all questions have been answered.

Buying signals, or indications that the buyer is ready to buy, can be evidenced both in the buyer's comments and nonverbally. Buying signals are also called **closing cues.**

Buyers' Comments

Customer's comments often are the best indication that they are considering commitment. A prospect will seldom say, "All right, I'm ready to endorse this product to our buying committee." Customers' questions about the product or terms of sale and comments in the form of requirements or benefit statements signal readiness to buy, as do their responses to trial closes.

Buyer Questions

Some examples of questions that signal readiness to buy are:

> If I do agree to go with this cooperative advertising program, do you have any ads already developed that I could use?
>
> Do you have any facilities for training our employees in the use of the product?
>
> How soon would you be able to deliver the equipment?
>
> What do we do next?

Not all questions will signal a readiness to buy, but if the question concerns implementing the purchase and points toward *when* the purchase is implemented, not *if,* the prospect is getting ready to buy.

Requirements

Requirements are conditions that have to be satisfied before a purchase can take place. For example:

We've got to have a cash discount for a supply order like this.

We will need to get this in weekly shipments.

Requirements that are stated near the end of the presentation are need statements that reflect a readiness to buy when they relate to how the purchase will be consummated.

Benefit Statements

Sometimes prospects offer their own benefit statements, such as:

Oh, I like the way this equipment is serviced—it will make it much easier on my staff.

Good, that color will match our office decor.

Such positive statements reflect strong feelings in support of the purchase, a sign that the buyer is ready.

Responses to Trial Closes

Salespeople can solicit such comments by continually taking the pulse of the situation with **trial closes,** or questions regarding the prospect's readiness to buy. Throughout the presentation, the salesperson should be asking questions such as:

How does this sound to you so far?

Is there anything else you would like to know at this point?

How does this compare with what you have seen of competing products?

Buyers' responses to such questions provide good guidance regarding when the salesperson should attempt to obtain commitment. The response also helps the salesperson ensure that the buyer agrees that the benefits will accrue and are important.

Nonverbal Cues

As in every phase of the presentation, nonverbal cues serve as important indicators of the customer's state of mind. While attempting to gain commitment, the salesperson should the use buyer's nonverbal signals to better identify areas of concern and

Do the two buyers on the left look like they are ready to commit to a purchase?

Courtesy Kimberly-Clark Corporation

see whether the buyer is ready to commit. Facial expressions most often indicate how ready the buyer is to make a commitment. Positive signals include eyes that are open and relaxed, face and mouth not covered with hands, a natural smile, and a relaxed forehead. The reverses of these signals indicate that the buyer is not yet ready to commit to the proposal.

Customers' actions also often indicate readiness to buy or make a commitment. For example, the prospective buyer of a fax machine may get a document and operate the machine or place the machine on the table where it will be used. The industrial buyer may refer to a catalog to compare specifications with competing products. A doctor, when told of a new drug, may pick up the pamphlet and begin carefully reading the indications and contraindications. A retailer considering whether to allow an end-of-aisle display may move to the end of an aisle and scan the layout. Any such actions may be signals for obtaining commitment; they should be viewed in the context of all available verbal and nonverbal cues.

HOW TO SUCCESSFULLY OBTAIN COMMITMENT

To obtain commitment in a nonmanipulative manner, salespeople need to follow several principles, including maintaining a positive attitude, letting the customer set the pace, being assertive instead of aggressive, and selling the right product in the right amounts.

Maintain a Positive Attitude

Confidence is contagious. Customers like to deal with salespeople who have confidence in themselves, their products, and their companies. On the other hand, unnecessary fear can be a self-fulfilling prophecy. The typist who fears making errors will make many; the student who fears essay exams usually does poorly; golfers who believe they will miss short putts usually do. So it is with salespeople: If they fear the customer will not accept their proposal, the chances are good they will be right.

One manager related the example of a salesperson selling laundry detergent who unsuccessfully tried to convince a large discount chain to adopt a new liquid version of the product. When the rep's sales manager stopped by the account later in the week to follow up on a recent stockout problem, the buyer related his reasons for refusing the liquid Tide: "Listen, I know you guys are sharp. You probably wouldn't come out with a new product unless you had tons of data to back up your decision. But, honestly, the sales rep who calls on me is always so uptight and apprehensive that I was afraid to adopt the new product! Don't you guys teach them about having confidence?"

Let the Customer Set the Pace

Attempts to gain commitment must be geared to fit the varying reactions, needs, and personalities of each buyer. Thus, the sales representative needs to practice adaptive selling. (See Chapter Six for a complete discussion of adaptive selling.)

Some buyers who react very slowly may need plenty of time to assimilate the material presented. They may ask the same question several times or show they do not understand the importance of certain product features. In these circumstances, the salesperson must deliver the presentation more slowly and may have to repeat certain parts. Trying to rush buyers is unwise when they show they are not yet ready to commit.

 As we discussed earlier in the book, buyers' decision-making styles vary greatly. Japanese and Chinese buyers tend to move more slowly and cautiously when evaluating a proposition. In contrast, buyers working for Fortune 500 firms located in the

This salesperson is just a little too aggressive; in handing her the pen, he hopes that she will take it and then use it to sign the order.

©Michael J. Hruby

largest U.S. cities often tend to move much more quickly. The successful salesperson recognizes such potential differences and acts accordingly.

Be Assertive, Not Aggressive

Marvin Jolson has identified three types of salespeople: aggressive, submissive, and assertive.[8] **Aggressive** salespeople control the sales interaction but often fail to gain commitment because they prejudge the customer's needs and fail to probe for information. Too busy talking to do much listening, they tend to push the buyer too soon, too often, and too vigorously. They might say, "I can't understand why you are hesitant," but they do not probe for reasons for the hesitancy.

    Submissive salespeople often excel as socializers. With customers they spend a lot of time talking about families, restaurants, and movies. They establish rapport quite effectively. They accept the customers' statements of needs and problems but do not probe to uncover any latent needs or opportunities. Submissive salespeople rarely try to obtain commitment.

    Assertive salespeople are self-confident and positive. They maintain the proper perspective by being responsive to customer needs. Rather than aggressively creating new "needs" in customers through persuasion, they look for buyers who truly need their products, then encourage them through questioning to provide information. Their presentations emphasize an exchange of information rather than a one-way presentation. Exhibit 12.2 summarizes the differences among assertive, aggressive, and submissive salespeople's handling of the sales interview.

Sell the Right Item in the Right Amounts

The chance of obtaining commitment improves when the right product is sold in the right amount. Although this principle sounds obvious, it often is not followed.

    For example, before attempting to sell two copiers, the office equipment sales representative must be sure that these *two* copiers, instead of only one copier or perhaps three, best fit the needs of the buyer's office. The chemical company sales repre-

EXHIBIT 12.2	How Aggressive, Submissive, and Assertive Salespeople Handle Sales Activities		
	Selling Style		
Selling Activity	Aggressive	Submissive	Assertive
Defining customer needs	Believe they are the best judge of customer's needs	Accept customer's definition of needs	Probe for need-related information that customer may not have volunteered
Controlling the presentation	Minimize participation by customer	Permit customer to control presentation	Encourage two-way communication and customer participation
Closing the sale	Overwhelm customer; respond to objections without understanding	Assume customers will buy when ready	Respond to objections, leading to somewhat automatic close

sentative selling to an industrial firm must know that one tank car of a chemical is more likely to fit the firm's needs than ten 55-gallon drums. The Johnson Wax sales rep who utilizes the firm's "Sell to Potential" program knows the importance of selling not too few units (or the store will run out of stock during the promotion) and not too many units (or the store will be stuck with excess inventory after the promotion). Customers have long memories; they will refuse to do business with someone who oversells, and they may also lack confidence in someone who undersells. The chances to obtain commitment diminish rapidly when the salesperson tries to sell too many or too few units or the wrong grade or style of product.

Also, salespeople should not rely on trial orders often. A trial order is no commitment, and all too often a buyer will agree to a trial just to get rid of the salesperson. Further, if any learning curve is necessary, a customer is unwilling to invest the time necessary to fully learn the product, thereby not fully realizing the benefits. The product will be rejected often because customers don't have time to give fair trials.

Salespeople are likely to sell the right product in the right amounts if they keep a service attitude. For example, Herb Burnap, sales representative for Moore Business Forms, recently figured out a way to save his account 35 percent of their annual business forms bill by combining information that was on two forms into one. Burnap rightly believes that, although the first sale may be smaller if the right product is sold in the right amounts, repeat sales and goodwill will always more than make up the difference.

EFFECTIVE
METHODS

"If closing is seen by so many sales experts as manipulative and insulting, are effective methods those that are manipulative but not insulting?" asked one of our students. It is a fair question, and the answer has two elements. First, the salesperson's purpose is to sell the right product in the right amounts. If the prospect does not need what is being sold, the salesperson should walk to the next door and start again. Thus, there is never a need to be manipulative. Second, in addition to selling only what the customer needs, the salesperson should also sell in a fashion consistent with the way the buyer prefers to buy. Therefore, the salesperson should gain commitment in a manner that will help the buyer make the choice. We use the word "choice" here to mean that the buyer can say *no*. Manipulative techniques are designed to reduce or eliminate choice; partnering methods are not.

Studying successful methods and techniques enables salespeople to help prospects buy a product or service they want or need. Buyers sometimes have a need or a want but still hesitate to buy the product or service that will satisfy it. For example, an industrial buyer for a candy manufacturer refused to commit to a change in sweeteners even though she had a need for a better raw material. Why? Because the sweetener rep had met with her on four separate occasions, and the buyer had difficulty remembering all that was said and agreed on. Had the salesperson used the appropriate method (the benefit summary method, discussed later in this section), commitment might have been obtained. We will explore several of the most important methods in this section.

Direct Request

The most straightforward, effective method of obtaining commitment is simply to ask for it. However, salespeople need to be wary of appearing overly aggressive when using this **direct request method.** It works best with decisive customers, such as drivers who appreciate getting down to business and not wasting time. Examples include:

> Can I put you down for 100 pairs of Model 63?
>
> Can we meet with your engineer next Thursday to further discuss this?
>
> Will you come to the home office for a hands-on demonstration?
>
> Can you call the meeting next week?
>
> Is it a deal?

Benefit Summary

Early in the interview, salespeople discover or reiterate the needs and problems of the prospect. Then, throughout the presentation, they show how their product can meet those needs. They do this by turning product or service features into benefits specifically for that buyer. As they present each benefit, they ask if that benefit meets the need. When using this approach, called the **benefit summary method,** the salesperson simply reminds the prospect of the agreed-on benefits of the proposal. This nonmanipulative method simply helps the buyer to synthesize points covered in the presentation to make a wise decision. For example, the salesperson attempting to obtain the buyer's commitment to recommend a proposal to a buying committee might say,

> You stated early in my visit that you were looking for a product of the highest quality, a vendor that could provide quick delivery, and adequate engineering support. As I've mentioned, our fasteners have been rated by an independent laboratory as providing 20 percent higher tensile strength than the closest competitor, resulting in a life expectancy of over four years. We also discussed the fact that our fasteners can be delivered to your location within 3 hours of your request, and that this holds true 24 hours a day. Finally, I discussed the fact that we have four engineers on staff whose sole responsibility is to work with existing customers in providing support and developing new specifications for new fasteners. Would you be willing to give this information to the buying committee along with your endorsement of the proposal?

One advantage of the benefit summary method over the direct request method is that the seller can help the buyer remember all the points discussed in the presentation. This becomes particularly important in long presentations and in selling situations involving several meetings prior to obtaining commitment. The salesperson cannot assume the buyer will remember all the major points discussed in the presentation.

Balance Sheet Method

Sometimes referred to as the *Ben Franklin method* because Franklin described using it to make decisions, the **balance sheet method** aids prospects who cannot make a decision even though no reason for their behavior is apparent. Such a prospect may be asked to join the salesperson in listing the pros and cons of buying now or buying later, of buying the salesperson's product or that of a competitor, or of buying the product or not buying it at all.

However, like many nonmanipulative sales techniques, this method can insult a buyer's intelligence if used inappropriately. The salesperson may start to obtain commitment with the following type of statement:

> You know, Mr. Thacker, Ben Franklin was like you, always anxious to reach the right decisions and avoid the wrong ones. I suppose that's how you feel. Well, he suggested taking a piece of paper and writing all the reasons for deciding *yes* in one column and then listing the reasons for deciding *no* in a second column. He said that when you make this kind of graphic comparison, the correct decision becomes much more apparent.

That close may seem manipulative. A more effective start may be to simply draw a *T* on a plain piece of paper, place captions on each side of the crossbar, and leave space below for the insertion of specific benefits or sales points. Then just ask the buyer to list pros and cons of making the purchase. For example, assume the product is National Adhesives' hot-melt adhesive used to attach paper labels to plastic Classic Coke bottles. Coca-Cola is currently using a liquid adhesive made by Ajax Corporation. In this situation, the *T* might look like this:

Benefits of Adopting National Adhesives' Hot-Melt Method	Benefits of Staying with the Ajax Liquid Adhesives

The salesperson may say something like "Making a decision like this is difficult. Let's see how many reasons we can think of for your going with the National Adhesive system." The salesperson would write the benefits (not features), in which the customer has shown interest on the left side of the *T*. Next, the salesperson would ask the customer to list reasons to stay with the Ajax adhesive on the right side. When completed, the T lists should accurately reflect all the pros and cons of each possible decision. At that point the buyer is asked, "Which method do you think is the wisest?"

When used properly, the balance sheet method can help hesitant buyers express their feelings about the decision, which gives the salesperson an opportunity to deal with those feelings. It is especially appropriate for a buyer who is an analytical, but would make less sense for an expressive. However, the balance sheet approach takes time and may appear "salesy," particularly if relatively unimportant benefits are considered to be equal to more important reasons not to buy. Also, the list of benefits of the product being sold will not always outnumber the list on the other side of the *T*.

Probing Method

In the **probing method,** sales representatives initially attempt to obtain commitment by another method, perhaps simply asking for it (the direct request method). If unsuccessful, the salesperson uses a series of probing questions designed to discover the reason for the hesitation. Once the reason(s) becomes apparent, the salesperson asks a what-if question (e.g., "What if I could successfully resolve this concern? Would you be willing to commit?"): An illustrative dialogue follows:

SALESPERSON Could we make an appointment for next week, at which time I would come in and do a complete survey of your needs? It shouldn't take more than three hours.

PROSPECT No, I don't think I am quite ready to take that step yet.

SALESPERSON There must be some reason why you are hesitating to go ahead now. Do you mind if I ask what it is?

PROSPECT I'm just not convinced that your firm is large enough to handle a customer of our size.

SALESPERSON In addition to that, is there any other reason why you would not be willing to go ahead?

PROSPECT No.

SALESPERSON If I can resolve the issue of our size, then you would allow me to conduct a survey?

PROSPECT Well, I wouldn't exactly say that.

SALESPERSON Then there must be some other reason. May I ask what it is?

PROSPECT Well, a friend of mine that uses your services told me that often your billing department sends him invoices for material he didn't want and didn't receive.

SALESPERSON In addition to that, is there any other reason for not going ahead now?

PROSPECT No, those are my two concerns.

SALESPERSON If I could resolve those issues right now, would you be willing to set up an appointment for a survey?

PROSPECT Sure.

This dialogue illustrates the importance of probing in obtaining commitment. The method attempts to bring to the table all issues of concern to the prospect. The salesperson does not claim to be able to resolve the issues but simply attempts to find out what the issues are. When probing has identified all of the issues, the salesperson should attempt to resolve them as soon as possible. After successfully dealing with the concerns of the buyer, the salesperson should then ask for a commitment.

There are many modifications of the probing method. One other way to achieve the same results is the following:

SALESPERSON Will you be willing to buy this product today?

PROSPECT No, I don't think so.

SALESPERSON I really would like to get a better feel of where you are. On a scale of 1 to 10, with 1 being absolutely no purchase and 10 being purchase, where would you say you are?

PROSPECT I would say I'm about a 6.

SALESPERSON If you don't mind my asking, what would it take to move you from a 6 to a 10?

 Also, it is important to always keep cultural differences in mind. For example, if a Japanese businesswoman wants to tell an American salesperson that she is not interested, she might state, "Your proposal would be very difficult" just to be polite. If the

Selecting the method with which to gain commitment requires an understanding of the buyer's culture.

Dick Berwin/ The Image Bank

seller attempts to use the probing method, the Japanese businesswoman may consider the seller to be pushy or a poor listener. In the same way, an Arab businessperson will never say *no* directly, a custom that helps either side avoid losing face.[9]

Alternative Choice

In many situations, a salesperson may have multiple options to present to a buyer. For example, Teo Schaars sells diamonds directly from cutters in the Netherlands to consumers in the United States. When he first started out, he would display several dozen diamonds on a purple damask–covered table. Sales were few until his father, a Dutch diamond broker, suggested that he limit his customers' choices; there were simply too many diamonds to choose from, overwhelming the buyer. Schaars found his father's comments to be wise advice. Now he spends more time probing about budget and desires, then shows only two diamonds at a time, explaining the key characteristics of each. Then he allows the customer to express a preference. Schaars may have to show half a dozen or more diamonds before a customer makes the final decision, but he rarely shows more than two at a time.

Other Methods

Literally hundreds of techniques and methods to obtain commitment have been tried. Exhibit 12.3 lists a number of traditional methods. Most of them, however, tend to be ineffective with sophisticated customers; nevertheless, all can be used in a nonmanipulative manner if appropriate. For example, the minor point close can be appropriate if there really is a need to make a choice between two options; what makes the method manipulative is the assumption that the minor choice is the equivalent to making the sale.

No method of obtaining commitment will work if the buyer does not trust the salesperson, the company, and the product. Gaining commitment should not require the use of tricky techniques or methods to force buyers to do something they do not want to do or persuade them to buy something they do not need. Trust, however, is a two-way commitment. Selling Scenario 12.1 presents an interesting turnabout that occurred when trust was lacking.

EXHIBIT 12.3	Some Traditional Closing Methods	
Method	**How It Works**	**Remarks**
Minor point close	The seller assumes it is easier to get the prospect to decide on a very trivial point than on the whole proposition: "What color do you like, blue or red?" If the prospects makes the minor decision, the seller assumes the sale is made and begins writing up the order.	This can upset a prospect who feels he or she is being manipulated. No one wants to feel that he or she has been tricked into making a commitment. Even unsophisticated buyers easily spot this technique.
Continuous *yes* close	Throughout the presentation, the seller constantly asks questions for which the prospect most logically would answer *yes*. By the end of the discussion, the buyer is so accustomed to saying *yes* that when the order is requested, the natural response is *yes*.	This method is based on self-perception theory. As the presentation progresses, the buyer begins to perceive himself or herself as being "agreeable." At the close, the buyer wants to maintain this self-image and almost unthinkingly says *yes*. Use of this method can destroy long-term relationships if the buyer *later* feels manipulated.
Assumptive close	The seller, without asking for the order, simply begins to write it up. A variation is to fill out the order form as the prospect answers questions.	This does not even give the buyer the courtesy of agreeing. It can be perceived as being very pushy and manipulative.
Standing-room-only close	The seller attempts to obtain commitment by describing the negative consequences of waiting. For example, the seller may state, "If you can't decide now, I'll have to offer it to another customer."	This can be effective if the statement is true. However, if the prospect really does need to act quickly, this should probably be discussed earlier in the presentation. An earlier discussion would tend to reduce possible mistrust and feeling of being pushed without apparent necessity.
Benefit-in-reserve close	First, the seller attempts to obtain commitment by another method. If unsuccessful, the seller says, "Oh, I forgot to tell you that if you order today I can offer you an additional 5 percent for your trade-in."	Although this method can be effective, it can also backfire easily. The buyer tends to think, "If I had agreed to your first attempt to obtain commitment, I would not have learned about this new enticement. What else do you have up your sleeves? If I wait longer, how much better will your offer be?" Use of this technique can also cause the buyer to seek additional concessions in every future sale attempt.
Emotional close	In this technique, the seller appeals to the buyer's emotions to close the sale. For example, the seller may say, "This really is a good deal. To be honest with you, I desperately need to secure an order today. As you know, I work on a straight commission basis. My wife is going to have surgery next week, and our insurance just won't cover. . ."	Many obvious problems arise with this method. It is an attempt to move away from focusing entirely on the salesperson's personal needs. It does not develop trust or respect.

IF COMMITMENT IS OBTAINED

The salesperson's job is not over when commitment is obtained. In fact, in many ways the job is just beginning. This section will describe the salesperson's responsibilities that accrue after the buyer says *yes*.

No Surprises

Customers do not like surprises, so now is the time to go over any important information they will need to fully enjoy the benefits of the product or service. For example, if selling life insurance and a physical is required, give the customer as much

SELLING SCENARIO 1 2 . 1

Seller's Remorse?

Salespeople occasionally run into a buyer who experiences "buyer's remorse," an immediate feeling that she or he shouldn't have bought. But Harold Bumpurs, manager of central purchasing at Plantation Foods, had a seller with remorse. He recalls, "We purchase natural gas and had done so for years from one vendor. There wasn't anything wrong with that vendor, but prices were rising and we wanted to lock in our cost with a year-long contract. So we began looking at proposals. A salesperson for another company called and said his company was wanting to start supplying companies like ours who use natural gas, and he was willing to give us an annual contract. He quoted a price, I took it before the Executive Committee, and they agreed to go ahead with it. So he faxed us a contract that morning, which we authorized and returned."

By day's end, the price of natural gas had risen 20 cents, a significant increase. More important, the rep had put no limit on the amount of gas Plantation could buy at the lower price. He immediately began faxing additional requirements and cost increases to the contract. "This guy didn't know us and didn't trust us," Bumpurs says. "He thought we would buy all the gas he had at the contract price and resell it at market price. Well, that's not our business; we wouldn't do that."

Since the vendor would not honor the agreement, Plantation filed legal action. Before the case came to trial, the price of gas had dropped below the contract price. So Plantation entered into an agreement with its original vendor and dropped the legal action.

As Bumpurs says, "Trust is an important element in any deal. Because of the trust we have with our vendors, I can't recall anyone who tried a tricky close. But this time, he didn't trust us, and therefore lost our business forever."

detail as possible to prepare them for that experience. Or if a company is going to lease a piece of heavy equipment, let the customer know that delivery will occur after a credit check and how long that credit check will take. No customer wants to be kept waiting in the dark, not knowing whether he or she will ever get the new product.

Confirm the Customer's Choice

Customers like to believe they have chosen intelligently when they make a decision. After important decisions, they may feel a little insecure about whether the sacrifice is worth it. Such feelings are called **buyer's remorse** or **postpurchase dissonance**.

Successful salespeople reassure customers that their choice was judicious. For example:

> I know you will enjoy using your new office machines. You can plan on many months of trouble-free service. I'll call on you in about two weeks to make sure everything is operating smoothly. Be sure to call me if you need any help before then.

Or:

> Congratulations, Mr. Jacobs. You are going to be glad you decided to use our service. There is no finer service available. Now let's make certain you get off to the right start. Your first bulletin will arrive Tuesday, March 2.

One way to help customers feel good about their decision is to assure them they have made an intelligent choice. Remarks such as the following may also be appropriate:

You've made an excellent choice. Other stores won't have a product like this for at least 30 days.

This is an excellent model you've chosen. Did you see it advertised in last week's *Time?*

Your mechanics will thank you for ordering these tools. You will be able to get your work out much faster.

Get the Signature

Often, the buyer's signature formalizes a commitment. Signing the order is a natural part of a well-planned procedure. The order blank should be accessible, and the signing should be treated as a routine matter. Ordinarily the customer has decided to buy before being asked to sign the order. In other words, the signature on the order blank merely confirms that an agreement has already been reached. The decision to buy or not to buy should not focus on a signature.

The salesperson needs to remember several important points: (1) Make the actual signing an easy, routine procedure; (2) fill out the order blank accurately and promptly; and (3) be careful not to exhibit any excess eagerness or excitement when the prospect is about to sign.

Show Appreciation

All buyers like to think their business is appreciated, even if they purchase only small quantities. Customers like to do business with salespeople who show that they want the business.

Salespeople may show appreciation by writing the purchaser a letter. This practice especially develops goodwill after large purchases and with new customers. Salespeople should always thank the purchaser personally; the thanks should be genuine but not effusive.

Cultivate for Future Calls

In most fields of selling, obtaining commitment is not the end of a business transaction; rather, it is only one part of a mutually profitable business relationship.[10] Obtaining commitment is successful only if it results in goodwill and future commitment. Harvey Mackay states:

> *My definition of a great salesperson is not someone who can get the order. Anyone can get the order if he or she is willing to make enough promises about price or delivery. A great salesperson is someone who can get the order—and the reorder—from a prospect who is already doing business with someone else.*[11]

Customers like to do business with salespeople who do not lose interest immediately after securing commitment. What a salesperson does after achieving commitment is called **follow-up.** As Frank DiCarlo, sales director for Calvin Klein, recognizes, "Making the sale is only the beginning." After making the sale, the salesperson must follow up to make sure the product is delivered when promised, set up appropriately, and so forth. We will talk more about this in later chapters. The point here is that the sale does not end with the customer's signature on the order form. Effective selling means building relationships with customers, not just going for the single sale.[12]

To be welcomed on repeat calls, salespeople must be considerate of all of the parties involved in buying or using the product. They must pronounce and spell all names correctly, explain and review the terms of the purchase so no misunderstandings will occur, and be sociable and cordial to subordinates as well as those in key positions. In addition, the buyer or user must get the service promised. The impor-

The salesperson is listening to a team of buyers while following up on a delivery.

Harry Sieplinga/HMS Images/The Image Bank

tance of this point cannot be overemphasized. Chapter Thirteen will provide detailed information about how to service the account and build a partnership.

IF COMMITMENT IS NOT OBTAINED

Naturally, the salesperson does not always obtain the desired commitment. The salesperson should never take this personally (which is easier said than done). Doing everything right does not guarantee a sale. Situations change, and customers who may have really needed the product when everything started may find that other priorities make a purchase impossible.

Thinking *it* Through

The buyer says "No!" and you suspect it is because she doesn't trust you. You have a lot riding on this sale, and you also believe you have the best solution for the buyer. What do you do?

This section describes some of the common reasons for failing to obtain commitment and offers practical suggestions for salespeople who encounter rejection.

Some Reasons for Failure

Wrong Attitudes

As discussed earlier in the chapter, salespeople need to have a positive attitude. A fear that obtaining commitment will be difficult may be impossible to hide. Inexperienced salespeople naturally will be concerned about their ability to obtain commitment; most of us have an innate fear of asking someone else to do anything. Some salespeople even fail to ask for the sale because if they never ask, they will never hear *no*. As a result, they always have more prospects but fewer customers than everyone else. But all salespeople know they need to focus on obtaining commitment to keep their jobs.

Some salespeople display unwarranted excitement when they see prospects are ready to commit. A salesperson who appears excited or overly eager may display nonverbal cues that suggest dishonesty or a lack of empathy. If this occurs, buyers may change their minds and refuse to commit.

One of the main reasons for salespeople's improper attitudes toward obtaining commitment is the historical importance placed on closing the sale. Closing has often been viewed as a "win-lose" situation (i.e., "If I get the order, I win; if I don't get the order, I lose"). Until salespeople see obtaining commitment as a positive occurrence for the buyer, these attitudes will persist.

Poor Presentation

Prospects or customers who do not understand the presentation or see the benefits of the purchase cannot be expected to buy. It is very important that the salesperson use trial closes (see Chapter Nine) and continually take the pulse of the interview.

A poor presentation can also be caused by haste. The salesperson who tries to deliver a 60-minute presentation in 20 minutes may skim over or omit important sales points. Forgoing the presentation may be better than delivering it hastily. Further, a sales presentation given at the wrong time or under unfavorable conditions is likely to be ineffective.

Another reason is lack of product knowledge. One study of purchasing agents found that 80 percent were dissatisfied with the level of product knowledge salespeople displayed![13] If the salesperson does not know what the product does, you can be certain the buyer will not be able to figure it out either.

Poor Habits and Skills

Obtaining commitment requires proper habits and some measure of skill. The habit of talking too much rather than listening often causes otherwise good presentations to fail. Knowing when to quit talking is just as important as knowing what to say. Some salespeople become so fascinated by the sound of their own voices that they talk themselves out of sales they have already made. A presentation that turns into a monologue is not likely to retain the buyer's interest.

Discovering the Cause

The real reasons for not obtaining commitment must be uncovered. Only then can salespeople proceed intelligently to eliminate the barriers. Some firms have developed sophisticated systems to follow up on lost sales. The BCI Consulting Group, acting as an independent third party, will perform this service for a firm's sales force. Salespeople supply BCI with names and phone numbers of buyers who failed to buy. BCI then contacts these individuals to obtain objective feedback on both the client's company and its competitors. The consultant generates a report that identifies the reason(s) the buyer decided not to buy.[14]

Suggestions for Dealing with Rejection

Maintain the Proper Perspective

Probably the inexperienced salesperson's most important lesson is that when a buyer says *no*, the sales process has not necessarily ended. A *no* may mean "Not now," "I need more information," "Don't hurry me," or "I don't understand." An answer of *no* should be a challenge to seek the reason behind the buyer's negative response.

In many fields of selling, the majority of prospects do not buy. The ratio of orders achieved to sales presentations may be 1 to 3, 1 to 5, 1 to 10, or even 1 to 20. Salespeople may tend to eliminate nonbuyers from the prospect list after one unsuccessful call. This may be sound practice in some cases; however, many sales result on the second, third, fourth, or fifth call. When an earlier visit has not resulted in commitment, careful preparation for succeeding calls becomes more crucial.

Another perspective is that when a buyer says *no* it is because the buyer is not yet fully informed; otherwise, the buyer would have said *yes*. This means that if the buyer has given the salesperson the opportunity to make a presentation, the buyer recognizes that a need exists or is going to exist. What has not happened yet is that match between the offering and the need. At the same time, however, *no* does not mean "Sell me again right now." It may mean "Sell me again later." Marty Lile, sales manager at Ritchie Pharmacal, believes this perspective helps salespeople remember that these prospects are still future customers and that the rejection isn't personal.[15]

The salesperson should have a clear objective for each sales call. When commitment cannot be obtained to meet that objective, the salesperson will often attempt to obtain commitment for a reduced request (a secondary or minimum objective). For example, the salesperson may attempt to gain a trial order instead of an actual order, although, as we discussed earlier, this should be offered as a last resort.

Recommend Other Sources

The sales representative using the consultative selling philosophy (as described in Chapter Six) may recommend a competitor's product to solve the prospect's needs. When doing this, the sales rep should explain the reasons why his or her product does not meet the prospect's needs and then provide the name of the competitive product. One salesperson for a welding supply company keeps a current list of competitive products. When a customer requests an item that the salesperson can't supply, he volunteers the name of a competitor who can. No one need feel sorry for the salesperson, though; he is extremely successful. "I haven't been squeezed out by a competitor in more than three years," he reports.[16]

After recommending other sources, the salesperson usually should ask the prospect for names of people who might be able to buy the seller's product. Also, the salesperson should emphasize the desire to maintain contact with the prospect in the event the seller's firm develops a competitive offering.

Good Manners Are Important

If obtaining commitment fails no matter what the reason, the salesperson should react good-naturedly. Salespeople have to learn to accept *no* if they expect to call on prospects again. Even if they do not obtain commitment, salespeople should thank prospects for their time. Arguing or showing disappointment gains nothing. The salesperson may plan to keep in contact with these prospects through an occasional phone call, a follow-up letter, or product literature mailings. One salesperson likes to make the following statement at the conclusion of any meeting that does not result in commitment: "I'll never annoy you, but if you don't mind, I'm going to keep in touch." Selling Scenario 12.2 describes how one salesperson has found that keeping in touch is important.

It is a good idea to leave something behind that will provide the prospect with a means of contacting the salesperson in the future. Vicki Whiteford, owner and salesperson for a courier service, leaves a Rolodex card with her name and number. "We figure even if everything else goes in the trash, they'll save the Rolodex card. . . . And if they get mad at their messenger [current courier service], they're likely to call us because our name is right in front of them."[17]

BRINGING THE INTERVIEW TO A CLOSE

Few buyers are interested in a prolonged visit after they commit. Obviously, the departure cannot be abrupt; the salesperson should complete the interview smoothly. Goodwill is never built by wasting the buyer's time after the business is concluded.

SELLING SCENARIO 12.2

Keep in Touch!

If there is one thing I have learned over the many years I have been selling, it is the importance of *persistence*. The computer systems we sell have extremely long sales cycles, sometimes approaching three years. We've even had prospects buy a competitor's system and use it for over a year before calling us back. Therefore, we have found it important to maintain contact with prospects, even if they give the order to another company. Our fragile egos often make this a difficult proposition.

The prospects must also be left with a way to "save face." We must not bludgeon them with "I told you so's." If they are having trouble with the competitor's system, they are now better prospects because they've learned that the least expensive solution may cost more in the long run. A lost sale simply means that the sales cycle has been extended. Besides, with computer technology becoming obsolete every three years, you will have another opportunity with each of them someday.

Source: Wayne B. Wilhelm, president, Computermax, personal correspondence, June 29, 1993; used with permission.

Remember that most sales take several calls to complete. If an order wasn't signed (and often this isn't even the objective of the call; see Chapter Eight) and the prospect wishes to continue considering the proposal, the salesperson should leave with a clear action plan for all parties. An example of the kind of dialog the salesperson might pursue is as follows:

SALESPERSON When will you have had a chance to look over this proposal?

BUYER By the end of next week, probably.

SALESPERSON Great, I'll call on you in about 1 1/2 weeks, okay?

BUYER Sure, set up something with my secretary."

SALESPERSON Is there anything else I need to do for you before that next meeting?

The salesperson should always make sure the next step is clear for both parties.

While taking her leave, this salesperson confirms that her buyer understands what will happen next and when she will return.

Sharon Hoogstraten

SUMMARY

Commitment cannot be obtained by some magical or miraculous technique if the salesperson has failed to prepare the prospect to make this decision throughout the presentation. Salespeople should always attempt to gain commitment in a way that is consistent with the objectives of the meeting. Obtaining commitment begins with the salesperson's contact with the prospect. It can succeed only when all facets of the selling process fall into their proper place. All sellers need to keep in mind the old saying "People don't buy products or services; they buy solutions to their problems!"

The process of obtaining commitment is the logical progression of any sales call. Commitment is important for the customer, the seller's firm, and the seller. Commitments should result in a win-win situation for all parties concerned.

Pricing is an important element of any sale, and is usually presented at the time of closing. Quantity discounts, payment terms, and shipping terms can affect the final price charged to the buyer as well as influence the decision.

There is no one "right" time to obtain commitment. Salespeople should watch their prospects closely and recognize when to obtain commitment. Successful salespeople carefully monitor customers' comments, their buyer's nonverbal cues and actions, and their responses to probes. Comments can be in the form of questions, requirements, benefits, and responses to trial closes.

To successfully obtain commitment, the salesperson needs to maintain a positive attitude, allow the customer to set the pace, be assertive rather than aggressive, and sell the right item in the right amounts. Engaging in these practices will result in a strong long-term relationship between buyer and seller.

No one method of obtaining commitment works best for each buyer. The direct request method is the simplest to use; however, the prospect often needs help in evaluating the proposal. In those instances, other methods may be more appropriate, such as the alternative choice, the benefit summary, the balance sheet method, or the probing method. No method of obtaining commitment will work if a buyer does not trust the salesperson.

If commitment is obtained, the salesperson should immediately assure the buyer that the choice was judicious. The salesperson should show genuine appreciation as well as cultivate the relationship for future calls.

If commitment is not obtained, the salesperson should analyze the reasons. Difficulties in obtaining commitment can be directly traced to wrong attitudes, a poor presentation, and/or poor habits and skills. Even if no commitment is obtained, the salesperson should thank the prospect for his or her time.

KEY TERMS

aggressive, 339
assertive, 339
balance sheet method, 342
benefit summary method, 341
buyer's remorse, 346
buying signals, 346
cash discount, 334
closing, 332
closing cues, 336

cumulative discount, 334
direct request method, 341
follow-up, 347
free on board (FOB), 334
postpurchase dissonance, 346
probing method, 342
requirements, 336
submissive, 339
trial close, 337

QUESTIONS AND
PROBLEMS

1. "The ABCs of closing are 'Always be closing.'" Another version is "Close early—close often." What is your reaction to these time-honored statements?

2. Harold Bumpurs (see Selling Scenario 12.1) says he has never noticed any tricky closes. His perception is due not to the smooth closing skills of the salespeople who call on him but to the total skill set they have developed. Prioritize a list of selling skills, from most important to least. How much time should be spent improving commitment-gaining skills as opposed to developing other skills? Why?

3. You are selling institutional refrigerators for use in school cafeterias, restaurants, and so on. After making a presentation that you think went rather well, you request the order and get this reply: "What you say sounds interesting, but I want some time to think it over." You answer, "Well, okay. Would next Tuesday be a good day for me to come back?" How can you improve on your answer?

4. One sales manager who worked for a refrigeration equipment company taught his salespeople the following close: Ask questions that allow you to fill out the contract. Assume the sale is made and hand the contract to the buyer, along with a pen. If the buyer doesn't immediately take the pen, drop it and make the buyer pick it up. Once the buyer has the pen in hand, he or she is more likely to use it to sign the contract, so just wait silently until the buyer does.

   a. Would you label this seller as assertive or aggressive?

   b. Is this a trick or merely dramatization?

   c. How would you respond to this behavior if you were the buyer?

5. You are one sale away from winning the top salesperson award with just one day left. Your boss tells you as you leave the office, "We're really counting on you to close a deal today! Win top rep in the country, and I'll double your bonus!" What impact will that have on your attempts to obtain commitment?

6. What makes a Cadillac worth more than a Chevrolet? How would you convince someone that it is worth more if she or he knew nothing about the various brands of cars? How would the buyer's lack of knowledge influence how you try to gain commitment?

7. A sales manager once told a salesperson, "You know that when Ms. Jacobs told you *no,* she was saying *no* to your proposal; she was not rejecting you personally." Why is understanding that statement vital to all salespeople?

8. One successful salesperson assumes an attitude of indifference toward whether or not a commitment is obtained.

   a. Could this indifferent attitude help in obtaining commitment? If so, how?

   b. Are there any dangers inherent in giving this impression?

9. One buyer stated, "All closing methods are devious and self-serving! How can a salesperson use a technique but still keep my needs totally in mind?" Comment.

10. Most of us have a natural fear of asking someone else to do something. What can you, as a student, do now to reduce such fear?

11. What would you say to a friend to gain his or her commitment to go on a spring break trip? Describe exactly what you would say to your friend, using each of the following methods (make any assumptions necessary):

    a. Alternative choice

    b. Direct request

    c. Benefit summary

    d. Balance sheet

    e. Probing

12. What laws govern the obtaining-commitment portion of a sales presentation? (Refer back to Chapter Three, if needed.) How can a salesperson stay within these laws while attempting to gain commitment?

13. A customer is willing to order 100 cases listed at $20 per case to get a 15 percent quantity discount. Terms are 2/10, n30. The customer pays five days after receiving the invoice. How much did the customer pay?

EXPLORING THE NET

Open three home pages, including at least one (but no more than two) of the following: (1) www.dowjones.com (2) www.lowes.com (3) and any home page of a company whose salesperson is profiled at the beginning of any chapter in this book.

When you surf the three pages, evaluate how each page asks for further action from you. Consider yourself a prospective buyer for a product or service that is offered and answer the following questions:

How do they ask you for further action?

How are they limited by the technology of the Internet? What advantages can a professional salesperson offer? Limit your response to the issue of gaining commitment.

CASE PROBLEMS

CASE 12.1
Steel Boy Inc.

Steel Boy Inc. makes and distributes watches for men and women. The firm is known for recreating designer watches and selling them at wholesale prices. Steel Boy's motto is "Designer quality at a fraction of the price."

    Lois Clark, a salesperson for Steel Boy, called on Jared Morris, a buyer for Kmart stores. The call objective was to have Jared agree to set up an appointment in the next several weeks with Lois and the full Kmart buying committee. The latter portion of their conversation follows:

LOIS The watches are packaged in clear plastic boxes, similar to the leading name brands. These watches are created to look and perform just as the originals. The only difference is the designer logo that appears on name-brand watches; instead, Steel Boy has its own logo, SB, appearing at the top of the watch.

JARED Are these watches really as good as the originals?

LOIS Quality is something that we at Steel Boy take very seriously. We have strong quality control standards and our own testing facility to ensure that our products can withstand the most extreme conditions.

JARED Your quality standards sound solid. I understand that you've got a good product, but how do you know that there will be a demand for this product in our stores?

LOIS You are currently carrying several name-brand watches, including Iron Man, Casio, and Timex. How are sales of those products?

JARED They are doing excellent. They are all heavily advertised, and people buy from us because we're cheaper than department stores.

LOIS Great! According to our research, your sales of those products will not decline if you decide to include our product. Actually, our product appeals more to lower- and middle-income consumers who would like to realize the benefits of wearing a designer watch but are not able to afford it.

JARED That's interesting, but how can I be sure that they will sell in our stores? Kmart is different than any other retailer in America, remember?

LOIS You're right. Kmart is different. You try your best to offer high-quality name brands at affordable prices. You attempt to satisfy both men and women of all income brackets. Steel Boy watches can help you reach those goals. We have had successful introductions at other, smaller regional chain discount stores. In fact, here's a letter from Jacob Baker at Super Discount World in Laredo, Texas.

JARED [*after reading the letter*] Okay, okay. Well, what about advertising? How will our customers know that we are carrying Steel Boy watches?

LOIS We are currently running ads for Steel Boy watches in *Sports Illustrated, People, Outdoor Life,* and *Texas Hunter* magazines. Also, once your chain has purchased 1,000 Steel Boy watches, our policy is to include your store's name in one of our magazine ads.

JARED That sounds pretty good. What happens if we overstock your product? Can we send it back?

LOIS After a three-month period, we will buy back any watches you would like to return at 90 percent of our cost. During the first three months, we hope to get a better handle on what brands Kmart customers are looking for. Does that sound okay?

JARED Not too shabby!

LOIS I would like to set up a meeting with the full buying committee of Kmart in the next several weeks. Do you think that would be possible?

JARED Sure, we could probably do that next Friday.

LOIS Will I have your endorsement at that meeting?

JARED We'll have to wait and see.

Questions

1. Lois used the direct request method of obtaining commitment. Was that appropriate? Why or why not?

2. Outline how you would attempt to obtain commitment, assuming you use the following methods (add any assumptions necessary to develop the outline):

   a. Benefit summary method.

   b. Balance sheet method.

   c. Probing method.

3. Although you have been provided with only a portion of the conversation, evaluate Lois's performance in terms of

   a. Selling benefits, not just features.

   b. Taking the buyer's pulse during the presentation.

   c. Using communication aids to strengthen communication.

   d. Responding to objections.

   e. Attempting to obtain commitment at the proper time.

CASE 12.2 Obtaining Commitment: A Prevideo Exercise

Brunswick Financial Services is an internationally recognized provider of diversified financial services. Founded over 50 years ago, Brunswick is now involved in stockbrokerage, mutual fund portfolios, and corporate and individual retirement programs.

Brunswick offers 15 different investment portfolios ranging from low risk and conservative to highly speculative. The more speculative the investment, the higher the risk and the greater the potential return on monies invested. Sales charges are based on a percentage of the amount of funds invested, plus a fixed annual management fee.

Brunswick has built a reputation on the high quality of service it provides for clients and for its prompt payment of retirement benefits. Brunswick is particularly proud of a government-approved application form that it uses, which speeds the process of initiating a retirement program.

In this video segment, Ann Clark, an account representative for Brunswick, is calling on David Johnson, founder and president of Johnson Foods, a manufacturer and distributor of gourmet food products. Prior to this meeting, Clark met with the company's comptroller, Joe Stone, about developing a proposal for a retirement program for Johnson's employees. Stone was very interested. He told her that it was an opportune time to start a pension plan for the tax benefits and the much-needed employee goodwill the plan would generate. He also told her that Johnson would certainly have the last word and was obstinate about even discussing the matter. Johnson is a very detail-oriented, somewhat distracted kind of person. Based on financial information received from Stone, Clark developed a written proposal that Stone reviewed. Johnson has repeatedly postponed meeting with Clark.

Following are the key features and benefits of Brunswick's proposal:

Features	Benefits
Fifteen investment funds with different levels of investment security and potential return	Allows investors to choose a fund that meets their investment criteria Helps to ensure superior return on investment
Simplified, government-approved form	Keeps set-up time to a minimum, usually less than two hours; reduces government approval time.
Forty years of pension experience	Eases penioners' transition into retirement Provides needed information
Investment advisers who discuss with the client company its investment goals and objectives	Increases confidence that money is invested in appropriate investment vehicles
Flexicon (an adjustable contribution schedule that allows for contributions of up to 15% of annual earnings)	Prevents investors from being locked into a fixed contribution schedule
Computerized benefits payment system	Ensures that retirees receive their checks in a timely manner

Questions

To help you think about how Clark might attempt to obtain commitment from Johnson in this call (assume the primary call objective is to have Johnson agree to set up a meeting for a formal presentation of Brunswick's offering), answer the following questions.

1. Outline how you would attempt to obtain commitment, assuming you use the following methods (add any assumptions necessary to develop the outline):
   a. Direct request method.
   b. Benefit summary method.
   c. Balance sheet method.
   d. Probing method.

2. Based on the limited information you have, which method do you think would be most appropriate?

3. Reread the case and be prepared to watch the videotape in class. Watch for the *actual* method Clark uses to obtain commitment. Evaluate her attempts to obtain commitment.

ADDITIONAL
REFERENCES

Badovick, Gordon J.; Farrand J. Hadaway; and Peter F. Kaminski. "Attributions and Emotions: The Effects on Salesperson Motivation after Successful vs. Unsuccessful Quota Performance." *Journal of Personal Selling and Sales Management*, Summer 1992, pp. 1–12.

Falvey, Jack. "For the Best Close, Keep an Open Mind." *Sales & Marketing Management*, April 1990, pp. 10, 12.

Gibson, W. David. "Holy Alliances!" *Sales & Marketing Management*, July 1993, pp. 85–87.

McCormack, Mark. "Customers Buy When They Want To." *Waco Tribune-Herald*, September 5, 1993, p. 1B.

Raymond, Mary Anne, and John F. Tanner, Jr. "Maintaining Customer Loyalty in Direct Sales: Toward a Model of Customer Loyalty." *Journal of Personal Selling and Sales Management*, Fall 1994, pp. 67–76.

Strutton, David, and James R. Lumpkin. "The Relationship between Optimism and Coping Styles of Salespeople." *Journal of Personal Selling and Sales Management*, Spring 1993, pp. 71–82.

Strutton, David; Lou Pelton; and John F. Tanner, Jr. "Shall We Gather in the Garden? The Effect of Ingratiatory Behaviors on Buyer Trust in Salespeople." *Industrial Marketing Management*, March 1996, pp. 151–62.

The relationship between a salesperson and a customer seldom ends when a sale has been made. In fact, salespeople are finding the building of relationships and even partnerships with customers increasingly important. Such relationships help to ensure that customers will select the salespeople's products and services the

Chapter Thirteen

Building Long-Term Partnerships

Some Questions Answered in this Chapter Are:

How should salespeople stay in contact with customers?

What sales strategies exist to sell to current accounts?

What trends are influencing long-term buyer-seller relationships?

What techniques are important to use when handling complaints?

next time they buy. This chapter provides insights into building a partnership with the buyer.

Future business can always be affected by elements beyond the control of the company or its sales representatives. However, one sure way to decrease future uncertainties lies in building solid, progressive business relationships with customers. These relationships, the topic of this chapter, may be developed through sound customer relations and proper servicing of accounts. The result of such relationships is additional selling opportunities.

PROFILE

After finishing college, Trey Morris landed his dream job: He went to work for the leading radio station in the Dallas/Ft. Worth metroplex as a salesperson and quickly became one of its top producers. Then came the opportunity to join a smaller, Christian radio station, KLTY, where he would have more impact and gain more responsibility. "Here I felt I could bring the full resources of the station to bear on the marketing problem my client has, rather than just sell advertising time," says Morris.

Morris tries to build a partnership by getting to know his client: "Getting to know them allows you to deliver the product or service that will turn them into a long-term partner. When building relationships with your clients, you must ask questions that will give them the opportunity to talk about specific problems, needs, and goals. Without specific information, you will never be able to satisfy their needs and consequently never develop a 'partner' customer. Asking the right questions before you make a sale will assist you in building that new client into a committed client."

"Without the ability to develop new, small clients into long-term, large clients, salespeople will be spending all of their time on one-hit deals. By building relationships with your clients, you can increase your sales by developing business you already have."

Another aspect of building relationships is the provision of continued service. Many salespeople fail because once they have sold their product or service, they move on to the next sale. In Morris's business, "Servicing a client after the sale separates me from my competition. Make it a practice to regularly talk to your clients, bringing them new ideas, services, or products. Make them feel like they are a 'special' client and that their business is important to you. Talk to them about their business—not yours! Give them an opportunity to talk to someone who is interested in their favorite topic of conversation: their business. By building strong re-

TREY MORRIS
KLTY Radio

lationships with your clients, you can develop a small new client into a committed large one."

One customer that grew with Morris's help is Equally Yoked Christian Singles, a dating service that opened an office in Dallas about two years ago. Morris recalls, "When I first met the owner of Equally Yoked, he planned on advertising on KLTY for their grand opening only. But by building a relationship with Equally Yoked, I was able to discover their problems, needs, and goals. With that information, I was able to develop a strategic marketing plan that would assist in solving their problems and reaching their goals."

At first, the relationship was shaky. Equally Yoked was hesitant to advertise and even more cautious about committing long term. "They started off very small, only spending a thousand dollars a month, but as the relationship developed, so did their confidence in KLTY and myself. I was able to increase their advertising budget by developing new marketing campaigns, promotional ideas, and research information. These new opportunities proved to Equally Yoked that I was concerned about their business and I wanted to see them succeed. My goal was to become a full-service marketing representative for Equally Yoked—a sustaining resource."

Over the last two years, Equally Yoked grew from a one-time advertiser with one small office to one of the largest advertisers on KLTY, with four offices across the metroplex. Morris says, "I meet with Equally Yoked at least three times a month, going over new ideas and analyzing the previous month's results. I no longer view Equally Yoked merely as a client but as a 'partner'. Therefore, I feel responsible for the growth and success of their business, and I am accountable for the results that KLTY generates."

Cultivating accounts such as Equally Yoked is one of the more rewarding elements of sales for Morris. "In the world of sales, we spend most of our time learning how to negotiate, question, and close. All of those skills are important to salespeople, but without the ability to develop new, small clients into long-term, large clients, salespeople will be spending all of their time on one-hit deals. By building relationships with your clients, you can increase your sales by developing business you already have."

Visit Our Website@
http://www.klty.com

THE VALUE OF CUSTOMERS

Ross/Flex, a Troy, Michigan, air and gas control maker, has never lost a customer. It has also become the dominant supplier in most of its accounts. For example, when Knight Industries needed a triple balance valve quickly, it requested designs from two of its regular suppliers, Ross/Flex and another company. Ross/Flex engineers worked directly with Jim Zaguroli, president of Knight, trading designs, prototypes, and ideas while the competitor's engineers worked on their own. The result? The Ross/Flex product was smaller and cheaper. Ross/Flex now has 100 percent of Knight's custom business and 70 percent of its off-the-shelf business.[1]

Many people believe the emphasis in selling is on getting the initial sale. For most salespeople, however, sales increases from one year to the next are due to increasing the revenue from existing accounts, not from getting new accounts. Even in industries where purchase decisions are made infrequently, salespeople gain a competitive advantage by maintaining partnering relationships with their customers, because when buying decisions need to be made, those customers look to their partners first. For example, when Turner Broadcasting purchases satellite time for television broadcasting from Hughes Telecommunications, the contract is for the entire life of the satellite (15 years or longer). Hughes may launch only a couple of satellites each year, but it is important that the Hughes salesperson maintain a high-quality relationship with Turner so that revenue is optimized through maximum customer satisfaction.

In this chapter, we will integrate the knowledge you have already gained in selling to new prospects with the material covered in Chapter Two on building partnerships so that you can learn how to sell to the same accounts over the long term. We will also discuss how to handle those situations where customers are unhappy.

Customers are, of course, the primary revenue source for companies. But many businesspeople do not fully understand the value of a customer. For example, if a company can retain only 2 to 5 percent more customers (instead of losing those customers to competition), the effect on the bottom line is the same as cutting costs by 10 percent.[2] Similarly, it takes an average of seven sales calls to close a first sale but only three to close a subsequent sale.[3] Thus, selling to satisfied customers not only costs less, but is also easier.

Customers are also worth more in terms of revenue than some salespeople recognize. For example, a car salesperson may think only of the immediate sale, but each customer is potentially worth hundreds of thousands of dollars in revenue over the salesperson's lifetime. Exhibit 13.1 illustrates the value of a small attorney's office over a 20-year period for just a few salespeople. For example, if an office equipment/supply salesperson sold all of the copiers needed during that 20-year period, total revenue would be at least $25,000. If the salesperson thinks only in terms of one sale, however, the customer is worth only about $5,000.

Thinking *it* Through	How much do you spend on gasoline each month? Now multiply that figure by 12. Assuming you live in the same neighborhood during the five years you will be in college, multiply that result by 5. That total is the amount of your gasoline purchases over your college career. Do you usually buy gasoline from one or two stations? If so, you are worth several thousand dollars as a customer of those stations! Is their service at a level equal to your value to them?

Successfully retaining customers is important to all companies. One study reported that 65 percent of the average company's business comes from current, satisfied customers. Another study found the cost of acquiring a new customer to be five times the cost of properly servicing a current customer and retaining that customer's business. Yet another study indicated that overall, customers are less satisfied than ever, so apparently many companies have failed to recognize the importance of customer satisfaction.[4]

Some industries are only now beginning to recognize the value of retaining customers because they lose customers as rapidly as they create new ones. As you can see in Exhibit 13.2, it is like trying to fill a pail with water when there is a hole in the bottom: The water leaks out as quickly as you pour it in. The cellular phone industry, for example, is experiencing a disconnect rate of 30 to 45 percent per year. Those companies must replace one-third to one-half of their customers each year just to stay even![5]

We have already discussed the importance of good service in generating referrals and of becoming a trusted member of the community in which your buyers operate so you can acquire more customers. The value of satisfied customers is so high that it makes good business sense to build the strongest possible relationships.

EXHIBIT 13.1 Selected Expenses for a Small Law Firm		
Item	Cost	Total
Copiers	5 @ $5,000	$25,000
Copying supplies	$50 per month	12,000
Fax machines	5 @ $2,000	10,000
Fax supplies	$20 per month	4,800
Telephone systems	3 @ $1,000	3,000
Other office supplies	$100 per month	24,000
Office furniture	$5,000	5,000
Total over 20 years		$83,800

BUILDING TRUST BUILDS PARTNERSHIPS

Trust is an important building block for long-term relationships. As discussed in Chapter Two, several types of relationships are possible between buyers and sellers. At one end of the spectrum are functional relationships, in which the buyer thinks of each purchase as a separate transaction. Previous experience with the seller is considered, but future purchases are not based on a commitment to the seller. In partnerships, buyers make commitments to purchase from sellers over the long term. They make these commitments because they believe they can trust the seller. Trust is a combination of five factors: dependability, competence, customer orientation, honesty, and likability. In this section, we will discuss each of these factors and how salespeople demonstrate their trustworthiness.

Dependability

Dependability, the buyer's perception that the salesperson, and the product and company he or she represents, will live up to promises made, is not something a salesperson can demonstrate immediately. Promises must be made and then kept. Early in the selling process, a salesperson can demonstrate dependability by calling at times agreed to, showing up a few minutes early for appointments, and providing information as promised.

Third-party references can be useful in proving dependability, especially if the salesperson has not yet had an opportunity to prove it personally. If the seller can point to a similar situation and illustrate, through the words of another customer, how the situation was resolved, dependability can be verified by the buyer. Some companies also prepare case studies of how they solved a particular customer's problem to aid salespeople in proving the company's dependability.

Product demonstrations, plant tours, and other special types of presentations can also illustrate dependability. A product demonstration can show how the product will work, even under difficult conditions. A buyer for component parts for appliances was concerned about one company's ability to produce the large volumes required. The salesperson offered a plant tour to prove that the company could live up to its promises of on-time delivery. When the buyer saw the size of the plant and the employees' dedication to making quality products, she was convinced.

The salesperson's prior experience and training can also be used to prove dependability. For a company (and a salesperson) to remain in business, there must be some level of dependability. Length of experience, however, is a weak substitute for proving dependability with action.

Competence can be proven by using accurate product information, as this ConAgra rep demonstrates to his buyer.

Courtesy Hunt-Wesson

As time goes on and the relationship grows, the buyer assumes dependability. For example, a buyer may say, "Well, let's call Sue at Mega. We know we can depend on her." At this point, the salesperson has developed a reputation within the account as dependable. But it doesn't stop there—reputations can spread beyond that account through the buyer's community. A reputation for dependability, however, can be quickly lost if the salesperson fails to continue to deliver as promised.

Competence

Salespeople demonstrate **competence** when they can show that they know what they are talking about.[6] As you learned in earlier chapters, knowledge of the customer, the product, the industry, and the competition are all necessary to the success of the salesperson. It is through the use of this knowledge that a salesperson demonstrates competency. For example, when a pharmaceutical representative can discuss the treatment of a disease in medical terms, the physician is more likely to believe the rep is medically competent.

Salespeople recognize the need to appear competent. Unfortunately, their recognition of the importance of competence may lead them to try to fake knowledge. Because buyers test the trustworthiness of a seller early in the relationship, they may ask questions just to see what the salesperson's response is.

Competence is demonstrated through the use of accurate information. Salespeople should never make up a response to a tough question; at the same time, salespeople should try to present information objectively. Buyers can tell when salespeople are exaggerating the performance of their products.

Kodak, which is reported to have the top sales force in scientific/photographic equipment, creates competence through intensive training. Each salesperson undergoes 90 days of training before being sent into the field. Once in the field, salespeople are continually fed a stream of information that they can use to aid their customers. The result is a highly competent sales force that works in partnership with retailers, helping them to run their businesses more successfully.[7]

Customer Orientation

Customer orientation is the degree to which the salesperson puts the customer's needs first. Salespeople who think only of making sales are sales oriented rather than customer oriented. Buyers perceive salespeople as customer oriented when sellers stress benefits and solutions to problems over features. Buyers who perceive that the product is tailored to their unique requirements are likely to infer a customer orientation. Stating pros and cons can be perceived as being customer oriented, because understanding the cons also indicates that the salesperson understands the buyer's needs.

Emphasizing the salesperson's availability and desire to provide service also indicates a customer orientation. For example, the statement "Call me anytime for anything that you need" indicates availability. Offering the numbers for toll-free hotlines, voice mail, and similar concrete information indicates a desire to respond promptly to the buyer and can serve as proof of a customer orientation.

Listening skills are essential for developing a customer orientation. Linda Zitka, a buyer for General Motors Acceptance Corporation, says this about Carrie Thomas, who sells for Duplex Products: "She picks up on things I never even realized I told her." Zitka appreciates the way Thomas keeps track of every detail and follows through. "When we had a little blip [problem] in the project, I felt that she understood my frustration. I get the feeling that it's her project as well as mine, that she's with me all the way."[8] This level of listening, listening to feelings as well as facts, is difficult but essential to building long-term relationships.

Honesty

Honesty is both truthfulness and sincerity. While honesty is highly related to dependability ("We can count on you and your word because you are honest"), it is also related to how candid a salesperson is. For example, giving pros and cons can increase perceptions of honesty.

Honesty is also related to competence. As we said earlier, salespeople must be willing to admit that they do not know something rather than trying to fake it; buyers consider salespeople who bluff to be dishonest.

A customer once asked, "Does your product SNA?" SNA was a new computer architecture that IBM had recently announced, but the salesperson represented a competing manufacturer. The salesperson replied, "No, not now, and I don't know if we will, but I can find out." The customer responded, "That's the first honest answer I've heard to that question." The salesperson eventually won a good portion of the customer's business, in part because she did not try to bluff her way through a tough question.

Partnering is such an important strategy that many salespeople overuse and misuse the term. One buyer said, "If I have one more vendor walk in the door and say they want to be my partner, I'll scream!" He believes salespeople use the term but do not change their actions or even listen seriously.[9] When a salesperson makes a claim, such as a desire to partner, and does not follow through, that person's honesty is called into question.

Likability

According to research, likability may be the least important component because most people can be "nice."[10] **Likability** refers to behaving in a friendly manner and finding a common ground between buyer and seller. While it is not as important as other dimensions, salespeople should still attempt to find a common ground or interest with the buyer.

Likability can also be influenced with personal communications such as birthday cards, hand-written notes, and so forth. Many businesses send Christmas cards

EXHIBIT 13.3

The Three Stages
between Awareness
and Dissolution
of Partnership Growth

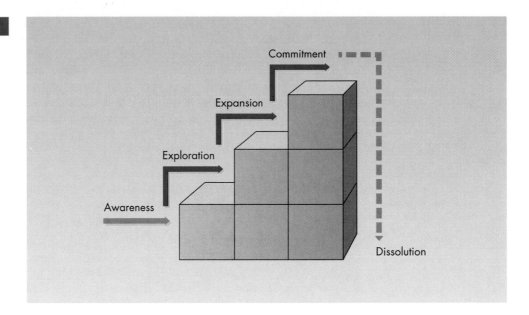

and gifts to all customers, but personal touches are needed for the gesture to be meaningful.

As you have probably noticed, the five dimensions of trust are highly interrelated. Honesty affects customer orientation, which also influences dependability, for example. Salespeople should recognize the interdependence among these factors rather than simply focusing on one or two. For example, at one time many salespeople emphasized only likability. In today's market, professional salespeople must also be competent, dependable, honest, and customer oriented.

As we discussed in Chapter Two, relationships go through several stages, beginning with awareness and ending in dissolution. In this chapter, we focus on the three stages between awareness and dissolution—exploration, expansion, and commitment—as illustrated in Exhibit 13.3. As you read the rest of the chapter, you will see how trust is built and maintained throughout the life of the partnership.

EXPLORATION

In the exploration stage, the relationship is defined through the development of expectations for each party. The buyer tests the seller's product, how the seller responds to requests, and other similar actions after the initial sale is made. A small percentage of the buyer's business is given to minimize the risk that the vendor cannot perform. When the vendor performs well, trust is developed, as is a personal relationship.

Beginning the relationship properly is important if the relationship is going to last a long time. Keep in mind that the customer is excited about receiving the benefits of the product as promised by the salesperson. If the customer's initial experience with the product or with the company is unfavorable, it may be extremely difficult to overcome. Beginning the relationship properly requires that the salesperson set the right expectations, monitor order processing, ensure proper use of the product, and assist in servicing the product.

Set the Right Expectations

The best way to begin a relationship is for each party to be aware of what the other expects. To a large degree, customers base their expectations on sales presentations.

Salespeople should make sure customers have reasonable expectations of product performance. If the salesperson exaggerates the capabilities of the product or the company, the customer will be disappointed. Admitting there has been a misunderstanding will not satisfy a customer who has registered a complaint. Avoiding complaints by setting proper expectations is best. Long-term relationships are begun by making an honest presentation of the product's capabilities and eliminating any misconceptions before the order is placed.

Monitor Order Processing

While many people may work on an order before it is shipped, the salesperson is ultimately responsible, at least in the eyes of the customer, for seeing that the product is shipped when promised. Salespeople should keep track of impending orders and inform buyers when the paperwork is delayed in the customer's plant. Orders placed directly with a salesperson should be transmitted to the factory immediately. Also, progress on orders in process should be closely monitored. If problems arise in filling the order, the customer should be informed promptly; on the other hand, if the order can be filled sooner than promised, the customer should be notified so that the proper arrangements can be made. For example, a carpet company was able to install sooner than planned in a hotel that was being renovated. Unfortunately, because the carpet was installed before some of the plumbing work was completed, the company had to remove and replace a section that was ruined by the plumbers.

Shipping delays often occur when customers use outdated information in placing orders. Salespeople can prevent these delays and other mistakes by making sure orders are accurate and complete. They should provide customers with the latest data sheets, product information, and descriptions of ordering procedures. Finally, they should review all orders for accuracy and completeness.

This United Stationers salesperson is working with the shipping department to make sure her customer's order is shipped promptly.

Courtesy United Stationers

Fortunately, computers have made the sales representative's job easier. Salespeople can use hand-held terminals and laptop PCs to check on inventory and/or the status of an order. Progressive firms have introduced automated order systems. Computers are now available that allow the customer to sign a pad on the computer; the signature is sent to the company electronically, avoiding delays that might result if the contract were mailed.

Some firms, such as GE and Baxter Healthcare, facilitate the automatic placement of orders by having customers' terminals talk to their own computers. This boosts the productivity of both the salespeople and the purchasing managers they call on. As a result, salespeople spend less time writing orders and more time solving problems; buyers save on ordering and inventory costs. Computerized communication for order placement is particularly useful when managing a customer's needs worldwide. Problems arising from elements such as time zones and language barriers are minimized.

Monitoring order processing and other after-sale activities is critical to developing a partnership. Studies continually show that buyers are displeased with most salespeople in this respect. One study indicated that failure to follow through after the sale was the buyers' second biggest complaint about salespeople (talking too much was first).[11]

Ensure Proper Initial Use of the Product or Service

Customer dissatisfaction can occur just after delivery of a new product, especially if the product is technical or requires special installation. Customers unfamiliar with the product may have problems installing or using it. They may even damage the product through improper use. Many salespeople visit new customers right after initial deliveries to ensure the correct use of the product. In this way, they can also help the customer realize the full potential benefits of the product.

In Bishop's Stortford, England, a Thermofrost representative trains a TESCO store manager in proper maintenance of a Thermofrost display cooler. Getting customers off to the right start is essential to building long and satisfying relationships.

Courtesy Parker Hannifin Corporation

Some buyers may be knowledgeable about how to use the basic features of a product or service, but if it is not operating at maximum efficiency, the wise salesperson will show the buyer how to get more profitable use out of it. Many firms have staffed a customer service department to aid salespeople in this task. It is still the salesperson's responsibility, however, to make sure the customer service department takes proper care of each new customer.

One former product manager for Olivetti reports that the company used to ship typewriters to the United States with a defective operator's manual. If the new owner followed the instructions exactly, there was no possible way to put in the ribbon. The manual was originally written in Italian, then poorly translated into English. To make matters worse, the product was redesigned, making the manual obsolete, but the company never changed it. In this situation, salespeople had to ask customers to call upon delivery of the product so they could demonstrate how to install the ribbon. In international sales, companies often try to get by with manuals that emphasize diagrams rather than words to avoid translation problems. In these situations, salespeople should follow up with a personal visit to make sure the customer gets off to a good start.

To be most effective, the salesperson should not wait until the user has trouble with the product and then point out remedies. The fewer the difficulties allowed to occur, the greater will be the customer's confidence in the salesperson and the product.

Handle Customer Complaints

Adjusting complaints is critical to developing goodwill and maintaining partnerships. Complaints can occur at any time in the partnering process, not just during the exploration stage. Handling complaints properly is always important, but perhaps even more so in the early stages of a partnership. Attempts to establish partner-

This Colgate salesperson is helping a Latin American dentist understand when to recommend a new mouthwash product.

Courtesy Colgate-Palmolive Company

ships often collapse due to shortsightedness in handling customer complaints. Some firms spend thousands of dollars on advertising but make the mistake of insulting customers who attempt to secure a satisfactory adjustment.

Complaints normally arise when the company and/or its products do not live up to the customer's expectations. Assuming the proper expectations were set, customers can be disappointed for any of the following reasons: (1) the product performs poorly, (2) it is being used improperly, or (3) the terms of the sales contract were not met. While salespeople usually cannot change the product or terms, they can affect these sources of complaints.

As we discussed earlier in this chapter, the cost of making the first sale is well known to be higher than the cost of repeat sales, so making every reasonable effort to keep customers in whom the company has invested time and money is good business. Also, many customers don't go to the trouble of complaining, so when a customer does attempt to secure satisfaction because of disappointment with a product or service, the company should view the complaint as an opportunity to prove that it is a reliable firm with which to do business.

One study showed that when a company fails in its dealings with a complainant, the latter will tell 10 people, on average, about the bad experience; those who are satisfied tell only four to five others. Also, for every dissatisfied person who complains, an estimated 50 more simply stop buying the product.[12]

Despite all the care manufacturers take to produce good products, unsatisfactory ones do find their way to the ultimate user or retailer. This inevitable situation, however, becomes alarming if the unsatisfactory products become too numerous.

Most progressive companies have learned that an excellent way to handle customer complaints is through personal visits by sales representatives. This means the salesperson may have total responsibility for this portion of the company's public relations. Salespeople who carry this burden must be prepared to do an effective job. Selling Scenario 13.1 illustrates how one salesperson with the responsibility and authority for customer service was able to turn a customer's complaint around.

Complaints cannot be eliminated; they can only be reduced in frequency. The salesperson who knows complaints are inevitable can learn to handle them as a normal part of the job. The following discussion presents some techniques for responding to complaints; Exhibit 13.4 provides an overview.

Encourage Buyers to Tell Their Story

Some customers can become angry over real or imaginary grievances. They welcome the salesperson's visit as an opportunity to voice complaints. Other buyers are less emotional in expressing complaints and give little evidence of irritation or anger, but the complaint is no less important.

In either case, customers need to tell their stories without interruption. Interruptions add to the irritation of emotionally upset buyers, making it almost impossible to arrive at a settlement that is fair to all parties concerned.

Customers want a sympathetic reaction to their problems, whether real or imagined. They want their feelings to be acknowledged, their business to be recognized as important, and their grievances handled in a friendly manner. An antagonistic attitude or an attitude that implies the customer is trying to cheat the company seldom paves the way for a satisfactory adjustment. You can probably relate to this if you have ever had to return a defective product or get some kind of adjustment made on a bill.

SELLING SCENARIO 13.1

Turning It Around

Sandy Garrett, manager of Personnel One Temporary and Permanent Placement in Tampa, Florida, held the phone away from her ear. The customer was shouting loud enough to be heard across the room.

"We deal with human beings; that's our product," notes Garrett. "And in this particular case, the people we sent to work for this account let us down. But as far as our client was concerned, it was Personnel One that let them down."

The client, a major insurance company headquartered in Tampa, had a data entry job that would take four temporary employees about three weeks to complete, including three days of training. Because of the training and the tight deadline, Garrett had asked for a three-week commitment from each person.

Unfortunately, one person's father died and she quit to be with her family. Another found a permanent job and quit, leaving two people to finish the job in less than two weeks. The customer wasn't interested, though, in why they left; the only thing the customer knew was that there was a deadline and it wasn't going to be met.

Garrett offered to come to the customer's office and discuss alternatives, but the customer wanted none of

that. "The last thing I heard before he hung up on me was, 'Sandy, we can't depend on Personnel One. We're going to another agency.'" But whether he wanted to see her or not, Garrett developed two possible solutions and drove straight to her client's office.

"He still didn't want to see me when I arrived," she said. "But I had two options and asked him to just look at them." She presented two options because she wanted him to think of the decision as a choice between Personnel One and Personnel One, not Personnel One and a competitor.

"Each option would take care of his biggest concern, which was getting people trained and productive in order to meet the deadline. And in each option, we absorbed any additional cost." Garrett also reminded her client of everything that Personnel One had done right. But she notes that "The biggest factor, though, was that I personally and immediately went to see him. He knew then how much his business meant to me."

Garrett kept the client and has since earned all of its temporary personnel business. "Turning around such a difficult client is a stressful challenge, but when you do it well, it is also intensely satisfying."

Good salespeople show they are happy the grievance has been brought to their attention. After the customer describes the problem, the salesperson may express regret for any inconvenience. An attempt should then be made to talk about points of agreement. Agreeing with the customer as far as possible gets the process off to the right start.

Determine the Facts

It is easy to be influenced by a customer who is honestly making a claim for an adjustment. An inexperienced salesperson might forget that many customers make their case for a claim as strong as possible. Emphasizing the points most likely to strengthen one's case is human nature. But the salesperson has a responsibility to his or her company, too. A satisfactory adjustment cannot be made until all the facts are known.

EXHIBIT 13.4

Responding to Complaints

- Encourage buyers to tell their story.
- Determine the facts.
- Offer a solution.
- Follow through with action.

Whenever possible, the salesperson should examine, in the presence of the customer, the product claimed to be defective. Encouraging the customer to pinpoint the exact problem is a good idea. If the defect is evident, this may be unnecessary. In other instances, making certain the complaint is understood becomes necessary. The purpose of getting the facts is to determine the cause of the problem so that the proper solution can be provided.

Experienced salespeople soon learn that products may appear defective when actually nothing is wrong with them. For example, a buyer may complain that paint was applied exactly as directed but repainting became necessary in a short time; therefore, the paint was no good. However, the paint may have been spread too thin. Any good paint will cover just so much area. If the manufacturer recommends using a gallon of paint to cover 400 square feet with two coats and the user covers 600 square feet with two coats, the unsatisfactory results are not the fault of the product. Or if an office equipment salesperson sells a fax machine that requires special paper, the machine is not at fault if the customer gets unsatisfactory results from a low-grade substitute paper.

On the other hand, salespeople should not assume product or service failure is always the user's fault. They need an open mind to search for the facts in each case. Defective material may have found its way to the dealer's shelves, the wrong merchandise may have been shipped, the buyer may have been overcharged, or the buyer may have been billed for an invoice that was already paid. The facts may prove the company is at fault. Also, some companies have the policy that the customer is always right, in which case there is no need to establish responsibility. There is still a need, however, to determine what the cause was so the right solution can be offered.

In this phase of making an adjustment, salespeople must avoid giving the impression of stalling. The customer should know that the purpose of determining the facts is to permit a fair adjustment, that the inquiry is not being made to delay action or avoid resolution.

Offer a Solution

After the customer tells his or her story and the facts are determined, the next step is to offer a solution. At this time, the company representative describes the process by which the company will resolve the complaint, and the rep should then gain agreement that the proposed solution is satisfactory.

Company policies vary, but many assign the responsibility for settling claims to the salesperson. Other companies require the salesperson to investigate claims and recommend a settlement to the home office. The proponents of both methods have good arguments to justify them. Some companies maintain that salespeople are in the best position to make adjustments fairly, promptly, and satisfactorily. This is especially true if the customer and salesperson are geographically distant from the home office. Others believe that permitting salespeople to only recommend a course of action assures the customer of attention from a higher level of management. Therefore, the customer will be more likely to accept the action taken. Companies holding the latter view also claim that for many technical products, the salesperson is not qualified to make a technical analysis of product difficulties.

Whatever the company policy, the customer desires quick action and fair treatment, and wants to know the reasons for the action. Most customers are satisfied if they quickly receive fair treatment. They must, however, be convinced of its fairness, and customers seldom are unless the reasoning behind the treatment is explained to them. Nothing discourages a customer more than having action postponed indefinitely or being offered vague promises. While some decisions may take time, the salesperson should try to expedite action. The opportunity to develop a partnership may be lost if the time lapse is too great, even though action is taken in the customer's favor.

Some salespeople make disparaging remarks about their own companies or managers. Blaming someone else in the company is a poor practice, because this can cause the customer to lose faith in both the salesperson and the company. Moreover, if the customer does not like the proposed solution, the salesperson trusted to make an adjustment or recommendation should shoulder the responsibility. Any disagreement on the action taken should be ironed out between the salesperson and the home office staff. When reported to the customer, the action, must be stated in a sound, convincing manner.

The action taken may vary with the circumstances. Some possible settlements when a product is unsatisfactory are

1. Replace the product without cost to the customer.
2. Replace the product and charge the customer for labor or transportation costs only.
3. Replace the product and share all costs with the customer.
4. Replace the product but require the customer to pay part of the cost of the new product.
5. Instruct the customer on how to proceed with a claim against a third party.
6. Send the product to the factory for a decision.

Occasionally customers make claims they know are unfair. Although they realize the company is not at fault, they still try to get a settlement. Fortunately, relatively few customers do this.

To assume a customer is willfully trying to cheat the company would be unwise. He or she may honestly see a claim as legitimate even though the salesperson can clearly tell that the company is not at fault. The salesperson does well, then, to proceed cautiously and, if any doubt exists, to treat the claim as legitimate.

A salesperson convinced that a claim is dishonest has two ways to take action. First, he or she can give the buyer an opportunity to save face by suggesting that a third party may be to blame. For example, if a machine appears not to have been oiled for a long time, a salesperson may suggest, "Is it possible that your maintenance crew neglected to oil this machine?" Second, the salesperson can unmask the fraudulent claim and appeal to the customer's sense of fair play. This procedure may cause the loss of a customer. In some cases, however, the company may be better off without that customer.

Answers to the following questions often affect the action to be taken:

- *What is the dollar value of the claim?* Many firms have established standard procedures for what they classify as small claims. For example, one moving and storage firm considers any claim under $200 to be too insignificant to investigate fully; thus, a refund check is issued automatically for a claim under this amount. Firms may also have a complete set of procedures and policies developed for every size of claim.

- *How often has this customer made claims?* If the buyer has instituted many claims in the past, the company may need to not only resolve the specific complaint but also conduct a more comprehensive investigation of all prior claims. Such a probe may reveal systematic flaws in the salesperson's company, product, or procedures. It may also spot similar deficiencies in the buyer's organization, or the salesperson may learn that the buyer is just hard to please and will complain regardless of the quality of the product or service.

- *How will the action taken affect other customers?* The salesperson should assume the action taken will be communicated to other prospects and customers. If the complaining customer is part of a buying community (discussed in Chapter Seven), chances are very good that others will learn about the resolution of the claim. Thus, the salesperson must take actions necessary to maintain a positive presence in that community, possibly even providing a more generous solution than the merits of the case dictate.

The solution that will be provided must be clearly communicated to the customer. The customer must perceive the settlement as being fair. When describing the settlement, the salesperson should carefully monitor all verbal and nonverbal cues to determine the customer's level of satisfaction. If the customer does not agree with the proposed course of action, the salesperson should seek ways to change the settlement or provide additional information as to why the settlement is fair to all parties.

Follow through with Action

A fair settlement made in the customer's favor helps to resell the company and its products or services. The salesperson has the chance to prove what the customer has been told for a long time: that the company will devote time and effort to keeping customers satisfied.

The salesperson who has authority only to recommend an adjustment must take care to report the facts of the case promptly and accurately to the home or branch office. The salesperson has the responsibility to act as a buffer between the customer and the company. After the claim is filed, contact must be maintained with the customer to see that the customer secures the promised settlement.

The salesperson also has a responsibility to educate the customer to forestall future claims. After a claim has been settled to the customer's satisfaction is a fine time to make some suggestions. For example, the industrial sales representative may provide a new set of directions on how to oil and clean a machine.

In two studies, buyers were asked to name the characteristics of excellent salespeople. The seller's ability to go to bat for the buyer within the seller's firm was the most important characteristic in one study and the second most important in the other.[13] Mike Rose, sales representative for Menasha Corporation, sells packaging materials. He was named a top 10 sales representative by *Purchasing* magazine because of the way he represents his buyers to his company. For example, one customer had a problem with boxes popping open in shipment. Rose observed the problem and recognized that the dyes his company was using caused the adhesive to fail. He returned to his own company and persuaded it to invest in new dyes so that the adhesives would keep the boxes closed.[14]

Many businesses have built great names by following the slogan "The customer is always right." Yet it often falls to the salesperson to make sure the company lives up to that slogan.

Achieve Customer Satisfaction

Although complaints always signal customer dissatisfaction, their absence does not necessarily mean customers are happy. Customers probably voice only 1 in 20 of their concerns. They may speak out only when highly dissatisfied, or a big corporation's buyer may not be aware of problems until the product users vent their frustration. Lower levels of dissatisfaction still hurt sales. Salespeople should continuously monitor customers' levels of satisfaction and perceptions of product performance.

When the customer is satisfied, an opportunity for further business exists. Complaints and dissatisfaction can occur at any time during the relationship; but during the exploration stage handling complaints well is one way to prove the salesperson is committed to keeping that customer's business. When customers sense such commitment, whether through the handling of a complaint or through other forms of special attention, they may be ready to move to the expansion stage.

EXPANSION

The next phase of the buyer-seller relationship is expansion. When a salesperson does a good job of identifying and satisfying needs and the beginnings of a partnership are in place, the opportunity is ripe for additional sales. Ross/Flex, for example, may have had only 10 percent of Knight's business at the start, but as trust developed, that percentage grew. With greater trust, the salesperson can focus on identifying additional needs and providing solutions. In this section, we discuss how to increase sales from current customers to expand the relationship. Keep in mind, however, that the activities of the exploration stage (monitoring order processing, handling complaints, etc.) still apply.

There are several ways to maximize the selling opportunity each account represents. These include generating reorders, upgrading, full-line selling, and cross-selling.

Generating Repeat Orders

In some situations, the most appropriate strategy is to generate repeat orders. For example, Cargill provides salt and other cooking ingredients to Kelloggs. The best strategy for the Cargill salesperson may be to ensure that Kelloggs continues to buy those ingredients from Cargill.

Several methods can be used to improve the likelihood of reorders. We will discuss each method in turn.

Be Present at Buying Time

One important method of ensuring reorders is to know how often and when the company makes decisions. For example, the salesperson who assisted your professor in choosing this textbook has already asked when book orders need to be in to the bookstore. The salesperson will then try to arrange a visit to take place just before that buying time.

Buyers do not always have regular buying cycles, which can make it difficult for salespeople to be present at buying time. In these situations, the seller still wants to be present in the buyer's mind. Two items that can help keep the seller present are catalogs and specialty advertising items. Catalogs are useful for buyers, who will usually refer to them when ready to buy. Specialty advertising items, such as pens or desk calendars, also aid buyers in reordering, especially if the 800 number is easy to find. Florida Furniture Industries has used desk calendars for over 60 years as a reminder for furniture store buyers of whom to call when inventories are low.

Help to Service the Product

Most products need periodic maintenance and repair, and some mechanical and electronic products require routine adjustments. Such service requirements offer salespeople a chance to show buyers that their interest did not end with the delivery of the product. Salespeople should be able to make minor adjustments or take care of minor repairs. If they cannot put the product back into working order, they must notify the proper company representative. They should then check to see that the repairs have been completed in a timely manner and to the customer's complete satisfaction.

As we will discuss in Chapter Seventeen, part of the salesperson's job is getting to know the company's maintenance and repair people. These repair people can act as the salesperson's eyes and ears when they make service calls. When a good relationship is established with service personnel, salespeople can learn of pending decisions or concerns and take the necessary action.

Salespeople should monitor parts shipments just as they would any order; in addition, they should supply up-to-date service manuals and place buyers' names on the service mailing list. In this way, bulletins on maintenance and repair reach the proper people. If the customer's maintenance department in the plant is well informed about the product, user complaints fall off dramatically.

Helping to service the product is just as important—and maybe more so—when the product is a service, as Michael Maynard of Azimuth Partners discovered. With one account, he kept trying to pitch new business after making a sale for a $20,000 project, but wasn't getting anywhere. He found that more postsale follow-up was needed to make sure the project was going smoothly and the data were being used fully. Only then could the customer see the benefits of additional work.[15]

Larry Dorfman, president and CEO of Atlanta-based Automobile Protection Corporation (APCO), administers extended service contracts that pay for automobile breakdowns. The car dealer may be APCO's customer, but the service department of the dealership is the users of the service. Dorfman trains his salespeople to first visit the service department when visiting a current account, because he believes that "until we service what we've already sold, we don't have the right to sell anything else."[16]

Thinking *it* Through	Some customers take advantage of salespeople by trying to have them perform almost all of the routine maintenance on a product for free. What can you as a salesperson do to curb such requests? How do you know where to draw the line?

Provide Expert Guidance

An industrial buyer or purchasing agent may need help in choosing a proper grade of oil or selecting a suitable floor cleaner. A buyer for a retail store may want help developing sales promotion ideas. Whether the buyer needs help in advertising, selling, or managing, good salespeople are prepared to offer worthwhile suggestions or services.

The salesperson usually prospers only if the buyer prospers. Obviously, unless buyers can use a product or service profitably or resell it at a profit, they have no need to continue buying from that product's seller. One expert suggests finding nonselling-related ideas to offer your customers. When you use your industry expertise to solve problems or develop opportunities for your clients that do not involve the sale of your product, you add value to the relationship, which can ultimately help you expand your business within the account.[17]

Many firms have developed a team approach to providing guidance and suggestions. For example, General Telephone & Electronics Corporation (GTE) uses a systems approach to help develop and maintain the communication systems of its major accounts. The Major Account Service Team (MAST) is composed of marketing (as chairperson), engineering, service, supply, and traffic representatives. This interdepartmental approach brings together all skills required to provide expert guidance and suggestions to meet the expanding and sophisticated needs of large customers.

Another salesperson named a top 10 sales representative by *Purchasing* magazine won the honor because of his expert guidance. John Paduch, now vice president of sales at American Supply Company of Gary, Indiana, saved one customer $1.4 million over five years through various ideas, such as showing how changing from stainless steel to cast iron pipes and valves saved $165,000 with no loss in quality. In addition, Paduch was able to assist the customer in reducing inventory by 47 percent. Such expert guidance led that customer to nominate John Paduch for *Purchasing's* top 10 sales rep award.[18]

UARCO's philosophy for success in the highly competitive field of selling business forms includes expert advice. Its forms management program makes the company a business partner with, rather than merely a supplier to, its major accounts. Customers are shown how to control the costs of buying and using forms by such practices as redesigning existing forms, grouping forms for more economical ordering, keeping records of quantities on hand and on order, and keeping track of the dollar value of the inventory. UARCO's customers welcome such advice, and the result is a high reorder rate.

Provide Special Assistance

Salespeople are in a unique position to offer many types of assistance to the buyer. This section will briefly mention a few of the types of assistance salespeople can and do provide to their customers.

Salespeople engage in many activities. For example, a Nabisco salesperson serves as a bagger during the grand opening of a new grocery store. Procter & Gamble salespeople help in resetting (determining where products should go on) the shelves whenever a grocery store decides to realign its shelf positions. Salespeople at Simmons help set up mattress displays in furniture stores. Makita power tool salespeople provide free demonstrations for customers of hardware stores. Most salespeople who sell to resellers will tidy up the shelves and physically restock them from the stockroom supplies. Salespeople also help train the reseller's employees in how to sell the products to the final consumers.

Gail Walker of Marquis Communications, a trade show and special events service agency, worked in the customer's booth at a trade show when one of the customer's salespeople got sick. She worked as hard as if she were one of the firm's employees. Providing such special assistance is one hallmark of excellence in selling. Good relationships are built faster and made more solid by the salesperson who does a little something extra for a customer, performing services over and above his or her normal responsibilities.

Upgrading

Similar to generating reorders is the concept of upgrading. **Upgrading,** also called *upselling,* is convincing the customer to use a higher-quality product or a newer product. The salesperson seeks the upgrade because the new or better product serves the needs of the buyer more effectively than the old product did.

Upgrading is crucial to companies like Digital Equipment Corporation. Digital launched the new Alpha AXP computer, and industry experts agree that for the new product to succeed, the company must secure upgrades from its old VAX products. Otherwise, as customers find needs for newer equipment, they will turn to IBM or Hewlett-Packard, and Digital may lose their business forever.[19]

When upgrading, it is a good idea to emphasize during the needs identification phase that the initial decision was a good one. Now, however, needs or technology have changed and the newer product fits the customer's requirements better. Otherwise, the buyer may believe that the seller is trying to take advantage of the relationship to foist off a higher-priced product.

Full-Line Selling

Full-line selling is selling the entire line of associated products. For example, a Xerox copier salesperson may sell the copier but also wants to sell the dry ink and paper the copier uses and a service contract. Or a Campbell Soup Company salesperson will ask a store to carry cream of potato soup as well as tomato soup.

When full-line selling, the emphasis is on helping the buyer realize the synergy of owning or carrying all of the products in that line. For example, the Xerox salesperson may emphasize the security in using Xerox supplies, whereas the Campbell rep will point out that sales for all soups will increase if the assortment is broader.

In selling to retailers, a current trend in the area of full-line selling is category management (discussed in greater detail in Chapter Fifteen). **Category management** is especially important in consumer packaged goods sales, such as processed foods sold to grocery stores. The salesperson from one supplier works closely with the retailer to create merchandising and marketing plans that will boost sales for the entire product category, including competitive brands. Salespeople who develop category management partnerships recognize that when they improve their customer's sales, their own sales improve too. For example, a Campbell Soup rep would help Kroger develop marketing plans to sell soup, including Progresso and Kroger's Cost-Cutter brands. These plans would include promotion schedules, pricing plans, and display ideas. The challenge for the salesperson is to increase category sales while raising profit for both Kroger and Campbell. It is a challenge that few suppliers have truly been able to meet.[20]

Cross-Selling

Cross-selling is similar to full-line selling, except the additional products sold are not directly associated with the initial products. For example, cross-selling occurs when the Xerox salesperson attempts to sell a fax machine to a copier customer or when a Campbell Soup Company rep sells spaghetti sauce to a soup buyer. Cross-selling involves leveraging the relationship with a buyer to identify needs for additional products. Again, trust in the selling organization and the salesperson already exist; therefore, the sale should not be as difficult as it would be with a new customer, provided the needs exist. One of the most unusual cross-selling situations is Moore Industries, which sells Filter Queen vacuum cleaners and Freedom Jet, a needleless insulin injector for diabetics. Salespeople try to sell Filter Queens to all Freedom Jet users and ask the Filter Queen users for leads on insulin-dependent diabetics.[21]

Cross-selling is an important strategy in some industries, such as banking. MasterCard salespeople are training employees at several major banks in how to cross-sell MasterCard, following a test that improved branch sales by 20 percent. When someone opens a new checking account or seeks a loan, the employee also recommends a MasterCard. While aimed primarily at improving consumer credit card

In Caracas, Venezuela, this Parker Hannifin salesman is demonstrating fluid connectors to a customer who already purchases other Parker products. Cross-selling opportunities like this one involve leveraging existing relationships in order to identify needs for additional products.

Courtesy Parker Hannifin Corporation

sales, the program will also help officers of the banks sell corporate cards to companies that are already clients of the banks.[22]

Some attempts at cross-selling, though, can resemble the initial sale, because the buying center may change. For example, the spaghetti sauce buyer may not be the same person who buys soups. If that is the case, the salesperson will have to begin a relationship with the new buyer, building trust and credibility.

Total Quality Management and Account Relationships

Many companies review their purchasing habits when they implement total quality management (TQM). Originating in the United States but first fully implemented in Japan, TQM means many things, but one area with tremendous implications for salespeople is purchasing. Companies espousing a TQM philosophy are reducing the number of vendors with whom they do business in order to demand higher quality and other benefits from partnership-type relationships (recall the discussion of buying trends in Chapter Four). The result is that some salespeople are finding receptive ears for full-line selling and cross-selling proposals, while others are losing business. For example, Xerox, including Fuji Xerox and Rank Xerox in Europe, reduced its number of vendors from 5,000 worldwide to 500 over a period of 10 years.[23] That means 4,500 salespeople lost what was probably their biggest account, while 500 salespeople increased their sales tremendously through full-line selling and cross-selling.

TQM also changes the way salespeople interact with their customers, because customers are also demanding greater quality. In a study by the Quality Research Institute, only 15 percent of customers surveyed reported that their vendors had adequate quality management procedures, but 73 percent of executives believe their own companies have instituted effective quality procedures. TQM suggests that customers should set quality standards and participate in continuous improvement programs, which means salespeople play an important role in ensuring that the voice of the customer is heard throughout the organization.

TQM and ISO 9000, a global quality standard, have increased global competition, making salespeople more important because of their role in satisfying customer needs. The TQM-driven trend to preferred supplier programs is strong. In only two years, the number of manufacturers with programs for developing preferred suppliers grew from approximately 67 percent to almost 80 percent.[24] In the next section, we will talk about how companies become preferred suppliers in the commitment phase of the relationship.

COMMITMENT

When the buyer-seller relationship has reached the commitment stage, there is a stated or implied pledge to continue the relationship, as we discussed in Chapter Two. Formally, this pledge may begin with the seller becoming a preferred supplier, which is a much greater level of commitment than those levels discussed in Chapter Twelve. While **preferred supplier** status may mean different things in different companies, in general it means the supplier is assured of a large percentage of the buyer's business and will get the first opportunity to earn new business.[25] For example, at Motorola, only preferred suppliers are eligible to bid on new-product programs.[26] Thus, *preferred supplier* is one term used for *partnership*.

What does it take to become a preferred supplier? To become a preferred supplier for Bethlehem Steel, the supplier must pass several criteria (listed in Exhibit 13.5). In some cases, a Bethlehem preferred supplier is a distributor, not a manufacturer. In these cases, the supplier and Bethlehem Steel work in tandem to find the best manufacturers at the lowest prices, with the result being increases in sales volume and better volume discounts. Bethlehem Steel gets the lowest price possible at the required service level, and the distributor makes more profit. Clearly this is a win-win opportunity.[27]

Note that upgrading, full-line selling, cross-selling, and handling complaints will continue to occur during the commitment stage. Because a commitment has been made by both parties to the partnership, however, expectations are greater. Handling complaints properly, appropriately upgrading or cross-selling, and fulfilling new needs are even more important because of the high level of commitment made to the partner.

EXHIBIT 13.5

Preferred Supplier Criteria for Suppliers to Bethlehem Steel

- Capability: The purchasing team examines manufacturing, shipping, and administrative capabilities. Because Bethlehem requires significant monitoring by suppliers, even paperwork is scrutinized.
- Organization: Are employees dedicated? Is the company flexible or bureaucratic? Can it change as we change?
- Financial health: Bethlehem reviews audited financial statements to determine if the supplier is managed well.
- Culture: Does the corporate culture fit with ours? Do we want the same things and do we work in similar ways? Can we get along?
- Willingness to commit: Suppliers must be willing to commit the resources necessary to serve the account. For many suppliers, this means a full-time representative on Bethlehem's site.
- Ethics: Is the supplier trustworthy?

Source: Adapted from Jean Graham, "A Simple Idea Saves $8 Million a Year," *Purchasing*, May 21, 1992, pp. 47–49.

Research has found that many buyers evaluate suppliers on criteria similar to those used by Bethlehem Steel.[28] While the salesperson may not have the ability to influence corporate culture, she or he plays an important role in managing the relationship and leading both sides into commitment.

Securing Commitment to a Partnership

When firms reach the commitment stage, elements in addition to trust become important. Trust may be operationalized in the form of shared risk, such as Baxter International's agreements with some customers to share savings or expenses for joint programs. Along with the dimensions of trust such as competence and dependability (similar to Bethlehem's capability) and honesty (or ethics), there must be commitment to the partnership from the entire supplying organization, a culture that fits with the buyer's organizational culture, and channels of communication so open that the seller and buyer appear to be part of the same company. GE and certain partners, for example, form cross-company teams to jointly solve problems or conquer opportunities.[29]

Commitment Must Be Complete

Commitment to the relationship should permeate both organizations, from top management to the secretary who answers the phone. This means devoting the resources necessary to satisfy the customer's needs, even anticipating needs before the buyer does. It is often the responsibility of the salesperson to secure commitment from his or her own company. Senior management must be convinced of the benefits of partnering with a specific account and be willing to allow the salesperson to direct the resources necessary to sustain the partnership. (In Chapter Seventeen, we will discuss building the internal partnerships the salesperson needs to coordinate those resources.)

Commitment also requires that all employees be empowered to handle the needs of the customer. For example, if the customer has a problem with a billing process,

Nestle's "Red Hot Sales Force" was created to build relationships with Thailand's rapidly developing supermarket industry.

C. Charlesworth/Saba

administration should be willing to work with the partner to develop a more satisfactory process. In a partnership, the customer should not have to rely on only the salesperson to satisfy its needs.

Communication

In the exploration stage, availability must be demonstrated (we already discussed the example of toll-free hotlines and voice to allow the seller's organization to respond quickly to customer calls). But in the commitment phase of a partnership, the seller must take a proactive communication stance. This means actively seeking opportunities to communicate at times other than when the salesperson has something to sell or a problem to resolve.

Partners are usually the first to learn of new products, often long before the rest of the market. Part of the commitment between suppliers and their customer partners is the trust that such early knowledge will be kept confidential. Partners want to know what is coming out soon so they can make appropriate plans. But what happens if the new product is delayed or needs to have some bugs worked out? Selling Scenario 13.2 describes just such a situation.

Salespeople should also encourage direct communication among similar functional areas. In previous stages, the two firms communicated through the buyer and the salesperson. If multilevel selling occurred, it occurred at even levels, that is, vice presidents talking to one another. But when two firms commit to a partnership, the boundaries between them, at least in terms of communication, should blur, as illustrated in Exhibit 13.6.

The buyer's production department, for example, should be able to communicate directly with the seller's engineering department rather than going through the salesperson, if they need to work on a change in the product design. While the salesperson would want to be aware of a product design change and ensure that engineering responded promptly to the customer's concern, direct communication means more accurate communication and a better understanding of the customer's needs. A better solution is more likely to result when there is direct communication.

Corporate Culture

Corporate culture is the values and beliefs held by senior management. A company's culture shapes the attitudes and actions of employees and influences the development of policies and programs.[30] For example, consider the following scene. In a large room with concrete floors are a number of cubicles built out of plywood. In each cubicle are a card table, two folding chairs, and a poster that says "How low can you go?" Such is the scene in Bentonville, Arkansas, the corporate headquarters of Wal-Mart, where salespeople meet their buyers for Sam's Club and Wal-Mart. That room reflects Wal-Mart's culture of the lowest possible price.

A similar culture of constantly seeking ways to drive down costs is necessary for a seller to develop a partnership with Wal-Mart. A single salesperson will not change a company's corporate culture to secure a partnership with a buyer, but the salesperson must identify the type of culture both organizations hold and make an assessment of fit. Although a perfect match is not necessary, the salesperson must be ready to demonstrate that there is a fit. Offering lavish entertainment to a Wal-Mart buyer, for example, would not demonstrate a fit. Telling the buyer that you are staying at a Circle-6 Motel might.

Underpromise and Overdeliver

Excitement was running at a fever pitch. For an entire year, executives at AlliedSignal were touting their plan to turn AlliedSignal into the leading supplier of automotive plastics. Well behind Du Pont's 47 percent market share with only 19 percent, AlliedSignal had developed a plan to deliver within 48 hours of any customer's request any amount of plastics to any location. With this kind of delivery, the company was confident it could capture market share by satisfying customers' just-in-time needs.

When the plan was launched, the salespeople visited key accounts, taking brochures and proposals that touted the plan. Then phase two of the marketing campaign would begin with a $15 million ad campaign. But just before the advertising campaign was to be launched, AlliedSignal pulled the plug and halted the campaign. A new group of executives responsible for managing production announced that the company was not yet capable of meeting that 48-hour promise, and therefore the campaign had to be scrapped.

But what about those key accounts that had already listened to presentations concerning the 48-hour delivery and were considering proposals? How would the sales force handle those?

To smooth things out, top AlliedSignal executives made joint calls with account representatives to those key accounts that were already considering contracts and purchases based on the new delivery promise. As one industry expert noted, it is far worse to promise and not deliver than to apologize and inform buyers of what they can reasonably expect, even if it means losing some business. And with some key accounts, joint 48-hour delivery plans are still being developed to meet their needs. What could have been a major disaster was avoided by being up-front with customers, working with them to solve their problems, and setting appropriate expectations.

Source: Laurie Freeman, "Beating a Strategic Retreat," *Advertising Age's Business Marketing*, October 1996, pp. 1, 44.

 Companies have often sought international partners as a way to enter foreign markets. Wal-Mart partnered with Cifra when Wal-Mart entered the Mexican market. Cifra provides distribution services and products to Wal-Mart for Sam's Club and Wal-Mart stores located in Mexico City, Monterrey, and Guadalajara. When partnering with companies from other countries, country culture differences as well as corporate culture differences can cause difficulties.

Though not attempting to change a company's culture, the salesperson who seeks a partnering relationship seeks change for both organizations. In the next section, we discuss what types of changes salespeople manage and how they manage those changes.

The Salesperson as Change Agent

In increasing revenue to grow in an account over time, the salesperson acts as a **change agent,** or a cause of change in the organization. Each sale may involve some type of change, perhaps a change from a competitive product or simply a new version of the old one. Partnering, though, often requires that change be made in both the buying and selling organizations. For example, earlier we discussed John Paduch, who saved his customer $1.4 million. To achieve those savings required that the buyer's company change the way it did business.

American Distribution Systems (ADS), a pharmaceutical distributor, and Ciba-Geigy, a pharmaceutical manufacturer, took six months to implement a joint operating plan that integrated systems of both companies. ADS created a cross-functional team that recreated ADS systems to function as part of Ciba-Geigy. At the same

EXHIBIT 13.6

Communication Lines
Are More Direct
between Partners

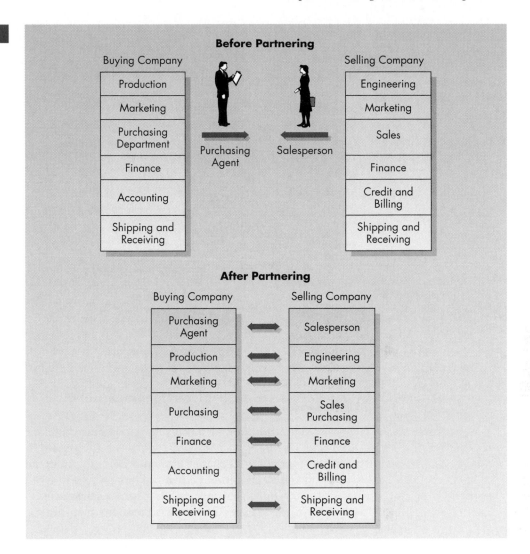

time, Ciba-Geigy had to share information and other resources to take full advantage of the benefits of the relationship. In this instance, both buyer and seller had to change significantly for the partnership to work.

Change is not easy, even when it is obviously beneficial. The objective is to manage change, such as changing from steel to iron pipe, in the buyer's organization while giving the appearance of stability. There are two critical elements to consider about change: the rate and the scope of change. The **rate of change** refers to how quickly the change is made; the **scope of change** refers to the degree to which the change affects the organization. Broad-scope changes affect many areas of the company, whereas narrow changes affect small areas. In general, the faster and broader the change, the more likely it will meet with resistance, as illustrated in Exhibit 13.7.[31]

To overcome resistance to change, the salesperson should consider several decisions. The first decision involves finding help in the buying organization for selling

EXHIBIT 13.7

Change and Resistance:
Resistance to Change Is
Greatest When the Scope
Is Broad and the Rate of
Change Is Fast.

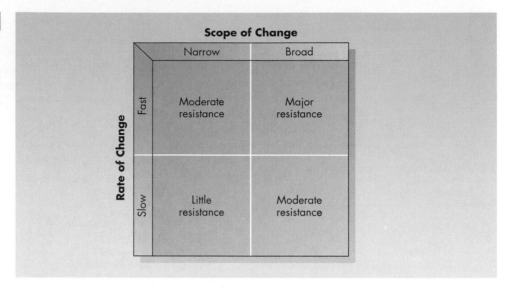

the proposal. Other important decisions are positioning the proposal, determining the necessary resources, and developing a time-based strategy.[32]

Champions

First, the choice of one or more champions must be made. **Champions,** also called *advocates or internal salespeople,* work for the buying firm in the areas most affected by the proposed change and work with the salesperson to make the proposal successful. These champions can build momentum for the proposal by selling in arenas or during times that are off limits to the salesperson. For example, a champion may sell for the salesperson during a company picnic in a casual conversation with a co-worker.

Salespeople can help potential champions by providing them with all of the knowledge they will need. Knowledge builds confidence; champions will have the courage to speak up when they are certain they know what they are talking about. Salespeople can also motivate champions to participate fully in the decision process by showing how the decision meets their needs as well as the overall needs of the company.

Positioning the Change

Positioning the change is similar to positioning a product in mass marketing, as you may have learned in a principles of marketing course. In this case, however, the salesperson examines the specific needs and wants of the various constituencies in the account to position the change for the greatest likelihood of success. For example, Benson Bakery makes bread for restaurants. It was considering the purchase of equipment that would allow it to make bread and freeze it at the request of Steak and Ale, one of its major accounts. Hobart, which manufactures such equipment, could have positioned its equipment as delivering the best quality end-product (marketing's concern) or as being the easiest to use and maintain (manufacturing's concern). Because manufacturing was not the key area in this decision, such a positioning may have been fatal.

Because salespeople are highly proactive in finding areas for improvement (or change) in their partners' organizations, positioning a change may determine who is involved in the decision. For example, suppose the IBM representative who calls on your school recognizes that the student computer labs are getting out of date. Is a proposal for new equipment primarily the domain of the computer services department, or is it the domain of faculty who teach computing classes? If the computer services department favors IBM but the users favor Apple, the IBM rep will be better served by positioning the change as the responsibility of the computer services department. Positioning the proposed change appropriately may spell success or failure for the proposal.

Determining the Necessary Resources

The customer's needs may be beyond the salesperson's expertise. For example, Fram, a maker of auto parts, may be working with CarQuest, an auto parts retailer, to develop a major advertising program that will highlight their growing partnership. Such a change may require some selling to the advertising department at CarQuest. The Fram account representative will use the expert advice of Fram's own advertising department, its marketing research department, and probably its marketing management as well. These experts may visit CarQuest with the account rep and aid in securing that change in CarQuest's advertising focus.

The salesperson must assess the situation and determine what resources are needed to secure the buyer's commitment. While the above example discusses allocation of personnel, salespeople have other resources, such as travel and entertainment budgets or sample supplies, that they manage. (We discuss how to build internal partnerships to effectively coordinate company resources in Chapter Seventeen.)

Developing a Time-Based Strategy

The salesperson must determine a strategy for the proposed change and set that strategy against a time line. This action accomplishes several objectives. First, the strategy is an outline of planned sales calls, with primary and minimum call objectives determined for each call. Second, the time line provides the salesperson with estimates of when each call should occur. Of course, objectives and planned times will change depending on the results of each call, but this type of planning is necessary to provide the salesperson with guidance for each call, determine when resources are to be used, and make sure each call contributes to the visionary objective, as discussed in Chapter Eight.

For example, the Fram salesperson may determine that calls need to be made on five individuals at CarQuest. A time-based strategy would indicate which person should be visited first and what should be accomplished during that visit, as well as the order of visits to the remaining four members of the buying center. The strategy would also alert the salesperson as to when the advertising personnel were needed. Exhibit 13.8 illustrates such a time line.

Common Problems to Avoid

A common belief is that once a customer has committed to a partnership, less work is needed to maintain that relationship. That belief, however, is untrue. When salespeople subscribe to that belief, they fall victim to one or more of the common prob-

EXHIBIT 13.8		Time Line for Fram/CarQuest Strategy			
Month 1	Month 2	Month 3	Month 4	Month 5	Month 6
Visit director of marketing • **Primary objective:** Determine marketing needs • **Minimum objective:** Secure permission to see merchandising manager and advertising manager	*Visit merchandising manager and advertising* • **Primary objective:** Secure support in principle	*Visit director of marketing* • **Primary objective:** Specify objectives for new advertising plan and secure commitment in principle	*Arrange tour of Fram facilities for VP of retail, marketing director, and advertising and merchandising managers*	*Submit plan to director of marketing for approval*	*Implement advertising program*

lems that can occur. As discussed in Chapter Two, the final stage for partnerships is dissolution, or break-up. Several potential problems, including maintaining few personal relationships, failing to monitor competitor actions, and complacency, can lead to dissolution.

Limited Personal Relationships

Salespeople tend to call on buyers they like; it is natural to want to spend time with friends. The result is that relationships are cultivated with only a few individuals in the account. Unfortunately for such salespeople, buyers may leave the organization, transfer to an unrelated area, or simply not participate in some decisions. Truly effective salespeople attempt to develop multiple relationships within an account.

One benefit of multiple relationships is that different champions can be selected for each proposal. Paul Kelly, a sales training consultant, suggests that after a proposal is decided on, the salesperson should review the process and identify the loudest opponent to the proposal in the buying organization. For the next proposal, the salesperson should solicit that person's support up front. The individual has already shown the courage and ability to fight for a position (even though it was against the salesperson's position), ideal qualities for a champion.[33]

Failing to Monitor Competitor Actions

No matter how strong the partnership is, competition will want a piece of the business. And no matter how good the salesperson is, there will still be times when the account is vulnerable to competitor action. Accounts are most vulnerable when a personnel change occurs (especially if the rep has developed relationships with a limited number of people in the account), when technology changes, or when major directional changes occur, such as a company starting a new division or entering a new market.

The successful salesperson, however, monitors competitor action even when the account seems invulnerable. For example, an insurance agency had all of the insurance business at a state university in Texas for over 10 years, but failed to monitor competitor action at the state capitol and lost the account when another insurance agency found a sympathetic buyer in Austin. The loss of this one account cut annual earnings by over 70 percent.

Monitoring competitor action can be as simple as checking the visitor's log at the front desk to see who has dropped by or keeping up with competitor actions and asking buyers for their opinions. Frequently, developing relationships with the many potential influencers in an account will also keep salespeople informed about competitor actions. As each person is visited, questions and comments about competitors will arise, indicating the activity level of competition.

Monitoring competition also means thinking about the benefits competition offers, what their products do, and what their selling strategies are.[34] When salespeople understand what the competitor offers, they can position their own company's unique capabilities more effectively. It is not enough to know where competitors have made calls; good salespeople also know what the competition is saying.

Complacency

Perhaps the most common thief of good accounts is complacency. In sales terms, **complacency** is assuming that the business is yours and will always be yours. It is failing to continue to work as hard to keep the business as you did initially to earn the business. Complacency was the root cause of the insurance salesperson's failure to monitor the competition.

Steven Berkey, sales manager at Victory Tube Company, continually reviews customer lists to see who is no longer placing orders in order to identify lost accounts. He also looks for significant drops in the amounts a customer orders, as this signals an account that is trying other vendors.[35]

To avoid complacency, salespeople should regularly audit their own customer service. Some of the questions a salesperson may want to consider are as follows:

- Do I understand each individual's personal characteristics? Do I have these characteristics in my computer file on each account?
- Do I maintain a written or computerized record of promises made?
- Do I follow up on *every* customer request promptly, no matter how insignificant it may seem?
- Do I follow up on deliveries, make sure initial experiences are positive, and ensure that all paperwork is done correctly and quickly?
- Have I recently found something new that I can do better than the competition?

We opened this chapter by discussing the value of customers. But just as a reminder, research indicates that customers are five times more likely to stop doing business with a company because of poor service.[36] While striving for excellence in relationships with customers is important, one millionaire salesperson says, "You beat 50 percent of the people in America just by working hard. You beat another 40 percent by being a person of honesty and integrity. . . . The last 10 percent is a dogfight in the free-enterprise system."[37] His words are a strong reminder of the importance of avoiding complacency in customer relationships.

SUMMARY

Developing partnerships has become increasingly important for salespeople and their firms. Salespeople can develop partnerships and generate goodwill by servicing accounts properly and by strategically building relationships. Both salespeople and buyers benefit from partnering.

Many specific activities are necessary to ensure customer satisfaction and develop a partnering relationship. The salesperson must maintain the proper perspective, remember the customer between calls, build perceptions of trust, monitor order processing, ensure the proper initial use of the product or service, help to service the product, provide expert guidance and suggestions, and provide any necessary special assistance.

Probably few opportunities exist to develop goodwill comparable to those provided by the proper handling of customer complaints. Sales representatives should encourage unhappy customers to tell their stories completely, fully, and without interruption. A sympathetic attitude to a real or an imaginary product or service failure cannot be overemphasized. After determining the facts, the salesperson should implement the solution promptly and monitor it to ensure that proper action is taken.

The appropriate solution will depend on many factors, such as the seriousness of the problem, the dollar amount involved, and the value of the account. A routine should be developed to make certain every step is followed to handle complaints fairly and equitably.

KEY TERMS

category management 377	dependability 362
champion 384	full-line selling 377
change agent 382	honesty 364
competence 363	likability 364
complacency 387	preferred supplier 379
corporate culture 381	rate of change 383
cross-selling 377	scope of change 383
customer orientation 364	upgrading 376

QUESTIONS AND PROBLEMS

1. How can a salesperson lose by overselling a customer?

2. Explain how the art of listening can be applied to a situation in which a customer makes a complaint. What can applying this art accomplish?

3. Your company has just introduced a new product. To determine if the product could perform a customer's application, you asked the head of the service department, who said that it would. But after delivery, it is clear that the new product will not perform that application. What should you do? Would it matter which stage of the relationship you and your customer were in?

4. Should a salesperson handle all complaints so that customers are completely satisfied? Explain why or why not. Would your answer change if you were in the exploration stage versus the commitment stage?

5. The soundest philosophy for building partnerships may be summed up in these words: "It's the little things that count." Identify six or eight "little things" a salesperson could do that will cost little or nothing but may be extremely valuable in building partnerships.

6. What is your reaction to the statement "The customer is always right"? Is it a sound basis for making adjustments and satisfying complaints? Can it be followed literally? Why or why not?

7. Your roommate or spouse complains that you don't do your share of the housework. Your friend complains that you never seem to have any free time anymore. What have you learned in this chapter that you could use to restore these relationships? If the answer is you have learned nothing, justify that answer. If you have learned useful techniques, explain how they would apply in those two situations.

8. How do you know when full-line selling, upgrading, or cross-selling strategies are appropriate?

9. What are the various ways a salesperson can provide a potential champion with knowledge to build confidence? What types of knowledge will the champion need?

10. At the beginning of the chapter, we mentioned how cellular phone companies have a high disconnect rate. Why do they lose so many customers? What can the salesperson do to avoid these problems?

11. We all know a store we used to do business with regularly but don't visit much any more. Think of one or two such establishments from your own experience. What could a salesperson for that store have done to keep your business? (Don't include a store that you stopped visiting because you moved away from the area.)

EXPLORING THE NET

Visit one of the following sites and explore it as though you were an organizational buyer or a partner for that organization's products or marketing programs.

www.disney.com

www.intel.com

www.microsoft.com

www.texaspension.com

www.wbap.com

1. What features do these sites offer to strengthen communication with the organization's customers? Do you think these home pages will move customers closer to partnering with the organization? Why or why not?

2. If you were a stockholder, how would your answers to question 1 change?

CASE PROBLEMS

**CASE 13.1
Ryder Truck
Rental–Leasing**

Ryder Truck Rental–Leasing is one of the largest truck-leasing companies in the United States, competing with Rollins for commercial rental and leasing. Unlike U-Haul, which rents primarily to consumers, Ryder's business comes from other businesses that either do not want to maintain their own fleets or use Ryder for those periods when they need more trucking capacity.

A special analysis of truck usage has revealed that some business executives with a long history of using Ryder have not used Ryder in the past nine months. Ryder knows these executives must be using a competitor or other means of transportation. To win back as many of them as possible, Ryder's management has instructed sales representatives to call on all dormant accounts or those that have not done business with Ryder in the past nine months.

Scott Eccles, who has been with Ryder for three years as a sales representative, selected the owner of a small manufacturing company, Dan Kemp, as his first contact. Eccles made an appointment with Kemp, and the following interview took place:

ECCLES Thought I'd stop around to see you, Mr. Kemp. Haven't heard your name mentioned lately.

KEMP And you won't hear my name mentioned around your place again either. I'm through using Ryder. I'm sick and tired of being kicked around by your outfit. The last time I used your trucks, I had a driver sitting for two days waiting for either repair or replacement. And when he did get back on the road, the truck wouldn't go over 50 miles an hour.

ECCLES How long ago did this happen?

KEMP You oughta know, it was the last time I used your company—probably 10 or 12 months ago. You people advertise reliability. But if the truth were known, it's got to be the worst I've ever experienced.

ECCLES Oh, it can't be as bad as all that!

KEMP You don't think so, eh? You ought to be the one to tell my best customer that her shipment is delayed. Her production line had to stop and wait for our parts to get there. They lost $30,000 in lost product. And you say, "It can't be as bad as all that."

ECCLES Well, of course, we are terribly sorry about it, and we are trying to cut down on that sort of thing.

KEMP I've heard that line before, but I haven't enough good customers to keep testing that statement. Moreover, you people just can't get a truck out here on time. I have two managers who ship by rental truck at least once a month. I've told them to take your competitor.

ECCLES Say, those new Fords of ours can beat anything they have to offer.

KEMP Says you, Mr. Eccles. My managers need trucks on time to get our products to our customers on time—oh, it's just not worth it.

ECCLES Well, Mr. Kemp, we are trying to cut down on delays. We are learning more about maintaining our newer equipment, and we feel that we are making headway.

KEMP I'm fed up with Ryder, and I'm not going to give you any more tries—not until you can really sell me that things are actually different. You haven't done a very good job so far.

Scott Eccles concluded the interview by saying he would certainly appreciate the opportunity to show that Ryder's service was all it was advertised to be.

Another Ryder sales representative, Jim Harris, was the luncheon speaker for a local Rotary Club when the club celebrated Transportation Day. He talked about the operations of Ryder in particular and about trucking problems in general. After the speech one of the Rotarians, Pam Pepper, congratulated Harris and said she enjoyed the talk. During the conversation, Harris learned that Pepper was a former Ryder customer but had become disgruntled and was no longer using Ryder.

Harris decided to call on Pepper. The following conversation took place about one week later:

HARRIS Ms. Pepper, it's kind of you to give me a hearing on your complaints about Ryder.

PEPPER Well, I felt I owed it to you after the way I criticized your company at our club the other day. You made a darn good speech, but when I thought about my experiences with Ryder, I got somewhat irritated.

HARRIS Tell me about the experience that led you to use our competitor.

PEPPER It wasn't one experience. It was a lot of the same old stuff over and over again. It was the repetition that got me down. I've used Ryder for nearly 20 years, and I've always thought the world of your management, to such an extent that I'm a stockholder. And I don't invest my money without thoroughly investigating and knowing the company.

HARRIS I'm sorry that you feel the way you do about our company, Ms. Pepper. Specifically what did you experience?

PEPPER Essentially I use a company like you for special situations, like when we have too many trucks down or at the end of our fiscal year to get extra shipments out. The last time I used Ryder, I had trouble getting enough trucks. Although a reservation was finally confirmed, when our drivers went to pick them up, your agents said there was no record of it. I'll bet I spent 20 to 30 minutes on the phone trying to get the reservation straightened out. They never did find any record of it and finally got us half of the trucks we needed about four hours later. But an hour with you people seems to be very unimportant. Also, your pricing plans are always changing. I'm never sure if our bills are accurate or if we're paying too much or too little. And frankly, I can't take that risk.

HARRIS You know, Ms. Pepper, if it weren't for the fact that we are getting those problems licked, I'd say you were justified in using other transportation.

PEPPER Getting them licked? How?

HARRIS In the first place, we have recently installed a new reservations system geared to our current needs. Under this setup, we can usually confirm your trucks' availability immediately. You make only one call. One call does it all.

In addition, we've simplified our pricing plan, and it hasn't changed for six months. It is part of a new billing system designed to make it easier for everyone involved. Not only does it make it easier for you to know if your bill is accurate, it saves us money in handling our accounts, which we've been able to pass along in the form of additional discounts for customers who use us regularly.

PEPPER That discount idea sounds great, and your "one call" is an answer to a shipping manager's prayer—if only it works.

HARRIS It works, all right. How about giving us a chance to prove it?

PEPPER (laughing): How about those delays? My customers can't wait for their products. We are using your competitors whenever possible, and your competitors aren't having any problems too.

HARRIS Well, I'm not going to deny we've had delays with our some of our equipment. The record isn't perfect yet, but we are way ahead of where we were only three months ago. How about giving us another try?

PEPPER And then have another truck break down? All rental trucks are not as reliable as the ones we own, but Ryder seems to be the worst.

HARRIS I'll admit we haven't got an enviable record on that score. We have been putting on a campaign all over our system to improve our maintenance, which should increase reliability. Management is trying its best to clean up that problem. If you will try Ryder, I'm sure you will find an improvement on that point, too.

PEPPER Well, you seem confident things are better. I'll tell you, I'll need a few trucks in about 10 days. I was going to use your competition, but I might try Ryder again. I'll call you as soon as I determine the exact date. But let me warn you, this is only a trial. I'm not going to use only your company until I see some real results. You've told me a good yarn. Now we'll see.

HARRIS Thank you. That's a fair arrangement. I'll call you early next week to learn if you have set a definite date for your shipment.

Questions

1. What do you believe were the specific weaknesses and strengths of Eccles's interview?

2. What strengths and weaknesses did you observe in Harris's interview?

3. Did Eccles or Harris do the better job? Why?

CASE 13.2
Fletcher Electric, Inc.

Molly Stevens, account manager for Fletcher, was pondering her next move with Tymco, her largest account. Fletcher manufactures a line of pumps, electric motors, and controls that are sold to companies that use Fletcher's parts in manufacturing all kinds of equipment. Tymco, a maker of street sweepers and other specialized industrial products, had purchased Fletcher controls for the last five years, but also purchased controls from several small distributors for specific applications when Fletcher's products could not meet the specifications. Stevens originally sold the controls by proving to the engineering department that Fletcher's quality could meet their specifications and demonstrating the controls' accuracy and long life. Then she convinced the purchasing agent that the pricing would be more stable with one major vendor than with multiple distributors. Since then, Stevens has heard no complaints about Fletcher's products. Tymco even allowed a trade magazine to write an article about Tymco's experience with Fletcher controls.

Early last year, Stevens persuaded the purchasing agent for Tymco to switch to Fletcher electric motors for several applications. Although engineering was not involved in this decision, Stevens had to prove to the purchasing agent that the products were as good as the ones they were currently purchasing. Stevens estimated that Fletcher had about 30 percent of the Tymco motor business, 30 percent went to Visa SA from Mexico, and the remainder of the business belonged to Smart & Company, which actually distributed several lines of electric motors imported from the Pacific Rim.

Last month, Stevens received a call from the director of engineering asking for a meeting to discuss some issues with Fletcher motors. She was delighted, because one of the Fletcher engineers had suggested combining Fletcher motors and controls and shipping the units as one assembly. Stevens believed such a meeting would be a perfect opportunity to present the new idea. She created and presented a proposal to the engineering department that, if accepted, would mean doubling Fletcher's share of the electric motor business. The proposal would require some redesign by Tymco, but the savings over two years would be more than the redesign costs. After that, Tymco could increase profits on those products by about 3 percent. But several engineers pointed out that Fletcher was unwilling to manufacture controls for all of Tymco's needs, and they were reluctant to make such a change with a company that was not willing to work more closely with them. In addition, one engineer seemed very unhappy that the purchasing department had switched to Fletcher motors. She thought the reject rate of 2 percent was too high; all of Tymco's other vendors were achieving fewer than 1 percent rejects. At the conclusion of the meeting, the director of engineering said to Stevens, "Molly, we've enjoyed a long and good relationship with Fletcher. And your idea is a good one. Right now, though, I don't think Fletcher is the company we should do that with. But we'll consider it and let you know."

Questions

1. In what stage of partnering is the relationship between Fletcher and Tymco?

2. Is there anything Stevens could have done to set the stage for better acceptance of her proposal?

3. What should she do right now? If her visionary objective is to develop a strategic partnership with Tymco, is it still realistic? What should she do to achieve that visionary objective?

ADDITIONAL REFERENCES

Brown, Stephen. "The Moderating Effects of Insupplier-Outsupplier Status on Organizational Buyer Attitudes." *Journal of the Academy of Marketing Science,* Summer 1995, pp. 170–81.

Cravens, Dave (ed.). *Journal of the Academy of Marketing Science,* Special Issue on Relationship Marketing, Fall 1995.

Dahlstrom, Robert; Kevin McNeilly; and Thomas Speh. "Buyer-Seller Relationships in the Procurement of Logistical Services." *Journal of the Academy of Marketing Science,* Fall 1996, pp. 110–24.

Dixon, Lance. "JIT II Favors Backdoor Selling." *Purchasing,* January 1994, p. 39.

East, Robert, and Kathy Hammond. "The Erosion of Repeat-Purchase Loyalty." *Marketing Letters* 7, (1996), pp. 163–71.

Farber, Barry, and Joyce Wycoff. "Relationships: Six Steps to Success." *Sales & Marketing Management,* April 1991, pp. 50–58.

Forenell, Claes; Michael Johnson; Eugene Anderson; Jaesung Cha; and Barbara Bryant. "The American Customer Satisfaction Index: Nature, Purpose and Findings." *Journal of Marketing,* October 1996, pp. 7–18.

Good, David. "Sales in the 1990s: A Decade of Development." *Review of Business,* Summer 1990, pp. 3–6.

Gronroos, Christian. "The Marketing Strategy Continuum: Towards a Marketing Concept for the 1990s." *Management Decision 29,* no. 1 (1991), pp. 7–13.

Hanan, Mack. Consultative Selling. New York: AMACOM, 1990.

Ingram, Thomas N. "Improving Sales Force Productivity: A Critical Examination of the Personal Selling Process." *Review of Business,* Summer 1990, pp. 7–12, 40.

Lengnick-Hall, Cynthia, "Customer Contributions to Quality: A Different View of the Customer-Oriented Firm." *Academy of Management Review* 21 (1996), pp. 791–824.

Lytle, John F. *What Do Your Customers Really Want?* Chicago: Probus Publishing, 1993.

Menon, Anil; Sundar G. Bharadwaj; and Roy Howell. "The Quality and Effectiveness of Marketing Strategy: Effects of Functional and Dysfunctional Conflict in Intraorganizational Relationships." *Journal of the Academy of Marketing Science,* Fall 1996, pp. 299–313.

Moore, Anne, and Bodo Schlegelmilch. "Improving Service Quality in an Industrial Setting." *Industrial Marketing Management,* February 1994, pp. 83–92.

"Partnering for Performance." *NAMA Journal,* Fall 1992, pp. 6–9.

Qualls, William, and Jose Rosa. "Assessing Industrial Buyers' Perceptions of Quality and Their Effects on Satisfaction." *Industrial Marketing Management* 24 (1995), pp. 359–68.

Raia, Earnest. "Quality Wins Out: The Shrinking Supplier Base." *Purchasing,* January 1994, pp. 93–95.

Stundza, Thomas. "More Dialog, Fewer Suppliers." *Purchasing,* January 1994, pp. 29–37.

Szymanski, David M. and Gilbert A. Churchill, Jr. "Client Evaluation Cues: A Comparison of Successful and Unsuccessful Salespeople." *Journal of Marketing Research,* May 1990, pp. 163–74.

Teas, Kenneth. "Expectations, Performance Evaluation, and Consumers' Perceptions of Quality." *Journal of Marketing,* October 1993, pp. 18–34.

Wilson, Larry. *Stop Selling, Start Partnering.* Essex Junction, VT: Oliver Wight Publications, 1994.

uilding on what you just learned in Part Three about partnering, this section
will cover specific types of selling situations. In Chapter Fourteen, you will
learn about one form of selling that continues to grow in importance: formal negotiations. Topics include premeeting planning, opening the session, strategies and
tactics, and how to effectively give and receive concessions.

Chapter Fifteen provides principles and guidance for the somewhat unique situation of selling to resellers. The chapter describes how salespeople aid resellers and

Part Four

Special Applications

discusses the role of supporting activities such as trade shows. Chapter Fifteen also
provides information about national account managers.

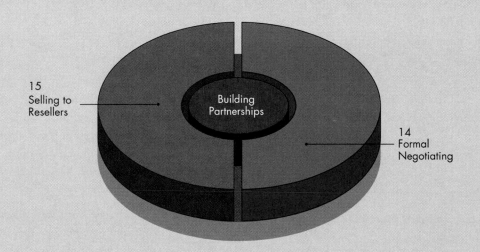

Chapter Fourteen

Formal Negotiating

We have all engaged in negotiations of some type. Most of these were informal (e.g., with your parents about attending a rock concert) and dealt with relatively minor issues, although they may have been intensely important to you at the time. This chapter discusses formal negotiations that occur between buyers

Some Questions Answered in this Chapter Are:

What is negotiation selling? How does it differ from nonnegotiation selling?

What items can be negotiated in selling?

What type of planning needs to occur prior to a negotiation meeting? How should a seller set objectives?

How can the negotiation session be effectively opened? What role does friendly conversation play?

What negotiation strategies and tactics do buyers use? How should negotiators respond?

What are the salesperson's guidelines for offering and requesting concessions?

and salespeople. The skills you will learn can also be used in your day-to-day negotiations with friends, parents, and people in authority positions.

PROFILE

Danny Cummings is a senior account representative at Wallace Computer Services, Inc. Wallace provides a wide range of information management, products, services, and solutions, most of which are business forms, labels, office products, computer supplies, ribbons and rolls, direct response printing, and commercial printing. Cummings recalled, "I had researched several companies in my job search and decided Wallace was the type of company I would like to work for and could be a valuable and successful contributor in the field of sales. After the usual processes and formalities, I walked into the sales office of Wallace Computer Services in Bloomington, Illinois, and started my career on February 10, 1986.

"As a sales representative, my number one objective was, and is, to increase the amount of product sold in my area over and above the last fiscal year. Therefore, I must know what I am selling and to whom I am selling. Without this knowledge and information, success is not possible. If I do not have the information available, the competition has the chance to get the upper hand.

"As a result of my determination and drive for knowledge and information, I was promoted to the Contract Division in 1987. This division of Wallace is primarily responsible for calling on national accounts. At that time, I had a customer base of four major accounts. Over the next six years these accounts more than doubled as a direct result of my efforts, earning me honors in the Wallace 100% Club and the Wallace Outstanding Performance Club. To generate the amount of sales I did in the past 11 years, a burning desire, almost an obsession, to succeed was and still is a requirement of the job. Sales is not like any other career; you are the only one who will make your sales.

"The customer was at a point where they needed to cut costs and improve services to their customers. I knew the WIN system was the answer. After six months of proposals, plant tours, and negotiations, Wallace was awarded the complete forms package."

"A true salesperson does all the work up front so the customer is completely comfortable with you, your company, and what you can provide for them. If you have prepared properly, there should be no unanswered questions. Know your customer. Know what they are doing now and what they need to do in the future. Know your customer better than they know themselves. The idea is to make sure you anticipate the customer's needs before they

DANNY CUMMINGS
Wallace Computer Services, Inc.

fully realize how much they need your product. Come to them with the idea before they search you out.

"Many times customers will ask you to prepare a proposal involving the capabilities you can provide to them. Several things you may want to include and that have been beneficial to me in the past are distribution, manufacturing, and order entry capabilities. Other important factors to consider are reporting, product management, pick and pack versus bulk packaging, and WIN (Wallace Information Network) abilities, which show your customer how well and in what manner you can supply them with information on their products.

"During the bid process, you are often up against several other suppliers of the same product. Many times you will be asked to give price quotes so the customer can compare you with the other suppliers. How quickly you can provide the information and how competitive you are is critical. This is where knowing your competition is just as important as knowing your customer.

"In the summer of 1993, I was offered a position to call on one of the nation's largest businesses, reducing my focus from four mid-size accounts to one large account. At that time, Wallace was on the outside looking in. Wallace had the business several years previously, but had lost the renewal to one of our biggest competitors. I had the chance to make history within Wallace or be just another salesperson. I liked the part about making history.

"The customer was at a point where they needed to cut costs and improve services to their customers. I knew the WIN system was the answer. After six months of proposals, plant tours, and negotiations, Wallace was awarded the complete forms package—a major turning point for the company as well as myself. I now work with a team of nine to promote and facilitate current business with this customer while continuing to look for avenues of growth."

Visit Our Website@
http://www.wallace.com

THE NATURE OF NEGOTIATION

The bargaining process through which buyers and sellers resolve areas of conflict and/or arrive at agreements is called **negotiation.** Areas of conflict may include minor issues (e.g., who should attend future meetings) as well as major ones (e.g., cost per unit, exclusive purchase agreements). The ultimate goal of both parties should be to reduce or resolve the conflict.

Two basic philosophies guide negotiations. In **win-lose negotiating,** the negotiator attempts to win all the important concessions and thus triumph over the opponent. This resembles almost every competitive sport you have ever watched. In boxing, for example, one person is the winner and the other is, by definition, the loser.

In the second negotiating philosophy, **win-win negotiating,** the negotiator attempts to secure an agreement that satisfies both parties. You have probably experienced social situations similar to this. For example, if you want to attend a football game and your friend wants to attend a party, you may negotiate a mutual agreement that you both attend the first half of the game and still make it to the party. If this arrangement satisfies both you and your friend, you have engaged in win-win negotiating.

The discussion in this chapter assumes that your goal as the salesperson is to engage in win-win negotiating. In fact, this entire book has emphasized partnering, which is a win-win perspective. Partners attempt to find solutions that benefit both parties because each is concerned about the other party's welfare.

However, the buyer may be using a win-lose strategy, whereby the buyer hopes to win all major concessions and have the seller be the loser. To help you spot and prepare for such situations, we discuss many of these tactics as well.

Negotiation versus Nonnegotiation Selling

How does negotiation differ from the sales presentations we have covered up to this point? In Chapters Eight through Twelve, we assumed that many factors are constants, that is, they cannot be changed. For example, the price of an Allsteel Office chair model K316 has been set at $395. The Allsteel salesperson will not lower that price unless, of course, the buyer agrees to purchase large quantities. Even then the buyer will receive just a standard quantity discount as outlined in the seller's price manual. In essence, the salesperson's price book and procedure manual form an inflexible set of rules. If the buyer objects, an attempt to resolve the conflict will occur by using techniques discussed in Chapter Eleven (e.g., the compensation method or the boomerang method).

In contrast, if the Allsteel seller enters formal negotiations with the same buyer, the price and delivery schedules will be subject to modification. The buyer neither expects nor wants the seller to come to the negotiation meeting with any standard price book. Instead, the buyer expects most policies, procedures, and prices to be truly negotiable.

Negotiations also differ from regular sales calls in that they generally involve more intensive planning and a larger number of people from the selling firm. Prenegotiation planning may go on for six months or more before the actual meeting takes place. Planning participants usually cover a wide spectrum of functional areas of the firm, such as production, marketing, sales, accounting, purchasing, and executive officers.

Finally, formal negotiations generally take place only for very large or important prospective buyers. For example, Quaker Oats might negotiate with some of the very large food chains, such as Jewel, Kroger, Safeway, and Cub Foods, but would not engage in a large, formal negotiation session with small local or "mom and pop" grocery stores. Negotiating is an expensive endeavor because it utilizes so much of so many important people's time. The firm wants to invest the time and costs involved in negotiating only if the long-term nature of the relationship and the importance of the customer justify the expense.

What Can Be Negotiated?

If the customer is large or important enough, almost anything can be negotiated. Salespeople who have not been involved in negotiations before often find it hard to grasp the fact that so many areas are subject to discussion and change. The following areas are often negotiated between buyers and sellers:[1]

Inventory levels the buyer must maintain.

Inventory levels the seller must keep on hand to be able to restock the buyer quickly.

Details about the design of the product or service.

How the product will be manufactured.

Display allowances for resellers.

Advertising allowances and the amount of advertising the seller does.

Formal negotiations usually involve multiple buyers and multiple sellers.

Photo courtesy of GMAC Financial Services

Sales promotion within the channel of distribution.

Delivery terms and conditions.

Retail and wholesale pricing points for resellers.

Prices and pricing allowances for volume purchases.

Amount and location of shelf positioning.

Special packaging and design features.

Service levels after the sale.

Disposing of unsold or obsolete merchandise.

Credit terms.

How complaints will be resolved.

Order entry and ease of monitoring orders.

Type and frequency of communication between the parties.

Performance guarantees and bonds.

In reality, no single negotiation session covers all of the areas listed. Each side comes to the bargaining table with a list of prioritized issues; only important points for which disagreement exists are discussed.

Are You a Good Negotiator?

All of us are negotiators; some of us are better than others. We have negotiated with parents, friends, professors, and, yes, sometimes even with opponents. However, the fact that you have engaged in many negotiations in your lifetime does not mean you are good at negotiating.

The traits necessary to successfully negotiate vary somewhat, depending on the situation and the parties involved. Some characteristics, however, are almost universal. For example, a good negotiator must have patience and endurance; after two hours of discussing the same issue, the negotiator needs the stamina and willingness to continue until an agreement is reached. Also, a willingness to take risks and the ability to tolerate ambiguity become especially critical in business negotiations because it is necessary to both accept and offer concessions during the meeting without complete information.

Successful salespeople do not always make great negotiators. In fact, "the art of negotiating—debating and brokering the merits of a sale—may be the most difficult skill for any salesperson to develop."[2] The unconscious reaction of most salespeople in negotiations often ends up being the opposite of the correct thing to do.[3] For example, what if, in preparation for the upcoming negotiation session, the customer asks for very detailed specifications about your product? Most salespeople would gladly supply reams of technical data, full glossy pictures, an offer of plant tours, and the like. The problem with that approach lies in the possibility that the customer will pick several features that he or she does not need and then pressure for price concessions (e.g., "Look, I don't need that much memory capacity and don't want to pay for something I'm not going to use. So why don't you reduce your price? I shouldn't have to pay for something I'm not planning on ever using!"). A salesperson who is a good negotiator would avoid this situation by supplying information to the customer only in exchange for the right to ask the customer more questions and thus gain more information.

People who fear conflict usually are poor negotiators. In fact, some negotiating strategies are actually designed to increase the level of conflict to bring *all* of the issues to the table and reach an equitable settlement. Along the same lines, people who have a strong need to be liked by all people at all times tend to make very poor negotiators. Other undesirable traits include being closed-minded, unorganized, dishonest, and downright belligerent.

According to Laurel G. Bellows, past president of the Chicago Bar Association, women have special strengths and weaknesses as negotiators.[4] She claims that women are great at building relationships but are less adept at confrontational negotiation meetings. Her advice for women is to be thoroughly prepared, make use of men's stereotypes about women ("let them treat you differently just because you are a woman"), use silence as a tool instead of always responding, get help from a mentor, and be a chameleon (smile, complain, be tough, be aggressive, pour the coffee, etc.).

Of course, cultural differences do exist.[5] For example, Brazilian managers believe competitiveness is more important in a negotiator than integrity. Chinese managers in Taiwan emphasize the negotiator's rational skills to a lesser extent than his or her interpersonal skills.

As the above discussion indicates, being a truly excellent negotiator requires a very careful balance of traits and skills. Take a moment and complete the questionnaire in Exhibit 14.1 to rate your negotiating skills.[6] Don't be discouraged by a low score. You cannot easily change personality traits, but the rest of this chapter will suggest ways to improve your skills.

EXHIBIT 14.1   Negotiation Skills Self-Inventory

Place a check by each item that accurately reflects your personality and traits on an average, normal day.

1. Helpful	20. Receptive
2. Risk taker	21. Easily influenced
3. Inconsistent	22. Enthusiastic
4. Persistent	23. Planner
5. Factual	24. Stingy
6. Use high pressure	25. Listener
7. Self-confident	26. Controlled
8. Practical	27. Think under pressure
9. Manipulative	28. Passive
10. Analytical	29. Economical
11. Arrogant	30. Gullible
12. Impatient	31. Afraid of conflict
13. Seek new approaches	32. Endurance
14. Tactful	33. Tolerate ambiguity
15. Perfectionist	34. Have strong need to be liked
16. Stubborn	35. Organized
17. Flexible	36. Honest
18. Competitive	37. Belligerent
19. Gambler	

How to score the checklist

All of the traits listed are positive except for the following negative traits: 3, 6, 9, 11, 12, 15, 16, 19, 21, 24, 28, 30, 31, 34, and 37. To arrive at a total score, give yourself one point for all positive traits and subtract one point for all negative traits. To interpret your total score: 19–22 excellent, 15–18 good, 11–14 fair.

Negotiations should occur in locations free of distractions. Because of frequent interruptions and the distractions of seeing other patrons, a restaurant is usually a poor place to conduct business.

Neil Selkirk/Tony Stone Images

PLANNING FOR THE NEGOTIATION SESSION

"Preparation and planning are the most important parts of negotiation,"[7] according to one expert source. In Chapter Eight, we discussed how to gather precall information and plan the sales call. All of that material is equally relevant when planning for an upcoming negotiation session—for example, learning everything possible about the buyer team and the buyer's organization.

The meetings the salesperson will have with the buyer prior to the actual negotiation session facilitate this learning. The buyer may also be, or have been, a customer of the salesperson, with the upcoming negotiation session designed to review contracts or specify a new working relationship. Even in such scenarios, negotiators will want to carefully review the players and learn as many facts about the situation as possible.

Location

Plan to hold the negotiation at a location free from distraction for both teams. A neutral site, one owned by neither party, is usually best; it removes both teams from interruptions by business associates, and no one has a psychological (e.g., "home court") advantage. Experienced negotiators find the middle of the workweek best for negotiations and prefer morning to afternoon or evening (because people are more focused on their jobs rather than after-hours and weekend activities).

Time Allotment

As you are probably aware, negotiations can take a tremendous amount of time. Some business negotiations take years to work out. But how much time should be set aside for one negotiation session? The answer depends on the negotiation objectives and the extent to which both sides will desire a win-win session. Studies have shown that high time pressure will produce nonagreements and poor outcomes when one or more side takes a win-lose perspective; but if both sides have a win-win perspective, high outcomes are achieved regardless of time pressure.[8]

Negotiation Objectives

Power is a critical element when developing objectives.[9] The selling team must ask, "Do we need them more than they need us?" "What part of our service is most valuable to them?" "Can they get similar products elsewhere?" In the optimal situation, both parties share balanced power, although this is rare in practice.

In developing objectives for the session, keep in mind that the seller will almost certainly have to make concessions in the negotiation meeting. Thus, setting several objectives, or positions, is extremely important. One successful negotiator sums it up well: "You must know what *you* want!"[10]

The **target position** is what your company hopes to achieve at the negotiation session. Your team should also establish a **minimum position,** the absolute minimum level you will accept. Finally, an **opening position**—the initial proposal—should be developed.

For example, for a Baxter salesperson negotiating the price for complete food service at a hospital, the target position could be $250,000, with a minimum position of $200,000 and an opening position of $300,000. In negotiations over service levels, the seller's opening position might be weekly delivery, the target position delivery twice a week, and the minimum position (the most the seller is willing to do) delivery three times a week.

To allow for concessions, the opening position should reflect higher expectations than the target position. However, the buyer team may consider a very high target position to be unrealistic and may simply walk away. You have probably seen this happen in negotiations between countries that are at war. To avoid this, negotiators must be ready to support that opening position with solid information. Suppose the opening position for a Colgate-Palmolive negotiating team is to offer the grocer a display allowance of $1,000 (with a target position of offering $1,500). The team must be ready to prove that $1,000 is reasonable.

One team of experts recommends that negotiators plan for the upcoming meeting by employing the **mini-max strategy**.[11] This approach helps sellers understand and then prepare for the trade-offs that will undoubtedly occur in the negotiating session. The negotiator must answer four planning questions:

What is the minimum that I can accept?

What is the maximum I can ask for without getting laughed out of the room?

What is the maximum I can give away?

What is the least I can offer without getting laughed out of the room?

When developing objectives, negotiators need to sort out all issues that could arise in the meeting, prioritizing them by importance to the firm. Then they develop a set of contingency plans to get a good idea, even before the meeting begins, of their reactions and responses to the buyer's suggestions. Talking this over beforehand helps the negotiation team avoid "giving away the store" during the heat of the negotiation session. It also allows the team to draw on the expertise of company experts who will not be present during the session.

The buyer team also develops positions for the meeting. Exhibit 14.2 presents a continuum that shows how the two sets of positions relate. With the positions illus-

Exhibit 14.2

Comparing Buyer and Seller Price Positions

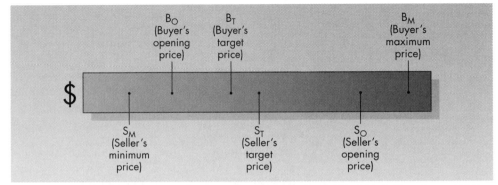

Note: See Howard Raiffa, *The Art and Science of Negotiation* (Cambridge, MA: Belknap Press, 1982), for a more complex discussion of the mathematical formulations designed to predict negotiation outcomes under various states.

Negotiating with IBM

Having International Business Machines Corporation (IBM) as a customer offers both enormous and obvious potential benefits. Purchase volumes can dwarf those of other major customers. For younger firms, an IBM contract often represents legitimacy—a springboard to recognition and respectability. And companies admitted to IBM's inner circle of favored suppliers may be rewarded with capital equipment, technical assistance, and even—on occasion—a role in IBM project planning.

But dealing with IBM also has a dark side. IBM has shrewdly structured its relationships with suppliers and potential suppliers to exploit fully its unique position as a high-volume, high-status purchaser. No other company demands as much. And no other company has so artfully refined the procedure for enforcing its demands.

Coming to Terms

Several suppliers make the point that IBM, particularly CCP (it's component purchasing group in Poughkeep-

sie), is fair in negotiating prices. Former Intel manager Jeffrey Miller, for instance, says that CCP was generally willing to pay more for products that exceeded industry standards.

But suppliers also picture IBM as an extremely tough negotiator that routinely wins serious and unusual contract concessions. "Count your fingers before and after every meeting with IBM," counsels James Porter, publisher of the annual *Disk/Trend Report.* Says Finis Conner, former vice chairman of Seagate Technology's board of directors, "IBM is a very tough negotiator because of their volumes and the leverage they can exert."

Companies that want IBM's business at any price are doomed to pay it. Companies willing to challenge IBM on contract terms and insist on purchase orders can gain some measure of protection. Also when IBM can turn to alternative sources of supply, the vendor is at an obvious disadvantage. But the supplier that has a unique product or technology or superior quality control must recognize and take advantage of its strengths.

---

trated, the parties can reach an agreement somewhere between the seller's minimum (S_M) and the buyer's maximum (B_M). However, if B_M fell to the left of S_M (had a lower maximum acceptable price), no agreement could be reached; attempts at negotiation would be futile. For example, if the buyer is not willing to pay more than $200 ($B_M$) and the seller will not accept less than $250 ($S_M$), agreement is impossible. In general, the seller desires to move as far to the right of S_M (as high a price) as possible and the buyer desires to move as far to the left of B_M (as low a price) as possible.

Negotiators need to try to anticipate these positions and evaluate them carefully. The more information collected about what the buyer hopes to accomplish, the better the negotiators will be able to manage the meeting and arrive at a win-win decision. Selling Scenario 14.1 discusses important aspects of anticipating these negotiating positions with an industry giant, IBM.

Negotiators create a plan to achieve their objectives. However, the chance of failure always exists. Thus, planners need to consider strategy revisions if the original plan should fail. The development of alternative paths to the same goal is known as **adaptive planning.**[12] For example, a firm may attempt to secure a premium shelf position using any of the following strategies:

- In return for a 5 percent price discount.
- In return for credit terms of 3/10, net 30.
- In return for a 50-50 co-op ad campaign.

SELLING SCENARIO 14.1 *(concluded)*

"It depends a lot on what the value of a product is to them. If you're the only guy that makes something they really need, you have a stronger position," says Jeffrey Miller of Adaptec.

Four times, according to Jim Watson, Quantum's vice president for marketing and sales, IBM and Quantum have sought to come to terms. Once says Watson, Quantum was told that its disk drives were acceptable but too expensive—about $100 to $125 too high per unit. IBM also wanted Quantum to invest in new plant and production equipment that, according to Watson's calculations, would have cost the Milpitas, California, firm $1.8 million. but IBM indicated that making such an investment still offered no guarantee of an IBM purchase order; the company would just have to take its chances. Then there was the matter of price reductions—which would be triggered not (as is generally the case) by the increasing volumes but simply by the passage of time. IBM also wanted Quantum to improve certain parameters in its standard products.

Quantum has declined to do business with IBM on IBM's terms. But Watson admits that he may wind up in business with IBM. The two companies continue to talk, and Watson reports that they are "coming closer and closer to amicable terms." If Quantum does eventually sign on with IBM, it will likely be under carefully negotiated terms that reflect the caution of the smaller company.

"It's always a high-risk thing to be selling to IBM, especially if you're thinking of a permanent marriage," concludes Porter. It would appear, though, that full and detailed awareness of the risks involved, a negotiating attitude every bit as tough and hardened as IBM's and a willingness to walk away from the wrong deal probably constitute the most comprehensive available insurance.

Source: Adapted from Norm Alster, "Supplying to IBM: The Obligations of Victory," *Electronic Business*, October 15, 1985, pp. 40–47. Used by permission of Reed Publishing, U.S.A.

The firm would attempt to secure the premium shelf position by using, for example, the first strategy; if that failed, it would move to the second strategy; and so forth. Fortunately, with laptop computers and software such as Excel® and Lotus 123®, negotiators can quickly calculate the profitability of various package deals for their firms.

Many firms will engage in a brainstorming session to try to develop strategies that will meet the firm's objectives. A **brainstorming session** is a meeting in which people are allowed to creatively explore different methods of achieving goals. Firms also use computer software, such as Negotiator Pro,[13] that is designed specifically to help salespeople prepare for negotiation sessions.

Once again, cultural differences exist. For example, Chinese and Russian businesspeople habitually use extreme initial offers, whereas Swedish businesspeople usually open with a price very close to their target position.[14]

Team Selection and Management[15]

So far we have discussed negotiation as though it always involves a team of both buyers and sellers. Usually this is the case. However, negotiations do occur with only two people present: the buyer and the salesperson.

Teams offer both pros and cons. Because of team members' different backgrounds, the group as a whole tends to be more creative than one individual could be. Also, team members can help one another and reduce the chances of making a "stupid" mistake. However, the more participants, the more time generally required to reach agreement. Also, team members may voice differing opinions among them-

It is important for the salesperson's team to prepare for an upcoming negotiation session. Remember that the buyer's team is also planning!

Chuck Savage/The Stock Market

selves, or one member may address a topic outside his or her area of expertise. Such things can make the seller's team appear unprepared or divisive.

In general, the seller should have a team the size of the buyer's team. Otherwise the sellers may appear to be trying to exert more power or influence in the meeting. Whenever possible, strive for the fewest team members possible. Unnecessarily large teams can get bogged down in details; also, the larger the team, the more difficult reaching a decision generally becomes.

Each team member should have a defined role in the session. For example, experts are often included to answer technical questions; executives are present as more authoritative speakers on behalf of the selling firm. Exhibit 14.3 lists the types of team members often chosen for negotiations. Many of these people take part in prenegotiation planning but do not actually attend the negotiation session.

Team members should possess the traits of good negotiators, although it often does not work out that way. For example, many technical experts have no tolerance for ambiguity and may fear conflict. As a result, the team leader needs to help them see clearly what their role is, as well as what they should *not* get involved in, during the session.

The team leader will manage the actual negotiation session. Because of their intimate knowledge of the buyers and their needs, salespeople often fill this post rather than the executive on the team. When selecting a team leader, the seller's management needs to also consider the anticipated leader of the buyer team. It is unwise to choose a leader for the selling team who may be intimidated by the buyer's leader.

The team usually develops rules about who will answer what kinds of questions, who should be the first to respond to a concession offered by the buyers, who will offer concessions from the seller's standpoint, and so on. A set of nonverbal and verbal signals is also developed so team members can communicate with one another. For example, they may agree that when the salesperson takes out a breath mint, all team members are to stop talking and let the salesperson handle all issues; or when the executive places her red book inside her briefcase, the team should move toward its target position, and the salesperson should say, "OK, let's look at some alternatives."

To ensure that team members really understand their respective roles and that all rules and signals are clearly grasped, the team should practice. This usually involves a series of videotaped role-play situations. Many firms, such as UARCO, involve their sales training department in this practice. Trainers, using detailed information supplied by the team, realistically play the roles of the buying team members.

	Title	Possible Role
EXHIBIT 14.3 People Who May Serve on the Selling Negotiation Team	Salesperson	Coordinates all functions.
	Field sales manager (district manager, regional manager, etc.)	Provides additional local and regional information. Secures necessary local funding and support for planning and presentations. Offers information on competitors.
	National sales manager/ vice president of sales	Serves as a liaison with corporate headquarters. Secures necessary corporate funding and staff support for planning and presentation. Offers competitor information.
	National account salesperson/national accounts sales managers	Provides expertise and support in dealing with large customer issues. Offers information about competitors.
	Marketing department senior executives, product managers, and staff	Provide suggestions for product/service applications. Supply market research information as well as information on packaging, new-product development, upcoming promotional campaigns, etc. Offer information about competitors.
	Chief executive officer/ president	Serves as an authority figure. Facilitates quicker decisions regarding changes in current policy and procedures. As a peer, can relate well with buyer's senior officers.
	Manufacturing executives and staff	Provide information on current scheduled production as well as the possibility/cost of any modifications in the schedule.
	Purchasing executives and staff	Provide information about raw materials inflows. Offer suggestions about possible quantity discounts from suppliers.
	Accounting and finance executives and staff	Source of cost accounting information. Supply corporate target returns on investment, cost estimates for any needed changes in the firm under various buying scenarios and information on order entry, billing, and credit systems.
	Data processing executives and staff	Provide information on current data processing systems and anticipated changes needed under various buying scenarios. Help ensure that needed periodic reports for the buyers can be generated in a timely fashion.
	Training executives and staff	Provide training for negotiation effectiveness and conduct practice role plays. Also provide information and suggestions on anticipated necessary buyer training.
	Outside consultants	Provide any kind of assistance necessary. Especially helpful if the firm has limited experience in negotiations or has not negotiated with this type of buyer before.

INDIVIDUAL BEHAVIOR PATTERNS

The team leader needs to consider the personality style of each member of both teams to spot any problems and plan accordingly. Of course, one method would be to sort the members into analyticals, amiables, expressives, and drivers based on the dimensions of assertiveness and responsiveness (see Chapter Six for a full discussion). Some leaders have developed personality profiles specifically for negotiations. We will now discuss one of the most widely used sets of negotiation profiles.

After studying actual conflict situations, a number of researchers arrived at a set of basic conflict-handling modes based on the dimensions of assertiveness and cooperativeness.[16] Exhibit 14.4 presents these five modes: competing, accommodating, avoiding, compromising, and collaborating. Note that these five styles are different than the social styles (drivers, amiables, expressives, and analyticals) we have been using throughout the book. Since all negotiations involve some degree of conflict, this typology is appropriate for use by salespeople preparing for a negotiation session.

People who resolve conflict in a **competing mode** are assertive and uncooperative. They tend to pursue their own goals and objectives completely at the expense of the other party. Often power oriented, they usually surround themselves with subordinates (often called "yes-men") who go along with their ideas. Team members who use the competing mode look for a win-lose agreement: they win, the other party loses.

Individuals in the **accommodating mode** are the exact opposite of competing people. Unassertive and highly cooperative, accommodators will neglect their own needs and desires to satisfy the concerns of the other party. In fact, they may seek a win-lose agreement, where they are the losers. Accommodators can be spotted by their excessive generosity; their constant, rapid yielding to another's point of view; and their obedience to someone else's order, even if it is obviously not something they desire to do.

Some people operate in the **avoiding mode,** an unassertive and uncooperative mode. These people do not attempt to fulfill their own needs or the needs of others. In essence, they simply refuse to address the conflict at all. They do not strive for a win-win agreement; in fact, they do not strive for any agreement.

The **compromising mode** applies to people "in the middle" in terms of cooperativeness and assertiveness. A compromiser attempts to find a quick, mutually acceptable solution that partially satisfies both parties. A compromiser gives up more than a competing person but less than an accommodating person. In many ways, the

EXHIBIT 14.4

Conflict-Handling
Behavior Modes

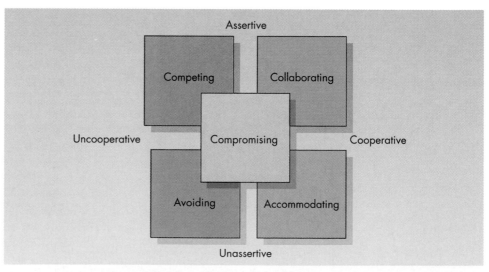

Source: Adapted from Kenneth Thomas, "Conflict and Conflict Management," in *The handbook of Industrial and Organizational Psychology,* ed. Marvin Dunnette (Skokie, IL: Rand McNally, 1976).

People exhibit different conflict-handling modes. Can you spot someone in this photo in the competing mode? The avoiding mode? The collaborating mode?

Mug Shots/The Stock Market

compromiser attempts to arrive at a win-win solution. However, the agreement reached usually does not maximize the satisfaction of the parties. For example, a compromising person might quickly suggest, "Let's just split the difference." Although this sounds fair, a better solution—one that would please both parties more—may be reached with further discussion.

Finally, people in the **collaborating mode** are both assertive and cooperative. They seek to maximize the satisfaction of both parties and hence to reach a truly win-win solution. Collaborators have the motivation, skill, and determination to really dig into an issue or a problem and explore all possible solutions. The best situation, from a negotiation standpoint, would be to have on both teams a number of people who generally use a collaborating mode.

As with the social style matrix described earlier, one person can exhibit different modes in different situations. For example, a buying negotiator who perceives that his or her position on an issue extremely vital to the long-term welfare of the company is correct may revert from a collaborating mode to a competing mode. Likewise, when potentially heavy damage could occur from confronting an issue, that same buyer might move to an avoiding mode.

Information Control

What do buyers do while selling teams engage in preparation? They prepare too! (Keep in mind that buyers have read as many books and attended as many seminars on negotiation as sellers have, because this training is one of their best negotitating tools.) They try to learn as much as they can about the seller's team and plans. This includes the seller's opening, target, and minimum positions. They also are interested in the seller's team membership and decision rules. As a result, the team leader needs to emphasize the need for security: Don't give everyone access to all information. In fact, many team members (e.g., technical support) do not need to have complete and exhaustive knowledge of all of the facts surrounding the negotiation.

As an example, one Fortune 500 firm was negotiating a $15 million deal with one of its customers.[17] The selling team's leader had to leave the room for a few minutes, and while he was gone the plant manager for the selling firm came in. The plant manager, though intending to do no harm, bragged about how his company had already invested $2 million in a prototype and retooling just to prepare for the customer's expected commitment. Needless to say, when the seller's team leader returned to the room, the buyer said he had *all* the information he needed. Two days later, the buyer was a very tough negotiator, armed with the knowledge that the seller had already commited to the project. It pays to control the flow of information!

THE NEGOTIATION MEETING

Before discussing what occurs in the negotiation meeting, we should note that some buyers will attempt to engage in a win-lose tactic of beginning to negotiate when the other party does not expect it. This tactic has been called **ambush negotiating** or **a sneak attack**.[18] It can occur during meetings prior to the negotiation meeting or even during installation of the new product. For example, during the first week of installation of a new computer system, the buyer may state, "We're going to have to renegotiate the price of this system. Since we signed that contract, we have learned of a new system being introduced by one of your competitors." The seller should never negotiate in such a situation until prepared to deal with the issue completely.

At the negotiation meeting, the buyer team and seller team physically come together and deliberate about topics important to both parties, with the goal of arriving at decisions. As mentioned earlier, this meeting usually has been preceded by one or more smaller buyer-seller meetings designed to uncover needs and explore options. Informal phone conversations probably were used to set some aspect of the agenda, learn about team members who will be present, and so on. Also, the negotiation itself may require a series of sessions to resolve all issues.

Preliminaries

Engaging in friendly conversation to break the ice before getting down to business is usually a good idea. Use this time to learn and use the names of all members on the buyer team. This is especially important in many international negotiation meetings. For example, Japanese businesspeople want to spend time developing a personal relationship before beginning negotiations. In fact, researchers have found that before negotiations begin, both sides must develop a working relationship that permits them to focus on the task.[19]

Every effort should be made to ensure a comfortable environment for all parties. Arranging ahead of time for refreshments, proper climate control, appropriate size of room, adequate lighting, and layout of furniture will go far to establish an environment conducive to negotiating.

Most negotiations occur at a rectangular table. Teams usually sit on opposite sides, with the leader of each team at the heads of the table. If possible, try to arrange for a round table or at least a seating arrangement that mixes members from each team together. This helps the parties feel they are there to face a common task and fosters a win-win atmosphere.

If the buyer team has a win-lose philosophy, expect all kinds of ploys to be used. For example, the furniture may be too large or too small or may be uncomfortable to sit in. The buyers may sit in front of large windows to force you to stare directly into sunlight. You may discover that the sellers' seats are all placed beneath heat ducts and the heat is set too high. You should not continue with the meeting until all unfavorable physical arrangements have been set right.

As far as possible, the selling team should establish a win-win environment.[20] This environment can be facilitated by avoiding any verbal or nonverbal threatening gestures, remaining calm and courteous, and adopting an attitude of investigation and experimentation. The leader might even comment:

> I can speak for my team that our goal is to reach agreements today that we can all be proud of. We come to this meeting with an open mind and look forward to exploring many avenues toward agreement. I am confident that we will both prosper and be more profitable as a result of this session.

Thinking
it
Through

What if you do everything in your power to establish a win-win attitude with the buyer team, but they insist on viewing the negotiation as a series of win-lose maneuvers? Since they won't play by win-win "rules," should you?

An **agenda,** a listing of what will and will not be discussed and in what sequence, is important for every negotiation session.[21] It helps to set boundaries and keeps everyone on track. Exhibit 14.5 offers an example of a negotiation agenda. The selling team should come to the meeting with a preliminary typed agenda. Don't be surprised when the buyer team also comes with an agenda; if they do, the first thing to be negotiated is the agenda itself. In general, putting key issues as late in the agenda as possible is advantageous. This allows time for each party to learn the other's bar-

EXHIBIT 14.5

Preliminary Negotiating
Session Agenda

Preliminary Agenda
Meeting between FiberCraft and Rome Industrial Inc.
Proposed New Spin Machine for 15 FiberCraft Plants
November 14, 1998

1. Introductions by participants.
2. Agree on the meeting agenda.
3. Issues:
   a. Who will design the new machine?
   b. Who will pay the costs of testing the machine?
   c. Who will have ownership rights on the new machine (if it is ever built for someone else)?
   d. Who will be responsible for maintaining and servicing the new machine during trial runs?
   e. Who will pay for any redesign work needed?
4. Coffee break.
5. Issues:
   a. How and when will the machines be set up in the 15 locations? Who will be responsible for installation?
   b. What percentage will be required for a down payment?
   c. What will the price be? Will there be any price escalation provisions? If not, how long is this price protected?
6. Summary of agreement.

gaining style and concession routines. Moreover, agreement has already been reached on the minor issues, which, in a win-win situation, supports an atmosphere for reaching agreement on the major issues.

General Guidelines

To negotiate effectively, the seller team must put into practice the skills discussed throughout this book. For example, listening carefully is extremely important. This involves not only being silent when the buyer talks but also asking good probing questions to resolve confusion and misunderstanding.

The team leader must keep track of issues discussed or resolved. During complicated negotiations, many items may be discussed simultaneously. Also, some issues may be raised but not fully addressed before someone raises a separate issue. The leader can provide great assistance by giving periodic status reports, including what has been resolved and the issues being discussed. More important, he or she can map out what still needs to be discussed. In essence, this mapping establishes a new agenda for the remainder of the negotiation session.

Once again, cultural differences are important in negotiations. For example, most Americans are uncomfortable with silence; most Japanese, on the other hand, are much more comfortable with extended periods of silence. Americans negotiating with Japanese businesspeople usually find this silence very stressful. Negotiators must prepare themselves for such probabilities and learn ways to reduce stress and cope in this situation.

Finally, keep in mind that during negotiations, people need to save face. **Face** is defined as the person's desire for a positive identity or self-concept. Of course, not all people strive for the same face (e.g., some want to appear "cool," some "macho," some "crass," etc.). Negotiators will at least try to maintain face and may even use the negotiation session to improve or strengthen this identity.[22]

Dealing with Win-Lose Negotiators

Many books have been written and many consultants have grown rich teaching both buyers and sellers strategies for effective negotiating. Unfortunately, many of these techniques are designed to achieve a win-lose situation. We will describe several to illustrate the types of tactics buyers might engage in during negotiations.[23] Such knowledge will help the negotiating team defend its position under such attacks.

Both buyers and sellers occasionally engage in the win-lose strategies described here. However, because we are assuming sellers will adopt a win-win perspective, this section will focus on how to handle buyers who engage in these techniques. Exhibit 14.6 presents an effective overall strategy for dealing with win-lose negotiators.

Good Guy–Bad Guy Routine

You have probably seen the **good guy–bad guy routine** if you watch many police movies or TV shows. A tough police detective interrogating the suspect gets a little rough. The detective uses bright lights and intimidation. After a few minutes, a second officer (who has been watching this) asks his or her companion to "go out and get some fresh air." While the tough detective (the "bad guy") is outside, the other detective (the "good guy") apologizes for his or her partner's actions. The good guy goes on to advise the crook to confess now and receive good treatment rather than wait and have the bad guy harass him or her some more.

EXHIBIT 14.6

What to Do
When the Buyer Turns
to Win-Lose Strategies

Detach yourself	Don't respond right away. Instead, give yourself time to think about the issue. Say something like "Hold on, I'm not sure I follow you. Let's go back over what you just said again." Use the time you have gained to rethink your positions and what would be in the best interests of both parties.
Acknowledge their position, then respond	In using this tool, you are trying to create a favorable climate for your response. You would start off by mentioning what you agree with by saying something like "Yes, you have a good point there when you said . . ." After agreeing, you then make your point. For example, you might conclude the example sentence with something like ". . . and I would like to make sure you continue to have minimal downtime. And for that to happen, you know, we really need to have someone from your firm attend the training. . . ." This tool is somewhat similar to the indirect denial and boomerang techniques discussed in Chapter Eleven.
Build them a bridge	To do this, you come up with a solution that incorporates the buyer's suggestion. For example, you might state, "Building on your idea, what if we . . ." or "I got this idea from something really neat you said at our meeting last Friday. . . ." Using this tool helps the buyer save face.
Warn, but don't threaten	Sometimes you may have to help the buyer understand the consequences of his or her position. For example, if the buyer indicates she or he must have a cheaper fabric for the furniture in an office building, you might say something like "I know how important the choice of fabric is to your firm's image, but if you choose that fabric, you won't achieve the image you're really looking for. How much will that cost you in lost clients who might not get a sense that you are very successful?" A warning is not the same thing as a threat. A threat is what will happen if you don't get *your* way; a warning is what will happen if they do get *their* way.

Sources: Jeff Tanner, "Partnering-Based Negotiations," *Exhibitor Times*, August 1994, pp. 38–39; William Ury, *Getting Past No: Negotiating with Difficult People* (New York: Bantam Books, 1991).

Negotiators often try the same routine. One member of the buyer team (the bad guy) makes all sorts of outlandish statements and requests:

> Look, we've got to buy these for no more than $15 each, and we must have credit terms of 2/10, net 60. After all the business we've given you in the past, I can't believe you won't agree to those terms!

Then another member of the buyer team (the good guy) takes over and appears to offer a win-win solution by presenting a lower demand:

> Hang on, Jack. These are our friends. Sure, we've given them a lot of business, but remember they've been good to us as well! I believe we should let them make a decent profit, so $15.50 would be more reasonable.

According to theory, the seller's negotiator is so relieved to find a friend that he or she jumps on the good guy's suggestion.

As an effective defense against such tactics, the selling team must know its position clearly and not let the buyer's strategy weaken it. (Obviously, the selling team needs the ability to spot a good guy–bad guy tactic.) A good response might be:

> We understand your concern. But based on all the facts of the situation, we still feel our proposal is a fair one for all parties involved.

Lowballing

You may also have experienced **lowballing.** Car dealers have used it for years. The salesperson says, "This car sells for $19,613." After you agree to purchase it, what happens? "Oh, I forgot to tell you that we have to charge you for dealer prep and destination charges, as well as an undercoating already applied to the car. So let's see, the total comes to $20,147. Gee, I'm sorry I didn't mention those expenses before!" Most people go ahead and buy. Why? They have already verbally committed themselves and do not want to go against their agreement. Also, they do not want to start the search process over again.

The technique is also used in buyer-seller negotiations in industrial situations. For example, after the sellers have signed a final agreement with the buyer team, one of the buyer team members says, "Oh, I forgot to mention that all of our new contracts must specify FOB destination and the seller must assume all shipping insurance expenses."

The best response to lowballing is to just say *no*. Remind the buyer team that the agreement has been finalized. The threat of lowballing underscores the importance of getting signatures on contracts and agreements as soon as possible. If the buyers insist on the new items, the selling team will simply be forced to reopen the negotiations. (Try this on car dealers too!)

A variation of lowballing, **nibbling,** is a small extra, or add-on, the buyer requests after the deal has been closed. Compared to lowballing, a nibble is a much smaller request. For example, one of the buyers may state, "Say, could you give us a one-time 5 percent discount on our first order? That would sure make our boss happy and make us look like we negotiated hard for her." Nibbling often works because the request is so small compared to the entire agreement.

The selling team's response to the nibble depends on the situation. It may be advantageous to go ahead and grant a truly small request that could be easily met. On the other hand, if the buyer team uses nibbling often, it may need to be restricted. Again, the best strategy is to agree on the seller's position before the meeting begins and set guidelines for potential nibbles. Often the seller grants a nibble only if the buyer agrees to some small concession in return.

Thinking *it* Through	Suppose you are in a very important negotiation session and one of your teammates makes a statement that is not true. What will you do or say? What are the consequences of your action?

Emotional Outbursts

How do you react when a close friend suddenly starts crying, gets angry, or looks very sad? Most of us think, "What have *I* done to cause this?" We tend to feel guilty, become uneasy, and try to find a way to make the person stop crying. That is simply human nature.

If a member of the buying team engages in an emotional outburst tactic, the seller should never respond in like fashion.

Bruce Ayres/Tony Stone Images

Occasionally buyer teams will appeal to your human nature by engaging in an **emotional outburst tactic.** For example, one of the buyers may look directly at you, shake his or her head sadly, slowly look down, and say softly,

> I can't believe it's come to this. You know we can't afford that price. And we've been good partners all these years. I don't know what to say.

This is followed by complete silence among the entire buyer team. They hope you will feel uncomfortable and give in to their demands. In an extreme case, one or more buyers would actually walk out of the room or begin to shout.

The selling team, once again, needs to recognize this behavior as the technique it is. Assuming no logical reason exists for the outburst, the negotiators should respond with a gentle but firm reminder of the merits of the offer and attempt to move the buyer group back into a win-win negotiating frame of mind.

Budget Limitation Tactic

In the **budget limitation tactic,** also called a **budget bogey,** the buyer team states something like the following:

> The proposal looks great. We need *every* facet of the program you are proposing in order for it to work in our business. But our budget allows us only $250,000 total, including all costs. You'll have to come down from $300,000 to that number, or I'm afraid we can't afford it.

This may be an absolutely true statement. If so, at least you know what you have to work with. Of course, claims of budget ceilings are sometimes just a ploy to try to get a lower price.

The best defense against budget limitations is to do your homework before going into the negotiation session. Learn as much as you can about budgets and maximums allowed. Have alternative programs or proposals ready that incorporate cost reduction measures. After being told of a budget limitation during the negotiation session, probe to make sure it is valid. Check the possibility of splitting the cost of the proposal over several fiscal years. Probe to find out if the buyer would be willing to accept more risk for a lower price or to have some of the installation work done by the buyer's staff. You can also help to forestall this tactic by working closely with the buyer prior to the negotiation meeting, providing reasonable ballpark estimates of the cost of the proposal.

Browbeating

Sometimes buyers will attempt to alter the selling team's enthusiasm and self-respect by **browbeating** them. One buyer might make a comment like the following:

> Say, I've been reading some pretty unflattering things about your company in *The Wall Street Journal* lately. Seems like you can't keep your unions happy or your nonunion employees from organizing. It must be tough to get out of bed and go to work every day, huh?

If the selling team feels less secure and slightly inferior after such a comment, the tactic was successful.

You should not let browbeating comments influence you or your proposal. That's easier said than done, of course. Presumably you were able to identify in prenegotiation meetings that this buyer had this type of personality. If so, you could prepare by simply telling yourself that browbeating will occur but you will not let it affect your decisions. If you can make it through one such comment, buyers usually will not offer any more because they can see that browbeating will not help them achieve their goals.

One response to such a statement would be to practice negotiation jujitsu.[24] In **negotiation jujitsu,** the salesperson steps away from the opponent's attack and then directs the opponent back to the issues being discussed. For example, the salesperson may say,

> We are concerned about our employees and are working to resolve all problems as quickly as we can. If you have any ideas that would help us in this regard, we would appreciate them. Now, we were discussing price . . .

Making Concessions

One of the most important activities in any negotiation is the granting and receiving of concessions from the other party. One party makes a **concession** when it agrees to change a position in some fashion. For example, if your opening price position was $500, you would be granting a concession if you agreed to lower the price to $450.

Based on many successful negotiations in a wide range of situations, a number of guidelines have been formulated to make concessions effectively:[25]

1. Never make concessions until you know all of the buyer's demands and opening position. Use probing to help reveal these.
2. Never make a concession unless you get one in return, and don't feel guilty about receiving a concession.
3. Concessions should gradually decrease in size. At first, you may be willing to offer "normal-size" concessions. As time goes on, however, you should make much smaller ones. This helps the prospect see that you are approaching your target position and are becoming much less willing to concede.

4. If a requested concession does not meet your objectives, don't be afraid to simply say, "No. I'm sorry, but I just can't do that."

5. All concessions you offer are tentative until the final agreement is reached and signed. Remember that you may have to take back one of your concessions if the situation changes.

6. Be confident and secure in your position, and don't give concessions carelessly. If you don't follow this advice, your buyers may have less respect for your negotiating and business skills. Everyone wants to conduct business with someone who is sharp and who will still be in business in the future. Don't give the impression that you are not and will not.

7. Don't accept the buyer's first attempt at a concession. Chances are the buyer has built in some leeway and is simply testing the water.

8. Help the buyer to see the value of any concessions you agree to. Don't assume the buyer will understand the total magnitude of your "generosity."

9. Start the negotiation without preconceived notions. Even though the buyers may have demanded certain concessions in the past, they may not do so in this negotiation meeting.

10. If, after making a concession, you realize you made some sort of mistake, tell the buyer and begin negotiating that issue again. For example, if you made a concession of delivery every two weeks instead of every four weeks but then realized that your fleet of trucks cannot make that route every two weeks, bring the issue back on the table for renegotiation.

11. Don't automatically agree to a "Let's just split the difference" offer by the buyers. Check out the offer to see how it compares to your target position.

12. If customer says something like "Tell us what your best price is and we'll tell you whether we are interested or not," remain noncommital. Respond with "In most cases, a price of $_ is the best we can do. However, if you want to make me a proposal, we'll see what we can do."[26]

13. Know when to stop. Don't keep trying to get and get and get *even if you are able.*

14. Use silence effectively. Studies have shown cultural differences in the negotiator's ability to use silence. For example, Brazilians make more initial concessions than Americans, who make more than the Japanese.[27]

The granting and receiving of concessions is often very complex and can result in the negotiations taking months or years to complete. Selling Scenario 14.2 describes some of the unusual concessions resulting from negotiations between Coca-Cola and the University of Minnesota, Twin Cities campus.

Recap of a Successful Negotiation Meeting

By setting the proper environment early in the meeting, you are well on your way to a successful negotiation. Remember to develop an agenda, and be aware of win-lose strategies that buyers may use. Offer concessions strategically.

When the session is over, be sure to get any negotiated agreements in writing. If no formal contract is possible, at least summarize the agreements reached.

Studies have shown that more cooperation exists if both sides expect future interactions.[28] Keep in mind that your goal is to develop a long-term partnership with your buyer. This process can be aided by being levelheaded, courteous, and, above all, honest. Also, do not try to get every concession possible out of your buyer. If

SELLING SCENARIO 14.2

U of M signs agreement with Coca-Cola

The University of Minnesota and Midwest Coca-Cola Bottling Corporation signed a 10-year partnership agreement in January, giving Coke exclusive soft drink vending rights for the Twin Cities campus. The agreement is expected to bring the University $28 million dollars, making it by far the most comprehensive and lucrative beverage contract ever signed by a higher education institution, according to McKinley Boston, vice president for student development and athletics. (The previous largest was a 10-year, $15-million deal between Penn State University and Pepsi-Cola.)

Of the $28 million, $15 million is guaranteed, $6 million of which will be donated up front and deposited into an endowment to support specific University objectives such as gender equity in athletics and campus life enhancements.

The agreement culminates a yearlong effort by the University to create a national model for beverage partnering in higher education. A University-wide beverage council was formed in January 1995 in anticipation of the June 30, 1996, expiration of the current contract with Pepsi. Its charge was to explore new ways of partnering to increase revenue to the institution in time of declining state and federal support.

When the University solicited bids in October, "both Coke and Pepsi responded with creative and aggressive proposals that addressed our financial as well as nonfinancial objectives," says Boston. Coke was ultimately chosen because their proposal represented "the best financial program with the least financial risk."

More than just a contract to sell soda, the partnership also allows for the University to tap into Coke's considerable marketing expertise in setting up programs aimed at making campus life more fun. Some ideas suggested in the Coke proposal include providing incoming freshmen with "goody bags" during orientation week and holding special spring break activities for students who stay in the Twin Cities area. Coke has also committed to sponsoring academic programs, such as internships and a speaker series on career development, as well as community programs, such as hiring University students to tutor inner-city junior high and high school students.

Source: Reprinted from *Kiosk,* February 1996, p. 2, the University of Minnesota's monthly faculty/staff newspaper.

you push too hard or too long, the buyer will get irritated and may even walk out. Never let this happen by being too greedy. Remember your goal: to reach a win-win settlement.

SUMMARY

This chapter described how to engage in win-win negotiating. It also described how buyers may engage in win-lose negotiating.

Almost anything can be negotiated. The areas of negotiation will depend on the needs of both parties and the extent of disagreement on major issues.

A successful salesperson is not necessarily a good negotiator. Important negotiator traits include patience and endurance, willingness to take risks, a tolerance for ambiguity, the ability to deal with conflict, and the ability to engage in negotiation without worrying that every person present will not be on one's side.

As in regular sales calls, careful planning counts. This involves choosing the location, setting objectives, and developing and managing the negotiating team. The salesperson does not act alone in these tasks but draws on the full resources of the firm.

Preliminaries are important in sales negotiation sessions. Friendly conversation and small talk can help to reduce tensions and establish some degree of rapport. Agendas help to set boundaries and keep the negotiation on track. Win-lose strategies that buyers use include a good guy–bad guy routine, lowballing, emotional outbursts, budget limitation, and browbeating. As much as possible, the salesperson should respond to any win-lose maneuvers calmly and with the intent of bringing the other side back to a win-win stance.

Concessions, by definition, will occur in every negotiation. Many guidelines have been established to help negotiators avoid obvious problems. For example, no concession should be given unless the buyer gives a concession of equal value. Also, any concessions given are not formalized until the written agreement is signed; thus, all concessions are subject to removal, if appropriate.

KEY TERMS

accommodating mode 408
adaptive planning 404
agenda 411
ambush negotiating 410
avoiding mode 408
brainstorming session 405
browbeating 416
budget bogey 415
budget limitation tactic 409
collaborating mode 408
competing mode 408
compromising mode 408
concession 416
emotional outburst tactic 415

face 412
good guy–bad guy routine 412
lowballing 414
mini-max strategy 403
minimum position 402
negotiation 398
negotiation jujitsu 416
nibbling 414
opening position 403
sneak attack 410
target position 402
win-lose negotiating 398
win-win negotiating 398

QUESTIONS AND PROBLEMS

1. What are the advantages of having a sales job that involves only selling by negotiation? What disadvantages could such a job have?

2. Think about recent encounters you either have had or have witnessed that involved negotiations. Did each party use a win-win perspective or a win-lose perspective? What clues did you use to make that determination?

3. Salesperson Jim Keyes enjoys meeting people and helping them solve their problems. Although he is excited when he obtains commitment, he really went into selling because he has a strong need to make friends and develop relationships. He is very patient and not averse to taking risks. Because his parents were in the military, he is accustomed to moving a lot and has developed a tolerance for ambiguity and new situations. Do you believe Jim will make a good negotiator? Why or why not?

4. "As a negotiator, solving your opponent's problem is your problem." Comment.

5. Assume you are going to have your fourth and final job interview with Camadon, an office equipment firm, next Friday. Knowledgeable friends have told you that since you "passed" the first three interviews, you will be offered the job during the fourth interview. Also, you know that Camadon likes to negotiate with its new hires.

   a. Think about your own needs and desires for your first job (e.g., salary, expense reimbursement, benefits, geographic location, promotion cycle).

   b. For each need and desire listed, establish your target position, opening position, and minimum position.

     c. Camadon has probably also developed positions that would meet each of your needs and desires. Describe how you might go about discovering these positions before next Friday's meeting.

6. Mary Joyner, a salesperson for Nabisco, is preparing for an important negotiation session with Kroger, a large, national food chain, regarding an upcoming promotional campaign. Her boss has strongly suggested that he attend the meeting with her. The problem is that her boss is not a good negotiator; he tends to get angry, is unorganized, and tries to resolve conflict by talking nonstop and thus wearing down the buyer team with fatigue. Her boss definitely has a win-lose negotiating philosophy. What should Mary do?

7. "You are the worst possible person to have negotiate for yourself. You care too much about the outcome. Always let someone else negotiate for you." State your reaction to this statement. What implications does it have in industrial sales negotiations?

8. During the negotiation session, buyers make all kinds of statements. What would be your response to the following, assuming each occurred early in the meeting?

     a. "We refuse to pay more than $3.20 each. That's our bottom line—take it or leave it!"

     b. "Come on, you've got to do better than that!"

     c. "You know, we're going to have to get anything we decide here today approved by our corporate management before we can sign any kind of a contract."

     d. "One of our buyers can't make it here for another hour. But let's go ahead and get started and see what progress we can make."

     e. "Tell you what, we need to see a detailed cost breakdown for each individual item in your proposal."

9. "Try to get a big concession from your opponent by giving away a small, insignificant concession yourself." Comment.

10. Negotiators have been known to lie during an important meeting. How can you tell whether or not buyers are lying? What should you do if you catch them telling a lie?

11. "If your opponent begins to use an unethical tactic, walk out of the room." Comment.

EXPLORING THE NET

Many people and firms will, for a fee, teach you how to be a better negotiator. Many of these have pages on the Web advertising their services. Search the Web for these pages. Although addresses for these sites might change a great deal, here are two you can try:

    http://www.fortune-group.com/RevGen/NEG.html

    http://web.wn.net/~usr/ricter/web/negotiation/goals.html

After finding two pages on the Web, answer the following questions.

1. To what extent do these training firms cover the topics discussed in this chapter? What additional topics do they cover? What topics do they not seem to cover?

2. Do you think the training that is described is tailored for salespeople or buyers? Why?

CASE PROBLEMS

CASE 14.1
Ingersoll-Rand*

Ingersoll-Rand is a 125-year-old worldwide company that produces a wide array of products, including industrial air compressors, architectural hardware, bearings and drivetrain components, golf carts and light-duty vehicles for off-road applications, road construction products, industrial pumps, loaders and excavators, and fastener-tightening systems. The firm is divided into nine separate operating groups. It has total annual sales of over $5 billion and more than 41,000 employees worldwide.

Guanta Kittikachorn is a salesperson for Ingersoll-Rand Pump Company in Thailand. This division offers pumps for industrial use and specialty pumps for process, power generation, and marine applications. Kittikachorn has a complete line of pumps she can sell, including centrifugal, diaphragm, reciprocating, rotary, and turbine pumps. She has been quite successful selling pumps to a number of businesses involved in chemical processing, construction, and fossil fuel generation plants.

Hat Yai Oil contacted Kittikachorn about four months ago to discuss its new oil refinery needs. The new refinery will produce gasoline, diesel fuel, and asphalt products. In six long meetings with the firm, Kittikachorn learned that Hat Yai needed more than 300 pumps to meet production needs. After carefully planning for the negotiation session, Kittikachorn and four other employees of Ingersoll-Rand (her sales manager, two design engineers, and the regional manager for her operating group) sat down to meet with negotiators from Hat Yai. Pibul Charusathien, the vice president of purchasing for Hat Yai, was the chief negotiator for his team.

The meeting began cordially, with both teams introducing their members and agreeing on an agenda for the meeting. After a few minutes of pleasant conversation, Charusathien made the following statement: "I'm glad we are here today, because I think this is a golden opportunity for both sides to win. I have been impressed with the product information that Guanta has shared with me. Your products seem to be top quality, which is something we demand. I've talked to several references that Guanta gave me information about, and they are all happy with the service and products they receive from you. Let me start the ball rolling by saying that we are willing to buy not only our pumps from you but also all of our air compressors and pneumatic cylinders from you. In fact, we would like to establish a partnership with Ingersoll-Rand by purchasing every item that you sell that we will have a need for. This assumes, of course, that you will give us a large discount off your list price. We are willing to enter into this agreement with you if you will give us a 40 percent discount across the board on every item that you sell. What do you say to that?"

Kittikachorn was stunned. In all of her premeeting sessions with Charusathien, he had never mentioned any arrangement like this. All of Ingersoll's planning had assumed the purchase of 300 pumps and nothing more. The situation was further compounded by the fact that Ingersoll-Rand is set up into different divisions, with each division having its own sales force. Charusathien's offer would involve at least four other divisions of her firm.

As she sat staring at her pencil, thinking hard, Charusathien spoke again: "I see I've caught you a little off guard. No? Well, if we're going to come to any agreement, we need to do it today. I have to move ahead and start ordering components for the new plant to ensure that everything will be ready when it is time to install. As you know, there are other firms that can supply these components." He paused, then smiled and continued, "I'll tell you what. We'll step out of the room and let your team discuss this. Okay? We'll be back in, say, an hour. Okay?"

*Information about the company was derived partly from the 1995 annual report of Ingersoll-Rand.

Questions

1. Evaluate the negotiation session to this point. How could Kittikachorn have better prepared for the meeting?

2. What should Kittikachorn do now? Be explicit, and give reasons for your answers.

CASE 14.2 Identifying Conflict-Handling Modes

This chapter describes a number of basic conflict-handling modes that people use in negotiation. These include competing, collaborating, compromising, avoiding, and accommodating.

Carefully reread the section that describes these modes. Then identify someone you know who falls into one of each of the five modes and answer the following questions for each person identified.

Questions

1. How do you know this person is "competing?" What specific behaviors of the person have you observed or heard about that support your assertion?

2. How do you (and/or others) interact with this person during a conflict situation? What do you do? How do you respond to this person's behavior? Is your approach effective?

3. Would you like to have this person on your team during an important negotiation session? Why or why not?

ADDITIONAL
REFERENCES

Alexander, Joe F.; Patrick L. Schul; and Denny E. McCorkle. "An Assessment of Selected Relationships in a Model of the Industrial Marketing Negotiation Process." *Journal of Personal Selling and Sales Management,* Summer 1994, pp. 25–39.

Batson, Bryan. "Chinese Fortunes: The Rewards of Marketing in China Can Be Great—but So Too Are the Challenges." *Sales & Marketing Management,* March 1994, pp. 93–98.

Cauthern, Cynthia R. "Moving Technical Support into the Sales Loop." *Sales & Marketing Management,* August 1990, pp. 58–61.

Chang, Kuochung, and Cherng G. Ding. "The Influence of Culture on Industrial Buying Selection Criteria in Taiwan and Mainland China." *Industrial Marketing Management,* 24 (1995), pp. 277–84.

Dawson, Roger. *Roger Dawson's Secrets of Power Negotiating.* Franklin Lakes, NJ: Career Press, 1995.

DeRose, Louis J. "Negotiating Value." *Sales & Marketing Management,* October 1990, pp. 108–9.

Falvey, Jack. "Team Selling: What It Is (and Isn't)." *Sales & Marketing Management,* June 1990, pp. 8–10.

Fisher, Roger, and William Ury. *Getting to Yes: Negotiating Agreement without Giving In,* 2nd ed. Boston: Houghton Mifflin, 1991.

Frank, Sergey. "Global Negotiating: Vive Les Differences!" *Sales & Marketing Management,* May 1992, pp. 64–69.

Gschwandtner, Gerhard. "How to Sell in France." *Personal Selling Power,* July/August 1991, pp. 54–60.

Hall, Lavinia, ed. *Negotiation: Strategies for Mutual Gain.* Newbury Park, CA: Sage Publications, 1993.

Joseph, W. Benoy; John T. Gardner; Sharon Thach; and Frances Vernon. "How Industrial Distributors View Distributor-Supplier Partnership Arrangements." *Industrial Marketing Management,* 24 (1995), pp. 27–36.

Karras, Chester L. *Give and Take: The Complete Guide to Negotiating Strategies and Tactics.* New York: Harper Collins, 1993.

Keller, Robert E. *Sales Negotiation Handbook.* Englewood Cliffs, NJ: Prentice Hall, 1988.

Kennedy, Danielle. "Let's Make a Deal: Successful Negotiations Are Based on Respect, Not Hard-Sell Tactics." *Entrepreneur,* October 1996. pp. 104–6.

Leritz, Len. *No-Fault Negotiating: A Practical Guide to the New Dealmaking Strategy That Lets Both Sides Win.* New York: Warner, 1987.

Morrison, William F. *The Prenegotiation Handbook.* New York: Wiley, 1985.

Nierenberg, Gerald I. *Negotiating the Big Sale: Super Strategies for Smart Dealmakers.* Berkeley, CA: Berkeley Publishing Group, 1992.

Richardson, Linda. *Winning Group Sales Presentations.* Burr Ridge, IL: Dow Jones-Irwin, 1990.

Royal, Weld. "Passport to Peril." *Sales & Marketing Management,* December 1994, pp. 74–78.

Selling to resellers—the trade—differs somewhat from other forms of selling. In this chapter, we explore those differences. (The answers to the questions below will sometimes also apply to industrial or institutional sales, but in a different manner.) By examining the arena of trade selling, you will understand more fully

Chapter Fifteen

Selling *to* Resellers

Some Questions Answered in this Chapter Are:

What is a reseller?

How does buying for resale differ from other forms of buying?

What common terms and conditions apply to such sales, and how do they affect sales?

How does a salesperson aid resellers in merchandising the product?

What role do trade shows and markets play in the sale of goods to the trade?

How do national accounts managers interact with field salespeople?

the role of the salesperson in marketing a product, both from a strategic, or executive, viewpoint and from the perspective of the field sales representative. Also, you will more fully understand the different roles salespeople play.

PROFILE

ConAgra is hardly a household name, but you probably know all its brands. Products such as Hunts Ketchup, Wesson Oil, and Healthy Choice foods make up just a few of the leading brands ConAgra manufactures and markets.

Julie Autry just finished her first year with ConAgra, after working for a year representing the Nexxus line of hair products following her graduation from SMU. "My primary function with ConAgra is to make sure that all products authorized by the retailer—Kroger, Albertsons, or Food Lion—are on the shelf and in the proper location so the consumer can purchase the product," Autry says. She visits each store in her territory every two weeks, checking the location of her products, the number of facings, and pricing information.

More important than selling large displays or pallets of products is ensuring the everyday availability of ConAgra products. Autry explains, "My number one priority is ensuring 100 percent distribution on all ConAgra products on every store call. We've found that more money is made when a product is displayed appropriately on the shelf and sold at the regular price than when the product is featured [in advertising] and displayed in a special endcap display. If the product is not available on the shelf, then the sale is lost." Selling displays or pallet quantities still plays an important role in supporting promotions, but having the product always in the right place and available is Autry's goal.

"Because they trust me and know that I don't oversell, they often go with what I suggest. I make their day much easier and their store much more profitable."

Healthy Choice foods are a good example. Healthy Choice leads its category with a 53 percent market share in the Dallas/Ft. Worth market. Therefore, Healthy Choice should have half or more of the freezer space, but may not lead the category's sales in a particular store. "From time to time, I enter a situation where the shelf space is not reflective of Healthy Choice's market share. This is where my job begins," Autry says. She knows that proper display of Healthy Choice will increase sales for the entire category. "Using data from IRI [an independent research company], I educate the manager on the whole premium dinner category. I present the latest DFW market share information, which tells the manager that by making a merchandising change [changing the allocation of shelf space], the store and ConAgra will benefit."

Not all ConAgra products are category leaders. Autry would not use that strategy to sell the ConAgra brand of chili, for example, because a competitor leads that market. In that case, "I

JULIE AUTRY
ConAgra

would make sure the product was in the store and in its proper location." She doesn't want that category leader taking her fair share of space for chili any more than she would allow Healthy Choice to have less than its fair share.

Autry recognizes the importance of building trust with her customers and always acting in their best interest: "Almost no other salespeople are in my customers' stores as frequently as I am. I am like another person on their staff, and they know that and trust me. That's one reason why I like working for ConAgra—we really work for our customers."

One function Autry helps her customers manage is inventory. "Food Lion has an automatic ordering system that orders our products via computer. When a product is sold, their computer decrements their inventory, and when it reaches a certain level, the computer orders more. But in most of my stores, the manager has to walk the aisle and enter orders into a hand-held computer, which takes up a lot of their time." During her visit to the store, Autry checks distribution and often generates a suggested order for her managers. "Because they trust me and know that I don't oversell, they often go with what I suggest. I make their day much easier and their store much more profitable."

What's next? Autry hopes to soon manage accounts like Kroger and Food Lion at the headquarters level as an account manager. "At

425

that level, I will work with accounts to develop cooperative advertising programs, special promotions, and also to gain acceptance of new products." In her short time with ConAgra, she has already received one promotion and successfully sold special promotions such as the Healthy Choice Mega Event. For now, she's happy with the challenge of boosting sales in the 42 stores that she visits every two weeks.

Visit Our Website@
http://www.crfi.com

Many people conjure up pictures of industrial salespeople selling the machinery that pounds away in a manufacturing plant or of a retail sales clerk assisting a shopper who is trying on a jacket. But selling to resellers may be a little harder to picture.

WHO ARE RESELLERS?

Resellers are all members of the channel of distribution that resell the product between the manufacturer and the user. Facilitators (e.g., banks, advertising agencies, transportation firms) would not be considered part resellers, but wholesalers, retailers, and other distributors fall under the broad umbrella of reseller.

Many people think of resellers in terms of consumer packaged goods; that is, selling to resellers involves getting a product on the shelf of a grocer or a discounter such as Wal-Mart. But this is actually only a small part of selling to resellers.

Titleist, for example, manufactures golf balls, clubs, and other products. Its sales force is responsible for assisting golf courses, pro shops, discount stores, and other retailers in merchandising and selling golf balls and other products. Titleist sells to golfers through retail outlets, as shown in Exhibit 15.1.

Broyhill, which manufactures furniture, provides another example. Its salespeople identify and sell Broyhill furniture to furniture retailers at annual furniture markets in High Point (North Carolina), Dallas, and Chicago. During the year, the reps assist their dealers in advertising, inventory management, and other merchandising tasks.

Selling to resellers may involve helping stores take inventory or assisting individual distributors merchandise products such as these WICOR pumps.

Jeff Zaruba/Tony Stone Images

Courtesy WICOR Inc.

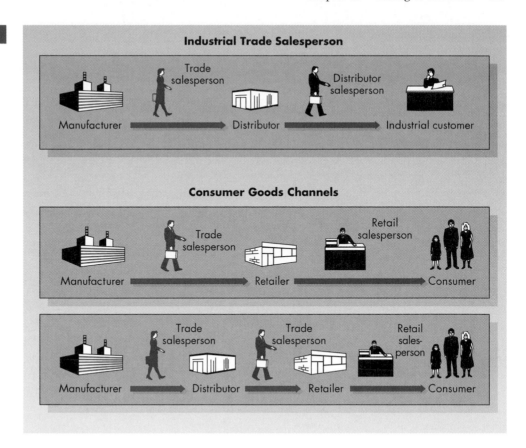

EXHIBIT 15.1

Where Trade
Salespeople Fit
in Channels of
Distribution

Not all trade selling involves selling consumer products through retailers. Agricultural equipment is also sold through dealers. Brazos Farm and Equipment is a John Deere dealer. In Brazos's showroom, a John Deere salesperson sets up displays of John Deere toy tractors, lawn and garden equipment, and farm equipment parts and accessories. The sales representative teaches Brazos salespeople how to sell John Deere tractors and farm implements. The rep also assists Brazos with the local advertising of Deere products. Dealers do not have to carry all of Deere's products or participate in all of Deere's marketing programs, but seeing that they do participate is the job of the Deere rep.

Industrial products are also sold through resellers, or distributors, particularly when selling in other countries. Canon, for example, is a Japanese manufacturer of copiers, laser printers, fax machines, and other office equipment. In the United States, Canon distributes these products through a network of dealers, and in Japan, it sells direct to users. In the United States, Canon reps call on dealers and train them in the selling and use of new products.

Resellers can be involved in the distribution of many types of products. Even when the final user is industrial or agricultural, salespeople are important to their reseller buyers. As you can see in Selling Scenario 15.1, resellers want to build partnerships with their suppliers.

**Resellers Offer
Sales Space**

Resellers provide an important element in the place function of marketing (remember the four Ps?). They offer selling space to manufacturers, and battling for that space is a primary point of competition among manufacturers. When resellers are

Salespeople are Important Partners!

Caralee Bradbury, manager of George's Casual and Western Wear, recognizes the importance of salespeople in helping her and her store be successful. "We make better business decisions with the aid of knowledgeable salespeople," she declares.

"Knowing my customer is essential," says Bradbury. She believes the salesperson must study the final buyer to discover what merchandise will see best. Vendor salespeople have access to different customer information than she does. When a partnership is formed and all partners share the information collected, all parties profit.

Bradbury notes that "Salespeople also bring imagination and fresh idea." Salespeople visit many stores daily and gather creative ideas from each store. The reseller, however, goes through the same routine each day. A salesperson is an outsider who can introduce new ways to produce business. "We trust our salespeople not to share our creative ideas with our direct competitors, but they call on many stores with which we don't compete. So in those situations, the salesperson can be a creative asset," Bradbury says.

Some of the creative ideas Bradbury has gotten from salespeople are anniversary sales, using joint promotions to create huge sales and customer giveaways, and other special events. "Salespeople also help us merchandise their products in our stores," she says. "When they understand our market, they can help us create the right in-store image that is supported by their marketing and really sells the product."

Bradbury depends on her salespeople for more than just creative ideas, however. She notes that sometimes a supplier does not want to accept returned defective merchandise. Then she depends on the salesperson to represent her case to the manufacturer. "The longer we work as a team, the more successful we both become because we understand each other. We're partners."

authorized dealers for a single company's products, shelf space is not a concern. For example, Hallmark salespeople sell cards and gifts to Hallmark store owners. But these same salespeople also sell to stores such as Kmart and HEB grocery stores, and have to compete with American Greetings and other card companies for the right to sell their cards.

For example, Kraft, Lipton, and Rice-a-Roni all manufacture a noodles alfredo product. Each manufacturer's salesperson desires the best shelf space possible, but the best space can go to only one product. The other products have to make do with less space or an inferior position. The grocery store wants to assign shelf space in a way that will maximize total noodles alfredo sales, but the three salespeople are interested only in their own brands' sales.

Al Summy, vice president of sales and service at Hallmark, says, "We're not selling to the retailer, we're selling through the retailer. We look at the retailer as the pipeline to the hands of consumers." This perspective means that when retailers make money with Hallmark cards, Hallmark has won the battle for space.[1]

Sometimes the battle is not ethical. One Noxell (Noxzema and Cover Girl cosmetics) rep described how she called on a pharmacy and discovered that her products were completely missing. A competitor had emptied the shelves of her products and moved them to the back room. The Noxell rep simply brought the lack of shelf space to the attention of the store manager and let him draw his own conclusions. The unethical competitor was later asked to remove his products.

Mind Share

In selling to industrial distributors, manufacturers often talk of the battle for space as a battle for mind share. **Mind share** is the degree to which a manufacturer's product receives attention from (occupies the mind of) the distributor. Industrial distributors may carry competing products that require some personal selling to the end user. In this case, the manufacturer wants its product recommended more often than the competitor's. When the products are sold at the user's site, the battle among manufacturers is for the distributor's mind share rather than shelf space.

For example, Panasonic manufactures electronic parts that other manufacturers use to make many types of products. It sells through distributors who also sell products produced by Panasonic's competitors. The distributors can recommend Panasonic or another product, and often there is no functional difference between the two. Panasonic would like to be the first brand recommended, that is, have the primary position in the mind of the distributor. As you will see later in this chapter, Panasonic and other manufacturers seek to increase mind share through training and special promotions to the trade.

Resellers Offer Resources

Resellers also offer their marketing resources to manufacturers. Together, resellers and manufacturers share marketing dollars to advertise. Resellers give manufacturers information about the market, what customers want, what the competition is doing, and other important data that help manufacturers respond to changing market conditions. Resellers also build displays, create special promotions, and perform other activities that help manufacturers achieve their goals. It is important that the salespeople who sell to resellers understand what resellers want so that mutual solutions can be achieved.

RESELLER BUYERS

Like all salespeople, salespeople who sell to resellers must convince their customers that the products and services offered will satisfy their needs. However, selling a product for resale differs in several ways from selling a product for personal or corporate use. The primary difference lies in the resellers' concern about their return on investment (ROI). All buyers focus on their ROI to some degree. For example, when you buy a suit, you want to make sure you will wear it often enough (the return) to justify the price (the investment). But resellers approach ROI a little differently.

The primary reason resellers approach ROI differently is that they deal with derived demand (discussed in Chapter Four). When resellers purchase a product for resale, they are concerned with whether their customers will also buy the product. Their ROI is based not on how well the product performs (such as how long the suit lasts) but on how well the product sells. Resellers have more control over both investments and revenue, which makes them more sensitive to differences in ROI when comparing proposals from several vendors.

To determine the projected ROI, resellers use a number of mathematical formulas. Resellers compare various profit projections by comparing their projected returns. One set of formulas they use is the strategic profit model. We will focus on those elements of the strategic profit model influenced by the salesperson.

Strategic Profit Model

The **strategic profit model** (SPM) is a mathematical formula used to examine the impact of strategic decisions on profit. Retailers and other resellers often use the SPM to evaluate such actions as adding another product or engaging in a promotion.

The SPM uses several financial ratios to evaluate the performance of the overall store. Our interest here is in the evaluation of a product or marketing program being sold to a retailer; the SPM also evaluates areas of performance that salespeople do not influence. Therefore, we are concerned only with gross margin ROI, or the portion of ROI related to the products the salesperson sells to the reseller (see Exhibit 15.2).

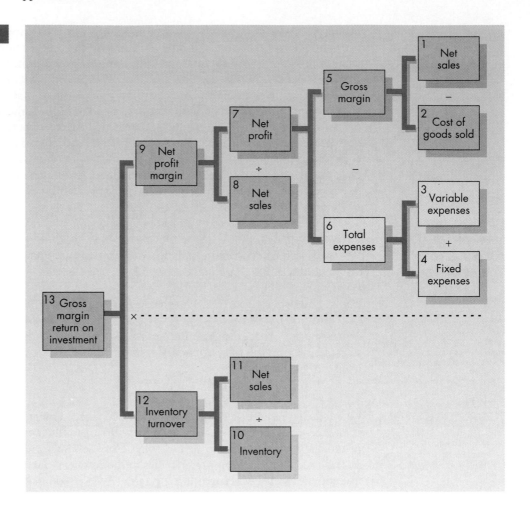

While discussing an evaluation of the future (i.e., "What if they adopt this product or program?"), we can use the same criteria to assess a current product or a prior program.

When evaluating a product or program, a reseller buyer focuses on three things: how many will be sold, at what profit, and how fast the product will sell. For example, when Jim O'Connell of Lego Systems meets with Wal-Mart to sell Legos, he is armed with data showing total sales, gross margin return on footage (the profit for the amount of space devoted to Legos), and inventory turnover for each store.[2] The Wal-Mart buyer uses this information to compare Legos' performance to objectives and to other products sold in the same category, such as Tinker Toys and Brio blocks.

Net Sales

Of great interest to the reseller buyer is how much sales revenue can be expected from a product or program. (When evaluating a product or program, reseller buyers express sales in dollars rather than units to evaluate the product or program's profitability.) However, total sales does not accurately measure sales; people return products because of damage, improper fit, or for no apparent reason, and these returns must be subtracted to calculate net sales. **Net sales,** for our purposes, is total sales minus returns, in dollars, represented by box 1 in Exhibit 15.2.

Another measure important to retailers is sales per square foot or sales per shelf foot (similar to what O'Connell refers to as gross margin return on footage). Of course, a John Deere dealer will not use this measure because space is not at a great premium, but the dealer will compare alternative uses of display space. In a grocery store or a department store, however, shelf and display space is a finite asset that has been filled to the maximum. Moreover, the nature of retailing dictates that only the fittest (most profitable) survive. Products are therefore evaluated by how well they use the space allocated to them.

The measure of how well products use space is the amount of sales dollars they generate. For example, if a retailer generates $50 per square foot in sales with Miami Fashion's products and generates only $45 with Suncoast, Miami Fashion will get more space; Suncoast may be eliminated entirely.

Net Profit Margin

The profit on the product, expressed as a percentage of sales, is the **net profit margin** (or simply *margin*). In mathematical terms,

Net profit margin = Net profit/Net sales

Net profit margin (box 9 in Exhibit 15.2) is influenced by the cost of goods sold (or the price charged to the reseller, box 2 in the Exhibit). Net profit margin is also influenced by the variable expenses (box 3), which can be affected by costs associated with reselling the product. As we will see later in this chapter, salespeople can reduce those costs by reimbursing the store and through other means. Thus, salespeople can influence net profit (box 7) in several ways, which can have a major impact on net profit margin.

Profit margin is an important factor when resellers consider a product or program. Many students confuse margin with markup, especially in practice role plays. **Markup** is the percentage of sales by which the price for the product is initially increased. Margin and markup are sometimes equal, but margin may be less if the retailer has to put the product on sale at a lower price because margin is not calculated until the product is sold. Markup is calculated only when the product is first put out for sale. The formula for markup is

Markup = (Price – Cost)/Price

The markdowns retailers take off the retail selling price also affect margin. When a retailer has a sale and says, "Everything is 15 percent off," it means everything is 15 percent off the regular retail price, not the cost to the store. Expenses are also calculated as a percentage of sales. Hence, to make it easier for buyers to calculate their profit margins, salespeople should quote profit margin in terms of suggested retail prices, not markup on the basis of retail cost.

For example, if Linz Jewelers buys a diamond ring for $1,000, it may sell the ring for $2,000. The markup is 100 percent when calculated as a percentage of cost: ($2,000 – $1,000)/$1,000. But profit margin is 50 percent: $1,000/$2,000 (multiply by 100 percent to convert to a percentage).

Vendors want their products on the shelves when the customer is there to buy, but retailers want the lowest possible inventory on hand to keep their costs low. So, vendors deliver more frequently, even sometimes daily.

Courtesy Borden, Inc.; photo by Michael Hart

Courtesy Dean Foods

Turnover

The reseller can use several types of turnover to evaluate performance, but the type of turnover of interest to salespeople selling to the reseller is inventory turnover. **Inventory turnover** measures how fast a product sells relative to how much inventory has to be carried. Inventory turnover (box 12 in Exhibit 15.2) measures how efficiently a reseller manages inventory. The reseller would like to have in the store only the amount needed for that day's sales because inventory represents an expense until it has been sold, but obviously receiving daily delivery is impossible for small retailers. Large retailers such as Wal-Mart do receive daily delivery of some products.

To fully understand the importance of inventory turnover, let's examine the impact inventory has on the overall ROI. Inventory (box 10) is often the largest current asset a store owns. (Other current assets would include accounts receivable, or customer purchases made on credit.) Inventory makes up most of total current assets. The larger the inventory, the lower the inventory turnover (box 12). The lower the inventory turnover, the lower the gross margin ROI (box 13). If we were to examine overall ROI and include other current assets, the effects would be similar. A low inventory turnover would still lower overall ROI.

Calculated by dividing net sales (represented by box 11 and the same as box 1) by inventory, the measure states the number of times the firm sold an amount equal to the inventory it carried. In mathematical terms,

Inventory turnover = Net sales/Inventory

A reseller does not necessarily want to push turnover to the highest possible level, most easily accomplished by reducing inventory. Several negative consequences could result, including stockouts, increased ordering costs due to more frequent ordering, higher shipping costs, and loss of quantity discounts. Lowering prices can also increase turnover but may reduce profits because gross margin (box 5) is lowered.

Improving Turnover

To improve inventory turnover, some resellers are working with manufacturers to develop efficient customer response systems. **Efficient customer response (ECR)** systems are distribution systems that drive inventory to the lowest possible levels, increase the frequency of shipping, and automate ordering and inventory control processes without creating the problems of stockouts and higher costs discussed earlier. Similar to just-in-time (JIT) systems in manufacturing, ECR systems improve efficiency throughout the distribution channel. Estimates are that $30 billion in waste could be cut from the grocery distribution channel alone if everyone adopted ECR.[3] Companies such as Bristol-Myers Squibb (makers of Excedrin and Nuprin) and Del-Monte also find that their billing is more accurate when they use ECR because they have better control over when goods are shipped and when invoices are mailed.[4] Orders are placed electronically, reducing manual errors, and some companies, such as Johnson & Johnson, link ECR to the ordering of their raw materials and their just-in-time manufacturing processes.[5]

Quick response, a similar term, refers to minimizing order quantities to the lowest level possible while increasing the speed of delivery to drive inventory turnover. It is accomplished by prepackaging certain combinations of products (*ECR* is primarily a grocery term, whereas *quick response* is used in other areas of retailing). Precision Fabric Group (PFG), an apparel manufacturer in North Carolina, even manufactures based on customer demand. If the retailer sells more of a certain color, it orders more of that color rather than a prepackaged combination, as is common in that industry. PFG can do this because it developed several weaving technologies that allow it to speed up the manufacturing process. Hence, it has a JIT manufacturing-through-retailing process.

Resellers use turnover to identify slow-selling merchandise, determine appropriate stock levels, and evaluate the buying process. Eliminating slow-moving goods, selling off excess inventory, and ordering at appropriate times can improve turnover. Turnover can also be improved by selecting reliable vendors. Less inventory is needed when the reseller does not have to carry extra stock in the event that a shipment is delayed. That is why ECR works best between partners; the partnership selection process (discussed in Chapters Two and Thirteen) would screen out vendors incapable of living up to the promises of ECR.

Electronic data interchange (EDI) is a computer-to-computer transmission of data from reseller to vendor and back. Resellers and vendors that practice ECR or quick response use EDI to transmit purchase orders and shipping information. For example, Martin Newman Shoes (a chain of 14 stores in Jacksonville, Illinois) tracks sales using computerized cash registers. When inventory of a particular shoe reaches a certain point, an order is generated to Brown Shoe, its primary vendor. Alternatively, if one store is out of a particular shoe, the same system can tell the store clerk which store has that shoe in stock and have the item sent directly either to the customer or to the store.[6]

Turnover varies widely for different products. Jewelry, hardware, and furniture stores have lower turnover rates than gas stations and grocery stores. As a result, the former need to make more profit from each sale and to maintain a wider assortment. Gas stations and grocery stores have lower margins but make up for that with higher unit sales volume.

Gross Margin ROI

When inventory turnover is multiplied by net profit margin, the buyer has determined the gross margin return on investment (box 13 in Exhibit 15.2). Note that this is a simplified version of ROI used to illustrate how a product is evaluated for purchase; overall ROI would include other assets and items not affected by a seller's program. If comparing two products, the buyer can insert the projected sales of each, the costs of each, the costs associated with reselling the products (less any support from the manufacturer), how much inventory must be kept on hand, and then calculate the return on investment. The choice would be made on the basis of which product had the better return on investment.

For example, Kmart was offered a large discount from a vendor if the vendor could begin shipping in bulk to Kmart's warehouses instead of directly to the stores. At first glance, the discount looked attractive because it lowered the cost of goods sold (box 2), which would improve gross margin (box 5) and thus improve net profit (box 7), net profit margin (box 9), and ultimately ROI (box 13). But Kmart would then incur other costs, such as increased shipping from its warehouses to the stores, increased handling to break the vendor's large shipments down to the amount needed for each store, and increased inventory. The first two costs would increase variable expenses (box 3), while increased inventory (box 10) would hurt total current assets (box 12), which would hurt inventory turnover (box 12). The overall result would be lower ROI (box 13). By forecasting these costs and applying the SPM, Kmart was able to avoid a costly decision.[7]

Other Factors to Consider

Unlike the hard financial aspects of reselling a product or evaluating the success of a marketing program, measuring the vendor's level of support is often not an objective process. Yet retailers and other resellers know that this element, the "soft" side of supplier selection, is as important as the hard, financial side. In fact, the two are often highly related.

The dimensions on which vendors are evaluated include reliability, turnaround, facilitating functions, information, credit, and ethics. Other dimensions are risk and investment. Image represents the buyer's total perception of all of these factors.

Dimensions of Image

Image can mean many things, especially when selling to the trade. We will discuss the image consumers hold of the selling firm as well as the image buyers have of the salesperson. Both are important to the buyer in vendor selection.

Image with Consumers   The image the consumer holds of a product is, the manufacturer hopes, the intended position. For example, Coca-Cola positioned Tab, a diet cola, as the "diet cola for women" because it contained calcium, something Diet Coke does not have. As another example, Procter & Gamble has positioned Crest toothpaste as a cavity fighter, whereas Close-Up is positioned as a whitening toothpaste that improves sex appeal. Those manufacturers hope consumers agree that Tab is a diet cola for women, Crest is a cavity fighter, and Close-Up whitens teeth and improves sex appeal. A store might not carry both Crest and Close-Up if the products had the same image.

What does this mean to a salesperson? It means the product's and the company's image in the marketplace must be consistent with the image the reseller wants to project. For example, a lawn and garden store that positioned itself as the lowest priced in town would not carry Snapper lawn mowers (premium-priced, high-quality products) but would carry Murray mowers (affordable, with fewer features). If the same store positioned itself on the basis of top quality and service, it would want to carry Snapper, not Murray. Therefore, salespeople should consider the fit between their company's image and a retailer's image when prospecting for new distributors.

Image in the Trade   The vendor also has an image in the trade. This image, based on how the company treats its distributors, is separate from the position the company strives for in the marketplace. In the Coca-Cola example, Tab has its image in the marketplace and Coca-Cola Company has an image among grocery stores separate from that for Tab. For example, Coca-Cola strives for an image of strong marketing support with its grocery store buyers.

Vendor image can be very important. For example, John Deere has a reputation among dealers of providing excellent support. This reputation made it easier for Deere to extend its product lines into lawn and garden equipment when times got tight in the agricultural market. New dealers for the new products were willing to invest in Deere because of that company's reputation for support.

When buyers evaluate a potential supplier's reputation, they consider questions such as the following:

- Is this company ethical? Does it fulfill its promises?
- Will the supplier stand behind its offerings?
- Is the supplier financially healthy? Will it be around to supply me over a period of time?
- Is this supplier innovative or conservative?
- Will I be treated fairly, that is, given fair access to discounts, marketing support, delivery, and credit terms?

Salespeople play a big role in how the territory views their companies. Each salesperson has the opportunity to build a reputation or tear it down. Often the little things build a reputation, just as the little things build a relationship. As you review the above questions, you can see that being professional in the way you conduct yourself can have a very positive impact on the reputation of your company.

Doing business with a reputable company reduces risk for the buyer. Companies want partners they can trust. Confidence in the decision to select a partner is greater when the buyer recognizes that the supplying company is reputable.

SELLING TO RESELLERS

How do salespeople use this knowledge to be more effective in their jobs? As a first step, they understand that customers, the resellers, will be interested in their return on investment—a function of their total sales for the product, their profit margins, and how fast the product will sell. Professional salespeople also understand how their own performance will be evaluated by buyers and how the buying process will work. Then salespeople must prepare to answer customers' questions and prove benefits for the buyer, using methods similar to the proof methods we discussed in Chapter Ten. Exhibit 15.3 lists the measures buyers use to consider their purchases and relates these factors to the proof processes salespeople use.

Using the SPM

Resellers evaluate many numbers and elements of marketing programs to make marketing and buying decisions. As you saw earlier, however, these evaluations boil down to three questions, often asked in this order:

- How much will sell (sales)?
- At what profit will it sell (margin)?
- How quickly and easily will it sell (turnover)?

The salesperson must show how the product will meet the reseller's needs on these three dimensions.

EXHIBIT 15.3	What Reseller Buyers Buy	How Salespeople Prove Benefits
Relationship between How Buyers Buy and Proof Processes	Net sales	Selling history
		Market share
	Net profit margin	Pricing terms
		Absorbing shipping costs
		Trade discounts
		Quantity discounts
		Promotional allowances
		Credit terms and financial discounts
		Marketing support
	Inventory turnover	Selling history
		Market share
		Third-party proof
	Image	Company history
		Turnaround

Proving Sales

An important point to remember when selling to resellers is that they deal with derived demand just as other organizational buyers do. Resellers are interested in whether their buyers will buy the product, not their own personal desire for the product. Students often forget this in practice presentations and spend too much time showing the buyer why the product is so wonderful, forgetting to tie those features back to the buyer's need for strong sales.

For example, Wayne Cimperman sells accessories for skiing and in-line skating, such as the Neck Wallet, a wallet that hangs around the skater's or skier's neck. In a meeting with one of the largest sports retailers in the Northeast, Cimperman discovered that while the buyer liked his Neck Wallet, the buyer already had thousands in stock from another supplier that were not selling. Cimperman diagnosed the problem as poor packaging; customers did not understand what the products were. Using data from similar chains, Cimperman showed how his Neck Wallets were outselling the competition five to one; but just as important, Cimperman showed how his packaging demonstrated product use to consumers. By proving that his product would sell, Cimperman became a major supplier to that chain of stores.[8]

Using Selling History

Salespeople often use past sales experience to gain future sales. **Selling history** refers to how well the vendor's product or line sold during the same season in the previous year. Selling history is the most important factor in vendor selection to department store buyers choosing clothing and accessories as well as housewares and appliances.[9] It is also important in other types of selling to resellers. For example, Mott's USA uses FastTrack sales automation software, TIPS promotion expense software, and data on market share and sales history from IRI to show how well its apple juice products sold in the past and to project the impact of promotion plans on future sales.[10] An example of how selling history might be presented appears in Exhibit 15.4.

EXHIBIT 15.4	Proposal for Budget Box Grocery Stores	
Using Selling History to Sell Margin	Last Spring's Off! Super Sales	This Spring's Deep Woods Off! Sell-Out
		New Off! product
	50¢ coupon	50¢ coupon
	$1 million national ad campaign	$1.3 million TV ad campaign
		$8 million print ad campaign
	You sold **50 cases**	You sell **70 cases**
	Profit **$736**	Profit **$1,1761**

A sales representative trying to secure distribution through a new outlet has no selling history with that prospect to prove the selling power of the product or program, but success with similar dealers or retailers can be used, as Cimperman did with the Neck Wallet. Be careful in such situations, however; you do not want to give away confidential information, such as how much your prospect's competitor is making. For example, you should not tell Macy's that Foley's sells 200 cases of your product per week. That would be unfair to Foley's, and unethical.

Using Market Share

One common method of proving that a product will sell is to show market share. **Market share** is the percentage of total market sales accounted for by one product. In mathematical terms,

Market share = Brand sales/Total product category sales

For example, to say that Banquet has a 40 percent market share means that 40 percent of all frozen meals are Banquet products. Market share is most often used for consumer packaged goods, because markets are easily defined by product categories and data concerning sales of various products are readily available. But market share may be less applicable in other industries, such as fashion goods and hardware, where markets may be poorly defined or data less readily available.

The way salespeople present market share information varies depending on the type of buyer being dealt with. For example, an amiable can be told that "everyone loves this product—in fact, it is the leading product in the market," whereas an analytical will want to see the actual percentage. Such percentages are available from marketing research firms. In consumer packaged goods, commonly used measures of market share are provided by BehaviorScan and Nielsen's Retail Index. These services provide the percentage of products sold, by brand, in various categories. A salesperson selling copiers to office suppliers, however, would use data from companies such as Datapro to support claims for market share. Other market research companies provide similar market data for hardware, soft goods (linens, clothing, etc.), furniture, and other products. However, as previously noted, a salesperson may be less likely to use those data in those markets.

Other proof sources of market share include test market results, third-party sources such as articles in trade magazines, and company data that indicate sales growth, average volume per retailer, and other information. These sources can indicate that market share is increasing and that the product is selling, especially in the

Banquet's sales brochure emphasizes sales data to show how stores will make more money with Banquet.

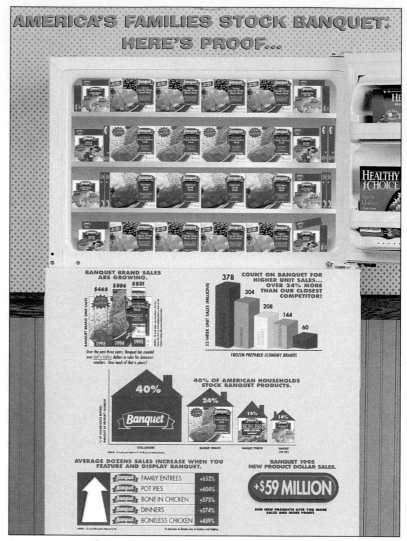

Courtesy ConAgra® Frozen Foods

case of a new product. As you can see in the accompanying photo, Banquet also included data to prove growing market demand for its products.

Selling Profit Margin

Net profit margin is the second most important factor considered by department store buyers. The importance of these two financial factors, selling history and margin, to department store buyers comes from the recognition that profits drive the store's activities. No matter how much a department store buyer likes a sweater, for example, if he or she thinks it will not sell or cannot be marked up enough to make a profit, the store will not carry it.

Terms and conditions of the sale also affect the seller's return. Knowledge of pricing, discounts, and credit policies is important because these policies affect the

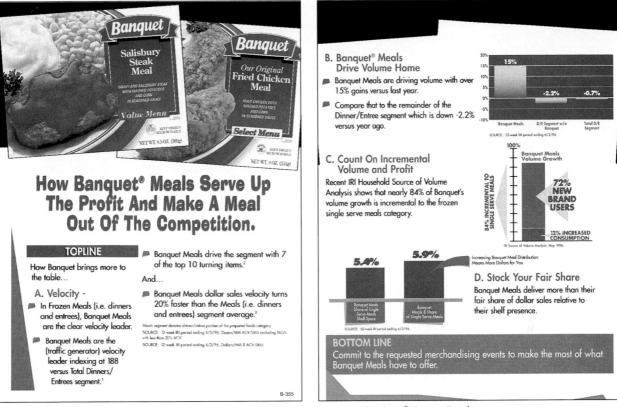

Courtesy ConAgra® Frozen Foods   Courtesy ConAgra® Frozen Foods

This part of the brochure includes market research data to help salespeople prove the brand's selling power.

buyer's actual cost and ROI. As we discussed in Chapter Twelve, if a salesperson misquotes a price, the selling company may be legally obligated to fill the order at that price, even if the rep and the company will lose money. However, price is just one component of the terms and conditions of sale, which often become important determinants for the buyer because they affect profit.

Pricing Terms

Among the most common expressions used in quoting price are list price, net price, suggested retail price, guaranteed price, and FOB price. **List price** is the quoted or published price in a catalog or price list from which buyers may receive discounts. **Net price** is the price buyers pay after all discounts and allowances have been subtracted. These would include quantity and other types of discounts that we will discuss shortly.

Suggested retail price is just that, the price at which the manufacturer suggests the store retail the product. The reseller, however, has no obligation to sell the product at that price. When presenting a product, the manufacturer's salesperson can suggest a retail price and base profit margin calculations on that price. However, to present margins and other sales-based information, the rep should also use any price the retailer has set. After all, that price is the one the retailer will use to make a decision.

Guaranteed prices are important to resellers during times of falling prices. For example, Apple may sell computers to retail stores at $500. If Apple decreases wholesale prices to $400 before a store can sell its inventory, the store has suffered an opportunity loss of $100 per computer. To encourage resellers to place larger orders, manufacturers may offer to protect the resellers' inventories with a guaranteed price. In our example, if Apple lowers its prices by $100, the retailer is refunded the $100 for each computer still in inventory. It would be the salesperson's job to verify the inventory and initiate the refund request.

The terms and conditions of sale include shipping costs. The seller who quotes an **FOB** (free on board—see Chapter Twelve) *origin price* agrees to load the goods on board a truck, freight car, or other means of transportation, but it may be up to the buyer to pay for transportation. On the other hand, an FOB *destination price* means shipping is included in the price.

Trade Discounts

Sometimes, the price a reseller will pay for a product is quoted in terms of a discount off of the list price, called a **trade discount**. For example, the manufacturer may offer the wholesaler a trade discount of 35 percent off.

Occasionally the manufacturer will sell directly to a retailer. If so, the retailer may be quoted a smaller trade discount, for example, 20 percent of the list price. The wholesaler's discount will then be taken off the resulting retailer's cost. Hence, if the trade discounts are expressed as 20 and 35, the retailer pays 80 percent of suggested retail and the wholesaler pays 35 percent less. Note that the wholesaler does not pay 45 percent of retail; the wholesaler's discount is taken from the retailer's cost. Exhibit 15.5 illustrates how the trade discount works. Trade discounts should provide a sufficient margin to cover the costs of the services rendered by the various intermediaries and to give the intermediaries a fair profit.

Most companies that use trade discounts classify their customers according to the trade discount allowed. However, when customers operate as both wholesalers and retailers, knowing which price to quote is difficult. Some manufacturers may then treat the trade discount as a quantity discount, offering the wholesale discount for larger orders and the retail discount for smaller quantities. Other manufacturers may give the customer only a retail discount, while still others may give the cus-

EXHIBIT 15.5 Trade Discount Example	Consumer pays retail price	←	Retailer pays wholesale price	←	Wholesaler pays manufacturer's price
	$10.00		$10.00 −2.00 (20% trade discount) $ 8.00 Retailer's cost: $8.00		$8.00 −2.80 (35% trade discount) $5.20 Wholesaler's cost: $5.20 Wholesaler's price: $8.00

Trade discounts are based on suggested retail price. Each discount is applied to the net price after previous discounts have been taken, beginning with the retail price and working back in the channel toward the manufacturer.

tomer the wholesale discount, depending on the overall level of sales for the customer's retail and wholesale operations.

Quantity Discounts

Quantity discounts, first discussed in Chapter Twelve, encourage large purchases by passing along savings resulting from reduced processing costs and should not be confused with trade discounts (which are designed to provide the reseller with profit). Quantity discounts are usually taken off the price after the trade discount is applied. Thus, if a trade discount of 20 percent were applied to a retail price of $10, the quantity discount would be applied to the trade price of $8. A quantity discount of 10 percent means the final price to the reseller would be $7.20.

Promotional Allowance

Manufacturers often offer special allowances if resellers agree to promote their products. Clorox may offer a special discount to grocery stores if they agree to offer a special price for Clorox liquid bleach, advertise the special price in the local paper, and permit the Clorox rep to build an end-of-aisle display of Clorox products. This allowance, usually offered as a discount off the regular price, is separate from any cooperative advertising allowance (which would be based on the cost of advertising, not the amount of product purchased) or any other discount. The grocery trade refers to promotional allowances as a **deal,** the promotional discount offered to the retailer. The product is said to be "on deal." This promotional discount may be a quantity discount or may be in addition to regular quantity discounts. In the above example, Clorox may have its products on deal, with an extra quantity discount for the retailer.

Credit Terms and Financial Discounts

As mentioned in Chapter Twelve, cash discounts are the last discount taken and, like the others, are not added to other discount percentages. A common discount is 2/10, n/30, which means the buyer can deduct 2 percent from the bill if it is paid within 10 days from the date of invoice; otherwise, the full amount must be paid in 30 days. Another common discount is 2/10, EOM, which means the 10-day period begins at the end of the month. In the earlier example, a bill for $7.20 with terms of 2/10, n/30, and received January 10 could be paid with $7.06 by January 20 or with $7.20 by January 31, but on February 1 the payment would be late.

 When selling to distributors in other countries, a company may ask customers to provide letters of credit. **Letters of credit** are like checks from a bank, except that the company cannot collect cash from a customer's letter of credit unless it is able to prove the customer did not pay for the merchandise. Letters of credit are the most common method of international payment.

Resellers frequently request **deferred datings,** which allow them to pay after the selling season, as an extra form of discount. In the golfing industry, for example, the big selling season is early spring. Golf pro shops ask to be billed at the end of the season, when they have sold enough products to be able to pay the bill. Consignment and buyback are similar. **Consignment** means the retailer makes no payment until after the product is sold, no matter when the sale takes place. A **buyback** is a guarantee to buy back any unsold merchandise. Most salespeople are reluctant to use these terms because there is no financial commitment from the buyer (because the buyer has no financial risk) to ensure that the product sells. Consignment is used most often in the fashion business, while buybacks are used in many settings.

Selling Turnover When proving the product will sell, the vendor also addresses turnover, or how quickly the product will sell. In addition, the vendor provides marketing support so that the product will sell faster. Marketing support from the vendor improves the efficiency of the reseller. Vendor advertising, for example, should lead to greater product recognition by the consumer. The reseller has less selling to do, because the vendor's advertising has already presold the consumer, thus improving turnover. Note that Banquet included its promotion schedule on the brochure its salespeople

A Banquet promotion calendar helps resellers make sure they have enough Banquet meals on hand to supply the added demand caused by successful promotions.

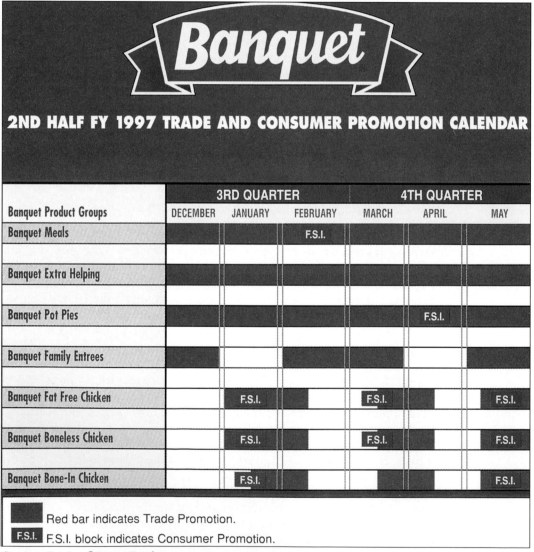

Courtesy ConAgra® Frozen Foods

use to sell the Banquet line, as the photo on page 442 shows. Buyers could rest assured that Banquet would help them sell the product, which should positively influence turnover.

In summary, we have seen the financial criteria on which product and marketing programs are evaluated. The financial needs of the reseller have been quantified to some degree, and you should have a better understanding of the ways to present a product's or program's financial capabilities.

Notice too, however, how support needs interact with financial needs. For example, turnover is determined in part by the level of inventory that must be carried. Inventory levels are affected by the level of service, specifically how promptly and reliably the company can deliver. How fast and how much a product sells will also be affected by the job the rep does in assisting the dealer or retailer in merchandising the product and by the effectiveness of the marketing program the rep helps to create.

Selling Image

How can a salesperson build the image of the company? Part of the proof will be in the pudding, or how well the salesperson serves prospects before they become customers. Returning phone calls, providing information or samples quickly, and delivering on promises will go a long way toward proving reliability.

If possible, salespeople should carry copies of business or trade periodical articles about the company. Salespeople should also maintain a file of letters from satisfied customers. When a customer thanks a salesperson for service, the salesperson should ask for a letter. The letter will allow the salesperson not only to document the level of service with other accounts but also prove his or her service skills to your management if the need arises.

Salespeople also sell image and prove it with company history. For example, if a salesperson discovers that the buyer prefers carrying the products of innovative companies, the salesperson should remind the buyer of past innovations that the company developed. Then, when presented with the current innovation, the buyer sees this new product as part of an overall history of innovation.

One word of caution: Many sellers get too wrapped up in discussing how wonderful their company is; they fail to make a connection to the buyer's needs, such as a concern about being treated fairly. Emphasizing one's company's reputation is most effective when buyers can relate that reputation to their needs.

Turnaround

An important dimension of service is turnaround. **Turnaround** is how quickly the seller delivers a product or service after the customer orders it. The term is also used to describe how quickly a seller responds to a customer. Elsewhere in this book, you have read about the top salespeople as rated by their customers. Frequently, these customers considered turnaround under difficult situations as one important criterion for performance.

Turnaround is often a function of salespeople's ability to plan and their relationships with others in the company. As we will discuss in Chapter Seventeen, salespeople need to develop strong relationships with colleagues in their companies' order entry, billing, credit, and shipping departments to provide the desired level of service to customers.

At the same time, however, salespeople must plan their activities and sales calls to provide plenty of lead time. If normal delivery is two weeks, for example, a salesperson would not want to wait to tell retailers about a promotion until two days be-

SELLING SCENARIO 15.2

Twin Peaks of the Baking Business

For Borden's baking goods division , the year is compressed between Thanksgiving and Christmas. These twin peaks comprise almost the entire year's worth of sales for Eagle Brand condensed milk, NoneSuch mincemeat, and other baking products, as well as such dairy products as Borden eggnog. But Americans are baking less, meaning that to boost sales, Borden had to gain at the expense of competitors.

Borden realized, though, that when a consumer needs one baking ingredient, she or he probably needs all ingredients. With that concept, Borden created a virtual company, a company called Premiere Partnership, that joined together the baking goods lines of Keebler Ready pie crust, Diamond walnuts, and Sun Maid raisins and Sunsweet dates. With each manufacturer paying about $500,000 for advertising, each gets the power of a $2 million campaign. The campaign includes a co-sponsored freestanding insert (FSI) ad; an account-specific, in-store-distributed, 16-page recipe book; and temporary price reductions to drive sales at retail.

Key to the success of the Premiere Partnership were the coordinated efforts of the four companies' sales forces. This was no small task, since Thanksgiving to Christmas is the key baking and selling season for all baking products companies and they all wanted extra space. Salespeople worked with their accounts to gain acceptance of the recipe book and convinced their accounts to feature the products and recipe book in the stores' ads. Salespeople also had to persuade buyers to build displays of products to support the promotion, as well as order in larger-than-usual quantities to avoid stockouts.

As clever as it was, the promotion could have failed without the complete support of the field salespeople. That support made the campaign a huge success. Instead of a twin-peak year, Borden and its Premiere Partners experienced one long, enjoyable plateau.

Source: Adapted from Daniel Shannon, "A Fully-Baked Idea," *PROMO: The Magazine of Promotion Marketing*, August 1996, p. 8.

fore it starts. Retailers will want to know at least two weeks in advance so they can receive sufficient inventories of the promoted product, build their displays, and so forth.

We have discussed throughout this text how salespeople build long-term partnerships and how important customer service and follow-up are in maintaining those partnerships. Turnaround can also apply to how quickly salespeople return phone calls and how promptly they handle credit requests and other problems. When customers know they can depend on the rep to turn their requests around on a timely basis, they will turn to that rep with more orders. As you can see in Selling Scenario 15.2, salespeople at Borden had to convince retailers of the expected success of the Premiere Partnership promotion so that the appropriate inventory could be ordered.

MERCHANDISE MARKETS, TRADE SHOWS, AND TRADE FAIRS

Another method of selling to resellers is to attend trade shows (see Chapter Six for a discussion of using trade shows for prospecting), trade fairs, and merchandise markets. Because these events are so important and are also used for selling to end users, we emphasize them in this chapter. In some cases, a manufacturer lives or dies by how well it does in these special selling situations. Keith Clark, a company that manufactures office products such as calendars, depends heavily on the annual national office products association show. Its salespeople report that selling year round is easier due to the impression the company makes on prospects at the show.

Merchandise Markets

Markets, short-term sales (usually only a few days) held in large buildings that create the aura of a huge mall, are an important part of selling to resellers. The Dallas Market Center, for example, hosts separate markets for children's wear, western apparel, linens, and other soft goods. The sellers are the manufacturers or distributors, and they sell only to resellers, not to the public. Sellers may lease showroom space permanently or only during the market weeks. If they lease space permanently, they usually bring buyers in during off-market periods or at times when no markets are being held.

Buyers visit many vendors during markets, selecting the products they will carry for the next season. In some industries, almost all sales to resellers occur during markets. These industries include hardware, clothing, toys, and furniture. The major furniture markets are held in Dallas, Chicago, and High Point, North Carolina. The biggest toy show is held annually in New York City. Major clothing markets are held for each season (such as fall and spring) in New York City, Atlanta, Paris, Dallas, and Los Angeles.

Trade Shows

Trade shows are short (usually less than a week), temporary exhibitions of products by manufacturers and distributors. Once the show is over, all vendors pack up and leave. Specialty Advertising Association International (SAAI), for example, holds its annual trade show in Dallas each year. Vendors at this show are all manufacturers looking for dealers for their products; the end users of the products are not admitted. Dealers make an entire year's worth of purchases at the SAAI show, so the show is a make-or-break situation for many manufacturers.

Comdex, the largest computer trade show in the world, is usually held in Las Vegas. Comdex differs from SAAI's show in that it has a dual audience: Vendors exhibit to end users (industrial consumers) as well as to resellers. Another show with a dual audience is Networld, a show for computer networking products. A recent sur-

Trade shows are a short, intense form of promotion important for many marketers who target business customers.

©IDEAS—Canada's Largest Residential Construction Show

vey of Networld exhibitors found that 40 percent of the vendors had promoting to dealers only as their primary objective, 40 percent were promoting to end users only, and 20 percent were looking for both dealers and end users. Successful trade shows reach qualified buyers that might not otherwise be reached, as illustrated in Exhibit 15.6.

Even firms that do not use resellers may have salespeople involved in trade shows. Many trade shows have only customers as their audience. For example, the National Association of Legal Secretaries is a professional organization that promotes the welfare of legal secretaries. When it holds its annual convention, it also invites manufacturers of office equipment and other products to exhibit wares. The trade show is an adjunct of the convention, with the audience composed entirely of end users.

Umax Technologies, a maker of computer scanners, exhibits at Comdex every year. Umax looks for potential retailers and commercial accounts at the show. At the 1996 Comdex, it hoped for 2,000 leads. It got 7,500 leads, balanced equally between resellers and users.[11]

Trade Fairs

In Europe, trade shows are called **trade fairs.** In Hanover, Germany, Europe's largest convention hall hosts many shows, including the Hanover fair, the European version of Comdex. This show attracts over half a million visitors from around the world and displays the products of 4,500 manufacturers from over 45 countries. Shows such as the Hanover fair can be extremely important for companies such as Microsoft and Novell when looking for local dealers and distributors in other countries.

Trade shows and markets, then, are two activities in which salespeople may engage, whether selling to resellers or to consumers. These shows provide excellent opportunities to locate prospects. Whereas the average number of calls needed to close a sale is 3.6 without trade shows, the average number of additional calls needed

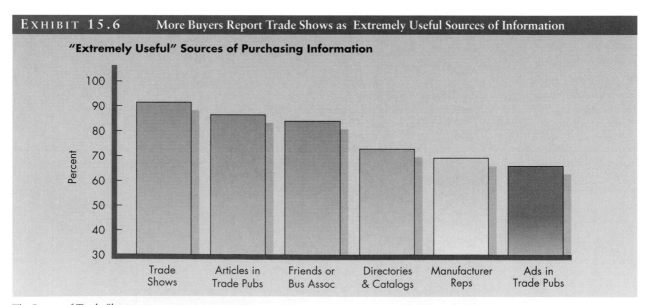

EXHIBIT 15.6   More Buyers Report Trade Shows as Extremely Useful Sources of Information

"Extremely Useful" Sources of Purchasing Information

The Power of Trade Shows
A Simmons MRB Study ©Trade Show Bureau

after exposure at a trade show is only 1.4. Thus, closing a sale costs $997 without a trade show and only $550 with a trade show, on average.[12] A company that employs an effective system to track visitors to its booth and uses that system to encourage prompt follow-up by salespeople can maximize the sales opportunities trade shows and markets offer.

REACHING THROUGH RESELLERS TO CONSUMERS

Manufacturers provide their salespeople with marketing programs that improve sales, margins, and turnover for retailers. Some programs involve special offers to the trade, called **trade promotions.** Other programs are more permanent and are designed to build partnerships with retailers.

Trade Promotions

While most successful trade promotions to consumers support retailers' efforts to build traffic, conflict between manufacturers and retailers can occur. Manufacturers are concerned primarily with sales of their products, whereas retailers are concerned not about the sales of a particular product but about the store's overall sales. Therefore, while manufacturers advertise and promote to sell their products, retailers advertise and promote to generate store traffic and sell anything. Manufacturers believe retailers do not always take full advantage of the consumer promotions manufacturers create, which is why they also offer promotions to the trade.

Objectives of Trade Promotions

Trade promotions have one or more general objectives, including

1. Gaining retailer support for a manufacturer's promotion.
2. Launching a new product.
3. Widening distribution, including getting new distributors, more shelf space, or better shelf space.

These objectives illustrate the dilemma trade promotions pose for most salespeople. Something is going to have to change in that store. Objective 1 means attention and resources must be diverted away from a current marketing program to the salesperson's program. Objectives 2 and 3 mean another product will have to be taken off the shelf or given less room.

A retailer's decisions often involve such trade-offs; being able to prove turnover and margins will help salespeople selling trade promotions to retailers. Trade promotions also work best when the manufacturer understands the retailers' advertising and promotion needs and works to satisfy those needs in a mutually beneficial way. For example, Kiwi, a manufacturer of footwear accessories such as shoe polish and athletic shoe cleaner, aids retailers in many ways, but the specific assistance given for a particular store depends on the store's needs. Merchandising materials that help to display the product in the store are supported by ads in sports magazines, and if the retailer also needs local advertising help, Kiwi can provide that too.[13]

Manufacturers use two major types of promotion strategies, often in tandem. The **pull** strategy is designed to stimulate demand among consumers for the manufacturer's product. The **push** strategy is used to stimulate sales efforts by the manufacturer's salespeople and/or the sales efforts by resellers.

Pull Promotions

Pull strategies are designed to pull consumers into the stores to buy the manufacturer's products. They include the use of national advertising campaigns, contests and sweepstakes for consumers, promotions such as the Pillsbury bake-off, and other means.

The importance of salespeople to a successful promotional campaign is illustrated by their actions when a manufacturer offers a coupon in a **freestanding insert (FSI)** (when you shake your Sunday paper, all of those coupon ads that fall out are FSIs). Creative salespeople will tell retailers that FSIs are coming up to secure a special display and plan inventory. Then the retailer can maximize the sales of that product with the coupon without affecting the store's profit margin.

Manufacturers may have a co-op advertising program as part of their pull strategy. With **co-op advertising** (short for *cooperative advertising*), the manufacturer will pay some of the store's advertising costs. The manufacturer may provide the advertisement original, and the retailer will simply insert its name and address into the ad. Alternatively, the retailer may combine several co-op ads into one large ad. While the co-op ad requires marketing effort by the retailer, it is not considered a push strategy because the ad's purpose is to pull people into the store. The retailer may be reimbursed for a percentage of the advertising costs or may be offered a discount off the price of the product.

Manufacturers in many businesses offer co-op advertising, but the consumer packaged goods industry is the heaviest user. Other users include the fashion industry, some hardware manufacturers such as Stanley and Black & Decker, and home appliance manufacturers.

Manufacturers may also combine co-op advertising with a national promotional campaign. When you see a manufacturer's ad that says "at participating dealers," you are seeing a national promotional campaign that depends on the salespeople securing the participation of resellers. Those salespeople may also help the participating dealers to properly display the promoted products and their in-store advertising to support the promotion. Free point-of-purchase displays may be a part of these trade promotions.

Push Trade Promotions

Salespeople and their companies often combine pull promotions with a program that encourages resellers to participate. Promotions that encourage reseller participation and support are push promotions. Push promotions include contests and extra incentives for the reseller's salespeople, special display incentives, and special pricing incentives.

Features Sometimes the manufacturer will offer additional discounts (called deals, as mentioned earlier) if the retailer will **feature** a product, that is, put the product on sale with a lower price, advertise it, and perhaps build a special display. When your grocery store advertises its weekly specials, those products are this week's features. For example, you may see an ad for Coke at $3.09 per 12-pack at your local grocery store. When you go into the store, you see a stack of Coca-Cola products at the end of the first aisle, with a sign hanging from the ceiling announcing the special price. The store benefits because Coca-Cola may have paid for the special attention through co-op advertising allowances and free point-of-purchase displays.

Salespeople play a major role in seeing that stores successfully feature their products. Neither the store nor the manufacturer wants to just sell at lower prices. Without the additional advertising and in-store promotion (through either an end-of-aisle display or some other special display), the sales volume will not increase enough to offset the lower price. The salesperson usually builds the display, sees that the retailer receives originals of any advertising, and ensures a proper inventory for the sale.

Deals can create problems. Sometimes retailers do not pass the savings on to their customers. Instead, because they can price the product for any amount, they keep the retail price at its regular level and pocket the extra earnings.

Similarly, the reseller may buy a larger-than-normal amount to take advantage of the lower price. At first glance, this seems reasonable. But some resellers may purchase an entire year's inventory at the low price, a practice called **buying forward.** Such a large order is much greater than what the manufacturer anticipated for the special promotion period. Buying forward can disrupt the manufacturer's production plans in relation to real demand, because the manufacturer expects orders to return to normal levels after the promotion period. But the reseller that bought forward places no more orders that year. Buying forward thus can create serious problems for manufacturers.

In spite of the reasons to avoid buying forward, and despite the growth of partnerships, buying forward is on the increase.[14] Salespeople can avoid the problem of buying forward if they resist the temptation to cut price to get the easy sale. Cumulative discounts can also help reduce buying forward because the buyer's lower price is based on total deliveries over a year. The motivation for buying more now is taken away because the lower price is not contingent on immediate delivery. Partnerships that include ECR can also limit the likelihood of forward buying because cost savings of ECR are lost. Those cost savings are based on low inventories, whereas buying forward raises the reseller's inventory levels.

Contests Some trade promotions are merely **contests** for the company's own salespeople. Top dealers may win trips to exotic places or be able to pick out merchandise from a catalog, paying with "dollars" earned through top sales performance. Some trade promotions actually reward the top salespeople of the reseller directly rather than the reseller. While a student at Baylor University, Robert Wagner worked part time for a local Montgomery Ward selling computers and stereos. During the Christmas season, he sold enough IBM computers to place among IBM's top 10 retailer salespeople, earning him an all-expenses-paid trip to the Super Bowl. These types of trade promotions are used when the retailer requires a personal selling effort.

Push Money Similar to contests are spiffs, or push money. Like a commission, **spiffs** or **push money (PM)** are paid directly to the retailer's salespeople by the manufacturer for selling the manufacturer's product. But the reseller's salespeople can earn PM only for a short period of time and for a specific product, unlike with a regular commission. Spiffs work well only when the promotion requires a personal selling effort by the retailer's salespeople.

Some retailers discourage the use of PM because they do not want products pushed on buyers and because the products may not be the best products for their customers. Other retailers frown on PM because they believe it diverts their sales staff's attention to products that may be less profitable to the store than others. Salespeople, however, may appreciate the opportunity to earn extra money.

Thinking *it* Through	How would you feel if you knew the stereo salesperson you were buying from could receive a spiff for selling you a particular product? Would you feel any differently if you knew that the salesperson was paid straight commission, no matter which product was sold?

PARTNERING WITH RESELLERS

Throughout this book, we have emphasized developing strategic partnerships with buyers whenever possible. Just as in all other selling arenas, selling to resellers has been revolutionized by the concept of partnerships. And, as you have seen in this chapter, partnering is important to strategies such as efficient customer response and quick-response systems. In this section, we'll take a closer look at two strategies related to partnering: training resellers and category management.

Training Resellers

An important dimension of partnering with resellers is training their sales staff. While not a promotion strategy per se, training the reseller may be necessary to enable a retailer's sales force to sell the product. The manufacturer's salespeople may be responsible for training the resellers' salespeople in how a product operates and how it should be sold.

For example, as mentioned earlier in this chapter, Kiwi has adopted a strategy of trade promotions involving advertising and merchandising. Its main competitor, SecondWind, uses an entirely different strategy, based primarily on training the trade. Part of the training is delivered through two free videos, one that trains the retailer on how to merchandise SecondWind products and one that focuses entirely on selling SecondWind shoe accessories at the time of a shoe sale (this is like asking if you want fries with your Big Mac). It is planning another video, one that teaches retail salespeople how to sell any specific product in its line of shoe cleaners, deodorizers, laces, insoles, cleats, and replacement spikes.[15]

In some situations, the salesperson needs to teach general selling skills first (the purpose of SecondWind's first sales training video). Some companies have product specialists to assist salespeople with the training task, but the responsibility lies solely with the salesperson in many cases. Without such training, the reseller's salespeople will not have the knowledge or confidence to successfully sell the product, and the resellers do not have the expertise to conduct the training themselves.

Training resellers is more important in situations requiring personal selling by the reseller. For example, office supply stores often sell office equipment and furniture. These products require active prospecting and selling skills that focus on needs satisfaction. The stores' salespeople need training so that they can sell the office equipment and furniture appropriate to the buyer's needs.

If customers require service, training may also be necessary. Sales clerks need to know the service procedures of the manufacturer so that the customer receives good service. Clerks may also be asked how something works or what is needed to solve a customer's problem (which is the purpose of the second sales training video from SecondWind). These situations may not require active selling, but a knowledgeable sales clerk can mean the difference between a satisfied customer and an irate ex-customer.

Hewlett-Packard dealers gather at the company's Mexico City training center for training on new products.

Keith Dannemillar/Saba

Category Management

Category management is a process by which retailers and manufacturers jointly plan and implement marketing programs to improve the performance of an entire product category (including competitive products) for mutual benefit.[16] Category management strives to maximize profits for the entire category (for the retailer) through efficiently using pricing, promotion, point-of-purchase merchandising, and other techniques. Perhaps the most important tool is information.[17] The supplier has information that was previously unavailable to the retailer through any other source. The retailer knew everything that went on in that store and therefore knew the impact of displays and special prices, but did not know the segmentation structure of the category's market, consumption trends, new product trends, and key influences on the category by region, market, or other division. Such information can be crucial to the success of a promotion strategy.

Category management has opened the communication channels.[18] By sharing such information in the form of fact-based presentations that educate buyers, salespeople and buyers create joint marketing and promotion programs. These joint programs are more effective than the old method in which each independently created a marketing program. But not just marketing programs are affected. Logistics, finance, and other phases of both companies' operations are affected by category management and partnership programs such as ECR.

One benefit of category management for the seller is that it can reduce forward buying for that salesperson's brand, but there is pressure to lower the usual price. With open communication, an average price can be agreed on that is more than a deal price but less than the regular price. The manufacturer will still save money because of more efficient manufacturing due to regular ordering, and can actually make more profit.

For example, a dried-fruit company examined market data (from IRI, a marketing research company) for Dallas and realized that one chain of stores accounted for 8.3 percent of all edible food sales but only 6.3 percent for dried fruits.[19] Closer examination revealed that raisins, the major component of the dried-fruit category, were selling at a rate half that of most other chains in the market. Further analysis indicated that raisin sales were actually decreasing at that chain, although increasing for the total market. What was the chain doing wrong?

By examining data from the retailer and comparing them to its own data, the company learned that 34.4 percent of all Dallas raisin sales are produced through promotions, but that amount fell to 15.3 percent at that particular chain. Additional data showed that the chain promoted raisins fewer times and less heavily than did other stores in the market. A joint review between the company and the chain resulted in a promotion program to improve raisin sales. One event in the program was a baking promotion that did not involve a specific raisin company's brand but was designed to simply increase raisin sales.

Category management began as a grocery store–consumer packaged goods strategy. This particular form of partnering, though, is spreading to other types of resellers such as Wal-Mart, sporting goods retailers, and others.

SUMMARY

Many students can easily picture how to sell a product to someone who will use it, but they have more difficulty understanding how to sell to resellers. Those who buy to resell, including wholesalers, distributors, and retailers, are called the *trade*. Resellers buy what sells, buy marketing support, and buy profits.

Industrial reseller salespeople speak of their battle as one for mind share. Each salesperson wants his or her product, rather than a competitor's, to be recommended whenever possible by the distributor's sales staff. Because the distributor's sales staff is key to selling the product to the user, mind share is more important than shelf space.

In evaluating products and vendors, resellers use the strategic profit model (SPM). This model evaluates a product or a store by examining net sales, net profit margin, and inventory turnover. When introducing a product or a program, salespeople can use selling history, market share, and similar products' results to prove how well a product can sell. Financial aspects such as the terms and conditions of the sale are also important.

Buyers also evaluate the product's image and the vendor's reputation. Reputation is often proven by taking care of the little things (as discussed in previous chapters).

Trade promotions are offered to resellers in an effort to stimulate sales. Pull strategies include advertising directly to the consumer, sponsoring contests, offering coupons, and the like. Push strategies include using push money, sponsoring contests for the retailer's salespeople, and building displays.

Merchandise markets, trade shows, and trade fairs can play a major role in a firm's sales efforts. In some industries, most sales are gained at a market. Trade shows and trade fairs are important when selling to certain types of industrial users, as well as to resellers and end users.

Training the trade, an important dimension of service in many industries, may be needed to enable resellers' salespeople to sell the product well. The manufacturer's sales rep often performs this task.

Selling to resellers involves different benefits, but many of the same principles still apply. Many people find personal fulfillment in the challenges and rewards of selling to the trade.

KEY TERMS

buyback 441
buying forward 449
category management 451
consignment 441
contests 449
co-op advertising 448
deal 441
deferred dating 441
efficient customer response (ECR) 432
feature 448
FOB 440
freestanding insert (FSI) 448
guaranteed price 440
inventory turnover 432
letters of credit 441
list price 439
market share 437
market 445

markup 431
mind share 428
net price 439
net profit margin 431
net sales 431
pull 447
push 447
push money (PM) 449
quick response 433
selling history 436
spiffs 449
strategic profit model (SPM) 429
suggested retail price 439
trade discount 440
trade fair 446
trade promotions 447
trade shows 445
turnaround 443

QUESTIONS AND PROBLEMS

1. Some students fail to see how anyone could get excited selling household cleaning products to resellers. But some people enjoy this job a great deal. What differences in the attitudes of the two groups might account for their different perspectives?

2. Is encouraging buyers to order a large quantity so they can get a better quantity discount always a good idea? Why or why not?

3. The list price for a child's outfit is $30. Your company offers trade discounts of 40 percent and 20 percent to retailers and wholesalers, respectively. If outfits are ordered in quantities greater than 5 dozen, wholesalers receive an extra 5 percent discount. A wholesaler places an order for 10 dozen. What does the wholesaler pay? If terms are 2/10, n/30, and the wholesaler pays in five days, what price does the wholesaler pay?

4. Profit and turnover seem to be two natural enemies. Discuss how the manufacturer's salesperson can influence both in a positive way for the reseller.

5. What types of point-of-purchase displays would be effective for promoting designer costume jewelry? Televisions? Fertilizer?

6. Assume you sell cleaning supplies. How would your presentation differ when selling to a store versus selling to a janitorial service company?

7. The most common complaint of resellers is a lack of support by vendors. Give your opinion as to why this is true.

8. Most insecticides are sold in spring and early summer. If you were an Ortho rep selling pesticides to retailers, what effect would seasonality have on your activities? What effect would an upcoming national ad campaign by Ortho have on your activities?

9. One problem with promotional discounts, such as the temporary price reductions described in Selling Scenario 15.2, is that some resellers do not pass them on to their customers but pocket the extra profit. Another problem with promotions in general occurs when some resellers do not participate. Why would resellers not participate fully in a manufacturer's promotional programs? What effect would this have on Borden's image and the images of its partners? The image of a nonparticipating grocery store?

10. What role do trade shows play in the overall marketing process? How does the role differ if one is selling through resellers rather than selling directly to users?

11. Discuss store loyalty versus brand loyalty. How would each affect the sales efforts of a manufacturer's salesperson? Would these concepts have any effect on a category management program?

12. How does category management differ from other forms of partnering? What impact do the buyer's customers have on any partnering relationship? How is technology used to manage categories and build partnerships?

EXPLORING THE NET

In the chapter, you read how salespeople who sell to resellers have to work with their customers to make sure sufficient inventory is available for special promotions. Check out one of the following home pages and look for these manufacturers' current promotions. Then list the benefits to the reseller who participates in that promotion. (If you have trouble finding a specific promotion, then use a new product announcement or other announcement.) When you list the benefits, be specific as to what you learned from the home page; don't assume 'more profit' as a benefit unless you can demonstrate how more profit is illustrated on the home page.

  alberto.com (Alberto VO5)

  brother.com

  calgon.com

  olympus.co.jp

  robertmondavi.com

After you have written out your benefits, then look at the home page of a reseller. Write a brief summary of your selling strategy to link the reseller's promotions to the manufacturer's.

  HEB.com

  kmart.com

  samsclub.com

  tandy.com

  wal-mart

CASE PROBLEMS

**CASE 15.1
Fairly Brushes**

Fairly Brushes offers several specialized cleaning brushes (such as a brush specially designed for washing cars), "Bag of Rags" for general cleaning, "Shop Towels" for use in the garage, and brooms. The company has been in business for over 20 years and enjoyed a growth rate of over 15 percent per year. The company does no advertising, nor has it offered co-op advertising in the past. In grocery stores, the products are set up in a standard 4-foot display that uses pegboard to allow for the varying heights of the brushes and brooms. In stores with an auto department, the company also displays the shop towels, chamoislike cloths, and other car-cleaning products.

Recently the company introduced a Bug Sponge. This sponge is covered with fishnet to provide extra scrubbing strength. Originally designed to clean bugs off cars, the sponges have a wide range of uses. They can be used for scouring in the kitchen or cleaning in the bathroom. Two sponges come in a small plastic bag with cardboard folded and stapled over the top; the unit can be hung on a pegboard.

As a sales representative for Fairly Brushes, you are planning tomorrow's activities. You want to call on the following stores:

Tusa Grocery. This is a small, family-owned grocery store in a poorer part of town. It currently has only the 4-foot display, with no separate auto products area.

Big Savings Grocery. You will call on the nongrocery item buyer for Big Savings, a four-store chain of mid-size grocery stores. These stores have the pegboard display in the auto section.

Brookshires. Brookshires, a regional discount chain, has 32 stores over a four-state area. Fairly is an approved vendor. You are calling on the only store in your territory that carries no Fairly products. The manager has told you he doesn't want Fairly because he already carries Maxi-Brush (a competitor) and doesn't want the hassle of two vendors. You have collected data to show that Fairly outsells Maxi-Brush in the other stores by an average of 10 percent.

Mac's Grocery. Mac's carries only Maxi-Brush in its 12 grocery stores. You called Mac's headquarters by phone because it isn't in your territory and found that all buying is done by local managers. They do not use an approved vendor list. When you visited this store last month, the manager did not have time to talk. She had never heard of Fairly, but did say you could come back when she had more time. You set up an appointment for tomorrow.

Questions

1. Keeping in mind why resellers buy, what strategies will you use to introduce the Bug Sponge (and/or Fairly) to these stores?

2. How will you maximize the number of facings for Bug Sponge in each store?

3. Assume the Tusa buyer is an analytical, the Big Savings buyer is an amiable, the Brookshires buyer is an expressive, and the Mac's buyer is a driver. How would you prove/dramatize the benefits for each buyer?

4. In what category does the Bug Sponge fit? What disadvantages would you face if you tried a category management program with each of these stores? How would you go about presenting a category management program?

**CASE 15.2
Electric City**

Bright and early on a Monday morning, Jill Cates found herself in the upstairs room at Cupp's, a local breakfast establishment. Cates is a salesperson for Electric City, a retail store that sells video and audio electronics. Recently, she closed a big sale with the psychology department of a local school with the help of Mario, her store manager. They sold over $100,000 of Sony video equipment to the school.

This morning all of the Electric City salespeople were there, along with Mario and a rep from Sharp (a Sony competitor), for a rare Monday morning sales meeting. Breakfast was on Sharp, and Cates found herself enjoying the eggs and bacon that she never seemed to have time to make for herself.

Near the end of the meal, the Sharp rep stood up at the head of the table. "Thank you all for coming here so early in the morning," she began, and was interrupted by a chorus of thank-you's for the breakfast from the salespeople. "Oh, you are all very welcome. The reason I asked Mario to bring you all together is that Electric City has long been a strong retailer for me and for Sharp products, and I wanted to first offer this breakfast as a thank-you for all of your hard work. Second, I wanted to tell you personally of an exciting sales incentive campaign that we have for the next month."

She walked over to an easel that had a large flipchart. As she pulled over the blank first page to reveal Sharp's slogan, "From Sharp minds come Sharp products," she said, "As you know, Sharp has kept new products coming that have really helped you make a lot of money." She flipped the page and pointed to several enlarged product photographs. "Here are several new products that will be arriving in your store around Thanksgiving, just in time for the Christmas season." She described each one, and each description was followed by applause.

"But as you know, we'll need room on the shelves for these products. That's why my company has authorized the first direct incentive program ever for you, the Electric City salespeople." She flipped the page to uncover a large dollar sign. "For each of the products on the list that Mario is passing out that you sell, Sharp will pay you an extra $25 spiff." The salespeople broke out into wild clapping and a few cheers. "And every rep who earns $100 in spiffs will also earn 100 points that can be used to purchase merchandise in the prize catalog that Mario is passing out." She was interrupted again by cheers.

Flipping the page to a picture of a sunny tropical beach, she continued, "The top rep in my district as of December 1 wins—are you ready for this?—a trip to the Bahamas!" The reps went wild.

The rest of the meeting involved strategies to switch customers from other products to Sharp, how to present features and benefits of various Sharp products, and all of the details of the contest.

Three days later, Cates was in the store demonstrating two stereos, a Sharp and a Moyashita. Mario had priced the Sharp so that it was now only a few dollars more than the Moyashita to help the salespeople move the Sharp.

"Gee, Jill, I really like the looks of the Moyashita," said the customer. The Moyashita did have a more futuristic look than the Sharp's more traditional lines.

"That's true, Bill, but looks aren't everything. If I were you, I'd have the Sharp for the sound it produces."

"I just don't hear the difference."

"Well, it is your decision, Bill. So you want to take the Moyashita?" Cates asked. Bill nodded *yes.* Even with the sale, Cates was slightly disappointed. She was having some difficulty pushing those Sharps compared to some of the other salespeople.

A couple of weeks later, the Sony rep called Cates at home. After some small talk and questions about the new video center in the sociology department, he asked Cates why Sony's sales were down at Electric City.

"Have you talked to Mario about that?" Cates asked.

"Yes, but I don't get a straight answer. I get the feeling he's hiding something."

"Well, we're having a contest on some other products," admitted Cates.

"Hmm. I wonder what it would take to make Sony a player. Well, thanks, Jill. And sell a few Sonys, okay?"

"Sure thing," replied Cates. After she hung up, she thought about the contest. She got out the catalog and leafed through it, thinking about what she wanted to win.

Questions

1. Did Cates do anything unethical in the above scenario?

2. Strategically, why is Sharp using the promotion program? What other reasons would cause it to use a push program?

3. Why would Mario agree to the promotion? How would it affect his relationships with other vendors?

4. Based on the success with the psychology department, the Sony rep believed he was building a partnership with Mario and Electric City. Now he's not so sure. What should he do?

ADDITIONAL REFERENCES

Ball, Benjamin. "Profit: The Common Denominator." *PROMO: The International Magazine for Promotion Marketing,* October 1993, p. 52.

Candler, Julie. "How to Choose a Distributor." *Nation's Business,* August 1993, pp. 45–46.

Chatterjee, Sharmila; Saara Hyvonen; and Erin Anderson. "Concentrated vs. Balanced Sourcing: An Examination of Retailer Purchasing Decisions in Closed Markets." *Journal of Retailing* 71, (1995), 23–46.

"Donnelly Reports Account-Specific Increase in Promotion Spending." *Sales and Marketing Strategies & News,* July/August 1993, p. 35.

Hoyt, Christopher W. "Co-Marketing Joins Marketing Lexicon." *PROMO: The International Magazine for Promotion Marketing.* March 1993, p. 90.

____ . "Co-Marketing Questions & Answers." *PROMO: The International Magazine for Promotion Marketing,* August 1993, p. 44.

Miller, Craig. "What Do Retailers Really Want?" *Potentials in Marketing,* June 1993, p. 36.

Schultz, Don E. *Strategic Advertising Campaigns.* Lincolnwood, IL: NTC Business Books, 1990.

Sharma, Arun. "The Persuasive Effect of Salesperson Credibility: Conceptual and Empirical Examination." *Journal of Personal Selling and Sales Management,* Fall 1990, pp. 71–80.

Smith, Kerry E. "Trade Promotion vs. Trade Spending, Part I." *PROMO: The International Magazine for Promotion Marketing.* February 1993, pp. 10–14, 32, 75.

____ . "Trade Promotion vs. Trade Spending, Part II." *PROMO: The International Magazine for Promotion Marketing,* March 1993, pp. 52–56.

Whittemore, Meg. "Trade Shows' Direct Appeal." *Nation's Business,* August 1993, pp. 48–50.

T his section discusses a little known but very important element of the profession of selling. Salespeople, by the very nature of their jobs, are managers, too. As you can see by the circle diagram, salespeople must manage their territory and their time, manage the resources within their companies, and manage their careers. In Chapter Sixteen, we discuss techniques salespeople use to manage their time and other resources effectively. Chapter Seventeen presents many of the company resources that salespeople manage, and discusses methods of building internal part-

Part Five

The Salesperson *as* Manager

nerships to deliver superior customer satisfaction. In Chapter Eighteen, you will learn valuable lessons for managing your career, beginning with how to get your career started. Even if you choose a career or an initial job outside of sales, you will find the information in this section useful for improving your effectiveness.

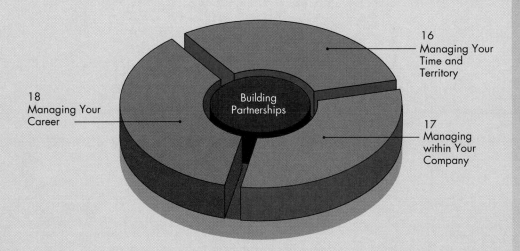

Chapter Sixteen

Managing Your Time *and* Territory

Some Questions Answered in this Chapter Are:

How should territories be managed?

Why is time so valuable for salespeople?

What can you do to "create" more selling time?

What should you consider when devising a territory strategy?

How should you analyze your daily activities and sales calls?

How can you evaluate your own performance so that you can improve?

Many salespeople work in the field, their only contact with the office by telephone, computer, and fax. Because no one tells them when to start working or when to quit for the day, they must be self-sufficient. Their success or failure depends on their own efforts.

Salespeople have more individual freedom than almost any other type of employee. With that freedom comes the responsibility to manage themselves. Self-management involves using their scarcest resource, time, to make the most of their other resources, their customers, and their skills.

PROFILE

As regional vice president for Texas Life Insurance Company's top territory in market penetration, Carroll Fadal places a high priority on time management. He has to—his region is the company's largest geographically but the smallest in market potential.

Covering a territory that spans the northwestern third of Texas and all of New Mexico, Fadal provides product and service to a diverse group of independent agents bound to Texas Life only by choice. Each independent agent is Fadal's customer, yet is free to sell any competitor's insurance product for which she or he is licensed. "When agents are free to pick and choose which companies they will use, it is imperative that I be in front of them on a regular basis," Fadal says. "Otherwise, you can lose your best people to someone else who gets in front of them with a hot idea."

Managing time is the easiest part of the equation. Operating on a schedule that takes him out of his office every other week, Fadal has at least 10 face-to-face meetings with his agents each year. "That makes a big difference in my region," he says. "In remote places such as Amarillo, Lubbock, and Espanola, New Mexico, agents aren't used to company officers being in their places of business that often. It really makes them feel important and helps cement the relationship."

> *"I always try to take them a new sales idea each time out, and I try to present it to them in an efficient fashion, never exceeding the allotted time unless it's their idea."*

It is that work—building the relationship—that Fadal sees as the key to managing his territory. "If the people with whom you work feel like you care about them beyond the amount of money they put in your pocket, they're less likely to be bowled over by the new kid on the block," he says. "I won't always have the lowest-priced product on the market, but if my agents know I will always go to the mat for them when they need service, price becomes a secondary issue. And the only way they'll know that is if I spend plenty of time listening to them to know what their needs are."

Building strong relationships takes time, which can present a problem when calling on busy, successful salespeople. That's why Fadal makes it a point to respect his agents' time and not waste it. "Before making the appointment, we send out a letter telling the agents exactly how much time we'll need," he says. "I always

CARROLL FADAL
Texas Life Insurance Company

try to take them a new sales idea each time out, and I try to present it to them in an efficient fashion, never exceeding the allotted time unless it's their idea." Each new sales idea he gives them means more sales for them, so they are willing to hear what he has to say.

Of course, relationships don't just happen in one-hour visits discussing sales ideas. To build relationships, Fadal always sprinkles in a few social events each year that also include agents' spouses. "We try to foster a team and family spirit among our producers," he explains. "When you're dealing with so many people who are also so widely scattered, you want to give them a place where they feel like they belong. Everybody's looking for a home, for a feeling of family. We see that as crucial to our success."

It must be working. With population and sales potential only half that of the next smallest territory, Fadal's western region is the only one in the company that exceeds the company's goal for market penetration. He now has his sights set on the bigger prize: number one in total production. At the moment, he's number two—and growing.

Visit Our Website@
http://www.texlife.com

Many salespeople view their sales job as though they were running their own small businesses. Like independent business owners, they have the freedom to establish marketing programs, advertising, and sales strategies while ringing up sales. For example, Gary Wolfe sells chemicals. He is responsible for deciding how his company's products will be advertised and promoted in central Texas, his territory. He arranges seminars for his prospects and is responsible for booking booth space at local business trade shows. Wolfe also decides which products to emphasize, the types of companies he will visit, and the strategies he will use to entice buyers to switch to his products. Just like the owner of a small business, Wolfe allocates marketing resources to generate the highest profit.

Also like a small-business owner, Wolfe has many demands on his time that can take him away from selling activities. Filling out paperwork, learning new products, and performing similar duties can take up a great deal of time.

Managing time and territory is often a question of how to allocate resources. Allocating resources such as time is a difficult management process, but when done well, it often spells the difference between stellar and average performance. Many times it is difficult to know what is really important and what only seems important. In this chapter, we will discuss how to manage your time. Building on what you have learned about the many activities of salespeople, we will also provide strategies for allocating resources among accounts, that is, managing your territory.

THE SELF-MANAGEMENT PROCESS

There are four stages in the self-management process in selling. The first stage is setting goals, or determining what is to be accomplished. The second stage is allocating resources and determining strategies to meet those goals. In the third stage, the salesperson implements the time management strategies by making sales calls, sending direct-mail pieces, or executing whatever action the strategy calls for. In the fourth and final stage, the salesperson evaluates performance to determine whether the goals will be reached and the strategies were effective or the goals cannot be reached and the strategies must change. This process is illustrated in Exhibit 16.1 and will serve as an outline for this chapter.

SETTING GOALS

The Need for Goals

The first step in managing any worthwhile endeavor is to consider what makes it worthwhile and what you want to accomplish. Salespeople need to examine their careers in the same way. Career goals and objectives should reflect personal ambitions and desires so that the individual can create the desired lifestyle, as illustrated

Sales managers often ask people to publicly state their sales goals because these managers recognize the importance of setting personal sales objectives.

Courtesy GMAC Financial Services

EXHIBIT 16.1

The Self-Management Process

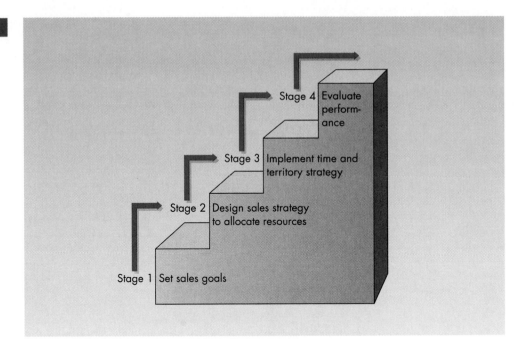

in Exhibit 16.2. When career goals reflect personal ambitions, the salesperson is more committed to achieving those goals.

To achieve career objectives, salespeople must set sales goals. These sales goals provide some of the means for reaching personal objectives. Sales goals also guide the salesperson's decisions as to which activities to perform, when to perform those activities, whom to see, and how to sell.

The salesperson who lacks goals will drift around the territory, wasting time and energy. Sales calls will be unrelated to objectives and may be minimally productive or even harmful to the sales process. The result will be poor performance and, eventually, the need to find another job.

In Chapter Eight, you learned that salespeople should set visionary, primary, and minimum call objectives so that the activities performed during the call will bring them closer to those objectives. The same can be said for setting sales goals: When sales goals are set properly and adhered to, the salesperson has a guide to direct activities.

The Nature of Goals

As you read in Chapter Eight, goals should be specific and measurable, reachable yet challenging, and time based. Goals should be *specific and measurable* so that the salesperson knows when they have been met. For example, setting a goal of making better presentations is laudable, but how would the salesperson know if the presentations were better or worse? A more helpful goal would be to increase the number of sales resulting from those presentations. The best goal would be a specific increase, such as 10 percent. Then there would be no question in the salesperson's mind as to the achievement of the goal.

Goals should also be *reachable yet challenging*. One purpose of setting personal goals is to motivate oneself. If goals are reached too easily, little has been accomplished. Challenging goals, then, are more motivating. But if the goals are too challenging, or if they are unreachable, then the salesperson may give up.

EXHIBIT 16.2

The Relationship of Goals

Career goals are devised from lifestyle objectives. Sales goals should reflect career goals. While activities lead to sales, performance goals are usually set first. Then, using conversion goals, activity goals are set.

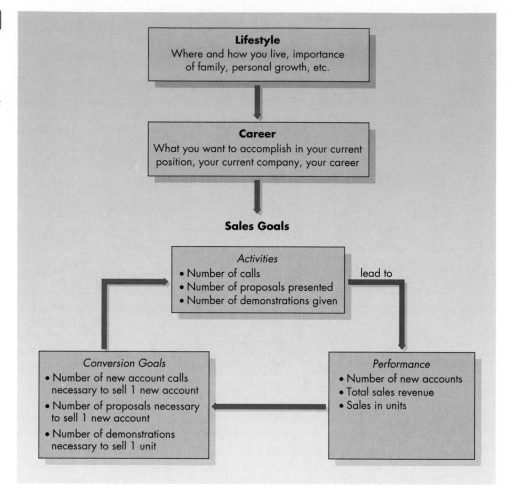

Goals should also be *time based;* that is, goals should have deadlines. Putting a deadline on the goal provides more guidance for the salesperson and creates a sense of urgency that can be motivating. Without a deadline, the goal is not specific enough and the salesperson may be able to drag on forever, never reaching the goal but thinking progress is being made. Imagine the motivational difference between setting a goal of a 10 percent increase in sales with no deadline and setting a goal of a 10 percent increase for the next month. In the first instance there is no sense of urgency, of needing to work toward that goal *now.* Without a deadline, the goal has little motivational value.

One problem some people have is periodically creating goals and then forgetting them. Goals should be *written down, then posted.* Probably not all goals should be posted in highly public areas, but the idea is to keep the goal in front of you so that it continues to direct your activities.

| Thinking *it* Through | What types of goals have you set for yourself in your college career? For specific classes? How would these goals meet the criteria of specific, and measurable, reachable yet challenging, and time based? How do you keep these goals in front of you? What would you do differently now? |

Establishing Sales Goals

Salespeople need to set three types of sales goals: performance, activity, and conversions. While many salespeople focus only on how many sales they get, setting all three types of goals is necessary to achieve the highest possible success.

Performance Goals

Goals relating to outcomes are **performance goals.** In sales, outcomes such as the size of a commission or bonus check, the amount of sales revenue generated or number of sales generated, and the number of prospects identified are common performance goals. For example, the rep in Exhibit 16.3 set a performance goal of $2,000 in commissions and another performance goal of eight sales. Revenue quotas are an example of goals set by the company, but each salesperson should also consider setting personally relevant goals. For example, you may want to set higher goals so that you can achieve higher earnings. People are more committed to achieving goals they set themselves. That commitment makes achieving them more likely. Performance goals should be set first, because attaining certain performance levels is of primary importance to both the organization and the salesperson.

Performance goals can also be less quantifiable, such as setting a goal of improving your presentation skills. But even that type of goal should be measurable in terms of how many customers agree to buy. Personal development goals, such as improving presentation skills, are important to long-term professional growth. Every person, whether in sales or other fields, should have some personal development goals. Reaching those goals will not only improve overall job performance but also increase personal satisfaction. Like all performance goals, however, these goals should meet the criteria of being specific, challenging, and time based.

Activity Goals

Salespeople also set activity goals. **Activity goals** are behavioral objectives: the number of calls made in a day, the number of demonstrations performed, and so on. Activity goals reflect how hard the salesperson wishes to work. The company may set some activity goals for salespeople, such as a quota of sales calls to be made each week. Exhibit 16.3 lists two activity goals: 240 sales calls per month and 12 calls per day.

All activity goals are intermediate goals; that is, achieving them should ultimately translate into achievement of performance goals. As Times Mirror Cable Television discovered by auditing sales performance, activity goals such as 10

EXHIBIT 16.3

Goal Calculations

Monthly earnings goal (performance goal):	$2,000
Commission per sale:	$250
$2,000 earnings ÷ $250 per sale = 8 sales	
Monthly sales goal (performance goal):	8
Closings goal (conversion goal):	10%
8 sales × 10 prospects per sale = 80 prospects	
Monthly prospect goal (performance goal):	80
Prospects per calls goal (conversion goal):	1 in 3
80 prospects × 3 calls per prospect = 240 calls	
Monthly sales calls goal (activity goal):	240
240 calls ÷ 20 working days per month = 12 calls	
Daily sales calls goal (activity goal):	12

prospecting calls per day are needed for the salespeople to achieve the overall performance goals. Activity goals help salespeople decide what to do each day, but those goals must ultimately be related to making sales.[1]

However, activity goals and performance goals are not enough. For example, a salesperson may have goals of achieving 10 sales and making 160 calls in one month. The salesperson may get 10 sales but make 220 calls. That salesperson had to work much harder than someone who managed to get 10 sales in only 160 calls. That is why salespeople should also set conversion goals.

Conversion Goals

Conversion goals are measures of salesperson efficiency. Conversion goals reflect how efficiently the salesperson would like to work, or work smarter. Unlike performance goals, conversion goals express relative accomplishments, such as the number of sales relative to the number of calls made or the number of customers divided by the number of prospects. The higher the ratio, the more efficient the salesperson. Exhibit 16.3 lists two conversion goals: closing 10 percent of all prospects and finding one prospect for every three calls. In our example above, a rep who made 10 sales while making 160 calls could sell 4 or 5 more by making 220 calls because that rep makes a sale every 16 calls.

Conversion goals are important because they reflect how efficiently the salesperson uses resources, such as time, to accomplish performance goals. For example, Freeman Exhibit Company builds custom trade show exhibits. Customers often ask for booth designs (called *speculative designs*) before making the purchase to evaluate the offerings of various competitors. Creating a custom booth design is a lot of work for a designer, and the cost can be high, but it does not guarantee a sale. If a salesperson has a low **conversion rate** for speculative designs, overall profits will be lowered because the cost for the unsold designs must still be covered. If the rep can increase the conversion rate, the overall costs for unsold designs will be lower, hence increasing profits.

Working harder would show up in an increase in activity; working smarter should be reflected in conversion goals. For example, a salesperson may be performing at a conversion rate of 10 percent. Reaching a conversion goal of 12 percent (closing 1 out of 8 instead of 1 out of 10) would reflect some improvement in the way the salesperson operates—some method of working smarter.

Measuring conversions tells salespeople which activities work best. For example, suppose a salesperson has two sales strategies. If A generated 10 sales and B generated 8 sales, the salesperson may think A is the better strategy. But if A required 30 sales calls and B only 20, the salesperson would be better off using strategy B. Thirty sales calls would have generated 12 sales with strategy B.

Comparing your performance with the best in your organization is a form of benchmarking.[2] Benchmarking can help you see where you are falling short. For example, if your conversion ratio of leads to appointments (the number of leads needed to get one appointment) is the same as that of the top seller but you are closing only half of your spec designs and that person is closing 80 percent, you know you are losing sales at the spec design stage. You can then examine what that person does differently to achieve the higher conversion ratio.

Setting Sales Goals

Performance and conversion goals are the basis for activity goals. Suppose a sale is worth $250 in commission. If a rep wants to earn $2,000 per month (a performance goal), eight sales are needed each month. If the salesperson sees closing 1 out of 10 prospects as a realistic conversion goal, a second performance goal results: The rep must identify 80 prospects to yield eight closings. If the rep can identify one prospect for every three sales calls (another conversion goal), 240 sales calls (an activity goal) must be made. Assuming 20 working days in a month, the rep must make 12 sales calls each day (another activity goal). Thus, activity goals need to be the last type of goals set because they will be determined by the desired level of performance at a certain rate of conversion.

Even though the conversion analysis results in a goal of 12 calls each day, that conversion rate is affected by the strategy the salesperson employs. A better strategy results in a higher conversion rate and better allocation of time, one of many important resources that must be allocated properly to achieve sales goals. We discuss how to allocate resources in the next section.

ALLOCATING RESOURCES

The second stage of the time and territory management process is to develop a strategy that allocates resources properly. These resources are allocated to different sales strategies used with different types of accounts with the purpose of achieving sales goals in the most effective and efficient manner possible. The process of allocating resources is very important for Bill Arend, sales representative for SOS Technology, as Selling Scenario 16.1 illustrates.

Resources to Be Allocated

Salespeople manage many resources. Some of these are physical resources, such as free samples, demonstration products, trial products, brochures, direct-mail budgets, and other marketing resources. Each of these physical resources represents a cost to the company, but to the salesperson they are investments. Salespeople consider physical resources as investments because resources must be managed wisely to generate the best possible return. Whereas financial investments may return dividends or price increases, the salesperson's investments should yield sales.

A key resource that salespeople manage is time. Time is limited, and not all of a salesperson's work time can be spent making sales calls. Some time must be spent in meetings, learning new products, preparing reports for management, and other nonselling duties. Thus, it is important to manage time wisely. As we will discuss in the next chapter, salespeople also coordinate many of the company's other departments to serve customers well. Salespeople must learn how to allocate these resources in ways that generate the greatest level of sales.

Where to Allocate Resources

For salespeople, the allocation of resources is often a question of finding the customers or companies that are most likely to buy, then allocating selling resources to maximize the opportunities they offer. As you may have learned in your principles of marketing course, some market segments are more profitable than others. And just as the company's marketing executive tries to determine which segments are more profitable so that marketing plans can be directed toward those segments, salespeople examine their markets to allocate their selling resources.

Cable & Wireless, for example, has achieved success in the highly competitive market of long-distance services sold to businesses by consistently going the extra mile for its customers. However, Cable & Wireless carefully chooses small-business customers for which it can add value and obtain more business. Each salesperson carefully quantifies the needs of the customer and then determines which accounts have sufficient potential to warrant building relationships with them.[3] Maximizing the opportunity means finding profitable ways to satisfy the greatest number of cus-

A Matter of Life and Death

Usually selling is not a matter of life and death. This is so even to Bill Arend who sells emergency response training and equipment to companies for SOS Technology. Yet, when Arend was working on the company's largest single sale, the prospect threw out an objection that seemed to kill the sale. OSHA requires companies to have trained CPR and first-aid personnel on site, and the prospect company had 59 locations around the country, with SOS units in only 6. So Arend walked in thinking he was going to easily add the other 53 when the customer said, "Bill, it appears from this Department of Labor memo that I don't have to have your equipment. In fact, it may be illegal. So I'd like to cancel all of our locations that have SOS."

Arens's first reaction was to sell. But when he saw that memo, he realized that trying to persuade the buyer that the memo was wrong was not the best approach. He recalls, "What I did was promise to find out more about it, because I had never seen the memo before." So Arend went to the Houston Public Library to do some research. He was up until after 2 am, working on a 30-page proposal documenting that the Department of Labor memo referred to a different product and illustrating the need for SOS products and service in all of the customer's 59 locations. "I felt like I was back in school and about to take the hardest final exam of my life."

Arend's research convinced the buyer. But then came the task of getting all 59 locations trained and the equipment installed as soon as possible—a time management nightmare. "The day after we trained the staff at one location, one of their customers had a heart attack. The staff was able to administer CPR and oxygen, saving his life" says Arend. "I hate to think what might have happened if I had put them off a day or two."

Yet that is the kind of total commitment it takes to prioritize activities. "My customers know that when I promise to act, I will act. At the same time, I don't make promises for my time that I don't think I can keep," Arend states. He knows, as well as his best customer knows, how important good time management is. In fact, it can be a matter of life or death.

tomers, but not necessarily everybody. In the following section, we discuss how to analyze the market to identify potential customers who are most likely to buy so that resources will be allocated properly.

Account Classification and Resource Allocation

Not all customers have the same buying potential, just as not all sales activities produce the same results. The salesperson has to concentrate on the most profitable customers and minimize effort spent with customers that offer little opportunity for profitable sales. The proportion of unprofitable accounts is usually greater than one would think. As a rule, 80 percent of the sales in a territory come from only 20 percent of the customers. Therefore, salespeople should classify customers on the basis of their sales potential to avoid spending too much time and other resources with low-potential accounts, thus helping to achieve their sales goals.

Customer management is not just a time management issue. Managing customers includes allocating all of the resources at the salesperson's disposal in the most productive manner. Time may be the most important of these resources, but salespeople also manage sample and demonstration inventories, direct-mail budgets, printed materials, and other resources.

ABC Analysis

The simplest classification scheme, called **ABC analysis,** ranks accounts by sales potential. The idea is that the accounts with the greatest sales potential deserve the

GoldMine is a contact management software package that helps salespeople keep track of their customers.

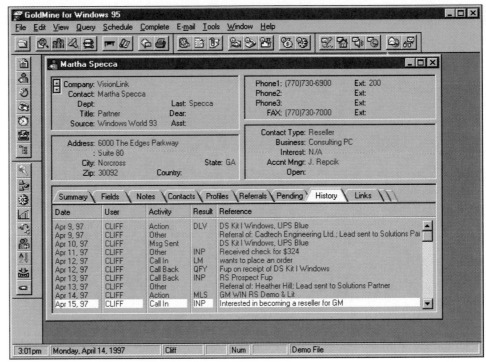

Courtesy GoldMine Software Corporation

most attention. Using the 80/20 rule, the salesperson identifies the 20 percent of accounts that (could) buy the most and calls those A accounts. The other 80 percent are B accounts, and noncustomers (or accounts with low potential for sales) are C accounts. This is how Marion/Merrell Dow classifies physicians and how Johnson Wax classifies retail stores. Federal Express studied buying habits of its customers and realized that 1 percent of its accounts generated 50 percent of revenue; it might call these A++ accounts! An example of an account analysis appears in Exhibit 16.4. As you can see, Sam Thompson has used estimated potential to classify accounts so that he can allocate sales calls to those accounts with the greatest potential.

Classification schemes can be used to generate call plans. Marion/Merrell Dow salespeople call on A physicians every two weeks, B physicians every six weeks, and C physicians only when they have nothing else to do (which is rare). This allows them to spend the most time with physicians who are heavy users of their products and account for the highest sales levels. ABC classification schemes work well only in industries that require regular contact with the same accounts, such as consumer packaged goods and pharmaceuticals. Some industries (e.g., plant equipment, medical equipment, and other capital products) may require numerous sales calls until the product is sold. After that sale, another sale may be unlikely for several years, and the number of sales calls may diminish. Then the A, B, and C classification may not be very helpful.

Salespeople in some industries find grid and market analysis methods more useful than ABC analysis. They have learned that simply allocating sales activities on the basis of sales potential may lead to inefficiencies. For example, satisfied customers may need fewer calls to maximize great potential than accounts of equal potential that are loyal to a competitor.

EXHIBIT 16.4   Account Classification

Salesperson: Sam Thompson   **A. Analysis of Call Pattern: 1997**

Customer Type	Number of Customers Contacted	Number of Calls	Average Calls per Customer	Sales Volume	Average Sales per Call
A	16	121	7.0	$212,516	$1,756
B	21	154	7.3	116,451	756
C	32	226	7.0	78,010	345
D	59	320	5.4	53,882	168
Total	128	821		$460,859	561

B. Annual Territory Sales Plan (dollars in thousands)

Account	Actual Sales			Estimated Potential	1998 Forecasted Sales	Number of Calls Allocated	Classification
	1995	1996	1997				
Allied Foods	$100	$110	$160	$250	$160	48	A
Pic N–Save	75	75	90	300	115	48	A
Wright Grocers	40	50	60	175	90	24	B
H.E.B.	20	30	30	150	30	24	B
Piggly Wiggly	10	10	25	100	55	18	C
Sal's Superstore	0	0	30	100	80	18	C
Buy-Rite	0	0	0	80	75	18	C
Tom Thumb	0	10	20	75	70	18	C
Apple Tree	0	5	12	60	60	12	D
Buy Lo	0	0	10	60	50	12	D
Whyte's Family Foods	10	8	9	50	40	12	D

Grid Analysis

The **sales call allocation grid** classifies accounts on the basis of the company's competitive position with an account along with the account's sales potential. As with ABC analysis, the purpose of classifying accounts using grid analysis is to determine which accounts are worth receiving more resources. Using this method, each account in a salesperson's territory falls into one of the four segments shown in Exhibit 16.5. The classification is determined by the salesperson's evaluation of the account on the following two dimensions.

First, the **account opportunity** dimension indicates how much the customer needs the product and whether it is able to buy the product. Some factors the salesperson can consider when determining account opportunity are the account's potential, growth rate, and financial condition. This rating is similar to the ABC analysis and is a measure of total sales potential. Again, the idea is that accounts with the greatest potential deserve the greatest resources.

Second, the **strength of position** dimension indicates how strong the salesperson and company are in selling the account. Some factors that determine strength of position are the present share of the account's purchases of the product, the attitude of the account toward the company and the salesperson, and the relationship between the salesperson and the key decision makers in the account. The strength of position

<table>
<tr><td></td><td colspan="2">Strength of Position</td></tr>
</table>

EXHIBIT 16.5		**Strength of Position**	

EXHIBIT 16.5

Sales Call
Allocation Grid

		Strong	Weak
Account Opportunity	**High**	*Segment 1* Attractiveness: Accounts are very attractive because they offer high opportunity, and the sales organization has a strong position. Sales call strategy: Accounts should receive a high level of sales calls because they are the sales organization's most attractive accounts.	*Segment 2* Attractiveness: Accounts are potentially attractive because they offer high opportunity, but the sales organization currently has a weak position with accounts. Sales call strategy: Accounts should receive a high level of sales calls to strengthen the sales organization's position.
	Low	*Segment 3* Attractiveness: Accounts are somewhat attractive because the sales organization has a strong position, but future opportunity is limited. Sales call strategy: Accounts should receive a moderate level of sales calls to maintain the current strength of the sales organization's position.	*Segment 4* Attractiveness: Accounts are very unattractive because they offer low opportunity, and the sales organization has a weak position. Sales call strategy: Accounts should receive minimal level of sales calls and efforts made to selectively eliminate or replace personal sales calls with telephone sales calls, direct mail, etc.

Source: Raymond W. LaForge, Clifford E. Young, and B. Curtis Hamm, "Increasing Sales Productivity through Improved Sales Call Allocation Strategies," *Journal of Personal Selling and Sales Management*, November 1983, pp. 53–59.

helps the salesperson understand what level of sales is likely in the account. The account opportunity may be tremendous, say, $1 million. But if the account has always purchased another brand, the salesperson's strength of position is weak and his or her real potential is something much less than $1 million.

The appropriate sales call strategy depends on the grid segment into which the account falls. Accounts with high potential and a strong position are very attractive, because the salesperson should be able to sell large amounts relatively easily. Thus, these attractive accounts should receive the highest level of sales calls. For example, if you have an account that likes your product and has established a budget for it, and you know the customer needs 300 units per year, you may consider that a segment 1 account (assuming 300 units is a high number) and plan to allocate more calls to that account. But if a competitor has a three-year contract with the account, you might be better off spending less time with that account. The account may buy 3,000 units per year, but you have little chance of getting any of that business. By classifying the account as a segment 2, you would recognize that the most appropriate strategy is to strengthen your position in the account. The sales call allocation grid, then, aids salespeople in determining where, by account, to spend time in order to meet sales goals.

The Grid and Current Customers   The sales call allocation grid is a great tool for analyzing current customers. Recall the value of a customer that was discussed in Chapter Thirteen; many businesses experience little or no profit in the first year of a customer's life. But over time, profit grows if the salesperson is able to grow sales in the account, find ways to reduce the cost to serve the account (for example, shipping more can mean reduced shipping costs), and so on.

In a landmark study of the paper and plastics industry, the key to a company's profit was found to be customer share, not market share. **Customer share** is the average percentage of business received from a company's accounts. The analysis of companies in that industry indicated that even if a company was the dominant supplier to a group of buyers, another company could be more profitable if it served fewer customers but had all of their business.[4]

Market Analysis

Salespeople who rely on new business can perform market analysis after the grid analysis. **Market analysis** is the evaluation of opportunity within segments in the overall territory (or market) to determine allocation of time and other resources. Market analysis is a process of looking for patterns in the types of accounts found in segments 1 and 2 of the grid analysis and can be helpful in determining prospecting and other selling efforts.

Grand Rapids Label puts market analysis to work.[5] The company first determines which accounts are the largest, then interviews each customer in detail. The responses are then transcribed and sent back to each customer for verification. Patterns and themes are then determined by Grand Rapids personnel who use the data to find out what buyers' wants and needs are and where Grand Rapids offers the greatest value. Then the company uses what it learned to guide sales strategies, such as where to prospect for accounts. If, for example, the company learned that small manufacturers have a certain set of needs that Grand Rapids can fill better than competitors, salespeople would then begin to prospect new accounts from small manufacturers.

Using the Computer for Account Analysis

Use of computers and sales force automation (SFA) software has grown tremendously over the last few years. Because sales involves face-to-face communication, companies have struggled with how to use computers to help salespeople become more productive. Account analysis is one area where computers have had a big impact.

The latest generation of sales automation software products is designed to let the salesperson know where each account stands in the selling cycle. In Chapter Seven, we discussed how accounts move through several stages, from lead to prospect to customer. These software products aid salespeople in determining which accounts are leads, which are prospects, and which are customers. The software can even be used to identify needs and recommend solutions.

For example, Northwestern National Insurance was processing about 27,000 applications for commercial insurance each year and declining half of them for a variety of reasons. For each of the 13,500 accepted applications, a personalized quote was prepared, and then half of those applicants would accept. Many sales were lost simply because the competition could produce a quote more quickly. Northwestern automated the process with astounding results. Not only was the cost reduced significantly (it cost $50 to turn down an application and $100 to produce a quote, so it cost $400 per sale just to get the pricing done), but the quicker turnaround improved the conversion ratio of quotes by 50 percent.[6]

BellSouth uses the Strategic Account Manager software package (Blackstone and Cullen, Atlanta, Georgia). With the aid of a computer, it diagrams the account's organization chart, which is useful in understanding decision processes. In addition, the software keeps track of what each area in the account purchases, records notes the salesperson makes after each call, and tracks personnel movement in the account. This account history is very useful in designing sales strategies as well as in determining customer share.

Minolta Business Systems compiles some of the data from its account management software for a market analysis. For example, if the company wants to know the organization size most likely to buy a certain product, it can extract that information from the database of account records that were entered by salespeople. Minolta can then use that profile to create a mailing or telemarketing campaign to noncustomers, to introduce them to that product. Those noncustomers that respond are profitable leads for the field salespeople.

Investing in Accounts

Planning such as grid and market analysis should result in more effective use of the opportunities presented by accounts. This relates to the improved use of time, which is allocated to the appropriate accounts. But developing good strategies entails more than developing good time-use plans; strategies require the use of other resources besides time.

Salespeople invest time, free samples or trials, customer training, displays, and other resources in their customers. Recall the free displays in the Banquet brochure in Chapter Fifteen; these were investments in supporting Banquet products. Pharmaceutical reps receive a limited number of free samples to distribute; account analysis enables them to use those samples where they should result in the largest sales. Market and grid analysis helps salespeople determine where to invest resources—samples, training aids, displays, and so forth. Sales costs, or costs associated with the use of such resources, are not always costs in the traditional sense but investments in an asset called customers. This asset generates nearly all of a firm's revenue. Viewed from this perspective, formulating a strategy to allocate resources to maintaining or developing customers becomes much more important.

IMPLEMENTING THE TIME MANAGEMENT STRATEGY

Time is a limited resource. Once spent, it cannot be regained. How salespeople choose to use their time often means the difference between superstar success and average performance. As former pro baseball player-turned-salesperson Carl Warwick says, "In baseball, you've got someone setting a schedule for you and telling what time the plane leaves and when the bus leaves. But sales was self-discipline from the time you woke up in the morning till you went to bed at night."[7] In this section, we discuss the value of a salesperson's time and how to plan for its efficient use.

The Value of Time

The old axiom "Time is money" certainly applies to selling. If you work eight hours a day for 240 days out of a year, you will work 1,920 hours that year. If you earn $30,000, each of those hours will be worth $15.63. An hour of time would be worth $20.84 if your earnings climbed to $40,000. Looking at your time another way, you would have to sell $208 worth of product per hour to earn $40,000 if you earned a 10 percent commission!

The typical salesperson spends only 920 hours in front of customers. The other 1,000 hours are spent waiting, traveling, doing paperwork, or in sales meetings. Thus, as a typical salesperson, you really have to be twice as good, selling $434 worth of products every hour to earn that $40,000 commission.

The lesson from this analysis is clear: Salespeople must make every hour count to be successful. Time is a resource that cannot be replaced if wasted. But salespeople can easily waste time; after all, no one really knows how they spend their time. They could be calling on customers or they might be playing tennis, taking extra coffee breaks, or engaging in social rather than business conversations with customers.

Thinking *it* Through	How do you plan your time now? What tools do you use to help you manage your time? How much of your time is planned by others, and how much of it are you free to allocate? What do you do to make sure you use your time wisely?

Daily Activity Planning

To be effective time planners, salespeople must have a good understanding of their own work habits. For example, some people tend to procrastinate in getting the day started, while others may want to knock off early. If you are a late riser, you may want to schedule early appointments to force yourself to get started. On the other hand, if your problem is heading for home too early, schedule late appointments so that you work a full day. The salesperson in Exhibit 16.6 has scheduled an early appointment to get the day started.

Guidelines

Salespeople need to include time for prospecting and customer care in their daily activities. Some minimize the time for such activities because they think sales do not occur on such calls, but prospects and happy customers feed future sales. IKON, an office equipment dealer, requires salespeople to handle customer care calls before 9 AM and after 4 PM and to schedule prospecting activities between 10 AM and noon and between 2 PM and 3 PM. Scheduled appointments are worked in when customers require them. The company bases these guidelines on its experience with buyers and when they are available.

Premier Industrial has a far different selling schedule. Its buyers are plant maintenance technicians who often arrive before the first shift, sometimes as early as 5:30 AM, to perform maintenance before the day's production begins. Premier expects its salespeople to begin prospecting at 5:30 AM, because buyers are available for cold calls at that hour.

Such planning guides are designed to maximize **prime selling time,** the time of day at which a salesperson is most likely to see a buyer. Prime selling time will vary depending on the buyer's industry. For example, a good time to call on bankers is late afternoon, after the bank has closed to customers. However, late afternoon is a bad time to call on physicians, who are then making rounds at the hospital or trying to catch up on a full day's schedule of patients. Prime selling time should be devoted to sales calls, with the rest of the day used for nonselling activities such as servicing accounts, doing paperwork, or getting information from the home office.

EXHIBIT 16.6	Sample Daily Plan				

Scheduling Worksheet

Day: Wednesday   **Date:** June 2   **Location:** Cincinnati

Hours	Appointments and Events	Type of Activity	Deadline	Estimated Time Involvement	Results Anticipated or Required
8:30	Jones Int'l	Sales call		60 min.	Make presentation to Dave Carey, VP eng. Demonstrate x35 tester.
10:00	D. Squares Systems	Service		20 min.	Drop off new catalog to Sue Jabbar in purchasing
10:45	Diamond Mfgr.	Sales call		15 min.	Deliver proposal to Jim O'Hara in purchasing. Pick up order
11:15	Quad Distributor	Service		15 min.	Get OK to work with new salespeople from Jill Conner
4:15	Write proposal for Wilkes Tool	Paperwork	Due 6/7	60 min.	Have manager review tomorrow morning.
5:15	Get sample for delivery tomorrow to Cube	Paperwork		5 min.	
5:20	Prepare schedule for tomorrow	Planning		10 min.	

Prime selling time can also vary from country to country. In the United States, prime selling time is usually 9 AM to 4 PM with the noon hour off for lunch. In Mexico, lunch starts and ends later, generally from 12:30 to 2:00 PM; offices may not close until 7 PM. In Great Britain, prime selling time starts later; a British Telecom rep may not begin making calls until 10 AM.

Planning Process

A process exists to help you plan your daily activities, with or without the aid of planning guides. This process can even help you now, as a student, take more control of your time and use it effectively.

As Exhibit 16.7 shows, you begin by making a to-do list. Then you determine the priority for each activity on your list. Many executives rank activities as A, B, or C, with A activities requiring immediate action, B activities being of secondary importance, and C activities being done only if time allows. You can correlate these A, B, and C activities with the A, B, and C accounts discussed earlier, as well as activi-

EXHIBIT 16.7

Activities Planning
Process

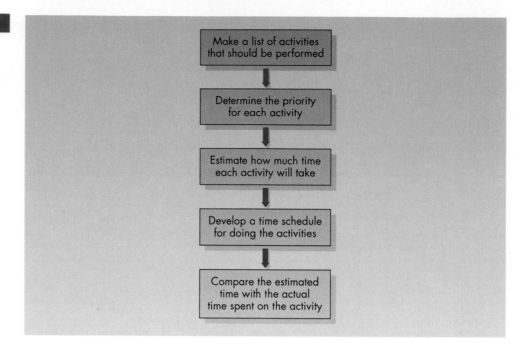

ties such as paperwork and training. Prioritizing activities helps you choose which activities to perform first.

Note, however, that there is a difference between activities that seem urgent and activities that truly are important. For example, when the phone rings, most people stop whatever they are doing to answer it. The ringing phone seems urgent. Sometimes activities such as requests from managers or even customers may have that same sense of urgency; the desire to stop and drop everything to handle the request is called the "tyranny of the urgent." Yet, like most phone calls, those requests may be less important than other tasks to be done. Successful businesspeople learn to recognize what is truly urgent and prioritize those activities first.

The next step in the planning process is to estimate the time required for each activity. In a sales situation, as we mentioned earlier, time must be set aside for customer care and prospecting. The amount of time depends on the activity goals set earlier and on how long each call should take. However, salespeople often have unique activities, such as special sales calls, demonstrations, customer training, and sales meetings, to plan for as well. Time must also be set aside for planning and paperwork.

The next step, developing an effective time schedule, requires estimating the amount of time such activities will require. As a follow-up, be sure to compare how long an activity actually took with how long you thought it would take. Such comparisons can help you plan more accurately in the future.

Using the Computer for Scheduling

Many of the same account management programs that salespeople use to identify and analyze accounts incorporate time-planning elements. This software can generate to-do lists and calendars through a tickler file or by listing certain customer types. A **tickler file** is a file or calendar that salespeople use to remember when to call specific accounts. For example, if customer A said to call back in 90 days, the computer would remind ("tickle") the salesperson in 90 days to call that customer. Or if the company just introduced a product that can knock out competitor B, then the computer can generate a list of prospects with products from competitor B; the salesperson then has a list of prospects for the new product. As you can see in Selling Scenario 16.2, many companies have enlisted the computer to help salespeople manage their territories.

Need for Flexibility

Although working out a daily plan is important, times will arise when the plan should be laid aside. You cannot accurately judge the time needed for each sales call, and hastily concluding a sales presentation just to stick to a schedule would be foolish. If more time at one account will mean better sales results, the schedule should be revised.

To plan for the unexpected, you should schedule a visit to the prime prospect first (in the terms discussed earlier, this would be an A account or activity); then the next best potential customer should be visited (provided the travel time is reasonable); and so forth. If an emergency causes a change of plans, at least the calls most likely to result in sales will have been made.

Making More Calls   Making daily plans and developing efficient routes are important steps toward better time use. But suppose you could make just one more call per day. Using our analysis from the beginning of this chapter and Exhibit 16.3, this would mean 240 more calls per year, which is like adding one more month to the year!

Some salespeople develop an "out Tuesday, back Friday" complex. They can offer many reasons why they need to be back in the office or at home on Monday and Friday afternoons. Such a behavior pattern, however, means the salesperson makes 20 to 30 percent fewer calls than a salesperson who works a full week. Scott Woolford, national sales manager at M.D. Industries, a health care supply company, took a big account away from a competitor on a Friday afternoon. The buyer had a problem with the competitor's delivery schedule, and Woolford was able to guarantee delivery the next day—Saturday. Working a full week really paid off for Woolford.[8]

To get the most out of a territory, the sales representative must make full use of all available days. For example, the days before or after holidays are often seen as bad selling days. Hence, while the competition takes those extra days off, the salesperson can be working and making sales calls they would miss. The same reasoning applies to bad weather: Bad weather reduces competition and makes things easier for the salesperson who doesn't find excuses to take it easy.

Salespeople can use certain techniques to increase the time they spend in front of customers selling instead of traveling. These are routing and zoning techniques.

Routing

Routing is a method of planning sales calls in a specific order to minimize travel time. Two types of sales call patterns, routine and variable, can be more efficient with effective routing. Using **routine call patterns**, a salesperson sees the same customers regularly. For example, Marion/Merrell Dow pharmaceutical salespeople's

Sales Force Automation Takes Off

In the 1980s, sales force automation (SFA) meant giving salespeople a word processing and spreadsheet package. The Gartner Group Inc. of Stamford, Connecticut, estimates that of $600 million spent on SFA, more than 80 percent was wasted. As one sales and marketing VP noted, SFA was a doomed-to-failure approach because the software did not affect the salesperson's productivity.

But today, SFA is getting a second chance. By combining pricing software with customer records and other programs that were once separate, companies are finding that their salespeople can make better decisions more quickly, often in front of the customer. For example, salespeople at Campbell Soup Company can check shipping dates, create customized promotions, and put together attractive pricing options based on their customers' needs while in the customers' offices.

Scott Salling, sales representative for Curtin Matheson Scientific, visited one buyer who immediately complained about how badly Salling's company had performed. With his laptop plugged into her phone and dialed into his company's mainframe, he showed her records documenting how all of her company's orders had been delivered the same or the next day. Her attitude changed completely.

Calvin Dill is a sales representative for Reckitt & Colman, the company that sells Lysol, Woolite, and French's mustard. Using Apollo software, he can design a store's layout. When he incorporates in the information he pulls from Data Server on the sales of his products and those of his competitors, he can truly manage food and household chemical product categories for that customer. A contact manager's tickler schedules his time and also keeps track of personal information and "hotbuttons," or key factors, for each buyer, which he uses to create a personalized presentation.

When Owens-Corning adopted SFA, salespeople were concerned that they would spend too much time feeding information into the system and not enough time selling. But SFA programs that work well not only free up time for selling, but they also provide information to make the salesperson manage that time more effectively. As one Owens-Corning sales manager noted, SFA helps salespeople "become real managers of their own business and their territories."

Sources: Emily Kay, "Selling Enters the Information Age," *Datamation*, May 1995; James G. Kimball, "Sales Automation Redux: Better Programs Lead to Second Chance," *Business Marketing*, September 1994, p. 2; Tony Seideman, "Who Needs Managers?" *Sales & Marketing Management*, June 1994, pp 15–17; Ginger Trumfio, "For the Love of a Laptop," *Sales & Marketing Management*, March 1995, pp. 31–33.

call plans enable them to see all important doctors in their territory at least once each six weeks. Certain types of doctors (those who see large numbers of certain types of patients) may be in the plan to be visited every two weeks. The salesperson repeats the pattern every six weeks, ensuring the proper call level.

Variable call patterns occur when the salesperson must call on accounts in an irregular order. In this situation, the salesperson would not routinely call on each account within a specified period. Routing techniques are useful, but the salesperson may not repeat the call plan on a cyclical basis.

The four types of routing plans, **circular routing, leapfrog routing, straight-line routing,** and **cloverleaf routing,** are illustrated in Exhibit 16.8. If a Marion/Merrell Dow rep used the cloverleaf method (with six leaves instead of four) for a routine call pattern, every sixth Tuesday would find that salesperson in the same spot. But a salesperson with variable call patterns could use the cloverleaf method to plan sales calls for an upcoming week and then use the straight-line method the next week. The pattern would vary depending on the demands of the customers and the salesperson's ability to schedule calls at convenient times.

EXHIBIT 16.8   Types of Routing Plans

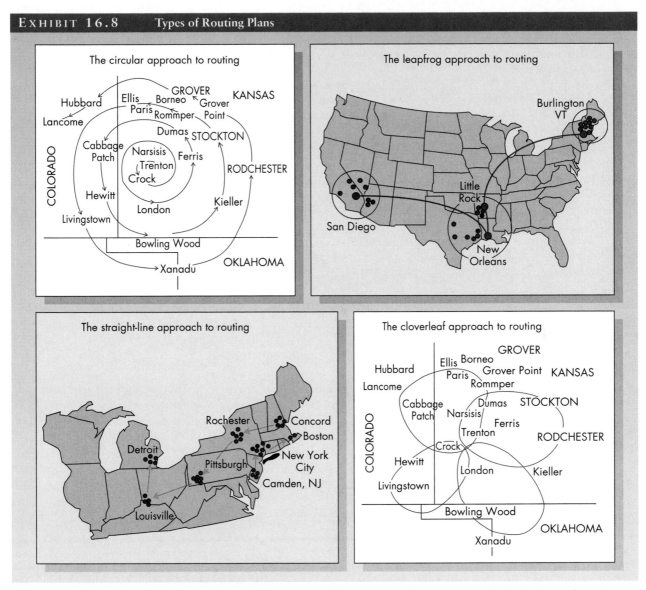

Source: Adapted from *Selling: The Personal Force in Marketing,* by W. J. E. Crissy, H. Cunningham, and Isabella Cunningham, Copyright 1977 by John Wiley & Sons, Inc. New York.

Zoning

Zoning is dividing the territory into zones, based on ease of travel and concentration of customers, to minimize travel time. First, the salesperson locates concentrations of accounts on a map. For example, an office supply salesperson may find that many accounts are located downtown, with other concentrations around the airport, in an industrial park, and in a part of town where two highways cross near a rail line. Each of those areas is the center of a zone. The salesperson then plans to spend a day, for example, in each zone. If the territory were zoned like the one in Exhibit 16.9, the salesperson might spend Monday in zone 1, Tuesday in zone 2, and so forth.

EXHIBIT 16.9

Zoning a Sales Territory
A salesperson may work
in zone 1 on Monday,
zone 2 on Tuesday,
and so forth.

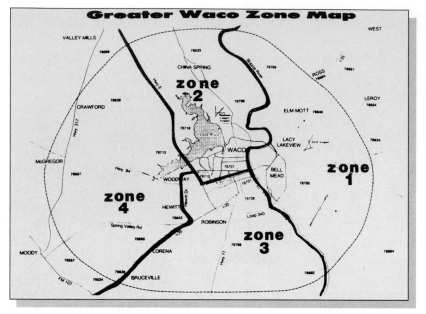

Source: *Waco Tribune Herald.*

Zoning works best for compact territories or for situations where salespeople do not call regularly on the same accounts. (In a large territory, such as the entire Midwest, a salesperson is more likely to use leapfrog routes, but the principle is similar.) By calling on customers that are in a relatively small area, travel time between calls can be minimized.

Salespeople can also combine zoning with routing, using a circular approach within a zone, for example. When zones are designed properly, travel time between accounts should be minimal.

Using Mail and Telephone

Customer contacts should not always be in-person sales calls. As many companies have learned, some sales objectives can be accomplished over the phone or through the mail. For example, some customer care calls can be handled by simply calling the customer and asking if everything is okay. The customer may appreciate the phone call more because it takes less time away from other pressing responsibilities. The salesperson may be able to make more customer care calls, increasing the number of contacts with customers. Keep in mind, though, that not all customer care activities should be handled by phone. Recall from Chapter Thirteen that there are many reasons, such as reorders and cross-selling, to continue to make sales calls in person to current customers.

Similarly, the telephone and direct mail can be used profitably when prospecting, as we discussed in Chapter Seven. More calls, or customer contacts, can be made equally effectively with judicious use of the mail and telephone.

**Handling
Paperwork
and Reports**

Every sales job requires preparing reports for management. All salespeople complain about such paperwork, but it is important. As we will discuss later, paperwork can provide information that helps a salesperson determine what should be improved. The information also helps management decide what types of marketing plans work and should be used again. Therefore, every salesperson should learn to handle paperwork efficiently.

Paperwork time is less productive than time spent selling to customers, so getting it completed in the least possible time is important. Salespeople can do several things to minimize the impact of paperwork on their prime selling time.

First, salespeople should think positively about paperwork. Although less productive than selling, it can increase their productivity and the productivity of the company's marketing programs by facilitating a detailed review of selling activities and marketing programs.

Second, salespeople should not let paperwork accumulate. We once knew of a salesperson who never did expense reports. He finally offered a summer intern 10 percent if she would complete his expense reports for the previous 12 months. This deal cost him $600; in addition, he was essentially lending the company $500 per month, interest free.

Routine reports should be completed daily. Nonproductive time (e.g., time spent waiting for a customer) can be used for paperwork. Call reports and account records should be updated immediately after the call so that important points are remembered and any follow-up actions can be planned.

Finally, salespeople should set aside a block of nonselling time for paperwork. It can be done more quickly if one concentrates on it and avoids interruptions. Setting aside a small amount of time at the beginning or end of each day for writing thank-you and follow-up notes and completing reports saves prime selling time for selling activities while ensuring that the salesperson keeps up with paperwork.

Using the Computer to Handle Paperwork

Many companies, such as IBM, provide their salespeople with laptop computers. These computers can be hooked up to the company's mainframe to access customer information and process other paperwork automatically. Salespeople who travel can then complete their paperwork while in a hotel, an airport waiting area, and other places. Salespeople calling on accounts overseas can also file reports or check the status of orders even though the home office may be closed due to time zone differences.

Computers can help international selling organizations operate smoothly by reducing communication barriers between the field and the home office. For example, Doug Loewe is the European marketing manager for CompuServe, managing a support staff in London and Munich, but his office is in New York. He answers about 50 e-mails a day from his overseas staff, whom he sees only about once every three months.[9] Computers and fax machines can give salespeople flexibility, enabling communication despite large differences in time.

Some account management packages include territory management capabilities. These packages allow salespeople to track their performance by calculating conversion rates, commissions, expenses, and other important figures. Such technology enables salespeople to file reports more quickly. Owens-Corning's insulation division developed a system called Field Automation Sales Team, or FAST. This system not only tracks customer information and provides quick access to product information but also allows salespeople to track their performance and automate all of their reports to management.[10]

Joe Davis receives 100 e-mails per day and answers each one personally. He uses a RadioMail, a service that allows him to receive or send e-mail to anyone, anytime, from any location, including the back seat of a cab. He admits that the main reason

Productive salespeople keep up with their paperwork at every opportunity, while waiting in a customer's lobby or in the car following a sales call.

West Stock

Sharon Hoogstraten

he began using wireless e-mail and other high-tech communication devices was for his own convenience, but now he believes he gains a competitive advantage by being able to communicate so quickly with any of his customers.[11]

Other companies use facsimile (fax) machines to transmit reports, contracts, disputed bills, and other paperwork. Faxes have the advantage over electronic mail of being able to send documents to anyone who has a fax machine, whereas electronic mail requires that the receiver be part of the same computer network. Fax machines can also scan and send written documents, including signatures, that electronic mail cannot send.

To manage your time wisely, you must exploit a scarce resource in the most effective manner possible. Your objective is to make as many quality calls as possible by reserving prime selling time for selling activities. Routing, zoning, goal setting, and other methods of planning and scheduling time will help you maximize your prime selling time.

EVALUATING PERFORMANCE

Being successful is a combination of how hard a salesperson works and how smart that salesperson works. Unlike in other jobs, however, the salesperson has a great deal of control over both how hard and how smart he or she works. Evaluating performance is the component of self-management that provides direction for how hard the salesperson should be working as well as an opportunity to determine what strategies work best.

Postcall Analysis

At the end of each call, many salespeople take a moment to write down what occurred and what needs to be done, perhaps using a printed form (see Exhibit 16.10) or entering the information into their computers' territory management program. Information such as customers' purchase volume, key people in the decision process, and current vendors is important to have, but so is information such as the fact that

EXHIBIT 16.10   Postcall Analysis Form

COMPANY NAME: _____   Date: _____
Contact name: _____   STATUS:
Decision Maker's Name:_____   A-Current Account
Office Address:_____   B-Current Prospects
                                   C-Competitor
    _____   D-Dormant
Office Phone: _____   E-Not Interested
First Contact Date: _____   INITIAL
Next Contact Date: _____   CONTACT:
                                   D-Direct Mail
Ranking: (Hot) 5 4 3 2 1 (Cold)   T-Telephone
Notes: C-Cold Call

COMPANY NAME: _____   Date:_____
Contact name: _____   STATUS:
Decision Maker's Name:_____   A-Current Account
Office Address:_____   B-Current Prospects
                                   C-Competitor
    _____   D-Dormant
Office Phone: _____   E-Not Interested
First Contact Date: _____   INITIAL
Next Contact Date: _____   CONTACT:
                                   D-Direct Mail
Ranking: (Hot) 5 4 3 2 1 (Cold)   T-Telephone
Notes: C-Cold Call

COMPANY NAME: _____   Date: _____
Contact name: _____   STATUS:
Decision Maker's Name:_____   A-Current Account
Office Address:_____   B-Current Prospects
                                   C-Competitor
    _____   D-Dormant
Office Phone: _____   E-Not Interested
First Contact Date: _____   INITIAL
Next Contact Date: _____   CONTACT:
                                   D-Direct Mail
Ranking: (Hot) 5 4 3 2 1 (Cold)   T-Telephone
Notes: C-Cold Call

COMPANY NAME: _____   Date: _____
Contact name: _____   STATUS:
Decision Maker's Name:_____   A-Current Account
Office Address:_____   B-Current Prospects
                                   C-Competitor
    _____   D-Dormant
Office Phone: _____   E-Not Interested
First Contact Date: _____   INITIAL
Next Contact Date: _____   CONTACT:
                                   D-Direct Mail
Ranking: (Hot) 5 4 3 2 1 (Cold)   T-Telephone
Notes: C-Cold Call

the buyer has three children who play soccer. The salesperson will need that information to remember the personal as well as professional side of the buyer during the next call.

Remember the plan you made for each sales call? That plan included one or more objectives. Postcall analysis should include reflecting on whether those objectives were reached. The professional salesperson not only looks for specific areas to improve but also evaluates the success of the overall sales call.

Activity Analysis   When planning their time, salespeople set certain activity goals. They use these goals not only as guidelines but also to evaluate their own performance. At the end of each day, week, and month, salespeople should review their activities in relation to the goals they set. For example, the salesperson might use a form such as the one in Exhibit 16.11 to compare goals with actual performance. Goals would be written down at the time they are set, say, Sunday evening when planning the following week. Then on Friday evening, the actual activities from each day would be tallied and totaled for the week, then written next to the goals. The salesperson could then evaluate whether more calls of a certain type are needed in the following week.

Merrill Lynch, for example, recommends that new brokers make 100 telephone calls each day (calls count even if no one answers). Frank Bugh, a new broker in central Texas, made 7,544 calls in his first 92 working days, or 82 calls per day. His goal is now 120 calls per day to bring his average up to 100 in the next quarter.

Many salespeople work out of their homes; even salespeople with company offices find a home office is a good place to catch up on paperwork or handle customer calls over the phone.

Jose Pelaez/The Stock Market

Performance Analysis

Salespeople also need to evaluate performance relative to performance goals set earlier. For example, they often evaluate sales performance in terms of percentage of quota achieved. Of course, a commission or a bonus check also tells the salesperson if the earnings goal was met.

An earnings goal can be an effective check for overall performance, but salespeople also need to evaluate sales by product type, as outlined in Exhibit 16.12. Salespeople who sell only part of the product line may be missing opportunities for cross-selling or full-line selling, which means they have to work harder to achieve the same level of sales as the salesperson who successfully integrates cross-selling and full-line selling in the sales strategy.

Productivity Analysis

Salespeople also need to identify which strategies work. For example, if using a certain strategy improved the ratio of appointments to cold calls made, that approach should be continued. Otherwise the salesperson should change it or go back to a previous approach. Frank Bugh, the Merrill Lynch broker, tried several approaches before settling on one that works well for him. Of course, Bugh keeps good records so he knows what works and what does not.

The conversion ratio, or number of sales per calls, is an important measure of effectiveness. Conversion ratios should also be calculated by account type; for example, a conversion ratio for type A accounts should be determined. Other conversion ratios can also pinpoint effective strategies and areas that need improvement.

SUMMARY

A sales territory can be viewed as a small business. Territory salespeople have the freedom to establish programs and strategies. They manage a number of resources, including physical resources such as sample inventory, displays, demonstration equipment, and perhaps a company vehicle. More important, they manage their time, their customers, and their skills.

EXHIBIT 16.11   Postcall Analysis Form

Rep Name:_____
Date:_____
Month:_____

	Goal / Actual	Goal / Actual	Goal / Actual	Goal / Actual	Goal / Actual	Goal / Actual	Goal / Actual	Goal / Actual
__to__								
__to__								
__to__								
__to__								
Total								

Remarks on this month's sales activities:

Action plan for next month:

Managing a territory involves setting performance, activity, and conversion goals. Salespeople use these goals to allocate time to various activities and to manage customers.

To manage customers well, the salesperson must analyze their potential. Accounts can be classified using the ABC method or the sales call allocation grid. These analyses tell how much effort should be put into each account. Market analyses then help to identify patterns within a territory. Salespeople can use these patterns to develop account sales strategies.

More calls (working harder) can be accomplished by moving nonselling activities, such as paperwork, to nonselling time. Also, selling time can be used more efficiently. For example, routing and zoning techniques enable the salesperson to spend more prime selling time in front of customers instead of behind the steering wheel of a car.

Effective planning of the salesperson's day requires setting aside time for important activities such as prospecting and still making the appropriate number of sales ap-

EXHIBIT 16.12	Evaluation Measure	Calculation	How to Use It
Sales Evaluation Measures	Conversion rate For total performance By customer type By product type	$\dfrac{\text{Number of sales}}{\text{Number of calls}}$	Are your strategies effective? Do you need to improve by working smarter (i.e., a better strategy to improve your hit rate)? Compare yours to your company and/or industry average.
	Sales achievement	$\dfrac{\text{\$ actual sales}}{\text{\$ sales goal}}$	Is your overall performance where you believe it should be? Are you meeting your goals? Your company's goals?
	Commission	$\dfrac{\text{\$ actual commission}}{\text{\$ earnings goal}}$	
	Sales volume (in dollars) By customer type		Where are you most effective? Do you need help with a customer type?
	By product category		Are you selling the whole line?
	By market share		How are you doing relative to your competition?
	By new customers		Are you building new business?
	By old customers		Are you servicing your accounts properly?
	Sales calls Prospecting calls Account calls Sales presentations Call frequency by customer type		Are your efforts in the right place?

pointments. Using the full workweek and employing technology such as telephones, computers, and fax machines can help the salesperson stay ahead of competition.

Finally, salespeople must manage their skills. Managing skills involves choosing how to make sales calls and improving the way one sells. Improvement requires that salespeople first understand what they do well and what needs improvement. Evaluating their performance can provide them with that insight.

KEY TERMS

ABC analysis 468
account opportunity 470
activity goals 465
circular routing 478
cloverleaf routing 478
conversion goals 466
conversion rate 466
customer share 472
leapfrog routing 478
market analysis 472

performance goals 465
prime selling time 474
routing 477
routine call patterns 477
sales call allocation grid 470
straight-line routing 478
strength of position 470
tickler file 477
variable call patterns 478
zoning 479

QUESTIONS AND
PROBLEMS

1. After reading the material in this chapter, a salesperson protests, "That's no fun. I like to play tennis every other afternoon. If I have to hustle every minute of every day, then forget it. I'll get another job!" What would you tell this salesperson?

2. Many companies call their salespeople "marketing representatives." Is this an accurate designation of their job? Why or why not? If not, when would it be an appropriate job title?

3. Compare and contrast the special problems of self-management for a computer salesperson who works in a computer store with those of a computer salesperson who only calls on customers in their offices.

4. Shakespeare wrote, "To thine own self be true." How would you apply this statement to your planning and development activities?

5. What factors are important for classifying customers? Why? How would these factors change depending on the industry?

6. Distinguish between routing and scheduling and between routing and zoning. Explain how routing and scheduling can interact to complicate the planning of an efficient day's work.

7. How might a pharmaceutical salesperson increase the number of calls made per day? A construction equipment salesperson? A financial services representative? A representative who sells golf clubs to retailers and pro shops?

8. Sales managers know that making more sales calls results in more sales. Should sales managers encourage salespeople to continually increase the number of calls made each week? Explain your answer.

9. One recruiter told a class that students are used to getting feedback on how they are doing every couple of months, but salespeople do not get a "final grade" until a year has gone by. He claims that students have a hard time making that adjustment when they enter the work world. What do salespeople do to know where they stand at any given time? What do you do now that helps you know where you stand in your classes?

10. Do you ever find yourself "burning the midnight oil" to study or finish an assignment? What self-management principles could you use to avoid "all-nighters"? Is there software you can use to help you manage your time as a student?

EXPLORING THE
NET

One of the most important topics in this chapter is developing an account strategy through understanding the potential or opportunity in an account. Assume that you sell computer software that improves the work of customer service departments. Access the following home pages and decide which account has the greatest opportunity. Justify your answer as to why you chose that company.

3M Corporation: www.3m.com

HEB Grocery: www.heb.com

General Foods: www.generalfoods.com

CASE PROBLEMS

CASE 16.1
ConAgra

ConAgra is a $5 billion annual sales company that most people haven't heard of, but they know all of the company's products—Wesson Oil, Wolf Brand Chili, Healthy Choice frozen dinners, among others. In a move designed to strengthen salespeople's ability to partner with key accounts, salespeople were given advertising budgets that enabled them to develop account-specific marketing strategies. From this budget, salespeople could "buy" point-of-purchase displays, co-op advertising, or whatever was necessary for key accounts.

Heidi Williams, a regional marketing representative for ConAgra, has two key accounts in her territory, HEB and Brookshire's. Both are family-owned grocery chains in central and southern Texas. HEB has recently made the decision to grow by saturating metropolitan areas with stores, and also has a reputation as one of the best at developing effective partnerships with manufacturers. Brookshire's is a highly profitable chain whose success is due to placing stores in smaller towns and rural areas. Therefore, while there is some overlap in certain markets, the two chains do not compete in most markets, although both cover the eastern half of Texas.

Williams is most concerned with her sales of Wesson cooking oil products and wants to develop a strategy. In the Dallas/Fort Worth area, Wesson is the number two cooking oil, second to Crisco, and has 25 percent of the market compared to Crisco's 34 percent. But Wesson has only 18 percent in HEB, compared to 21 percent for the HEB brand and 32 percent for Crisco, and 16 percent in Brookshire's, well behind Crisco's 35 percent and Mazola's 22 percent. Dollar volume for Wesson is just about equal between the two chains. Overall cooking oil sales are rising nationally at a rate greater than 8 percent per year, with vegetable oils controlling over 51 percent of that market. If Williams is unsuccessful in getting a larger share, Wesson could end up a nonplayer in the central and southern parts of Texas.

HEB   The buyer for HEB is Bill Jorgensen. In the past 12 months, HEB has featured its store brand of cooking oil four times and Crisco three times. The Crisco features have included special end-of-aisle displays, a feature in HEB's newspaper advertisement, and a lower price coinciding with FSI drops by Crisco. The HEB specials have been only newspaper advertising as far as Williams could tell. She has had a hard time convincing Jorgenson to work with ConAgra, particularly in categories where HEB has its own product. Jorgenson likes to feature category leaders or HEB brands. He also prefers cross-promotions that tie in other products. But as far as Williams can tell, he has not assigned Crisco the responsibility of managing the cooking oil category.

Brookshire's   David Brookshire is the buyer for Brookshire's. Recently he and Williams did a promotion that tied together ConAgra's Mexican food lines (Rosarita, Patio, and Wolf Brand Chili). The promotion was extremely successful, boosting sales for those products by an average of 16 percent and generating net new sales of 7 percent (meaning that sales for the categories increased 7 percent after subtracting decreases in competitors' in-store sales). Over the past year, Brookshire's also featured Crisco in conjunction with Crisco's FSIs and featured Mazola once in a special promotion for all of Mazola's products. Brookshire's likes cross-promotions but has been very slow to adopt the concept of category management; Williams is not aware of any category management programs, although David has asked her opinion on the topic.

Questions

1. Assess the two accounts in terms of the sales call allocation grid. Justify your evaluation using information from the case.

2. What percentage of your marketing budget would you allocate to each account? Assume you must spend all of your budget on only these two accounts. Justify your allocation.

3. Assume you are planning to visit each store. Outline your plan for the sales call, making sure to set objectives. List SPIN questions designed to identify what each buyer wants in a marketing plan from you (i.e., how they want to spend those dollars).

*Some of the information in this case is from the ConAgra, Inc., 1995 annual report; some is from recruiting materials used by ConAgra. However, all information concerning HEB and Brookshire's was created for this case for the purpose of class use and does not reflect actual sales within those stores.

**CASE 16.2
Northern Farm
Equipment: A Day
with a Farm
Equipment
Salesperson**

"We sell a lot of farm equipment throughout this river bottom area," said Bob Hart, sales representative for Lang Implement Company, the Northern Farm Equipment Company dealer in Quincy, Illinois. Hart's territory lies on both sides of the Mississippi, in Illinois and Missouri. He covers it in a Northern pickup truck so he can go right out to his prospects when they are working in the field. Hart often meets his customers in an open-collar shirt, a leather jacket, and a felt hat that he rarely removes. In fact, Hart usually dresses more like one of his customers than a sales representative. He knows the problems of his customers, and he talks their language. He is proud of his ability to "run a tractor around a barnyard and tell pretty well by the sound whether or not the rear end is OK."

Hart has spelled out some of his ideas on selling farm equipment:

The first thing I do is get around to enough doors and barn lots to find a person interested in buying something. During this time of year, there may be weeks when I'm never in the office except in the morning before I start out on my calls. If you expect to sell farm equipment, you have to go out to the customer. And I usually have plenty of customers to call on. I do, however, want to spend some time in the store. A person who tends to business in the store can sell a lot of equipment and get a good many leads for future action.

When you go to some farmers, you can sit and talk all day if you want, and then they'll invite you in for dinner. It's a great temptation to waste time this way when you're out in the country. When I drive into a place, I always assume the customer is as busy as I am, so 30 minutes is about as long as I stay. I follow a plan of talking business while I'm there, and when I see it's time to leave, I leave. Often I stop at one place and find that my customer is not going to buy anything. But sometimes the customer will say, "Hart, you ought to go down the road and see Albert Fowler. He's planning on buying a new tractor. Now don't you tell him I told you, but I heard that the John Deere people were out there the other day." When I get a lead like this, instead of going directly to Fowler's place, if he's a next-door neighbor I go down the road, and then maybe the next morning I stop at the Fowler farm. If he doesn't say anything about the tractor deal, I pass the time of day with him for awhile. Then our conversation naturally drifts into a discussion about his tractor.

If customers want to buy something that I don't think they should buy because it doesn't fit their needs, I always try to talk them out of it. I may lose an immediate sale by doing this, but in the long run I have found that this procedure pays big dividends. The only time I mention anything about a competitive tractor is when the customer brings the subject up first. I prepare myself for such an occasion by studying up on the literature of all competitive machines.

Whenever you try to talk about everything on a tractor, you get your customer confused. I usually stress one or two major features, such as fuel efficiency or the 24-speed transmission. After I get the customer sold on that, I mention the hydraulic system, which has special features on our tractors.

When I drive from one customer's place to the next, I usually listen to the car radio. This is very helpful, as I always pick up the community news and the market information everybody is talking about. A lot of people will tell you that the price of hogs or cattle dropped off yesterday and they don't know if they ought to buy anything from you. But if you catch that market news, maybe you can answer right back that they went up 50 cents today.

By putting selling techniques such as these into practice, Bob Hart has helped Lang Implement Company stay in the running with the best of its seven competitors in Quincy.

Hart drove 60 miles on March 4, spending the morning in Missouri and the afternoon in Illinois. He made eight calls and talked to two customers at the store. His efforts bore some fruit, but the day also produced its share of blind alleys and frustrations. Arriving at one stop, he learned that the farmer had gone into Quincy to see him. Efforts to find another farmer at the grain elevator ended in failure. He found Harvey Ireland ringing pigs and had to talk business with him above the pigs' shrill, incessant squealing. Ireland finally decided not to deal.

Right after lunch, Hart drove up to see Glenn Mugdalen (who was in partnership with his brother, Orville) about the possibility of trading for a baler. Glenn's wife, Martha, came out to meet him when she heard the dog bark.

BOB What do you have Glenn doing today?

MARTHA Well, he's sowing clover seed.

BOB What's he doing sowing clover seed, as muddy as it is?

MARTHA Well, I tell you, he looked like a mud turtle. But he's sowing clover seed.

BOB What have Orville and Glenn decided on that baler?

MARTHA You go over and see Orville. Have you been over there?

BOB No, I haven't.

MARTHA He has all the statistics, and I think when you get over there, you'll get your answer.

BOB Thank you a lot, Martha. I'll go right over to see Orville to find out what was decided on that baler.

Hart found Orville preparing to go into the fields with fertilizer. They passed the time of day before Hart got down to business.

BOB I stopped over at Glenn's and talked with Martha. She said you had all the answers about the baler.

ORVILLE Yes, sir. Well, I wish I did know all the answers about the baler.

BOB If you go ahead and trade balers with us now, it'll help us to get rid of the used one.

ORVILLE After thinking it over, we just kind of thought we'd be better off by having this one fixed.

BOB You want us to pick it up, then?

ORVILLE I believe so.

BOB We can pick it up anytime. That's all right with us if you want to fix it and don't want to trade. And while we've got it down there fixing it, you might take a notion to go ahead and trade.

ORVILLE That's right. I believe that's about as good a way as any to do it.

BOB Another thing. I want to see what we can do on that tractor deal . . .

But 15 minutes of earnest talk in Orville's barnyard failed to bring the two men to terms on anything but repairing the baler (although a few days later, Orville did buy a new, fast hitch for his tractor).

Bob Hart's conversion rate was considerably less than eight for eight on March 4. But every minute he wasn't on the road, he was selling. He made two sales on March 4. Both were corn planters. One of the buyers came to him at the store after he made a pitch at the farm. He made the other sale because he went out after it.

Bill Adams owns 400 acres near LaGrange, Missouri, about 12 miles from Quincy. Hart had talked to him before about buying a new eight-row planter, using his old John Deere planter as a trade-in. Hart had also agreed to sell Adams's old crawler for him. On the morning of March 4, Hart crossed the river to LaGrange and found Adams at the wheel of his Case-IH tractor, hauling feed. The following conversation ended in a sale:

BOB You know what I stopped for. We're going to trade that John Deere corn planter for that new Northern.

BILL Just as soon as you sell that crawler.

BOB They pick it up yet?

BILL Nope.

BOB Well, they're going to pick it up. Now listen. On that cash part of it, you know, we're not going to worry about that. But corn planting may be over before we get that crawler sold, and you know you want that new planter. What do you say we trade this morning?

BILL I have to get some cash—that's all there is to it.

BOB I know you haven't bought anything yet for which you haven't paid cash. But here's our point on the planter. What we're in a hurry for is to get the used one sold because you can wait too long and then you'll have to carry it over another year. That's when you lose money. How long would I have to carry you?

BILL You might have to carry me till harvest.

BOB Aw, I don't think so. You know you're going to buy that planter.

BILL Oh, I can get by.

BOB Doggone it, I'd sure like to trade with you. I want to look at that planter of yours again.

At this point, Hart went into a shed to check the trade-in planter. When he came out, Adams waited while Hart returned to his pickup to do some figuring. The conversation began again when Hart finished.

BOB Well, here's what I'll do. I'll bring that new planter over here for $9,300.

BILL $9,300. Hmm. Let's see how you figured, Bob.

BOB That's putting a lot of money in your planter.

BILL You're taking that forage harvester in on that, aren't you, Bob—for $1,200?

BOB No. Doggone it, I can't. [*Short pause*]

BILL You're still asking a lot of money, Bob.

BOB But that's giving you an awfully good deal on the planter too, you must remember. If you keep yours, you're going to have to put runners on it. Six of them—that's $270. With this new one, you'd be getting a high-speed planter that will plant accurately.

BILL Is that a good hill-drop planter?

BOB It sure is. It'll hill drop 211 hills a minute. In other words, if you're spacing 40 inches apart, it'll hill drop at 6 miles an hour and put 95 percent of the grain in a hole the size of a silver dollar. Also, think of the productivity gain in upgrading from your current six-row unit to this eight-row. You'll cover one-third more with each pass. [*Long silence while Bill Adams thinks it over*]

BILL That's a lot of money, Bob. It's a good trade, but . . . [*Another long pause*]

BOB You can see our point. Here it is, the fourth of March, and people are buying this equipment now. We don't want to wait around too long. [*Another pause*]

BILL Aw, I don't know. You always make me a good deal, Bob.

BOB Sure I do. Why don't you let me write the order this morning? Let's see, that price is $14,500. I'm giving you $5,200 on your planter. That's $9,300 difference.

BILL By the time this thaw is over, I'm liable to have to put all that money for a planter into gravel for these roads.

BOB Well, you don't have to pay for that planter today. Tell me when you would pay for it.

BILL [*pausing*] Reckon I can get the job done with that planter?

BOB I know you can, because we'll come out and get it started for you.

BILL Are you going to get somebody over here to get the fuel injectors on this tractor straightened out?

BOB Sure, I'll get it fixed for you—get somebody out here right away. Can you pay me by April 15? That wouldn't crowd you any, would it?

BILL Give me until the 15th of May. That'll give me a chance to sell some of the bred heifers.

BOB OK, let me write it up. [*At this point, Bob begins to write*]

BILL Better give me $5,500 for my planter, Bob.

BOB I'm giving you $5,200.

BILL Well, I know, but it looks so much better.

BOB Well, OK. You just sign here. And thanks a lot to you, Bill. I'm sure you'll be happy about it.

"The greatest thing we've got to sell is goodwill," Bob Hart says. "If we keep the customer's goodwill, we'll keep our fair share of the business. Courtesy calls pay real dividends in this business. About 80 percent of Lang Implement's sales are repeat business. The first sale to a person is a hard one to make. The next one comes easier, and the one after that even easier. By this time, the customers come back because they like the way they've been treated."

Questions

1. How well do you think Bob Hart utilized his time on March 4? What, if any, suggestions would you make to Hart to improve his efforts?

2. If you were Bob Hart, what criteria would you use to evaluate the effectiveness of your sales efforts in that territory?

ADDITIONAL REFERENCES

Campanelli, Melissa, "Automation: On the Right Track," *Sales & Marketing Management,* August 1995, pp. 46–51.

Clayton, Carl K. "How to Manage Your Time and Territory for Better Sales Results." *Personal Selling Power,* January 1990, p. 46.

Kay, Emily. "Selling Enters the Information Age." *Datamation,* May 1995 (http://www.datamation).

Klein, Matthew H. "Move Over, Indiana Jones!" *Sales & Marketing Management,* February 1990, pp. 88–89.

Messer, Carla; Michael Lyons; and James Alexander. "Classifying Your Customers." *Sales & Marketing Management,* July 1993, pp. 42–43.

Parasuraman, A. "An Approach for Allocating Sales Call Effort." *Industrial Marketing Management,* Winter 1987, pp. 75–79.

PSP Editors. "Seven Thieves of Time That Can Steal Your Sales Away." *Personal Selling Power,* January 1990, pp. 48–49.

Sauers, Daniel A.; James B. Hunt; and Ken Bass. "Behavioral Self-Management as a Supplement to External Sales Force Controls." *Journal of Personal Selling and Sales Management,* Summer 1990, pp. 17–28.

Schiffman, Stephan. "Prospect Management: Avoiding the Ups and Downs of Sales." *American Salesman,* September 1989, pp. 3–5.

Sharma, Arun, and Michael Levy. "Categorization of Customers by Retail Salespeople." *Journal of Retailing,* 1995, pp. 71–81.

Swenson, Michael J., and Adilson Parrella. "Cellular Telephones and the National Sales Force." *Journal of Personal Selling and Sales Management,* Fall 1992, pp. 68–74.

Taylor, Thayer C. "From Selling Aid to Taskmaster." *Sales & Marketing Management,* May 1991, pp. 69–73.

Trumfio, Ginger, "For the Love of a Laptop," *Sales & Marketing Management,* March 1995, pp. 31–33.

Weeks, William A., and Lynn R. Kahle. "Salespeople's Time Use and Performance." *Journal of Personal Selling and Sales Management,* Winter 1990, pp. 29–38.

Because salespeople manage and coordinate many elements of the firm's marketing mix, they are often called territory managers. And, of course, they work with and can themselves become sales managers. In this chapter, we explore how salespeople manage their work within their companies to achieve their sales goals and create customer satisfaction.

Chapter Seventeen

Managing *within* Your Company

Some Questions Answered in this Chapter Are:

What areas of the company work with salespeople to satisfy customer needs?

How do salespeople coordinate the efforts of various functional areas of the company?

How do salespeople work with sales managers and with sales executives?

How do company policies, such as compensation plans, influence salespeople?

How do salespeople work within the company to resolve ethical issues?

What is the organizational structure, and how does it influence salesperson activities?

As you read in the previous chapter, to be a successful salesperson required that salespeople manage time and territory. But success also requires that salespeople manage their companies' resources to satisfy customers by coordinating the companies' manufacturing, shipping, customer service—even the sales managers—to fulfill customers' needs.

PROFILE

Like a whirling dervish, Ron Williams feels he spins around and around. As a national accounts director at Champion Products, a sports apparel company, Williams often finds himself selling *for* Champion at one moment and selling *to* Champion at the next. As he puts it, "I find myself selling the needs of the customer to senior management, manufacturing, merchandising, and other parts of the company every day."

Williams has worldwide responsibility for merchandising Champion products through key sporting goods companies such as Foot Locker. It may seem natural for Champion to do whatever customers want, but sometimes what they want may conflict with Champion's goals or methods of operation. "That's why I am constantly proving to our executives or manufacturing people or whoever needs to change that it is essential for us to take care of my customer's needs," Williams says.

"I find myself selling the needs of the customer to senior management, manufacturing, merchandising, and other parts of the company every day."

Williams's efforts are supported by local, independent sales agents who call on Foot Locker in the local mall. Champion also has regional sales managers who help the agents by providing training and support. But these salespeople and sales managers don't have to do what Williams says. "My goal is to develop partnerships where we all win, whether it is just me and the buyer, or the sales agent, the manager, and the whole chain of buyers," he explains. When Williams can create or broker the partnership between the local salesperson, that person's manager, and the local store manager, he is certain the plans he created with the central buying office will be fulfilled.

RON WILLIAMS
Champion Products

Those plans might include special merchandising and advertising plans, a gift-with-purchase plan, or other promotion. When putting these plans together, Williams has to create a plan that satisfies his customer's needs as well as the needs of various departments within Champion. "Many times, when I am working with my own advertising or merchandising people, I am the customer, I am Foot Locker," he says. When he is successful in representing his customer, it opens new selling opportunities. "Some Champion apparel is available only through Foot Locker. Those products were co-designed by my customer and my merchandising people."

Williams says, "It all boils down to making Champion work for the customer. I'm the one who has to make sure the order gets in on time for manufacturing to schedule it, for purchasing to order the material at a good price, and so our billing system can generate an invoice to get to the customer at the right time. Then I've got to get the products shipped to the customer so they arrive when our advertising campaign hits the market." As he says, "This job is like running my own business!"

BUILDING
INTERNAL
PARTNERSHIP

To effectively coordinate the efforts of the many areas of a company, the salesperson must develop partnerships with the individuals in those areas. **Internal partnerships** are partnering relationships between a salesperson and another member of the same company. These partnerships should be dedicated to satisfying customer needs.

The Importance
of Internal
Partnerships

By definition, a sales representative represents something. Students often think the title means the salesperson represents only a company or a product, but at times the salesperson must represent the customer to the company. For example, the salesperson may have to convince the warehouse manager to ship a customer's product next to meet a special deadline. The salesperson does not have the authority to order the manager to ship the product, but he or she must use persuasion. Or the rep may have to negotiate with production to get a product manufactured to a customer's specifications. Sometimes success in landing a sale may depend on the salesperson's ability to manage such company efforts.

This ability to work with groups inside the company can directly affect the rep's pocketbook. One of the authors, while selling for a major corporation, had an opportunity to earn a large bonus by making 30 sales. He had 31 orders, but a sale wasn't a sale until the product was delivered. Unfortunately, two orders were delivered after the deadline, and he did not get the bonus. In tracking down the slow deliveries, the hapless salesperson learned that the order entry clerk had delayed processing the orders. A little probing uncovered the reason: She was upset with the way he prepared his paperwork! Her performance was evaluated on how quickly an order was delivered, but his sloppy paperwork always slowed her down and got her into trouble. Delaying work on his orders was her way of getting his attention.

It surely worked! For several months after that, he enlisted her help in filling out the paperwork properly before he turned it in. After that, she never had a problem with his orders. And, when necessary to meet a customer's requirements, she would prioritize his orders.

The Role of Sales in Learning Organizations

Salespeople not only sell a company, its products, and its services to customers; they must also sell their customers' needs to their companies. Carrying the customer's voice across a learning organization is one of the most important functions of the sales force. While many learning organizations work to increase the customer contact time for support personnel so that those personnel will better understand customers, often the only person who really understands what the customer needs and why is the salesperson. That salesperson must communicate the customer's wants and needs to all who can potentially satisfy them. The salesperson's ability to carry the voice of the customer across the learning organization is key to the success of any firm.[1]

In addition, salespeople must adapt to satisfy the needs and desires of those who influence their performance. Salespeople who develop strong partnerships are successful because they understand the needs of their partners. Selling Scenario 17.1 describes a salesperson who has been successful with the help of internal partners because he has nurtured relationships with others in his company.

Selling Internally

To service customers well, salespeople must often rely on personnel in other areas of the firm to do their respective jobs properly. But how well those other employees assist salespeople may be a function of the relationship the salesperson has already

SELLING SCENARIO 17.1

What's "with-it?"

"She kept saying she wanted something 'with-it,'" says Alan Wester, vice president of sales at Freeman Exhibit Company in Dallas, a company that builds trade show exhibits. "She'd say something like 'We don't want the Jetsons, we want high-tech but not metal—with-it, you know? A with-it type of exhibit, not some ole fogey thing, a with-it thing.' If we hadn't had the design director there to talk over what she meant by *with-it*, I don't think we'd have gotten that business."

In Wester's business, custom exhibits are designed and presented to potential clients who select from among the offerings of several companies. "The salesperson has to fully understand the customer's requirements and then be able to communicate those requirements to the designer," he explains. "Then, once a preliminary design is created, the account coordinator determines what it costs us to build the exhibit and puts the price on it. Then we make the presentation to the client, and hopefully they choose our proposal."

After the client orders the exhibit, production takes over and actually builds it.

"The best reps are those that have strong relationships with design, production, and the account coordination staff," claims Wester. "By creating a team to serve the customer and involving the customer with the team during the decision process, we are abler to get the customer to buy in incrementally. So when the designer shows some preliminary sketches to the buyer, he can check to see if those designs are *with-it*."

Wester believes that "In the organizations that do this [build teams between sales and the rest of the firm] the best, they nurture those teams. People have the information to manage activities, but creating the environment for productive relationships is a vital component. It won't happen without someone saying this is valuable and nurturing those relationships. And it has to be done via example, actually participating—not dominating or telling, but doing."

established with them. That relationship should be a partnership, just like the one the salesperson wants to establish with customers. To establish the appropriate partnership, the salesperson must invest time in understanding the customer's needs and then work to satisfy those needs.

As summarized in Exhibit 17.1, the first step is to recognize that it is *the salesperson's responsibility* to develop relationships with other departments. Rarely do other departments have an incentive to take the initiative. Salespeople who have the attitude "They should help me because it is their job to serve me" are frustrated by

---

EXHIBIT 17.1

Seven Principles of Selling Internally

1. Understand that it's your problem. Accept responsibility for gaining the support of the internal staff.
2. Appeal to a higher objective.
3. Probe to find out and understand the personal and professional needs of the internal customer.
4. Use arguments for support that adequately address internal customers' needs as well as your own.
5. Do not spend time or energy resenting the internal customers' inability to understand or accept your sense of urgency. Rather, spend this time fruitfully by trying to figure out how you can better communicate your needs in a manner that will increase the internal customers' sense of urgency to the level you need.
6. Never personalize any issues.
7. Be prepared to negotiate.

the lack of support they receive. The better perspective is "How can I serve them so we can serve the customer better?"

Learning organizations have a common vision, or a shared view of what goals are important and how those goals will be achieved. When appropriate, *an appeal to common objectives* and the shared vision can encourage partnering behavior with others in the organization.[2] For example, saying something like "This request is in line with the corporate customer satisfaction goals" can help the internal partner recognize the impact of the request on the company's goals.

Use questioning skills such as SPIN to understand the personal and professional needs of personnel in other departments. Salespeople have excellent communication skills but sometimes fail to use these skills when dealing with internal customers and support groups. SPIN and active listening are just as important to understanding the needs of colleagues as they are to satisfying customer needs. For example:

SALESPERSON What do you do with these credit applications? (*Situation*)

CREDIT REP We key the information into the computer system, and then it is processed by a credit company each night. The next morning, we get a report that shows who has been approved and who hasn't. That's why it is so important to have a clean copy.

SALESPERSON So the quality of the copy we give you is a problem? (*Problem*)

CREDIT REP That's right.

SALESPERSON What happens when you can't read the copy we give you? (*Implication*)

CREDIT REP We put in incorrect information, which can result in a customer's credit application being rejected when it should have been accepted.

SALESPERSON What happens when that happens? (*Implication*)

CREDIT REP That's when we call you. Then we get the right information and reenter it. But we get in trouble because the approval cycle was made longer and you know that the goal is to have a customer's order shipped in three days. We can't meet that goal if we're still working on their credit application.

SALESPERSON So you need legible applications—and probably typewritten would be better than handwritten, right? (*Needs payoff*)

CREDIT REP Yes, that would help a lot.

Keep in mind too that the salesperson cannot simply order a colleague to do what the salesperson wants, such as approving a customer's credit application. But if a salesperson can show that doing what he or she wants will also meet the needs of the colleague, the salesperson is more likely to receive the desired aid. Just as in selling to the external customer, persuasion requires that the other person's needs be met as well as the salesperson's. *Show how their needs can be met* while meeting your needs and those of your customer. For example, if a salesperson can show a plant manager how an expedited order will result in a higher profit margin, thereby more than covering the plant manager's higher costs and helping that manager make production targets, both the plant manager's needs and the customer's needs will be met.

People from other departments, except for billing and customer service, do not have direct contact with the customer. Therefore, they do not feel the same sense of urgency the customer or the salesperson feels. Successful internal sellers can *commu-*

nicate that sense of urgency by relating to the needs of the internal customer. Just as with external customers, salespeople need to communicate the need to act now. Salespeople do this by securing commitment to the desired course of action. Also, just as with external customers, the salesperson should be sure to say "thank you" when someone agrees to provide the support requested.

Selling to internal customers also means *keeping issues professional*. Personal relationships can and should be developed. But when conflicts arise, focus on the issue, not the person. Personalizing conflict makes it seem bigger and harder to resolve. For example, rather than saying, "Why won't you do this?" ask, "If you can't do this, how can we resolve the customer's concern?" This type of statement focuses the other individual on resolving the real problem rather than arguing about company policy or personal competence.

Be prepared to negotiate. Remember from Chapter Fourteen that negotiation is a set of techniques to resolve conflict. Conflicts between salespeople and members of the firm representing other areas will occur, and negotiation skills can be used to respond to conflict professionally.

Salespeople must work with many elements of their organization. In fact, few jobs require the boundary-spanning coordination and management skill that the sales job needs. In the next section, we will examine the many areas of the company with which the salesperson works, what their needs are, and how they partner with the salesperson to deliver customer satisfaction.

COMPANY AREAS IMPORTANT TO SALESPEOPLE

The sales force interacts with many areas of the firm. Salespeople work with manufacturing, sales administration, customer service, and personnel. In some industries requiring customization of products, engineering is an important department for salespeople. Finance can get into the picture as well when that department determines which customers receive credit and what price is charged. In addition, salespeople work with members of their own department and the marketing department.

Manufacturing

Grafo Regia S.A. is a packaging and labeling firm in Monterrey, Mexico. Its clients include companies such as Kellogg, and it prints labels and boxes that are used around the world. A key competitive advantage for Grafo Regia is its ability to deliver small or large orders faster than their competitors. Because the primary competitive advantage is based on manufacturing, the sales managers and salespeople spend a great deal of time in the factory learning the manufacturing processes. More important, these salespeople have established personal relationships with workers at every level in the plant. Salespeople even play on manufacturing softball teams in a local corporate league, even though they may have to fly home from Kellogg's headquarters in Battle Creek, Michigan, to make a game.

These personal relationships enable Grafo Regia to respond much more quickly to customer needs. If Kellogg needs to change a Frosted Flakes package to include a promotion involving David Robinson (a basketball player for the San Antonio Spurs) just for the San Antonio market, Grafo Regia can do it faster than anyone else. One main reason is that manufacturing and sales are on the same team and are not viewed as separate entities.

In general, manufacturing is concerned with producing product at the lowest possible cost. In most cases, this means they want long production runs, little customization, and low inventories. Customers, however, want their purchases shipped immediately and custom-made to their exact specifications. Salespeople may have to

Scott Wanner

Chuck Keeler/Tony Stone Images

Salespeople who develop partnerships with people in areas such as shipping and manufacturing can count on their internal partners' support when they need it.

negotiate compromises between both manufacturing and the customer. Salespeople should also develop relationships with manufacturing so that they can make accurate promises and guarantees to customers.

Administration

The functions of order entry, billing, credit, and employee compensation require that each company have an administrative department. This department processes orders and sees that the salesperson gets paid for them. Employees in this area (as discussed earlier) are often evaluated on how quickly they process orders and how quickly the company receives customer payment. Salespeople can greatly influence both processes and realize substantial personal benefit for themselves.

The credit department is an important part of administration. Understanding the needs of the credit department and assisting it in collecting payments can better position the salesperson to help customers receive credit later. A credit representative who knows you will help collect a payment when a problem arises is more likely to grant credit to one of your customers. Some companies do not pay commission until after the customer has paid to ensure that salespeople sell to creditworthy accounts. These companies, such as Force Computers in San Jose, California, believe a close working relationship between sales and credit is critical to the financial health of the company.[3]

Shipping

The scheduling of product shipments may be part of sales administration or manufacturing, or it may stand alone. In any case, salespeople need the help of the shipping department. When salespeople make special promises to expedite a delivery, they actually must depend on shipping to carry out the promise. Shipping managers focus on costs, and they often keep their costs under control by planning efficient shipping routes and moving products quickly through warehouses. Expedited or special-handling deliveries can interfere with plans for efficient shipping. Salespeople who make promises that shipping cannot or will not fulfill are left with egg on their faces. John Munn, a Coca-Cola key accounts representative, will help load and drive a delivery truck when one of his accounts needs an expedited shipment so that his promise is fulfilled with minimal interruption in the warehouse.

Customer Service

Salespeople also need to interact with customer service. Perhaps this is obvious, but many salespeople arrogantly ignore the information obtained by customer service representatives. A technician who fixes the company's products often goes into more customers' offices or plants than the salesperson does. The technician has earlier warning concerning a customer's switch to a competitor, a change in customer needs, or failure of a product to satisfy. For example, if an IBM technician spies a new DEC computer in the customer's office, the technician can ask if the DEC unit is on trial. If a good working relationship exists between the technician and the salesperson, the technician will warn the salesperson that the account is considering a competitive product. Close relationships and support of customer or technical service representatives means not only better customer service but faster and more direct information flow to the salesperson. This information will help the salesperson gain and keep customers.

Salespeople, in turn, can help customer service by setting reasonable expectations for product performance with customers, training customers in the proper use of the product, and handling complaints promptly. Technicians are evaluated on the number of service calls they make each day and how long the product works between service calls, among other things. Salespeople can reduce some service calls by setting the right expectations for product performance. Salespeople can also extend the amount of time between calls by training customers in the proper use of the product and in preventive maintenance. An important by-product of such actions should be higher customer satisfaction.

Marketing

Sales is part of marketing in some firms and separate from marketing in others. Marketing and sales should be highly coordinated because their functions are closely related. Both are concerned with providing the right product to the customer in the most efficient and effective manner. Sales acts as the eyes and ears of marketing, while marketing develops the promotions and products that salespeople sell. Salespeople act as eyes and ears by informing the marketing department of competitor actions, customer trends, and other important market information. Marketing serves salespeople by using that information to create promotional programs or design new products. Marketing is also responsible for generating leads through trade show exhibiting, direct-mail programs, advertising, and public relations.

Sales

Within any sales force, there may be several types of salespeople. As you learned in earlier chapters, global account managers may work with the largest accounts while other representatives handle the rest of the customers, and the salesperson must interact with certain sales executives and sales managers. How these people work together is the subject of the next section.

PARTNERS IN THE SALES ORGANIZATION

The sales function may be organized in many different ways, but no matter how it is organized, it is rarely perfect. Usually some customer overlap exists among salespeople, meaning several salespeople have to work together to serve the needs of one account. Customer needs may require direct customer contact with the sales executive as well as the salesperson. At the same time, the salesperson must operate in an environment that is influenced by the policies and procedures created by that same sales executive and executed by the salesperson's immediate manager. In this section, we examine how the activities of sales management affect salespeople.

Sales Management

Within sales management, salespeople should understand the roles of both sales executives and field sales managers. Salespeople who are able to develop partnerships with their managers will have more resources available to them to perform at a higher level.

The Sales Executive

The sales executive is the manager at the top of the sales force hierarchy. This person is a policymaker, making decisions about how the sales force will accomplish corporate objectives. Sales executives play a vital role in determining the company's strategies with respect to new products, new markets, sales forecasts, prices, and competition. They determine the size and organization of the sales force, develop annual and long-range plans, and monitor and control sales efforts. Duties of the sales executive include forecasting overall sales, budgeting, setting sales quotas, and designing compensation programs.

Size and Organization of the Sales Force   The sales executive determines how many salespeople are needed to achieve the company's sales and customer satisfaction targets. In addition, the sales executive must determine what types of salespeople are needed. For example, it is the sales executive who determines whether global account management is needed. Many other types of salespeople can be selected, which we will discuss later in this chapter. For now, keep in mind that the sales executive determines the level of customer satisfaction necessary to achieve sales objectives and then designs a sales force to achieve those goals. How that sales force is put together is important, because salespeople often have to work together to deliver appropriate customer service and successfully accomplish sales goals. We will also discuss different organizing mechanisms when we discuss integrative selling.

Forecasting   Sales executives use a number of techniques to arrive at sales forecasts. One of the most widely used techniques is **bottoms-up forecasting,** or simply adding each salesperson's own forecast into a forecast for total company sales. At each level of management, the forecast would normally be adjusted based on the manager's experience and broader perspective. This technique allows the information to come from the people closest to the market: the salespeople. Also, the forecast comes from the people with the responsibility for making those sales. But salespeople tend to be optimistic and may overestimate sales, or they may underestimate future sales if they know their bonuses depend on exceeding forecasts or if they think their quotas will be raised.

Salespeople are especially important to the forecasting process when the executive is attempting to forecast international sales.[4] Statistics used in the United States to forecast sales are often not available in other countries or, if available, may be unreliable. Therefore, the only reliable forecasting mechanism is the salesperson's own idea of what can be sold. For example, Harley-Davidson depends heavily on its salespeople in other countries for accurate forecasts of motorcycle sales. Harley-

Davidson's international sales are more than 20 percent of total sales, making such forecasts important to its planning. Salespeople are the most important source of market information in international markets.

Expense Budgets   Managers sometimes use expense budgets to control costs. An expense budget may be expressed in dollars (e.g., the salesperson is allowed to spend up to $500) or as a percentage of sales volume (e.g., expenses cannot go over 10 percent of sales). A regional manager or salesperson may be awarded a bonus for spending less than the budget allocates. However, such a bonus may encourage the salesperson to underspend, which could hurt sales performance. For example, if a salesperson refuses to give out samples, customers may not be able to visualize how the product will work; thus, some may not buy. The salesperson has reduced expenses but hurt sales.

While salespeople may have limited input into a budget, they do spend the money. Ultimately it is the salesperson's responsibility to manage the territorial budget. The salesperson not only has control over how much is spent and whether expenditures are over or under budget but, more important, decides where resources are placed. Recall from Chapter Sixteen that these resources, such as samples and trial units or direct mailers, are investments in future sales. If used unwisely, the salesperson may still meet the expense budget but fail to meet his or her sales quota.

Control and Quota Setting   The sales executive faces the challenge of setting up a balanced control system that will encourage each sales manager and salesperson to maximize his or her individual results through effective self-control. As we have pointed out throughout this text, salespeople operate somewhat independently. However, the control system management devises can help salespeople manage themselves more effectively.

Quotas are a useful technique for controlling the sales force. A **quota** represents a quantitative minimum level of acceptable performance for a specific time period. A **sales quota** is the minimum number of sales in units, and a **revenue quota** is the minimum amount of sales revenue necessary for acceptable performance. Often sales quotas are simple breakdowns of the company's total sales forecast. Thus, the total of all sales quotas equals the sales forecast. Other types of quotas can also be used. Understanding quotas is important to the salesperson because performance relative to quota is evaluated by management.

Profit quotas or **gross margin quotas** are minimum levels of acceptable profit or gross margin performance. These quotas motivate the sales force to sell more profitable products or sell to more profitable customers. Some companies assign points to each product based on the product's gross margin. More points are assigned to higher-margin products. The salesperson can then meet a point quota by selling either a lot of low-margin products or fewer high-margin products. For example, assume an office equipment company sells fax machines and copiers. The profit margin (not including salesperson compensation) on copiers is 30 percent but only 20 percent on fax machines. Copiers may be worth 3 points each, while faxes are worth 2. If the salesperson's quota is 12 points, the quota can be reached by selling four copiers, or six faxes, or some combination of both.

Activity quotas, similar to the activity goals we discussed in the last chapter, are minimal expectations of activities for each salesperson. These quotas are set by the company to control the activities of the sales force. This type of quota is more important in situations where the sales cycle is long and sales are few, because activities can be observed more frequently than sales. For example, for some medical equipment, the sales cycle is longer than one year and a salesperson may sell only one or two units each quarter. Having a monthly sales target in this case would be inappropriate, but requiring a certain minimum number of calls to be made is reasonable. The assumption made by management is that if the salesperson is performing the proper activities, sales will follow. Activities for which quotas may be established include number of demonstrations, total customer calls, number of calls on prospects, or number of displays set up.

Thinking *it* Through	How would you respond if you felt you were making as many calls as possible during the workweek, yet your manager demanded that you make more? The manager's reasoning is that if you make more, you will sell more. How would your response change if you were not meeting your sales quota? If you were selling twice your sales quota?

Compensation and Evaluation   An important task of the sales executive is to establish the company's basic compensation and evaluation system. The compensation system must satisfy the needs of both the salespeople and the company. You, as a salesperson, need an equitable, stable, understandable system that motivates you to meet your objectives. The company, however, needs a system that encourages you to sell products at a profitable price and in the right amounts.

Salespeople want a system that bases rewards on efforts and results. Compensation must also be uniform within the company and in line with what competitors' salespeople receive. If competitors' salespeople earn more, you will want to leave and work for that competitor. But your company expects the compensation system to attract and keep good salespeople and to encourage you to do specific things. The system should reward outstanding performance while achieving the proper balance between sales results and costs.

Compensation often relates to quotas. As with quotas, salespeople who perceive the system as unfair may give up or leave the firm. A stable compensation system ensures that salespeople can reap the benefits of their efforts, whereas a constantly changing system may lead them to constantly change their activities but never make any money. A system that is not understandable will be ignored.

The sales executive decides how much income will be based on salary or incentive pay. The salesperson may receive a **salary,** a regular payment regardless of performance, or **incentive pay,** which is tied to some level of performance. There are two types of incentives: commission and bonus. A **commission** is incentive pay paid for an individual sale, whereas a **bonus** is incentive pay given for overall performance in one or more areas. For example, a bonus may be paid for acquiring a certain number of new customers, reaching a specified level of total sales in units, or selling a certain amount of a new product.

Sales executives can choose to pay salespeople a straight salary, a straight commission, or some combination of salary, commission, and/or bonus. Most firms opt for some combination of salary and bonus or salary and commission. Fewer than 4 percent pay only commission, and slightly fewer than 5 percent pay only salary. Exhibit 17.2 illustrates how the types of compensation plans would work.

Under the **straight salary** method, a salesperson receives a fixed amount of money for work during a specified time. The salesperson is assured of a steady income and can develop a sense of loyalty to customers. The company also has more

EXHIBIT 17.2

How Different
Types of Compensation
Plans Pay

Month	Sales Revenue	Amount Paid to Salesperson			
		Straight Salary	Straight Commission*	Combination†	Point Plan
January	$50,000 6 copiers 10 faxes	$3,500	$5,000	$1,500 (salary) 3,000 (commission) 4,500 (total)	$3,800
February	$60,000 6 copiers 15 faxes	3,500	6,000	1,500 (salary) 3,600 (commission) 5,100 (total)	4,800
March	$20,000 2 copiers 5 faxes	3,500	2,000	1,500 (salary) 1,200 (commission) 2,700 (total)	1,600

*Commission plan pays 10% of sales revenue.

†Commission portion pays 6% of sales revenue.

Note: Copiers are worth 3 points, faxes are worth 2, and each point is worth $100 in commission. Also, the commission rates are used for example purposes only to illustrate how compensation schemes work. Point plans, for example, do not necessarily always yield the lowest compensation.

control over the salesperson. Because income does not depend directly on results, the company can ask the salesperson to do things in the best interest of the company, even if those activities may not lead to immediate sales. Straight salary, however, provides little financial incentive for salespeople to sell more. For example, in Exhibit 17.2, the salesperson receives $3,500 per month, no matter how much is sold.

Straight salary plans are used when sales require long periods of negotiation, when a team of salespeople is involved and individual results cannot be measured, or when other aspects of the marketing mix (e.g., advertising) are more important than the salesperson's efforts in generating sales (e.g., in trade selling of consumer products). Most sales trainees also receive a straight salary.

A **straight commission** plan pays a certain amount per sale, and includes a base and a rate but not a salary. The **commission base,** the item from which commission is determined, is often unit sales, dollar sales, or gross margin. The **commission rate,** which determines the amount paid, is expressed as a percentage of the base (e.g., 10 percent of sales or 8 percent of gross margin) or as a dollar amount (e.g., $100 per sale). Exhibit 17.2 illustrates two straight commission plans, one that pays 10 percent of sales revenue and a point plan that pays $100 per point (using the copier and fax example we discussed previously).

Commission plans often include a draw. A **draw** is money paid to the salesperson against future commissions, in essence a loan that guarantees a stable cash flow. For example, a salesperson receives a draw of $1,000 per month. If the salesperson earns less than $1,000 in commissions during one month, he or she will still receive $1,000. The difference between the earned commission and the draw will be paid back in months when the salesperson earned over $1,000. Exhibit 17.3 presents an example.

Straight commission plans have the advantage of tying the salesperson's compensation directly to performance, thus providing more financial incentive. However, salespeople on straight commission have little company loyalty and certainly are less willing to perform activities, such as paperwork, that do not directly lead to sales.

EXHIBIT 17.3

An Example
of a Draw
Compensation Plan

Month	Draw	Commission Earned	Payment to Salesperson	Balance Owed to Company
January	$1,000	$ 0	$1,000	$1,000
February	1,000	1,500	1,000	500
March	1,000	2,000	1,500	0

Xerox experimented with such a plan but found that customer service suffered, as did company loyalty among salespeople.

Companies that do not emphasize service to customers or do not anticipate long-term customer relationships (e.g., a company selling kitchen appliances directly to consumers) typically use commission plans. Such plans are also used when the sales force includes many part-timers, because part-timers can earn more when their pay is tied to their performance. Also, part-timers may need the extra motivation straight commission can provide.

Under a bonus plan, salespeople receive a lump-sum payment for a certain level of performance over a specified time. Bonuses resemble commissions, but the amount paid depends on total performance, not on each individual sale. Bonuses, awarded monthly, quarterly, or annually, are always used in conjunction with salary and/or commissions in combination plans. For example, a bonus could be added to any of the compensation plans illustrated in Exhibit 17.2.

Sales executives frequently combine two or three of the basic methods to form the compensation plan. **Combination plans,** also called *salary-plus-commission,* provide salary and commission and offer the greatest flexibility for motivating and controlling the activities of salespeople. The plans can incorporate the advantages and avoid the disadvantages of using any of the basic plans alone. Note in Exhibit 17.2 that the straight salary plan pays a higher salary than the combination plan, but the difference can be offset by the incentive portion.

The main disadvantage of combination plans lies in their complexity. Salespeople confused by this complexity could unknowingly perform the wrong activities, or sales managers could unintentionally design a program that rewards the wrong activities. Using the office equipment example above, if faxes and copiers were worth the same commission (for example, $100 per sale), the salesperson would sell whatever was easiest to sell. If faxes were easier to sell than copiers, the firm may make less money because salespeople would expend all of their effort selling a lower-profit product unless the volume sold made up for the lower margin. Even then, however, the firm may be stuck with a warehouse of unsold copiers.

Management uses salary-plus-commission plans to motivate salespeople (through commissions) to increase revenues while continuing to perform nonselling activities (paid for with salary) such as customer service. When management wants to develop long-term customer relations, salary-plus-bonus plans are used so that less emphasis is placed on getting new (and commissionable) sales. Bonus plans are also used when the sales effort involves a team of people.

Thinking
it
Through

As a buyer, under which plan would you prefer your salesperson to work? Which would you prefer if you were a salesperson? What conflicts might occur between buyer and seller because of the type of compensation plan?

Field Sales Managers

Salespeople report directly not to a sales executive but to a field sales manager. **Field sales managers** hire salespeople, evaluate their performance, train salespeople, and perform other important tasks. Salespeople find it useful to partner with their managers, because the managers often represent the salespeople to other parts of the organization. Also, the salesperson often has to sell the manager first on any new idea before the idea can be pitched to others in management. Building a partnering relationship with managers can go a long way toward getting ideas accepted.[5]

Evaluating Performance Field sales managers are responsible for evaluating the performance of their salespeople. The easiest method of evaluating performance is to simply add up the amount of sales that the salesperson makes. But sales managers must also rate their salespeople's customer service level, product knowledge, and other, less tangible aspects. Some companies, such as Federal Express, use customer satisfaction surveys to evaluate salespeople. In other companies, the manager rates each salesperson, using evaluation forms that list the desired aspects. (An example of an evaluation form appears in Exhibit 17.4.) Such evaluations help managers determine training needs, promotions, and pay raises.

The records and reports salespeople submit also play an important role in communicating their activities to the sales manager. The manager then uses these reports to evaluate performance in a manner similar to the way the salesperson would. But these written reports are not enough; sales managers should also make calls with salespeople to directly observe their performance. These observations can be the basis for recommendations for improving individual performance or for commending outstanding performance. Other information, such as customer response to a new strategy, can be gained by making calls. This information should be shared with upper management to improve strategies.

Training The sales manager trains new hires and provides refresher training for experienced salespeople. To determine what refresher training they need, managers often use information gathered while observing salespeople making sales calls. Content of training for new salespeople may be determined by a sales executive, but the field sales manager is often responsible for carrying out the training.

EXHIBIT 17.4 Behavioral Observation Scale (BOS)	Almost Never						Almost Always
1. Checks deliveries to see if they have arrived on time.	1	2	3	4	5	6	7
2. Files sales reports on time.	1	2	3	4	5	6	7
3. Uses promotional brochures and correspondence with potential accounts.	1	2	3	4	5	6	7
4. Monitors competitor activities.	1	2	3	4	5	6	7
5. Brushes up on selling techniques.	1	2	3	4	5	6	7
6. Reads marketing research reports.	1	2	3	4	5	6	7
7. Prospects for new accounts.	1	2	3	4	5	6	7
8. Makes service calls.	1	2	3	4	5	6	7
9. Answers customer inquiries when they occur.	1	2	3	4	5	6	7

Professional salespeople constantly seek to upgrade their selling skills. This salesperson for Flair Personnel is receiving some pointers from his sales manager.

Courtesy MSI International, Atlanta, Georgia; photo by Ann States

Most experienced salespeople welcome training when they perceive that it will improve their sales. Unfortunately, training is often viewed as an inconvenience that takes away from precious selling time. Additional sales training can be useful when the organization makes a real commitment to it. Follow-up in the field is often necessary to assist the experienced salesperson in practicing what was learned in the training session. If the commitment isn't there from the company, the experienced rep is likely to slip back into old habits.

You should continue to welcome training, no matter how successful you are. It always offers the opportunity to improve your performance, or at least achieve the same level with less effort. Also, as you will see in Chapter Eighteen, continuing to learn is important to the salesperson who is part of a learning organization.

Managing Ethics in Sales

Salespeople, particularly those within certain industries, have earned a reputation that is unfavorable. Most salespeople, though, want to act ethically. Because we have emphasized throughout this book methods of selling that help people solve problems and satisfy needs, we believe it is important to understand what companies do to encourage ethical behavior and how salespeople should work with their sales management partners to choose ethical options. First, we will discuss the sales executive's role in making ethics policy. Then we will cover the roles of the field sales manager and the salesperson in implementing that policy.

Ethics and the Sales Executive

Part of a sales executive's job is to determine corporate policy concerning what is considered ethical and what is not and how unethical behavior will be investigated and punished. In addition, the sales executive must ensure that other policies, such as the performance measurement and compensation policies, also support the ethics of the organization. When performance measurement and compensation policies reward only outcomes, there may be a greater tendency on the part of salespeople to act unethically because of pressure to achieve and a culture supporting the credo "the end justifies the means." But when behavioral performance measurement systems are also in place, the compensation system can reward those who do things the right way.[6] While unethical behaviors may result in short-term gain (and therefore may accidentally be rewarded in an outcome-only compensation scheme), they can have serious long-term effects.

Sales executives must therefore develop a culture that creates behavioral norms regarding how things should be done and what behaviors will not be tolerated. Such a culture can be enhanced through the development of formal policy, training courses on ethics, ethics review boards, and an open-door policy. **Open-door policies** are general management techniques that allow subordinates to bypass immediate managers and take concerns straight to upper management when the subordinates perceive a lack of support from the immediate manager. Open-door policies enhance an ethical culture, because salespeople can feel free to discuss troublesome issues that involve their managers with someone in a position to respond. Ethics review boards may function in the same way, providing expert advice to salespeople who are unsure of the ethical consequences of an action. **Ethics review boards** may consist of experts inside and outside the company who are responsible for reviewing ethics policies, investigating allegations of unethical behavior, and acting as a sounding board for employees. Sales executives play an important role in determining how the corporate culture will support ethical activity by salespeople.

Salespeople also have the right to expect ethical treatment from their company. Fair treatment concerning compensation, promoting policies, territory allocation, and other actions should be delivered. Compensation is probably the area with the most common concerns, although problems can arise in all areas. Compensation problems can include slow payment, hidden caps, or compensation plan changes after the sale.

For example, one company paid its salespeople a straight commission of about 10 percent. When a salesperson sold one major account $11 million worth of product, the company changed her commission plan to a salary plus commission to cut her payment. In another example, a company refused to pay a salesperson all of his commission because he earned more than the vice president of sales. The company claimed there was a **cap,** or limit, on earnings. Caps are not unethical; what was unethical was that the salesperson was not made aware of the cap prior to selling. Although some problems do occur, most companies want to hire and keep good salespeople, and most businesspeople are ethical.

Thinking *it* Through	Should schools have ethics review boards? What advantages would such boards have for the student? For the teacher? Would salespeople reap the same types of benefits if their companies had ethics review boards?

Ethics and the Field Sales Manager

Salespeople often ask managers for direction on how to handle ethical problems, and the sales manager is usually the first person to investigate complaints of unethical behavior. Field sales managers can provide a role model for salespeople by demonstrating ethical behavior in role plays during training or when conducting sales calls in the field. Sales managers should also avoid teaching high-pressure techniques and manipulative methods of selling.

Responding to Unethical Requests   Salespeople, however, may find themselves facing a sales manager who encourages them to engage in unethical behavior. When that situation occurs, a salesperson has several options to choose from to avoid engaging in such behavior.[7] Perhaps the most obvious option is to find another job, but that is not always the best solution. If the organizational culture supports the unethical request, however, finding another job may be the only choice. Exhibit 17.5 lists choices available to the salesperson.

Another choice is to blow the whistle, or report the unethical request, if the salesperson has adequate evidence (if adequate evidence is not available, sometimes simply threatening to blow the whistle may work). If this choice of action is followed, the salesperson must be ready to accept a perception of disloyalty, retaliation by the manager, or other consequences. However, if senior management is sincere in efforts to promote ethical behavior, steps should be taken to minimize those negative outcomes. If an open-door policy or an ethics review board exists, the salesperson can take the concern to higher levels for review. For example, the salesperson could say, "I'm not sure that is appropriate. I'd like to get the opinion of the ethics review board." If the action is unethical, the sales manager may back down at that point. It is also possible that the manager will try to coerce the salesperson into not applying to the ethics review board; if that is the case, another course of action may prove to be a better choice.

Another strategy is to negotiate an alternative. This response requires that the salesperson identify an alternative course of action with a high probability of success. For example, if a sales manager tells the salesperson to offer a prospect a bribe, the salesperson should be prepared to prove that a price reduction would be just as effective. Similar to negotiation is to simply ignore the request. The salesperson may say to the manager that the request was carried out, when in fact it was not; the potential problem with this is that the salesperson has admitted to carrying out an unethical act (even though she or he did not), which can lead to future problems. Finally, the salesperson can simply deny the request. Denial can be a dangerous action in that it opens the salesperson to possible retaliation, particularly retaliation that is not obviously linked to the denial, such as denying access to training or reducing the size of the salesperson's territory.

The salesperson's choice of action will depend on how much proof is available, what alternative actions to the unethical action exist, and the type of relationship

---

EXHIBIT 17.5

Strategies for Handling Unethical Requests from a Manager

- Leave the organization, or ask for a transfer.
- Negotiate an alternative course of action.
- Blow the whistle, internally or externally.
- Threaten to blow the whistle.
- Appeal to a higher authority.
- Agree to the demand, but fail to carry it out.
- Deny to comply with the request.
- Ignore the request.

with the manager. Other factors to consider are the ethical climate of the organization, whether an open-door policy exists, and similar factors. The salesperson, however, is always in control of his or her behavior. Never should a salesperson rationalize away a behavior by placing responsibility on the sales manager.

Salespeople as Partners

Many types of salespeople exist, including telemarketing representatives, field salespeople, product specialists, and account specialists. Often there is some overlap in responsibilities; when overlap occurs, companies should have policies that facilitate serving the customer.

Geographic Salespeople

Most sales departments are organized geographically. A **geographic salesperson** is assigned a specific geographic territory in which to sell all of the company's products and services. Companies often combine geographic territories into larger branches, zones, or regions. For example, Eli Lilly has geographic regions that include 50 or more salespeople. Each Lilly salesperson has responsibility for a specific geographic area. For example, one rep may call on physicians in a portion of Dallas, using zip code boundaries to determine the territory; that rep may have all physicians in zip codes 75212, 75213, 75218, 75239, 75240, and 75252. Geographic salespeople also work with other types of salespeople, which we will discuss.

Account Salespeople

There are several ways companies may organize salespeople by account. The most extreme example would be to give a salesperson the responsibility to sell to only one company but responsibility for every location of that company in the country or the world. In another common form of specialization, some salespeople develop new accounts while others maintain existing accounts. Developing new accounts requires different skills than maintaining an already sold account. One RCA radio communications division uses field salespeople to develop new accounts and a telemarketing sales force to maintain the accounts. The field salespeople must identify prospects from noncustomers and sell the product. Once the RCA product has been installed, the account becomes the responsibility of the telemarketing sales force.

Similar customers often have similar needs, whereas different types of customers may have very different needs for the same product. In such cases, salespeople may specialize in calling on only one or a few customer types, although they sell the same products. AT&T's Global Information Systems division has different sales forces for calling on manufacturing companies, retailers, and financial companies. Andritz, an international heavy machinery company, has salespeople who sell only to paper producers and other salespeople who sell only to wastewater treatment plants, even though the same product is being sold. Some Procter & Gamble salespeople call on central buying offices for grocery store chains; others call on food wholesalers.

Companies also divide their customers on the basis of size. Large customers, sometimes called **key accounts,** may have a salesperson assigned only to that account; in some cases, a small sales force is assigned to one large account. Amdahl, a computer and telecommunications company, has an account executive, a systems engineer, and a customer support representative assigned to each of certain large accounts.

This Hewlett-Packard major account team is planning a product proposal for a new computer system.

Courtesy Hewlett-Packard Company

In other firms, one company executive coordinates all of the salespeople who call on an account throughout the nation or the world. These executives are called **national account managers (NAM)** or **global account managers (GAM)**. These account managers are more than salespeople; they are business executives. As Unisource, a distribution company in Valley Forge, Pennsylvania, discovered, partnering with global accounts requires executive-level account management.[8]

Global account managers manage large teams of salespeople. John Slattery, for example, is Xerox's global account manager for the AT&T account. He works with over 200 local Xerox people located in district offices around the world, as well as service specialists assigned to AT&T and other global accounts.[9]

The local geographic rep's responsibility may involve coordinating delivery with the local customer. This coordination may also require customer training on the product or working with a local store manager to set up displays, plan inventories, and so on. Local reps should also look for sales opportunities in the customer's location and provide this information to the GAM. They often become the eyes and ears of the GAM and provide early notice of opportunities or threats in the account, just as a service rep does for the geographic rep. IBM found that local reps did not want to work with GAMs because there was no compensation for servicing those accounts. So IBM completely revamped the compensation plan to encourage local reps' participation in global account selling and service.[10] GAMs often report directly to the vice president of sales or to a director of global sales, as illustrated in Exhibit 17.6, but work with geographic reps.

Note, however, that house accounts differ from key accounts. As described in Chapter Seven, a **house account** is handled by a sales or marketing executive in addition to that executive's regular duties, and no commission is paid on any sales from that account. House accounts are often key accounts, but not all key accounts are house accounts. The main point is that house accounts have no "true" salesperson. Wal-Mart has negotiated to be a house account with some suppliers on the basis that

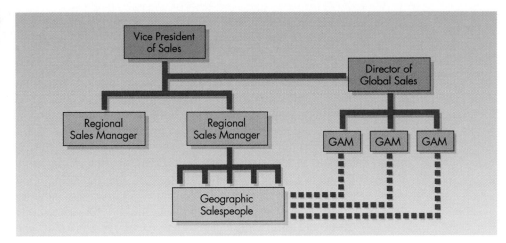

EXHIBIT 17.6

GAMs in the Sales Force
Although GAMs and geographic salespeople have different immediate managers, they still work together. GAMs coordinate the efforts of geographic reps within local buying offices of global accounts.

Wal-Mart will save money when the suppliers pass on the salesperson's commission or salary savings. General Dynamics attempted the same strategy when buying, but abandoned it when it realized that lower costs also meant reduced service.

Product Specialists

When companies have diverse products, their salespeople often specialize by types of products. Johnson & Johnson, which sells baby products, has two specialized sales forces: the disposable-products sales force and the toiletries products sales force. Hewlett-Packard has separate sales forces that specialize in selling computers, electronic test instruments, electronic components, medical test equipment, or analytical test equipment. Each sales force has its own regional, district, and area sales managers. Insuror's of Texas has salespeople who specialize in auto insurance, others who specialize in homeowner's insurance, and still others who specialize in medical and disability insurance. However, all of Insuror's salespeople operate under the same sales management structure. Irrespective of the management structure, sometimes the technical knowledge requirements are so great that organizing territories by product makes sense.

In addition to having management responsibilities similar to those for geographic reps, product salespeople must coordinate their activities with those of salespeople from other divisions. Success can be greater for all involved when leads and customer information is shared. For example, a Hewlett-Packard test instrument salesperson may have a customer who is also a prospect for electronic components. Sharing that information with the electronic components rep can help build a relationship that can pay off with leads for test instruments.

Inside versus Outside

Our discussion to this point has focused on outside salespeople, called **field salespeople,** that is, salespeople who sell at the customer's location. **Inside salespeople** sell at their own company's location. Inside salespeople may handle walk-in customers or telemarketing salespeople, or they may handle both duties. For example, a plumbing supply distributor may sell entirely to plumbers and employ inside salespeople who sell to those plumbers who come into the distributorship to buy products.

As we discussed in Chapter Seven, some telemarketing salespeople are used to provide leads for field salespeople. But there are other types of telemarketing salespeople, including account managers, field support reps, and customer service reps.[11] A telemarketer who is an account manager has the same responsibilities and duties a field salesperson does, except that all business is conducted over the phone. Hewlett-Packard's test and measurement group, for example, has 40 account telemanagers, with accounts ranging from small electronics manufacturers to Fortune 100 companies.[12]

A **field support rep** is a telemarketer who works with field salespeople and does more than prospect for leads. The field support rep may also cross-sell, upgrade, or seek reorders. Together with field salespeople, field support reps develop account strategies, handle customer concerns, and perform similar duties. We will discuss these representatives further when we discuss team-selling strategies shortly.

Customer service reps are in-bound salespeople who handle customer concerns. **In-bound** means they respond to telephone calls placed by customers, rather than **out-bound,** which means the telemarketer makes the phone call (prospectors, account managers, and field support telemarketers are out-bound reps). For example, there is an 800 telephone number on the back of a tube of Crest toothpaste. If you call that number, you will speak with an in-bound customer service rep.

Sales Teams

A growing number of companies are adopting a team approach to sales.[13] Amdahl's team approach to some key accounts is an example of a sales team. This concept is being used by companies that recognize they can best build partnerships by empow-

Baxter's new team-selling approach for hospital supplies is designed to make it easier for hospitals to coordinate their business with Baxter. Where the company has used a team approach, sales have increased 50 percent faster than in hospitals the company serves in a traditional fashion.

Courtesy Bellini Design; photo by Will Panich

ering one person, the account manager, to represent the organization. In **team selling,** a group of salespeople support a single account. Each person on the team brings a different area of expertise or handles different responsibilities. As you see in Exhibit 17.7, each specialist can be called on to team up with the account managers.

Before adopting team selling, companies may have had one salesperson for each product line. Xerox, for example, once had separate copier, duplicator, supplies, telecopiers (fax), printer, computer workstation, and communication network salespeople all calling on the same buyer. These reps would pass one another in customers' lobbies without recognizing one another. Customers grew tired of seeing as many as seven salespeople from Xerox. Now one account manager calls on the buyer, and brings in product specialists as needed.

Xerox uses permanent teams, whereas Dendrite International, a software company, forms teams as needed. The company may involve as many as 50 employees over the 12-month cycle of any given sale. In both cases, though, salespeople are responsible for coordinating the efforts of the specialists and determining who is brought in and at what point in the sale.[14] A similar situation occurs at Central Transportation Systems, as Selling Scenario 17.2 illustrates.

In an extension of team selling, **multilevel selling,** members at various levels of the sales organization call on their counterparts in the buying organization. (As charted in Exhibit 17.8, for example, the vice president of sales calls on the vice president of purchasing.) Multilevel selling can take place without a formal multilevel sales team if the account representative requests upper-level management's involvement in the sale. For example, you may ask your company's vice president of sales to call on the vice president of operations at a prospect's company to secure top-level support for your proposal.

Another type of sales team is made up of the field rep and the field support rep (see Exhibit 17.9). Some companies use one telemarketer for each field salesperson,

Team-Selling Organization
In team selling, product specialists work with account managers. Account managers have total account responsibility, but product specialists are responsible for sales and service of only a limited portion of the product line, and may work with several account managers.

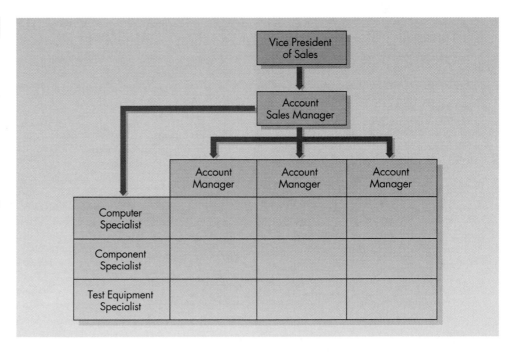

Creating a Virtual Selling Team

Team selling is a strategy that has helped many companies, such as Xerox and Wachovia, leverage strength in one area of an account to grow revenue in other areas. But small companies cannot always create the kind of permanent structure that Xerox or Wachovia has. In cases where the demand varies too greatly from situation to situation, many companies create a virtual team culture, such as that developed at Central Transportation Systems. A virtual team is one brought together by technology to bring the expertise of many individuals to bear on a single account.

Central is an agent for United Van Lines, representing the moving and storage company all across Texas. Most people may not think of sales agents for van lines (Central does not haul freight but acts as an agent for

United's freight services) as high-tech companies, but it takes a great deal of expertise to move goods reliably and profitably, expertise that may not always be right in the next office. But Central contracts for United to move office furniture when companies relocate, household goods when companies relocate their personnel or when people move on their own, and trade show equipment for companies. Technology and virtual teamwork are needed to bring it all together.

Central's virtual team strategy is driven by the many different decision makers that reside in each account due to the diverse services that Central offers. According to Dick Crovisier, sales manager for the company's Austin location, a company is likely to have a different decision maker for each service. "The per-

whereas other companies have several salespeople working with a telemarketer. The telemarketer performs as many selling tasks as possible over the telephone. But when a sales call is needed at the customer's location, the field support rep makes the appointment for the field rep. Good communication and joint planning are necessary to avoid overbooking the field rep, as well as to prevent duplication of effort.

Technology and Teamwork

Technology has greatly facilitated the growth of teams, because technology provides quick communication to anyone in the world. Technology also enables communication among people in different time zones, as conversations can be conducted via e-mail over a period of days, with none of the parties required to be in the office or on

---

EXHIBIT 17.8

Forming Sales Teams for Multilevel Selling

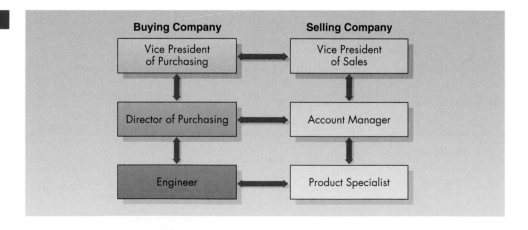

S E L L I N G   S C E N A R I O   1 7 . 2   *(concluded)*

son who handles trade shows is probably in the marketing department, while the human resources manager may work with us for employee residential moves, and yet another manager from another department may request our heavy machinery moving services," says Crovisier. "Although ordinarily one account rep might be responsible for all of the account's business, sometimes expertise of other salespeople is required to handle the needs of each department."

Accounts are assigned to specific account managers, usually based on whoever sells the account first. But account managers bring in colleagues when their expertise is required to create an ad hoc, or temporary, team. Crovisier says, "Our account managers are professionals, so they have the authority to make their own decisions, but they also have the responsibility to bring in the business. Once we have a portion of an account's business, our salespeople want to leverage our performance in that area to gain the rest of the account's work. We might have as many as four salespeople working with the account, coordinated by the original account manager." Sometimes those salespeople are in different cities, so using e-mail, intranet, and fax, a virtual team is created that can share account information and expertise to grow revenue within the account.

Crovisier believes that "Part of my job is to make sure that my salespeople are using their talents wisely. Each salesperson brings unique gifts, knowledge, and skills to the job. One of the aspects I like most about my job is helping each one achieve as much as he or she possibly can while also contributing the most to our team." With technology making communication easier, contributions to the team can be much greater.

the phone at the same time. E-mail is used to keep the sales team informed, and some companies even communicate with customers via e-mail.

Fallon McElligott is one of the fastest-growing advertising companies. When it made the pitch to win McDonald's Arch Deluxe advertising campaign, it used a presentation that had been created by eight account supervisors from different areas of the firm. Moreover, most of the shared creative work was conducted electronically.[15] Each account manager would work on the presentation, then share the document with others. And yes, the company did win the Arch Deluxe account!

Mettler-Toledo Inc., an industrial scale company, uses technology for all of the usual reasons: increased productivity, better account information, and so forth. One benefit has been that sales managers are much more aware of what is happening in each account, making their contribution more valuable. Salespeople and sales managers alike report that teamwork has been enhanced by the ability to communicate electronically.[16]

EXHIBIT 17.9

Inside/Outside Sales Team

Sometimes an inside rep or a field support rep works with accounts over the phone while his or her partner, the field rep, makes calls at the customer's location.

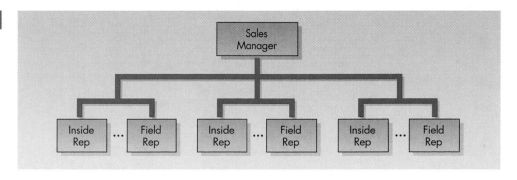

SUMMARY

Successful salespeople manage resources and build internal partnerships—partnerships with people in order entry, credit, billing, and shipping, as well as sales and marketing. These partnerships allow salespeople to keep the promises they make to customers when someone else must carry out those promises.

Salespeople in learning organizations also have a responsibility to carry the voice of the customer to other areas of the organization. Successful learning organizations are more adept at adapting to changing customer needs and developing successful products when salespeople fulfill their role of speaking for the customer.

In the sales organization, salespeople work with and for a sales executive and a field sales manager. The sales executive determines policy and maintains financial control over the sales organization. Salespeople participate in the development of forecasts that the sales executive uses in the planning process.

Another policy decision involves the method of compensation for the sales force. The four basic methods are straight salary, straight commission, bonus, and a combination plan. Straight commission plans provide strong financial incentive for salespeople but leave the company with little control over their activities. Salary plans give greater control to the company but offer less incentive for salespeople to work hard.

Sales executives are also responsible for creating a culture that supports ethical activities. Policies (e.g., open-door policies) can encourage salespeople to act ethically. Ethical review boards are also useful in reviewing ethics policies, investigating potential ethics violations, and counseling salespeople who have concerns about the ethics of possible actions. Sometimes, however, salespeople face unethical requests from their managers. If that occurs, salespeople can choose from several courses of actions, such as blowing the whistle or appealing to an ethics review board.

Partnerships must be built within the sales force, too. Some examples include team selling with product specialists, inside and outside teams, and multilevel selling.

KEY TERMS

activity quota 503
bonus 504
bottoms-up forecasting 502
cap 509
combination plans 506
commission 504
commission base 505
commission rate 505
customer service rep 514
draw 505
ethics review board 509
field sales manager 507
field salespeople 513
field support rep 514
geographic salesperson 511
global account manager (GAM) 512
gross margin quota 503
house accounts 512

in-bound 514
incentive pay 504
inside salespeople 513
internal partnerships 496
key accounts 511
multilevel selling 515
national account manager (NAM) 512
open-door policy 509
out-bound 514
profit quota 503
quota 503
revenue quota 503
salary 504
sales quota 503
straight commission 505
straight salary 504
team selling 515

QUESTIONS AND PROBLEMS

1. Your largest and most faithful customer wants its order shipped early. You could do that, but it would mean that a new, small account's order would be delayed. What will you do? In another situation, you have an order from an account with the potential to be your

biggest. But shipping tells you the product will be delayed one week, and credit refuses to allow the customer to pay COD on the first order, which is what the customer specifically requested. What will you do? What could you have done to prevent these problems from occurring?

2. A company that rents office equipment to businesses pays its salespeople a commission equal to the first month's rent. However, if the customer cancels or fails to pay its bills, the commission is taken back, even if the customer cancels 10 months later. Is this fair? Why or why not? Why would the company have this plan?

3. What is the role of the geographic salesperson in a national or global account? Assume you are a NAM. What would you do to ensure the support of geographic reps? How would that support differ if you were a product specialist and worked in a team situation? How would you get support of the account manager?

4. Consider your own experience in group work at school. What makes groups effective? How can you translate what you have learned about group work into managing a sales team?

5. To what extent should salespeople be allowed to manage themselves? What risks do you take as a sales manager when you allow self-management among salespeople? How can you minimize those risks?

6. Explain how compensation plans can create conflict among salespeople. How can companies alter compensation to influence customer care activities, increase prospecting activities, or increase prices?

7. Assume your sales manager is working with you to evaluate your performance. As the sales call progresses, your manager begins to take over and ultimately dominates the call. Why might this occur? How would you handle it?

8. An experienced salesperson argues against salaries: "I don't like subsidizing poor performers. If you paid us straight commission, we'd know who could make it and who couldn't. Sure, it may take awhile to get rid of the deadwood; but after that, sales would skyrocket!" Explain why you agree or disagree with this statement.

9. It took you four months to find a job, and you were almost out of money, when you finally landed your position. But today your boss asked you to do something unethical. You aren't sure what the corporate culture is yet because you are new at the company. How do you respond?

10. Does a salesperson's role differ in a learning organization from what it might be in an organization that does not value learning? Explain.

EXPLORING THE NET

Xerox Corporation, The Document Company, has long been an advocate of team selling. Access their home page and see if you can determine how a team is organized. How can a salesperson use this home page to stay current with what the company is doing? Give a specific example of information you could use as a rep from your own company's home page.

Xerox corporation: www.xerox.com

CASE PROBLEMS

CASE 17.1
Ben Franklin
Processors

Ben Franklin Processors, a manufacturer of medical testing equipment, has the following compensation program. Reps are paid a $1,500 draw per month, with straight commission paid on a point system and a bonus based on quota performance. The Kitometer is the latest product introduced by Ben Franklin and does much the same thing as the Mixometer, but 30 percent faster and with greater accuracy. The point system is shown in the following table:

Table 1

Product	Points/Sale	Quota
Kitometer	50	4 (units per month)
Mixometer	40	5
Plethysmograph	35	6
Quadramograph	25	8
Duplex scanner	5	45

Reps are paid $5 per point, or $5,175 plus a bonus of $500, if they sell quota for each product, for a total of $5,675. The total number of points to reach each month is 1,035, but they have to reach quota for each product to get the bonus. The following tables show the performance of the district:

Table 2

Product	Quota	Number Sold
Kitometer	40	22
Mixometer	50	78
Plethysmograph	60	63
Quadramograph	80	82
Duplex scanner	450	479

Table 3

Name	Kitometer	Mixometer	Plethysmograph	Quadramograph	Duplex Scanner	Total Points
Chonko	5	6	7	9	53	1,225
Dunn	1	7	5	8	45	930
Easley	0	6	5	8	44	835
Cooper	1	8	6	8	48	1,020
Madden	1	7	7	8	47	1,010
Moore	3	11	7	9	52	1,320
Roberts	2	9	7	11	46	1,210
Weeks	2	8	6	7	48	1,045
Johnson	3	8	7	6	48	1,105
Davis	4	8	6	8	48	1,170
TOTAL	22	78	63	82	479	

Table 4

Sales call	Kitometer	Mixometer	Plethysmograph	Quadramograph	Duplex Scanner	Total sales calls:
Quota	20	20	10	10	10	70
Roberts	28	17	11	9	10	75
Weeks	24	24	8	8	7	71
District average	27.2	18.6	9.5	10.4	9.7	75.4

Questions

1. Evaluate the district's sales performance. Draw conclusions (e.g., just where are we doing well? Doing poorly?) but don't fix anything yet. Justify your conclusions.

2. Compare Roberts's and Weeks's performances. What are some possible explanations for the poor Kitometer sales?

3. The VP of sales says the problem is a compensation plan problem. How would you fix it?

4. The company is planning to create a new position, called product specialist. This salesperson will work with territory salespeople and will have a sales quota for Kitometers only. The product specialist salesperson will work with one sales team (8 to 12 salespeople) and, once a territory rep has identified a Kitometer prospect, the rep will bring in the product specialist. How should the compensation plan be adjusted? Why?

5. The VP of sales managed to get the product specialist idea approved by the CEO even though the CEO argued that the salespeople were just too lazy to make the effort to sell the Kitometer. Lower the compensation on it to the territory reps, and everyone will sell the Mixometer at its lower price, the CEO says. The best way to get more Kitometer sales is to cut compensation on Mixometers to 20 points. What do you think should be done? Why?

**CASE 17.2
Structural Steel
Industries**

It was nearly 5:00 on Friday afternoon when Charlie got the call from Laredo Construction. "Charlie, you gotta get someone out here now!" hollered Jack Belmont, owner of Laredo Construction. "You people tried to slip some foreign steel into our job, and now we gotta rip it all out. But we aren't going to do it. You are, and it better be done by Monday!"

Charlie could tell that Jack was furious, and he had every right to be. Jack's company was building a major complex at the naval base in San Diego. Because it was a job for the federal government, the specs called for all U.S. steel. Somehow steel from Structural Steel's Mexican supplier had been mixed with the domestic steel and sent to Laredo. If a Navy inspector had seen it, Jack might even have had to forfeit a performance bond.

Structural Steel Industries (SSI) is a division of a larger steel fabricator. Steel fabricators take stock steel and make it into products. Miscellaneous steel fabricators, such as SSI, make custom steel components. SSI takes I-beams and other stock steel products and prepares them for assembly at a construction site. It cuts the steel to size, drills the holes for the rivets, and makes special beams and other steel products customized for specific buildings.

The company, a small division, employs 45 welders and production workers (including a plant manager and four supervisors), 10 employees in shipping (including the shipping manager), two engineers, three salespeople, three project managers who work with salespeople and engineers to prepare bids, one controller, two secretaries, and Charlie (the chief executive officer).

Everyone from the plant supervisors on up (see Exhibit A) talks with customers directly. Because the jobs are custom, a lot of communication takes place among the contractor, the architect, and SSI to make sure everything is done just right.

In addition to a high degree of customer contact, each job requires a great deal of communication within SSI. As the flowchart in Exhibit B shows, all areas of the organization must interact throughout the project to ensure that SSI meets customer specifications.

After dealing with Jack, Charlie hung up the phone and buzzed Mary Longren, the project manager for Laredo's project. "Mary, who worked on the Laredo project?" Charlie queried.

"I did. Why?" she replied.

"I know you did. I meant who was the engineer and who inspected the goods before shipping? I just heard from Jack Belmont. Seems as though some of the steel was from a Mexican mill."

"Oh great, just what we need! When is he building the structure?" she asked.

"He's already started. He wanted us to go to San Diego and rip the material out ourselves, but I've got him calmed down somewhat," Charlie replied.

EXHIBIT A	Patterns of Nonverbal Expression

"Was it all Mexican steel?"

Charlie sighed. "No, only about 40 percent. The good news is that only about half of that was installed before they realized the problem. But they can't do anything until we ship the right steel."

Mary muttered something that Charlie didn't quite catch. Then she said, "OK, I'll go get Manuel and Mark and get manufacturing going." Mary hung up the phone and then slapped her desk in disgust. To the ceiling she said, "Why can't we get this right? Is it that difficult?" She left her office to find Manuel, the production manager, and Mark, the shipping manager.

She quickly located the two among a crowd at the break lounge. She glanced at her watch; it was a few minutes after 5:00. Mark and several others were laughing loudly as Manuel described his weekend plans.

"You can forget those plans," interrupted Mary. "Laredo called. It seems that 40 percent of the steel we shipped was from a Mexican mill. That's a federal job, so it all has to be domestic steel."

"Well, we can get to it next week," Manuel replied, with his hands on his hips.

" 'Fraid not, Manuel. Charlie wants it out this weekend."

"No way, Mary! We can't get all of that done this weekend. That was a full-week job." Manuel was almost shouting.

Exhibit B

Process for Filling
an Order

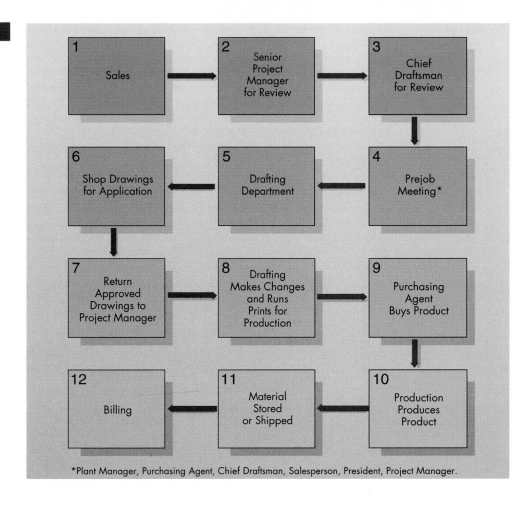

*Plant Manager, Purchasing Agent, Chief Draftsman, Salesperson, President, Project Manager.

"Then we'll just have to get out what we can," she stated, noticing that Mark was smirking. "You can forget your weekend plans too, pal. You've got to get us domestic steel and get this shipped to San Diego as soon as a truckload is ready."

"Well, we'll just see about that," said Mark, slamming a Coke can into a trash container. "C'mon Manuel, let's go see Charlie." The two walked off, talking animatedly to each other. A few production workers got up and started to walk out.

"Hey, you guys can just wait right there!" yelled Mary. "You are going to get plenty of overtime today. And if you don't want it, Charlie will help you find another place to work." One worker acted as if he didn't hear and kept right on going. Two turned around and returned to the break area.

On Monday, Angela Davis, the salesperson who handled the Laredo account, called Charlie. "I got your message, boss. What's up?" she asked.

"Laredo got Mexican steel. We've managed to ship a little more than half of the stuff he had already installed, but it will be Wednesday before the final shipment goes out."

"That's just terrific. What's the matter with those people in manufacturing? Can't they read specs?" Angela asked. Laredo wasn't her largest customer, but it was one of her biggest, a class-A account.

"Well, Angela," Charlie replied, pausing for effect, "it wasn't on the specs. Nothing manufacturing got said domestic only."

"But they should have known. It was a federal job!" she protested.

"Why should they have known? Anyway, you better call Jack Belmont and let him know what's happening. I'll let you talk to Mark next so you can get the full shipment schedule." Charlie transferred Angela to Mark. As Charlie hung up, he wondered where he was going to make up for the loss he was taking on the Laredo project.

Angela was in no mood for polite conversation when she finally reached Jack at the construction site. "Jack, this is Angela. Have you received the first emergency shipment yet?"

"No, we haven't. But it better get here soon. My guys are just sitting around." Jack sounded grim.

"You should get it any time now. I talked to Mark, and it went out about 5:00 this morning, so it should be there by 9:00."

"Look, Angela. If it isn't here by 9:00, you might as well keep it. I can't afford to do business with you people any longer." The line went dead as Jack hung up. Angela slumped against the wall of the pay phone booth, wondering what could go wrong next.

Questions

1. Who was primarily responsible for the Laredo project mistake? Who else was responsible? Why?

2. What can be done to prevent these problems in the future, and who should make those corrections?

3. Identify the managers who would be involved in a project and discuss what their priorities would be (e.g., the engineer would be most interested in the design itself).

ADDITIONAL REFERENCES

Campanelli, Melissa. "Sound the Alarm!" *Sales & Marketing Management,* December 1994, pp. 20–25.

Cauthern, Cynthia R. "Moving Technical Support into the Sales Loop." *Sales & Marketing Management,* August 1990, pp. 58–61.

Cravens, David. "The Changing Role of the Sales Force." *Marketing Management,* Fall 1995, pp. 49–57.

DeConinck, Jim; Ronald Stephens; and Richard Foster. "Variables That Influence Intentions to Discipline and Reward Ethical and Unethical Sales Behavior." *American Business Review,* January 1995, pp. 99–105.

Deeter-Schmelz, Dawn, and Rosemary Ramsey. "A Conceptualization of the Functions and Roles of Formalized Selling and Buying Teams." *Journal of Personal Selling and Sales Management,* Spring 1995, pp. 47–60.

D'Innocenzo, Len, and Jack Cullen. "Chameleon Management." *Personal Selling Power,* January/February 1995, pp. 60–61.

Hartline, Michael, and O. C. Ferrell. "The Management of Customer Contact Service Employees: An Empirical Investigation." *Journal of Marketing,* October 1996, pp. 52–70.

Kurland, Nancy B. "Ethics, Incentives, and Conflicts of Interest." *Journal of Business Ethics 14,* (1995), pp. 465–75.

Morris, Michael H.; Ramon Avila; and Eugene Teeple. "Sales Management as an Entrepreneurial Activity." *Journal of Personal Selling and Sales Management,* Spring 1990, pp. 1–15.

Mutert, Cara. "Surfing Salespeople Have an Edge." *Sales and Marketing Strategies & News,* September 1996, pp. 53–56.

Royal, Weld. "Scapegoat." *Sales & Marketing Management,* January 1995, pp. 62–69.

St. John, Caron H. and Earnest H. Hall, Jr. "The Interdependency between Marketing and Manufacturing." *Industrial Marketing Management,* Fall, 1991, pp. 223–29.

Weisendanger, Betsy. "Team." *Selling,* April 1996, pp. 45–53.

Chapter Eighteen

Managing Your Career

In this chapter, you will find the answers to many questions concerning how to start and develop a successful career in sales and marketing. Your first sale will involve selling yourself to land that first position. But job searching is not always selling. As you will see, other activities are also necessary during the hiring

Some Questions Answered in this Chapter Are:

What entry-level jobs are available to new college graduates?

Where do I find these jobs?

How should I go about getting interviews, and what should I do when I have an interview?

What selection procedures besides interviews might I go through?

What career paths are available in sales?

How can I prepare myself for a promotion into management?

process. That hiring process can be repeated each time you are considered for a promotion. Whether you decide to enter sales as a career or use it as a launching pad for a career in marketing, or if you decide you are better suited for another career, this chapter will help you get started.

PROFILE

Most marketing students begin their careers in sales. Whether their career goals are to stay in sales or move into management, most find sales a great place to start. Lori Liles is no exception to that rule, except that her start was probably a little stronger than most.

Liles recalls, "When I was a sophomore at Baylor University, I decided to pursue a career in sales. At that time, I thought it was a great place to get in on the ground floor and learn about a company. My goals are to progress into sales management and on to upper-level management positions." She believes the broad-based learning of the company that sales requires will help her reach those goals. "The people (customers) you work with in sales are usually management level, and I thought this exposure would help me to mature in business," she says.

An important element in the decision was that she would be paid for her results, not just earn a salary. "I learned that as a new college graduate, the earnings potential in sales is greater than most other entry-level positions. People whom I respect told me that in sales you are paid for your results. Also, I was told that you are recognized for your individual accomplishments. All of these attributes appealed to me at the time."

> *"I thought it [a career in sales] was a great place to get in on the ground floor and learn about a company. My goals are to progress into sales management and on to upper-level management positions."*

How did Liles get a stronger start? "To try to differentiate myself from others entering the job market at the same time, I did internships in sales with Xerox Corporation and Neiman Marcus." Liles also represented Baylor in the North American Sales Cup, a sales competition held in Montreal. "The Sales Cup experience alone taught me more than I ever imagined," she says. Liles is too modest to say it, but she won the competition, beating top sales students from Canada and Mexico. She received a cash prize and trophy, but her big payoff came in the form of multiple sales offers before she graduated.

Liles accepted a position with AT&T as a field sales representative calling on business clients. AT&T has a 90-day training course that includes product knowledge and sales techniques, so Liles got the ground-floor knowledge she wanted. "My first year was a period of rapid self dev-

LORI LILES
AT&T

elopment as I learned to build relationships with customers and to grow AT&T's revenue through consultative selling," she says.

She also learned firsthand the roller coaster of emotions salespeople experience: "One was excitement when I closed an order and got a good commission check, and the other was disappointment when I did not get an anticipated sale." The good news is that the excitements well exceeded the few disappointments.

How did her first year go? "I ended my first year at over 110 percent of sales quota and was rewarded with two raises and a promotion. I made more money this past year than I ever thought I would when I was in college." She also loves showing off the new car she was able to purchase.

"I think sales was a good decision for me," Liles says. "I have learned and matured more in this past year from my job experiences than I ever imagined. I am confident that any successes experienced during the remainder of my career, can be attributed to my invaluable sales experience."

Visit Our Website@
http://www.att.com

Landing that first career position is an exciting moment! However, the job search is just the first task in managing your career. Like the chess player who is thinking two or three moves ahead, you too must think ahead about later opportunities. Also like the chess player, you must maintain some flexibility so that you do not checkmate your career if one strategy does not work.

Sales is a great place to begin a career. Salespeople gain firsthand customer knowledge that they use to be successful in later positions. Because salespeople must represent the entire company, they learn about many aspects of the business as well as many of the people in various parts of the company. All of this knowledge can be put to use later as your career progresses.

OPPORTUNITIES IN SELLING

Selling offers many opportunities. About 3.4 million people are engaged in nonretail sales, with nearly a million new jobs expected in the next decade.[1] The *Occupational Outlook Quarterly* projects growth in manufacturing sales to range between 21 and 35 percent between now and 2005.[2] Professional sales is second only to grade school teaching in new-job growth. As you can see in Exhibit 18.1, there is strong growth in many sectors for new salespeople.

The number of sales positions is growing at a rate faster than for other types of positions, with 40 percent of companies reporting that they plan to add salespeople in the next 12 months.[3] This fast-paced growth bodes well for marketing students, because most will begin their careers as salespeople. Corporate executives clearly recognize the importance of selling experience in any marketing career. You may recall the quote in an earlier chapter from Frank Cary, former chairman of the board of IBM, recommending selling as a great place to begin a career. Many people have also found career satisfaction by staying in sales throughout their working lives.

Whether the career is sales or any other field, there are similar questions to consider when searching for a job. We will focus these questions, however, on the search for a sales position. We will also explore how to land the first position. In that discussion, we will examine how companies make hiring decisions. We will conclude with tips on how to build selling and management skills while managing a career.

International opportunities are unlikely for most entry-level salespeople, but some entry-level marketing or sales positions can lead to international sales. Students who seek international opportunities may do well to begin with foreign companies doing business in the United States. International opportunities are also more likely with small companies already engaged in international business, especially for

---

EXHIBIT 18.1		Number of Jobs
New Jobs in Sales	Source	(in thousands)
	Sales and commodities	212
	Sales, mining, manufacturing, and wholesale	209
	Sales, retail durables and services	156
	Insurance sales	31
	Real estate sales	28

Source: U.S. Department of Labor, *Occupational Outlook Quarterly*, Spring 1993, pp. 13–23.

salespeople who have proven their abilities in a domestic sales position. Students who desire international sales should prepare themselves by learning the language of the people with whom they would like to do business and participating in exchange or foreign study programs. There is no substitute for living in a culture to learn it.

MAKING A GOOD MATCH

The keys to being successful and happy lie in finding a good match between what you need and desire in a position and the positions companies offer. The first step, then, is to understand yourself, what you need and what you have to offer. Then you must consider what each company needs and what each has to offer. As Exhibit 18.2 illustrates, a good match means your needs are satisfied by what the company offers and what you offer satisfies the company's needs.

Understanding Yourself

Shakespeare said, "To thine own self be true," but to be true to yourself, you must know who you are, what you need, and what you can offer others. Knowing these things about yourself requires substantial self-examination. We will pose some questions that can help you follow Shakespeare's suggestion.

Understanding Your Needs

The first step to making a good match between what you have to offer and a company's position is to determine what it is you need. Important questions to consider include the following:

1. *Structure.* Can you work well when assignments are ambiguous, or do you need a lot of instruction? Do you need deadlines that others set, or do you set your own deadlines? If you are uncomfortable when left on your own, you

---

EXHIBIT 18.2

A Good Match between Salesperson and Company

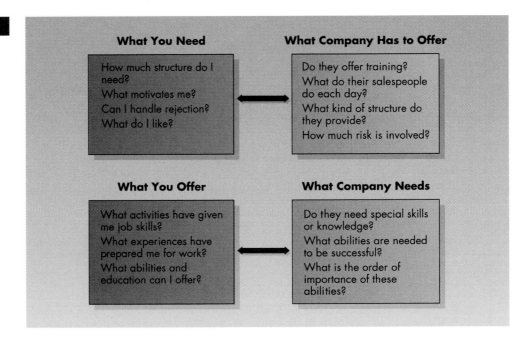

What You Need
How much structure do I need?
What motivates me?
Can I handle rejection?
What do I like?

What Company Has to Offer
Do they offer training?
What do their salespeople do each day?
What kind of structure do they provide?
How much risk is involved?

What You Offer
What activities have given me job skills?
What experiences have prepared me for work?
What abilities and education can I offer?

What Company Needs
Do they need special skills or knowledge?
What abilities are needed to be successful?
What is the order of importance of these abilities?

Many companies, such as Coach, sell their products to other companies to be used as incentives for superior sales performance. A company may offer the salespeople so many points for each sale, which can be redeemed for Coach products.

WHAT BETTER WAY TO ACKNOWLEDGE SUPERIOR
WORK THAN WITH A SUPERIOR GIFT?

COACH leathergoods make superb incentive gifts because

their exceptional quality and fine craftsmanship both embody

and reward high standards of performance.

Choose from our renowned collection of briefcases,

business accessories, handbags and a wide range of durable

travel pieces. Handcrafted of the finest

natural leather, these simple

designs look wonderful

when new and acquire a rich patina over time. Coach

leathergoods are American classics that promise to endure.

COACH

*For more information or a complimentary corporate catalogue,
please call 800-356-0301.*

©1996 Coach. Coach is a registered trademark.

may need structure in your work life. Many sales positions, such as missionary and trade sales, are in a structured environment with well-defined procedures and routines. Other positions require the salesperson to operate with little guidance or structure.

2. *Motivation.* Will financial incentives, personal recognition, or simply job satisfaction get you going? Probably it will be some combination of the three, but try to determine the relative value of each to you. Then you can weigh compensation plans, recognition programs, and other factors when considering which sales position is right for you. You may want to review the section on compensation plan types in Chapter Seventeen to aid you in determining which plan would best suit your needs.

3. *Stress and rejection.* How much can you handle? Are you a risk taker, or do you prefer more secure activities? What do you do when faced with stress? With rejection? These are important questions in understanding what you need from a sales position. For example, capital equipment sales jobs can be high-stress positions because sales are few and far between. Other jobs may require you to wade through many rejections before landing a sale. If you thrive on that kind of challenge, the rewards can be very gratifying. Other

sales positions, though, involve working only with current customers, and salespeople incur little outright rejection. Every grocery store, for example, will carry at least some of Procter & Gamble's products.

4. *Interest.* What do you find interesting? Mechanical or technical topics? Merchandising? Art or fashion? You cannot sell something that bores you. You would just bore and annoy the customer.

Understanding What You Have to Offer

Other questions that can help you understand the person you are may be available through your college's placement center. You must also take inventory of what you bring to the job:

1. *Skills.* What activities and experiences provided you with certain skills? What did you learn from those experiences and your education that you can apply to a career? Keep in mind that it is not the activities in which you participated that matter to hiring companies; it is what you learned by participating that counts.

2. *Knowledge.* College has provided you with many areas of knowledge, but you have also probably learned much by participating in hobbies and other interests. For example, you may have special computer knowledge that would be useful in selling software, or you may have participated in a particular sport that makes you well suited to sell equipment to sporting goods stores.

3. *Qualities and traits.* Every person is different and has a unique personality. What part of your personality adds value for your potential employer? Are you detail oriented and systematic? Are you highly creative? In other words, what can you bring to the job that is uniquely *you?*

Your answers to these questions will provide you with a list of what you have to offer companies. Then, when you are in an interview, you can present those features that make you a desirable candidate.

When to Ask These Questions

Unfortunately, many students wait until just before graduation before seriously considering what type of career they desire. According to our career services director, students who start a search while in school will find a job three times faster than those who start after graduation. While it is not always realistic to expect every student to map out a life plan prior to senior year, asking questions such as these as early as possible can guide a student to better course selection, better use of learning opportunities, and, ultimately, a better career decision. Then the student can begin actively searching for the job at the beginning of the senior year so that graduation signals the beginning of a career, not a career search.

Understanding the Company

While developing a good feel for who you are and what you have to offer companies, you should also explore what is available and the companies that offer those positions. As you can see in Exhibit 18.3, there are numerous sources of information regarding those positions and growth opportunities in various industries and specific companies. Don't forget, though, that the best sources are personal; be sure to talk over job opportunities with friends, friends of your parents, and your professors. Use

	Source	Example
EXHIBIT 18.3 **Sources of Job Information**	Government	*U.S. Industrial Outlook*
	Research services	*Standard & Poor's Industry Surveys*
	Industry associations	Christian Booksellers' Association
	Professional organizations	Sales and Marketing Executives International
	General magazines	*Business Week, Money Magazine*
	Trade magazines	*Sales & Marketing Management,* SELLING
	Placement services	University placement office; nonfee private agencies such as Personnel One
	Personal sources	Friends, relatives, industry association executives at trade shows, recruiters at career fairs

term papers as an excuse to call professionals in a field that interests you. Join trade and professional associations now, as these offer great networking opportunities. As someone who has studied sales, you should use your prospecting skills, too. Let's discuss how to evaluate what you learn about the companies and their positions.

What the Company Has to Offer

When you meet a salesperson or sales manager, you should ask about compensation and recognition programs, training, career opportunities, and other information to determine whether the company truly offers benefits to satisfy your needs. You should also explore daily activities of the salesperson, likes and dislikes about the job, and what that person thinks it takes to be successful. This information will help you determine if a match exists.

For example, if you need structure, you should look for a sales position in which your day is structured for you. Any industry that relies on repeated sales calls to the same accounts is more likely to be highly structured. Industries with a structured sales day include consumer packaged goods sales (Procter & Gamble, Quaker Oats, etc.) and pharmaceutical sales (Marion/Merrell Dow, Eli Lilly Company, etc.). Even these sales positions, however, offer some flexibility and independence. Office and industrial equipment sales provide much less structure when the emphasis is on getting new accounts.

Knowing your comfort level with risk and your need for incentives should assist you in picking a company with a compensation program that is right for you. If you need the security of a salary, look for companies in trade sales, some equipment sales, or missionary sales. But if you like the risk of straight commission, which can often be matched with greater financial rewards for success, explore careers in such areas as convention sales, financial services, and other straight commission jobs.

Other factors to consider may include the size of the company and its promotion policies, particularly if the company is foreign. Many companies have a "promote from within" policy, which means that whenever possible they will fill positions with people who already are employees. Such policies are very attractive if you seek career growth into management. A company that is foreign owned, however, may prefer to staff certain positions with people from its home country.

Take advantage of interests you already have. If you are intrigued by medical science, seek a medical sales position. If merchandising excites you, a position selling to the trade would be appropriate. A bar of soap by itself is not exciting, but helping customers find ways to market that bar of soap is.

Courtesy MacCormac College

Courtesy MacCormac College

Career fairs, such as this one at MacCormac College, are great opportunities to find out what companies have to offer.

Important Trends   An important trend is the increasing use of on-the-job training, or at least delaying formal training. Many companies are providing little sales training at the start, emphasizing product and company knowledge in its place and reducing the initial training time to a few days or a week. Then, after six months or so in the field, the new rep is brought in for sales training. The thinking behind this strategy is that some aspects of sales training have little impact unless the trainee has a better understanding of what happens in the field. Do not automatically drop a company from consideration if it follows this policy; many of our graduates report that it works well.

Another important trend is the growing use of interns. Both General Mills and Union Carbide, two very different companies, report that their goal is to hire half of their new salespeople from their own college intern program. Interns learn corporate culture and have a much more realistic set of expectations when hired as salespeople, factors that these and other companies have found to be important in ensuring a good match.

What the Company Needs

At this point in your job search, you may have narrowed your selection to a group of industries or companies. At a minimum, you have a good picture of what a company should offer to land you as a salesperson. The next step is to find a company that needs you. Finding out what a company needs will require some research, but you will find it to be fun and rewarding.

Many Fortune 500 companies have changed their hiring policies for entry-level positions. In the past, they recruited heavily at college campuses for beginning salespeople. Today some of those companies, such as Xerox Corporation, hire only experienced salespeople. However, many excellent opportunities exist in small companies. Selling Scenario 18.1 discusses one salesperson's experience in entry-level selling for two small businesses.

*Big or Small—
A State of
Mind?*

Wade Hallisey works for a company that many people haven't heard of: Rollins Leasing. Though it is traded on the New York Stock Exchange, employs 2,600 people, and generates $400 million in revenue a year, Rollins does not enjoy the name recognition among the general public that competitors such as Ryder Truck Leasing or Penske do. But according to Hallisey, Rollins does have a reputation where it counts: with its customers.

"Ask anyone in the business, and they'll tell you that Rollins is the most professional leasing company," says Hallisey. He attributes that reputation to small-company flexibility and family pride. "The Rollins family still owns over 20 percent of the company, so they instill a personal pride in providing customer service. And we've always run lean [with few layers of management], which gives me greater flexibility in meeting my customers' needs."

Hallisey also likes the structured freedom at Rollins. "They provide me with goals, sales strategies, and excellent training, but they also give me the freedom to serve my market as I see fit. I think that is one benefit that a company of this size can provide."

But not all small companies are wonderful to work for. His first experience lasted only three months. "Training consisted of being introduced to everyone in the home office. I had no clear idea of how they wanted me to sell the product." Hallisey also reports that the company had no clear organization chart; responsibilities and authority were so ill defined in the corporate office that he was unsure who his boss was. Quickly he learned that the company also had different ethical standards than those he was willing to accept. Because of a conflict over the way a customer was treated, he left the company.

"After leaving them, I was more interested in a company with more square footage vertically than horizontally—in other words, I wanted to work on the 16th floor of a major corporation instead of on the shop floor of truck leasing company," he says. "But I've learned that it takes professional selling to sell a $20,000 leasing contract on the shop floor, and I've also realized that I get a great deal of satisfaction when I do close those big deals." As Hallisey says, "We may be small, but we're solid. And I'm building a solid sales career with Rollins."

In general, companies look for three qualities in salespeople: good communication skills, self-motivation, and a positive and enthusiastic attitude.[4] Al Lynch, CEO of JCPenney International, adds to this list quantitative skills and an ability to ask the right questions.

Companies in certain industries may also desire related technical skills or knowledge, such as medical knowledge for the field of pharmaceutical sales or insurance knowledge to enter that field. All companies will need salespeople with computer skills, because the computer is increasingly being used to track and manage accounts, communicate internally, and perform other important activities.[5] If you desire to enter a field requiring specialized knowledge or skills, now is the time to begin acquiring that knowledge. Not only will you already have the knowledge when you begin to search for a position; you will also have demonstrated self-motivation and the right kind of attitude by taking on the task of acquiring that knowledge and skill.

THE RECRUITING PROCESS

Early in this book, we discussed the buying process so that you would understand the purchase decision buyers make. Now we will look at the recruiting process so that you will understand how companies will view you as a candidate for a sales job or any other position.

Selecting
Salespeople

In recent years, companies have made considerable progress in screening and selecting salespeople. Most have discarded the myth that there is a "sales type" who will be successful selling anything to anybody. Instead, they seek people who match the requirements of a specific position. To do this, they use a number of methods to gain information and determine whether a good match will be made.

Applicant Information Sources

To determine whether a match exists between the job requirements and the applicant's abilities, information about the applicant must be collected. Companies use five important sources of information: application forms, references, tests, personal interviews, and assessment centers. We will discuss each of these sources from the perspective of the company so that you can understand how they are used to make hiring decisions. We will also discuss how you should use these sources of information so that you can present yourself accurately and positively.

The **application form** is a preprinted form that the candidate completes. You have probably already filled these out for part-time jobs you have had. The form should include factual questions concerning the profile the company established for the position. Responses on the form are also useful for structuring the personal interview. Resumés provide much of the same information application forms do, but are often too individualized for easy comparison. For this and other reasons, companies must supplement resumés with an application form (we will discuss resumés in greater detail later in this chapter).

Contacting **references,** or people who know the applicant, is a good way to validate information on the application form. References can also supplement the information with personal observations. The most frequently contacted references are former employers. Other references are co-workers, leaders of social or religious organizations, and professors. You should be aware that some organizations try to develop relationships with faculty so that they can receive leads on excellent candidates before visiting the placement office. Professors recommend students who have demonstrated in class the qualities the recruiting companies desire.

When you select references, keep in mind that companies want references that can validate information about you. Choose references that provide different information, such as one character reference, one educational reference, and one work-related reference.

Experienced sales managers expect to hear favorable comments from an applicant's references. More useful information may be contained in unusual comments, gestures, faint praise, or hesitant responses that may indicate a problem. Before you offer someone's name as a reference, ask that person for permission. At that time, you should be able to tell whether the person is willing to give you a good recommendation.

Intelligence, ability, personality, and interest **tests** provide information about a potential salesperson that cannot be obtained readily from other sources. Tests can also correct misjudgments made by sales managers who tend to act on "gut feelings." While tests were widely criticized in the early 1980s for failing to predict success better than other sources, recent studies indicate that personality and interest tests are growing in popularity once more, in part due to their improved predictive power.[6]

Several types of tests may be given. H. R. Challey Inc. designs tests to determine a person's psychological aptitude for different sales situations. IBM requires sales candidates to demonstrate technical aptitude through a test. Many companies require candidates to pass a math test because of the importance of calculating price correctly. Still other tests indicate a candidate's ethical nature. Companies may require candidates to take tests in all of these categories before offering a position.

The important point to remember about tests is to remain relaxed. If the test is a valid selection tool, you should be happy with the outcome no matter what it is. If you believe the test is not valid, that is, does not predict your ability to succeed in that job, you may want to present your feelings to the recruiter. Be prepared to back up your line of reasoning with facts and experiences that illustrate you are a good candidate for the position.

Interviews, or personal interaction between recruiter and candidate, are an important source of information for recruiters. Companies now give more attention to conducting multiple interviews in the selection process because sometimes candidates show only slight differences. Multiple interviews can improve a recruiter's chances of observing the differences and selecting the best candidate. We will discuss interviews in more detail later in the chapter.

Companies sometimes evaluate candidates at centrally located **assessment centers.** In addition to being used for testing and personal interviews, these locations may be used to simulate portions of the job. Simulating the job serves two purposes. First, the simulation provides managers with an opportunity to see candidates responding to a joblike situation. Second, candidates can experience the job and determine whether the job fits them. For example, Merrill Lynch sometimes places broker-candidates in an office and simulates two hours of customer telephone calls. As many as half of the candidates may then decide that being a stockbroker is not right for them, and Merrill Lynch can also evaluate the candidates' abilities in a lifelike setting.

Companies will use many sources of information in making a hiring decision, perhaps even asking for a copy of a videotaped presentation you may make for this class. These sources are actually selling opportunities for you. You can present yourself and learn about the job at the same time, continuing your evaluation of the match.

Selling Your Capabilities

With an understanding of the recruiting process from the company's point of view, you can create a presentation that sells your capabilities and proves you have the skills and knowledge they want. Preparing the resumé, gaining an interview, and presenting your capabilities in the interview are important activities that require sound planning to present yourself effectively.

Preparing the Resumé

The resumé is the brochure in your marketing plan. As such, it needs to tell the recruiter why you should be hired. Recruiters scan a resumé for only 20 seconds before deciding whether to study it more carefully.[7] Whether you choose the conventional style or the functional style of resumé, the purpose is to sell your skills and experience.

Conventional Resumés   **Conventional resumés** are a form of life history, organized by type of experience. The three categories of experience most often used are educational, work, and activities/hobbies (see the example in Exhibit 18.4). Although it is easier to create conventional resumés, it is also easier to fail to emphasize important points. To avoid making this mistake, follow this simple procedure:

EXHIBIT 18.4

Conventional Resumé
Example

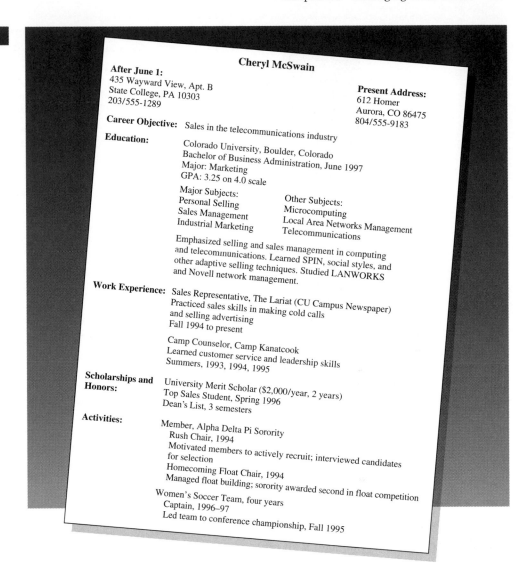

Cheryl McSwain

After June 1:
435 Wayward View, Apt. B
State College, PA 10303
203/555-1289

Present Address:
612 Homer
Aurora, CO 86475
804/555-9183

Career Objective: Sales in the telecommunications industry

Education:
Colorado University, Boulder, Colorado
Bachelor of Business Administration, June 1997
Major: Marketing
GPA: 3.25 on 4.0 scale

Major Subjects:
Personal Selling
Sales Management
Industrial Marketing

Other Subjects:
Microcomputing
Local Area Networks Management
Telecommunications

Emphasized selling and sales management in computing
and telecommunications. Learned SPIN, social styles, and
other adaptive selling techniques. Studied LANWORKS
and Novell network management.

Work Experience: Sales Representative, The Lariat (CU Campus Newspaper)
Practiced sales skills in making cold calls
and selling advertising
Fall 1994 to present

Camp Counselor, Camp Kanatcook
Learned customer service and leadership skills
Summers, 1993, 1994, 1995

**Scholarships and
Honors:**
University Merit Scholar ($2,000/year, 2 years)
Top Sales Student, Spring 1996
Dean's List, 3 semesters

Activities:
Member, Alpha Delta Pi Sorority
Rush Chair, 1994
Motivated members to actively recruit; interviewed candidates
for selection
Homecoming Float Chair, 1994
Managed float building; sorority awarded second in float competition
Women's Soccer Team, four years
Captain, 1996–97
Led team to conference championship, Fall 1995

- List education, work experience, and activities.

- Write out what you gained in each experience that will help you prove you have the desired qualities.

- Emphasize what you learned and that you have the desired qualities under each heading.

For example, the resumé in Exhibit 18.4 is designed for a student interested in a sales career. Note how skills gained in this class are emphasized in addition to GPA and major. The candidate has also chosen to focus on customer service skills gained as a camp counselor, a job that a recruiter would otherwise overlook. Rather than just listing herself as a member of the soccer team, the candidate highlights the leadership skills she gained as captain.

Functional Resumés   **Functional resumés** reverse the content and titles of the conventional resumé, organizing by what the candidate can do or has learned rather

EXHIBIT 18.5

Functional Resumé
Example

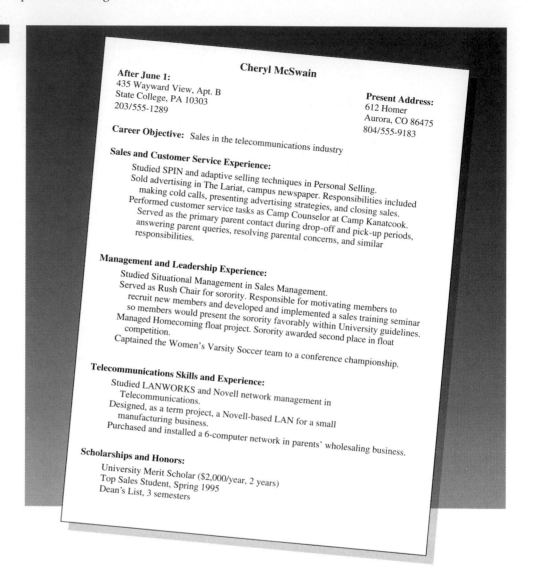

Cheryl McSwain

After June 1:
435 Wayward View, Apt. B
State College, PA 10303
203/555-1289

Present Address:
612 Homer
Aurora, CO 86475
804/555-9183

Career Objective: Sales in the telecommunications industry

Sales and Customer Service Experience:

Studied SPIN and adaptive selling techniques in Personal Selling.
Sold advertising in The Lariat, campus newspaper. Responsibilities included making cold calls, presenting advertising strategies, and closing sales.
Performed customer service tasks as Camp Counselor at Camp Kanatcook.
Served as the primary parent contact during drop-off and pick-up periods, answering parent queries, resolving parental concerns, and similar responsibilities.

Management and Leadership Experience:

Studied Situational Management in Sales Management.
Served as Rush Chair for sorority. Responsible for motivating members to recruit new members and developed and implemented a sales training seminar so members would present the sorority favorably within University guidelines.
Managed Homecoming float project. Sorority awarded second place in float competition.
Captained the Women's Varsity Soccer team to a conference championship.

Telecommunications Skills and Experience:

Studied LANWORKS and Novell network management in Telecommunications.
Designed, as a term project, a Novell-based LAN for a small manufacturing business.
Purchased and installed a 6-computer network in parents' wholesaling business.

Scholarships and Honors:

University Merit Scholar ($2,000/year, 2 years)
Top Sales Student, Spring 1995
Dean's List, 3 semesters

than by types of experience. As you can see in Exhibit 18.5, an advantage of this type of resumé is that it highlights more forcefully what the candidate can do.

When preparing a functional resumé, begin by listing the qualities you have that you think will help you get the job. Narrow this list to three or four qualities, then list activities and experiences that prove that you have those skills and abilities. The qualities are the headings for the resumé, while the activities and experiences provide evidence that you really do have those qualities. One difficulty with this type of resumé is that one past job may relate to several qualities. If that is the case, emphasize the activity within the job that provided you with the experience for each specific quality.

The Career Objective As you have probably noticed, both sample resumés list a career objective. The career objective is important because it identifies immediately the desired position. One question many students ask is what to do when interviewing for several types of positions, for example, interviewing for retail management with one company and for sales with another. The solution is to create several resumés, each listing a different objective, then use whichever version is most appropriate for a particular company. The worst solution is not to use one; potential employers then have to guess what you want.

Gaining the Interview

Students should begin examining different industries as early as possible, as we suggested earlier. As graduation looms closer and the time for serious job hunting arrives, your knowledge of the industries and companies that interest you will put you a step ahead. You will also understand the process the company will go through in searching for a new salesperson.

Using Personal Contacts   More important, you have already begun to make personal contacts in those fields—contacts you can now use to gain interviews. The same salespeople and sales managers who gave you information before to help you with term projects will usually be happy to introduce you to the person in charge of recruiting. Contacts you made at job fairs and trade shows can also be helpful.

Thinking *it* Through	**M**any students feel uncomfortable asking for favors from people they barely know. How can you overcome such feelings of discomfort? Why would someone want to help you find places to interview? What obligations do you have to people who provide you with the names of job contacts?

Using Employment Advertisements   Responding to newspaper advertisements can also lead to job interviews. You will need to carefully interpret employment advertisements and then respond effectively to them.

All ads are designed to sell, and employment ads are no exception. But what sounds great on paper may not be wonderful in reality. Here are some phrases often found in such ads and how you should interpret them:[8]

Independent contractor: You will work on straight commission with no employee benefits. You will probably receive no training and little, if any, support.

"Earn up to $____" (another variation is "Our top rep made $100,000 last year"): You need to know what the average person makes and what the average first-year earnings are, not what the top rep made or the upper limit. Another variation is "Unlimited income" (see "Independent contractor"). The job could still be desirable, but you need to find out what reality is before accepting a position.

"Sales manager trainee": This is another title for sales representative. Don't be put off or overly encouraged by high-sounding titles.

"Bonuses paid weekly": Other versions include "Daily commissions" or "Weekly commissions." These are high-pressure jobs and probably involve high-pressure sales.

"Ten salespeople needed now!": That's because everyone quit. This company uses salespeople, then discards them.

In an ad, you should look for two things: what the company needs and what it has to offer. The company should provide concrete information concerning training, compensation plan (although not necessarily the amount), amount of travel to expect, and type of product or service you will sell. You should also expect to find the qualifications the company desires, including experience and education. If you do

Want ads can be a good source of job leads, but care should be taken when interpreting claims made in some ads.

©Michael J. Hruby

not have the experience now, call and ask how to get the experience. Be specific: "What companies should I pursue that will give me the experience you are looking for?"

Responding to Advertisements   Many ads will ask you to write and may have a blind box number. A blind box number is given when the company name is not included in the ad; the box number is usually at the address of the newspaper. For example, the ad may say to send a resumé to Box 000, care of the *Dallas Morning News.* Don't be put off by the lack of company name; the ad may be placed by a company such as IBM that would otherwise receive a large number of unqualified applicants. Companies use blind box numbers for many legitimate reasons.

Writing the Cover Letter

When you write in response to an ad, you are writing a sales letter. Like any sales letter, it should focus on what you can do for them, not what you expect from them. The letter should start with an attention-getter. Here is one example:

> *In today's economy, you need someone who can become productive quickly as a territory representative. Based on your ad in the* Dallas Morning News, *I believe that I am that person.*

This attention-getter is direct, focused on a probable need, and includes a link to the ad. The probability of getting a response to this attention-getter is far greater than if you simply said:

> *Please consider me for your territory representative position, advertised in the* Dallas Morning News.

This is because the attention-getter tells why you should be considered.

The body of the letter should center on two or three reasons you should be hired. For example, if you have the qualities of self-motivation and leadership, devote two paragraphs relating each to the position. Use your resumé as proof. For example:

A territory representative position often requires self-motivation. As you can see from the attached resumé, I demonstrated self-motivation as a sales representative for the campus newspaper, as a volunteer for the local food bank, and as a member of the Dean's Honor Roll during two of the last four semesters.

The letter should close with a request for action. Ask for an interview and suggest times you are available. For example:

Please call me to arrange an interview. My schedule allows me to meet with you on Tuesday or Thursday afternoon.

An alternative is to state that you will call:

I will call you early next week to discuss my potential as a salesperson for XYZ Corporation.

No response does not necessarily mean you have been rejected; follow up with a phone call if you do not hear anything within a week. One student got a job because he called to verify that the sales manager had received his resumé. She had never seen it but was impressed enough with the student's phone call to arrange an appointment. Sometimes letters are lost or delayed, and you would not want a company to miss out on the opportunity to hire you because of the mail!

The Interview

Many students do not realize how much competition exists for the best entry-level sales positions, or perhaps they do not know what companies look for in new employees. Students often act as though they are shopping for a job. Job shoppers, however, are not seriously considered by recruiters, who are usually astute enough to quickly pick up on the student's lack of interest. If the job shopper does become interested, it is probably too late because the recruiter has already discounted this applicant. Like it or not, you are really competing for a job. As in any competition, success requires preparation and practice.

Preparing for the Interview   Students who know something about the company and its industry lead the competition. You have already looked for company and industry information in the library, in business reference books, and in periodicals. You have also interviewed the company's customers, salespeople, and sales managers. You can use this knowledge to demonstrate your self-motivation and positive attitude, two of the top three characteristics sales managers look for in sales candidates. The third top characteristic, communication skills, you will find easier to demonstrate with the confidence you gain from proper preparation.

In addition to building knowledge of the "customer," you must plan your responses to the questions you will be asked. Exhibit 18.6 lists standard questions you might hear.

Scenario questions are very popular with recruiters. These questions ask what the candidate would do in a certain situation involving actions of competitors, for example, "What would you do if a customer told you something negative about your product that you knew to be untrue, and the customer's source of information

EXHIBIT 18.6	1. What are your long-range and short-range goals and objectives? When and why did you establish these goals, and how are you preparing yourself to achieve them?

Frequently Asked Interview Questions

1. What are your long-range and short-range goals and objectives? When and why did you establish these goals, and how are you preparing yourself to achieve them?
2. What do you consider to be your greatest strengths and weaknesses?
3. Why did you choose the career for which you are preparing?
4. How do you think a friend or professor who knows you well would describe you?
5. Why should I hire you?
6. In what ways do you think you can make a contribution to our company?
7. Do you think your grades are a good indication of your academic achievement?
8. What major problem have you encountered, and how did you deal with it?
9. What do you know about our company? Why are you seeking a position with us?
10. If you were hiring a graduate for this position, what qualities would you look for?

Source: Baylor University Career Services Center.

was your competitor?" This scenario question tests ethics regarding competitors and the ability to handle a delicate situation. Other such questions test the candidate's response to rejection, ability to plan, and other characteristics. You can best prepare for these types of questions with this class and by placing yourself in the situations described in the cases and exercises in this book. You may also want to review the questions at the ends of the chapters.

Sales has several unusual characteristics, such as travel, that influence the type of questions asked. For example, if significant travel is a part of the position, you may be asked something such as: "Travel is an important part of this job, and you may be away from home about three nights per week. Would you be able and willing to travel as the job requires?" However, questions such as "What is your marital status? Do you plan to have a family? Will that affect your ability to travel?" are illegal, and you do not have to answer them. Exhibit 18.7 lists some questions that are illegal, as well as legal questions that you may have to answer.

At some point during the interview, the recruiter will ask if you have any questions. In addition to using the standard questions concerning pay, training, and benefits, you should prepare questions that are unlikely to have been answered already. For example, suppose your research has uncovered the fact that the company was recently awarded the Malcolm Baldrige Award for Quality; you might plan to ask what the company did to win that award.

You may also want to plan questions about the interviewer's career, how it got started, and what positions he or she has held. These questions work best when you are truly interested in the response; otherwise, you might sound insincere. Answers to these questions can give you a personal insight into the company. Also, you may often find yourself working for the interviewer, so the answers to your questions may help you decide whether you like and can work with this person.

Other important subjects to ask about are career advancement opportunities, typical first-year responsibilities, and corporate personality. You also need to know how financially stable the company is, but you can find this information for public firms in the library. If the firm is privately owned, ask about its financial stability.

Finally, it may seem trivial, but shine your shoes! You are interviewing for a professional position, so look professional. A student once showed up for an interview dressed in cut-off shorts and a T-shirt. The interviewer assumed the student didn't care enough to dress for the interview and ended the interview before it began. If you do not look the part now, they will not see you in the part.

EXHIBIT 18.7

Examples of Legal and Illegal Questions

Subject	Legal Questions	Illegal Questions
Name	Have you ever used another name?	What is your maiden name?
Residence	Where do you live?	Do you own or rent your home?
Birthplace or national origin	Can you, after employment, verify your right to work in the United States?	Where were you born? Where were your parents born?
Marital or family status	Statement of company policy regarding assignment of work of employees who are related. Statement of company policy concerning travel, Can you accept this policy?	With whom do you reside? Are you married? Do you plan a family?
Arrest or criminal record	Have you ever been convicted of a felony? (Such a question must be accompanied by a statement that a conviction will not necessarily disqualify the applicant.)	Have you ever been arrested?

Source: Baylor University Career Services Center. See also Wayne Barlow "Pre-Employment Interviews: What You Can and Cannot Ask." *Personnel Journal*, January 1996, p. 99.

During the Interview

The job interview is much like any other sales call. It includes an approach, needs identification, presentation, and gaining commitment. There are, however, several important differences because both parties are identifying needs and making presentations.

Many colleges offer career and placement counseling, with companies coming to campus to find new salespeople. This student is seeking advice from a DePaul University counselor.

Sharon Hoogstraten

The Approach   Social amenities will begin the interview. You will not need the same type of attention-getter that you would on a cold call. However, you may want to include an attention-getter in your greeting. For example, use a compliment approach, such as "It must be very exciting to work for a Malcolm Baldrige Award winner."

Needs Identification   One difference between sales calls and job interviews is that both parties have needs they have individually defined before the meeting (in a sales call, SPIN helps you to assist the buyer in defining needs). Questions such as "Are you willing to relocate" are used not to define needs so much as to determine whether the company's needs will be met. You should prepare questions that will help you learn whether the company's offer will meet your needs.

Take notes during the interview, especially when asking about the company, so that you can evaluate whether your needs will be met. Carry a portfolio with extra resumés and blank paper and pen for note taking. You may want to ask, "Do you mind if I take notes? This information is important to me, and I don't want to forget anything."

Try to determine early whether your interviewer is a sales manager or a personnel manager. Personnel managers may have a difficult time telling you about the job itself, its daily activities, and so forth; they may be able to outline only things such as training and employee benefits. Sales managers, however, can tell you a lot about the job, perhaps to the point of describing the actual territory you will occupy.

Personnel managers do not like being asked about salary; you will find that many people will advise you not to ask about money on the first interview. On the other hand, you are making an important decision. Why waste your time or theirs if the salary is much lower than your other alternatives? Sales managers are less likely to object, but just in case you may want to preface a question about earnings by saying, "Compensation is as important a consideration for me as training and other benefits when making a decision. Can you tell me the approximate earnings of a first-year salesperson?" You will probably get a range rather than a specific figure. You could also wait until a later meeting to ask about earnings.

People who prefer security desire compensation plans with an emphasis on salary. Other people like the potential rewards of straight commission. If either is important to you, ask about the type of compensation plan in the first meeting. For example, you should ask, "What type of compensation plan do you offer: salary, straight commission, or a combination of salary plus commission or bonus?"

Presentation   Features alone are not persuasive in interviews, just as features alone do not persuade buyers to purchase products. The U.S. Army recruiting command uses a technique to sell the army that can be useful in interviewing. The technique is called **FEB**, which stands for feature, evidence, benefit. For example, Cheryl Mc-Swain (see Exhibit 18.4) might say, "I was a camp counselor for two summers at Camp Kanatcook (F), as you can see on my resumé (E). This experience taught me customer service skills that you will appreciate when I sell for you (B)."

If asked to describe yourself, use features to prove benefits. Recruiters will appreciate specific evidence that can back up your claims. For example, if you say you like people and that is why you think you would be a good salesperson, be prepared to demonstrate how your love of people has translated into action.

Many students now carry portfolios into interviews. A **portfolio** is an organized collection of evidence of one's career.[9] For example, a portfolio might contain letters of reference and a resumé, but would also carry thank-you letters from customers, a paper on an internship, a strategic plan created for a business policy class, or even photographs of the homecoming float for which you were chairperson. Portfolios are one method of offering proof that you can deliver benefits.

Thinking *it* Through	How would you describe yourself in terms of features? What would go in your portfolio to prove your features? What needs would be satisfied by those features so they could become benefits?

Keep in mind that the interviewer also will be taking notes. Writing answers down takes the interviewer longer than it takes for you to speak. Once the question is answered sufficiently, stop and allow the interviewer time to write. Many applicants believe they should continue talking; the silence of waiting is too much to bear. Stay silent, however; otherwise, you may talk yourself out of a sale.

Gaining Commitment   If interviewing for a sales position, one that will probably require skill at gaining commitment, sales managers will want to see if the candidate has that skill. Be prepared to close the interview with some form of gaining commitment, for example, "I'm very excited about this opportunity. What is our next step?"

Be sure to learn when you can expect to hear from the company, confirm that deadline, and write it down. You may want to say, "So I'll receive a call or a letter within the next two weeks. Let's see, that would be the 21st, right?"

Asking for commitment and confirming the information signals your professionalism and your organizational and selling skills.

Special Types of Interviews   You can face many types of interviews: disguised interviews, stress interviews, and panel interviews, among others. **Disguised interviews,** or interviews in which the candidate is unaware that the interviewer is evaluating the candidate, are common at college placement offices. In the lobby you may meet a **greeter,** probably a recent graduate of your college, who will try to help you relax before a scheduled interview and offer you an opportunity to ask questions about the job and the company. Although you can obtain a lot of good information from a greeter, you may want to save some questions for the real interview. You may also want to repeat some questions in the interview to check for consistency. Keep in mind that the greeter is also interviewing you, even though the meeting seems like friendly conversation. Keep your enthusiasm high and your nerves low.

A **stress interview** is designed to place the candidate under severe stress to see how the candidate reacts. Stress interviews have been criticized as being unfair because the type of stress one experiences on a job interview often differs from the type of stress one would actually face on the job. Using one stress interview tactic, the interviewer asks the applicant to reveal something personal, such as a time when the person felt hurt. Once the situation has been described, the interviewer may mock the applicant, saying the situation wasn't that personal or that hurtful and surely the applicant can dig deeper. Another stress tactic is to ask the interviewee to sell something such as a pencil or a table.

You probably will not see stress interviews at a college placement office, but you could face one at some point in the job-hunting process. You may find it

Panel interviews require special tactics by the candidate to keep all interviewers involved.

Sharon Hoogstraten

helpful to deal with a stress interview by treating it as a game (e.g., say to yourself, "She's just trying to stress me out; I wonder how far she will go if I don't react"). Of course, you may simply refuse to play the game, either by terminating the interview or by changing the subject. If you terminate the interview, you will probably not get the job.

In **panel interviews,** you will encounter multiple interviewers. During a panel interview, try to make eye contact with each interviewer. Keep your eyes on each person for at least three seconds at a time; anything less than that and you are simply sweeping the room. When asked a question, begin your answer by directing it to the questioner, but then shift your attention to the group. By speaking to the group, you will keep all interviewers involved and avoid a two-person conversation.

Group interviews are similar to panel interviews, but include several candidates as well as several interviewers. Group interviews may take place in a conference room or around a dinner table. If you find yourself in a group interview, avoid trying to top the stories of the other candidates. Treat social occasions during office or plant visits as interviews, and avoid alcohol or overeating. As with stress interviews, the key is to maintain your cool while being yourself. You cannot do that if you overindulge.

Follow-Up   Regardless of the type of interview, you should send a thank-you note shortly afterward. Send one to the greeter, if possible (thus, you will probably want to get this person's business card). If you had a panel interview, find out who the contact person is and write to that person. After thanking the person in the first paragraph, write a paragraph that summarizes the interview. Focus your summary on the reasons you should be hired. In the final paragraph, reiterate your thanks and end with an assumptive statement, such as "I look forward to seeing you again."

If you do not hear by the target date, contact the person. Call if the interviewer was a sales manager; write if a personnel manager spoke with you. Sales managers will appreciate the saleslike perseverance; personnel managers may not. Within another week, call the personnel manager also. Simply ask for the status of your application rather than whether or not you got the job. The process of deciding may have taken longer than expected, or other delays may have arisen. You need to know where you stand, however, so that you can take advantage of alternatives, if possible.

Interviewing Never Ends

Even if you spend your entire career with one company, your job interviewing days are not over once you land that first job; you will interview for promotions as well. Some companies even interview candidates for admission to management development programs. The same techniques apply in all of these cases. You will still need to prepare properly, conduct the interview professionally, close for some level of commitment, and follow up.

MANAGING YOUR CAREER GOALS

Mary Kay Cosmetics encourages its salespeople to plan family time first, religious time second, and Mary Kay time third. This company recognizes the importance of sales employees leading a balanced life. As independent salespeople, they could easily allow their jobs to run their lives rather than maintaining control. But with the company's encouragement, they set time aside to keep their lives balanced.

An important aspect of career management is to set life-based objectives, then use those to determine your career objectives. A manager at MSI Steel keeps a photo of a ranch on his desk. It is not his ranch, but it resembles the one where he wants to raise his family. Keeping this life-based objective in front of him has helped him make career decisions. Career decisions must be compatible with family and personal objectives.

You may want to run the marketing operations of a company. Keeping that, or any, objective in mind and remembering your reasons for setting that objective will help you map out a career with which you can be happy.

Making the Transition from College to Career

That first year after college is a unique and important time in anyone's life. How this transition is handled can have a big influence in reaching success or experiencing disappointment. Although a life's work is not created or ruined in the first months, a poor start can take years to overcome. It is not just a matter of giving up student attitudes and behaviors; making the transition also requires taking the time to understand and earn the rights, responsibilities, and credibility of being a sales professional[10] (see Selling Scenario 18.2).

Many new hires want to make a great first impression so they charge ahead, and fail to recognize that the organization was there long before they were and has already developed its own way of doing things. The first thing to do is to learn the organization's culture, its values, and the way things are done there.

Thinking *it* **Through**	During your first year at your school, you became part of the school's culture. How did you learn about the school's culture and values? How can you apply that learning process to your first job?

Another important aspect of the first year is the fact that you are under a microscope. Your activities are watched closely as management and your peers try to decide whether you are someone on whom they can depend. Demonstrate a mature

SELLING SCENARIO 18.2

*Sales
Bloopers*

The first year in anyone's career can be exciting, especially in sales, when closing those first big deals is thrilling. On the other hand, the first year is filled with gaffes and bonehead mistakes, things you wish had never happened.

Katie Sarantakes joined Wallace Computer Services immediately upon graduating in 1995. "Shortly after I got my territory, I took a customer to lunch," she recalls. "Unfortunately, I was still new to Dallas and got hopelessly lost. I took a wrong turn and ended up going the wrong way down a one-way street. My customer was not too concerned, as there wasn't much traffic. But he got pretty scared when I made another wrong turn over a curb and onto Dallas's new light-rail mass transit system. Dodging cars was one thing—dodging trains was another!"

Bill Maxwell was a new college graduate and a new husband with little money when he got his first sales job. So he borrowed $1,000 from his parents to buy several business suits. "I found one suit that I really liked, so I got it in two different colors," he says. Getting dressed in the dark so as not to wake his wife, he didn't realize that the pants he put on didn't match the coat until he was in a customer's office. "It's hard to impress someone that you can handle the details of satisfying their needs when you can't dress yourself!" Still, Maxwell says the customer laughed along with him, told stories of his own newlywed days, and eventually purchased from him.

Jeff Ducate was the top rep in 1993 for the San Antonio Convention and Visitor's Bureau after joining the bureau in 1992. He recalls, "My job is to bring conven-

tions to San Antonio, and many of my accounts are located in Washington, DC, and Chicago. I planned an entire week of sales calls in Chicago and flew up on Sunday so I could begin making calls early Monday morning. But in the middle of Monday morning, I realized my lunch appointment was with an account located in DC, so I called and rescheduled. When I visited them in DC, I took them to dinner. But the restaurant would not accept Visa, only American Express, which I did not have. So while they waited, I took a cab back to the hotel, cashed a check, and then returned so I could pay the bill with cash. They are one of my best accounts now, but they won't let me forget those first two mistakes!"

Jim Murray also sells in San Antonio, representing the Hilton Hotel located on the San Antonio River. The famous Riverwalk is a popular attraction, especially at night. After a few drinks in the hotel bar, Murray and his customer decided to stroll the walk. Unfortunately, the customer walked straight out of the hotel and into the river. Murray grabbed him by his belt and kept him from taking a complete bath. "It dampened his spirits a little bit, but his company still does business with us," notes Murray.

Each one of these salespeople has achieved significant early success, but not without a mistake or two along the way. "It didn't seem funny at the time," says Jeff Ducate, "but when you do something silly and you still win the account, you realize you can relax and not worry about being perfect all of the time. The mark of a true professional is how you overcome mistakes, not whether you never make one."

willingness to learn, plus respect for those with experience. Part of this mature willingness to learn means you hold your expectations in check and keep your promotion hopes realistic. Remember too that recruiters tend to engage in puffery when presenting the opportunities and benefits of a company. While the recruiter said it may be possible to earn a promotion in six months, the average may be much longer.

Seek a partnership with your manager. While partnership implies a peer-level relationship and you do not have the experience to be a true peer with your manager, use the same partnering skills with him or her that you would use with customers. Find out what your manager needs and wants, and then do it. Keep in mind that every workday is a test day, except that you sometimes write the questions. Just like your professor, your manager wants the answers, not the problems. Provide your boss with solutions and you will be well on the way to a partnership. Keep in mind, however, the need to respect your manager's position and experience, as discussed earlier.

You **Manage Your Career**

Managing your career wisely will require conscious effort on your part. You are the person in your company to whom your career means the most. Many companies have recognized that ownership of development belongs to the person, not to the company, and have turned training into self-directed development programs.[11] Even if your company has not formalized development into a self-directed program or if the development program does not provide you with many options, take the time and effort to invest in yourself so that you can grow in your career.

Life-long learning is important in today's learning organization. AT&T, for example, spends $1 billion annually on learning.[12] While many companies have downsized, it is the versatile, well-educated employee who not only keeps a job but grows a career.

Many people consider life-long learning to be an important factor in not only improving your position but also enjoying what you do. Once you have a position within an organization, your objective will be to develop yourself to both get a promotion and be successful in that promotion. (To get the promotion after that, you will need to do well in the job you are seeking.) You should take several significant actions in each position along the way. The first action is to understand the options that you have, because sales can often lead to many different positions.

Dual Career Path

When you start out in sales, many career options are open. Career paths can alternate between sales and marketing or follow a route entirely within sales or entirely within marketing. You may even wind up as chief executive officer of a major global corporation. To exemplify how you might pursue various positions, Exhibit 18.8 depicts the career path for salespeople at Wallace Computer Services. Note that in addition to sales management opportunities, they have opportunities in marketing and product development that all begin in sales.

EXHIBIT 18.8

Career Path at Wallace Computer Services

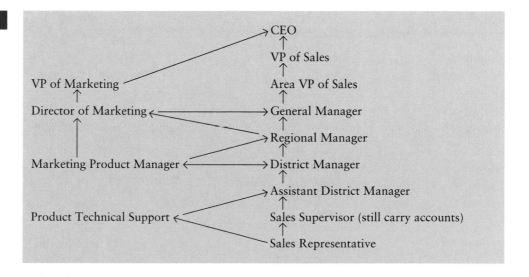

Learn Your Current Job

Learn all you can about the job you have now. Many people want promotions as fast as they can get them, regardless of their readiness. But consider that you will probably be managing people holding your current job. To be truly effective as their manager, you should learn all you can about the job while in the best position to do so: while you are one of them.

Learn the Job You Want Next

A manager once said, "In order to become a manager, you must first be a manager." He meant that promoting someone is easier when that person already has the characteristics the position requires—that is, already acts like a manager—rather than having only potential. A recent study of Fortune 500 firms and their promotion practices supports his statement. Of the 11 characteristics the firms said were crucial to effective sales management, 10 must exist for a promotion to take place (see Exhibit 18.9 for a list of the characteristics).

Several ways exist for you to learn about the job you desire. First, solicit the help of people who hold the job now. Many companies expect managers to develop their people. Take advantage of that fact; ask for the help of such managers. Find out what they did to prepare themselves and what you should do.

Second, volunteer to take on special projects that will demonstrate your leadership and organizational abilities. Taking projects off the hands of your manager can also give you an opportunity to see what responsibilities he or she has. Look for ways you can contribute to the overall sales team to show your commitment to the organization, your ability to lead and develop others, and your management skills.

Developing Your Skills

Years of hard work and frustration usually preceded "overnight" successes. Rarely does true overnight success occur. More often success results from years of practice, limited success and unlimited failure, and determination to persevere. This is as true in sales as in any profession.

To improve their selling skills and raise their level of earnings, salespeople must constantly seek new ways to perform. But salespeople must also know what they do

---

EXHIBIT 18.9

Traits Crucial for Sales Management
Ten of the top 11 must have been demonstrated on the person prior to promotion.

Trait*	Must Exist prior to Promotion
1. Motivation	X
2. Human relations skills	X
3. Higher than average energy	X
4. Ambition	X
5. Human interaction	X
6. Persuasiveness	X
7. Behavior flexibility	X
8. Perception of threshold social cues	X
9. Intellectual ability	X
10. Personal impact	X
11. Tolerance of uncertainty	X

*Listed in order of most frequently agreed as crucial to least frequently agreed.

Source: Based on responses of Fortune 500 companies in a 1989 survey. See Donald Guest and Havva Meric, "The Fortune 500 Companies' Selection Criteria for Promotion to First Level Sales Management: An Empirical Study," *Journal of Personal Selling and Sales Management*, Fall 1989, pp. 47–58.

that already works! They need to evaluate their performance, looking for ways to improve their sales presentations.

Sources of Improvement

Most companies continue to train their salespeople after basic sales training, but most training of experienced salespeople is product related rather than sales skills related. If you want to improve your selling skills, you may have to actively seek assistance.

The first place to start is with the field sales manager. When that person works with you in your territory, solicit feedback after each call. During these curbside conferences, you can learn a great deal about what you are doing from an objective observer. One warning, however: Make sure your manager only observes during the sales call and does not try to get into the act! As we discussed in the previous chapter, many sales managers are ex-salespeople who get excited in the heat of battle and may try to take over the sales call.

Peers provide another source. Who is successful in the company? When gathered together for a sales meeting, many successful salespeople pick one another's brains for new ideas and strategies. Offer to work with them *in their territories* for a day or so in order to learn from them. In most situations, they will be flattered and helpful. Clairol, for example, has a mentoring program that matches up successful salespeople with younger reps. They, like many others, have found that this arrangement benefits both the mentor and the protégé.[13] Noncompeting salespeople in professional organizations such as Sales and Marketing Executives, an international organization of salespeople and marketing managers, will also be flattered to share their tips with you.

Bookstores offer a wealth of material for developing sales skills. Many good books remind salespeople of the basics of selling and present advanced methods of selling and negotiating. Be sure to save this book too, as you will want to refer to it when you are in the field.

Sales seminars and cassette tapes are also available. Seminars, such as those offered by Dale Carnegie, Wilson Learning, and Tom Hopkins, can be very motivating. However, many experienced salespeople desire more than just motivation; they look for seminars that also teach new ways to present and gain commitment, as well as other sales skills. When they cannot attend the seminar, they purchase cassette tapes. They can listen while driving, using what would have been unproductive time to improve their skills.

In this course, you have begun to develop your interpersonal persuasion, or selling, skills. Whether or not you plan a career in sales, you owe it to yourself to continue to develop these skills.

Managing Stress

Selling can be a stressful career. For example, with three days left in the month, Richard Langlotz, a sales manager at Minolta Business Systems, faced a sales team that lost $100,000 in business. One sale alone, worth $60,000, would have made the team's quota, but that account delayed its order for a few months. The rest decided to go with the competition. Suddenly it looked as though Langlotz was going to finish the month at only 50 percent of quota. To top it off, one of his salespeople quit. What did he do? "I took my sales team to a pizza place," Langlotz says. He thought about calling a meeting and getting tough with his team, but he realized they already had enough stress and didn't need any more from him. At the pizza parlor, without any prompting from him, each salesperson examined his or her prospect lists and determined how the team was going to move sales forecasted for the next month into the current month. While they didn't recover the entire $100,000, they did sell enough to cover the team's quota. For more on how Langlotz has faced stress, see Selling Scenario 18.3.

Meeting quota is the most stressful part of the job, according to one survey. Phil Warnke, senior sales consultant at Learning International, says, "If I don't sell, I don't eat."[14] Many salespeople liken sales to a roller coaster ride, with great emotional highs when sales are good but emotional lows when sales are poor.

Stress can also be caused by factors in a salesperson's personal life, such as divorce, death of a loved one, and other events. Many dual-income couples face additional stress when both are in sales, one or both travels, and they have children. Coping with the requirements of a family and two jobs can place stress on the marriage as well as on the individual. One couple, Rick and Cindy Rutter, who had one set of twins and twin careers, were shocked mightily when they found out a second set of twins was on the way! But their companies have been very willing to accommodate the needs of their family. In addition, the Rutters have found that sales offers them both the flexibility they need to meet their financial needs and still have time for their children.[15]

For some people, coping with stress results in changing jobs.[16] Changing jobs may be the right thing for some people to do. Others turn to less healthy releases, such as absenteeism, drugs, alcohol, and so forth. All jobs have some stress; managing that stress is important to leading a happy and healthy life. However, managing stress does not always mean removing the cause of stress. Sometimes, as with the loss of a loved one, most people find they must manage the influence that causes of stress have over them.

Situational Stress

Situational stress is short-term anxiety caused by a situational factor.[17] You may face situational stress when waiting to make a sales presentation for your class, for example. The best strategy to deal with situational stress is to leave the situation or re-

Exercise is one way to reduce stress.

©Venning/Stock Imagery

A Wake-Up Call

He had just swallowed the last of the barium sulfate the nurse told him to drink when he realized what he had always heard was true: Life is too short to work in a career you don't enjoy, regardless of how much you make. Now, faced with the beginnings of gastrointestinal problems, he was going to do something about it. After the X-rays were taken he went back to his office and wrote his resignation letter. Finally he would do what he always wanted to do: sell.

Eight-plus years before that day Richard Langlotz, fresh out of the Air Force, went to work as a store clerk at a 7-Eleven. His plan was to finish his marketing degree and go into sales. But Southland Corporation offered him a job in its management team. After four years in the Air Force and three years working as a clerk, the money looked good. He was about to get married, so the opportunity to build on the three years he had at Southland looked like a great career move. Besides, he could always finish his degree at night and join the marketing department at Southland. He spent the next five years gaining a reputation as a top-notch field manager.

Now, at age 34 and suffering from stomach problems, Langlotz changed careers. He finished his mar-

keting degree but found out that companies were not interested in a 34-year-old seeking an entry-level sales position. Finally, Langlotz got a position with Minolta Business Systems selling copiers.

It didn't take long for Langlotz to verify what he knew all along. His experiences in management and in the Air Force were going to help. He had learned about people, the decision-making process, and what it took to make a good business decision. The first few months were typical for a new salesperson; however, beginning in the fourth month, Langlotz's sales skyrocketed. He ended his first year at Minolta with a 400 percent increase in his territory, was promoted through three sales positions, and made Minolta's President's Club. After 15 months with Minolta, he was promoted to branch sales manager.

In looking back, Langlotz says, "I was able to apply my experiences from the service and Southland to selling situations. Understanding business and people helped me understand the true needs of my customers and better help them with the decision-making process. It's hard to believe that I actually get paid to do this. To top it off, I haven't had a stomach problem since I came to Minolta."

move the situational factor causing the stress, but that cannot always be done. You cannot, for example, simply tell your instructor that you are too stressed to sell in class today so you are leaving! One technique for managing situational stress is to imagine that the situational factor has been removed (see Exhibit 18.10 for more ideas). In class, imagine that you have already finished your role play. Mentally consider that feeling of relief you get when you know you have done a job well. Sometimes imaging success can reduce feelings of stress.

In sales, situational stress may be caused by impending presentations, deadlines for closing orders (as in Richard Langlotz's case), and similar situations. Situational stress can cause stage fright in even the most experienced salespeople. One price of success is that situational stress will continue to occur, but successful salespeople learn to control their feelings of situational stress.

Felt Stress

Felt stress is longer term in nature than situational stress because the causes are more enduring. **Felt stress** is psychological distress brought about by job demands or constraints encountered in the work environment.[18] Perhaps the most common form of felt stress is **role stress,** or feelings of stress caused by a lack of role accuracy. **Role**

EXHIBIT 18.10

Coping with
Situational Stress

Imaging: Close your eyes and imagine yourself past the source of stress. Try to feel the actual sensation of what it will be like when the stress is gone.

Exercise: Exercise can moderate feelings of stress. When situational stress occurs over a period of time, set time aside for exercise breaks.

Breaks: Take a walk, phone a friend, or anything else. If working on a stressful project, take regular stress breaks. Combine imaging techniques with breaks to increase the stress-reducing power of breaks.

Rest: In addition to breaks, be well rested when the situation arises. If you have a major presentation, get a good night's rest beforehand.

Prepare: If the situation involves future performance, prepare and practice. Prepare for every contingency, but don't let the tension build by thinking only of things going wrong.

Recover: Plan time for the post-situation recovery before you charge into the next high-stress situation. Doing two major presentations in one day, for example, may not provide you with the recovery time you need to do well in the second presentation.

accuracy refers to the degree to which the salesperson's perceptions of the sales role are correct.[19]

Role stress is brought about by role conflict and/or role ambiguity. **Role conflict** occurs when two partners demand incompatible actions of the salesperson. For example, a customer wants higher levels of service from the salesperson, whereas the sales manager wants the salesperson to spend time working with new accounts. Conflict occurs because the salesperson does not have time for both. **Role ambiguity** occurs when the salesperson is not sure what actions are required. The salesperson may not be sure what is expected, how to achieve it, or how performance will be evaluated and rewarded.

In general, the best way to handle role stress is to increase role accuracy (see Exhibit 18.11 for specific ideas). When the problem is role ambiguity, simply asking for further instruction or reviewing training materials may be helpful. Coaching and other management support can also be requested.

Role conflict and role ambiguity, however, require prioritizing activities. In the example of the salesperson who feels stress due to conflict between the customer's and the manager's demands, the salesperson must decide whose needs will be met. Once that decision is made, further stress can be avoided by refusing to dwell on the conflict. Note that the conflict is still there (both parties have conflicting demands), but the effect on the salesperson is minimized.

In either case, a strong partnership with the sales manager can greatly aid in reducing stress. When a partnership is formed between a sales manager and a salesper-

EXHIBIT 18.11

Reducing Role Stress

Prioritize: Set your own priorities so that when different people place conflicting expectations on you, your preset priorities determine where your actions will go.

Seek Support: Enlist support of your priorities from your spouse, your manager, and other key people. By focusing on goals and priorities, you can reduce conflict over specific activities.

Reset Expectations: By prioritizing and seeking support, you can reset expectations of various constituencies so that they are in harmony. Communicate and gain agreement on what you are capable of doing so that others' expectations of you are realistic.

Act and Move on: Once you have made a decision to act, don't dwell on the conflict. Act and move on.

son, the salesperson has a better understanding of the demands of the job, which activities should receive priority, and how the job should be performed. Partners also have access to more resources and more information, which can help remove some of the organizational constraints that can bring about stress.[20]

Strong sales skills can also reduce feelings of stress. Mastery of the job will reduce feelings of stress because the salesperson is in control of the situation.

Thinking *it* Through	What stresses you out now? How do you deal with it? What healthy ways to handle stress do you use? What are some ways you respond to stress that may not be so healthy?

SUMMARY

A sales career offers many opportunities for growth and personal development, but that career has to start somewhere. That is the purpose of the job search: to find a good match between what you need and have to offer and what a company needs and has to offer.

To achieve a match that results in mutual satisfaction, you must first understand who you are, specifically what you need and what you have to offer. You can ask yourself a number of questions to stimulate your thinking about the type of person you are and what you will need from a sales position. In addition, as you review your experiences in school, work, and other activities, you can identify the skills and characteristics that you have to offer.

Finding industries and companies with the characteristics you desire will require you to apply your marketing research skills. The library contains many sources of information that will help you. Personal sources can also be useful in providing information as well as leads for interviews.

Sources for job interviews include the campus placement office, personal contacts, and advertisements. Resumés are personal brochures that help to sell a candidate. Writing effective cover letters will help you get interviews off campus, while the interview itself is similar to a sales call. Plan questions that demonstrate your knowledge of and interest in the company. Also, plan to ask for information that will help you make your decision. Follow up after the interview to demonstrate your desire and perseverance.

You are the person in the company to whom your career means the most. This means you must actively manage your own career. Set career goals that are compatible with family and personal objectives. Keeping the reasons for these career goals in front of you will enable you to make better decisions.

Learn the job you have now. You may someday manage people who have this job; the better you know it, the better you will be at managing it. To become a manager, you must first be a manager. Learn the manager's job as well, and volunteer for activities and projects that will let you demonstrate your management ability.

Stress can occur in any job. Situational stress is short term, whereas felt stress is longer term. For many people, the key to managing stress is to reduce the influence stressors have, because the causes of stress often cannot be eliminated.

Sales offers a challenging and exciting career. The opportunities are so varied that virtually every type of person can probably fit into some sales position. Even if you choose a career in another field, take advantage of the material in this chapter. You should find these job search and career management tips helpful in any field. Good luck!

KEY TERMS

application form 535
assessment center 536
conventional resumé 536
disguised interview 545
FEB 544
felt stress 553
functional resumé 537
greeter 545
group interview 546
interviews 536

panel interview 546
portfolio 544
references 535
role accuracy 553
role ambiguity 554
role conflict 554
role stress 553
situational stress 552
stress interview 545
tests 535

QUESTIONS AND PROBLEMS

1. The chapter contained questions you should ask yourself to understand your needs. Answer those questions now. What else should you consider?

2. Some people recommend signing up for as many interviews as possible, reasoning that the experience will be helpful when you find a company with a job you really want. (And who knows? You might find a job you like.) Is this ethical? Why or why not? Are companies ethical when they come to campus and interview, even though a job is not available, just to maintain a presence on campus?

3. What would you do differently if you were being interviewed by an amiable, a driver, an analytical, or an expressive? What about a panel interview with one driver and one amiable? One analytical and one expressive?

4. Is a resumé the only document you should take into an interview? What other things might be helpful in documenting your capabilities?

5. Analyze yourself. List your strengths and weaknesses. What type of sales would best suit you? Why? Are you qualified for that job? If not, what do you need, and how would you go about getting it?

6. How would you express your career objective in one sentence? If you are thinking of two or more industries, rewrite the career objective as you would for a resumé to be sent to recruiters in each industry.

7. Answer the questions in Exhibit 18.6 as you would in a sales job interview.

8. Your summer internship in a sales job was a very bad experience. Your biggest complaint was that the sales manager seemed incompetent. In spite of this negative experience, you like sales, so you are interviewing for a sales position. What would you say if asked why you do not seek full-time employment with the summer internship firm?

9. You walk into an interview and the recruiter says, "A job interview is simply another sales call, only this time you are selling yourself instead of a product or service. So sell me." Do you agree with the recruiter—are interviews just a sales call? Why or why not? How would you sell yourself in this situation?

10. How does partnering reduce stress? Could multiple partnerships lead to role conflict? If so, what should the salesperson do when such conflict arises?

EXPLORING THE NET

Visit either www.jobtrak.com/jobsearch_docs/indoutlk.html or stats.bls.gov:80/ocohome.htm and look for information on trends in an industry where you would like to work. Then open the site www://marketingjobs.com/ (for sales and marketing jobs only) www.monster.com, www.jobtrak.com/jobs, or rescomp.stanford.edu/jobs and find two jobs that interest you.

1. Visit the companies' home pages and report what you learned about the companies.

2. Summarize what aspects of those jobs (and that industry) make them attractive to you based on what you learned from the Web pages.

CASE PROBLEMS

**CASE 18.1
CHARLIE ROE'S
INTERVIEW**

At 8:45 AM, Charlie Roe arrived at his campus placement center for a 9:00 interview. He was surprised to be greeted by Katie McNichols, whom he had known when she was in a marketing class. This conversation followed.

KATIE Charlie, good to see you! I see that you are interviewing with us today." [*Shakes Charlie's hand and offers him a chair in the lobby*]

CHARLIE Katie! Hi, how are you? I didn't know you were with Health Images. I've got the 9:00 spot.

KATIE Great! I started with Health Images right after graduation, and it has been a great six months. Tell me, are you interviewing with many medical firms or just Health Images?

CHARLIE I'm very interested in pharmaceuticals, but I know that Health Images is doing real well. So I thought that I should consider all medical companies. One of the physicians at a sports medicine center recommended Health Images. She said that your company does MRI scans for the NFL, as well as here at the university.

KATIE That's right, we do! I'm glad to hear that others agree we are one of the best." [*Leans a little closer*] Look, just relax in the interview. Health Images really likes to get people from State, and I'm sure you will do well. [*Looks up at the entrance of an older man.*] Oh, here's Mike Mayfield, my sales manager. He'll be interviewing you today. Mike, here's an old friend of mine, Charlie Roe.

MIKE [*stepping forward and offering his hand*] Charlie, it's nice to meet you.

CHARLIE [*shaking his hand firmly*] It's nice to meet you, too, Mr. Mayfield. [*Turning to Katie*] Katie, it was good to see you again. Perhaps we'll talk some more later. [*Charlie and Mike seat themselves in the interviewing room; Mike opens a notebook*]

MIKE Tell me about yourself, Charlie.

CHARLIE I'm the oldest of three children, and we were raised in a small town in the eastern part of the state. As a kid, I was very interested in soccer and wanted to be an Olympic soccer player. But an ankle injury ended my soccer career. Still, I learned a lot about self-discipline and the importance of hard work to achieve success, and I am still involved in soccer as a coach for a youth team. I chose State because it offers a strong marketing program. Marketing, and sales especially, seems to me to be a place where your success is directly related to your efforts. And I believe that more strongly now that I have taken the marketing courses here at State.

MIKE [*writing furiously in his notebook*] I see. [*Momentary silence as he finishes his notes, then looks up*] Tell me about a time when you were the leader of a group and things were not going your way. Perhaps it looked as if the group wasn't going to meet your objectives. What did you do?

CHARLIE Let's see. There was the time when we were working on a group project for my marketing research class. Understand, though, that we had not elected a formal leader or anything. But no one in the group really wanted to do the project; they all thought research was boring. So at a group meeting, I suggested we talk about what we liked to do in marketing. After all, we were all marketing majors. Each person talked about why they had chosen marketing. Then I framed the project around what they wanted out of marketing. When they looked at it as a marketing project instead of a research project, it became something they wanted to do.

MIKE Did you get an A?

CHARLIE No, we got a B+. But more important, we were the only group that had fun, and I think we learned more as a result.

The interview went on for nearly 30 minutes. Charlie thought he had done fairly well. He stopped in the lobby to write down his impressions and record Mike's answers to his questions about the company. He smiled at Katie, who was talking to another applicant.

Questions

1. What did Charlie do right? Why was that right? What did he do wrong? Why was that wrong?

2. What was Katie's purpose at the interview? What do you think Katie could tell Mike about Charlie?

3. Health Images is a publicly traded company, trading on the NYSE under the symbol HII. What sources of information could Charlie use to learn about the company? What information should he expect to get from those sources?

CASE 18.2
The Sunday
Classifieds

Last Sunday, the following ads appeared in your local paper:

SALESPERSON NEEDED NOW
Local territory selling packaging products to manufacturers. Straight salary plus bonus, car allowance, full med & dent. No overnight. Exp. preferred, 3 mo. training. Fax resumé to: John Comacho, Walton Packaging Co. (817) 555-2412.

SALES PROFESSIONAL NEEDED
Selling network systems to small businesses. 20% travel. Opening new market. Sales exp. helpful, not nec. Must have some computer or telephone exp., college degree. 6 mo. tng. in NY. Co. car. Straight sal. first yr., sal. plus comm. after. Send resumé to Ms. R. Weinberg, DIY Computers, P.O. Box 17, NY, NY, 10017.

Questions

1. What characteristics do you have that might work well in these positions? What characteristics do you think are necessary to be successful in these jobs? Why?

2. John Comacho called and wants to interview you tomorrow. You never heard of the company until you saw the ad. How will you learn more about it?

3. It turns out that Walton is a division of a U.S.–based Fortune 500 company, whereas DIY is a distributor for several Japanese manufacturers. Walton employs 535 salespeople; DIY employs 47 salespeople. What are the advantages and disadvantages of working for Walton? For DIY?

ADDITIONAL
REFERENCES

Amin, Sammy; Abdalla Hayajneh; and Hudson Nwakanma. "College Students' Views of Sales Jobs as a Career: An Empirical Investigation." *American Business Review,* June 1995, pp. 54–60.

Barner, Robert. "Seven Changes That Will Challenge Managers—and Workers," *The Futurist,* March/April, 1996, pp. 14–18.

Boone, Louis, and John Milewicz. "Is Professional Selling the Route to the Top of the Corporate Hierarchy?" *Journal of Personal Selling and Sales Management,* Spring 1989, pp. 42–54.

Bowers, Michael; Thomas Powers; and Pamela Spencer. "Characteristics of the Salesforce in the US Healthcare Service Industry." *Journal of Services Marketing* 8, no. 4, (1994), pp. 36–49.

Brown, Steven; Thomas Leigh; and Martin Haygood. "Salesperson Performance and Job Attitudes." in *The Marketing Manager's Handbook,* Chicago: Dartnell, 1994.

Dalrymple, Douglas J., and William M Strahle. "Career Path Charting: Framework for Sales Force Evaluation." *Journal of Personal Selling and Sales Management,* Summer 1990, pp. 59–72.

Gable, Myron; Charles Hollan; and Frank Dangello. "Increasing the Utility of the Application Blank: Relationship between Job Application Information and Subsequent Performance and Turnover of Salespeople." *Journal of Personal Selling and Sales Management,* Summer 1992, pp. 39–56.

Ganesan, Shankar; Barton A. Weitz; and George John. "Hiring and Promotion Policies in Sales Force Management: Some Antecedents and Consequences." *Journal of Personal Selling and Sales Management,* Spring 1993, pp. 15–26.

Pitt, Leland F., and B. Rameseshan. "Realistic Job Information and Salesforce Turnover: An Investigative Study." *Journal of Managerial Psychology* 10 (1995), pp. 29–36.

Royal, Weld F. "Pleading Their Case (Salespeople's Top 5 Complaints about Selling)," *Sales & Marketing Management,* February 1995, pp. 50–57.

Russ, Frederick, and Kevin McNeilly. "Links among Satisfaction, Commitment, and Turnover Intentions: The Moderating Effect of Experience, Gender, and Performance." *Journal of Business Research* 34 (1995), pp. 57–65.

Sparks, John R., and Mark C. Johlke. "An Experimental Investigation of Personal Selling Job Attributes and Their Effects on Job Desirability." Developments in Marketing Science 18, Roger Gomes ed., Academy of Marketing Science, 1995, pp. 139–143.

Stevens, Cynthia Kay, and Amy L. Kristof. "Making the Right Impression: A Field Study of Applicant Impression Management during Job Interviews." *Journal of Applied Psychology,* October 1995, pp. 587–606.

Swenson, Michael J.; William R. Swinyard; Frederick W. Langrehr; and Scott M. Smith. "The Appeal of Personal Selling as a Career: A Decade Later." *Journal of Personal Selling and Sales Management,* Winter 1993, pp. 51–64.

Swift, Cathy; Jane Wayland; and Robert Wayland. "The Americans with Disabilities Act 1990: Guidelines for Industrial Sales Managers," *Journal of Business and Industrial Marketing* 9, no. 3 (1994), pp. 30–37.

"Women Sales Managers Speak Out, Volume III," *Personal Selling Power,* March 1994, pp. 84–85.

Wotruba, Thomas; Edwin Simpson; and Jennifer Reed-Draznick. "The Recruiting Interview as Perceived by College Student Applicants for Sales Positions." *Journal of Personal Selling and Sales Management,* Fall 1989, pp. 13–24.

Role Play Cases

This section provides a practical tool for developing your selling skills. Your professor will probably assign you a selling scenario to role play in class. In this section, you will find information on the role plays.

We have also included some helpful information on how to prepare for role plays, as well as how to make constructive, helpful comments on the role plays you will observe.

Have fun!

How to Prepare for Role Plays

Preparing for role plays will depend somewhat on the topic of the role play. Some of the role plays will involve only part of the sales call. We will assume, however, that you are preparing for a complete sales call.

The first step is to organize your information. What do you know about this buyer? Do you know anything about his or her social style? What activity has there been in this account? What do you know about this type of customer? For example, if you are calling on a convenience store, what do you know about convenience stores in general as they relate to your product (e.g. do they usually carry your product)?

The next step is to write down your call objectives. Include primary, minimum, and visionary objectives.

Next, write a list of possible needs. Based on what you know about the person on whom you are calling, the account's buying history, and the type of account, what do you think he or she might need? How would he or she go about making the decision, and how would that person make the purchase (finance, pay cash, order by phone, etc.)?

Based on that information, you can begin to prepare for the content of the sales call. Develop open/closed or SPIN questions designed to develop those needs. Anticipate what aspects of that person's situation would create a problem that would lead to a need.

Examine your product and your promotions. What features will resolve those needs? What promotions will help the person buy? Then develop phrases that present benefits, that is, tie features to needs. Also, gather any materials you can use; prepare testimonial letters, brochures, contracts, and any other support documents. You may also want to make a business card to have something to hand to the buyer.

Make a list of all the objections you can think of. Then develop responses to those objections. Plan how you will obtain commitment, based on your call objectives. Then memorize your approach. Many students tell us they are extremely nervous just before a role play (we'll deal with that some more later). One way to handle this is to memorize your opener, all the way up to SPIN. Once you get that far, you will forget about the camera and the class watching you and you can settle down.

Now practice the rest of the role play. You can practice your presentation out loud in front of the mirror or a friend. One word of caution, though: Not all of your presentation will be needed, because you will prepare for needs that may not exist. Don't go through the whole thing for the buyer during the actual sales call; just use the parts you need.

Mentally role play, playing a constant "what if?" game. What if the buyer says this; how will you respond? What if the answer to a situation question is that; what will you do then? You won't cover all of the possibilities, but you will be a lot better prepared for what actually does happen.

Now a word on nerves. We've already discussed one technique (memorizing the approach) for handling nerves. Another technique is designed to help you remain calm. Students often worry about the role play, causing stress and nerves to build up. You can minimize this by imagining yourself being finished. Think about how good it will be to walk out of the classroom, done with the sales call. Or think about what you have planned for that evening, weekend, or whenever. Or think about one of your favorite places and what it must be like to be there right now. These thoughts will keep your mind off the role play so that stress won't build up.

Be sure to arrive to class early on the day of your role play so you won't feel rushed. Also, *remember to take all your visuals and blank videotape (if required) to class!*

Just before you begin the role play, take a deep breath, think about your opener, and smile. Aspiring concert pianists are taught to sit down and place their hands in their lap, then begin. This keeps them from rushing the beginning of the first piece. You don't want to rush, either.

Finally, if you are being videotaped, be sure to watch your tape after you're done and evaluate your performance. An unplayed videotape is of no value at all.

Good luck, and have fun.

How to Make Comments on Role Plays

As a student observer, you may be asked to evaluate your peers' performances, and your evaluations may become part of their grade. Whether or not your evaluation is averaged into their final grade, it is important for their development, and yours, that you do a good job.

As you watch role plays for the purpose of providing feedback, you will find yourself learning more about the art of selling. You will observe and think of ways to phrase ideas better, handle different types of customers, and develop strategies for persuading others. But this requires that you observe carefully.

Identify what the person actually did. It is best if you can identify the technique used. For example, you recognize an objection-handling method as the feel-felt-found technique. Identifying what you saw serves two purposes: First, you have to learn the techniques (which will help you on exams and in your own role plays); second, you can discuss the technique more appropriately after the role play.

Then note whether or not the technique was appropriate. How did the buyer respond? How would you have

responded if the technique was used on you? Was the technique appropriate for the situation, for the buyer's social style, and for the product?

Finally, think about what you would have done if the technique was not appropriate. During the role play, you won't have time for anything but writing down what the person actually did. But in the moments afterward, you can contemplate alternative approaches.

Your comments to the seller, then, can be phrased in this manner. When the student used a technique or offered a phrase that you don't think was the best one possible, use this formula: First, identify what the person did and discuss why it was inappropriate or less than optimal. Then offer an alternative and present why you think it is better. Finally, end with a comment about something the person did that was good. Even if you don't observe any problems, you can still comment on what was good.

Keep in mind that immediately after a presentation, the seller's emotions are strongest. The person is usually convinced that the presentation was awful and there was nothing good about it. Find something positive about which to comment. Everyone does something well in every role play. You can really boost someone's confidence if you can find that one good thing and hold it up for the person to see. Then she or he will be more receptive to instructional comments.

ROLE PLAY CASE 1   Wilson Hammer® Tennis Racquets*

Wilson Sporting Goods Company includes three divisions—Racquet Sports, Team Sports, and Golf—and is a world leader in all three areas. Its core products include tennis racquets, tennis balls, tennis shoes, footballs, basketballs, baseball gloves, golf clubs, and golf balls. Wilson has 3,208 employees worldwide, 2,748 employees in the United States and 460 outside the United States. Wilson is now owned by Amer Group, Ltd., in Helsinki, Finland. Wilson's distribution center for tennis racquets is located in Clearfield, Utah.

Wilson started out as a part of Ashland Manufacturing Company, a subsidiary of a meat-packing firm. At that time, it was primarily an outlet for meat packing by-products such as violin strings, surgical sutures, and tennis racquet strings. In 1914, Thomas E. Wilson was selected to run the business. Wilson actively expanded the firm, adding baseball gloves, leather balls, and golf bags. By the end of World War II, Wilson was the largest sporting goods manufacturer in the United States. It has continued to grow aggressively since then.

In 1967, Wilson introduced the T-2000, a light steel racquet that vaulted Jimmy Conners to the spot of number one tennis player in the world. It also introduced the end of the era for wood racquets because the steel racquets were more durable and allowed players to hit with more power. The T-2000 broke all previous sales records for tennis racquets.

In 1987, Wilson developed the Profile racquet, creating a new form of racquet known as "widebodies." By increasing the area of the face of the racquet, the sweet spot grew significantly; this allowed players a greater chance of getting off a good shot.

---

*Sales literature and brochures from Wilson. All racquet names are registered trademarks.

In 1990, Wilson introduced the Profile 2.7 Hammer System racquet. The unique feature of this product was the reduction in weight in the racquet's handle without decreasing the weight of the head, providing an effect like a hammer. Weighing less than 10 ounces, the Hammer has one of the biggest sweet spots of any racquet on the market.

In 1993, Wilson improved the Hammer line by introducing the Sledge Hammer 3.8si performance racquet. This racquet eliminated more weight in the racquet handle and introduced a different head shape and fan string pattern. The new racquet weighed only 9.2 ounces.

A number of world-class tennis players are Wilson endorsers. These include Jim Courier, Stefan Edberg, Richard Krajaicek, Chris Evert, Lindsay Davenport, Chanda Ruben, Todd Woodbridge, Tim Gullickson, Rick Macci, Jack Kramer, Peter Burwash, and Vic Braden. Wilson keeps these players happy by spending effort on research and development for the tennis racquet line. Wilson holds more patents than any other racquet company on the market.

There are four general types of tennis players: beginner youth, intermediate, recreational, and club level. Wilson has a racquet for every tennis player. Some of its Hammer models include the Hammer 2.7si (good for players with steady swings and short, compact strokes; the number one selling racquet in pro and specialty shops since its introduction; retails at $280), the Sledge Hammer 3.8 (the ultimate in power and control; retails at $319), the Hammer 4.0si (good for players with moderate to fast swing speeds and full strokes; offers medium power; retails at $240), the Hammer 5.0si (good for players with fast swing speeds and very full strokes; retails at $210), the Hammer 5.2si (good for top-level players who have a fast swing speed and very full strokes, and want a heavier hammer; retails at $220), and the Hammer 6.2si (good for players with very fast swing speeds, and long stroke styles; retails at $170). Wilson also offers the Pro Staff line for professionals (e.g., Pro Staff Class 4.2, Original Pro Staff 6.1si, and Pro Staff Classic 6.1si, Pro Staff Tour Class 6.6si, Pro Staff Classic 7.5 si, and Pro Staff Lite 5.8si) and a line of junior racquets (e.g., Hammer 26, Pro Staff 26, Courier 26, Photon, Court Force, and Rak Attak).

As one example, some features of the Hammer 6.2si include the following:

Construction of 60% graphite, 40% fiberglass.

Average weight strung is 9.75 ounces.

Medium power level.

Patented Hammer Weighting System®. (The balance of the weight is toward the head of the racquet. This moves the sweet spot higher up the frame.)

Patented Dual-Taper Beam® cross section. (When looking at the head of the racquet from the side, you will notice that it is thin at the top, wider at the middle, and thin at the bottom. This makes the head stiffer at its widest point, offering more stability.)

Patented Stiffness—6.2si.(The stiffer the racquet is, the faster the ball will fly off the racquet. Lower numbers mean stiffer frames.)

Perimeter Weighting System®. (Weights have been added at the 3 o'clock and 9 o'clock positions [from the perspective of looking at the face of the racquet]. This adds stability when the player has off-center hits.)

Cushion-Aire® sponge grip.

Benefits of these features of the Hammer 6.2si include the following:

Large and higher sweet spot. (The sweet spot is the part of the racquet's face that gives you the most power and control. The larger this is, the better.)

Lightweight.

Very maneuverable.

Virtually no shock or vibration on impact.

Consistent power across the racquet face.

Unmatched directional control. (This means that you have more accuracy in hitting the ball where you want it to go.)

Improved stability and playability.

Greater cushion and absorption, faster-drying grip.

The tennis racquet market has experienced strong growth for several reasons. First, innovation in racquet technology has made older narrow-body racquets obsolete. Second, more people are participating in the game of tennis. This is due to several factors, including the development of strong national and regional tennis programs. Beginning in 1994, Wilson joined the United States Professional Tennis Association (USPTA) to coordinate programs for young children (from entry-level to advanced instructional activities for highly skilled youths).

There are many manufacturers and models of tennis racquets to choose from. Some of the stronger competitors (all of which offer high-tech, wide-head models) include Prince, Head, Dunlop, Spalding, and Donnay. Other competitors include Pro Kennex, Wimbledon, Donnay, Esstusa, Volkl, Yonex, Rossignol, Yamaha, Amerpro, Mizuno, Fox, Slazenger, and Fischer.

One of the strongest competitors is Prince, which offers Extender Series and Precision Series racquets. These racquets come in graphite (and graphite-composite) designs, and some weigh as little as 9.5 ounces. Like Wilson, Prince offers a wide array of styles for every type of player profile. Some tennis stars who endorse Prince include Michael Chang, Jimmy Conners, Andrei Medvedev, Jana Novotna, Luke and Murphy Jensen, Lim Xiao Qing, Thomas Stuer-Lauridsen, Peter Nicol, and Cassie Jackman. Although individual racquets vary, Prince and Wilson sell for about the same price points.

For purposes of this case, assume that most racquets (both Wilson's and competitor's) retail at about 60 percent over wholesale costs. Retailers can purchase Hammer models from Wilson at the following rates off the suggested retail selling prices listed earlier:

1–25 units	60% off
26–100 units	65% off
Over 100 units	70% off

Wilson does not allow any returns for unsold merchandise. In terms of promotion, Wilson has lined up a strong program of advertisements in tennis magazines, and during television broadcasts of important tennis matches, endorsements by many leading tennis stars, and a full array of point of purchase materials.

At the time this role play was written, Wilson was offering a toll-free number for those interested in learning more about its racquets (1-800-WIN-6060). Also, students may want to visit Wilson Web pages. Tennis page: http://www.wilsonsports.com/wilson/Tennis/tennismain.html. Main home page: http://www.wilsonsports.com/wilson/index.html. Competitors also have Web pages; for example, the home page for Prince is http://www.princetennis.com/. (These were accurate at press time, but students should be aware that firms often change their page sites.)

Situations

Situation 1

You are a new salesperson for Wilson calling on a small tennis shop. You have never called on this particular shop before (because you never seemed to have time to stop there), but have sold to several larger tennis shops in the same town. You don't know anything about the shop or its primary market. Your objectives are to introduce yourself, tell the owner about the Hammer line of tennis racquets, and secure an order for two Hammer racquets (to generate customer interest in the line of racquets).

Situation 2

You are a salesperson for Wilson calling on Sportmart, Inc., a national chain selling sporting goods. Sportmart has purchased Wilson tennis racquets in the past (including some of your Hammer models) and, to the best of your knowledge, is happy with its sales. Sportmart has also purchased many of Wilson's other products (tennis balls, tennis shoes, footballs, basketballs, baseball gloves, and golf balls). Your objective is to sell Sportmart 500 Hammer 6.2si racquets for the upcoming tennis season.

Situation 3

You are a new salesperson for Wilson calling on the head pro at the Outlast Tennis Camp in upstate New York. Outlast offers a wide range of tennis instruction, including week-long, two-week, and three-day camps. Outlast also offers custom-training packages designed for executives and corporations. Outlast maintains a well-stocked pro shop, including racquets, strings, grips, shoes, clothing, and bags. Although Outlast does carry some Wilson racquets, it is obvious that Prince is the dominant racquet there. Prince has more shelf space and better visibility in the pro shop. Most of the posters on the walls are of Prince racquets. This will be your first call on the head pro and on Outlast. Due to its location, you won't have an opportunity to walk through the pro shop before your appointment. You are new to the territory, and the old rep didn't leave many notes about the account. Your sales manager simply said, "For some reason Outlast just doesn't seem to like us." Your objective for this call is to introduce the pro to the Hammer 6.2si and secure an order for five units.

Situation 4

You are a salesperson for Wilson calling on Dave's Sport Shop, a small chain of five sporting goods stores located in Denver. Dave's continually updates the store's product lines to keep up with the current trends in the tennis market. You have called on the tennis buyer from Dave's before and get along well with that person. The tennis buyer has always been interested in your latest lines but has never purchased as many units as you would have liked Dave's to buy. Your objective for this call is to introduce the Hammer 6.2si to the tennis buyer and secure an initial order for 25 units.

Situation 5

You are a summer college intern for Wilson. You are on the tennis team at your college and use a Wilson Hammer 5.0si. During the summer, Wilson is having you make calls on tennis clubs in a five-county area. Today you will be calling on the president of a local tennis club that caters to serious tennis players who are also corporate executives. Your goal is to schedule a day and time when you can make a short (20-minute) presentation to the club's members about the Hammer line. You know nothing else about the club or when its meetings (if any) are held.

ROLE PLAY CASE 2   Clorox Formula 409

You just took over a new territory today, June 1 (remember that date), and you sell Clorox Formula 409 cleaning products. You have three types of products: All Purpose cleaner, Pro 409, and Glass & Surface 409. All products are available in 22-, 32-, and 64-ounce economy refills. (Note: Clorox adds new products from time to time. You are responsible for visiting a store and you can use any information you learn, such as new scents, new products, and any pricing or advertising you see.) The 22- and 32-ounce sizes come 24 to the case, while the refills are 12 to the case.

Retail Accounts

- Pricing: $36.00 per case

Suggested Retail	All Purpose	Pro 409	Glass & Surface 409
22 oz. size	$2.49	$3.49	$3.49
32 oz. size	$3.99	$4.99	$4.99
Economy refill	$4.99	$5.99	$5.99

- 2 percent discount for 10 cases (one size and type only).
- 5 percent discount for pallet (50 cases, any mixture of size and type by the case—*you cannot mix or match within a case on any order*).

Industrial Accounts
- 5 percent discount for case contract, agreeing to purchase 50 cases over a 12-month period, with minimum shipment of 3 cases per order. Any type or size counts. (Note: If customer fails to purchase 50 cases over the 12-month period, he or she is rebilled the difference between the discount and the single-case price.)
- 7 percent discount for pallet order (50 cases in one shipment).

June 1 Promotions Announcement

Retail Promotions

Pallet pack: An end-of-aisle display of 50 cases, containing a mix of all sizes and scents, with a 7 percent discount.

Advertising: A freestanding insert coupon of 50 cents off large-size cans on Sunday, June 14, plus a $1 million TV ad campaign from June 10 to June 28. This ad is going in the paper whether or not your customer buys. You cannot add your customer's name to this ad.

Forty percent reimbursement to retailer of ad costs for up to 1/4 page of a display ad bought by the retailer featuring Formula 409. For example, if the retailer bought a full-page ad and devoted 1/4 of that space to Formula 409, the retailer would receive 40 percent times 1/4 of the page cost. If the retailer devoted 1/8 of the page to Formula 409, the retailer would get 40 percent of 1/8 of the page cost back from the company.

Preferred Retailer Program: For small retailers with little local competition (rural retailers)—order 10 cases of the 32-ounce size (any combination of types), plus feature the product in a newspaper ad, and the retailer receives a 4 percent discount plus ad reimbursement (see above).

Industrial Promotions

New industrial customers: 10 percent off new case contracts (instead of 5 percent).

Current case contracts: Receive an extra 5 percent off orders of 10 cases received by June 30 (cannot be applied to new case contracts; the most anyone can take off one order is 10 percent).

Preferred industrial customer program: All orders by June 30 of five cases or more by customers that are not on case contract receive a 5 percent discount.

Competitor Information

Your company has given you the following information about your product versus competitors:

Industrial pricing varies greatly and market share isn't available on a local basis; however, Formula 409 is the largest national seller. If an off-brand is used, probe regarding scent, cleaning ability, and residue. Delivery cost may be extra for other brands, but delivery is always included for Formula 409.

Retail Brand	Market Share	Cost per Case	Suggested Retail Price	Discounts
Formula 409	22%	$36	22 oz. $2.49	Yes, quantity and advertising
All Purpose			32 oz. $3.99	
			64 oz. $4.99	
Spic & Span	18%	Approx. $36	22 oz. $2.49	
			32 oz. $3.99	Yes, quantity and advertising
Fantastik	20%	Approx. $32	20 oz. $2.29	
Others	40% (total)	$28–$34 (avg.)	22 oz. $1.99 to $2.39	No discounts or advertising

Customer Situations: Resellers

Situation 1: Buy-Lo Foodstores, 24 Stores in Your Territory

Purchase history: 1/10/9X: One case each size and type. Drop shipped directly to each store. 3/05/9X: One case of 32 oz. All Purpose and one case of 32 oz. Glass & Surface shipped directly to 12 stores.

Other information: No co-op advertising using Formula 409 this year. Also carries Spic & Span and Fantastik, as well as a store brand.

You have an appointment with the HBA (health and beauty aids) buyer set up by the previous rep.

Situation 2: Safeway Grocery Stores, Five Stores in Your Territory

Purchase history: 2/15/9X: Five cases 32 oz. All Purpose only. Shipped to Safeway's warehouse.

Other information: None available.

You have an appointment with the non-grocery items buyer.

Situation 3: QwikStop, 18 Convenience Stores in Your Territory

Purchase history: None.

Other information: The regional buyer sees reps for new products on Fridays, so you are dropping in Friday morning.

Situation 4: Metro Hotel/Motel Supply

Purchase history: This account has never purchased Formula 409 before.

Other information: You have notes from the previous rep indicating that this account carries a lot of no-name brands.

Situation 5: Bill's Grocery in a Small Rural Town

Purchase history: 1/05/9X: One case, All-Purpose 32 oz.

Other information: Order was taken through telemarketing. Doesn't look like previous rep ever visited this store.

Industrial Situations

Situation 1: Trinity Park Plaza (16-Story Office Building)

Purchase history: 1/01/9X: Five cases—All Purpose refills. 2/06/9X: Seven cases—All Purpose refills. 3/21/9X: Four cases—All Purpose refills (phone order). 4/04/9X: Five cases—All Purpose refills 5/20/9X: Six cases—All Purpose refills (phone order).

Other information: No case contract.

You have an appointment today for 3:00.

Situation 2: Morris Business Forms (Manufacturing Facility with Large Office Building in Front)

Purchase history: None.

Other information: None.

You have no appointment, but have located the purchasing agent's name, and you plan to drop in.

Situation 3: Metro Maintenance

Purchase history: Purchased 5 cases per month of All Purpose refills from November of last year through March of this year.

Other information: A note from the previous rep says, "Switched to Spic & Span—likes the other rep better."

Situation 4: Lexington Inn

Purchase history: Purchased 3 cases of All Purpose refills in March.

Other information: You have a note dated 5/5 from the previous rep that says, "What a jerk! Bought SprayNine yesterday—no sale for me."

Situation 5: Buck's Janitorial Services

Purchase history: None.

Other information: You've heard they perform cleaning services for two major manufacturers in town. You called to make an appointment, and the purchasing agent's secretary said to drop in on Friday because the purchasing agent sees all new salespeople then.

Notes

Chapter 1

1. Linda Corman, "Look Who's Selling Now," *Selling*, July/August 1996, pp. 49–53. 2. Stanley Slater and John Narver, "Marketing Orientation and the Learning Organization," *Journal of Marketing*, July 1995, pp. 63–74; James Sinkula, "Market Information Processing and Organizational Learning," *Journal of Marketing*, January 1994, pp. 35–45; David Garvin, "Building a Learning Organization," *Harvard Business Review*, July/August 1993, pp. 78–90. 3. Tom Richards, "Seducing the Customer—Dale Ballard's Perfect Selling Machine," *Inc.*, April 1990, pp. 96–98. 4. Martin Everett, "Selling's New Breed: Smart and Feisty," *Sales & Marketing Management*, October 1989, pp. 52, 54. 5. Troy Festervand, James Lumpkin, and Gerald Skelly, "Strategic Intelligence Systems and the Salesforce," in *Development in Marketing Science*, ed. Roger Gomer (Coral Gables, FL: Academy of Marketing Science, 1995), p. 155. 6. Philip Kotler, *Marketing Management: Analysis, Planning, Implementation and Control*, 9th ed. (Englewood Cliffs, NJ: Prentice Hall, 1997). 7. Debra Miller and Patrica Rose, "Integrated Communications: A Look at Reality Instead of Theory," *Public Relations Quarterly*, March 1994, pp. 13–23; Don Schultz, Stanley Tannebaum, and Robert Lauterborn, *Integrated Marketing Communications: Putting It All Together & Making It Work*. (Lincolnwood, IL: NTC Business Books, 1992). 8. Nancy Arnott, "Printing Money," *Sales & Marketing Management*, February, 1995, pp. 64–67. 9. Christen Heide, *Dartnell's 29th Sales Force Compensation Survey 1996–97* (Chicago: The Dartnell Corporation, 1996), pp. 176–77. 10. "How Firms in Mexico Reach Isolated Rural Villages," *Business Latin American*, September 9, 1991, pp. 289–95. 11. William Keenan, Jr., "America's Best Sales Forces: Six at the Summit," *Sales & Marketing Management*, June 1990, pp. 72–73. 12. Thayer Taylor, "Selling in the Future," *Sales & Marketing Management*, June 1992, p. 60. See also Arthur Bragg, "Getting Face-to-Face with Customers," *Sales & Marketing Management*, February 1991, pp. 44–48. 13. Tom Dellecave Jr., "Getting the Bugs Out," *Sales & Marketing Management, Road Warrior: A Sales Automation Supplement*, December 1995, p. 27. 14. Leonard Berry, "Relationship Marketing of Services—Growing Interest, Emerging Perspectives," *Journal of Academy of Marketing Science*, 23 (1995), pp. 236–45. 15. Barton Weitz, "Effectiveness in Sales Interactions," *Journal of Marketing*, Winter 1981, pp. 85–103. 16. Harish Sujan, Barton Weitz, and Nirmalya Kumar, "Learning Orientation. 17. John Hill and Arthur Allaway, "How U.S.-based Companies Manage Sales in Foreign Countries," *Industrial Marketing Management*, February 1993, pp. 7–16; Brian Flynn, "The Challenges of Multinational Sales Training," *Training and Development Journal*, November 1987, pp. 54–56. 18. Barton Weitz, Harish Sujan, and Mita Sujan, "Knowledge, Motivation, and Adaptive Selling: A Framework for Improving Selling Effectiveness," *Journal of Marketing*, October 1986, pp. 174–91; Rosann Spiro and Barton Weitz, "Adaptive Selling: Conceptualization, Measurement, and Nomological Validity," *Journal of Marketing Research*, February 1990, pp. 61–69; Fred Morgan and Jeffrey Stoltman, "Adaptive Selling—Insights from Social Cognition," *Journal of Personal Selling & Sales Management*, Fall 1990, pp. 43–54. 19. Gerhard Gschwandtner, "Donald Trump: 13 Blueprints for Achievement," *Personal Selling Power*, November 1993, p. 19. 20. Daniel Goleman, *Emotional Intelligence* (New York: Bantam Books, 1995). 21. Perri Capwell, "Are Good Salespeople Made or Born?" *American Demographics*, July 1993, pp. 12–13. 22. "The 1996–97 Job Outlook in Brief," *Occupational Outlook Quarterly*, Spring 1996, pp. 22–37. 23. Heide, *Dartnell's 29th Sales Force Compensation Survey*, p. 182. 24. Michele Marchetti, "Are You Making Enough Money?" *Sales & Marketing Management*, October 1996, pp. 56. 25. Louis Boone and John Milewicz, "Is Professional Selling the Route to the Top of the Corporate Hierarchy?" *Journal of Personal Selling and Sales Management*, Spring 1989, pp. 42–54. 26. Nancy Arnott, "I'd Rather Be Selling," *Sales & Marketing Management*, July 1995, pp. 77–83; Bill Kelley, "Who Says You Can't Go Home Again?" *Sales & Marketing Management*, September 1989, p. 39.

Chapter 2

1. Jaclyn Fierman, "The Death and Rebirth of the Salesman," *Fortune*, July 25, 1994, p. 80. 2. This section draws heavily on Thomas Wotruba, "The Evolution of Personal Selling," *Journal of Personal Selling and Sales Management*, Summer 1991, pp. 1–12. 3. Nancy Arnott, "Selling a Relationship," *Sales and Marketing Management*, January 1995, p. 14 ; R. Rehfeld, "How Large Companies Buy," *Personnel Selling Power* 13 (1993), pp. 26–33. 4. Thomas Forbes, "Top Guns," *Selling*, October 1993, p. 59. 5. Kevin Sullivan, Richard Bobbe, and Martin Strasmore, "Transforming the Salesforce in a Mature Industry," *Management Review*, June 1988, pp. 46–49. 6. Sandy Jap and Barton Weitz, "A Taxonomy of Long-Term Relationships" (Working paper, College of Business Administration, University of Florida, 1996); F. Robert Dwyer, Paul Schurr, and Sejo Oh, "Developing Buyer-Seller Relationships," *Journal of Marketing*, April 1987, pp. 11–27. 7. B.G. Yovonvich, "Partnering at Its Best," *Business Marketing*, March 1992, p. 36. 8. T. Hendrick and L. M. Ellram, *Strategic Supplier Partnerships: An International Study* (Tempe, AZ: Center for Advanced Purchasing Studies, 1993). 9. Robert Sharoff, "Starbucks Sells United a Special Blend," *Selling*, May 1996, p. 12. 10. Manohar U. Kalwani and Narakesari Narayandas, "Long-Term Manufacturer-Supplier Relationships: Do They Pay Off for Supplier Firms?" *Journal of Marketing*, Winter 1995, pp. 1–3; Robert Krapel, Deborah Salmond, and Robert Spekman, "A Strategic Ap-

proach to Managing Buyer-Seller Relationships," *European Journal of Marketing* 25 (1991), pp. 22–37; B. G. Yovovich, "Do's and Don'ts of Partnering," *Business Marketing,* March 1992, pp. 38–39; and "Smart Selling: How Companies Are Winning over Today's Tough Customers," *Business Week,* August 3, 1992, pp. 46–52. 11. Barry Rehfeld, "How Large Companies Buy," *Personal Selling Power,* September 1993, pp. 31–32. 12. Company documents. 13. Lisa Ellram, "Partnering Pitfalls and Success Factors," *International Journal of Purchasing and Materials Management,* April 1995, pp. 36–44. 14. "Taking Aim at Tomorrow's Challenges," *Sales & Marketing Management,* September 1991, p. 80. 15. "Pritchett on Quick Response," *Discount Merchandiser,* April 1992, p. 64. 16. John Swan and Johannah Nolan, "Gaining Customer Trust: A Conceptual Guide for the Salesperson," *Journal of Personal Selling & Sales Management,* November 1985, pp. 39–48; John Swan, I. Fred Trawick, David Rink, and Jenney Roberts, "Measuring Dimensions of Purchaser Trust of Industrial Salespeople," *Journal of Personal Selling and Sales Management,* May 1988, pp. 1–9. 17. John Hawes. "To Know Me Is to Trust Me," *Industrial Marketing Management,* July 1994, pp. 215–19; Frank Sonnenberg, "Trust Me . . ., Trust Me Not," *Journal of Business Strategy,* January/February 1994, pp. 14–16; Dennis Bialeszewski and Michael Giallourakis, "Perceived Communication Skills and Resultant Trust Perceptions within the Channel of Distribution," *Journal of the Academy of Marketing Science,* Spring 1985, pp. 206–17; Christine Moorman, Gerald Zaltman, and Rohit Deshpande, "Relationships between Providers and Users of Market Research: The Dynamics of Trust within and between Organizations," *Journal of Marketing Research,* August 1992, pp. 314–28. 18. Edmund Lawler, "Building Relationships," *Business Marketing,* August 1992, p. 34. 19. James Morgan and Susan Zimmerman, "Building World Class Supplier Relationships," *Purchasing,* August 16, 1990, p. 2. 20. Don McCreary, *Japanese–U.S. Business Negotiations* (New York: Praeger, 1986); Frank Acuff, "Negotiating in the Pacific Rim," *The International Executive,* May 1990, p. 21. 21. Yovonvich, "Partnering at Its Best," p. 37. 22. Erin Anderson and Barton Weitz, "The Use of Pledges to Build and Sustain Commitment in Distribution Channels," *Journal of Marketing Research,* February 1992, pp. 18–34. 23. Rahul Jacob, "Struggling to Create an Organization for the 21st Century," *Fortune,* April 3, 1995, pp. 90–99. 24. Patricia Sellers, "How to Remake Your Sales Force," *Fortune,* May 4, 1992, p. 103. 25. Ibid. 26. Laura Litvan, "Increasing Revenues with Repeat Sales," *Nation's Business,* January 1996, pp. 36–37. 27. Ira Sanger, "IBM Leans on Its Sales Force," *Business Week,* February 7, 1994, p. 110. 28. Tom Dellecave, Jr., "Getting the Bugs Out," *Sales & Marketing Management, Road Warrior: A Sales Automation Supplement,* December 1995, p. 27. 29. "Professionalism in Selling," *Personal Selling Power,* January/February 1993, pp. 21–24 and Gerhard Gschwandtner, "Sales Trainers Face the Future of Professionalism in Selling," *Personal Selling Power,* March 1993, pp. 28–31. 30. Harish Sujan, Barton Weitz, and Nirmalya Kumar, "Learning Orientation, Working Smart, and Effective Selling," *Journal of Marketing,* July 1994, pp. 39–52.

Chapter 3

1. Ralph Clark and Alice Lattal, " The Ethics of Sales : Finding an Appropriate Balance," *Business Horizons,* July/August 1993, pp.

66–69. 2. Frank Sonnenberg, "Trust Me . . ., Trust Me Not," *Journal of Business Strategy,* January/February 1994, pp. 14–16; Scott Kelley and Michael Dorsch, "Ethical Climate, Organizational Commitment, and Indebtedness among Purchasing Executives," *Journal of Personal Selling and Sales Management,* Fall 1991, pp. 55–65; I. Fredrik Trawick, John Swan, Gail McGee, and David Rink, "Influence of Buyer Ethics and Salesperson Behavior on Intention to Choose a Supplier," *Journal of the Academy of Marketing Science,* Winter 1991, pp. 17–23; Rosemary Lagace, Robert Dahlstrom, and Jule Assenheimer, "The Relevance of Ethical Salesperson Behavior on Relationship Quality: The Pharmaceutical Industry," *Journal of Personal Selling and Sales Management,* Fall 1991, pp. 39–47. 3. Gregory Gundlach and Patrick Murphy, "Ethical and Legal Foundations of Relational Marketing Exchanges," *Journal of Marketing,* October 1993, pp. 35–46; Gregory Gundlach, "Exchange Governance: The Role of Legal and Nonlegal Approaches Across Exchange Processes," *Journal of Public Policy & Marketing,* Fall 1994, pp. 246–58. 4. Debra Haley, "Sales Management Students vs. Business Practitioners: Ethical Dilemmas and Perceptual Differences," *Journal of Personal Selling and Sales Management,* Spring 1992, pp. 60–63; Pratibha and James Kellaris, "Toward Understanding Marketing Students' Judgement of Controversial Personal Selling Practices," *Journal of Business Research,* June 1992, pp. 313–28. 5. Thomas Wotruba, "A Comprehensive Framework for the Analysis of Ethical Behavior, with a Focus on Sales Organizations," *Journal of Personal Selling and Sales Management,* Spring 1990, pp. 29–42; Anusorn Singhapakdi and Scott Vitell, "Analyzing the Ethical Decision Making of Sales Professionals," *Journal of Personal Selling and Sales Management,* Fall 1991, pp. 2–12; K. Douglas Hoffman, Vince Howe, and Donald Hardigree, "Ethical Dilemmas Faced in the Selling of Complex Services: Significant Others and Competitive Pressure," *Journal of Personal Selling and Sales Management,* Fall 1991, pp. 13–25. 6. Bristol Voss, "Eat, Drink, and Be Wary," *Sales & Marketing Management,* January 1991, pp. 49–57; David Finn and William Moncrief, "Salesforce Entertainment Activities," *Industrial Marketing Management,* November 1985, p. 230. 7. Fiona Gibbs, "To Give or Not to Give," *Sales & Marketing Management,* September 1994, p. 136. 8. I. Fredick Trawick, Fred Morgan, and Jeffery Stoltman, "Influence of Buyer Ethics and Salesperson Behavior on Intention to Choose a Supplier," *Journal of the Academy of Marketing Sciences,* Winter 1991, pp. 17–24. 9. Bill Kelley, "When a Key Person Leaves for a Competitor," *Sales & Marketing Management,* February 1988, pp. 48–50. 10. Leslie Fine, David Shepherd, and Susan Josephs, "Sexual Harassment in the Sales Force: The Customer Is NOT Always Right," *Journal of Personal Selling and Sales Management,* Fall 1994, pp. 15–30. 11. S. J. Vitell and L. J. Grove, "Marketing Ethics and the Technique of Neutralization," *Journal of Business Ethics,* 1987, pp. 433–38. 12. "Putting the Fear of Crime into Corporations," *Business Week,* March 12, 1990, p. 35; "Soon, Corporate Crime May Really Not Pay," *Business Week,* February 12, 1990, p. 36. 13. Alexander Simonson and Morris Holbrook, "Permissible Puffery versus Actionable Warranty in Advertising and Sales Talk: An Empirical Investigation," *Journal of Public Policy & Marketing,* Fall 1993, pp. 216–33. 14. Karl Boedecker, Fred Morgan, and Jeffrey Stoltman, "Legal Dimensions of Salespersons' Statements: A Review and Managerial Suggestions," *Journal of Marketing,* January 1991, pp. 70–80. 15. Kathleen Getz, "International Codes of Conduct:

An Analysis of Ethical Reasoning," *Journal of Business Ethics* 7 (1990), pp. 567–77; Sak Onkvisit and John Shaw, "International Corporate Bribery: Some Legal, Cultural, Economic, and Ethical–Philosophical and Marketing Considerations," *Journal of Global Marketing* 42 (1991), pp. 5–20. 16. This section is drawn from Thomas Donaldson, "Values in Tension: Ethics Away from Home," *Harvard Business Review*, September/October 1996, pp. 48–62; Thomas Donaldson and Thomas Dunfee, "Toward a Unified Conception of Business Ethics: Integrative Social Contract Theory," *Academy of Management Review*, April 1996, pp. 123–56.

Chapter 4

1. Michael Levy and Barton Weitz, *Retailing Management*, 3rd ed. (Burr Ridge, IL: Richard D. Irwin, 1997), Chapters 10–12. 2. U. S. Department of Commerce, *Statistical Abstract of the United States*, 115th ed. (Washington, DC: U.S. Government Printing Office, 1995), p. 115. 3. *Selling to Government Markets: Local, State, and Federal* (Cleveland: Government Product News, 1991); Mary Beth Marklein, "Selling to Uncle Sam," *Nation's Business*, March 1991, p. 29. 4. Erskine Bowles, "Uncle Sam on RAM," *Entrepreneur*, August 1993, p. 138. 5. See Scott Ward and Frederick E. Webster, Jr., "Organizational Buying Behavior," in *Handbook of Consumer Research and Theory*, ed. T. S. Robertson and H. Kassarjian (Englewood Cliffs, NJ: Prentice Hall, 1991), pp. 419–58. 6. Shirley Cayer, "Low Key, but Savvy," *Purchasing*, October 1989, p. 54. 7. Daniel Glick, "The Magic of 'Mr. Spud,'" *Newsweek*, November 27, 1989, p. 63. 8. The classic study of organizational buying is in Patrick Robinson, Charles Faris, and Yoram Wind, *Industrial Buying and Creative Marketing* (Boston: Allyn & Bacon, 1967). For a description of how John Deere used an understanding of the buying process to build sales, see Norton Paley, "Cultivating Customers," *Sales & Marketing Management*, September 1994, pp. 31–32. For an interesting comparison of organizational buying in other countries, see Johan Roos, Ellen Veie, and Lawrence Welsch, "A Case Study of Equipment Purchasing in Czechoslovakia," *Industrial Marketing Management*, August 1992, pp. 257–63, and Tomasz Domanski and Elizabeth Guzek, "Industrial Buying Behavior: The Case of Poland," *Journal of Business Research*, January 1992, pp. 11–18. 9. Donald Barclay, "Organizational Buying Outcomes and Their Effects on Subsequent Decisions," *European Journal of Marketing* 4 (1992), pp. 48–64. 10. Philip Burger and Cynthia Cann, "Post-Purchase Strategy: A Key to Successful Industrial Marketing and Customer Satisfaction," *Industrial Marketing Management*, Summer 1995, pp. 60–65. 11. For a revised and expanded taxonomy of buying situations, see Michele Bunn, "Taxonomy of Buying Decision Approaches," *Journal of Marketing*, January 1993, pp. 38–56. See Erin Anderson, Barton Weitz, and Wujin Chu, "Industrial Purchasing: An Empirical Exploration of the Buy-Class Framework," *Journal of Marketing*, Fall 1987, pp. 71–86, for another empirical study of buying decision types. 12. Barry Rehfeld, "How They Buy," *Personal Selling Power*, September 1993, p. 3. 13. Robert McWilliams, Earl Naumann, and Stan Scott, "Determining Buying Center Size," *Industrial Marketing Management*, February 1992, pp. 43–50; Ajay Kohli, "Determinants of Influence in Organizational Buying: A Contingency Approach," *Journal of Marketing*, July 1989, pp. 50–65; Melvin Mattson, "How to Determine the Composition and Influence of a Buying Center,"

Industrial Marketing Management, August 1988, pp. 204–14. 14. Martin Everett, "This Is the Ultimate in Selling," *Sales & Marketing Management*, August 1989, pp. 32–37. 15. I. Fredrick Trawick, John Swan, and David Rink, "Back-Door Selling: Violation of Cultural versus Professional Ethics by Salespeople and Purchaser Choice of Supplier," *Journal of Business Research*, Summer 1988, pp. 299–309. 16. "How to Use Chinese Culture to Your Advantage," *Personal Selling Power*, January/February 1994, p. 19. 17. Kevin Kelley and Zachary Schiller, "Cut Costs or Else," *Business Week*, March 22, 1993, pp. 28–29. 18. D. Greising, "Quality: How to Make It Pay,". *Business Week*, August 8 1994, pp. 54–59; V. D. Hunt. *Managing for Quality: Integrating Quality and Business Strategy* (Burr Ridge, IL: Richard D. Irwin, 1993). 19. B. A. Spencer, "Models of Organization and Total Quality Management: A Comparison and Critical Evaluation," *Academy of Management Review* 19 (1994), pp. 446–71. 20. Elizabeth Ehrlich, "The Quality Management Checkpoint," *International Business*, May 1993, pp. 56–58. 21. David Sprague, "Adding Value and Value Analysis to TQM," *Journal for Quality and Participation*, January/February 1996, pp. 70–72; James Carbone, "VA for Some More Important Than Ever," *Purchasing*, June 20, 1996, p. 30. 22. Tony Henthorne, Michael LaTour, and Alvin Williams, "How Organizational Buyers Reduce Risk," *Industrial Marketing Management*, February 1993, pp. 41–48: Robert Settle and Pamela Alreck, "Risky Business," *Sales & Marketing Management*, January 1989, pp. 48–52; Christopher Puto, Wesley Patton, and Ronald King, "Risk Handling Strategies in Industrial Vendor Selection Strategies," *Journal of Marketing*, Winter 1985, pp. 89–98. 23. Donald Jackson, Janet Keith, and Richard Burdick, "The Relative Importance of Various Promotional Elements in Different Industrial Purchase Situations," *Journal of Advertising*, Fall 1988, pp. 216–22. 24. Michael Morris, Ramone Avila, and Alvin Burns, "The Nature of Industrial Source Loyalty: An Attitudinal Perspective," in K. D. Bahns, ed., *Developments in Marketing Science*, Vol. II (Miami: Academy of Marketing Sciences, 1988), pp. 333–37. 25. Elizabeth Wilson, "The Relative Importance of Supplier Selection Criteria: A Review and Update," *International Journal of Purchasing and Materials Management*, June 22, 1994, pp. 35–42; John N. Pearson and Lisa M. Ellram , "Supplier Selection and Evaluation in Small versus Large Firms, " *Journal of Small Business Management*, October 1995, pp. 53–58. 26. Tim Minahan, "Purchasing Execs Take Shears to Corporate Costs," *Purchasing*, May 23, 1996, pp. 22–24. 27. S. Tully, "Purchasing's New Muscle," *Fortune*, February 1995, pp. 75–83; Clarissa Cruz, "Buyers Take a Lead Role in Setting Corporate Strategies," *Purchasing*, May 9, 1996, pp. 31–33; Larry Smeltzer and Sanjay Goel, "Sources of Purchasing Managers' Influence Within the Organization," *International Journal of Purchasing and Materials Management*, Fall 1995, pp. 2–11. 28. Edith Cohen, "A View from the Other Side," *Sales & Marketing Management*, June 1990, pp. 108–9. Copyright June 1990. 29. Andy Cohen, "Planning National Accounts to Get a National Footing," *Sales & Marketing Management*, April 1996, pp. 76–77. 30. Kurt Salmon Associates, *Efficient Consumer Response: Enhancing Consumer Value in the Grocery Industry*, Research Department (Washington, DC Food Marketing Institute, 1993). 31. Claudia Pragman, "JIT II: A Purchasing Concept for Reducing Lead Times and Gaining Competitive Advantage," *Business Horizons*, (July 1996), pp. 54–66; Jitendra Chhikara and Elliott N. Weiss, "JIT Savings—Myth or Reality?" *Business*

Horizons, May/June 1995, pp. 31–42. 32. Susan Fiorito, Eleanor May, and Katherine Straughn, "Quick Response in Retailing: Components and Implementation," *International Journal of Retail and Distribution Management,* May 1995, pp. 12–18. 33. John W. Verity, "Invoice? What's An Invoice?" *Business Week,* June 10, 1996, p. 54; Ned Hill and Michael Swenson, " The Impact of Electronic Data Interchange on the Sales Function," *Journal of Personal Selling and Sales Management,* Summer 1994, pp. 79–87. 34. Robert Reich, "The Myth of 'Made in the USA,'" *The Wall Street Journal,* July 5, 1991, p. A6. 35. Sana Siwolop, "Outsourcing: Savings Are Just the Start, "*Business Week,* May 13, 1996, p. 40. 36. Thomas Stundza, "More Dialog with Fewer Suppliers," *Purchasing,* January 13, 1994, pp. 29–37; Sang-Lin Han, David T. Wilson, and Shirish Dant, "Buyer-Supplier Relationships Today," *Industrial Marketing Management,* November 1993, pp. 331–38; Martin Stein, "The Ultimate Customer-Supplier Relationship at Bose, Honeywell, and AT&T," *National Productivity Review* Autumn 1993, pp. 543–48.

Chapter 5

1. William Nickels, Robert Evert, and Ronald Klein, "Rapport Building for Salespeople: A Neuro-Linguistic Approach,*" Journal of Personal Selling and Sales Management,* November 1983, pp. 1–7. 2. Robert Peterson, Michael Cannito and Steven Brown, "An Exploratory Investigation of Voice Characteristics and Selling Effectiveness," *Journal of Personal Selling and Sales Management,* Winter 1995, pp. 1–16. 3. Camile Schuster and Jeffrey Danes, "Asking Questions: Some Characteristics of Successful Sales Encounters," *Journal of Personal Selling and Sales Management,* May 1986, pp. 17–28. 4. Monci Jo Williams, "America's Best Salespeople," *Fortune,* October 26, 1987, pp. 128–29. 5. Stephen Castleberry and C. David Sheppard, "Effective Interpersonal Listening and Personal Selling," *Journal of Personal Selling & Sales Management,* Winter 1993, pp. 35–50; Om Kharbanda and Ernest Stallworthy, "A Vital Negotiating Skill," *Journal of Managerial Psychology* 6 (1991) pp. 6–9, 49–52. 6. C. Barnum and N. Wolniansky, "Taking Cues from Body Language," *Management Review,* June 1989, p. 59; David Stewart, Sid Hecker, and John Graham, "It's More Than What You Say: Assessing the Influence of Nonverbal Communication in Marketing," *Psychology and Marketing,* Winter 1987, pp. 302–22; Allan Pease, *Signals: How to Use Body Language for Power, Success and Love* (New York: Bantam, 1984). 7. Paul Ekman, *Telling Lies* (New York: Norton, 1985). 8. Paul Ekman and Wallace Friesen, *Unmasking the Face: A Guide to Recognizing Emotions from Facial Expressions,* 2nd ed. (Englewood Cliffs, NJ: Prentice Hall, 1984). 9. This section and the following section rely heavily on Gerhard Gschwandtner and Pat Garnett, *Non-Verbal Selling Power* (Englewood Cliffs, NJ: Prentice Hall, 1985). 10. David Urban, "Neuro-Linguistic Programming Revisited: A Critical Literature Review and Its Implications for Sales," in Terry Childers et al. (eds.), *AMA Winter Educators Conference: Marketing Theory and Practice* (Chicago: American Marketing Association, 1991), pp. 212–19. 11. "The Eyes Have It!" in Philip Cateora, *International Marketing,* 8th ed. (Burr Ridge, IL: Richard D. Irwin, 1996), p. 541. 12. "Some Gestures Not Necessarily A-OK Abroad," *Houston Post,* February 12, 1989, p. A34. 13. Gerhard Gschwandtner, "Lies and Deception in Selling," *Personal Selling Power,* 15th Anniversary Issue, 1995, pp. 62–66. 14. John Anderson, " Mind Games: The Secret of NLP," *Selling,* July/Auguest 1994, pp. 59–65. 15. Michael McCaskey, "The Hidden Messages Managers Send," *Harvard Business Review,* November/December 1979, p. 147. 16. T. J. Becker, "Put 'High Touch' in High Tech," *Selling,* December 1995, pp. 53–57. 17. See James McElroy, Paul Morrow, and Sevo Eroglo, "The Atmospherics of Personal Selling," *Journal of Personal Selling and Sales Management,* Fall 1990, pp. 31–42; Edward T. Hall, *The Hidden Dimension* (Garden City, NY: Doubleday, 1966). 18. Anne Phaneuf, "Decoding Dress Codes," *Sales & Marketing Management,* September 1995, pp. 138–39; Jan Gelann, "How to Make a Great First Impression," *Selling,* July/August 1995, pp. 58–65; Tony Henthorne, Michael LaTour, and Alvin Williams, "Initial Impressions in the Organizational Buyer-Seller Dyad: Sales Management Implications," *Journal of Personal Selling and Sales Management,* (Summer 1992), pp. 57–65; Betsy Wiesendanger, "Do You Need an Image Consultant?" *Sales & Marketing Management,* May 1992, pp. 30–33, 36; John Molloy, *New Dress for Success* (New York: Warner, 1988). 19. "Sales Is Dressing Down," *Sales & Marketing Management,* August 1995, p. 33. 20. Anne Phaneuf, "The Catch-22 of Dress-Down Days," *Sales & Marketing Management,* August 1995, p. 33. 21. John Hill, Richard Still, and Unal Boya, "Managing the Multinational Salesforce," *International Marketing Review* 8 (1991), pp. 19–31. 22. D. Riddle and Z. Lonham, "Internationalizing Written Business English: Twenty Propositions for Native English Speakers," *Journal of Language for International Business,* Spring 1985, pp. 45–48. 23. *Doing Business in the New Europe* (New York: American Express and Lufthansa, 1991). 24. "Training for International Sales," *Sales & Marketing Management,* June 1996, p. 72.

Chapter 6

1. For another view of sales presentations, see Marvin Jolson, "Canned Adaptiveness: A New Direction for Modern Salesmanship," *Business Horizons,* January/February 1989, pp. 7–12. 2. James Lukaszewski and Paul Ridgeway, "To Put Your Best Foot Forward, Start by Taking These 21 Simple Steps," *Sales & Marketing Management,* June 1992, pp. 84–86. 3. Barton Weitz, Harish Sujan, and Mita Sujan, "Knowledge, Motivation, and Adaptive Behavior: A Framework for Improving Selling Effectiveness," *Journal of Marketing,* October 1986, pp. 174–91. 4. "What Is the Best Advice on Selling You Have Ever Been Given?" *Sales & Marketing Management,* July 1988, p. 8. 5. Ibid. 6. Daniel Smith and Jan Owens, "Knowledge of Customers' Customers as a Basis for Sales Force Differentiation," *Journal of Personal Selling and Sales Management,* 15 (Summer 1995), pp. 1–15. 7. Edith Cohen, "A View from the Other Side," *Sales & Marketing Management,* June 1990, p. 112. 8. "For Levi's, a Flattering Fit Overseas," *Business Week,* November 5, 1990, p. 76. 9. Charles Gengler, "A Personal Construct Analysis of Adaptive Selling and Sales Experience," *Psychology and Marketing,* July 1995, pp. 287–304; Carolyn Predmore and Joseph Bonnice, "Sales Success as Predicted by a Process Measure of Adaptability," *Journal of Personal Selling and Sales Management,* Fall 1994, pp. 56–65; Harish Sujan, Mita Sujan, and James Bettman, "Knowledge Structure Differences between Effective and Less Effective Salespeople," *Journal of Marketing Research,* February 1988, pp. 81–86; David Szymanski, "Determinants of Selling Effectiveness: The Importance of Declarative Knowledge to the Personal Selling Concept," *Journal of*

Marketing, January 1988, pp. 64–77; Leslie Fine, "Refining the Concept of Salesperson Adaptability," in Chris Allen et al. eds., *Marketing Theory and Applications* (Chicago: American Marketing Association, 1992), pp. 42–49. 10. Robert Trotter, "The Mystery of Mastery," *Psychology Today,* July 1986, pp. 32–38. 11. Sarah Mahoney, "Beware the Killer Pitch," *Selling,* April 1996, pp. 76–77. 12. Linda Gorman, "Send in the Marines," *Selling,* May 1995, p. 65. 13. David Merrill and Roger Reid, *Personal Styles and Effective Performance* (Radnor, PA: Chilton, 1981); Robert Bolton and Dorothy Bolton, *Social Style/Management Style* (New York: AMACOM, 1984). 14. V. R. Buzzotta and R. E. Lefton, "What Makes a Sales Winner?" *Training and Development,* November 1981, pp. 70–73. 15. Gerald Manning and Barry Reece, *Selling Today: A Personal Approach,* 6th ed. (Boston: Allyn & Bacon, 1996), pp. 85–94. 16. Howard Stevens, "Matching Sales Skills to Customer Needs," *Management Review,* June 1989, pp. 44–47. 17. See Paul Petach, "Picking the Pitch for the Prospect, by Computer," *Business Marketing,* October 1988, pp. 78–81; Robert Collins, "Artificial Intelligence in Personal Selling," *Journal of Personal Selling and Sales Management,* May 1984, pp. 58–66; Arlyn Rubash, Rawlie Sullivan, and Paul Herzog, "The Use of an 'Expert' to Train Salespeople," *Journal of Personal Selling and Sales Management,* August 1987, pp. 49–56; Hubert Hennessey, "Accelerating the Salesperson Learning Curve," *Journal of Personal Selling & Sales Management,* November 1988, pp. 77–82.

Chapter 7

1. Office of Management and Budget, "Prompt Payment: 1989 Report to Congress," as reported in *Inc.,* July 1990, p. 95. 2. Danielle Kennedy, "Screen Test: Qualify Prospects by Asking the Right Questions," *Entrepreneur,* August 1996, p. 86. 3. Martin Everett, "Systems Integrators: Marketing's New Maestros," *Sales & Marketing Management,* November 1990, pp. 50–60. 4. See Jay Conrad Levinson, "Referred Customer," *Entrepreneur,* April 1996, p. 82. 5. Nanci McCann, "One Happy Customer Leads to Another," *Selling,* November 1994, p. 21. 6. "Sales Talk²," *Sales and Marketing Strategies and News,* June/July 1996, p. 62. 7. "Sales Talk²," *Sales and Marketing Strategies and News,* January/February 1996, p. 62. 8. Neil Baum, "Secrets to Lasting Rapport," *Personal Selling Power,* March 1993, p. 55. 9. Howard Davies, Thomas K. P. Leung, Sherriff T. K. Luk, and Yiu-hing Wong, "The Benefits of 'Guanxi'," *Industrial Marketing Management,* 24 (19), pp. 207–14. 10. See, for example, Ginger Trumfio, "Cultivating Your Network," *Sales & Marketing Management,* January 1994, p. 57; Kristen Richards, "Networking: Expanding Circles of Influence," *Sales & Marketing Management,* December 1994, p. 88; Charlotte Mulhern, "Talking Shop: To Keep Your Business Competitive, Tap into the Power of Networking," *Entrepreneur,* May 1996, pp. 174–77. 11. See, for example, Edward Nash, "Prospecting for Leads: Database Marketing Can Help Your Advertising Build Image and Produce Traceable Sales at the Same Time," *Sales & Marketing Management,* February 1994, p. 33; Michael K. McClellan, "Fishing for Leads, Catching Sales: Integrating Direct Marketing and Sales Will Maximize Productivity," *Agri Marketing,* June 1993, pp. 22–25. 12. For another example of using direct mail to generate leads, see Duncan Maxwell Anderson, "Smart-Bomb Selling: Use Information Technology to Home in on Hot Prospects," *Selling,*

May 1996, p. 47. 13. "Response Cards Enter the Electronic Age," *Sales and Marketing Management,* April 1990, p. 27. 14. Road Warrior, "The King of E-Mail," *Sales & Marketing Management,* December 1994, pp. 13–16. 15. Betty Wiesendanger, "Are Your Salespeople Trade Show Duds?" *Sales & Marketing Management,* August 1990, pp. 40–46. See also Susan Greco, "Stretching the Trade Show Budget," *Inc.,* May 1992, p. 83. 16. See John F. Tanner, Jr., "Adaptive Selling at Trade Shows," *Journal of Personal Selling and Sales Management,* Spring 1994, pp. 15–23; Ginger Trumfio, "The Do's and Dont's of Boothmanship," *Sales & Marketing Management,* September 1994, p. 54; Joseph Conlin, "Bazaar Behavior: Sure Your Trade Show Exhibit Attracts Attention, But Does It Attract Quality Leads?" *Sales & Marketing Management,* June 1995, pp. 78–81. 17. See also Tom Richman, "A Seminar of One," *Inc.,* December 1991, p. 153; Jay Finegan, "Reach Out and Teach Someone," *Inc.,* October 1990, pp. 112+. 18. Richard R. Szathmary, "What's in a List?" *Sales & Marketing Management,* October 1992, p. 114. 19. Cyndee Miller, "North American Marketers Await Trade Pact: U.S. Companies Eager to Head South," *Marketing News* 27 no. 10 (1993), pp. 1+. 20. For example, see Teri Lammers, "The Pacific Rim on a Shoestring," *Inc.,* June 1991, pp. 122–23. 21. "Salespeople 'Hate' Making Cold Calls," *American Salesman,* May 1989, pp. 6–7. But not *everyone* hates them. See, for example, the story of Chuck Piola, who has made 15,000 cold calls and loves them, in Jay Finegan, "King of Cold Calls," *Inc.,* June 1991, pp. 101–7; and Melissa Campanelli, "The King of Cold Calls Goes on Call," *Sales & Marketing Management,* November 1993, p. 10; Danielle Kennedy, "Fire Up! In a Sales Slump? Turn Up the Heat on Your Cold Calls," *Entrepreneur,* May 1996, p. 88. 22. Francy Blackwood, "Out of the Cold: Banned from Cold Calling, Amex Financial Reps Have Had to Warm Up to Referrals," *Selling,* May 1996, pp. 22–24. 23. See also Susan Greco, "Using Others to Sell Your Products," *Inc.,* August 1991, p. 81. 24. Martin Everett, "How Outsiders Can Get You Inside," *Sales & Marketing Management,* February 1990, pp. 56–57. 25. Interested readers can learn more about the rule from "New Federal Trade Commission Rule to Protect Consumers from Deceptive and Abusive Telemarketing Practices," August 16, 1995, located on the FTC World Wide Web home page at http:/www.ftc.gov/. 26. Michele Marchetti. "Prospecting: Finding Hot Leads," *Sales & Marketing Management,* March 1996, p. 44. 27. Paul B. Brown, "Building Sales: How to Make Every Marketing Dollar Count," *Inc.,* March 1991, pp. 98-99. See also Ernan Roman, "Integrated Direct Marketing: Managing the Mix," *Sales & Marketing Management,* May 1991, pp. 82–87. 28. Danielle Kennedy, "Perfect Pitch: Writing Sales Materials That Sing," *Entrepreneur,* June 1996, pp. 98–101. 29. Jerry Fisher, "Fan Mail: Want Your Sales Letter to Get Past the Gatekeeper? Have a Loyal Client Write It for You," *Entrepreneur,* July 1996, pp. 94–96. 30. Richard Edwards, "Direct Mailing—Making It More Effective," *American Salesman,* April 1990, pp. 16–19. 31. Tom Richman, "A Good Name Is Hard to Find," *Inc.,* July 1991, p. 69. 32. "A Company of Lead Generators," *Inc.,* September 1987, p. 111. See also Susan Greco, "Using Service Reps to Generate Leads," *Inc.,* May 1992, p. 141. 33. Albert G Holzinger, "Selling in the New Europe," *Nation's Business,* December 1991, pp. 18–24. 34. Mark H. McCormack, *What They Still Don't Teach You at Harvard Business School* (New York: Bantam Books, 1989), pp. 26–27. 35. William E. Gregory, Jr., "Time to Ask Hard-Nosed Questions," *Sales & Marketing Management,*

October 1989, pp. 88–93. 36. For example, see Kevin Reichard and Kathy Yakal, "Share the Wealth," *PC Magazine,* August 1995, pp. 243–77. Also, *Sales & Marketing Management* devotes at least one special issue each year to changes in technology that affects salespeople. 37. Kristin Dunlap Godsey, "Sell Yourself: This Sales Technology Expert Practices What He Preaches," *Selling Success,* May 1996, pp. 51–52. 38. Robyn Griggs, "Taking the Leads," *Sales & Marketing Management,* September 1995, pp. 40–48. 39. See David M. Szymanski and Gilbert A. Churchill, Jr., "Client Evaluation Cues: A Comparison of Successful and Unsuccessful Salespeople," *Journal of Marketing Research,* May 1990, pp. 163–74. 40. Stanley F. Slater and John C. Narver, "Market Orientation and the Learning Organization," *Journal of Maketing,* July 1995, pp. 63–74. 41. Dennis Fox, "The Fear Factor: Why Traditional Sales Training Doesn't Always Work," *Sales & Marketing Management,* February 1992, pp. 60–64. 42. Griggs, "Taking the Lead," p. 47. 43. Ginger Trumfio, "Sales Secrets to Take to the Grave," *Sales & Marketing Management,* January 1994, p. 57.

Chapter 8

1. Edward O Welles, "Quick Study," *Inc.,* April 1992, pp. 67–76. 2. See Arun Sharma and Rajnandini Pillai, "Customers' Decision-Making Styles and Their Preference for Sales Strategies: Conceptual Examination and an Empirical Study," *Journal of Personal Selling and Sales Management,* Winter 1996, pp. 21–33. 3. See Harvey Mackay, *Swim with the Sharks without Being Eaten Alive* (New York: Morrow, 1988), pp. 25–34. 4. In fact, sellers who wish to emphasize value-added selling must begin adding value even in the planning stage of the sales cycle. See Thayer C. Taylor, "Are Sellers Prepared for Added-Value?" *Sales & Marketing Management,* September 1994, p. 40. 5. See Daniel C. Smith and Jan P. Owens, "Knowledge of Customers' Customers as a Basis of Sales Force Differentiation," *Journal of Personal Selling and Sales Management,* Summer 1995, pp. 1–15. 6. Martin Everett. "Know Why They Buy," *Sales & Marketing Management,* December 1994, pp. 66–71. 7. See Cassandra Cavanah, "For Your Information: CD-ROM's Put a World of Facts and Figures at Your Fingertips," *Entrepreneur,* July 1996, pp. 46–49. 8. NEXIS is a leading source of national and international news and information for professionals and is provided by Mead Data Central, Inc., Dayton, Ohio 1-800-227-4908. 9. Kristen Richards. "Researching Prospects On-Line," *Sales & Marketing Management,* December 1994, p. 49. 10. "Sales Talk," *Sales & Marketing Management,* March 1990, p. 120. 11. For an excellent summary, see Linda Corman, "The Selling Guide to Getting the Inside Story," *Selling,* April 1995, pp. 56–63. 12. For information, see the service's home page at http://www.infosage.ibm.com. 13. Madelyn R. Callahan, "Tending the Sales Relationship," *Training and Development,* December 1992, p. 34. 14. Harvey B. Mackay, "The CEO Hits the Road (and Other Sales Tales)," *Harvard Business Review,* March/April 1990, p. 32. 15. Neil Rackham, *Major Account Sales Strategy* (New York: McGraw-Hill, 1989), p. 39. 16. See Brian Koon Huat Low, "Long-Term Relationships in Industrial Marketing," *Industrial Marketing Management,* 25 (1996), pp. 23–35. 17. Porter Henry, *Secrets of the Master Sellers* (New York: AMACOM, 1987), p. 72. 18. Jack Falvey, "Without a Goal for Every Call, a Salesperson Is Just a Well-Paid Tourist," *Sales & Marketing Management,* June 1989, p. 92. 19. I. Martin Jacknis, "Multiple Choice: Why Your Salespeople Should Have Not One, but Three Objectives Every Time They Make a Call," *Inc.,* December 1987, p. 184. 20. John P. Kirwan, Jr., "The Precision Selling Payoff," *Sales & Marketing Management,* January 1992, pp. 59–61. 21. Jim Hersma, personal correspondence; used with permission. 22. "Should Salespeople Go over the Heads of Purchasing Agents?" *Sales & Marketing Management,* May 1992, p. 14. 23. Terry Booten, "How to Crack a New Account," *Executive Female,* July/August 1992, p. 18. 24. Rackham, *Major Account Sales Strategy,* p. 39. 25. Ibid., p. 30. 26. Nancy J. Adler, *International Dimensions of Organizational Behavior* (Boston: Kent Publishing, 1986), p. 33. 27. Nanci McCann, "For Their Own Good, as Well as Yours: If You Can Offer Real Benefits, Someone Should Really Hear about Them," *Selling,* April 1995, pp. 23–24. 28. See Michele Marchetti, "Dial 'R' for Rudeness," *Sales & Marketing Management,* December 1995, p. 33; Danielle Kennedy, "Fire Up!" *Entrepreneur,* May 1996, pp. 88–91. 29. Melissa Campanelli. "Welcome to Voice Mail Hell," *Sales & Marketing Management,* May 1995, pp. 98–101; T. J. Becker, "How to Put 'High Touch' in High Tech," *Selling,* December 1995, pp. 53–57. 30. Nanci McCann, "Protocol," *Selling,* October 1994, p. 24. 31. Joan Guiducci, "Power Calling," *Bank Marketing,* March 1993, pp. 40–41.

Chapter 9

1. Of course, many aspects of first impressions are outside the control of the salesperson. See, for example, Tony L. Henthorne, Michael S. LaTour, and Alvin J. Williams, "Initial Impressions in the Organizational Buyer-Seller Dyad: Sales Management Implications," *Journal of Personal Selling and Sales Management,* Summer 1992, pp. 57–65. The authors found that different first impressions were formed as a function of race and gender. 2. Ann Marie Sabath, "When Your Salespeople Are Rough around the Edges," *Sales & Marketing Management,* February 1991, p. 88. 3. See "Serve and Ye Shall Get," *Personal Selling Power,* March 1993, p. 40. 4. Dale Carnegie, a noted sales training consultant, would disagree with this advice. He suggests that not offering a handshake shows a lack of assertiveness. 5. Danielle Kennedy, "Worldly Wise: In a Global Economy, Cross-Cultural Sensitivity Can Make or Break the Sale," *Entrepreneur,* March 1996, pp. 86–89. 6. John R. Graham, "The 'Good Old Days' Are Gone Forever: Seize the Opportunities for Change," *Personal Selling Power,* March 1993, p. 49. 7. Kevin Daley, "Socrates on a Sales Call," *Marketing News,* May 6, 1996, p. 4. 8. "Shame and Fortune: Learning from Entrepreneurial Nightmares," *Entrepreneur,* December 1995, p. 18. 9. Ken Delmar, *Winning Moves* (New York: Warner, 1984), p. 4. 10. Christopher McGinnis, "Sign Language," *Entrepreneur,* December 1995, p. 59. 11. Fiona Gibb. "Don't Forget the Customer," *Sales & Marketing Management,* April 1995, p. 81. 12. Neil Rackham, *SPIN Selling* (New York: McGraw-Hill, 1988). 13. Kevin J. Corcoran, Laura K. Peterson, Daniel B. Baitch, and Mark Barrett, *High Performance Sales Organizations: Best Sales Practices from Global Leaders* (Burr Ridge, IL: Irwin Professional Publishing, 1995), pp. 45–47. 14. Arthur Bragg, "Put Your Program to the Test," *Sales & Marketing Management,* February 1990, p. 10. 15. Arun Sharma and Douglas M. Lambert, "How Accurate Are Salespersons' Perceptions of Their Customers?" *Industrial Marketing Management,* 23 (1984), pp. 357–65. 16. See Calman P. Phillips, "The Not-So-Sweet Sound of Sales Talk," *Training,* September 1988, pp. 56–62. 17. Brian Tracy, "Stop Talking . . . and Start Asking Ques-

tions," *Sales & Marketing Management,* February 1995, pp. 79–87. 18. Rackham, *SPIN Selling.* 19. Sergey Frank, "Global Networking: Vive Les Differences!" *Sales & Marketing Management,* May 1992, p. 66. 20. For another example, see Nanci McCann, "When All Else Fails: You've Presented Every Benefit-Except the One That Matters to the Customer," *Selling,* May 1996, pp. 19–20. 21. See Richard Whiteley, "Are You Driven to Action?" *Sales & Marketing Management,* June 1994, pp. 31–32; Francy Blackwood, "It's All in the Packaging," *Selling,* April, 1995, pp. 34–36. 22. Ray Hanson, personal correspondence, used by permission. 23. See Josh Gordon, "Making a Sales Presentation Work," *Folio,* March 1992, pp. 91–92. 24. See Daniel A. Sauers, "Limber Up Mentally before Big Sales Presentations," *Marketing News,* March 19, 1990, p. 10. 25. Richard Whiteley, "How to Push Customers Away," *Sales & Marketing Management,* February 1994, pp. 29–30. 26. Nancy J. Adler, *International Dimensions of Organizational Behavior* (Boston: Kent Publishing, 1986), p. 55. 27. John J. Withey and Eric Panitz, "Face-to-Face Selling: Making It More Effective," *Industrial Marketing Management,* vol. 24 (1985), pp. 239–46. 28. See, for example, Jon Hawes, "To Know Me Is to Trust Me," *Industrial Marketing Management,* vol. 23 (1984), pp. 215–19. 29. Credibility can be influenced by many factors. For example, see John Tsalikis, Oscar W. DeShields, Jr., and Michael S. LaTour, "The Role of Accent on the Credibility and Effectiveness of the Salesperson," *Journal of Personal Selling and Sales Management,* Winter 1991, pp. 31–41. They found that, for an American audience, using a standard American accent resulted in more credibility than did Greek-accented English. See also Frank K. Sonnenberg, "If I Had Only One Client," *Sales & Marketing Management,* November 1993, pp. 104–7. 30. Jim Hersma, personal correspondence; used with permission. 31. John E. Swan, I. Fredrick Trawick, and David W. Silva, "How Industrial Salespeople Gain Customer Trust," *Industrial Marketing Management,* 1985, pp. 203–11. 32. Richard Whiteley, "Do Selling and Quality Mix?" *Sales & Marketing Management,* October 1993, p. 70. 33. Margie Markarian, "Cultural Evolution," *Sales & Marketing Management,* May 1994, pp. 127–28. 34. Todd Graf, personal correspondence; used with permission. 35. Tracey Brill, personal correspondence; used with permission. 36. This section was developed from Stewart A. Washburn, "Daniel in the Lion's Den: Selling to Groups," *Journal of Management Consulting,* Spring 1992, pp. 9–19; Steve Zurier, "Making Group Presentations Pay Off: The Goal Is to Reach Several Buying Influences at Once," *Industrial Distribution,* June 1989, p. 41; Joseph Conlin, "Teaming Up," *Sales and Marketing Management,* October 1993, pp. 98–104; Richard G. Ensman, Jr., "How to Participate in a Meeting," *Ideas,* October 1992, pp. 11–12. 37. Barbara L. Breaden, *Speaking to Persuade,* (Fort Worth, TX: Harcourt Brace College Publishers, 1996). 38. Stanley F. Slater and John C. Narver, "Market Orientation and the Learning Organization," *Journal of Marketing,* July 1995, pp. 63–74.

Chapter 10

1. Michele Marchetti. "That's the Craziest Thing I Ever Heard," *Sales & Marketing Management,* November 1995, pp. 76–82. 2. See Bob Boylan, "Insuring Effective 'Re-Presentation'" *Business Marketing,* January 1993, p. 59. 3. Fiona Gibb, "Getting It Right the First Time," *Sales & Marketing Management,* March 1995, p. 49. 4. See Mauri Edwards, "Now Presenting . . . " *Sales &*

Marketing Management, November 1992, pp. 23–26. 5. This section is based on information from Frank K. Sonnenberg, "Presentations That Persuade," *Journal of Business Strategy,* September–October 1988, pp. 55–58; Jack Falvey, "Does Your Company Need First Aid for Its Visuals?" *Sales & Marketing Management,* July 1990, pp. 97–99; Richard Kern, "Making Visual Aids Work for You," *Sales & Marketing Management,* February 1989, pp. 45–48. 6. Thayer C. Taylor, "Mapping Out a Strategy," *Sales & Marketing Management,* February 1994, pp. 51–56. 7. Anne M. Phaneuf. "Is It Really Better to Give?" *Sales & Marketing Management,* September 1995, pp. 95–104. 8. Andy Cohen, "A New Surgical Tool," *Sales & Marketing Management,* September 1994, p. 50. 9. Pricilla C. Brown, "How to Project the 'Big Picture,'" *Business Marketing,* January 1993, p. 56. 10. See, for example, Ginger Trumfio, "The Future Is Now," *Sales & Marketing Management,* November 1994, pp. 74–80; Ginger Trumfio, "Ready! Set! Sell!" *Sales & Marketing Management,* February 1994, pp. 82–84; Tom Dellecave, Jr., "Now Showing: New Multimedia Tools Put Sound, Video, and Graphics at Your Sales Reps' Fingertips," *Sales & Marketing Management,* February 1996, pp. 68–72; Francy Blackwood, "Present Your Best Case," *Selling,* January/February 1995, pp. 26–28; Wilder, Claudyne and David Fine, *Point, Click and Wow: A Guide to Brilliant Laptop Presentations,* San Diego: Pfeiffer and Co., 1996. 11. Dona Z. Meilach, "Resources on the Road," *Presentations,* August 1996, pp. 14–20. 12. Kate Bertrand, "The Presentation Sensation: Multimedia Technology Provides New Impact," *Business Marketing,* June 1992, p. 32. 13. See Bristol Voss, "Sales Tools: A Presentation Update," *Sales & Marketing Management,* November 1992, pp. 96–97. 14. See, for example, Thomas Leech and Leslie Johnson-Leech, "18 Tips for Making Your Next Presentation Less Stressful," *Presentations,* July 1996, pp. 10–11. 15. See Carl Quintanilla, "Tractor Dealers Get Down in the Dirt Promoting Machines," *The Wall Street Journal,* July 16, 1996, pp. 1+. 16. Don Wiley, "What's the Etiquette of the RFP?" *Communication News,* October 1990, p. 20. 17. Melissa Campanelli, "Writer's Block: Writing Proposals Can Be the Easiest Part of the Sales Cycle," *Sales & Marketing Management,* September 1995, p. 114. 18. "Setting Sights with Statistics," *Sales & Marketing Management,* September 1995, pp. 32–33. 19. Information from this section was gathered from a number of sources, including Mack Hanan, *Consultative Selling: The Hanan Formula for High-Margin Sales at High Levels* (New York: AMACOM, 1990).

Chapter 11

1. Richard Kern, "The Art of Overcoming Resistance," *Sales & Marketing Management,* March 1990, p. 101. 2. Saul W. Gellerman, "The Tests of a Good Salesperson," *Harvard Business Review,* May/June 1990, p. 68. 3. See Roger M. Pell, "The Road to Success Is Paved with Objections," *Bank Marketing,* February 1990, pp. 16–17. 4. *Increase Your Selling Power* (Pittsburgh: Westinghouse Electric Corporation), sec. 3, pp. 4–5. 5. See Gordon Bethard, "Clarify the Question Before You Answer It," *Agri Marketing,* January 1990, pp. 74–75. 6. Joseph P. Vaccaro and Derek W. F. Coward, "Managerial and Legal Issues of Price Haggling: A Sales Manager's Dilemma," *Journal of Personal Selling and Sales Management,* Summer 1993, pp. 79–86. 7. Steve Zurier, "How to Overcome Price Objections: Salespeople Can Fight Back by Selling Value," *Industrial Distribution,* March

1990, p. 55. 8. Personal correspondence; name of firm and industry withheld by request. 9. See Alan Cimberg, "Overcoming Price Objections," *Small Business Reports,* July 1990, pp. 2–6; Minda Zetlin, "Kicking the Discount Habit: Teach Your Salespeople to Stop Leaving Money on the Table," *Sales & Marketing Management,* May 1994, pp. 102–6; Nanci McCann, "Protocol," *Selling,* July/August 1994, pp. 77–78. 10. Tracey Brill, personal correspondence; used with permission. 11. See Sergey Frank, "Global Negotiating: Vive Les Differences!" *Sales and Marketing Management,* May 1992, p. 64.

Chapter 12

1. "No More Commando Selling," *Sales & Marketing Management,* May 1986, pp. 29–30. 2. Jack Falvey, "For the Best Close, Keep an Open Mind," *Sales & Marketing Management,* April 1990, pp. 10, 12. 3. Tim Conner, "The New Psychology of Closing Sales," *American Salesman,* September 1987, p. 25. 4. Neil Rackham, *Spin Selling* (New York: McGraw-Hill, 1988), pp. 19–51. 5. John Graham, "A Three-Step Sales System," *Personal Selling Power,* November/December 1994, pp. 62–63. 6. Tom Dellecave Jr., "Missing Link," *Sales & Marketing Management,* August 1996, pp. 94–95. 7. Russ Berry, "You're Always Selling," Presentation as Executive in Residence, Baylor University's Center for Professional Selling, October 19, 1995. 8. Marvin A. Jolson, "Selling Assertively," *Business Horizons,* September/October 1984, pp. 71–77. 9. See Sergey Frank, "Global Negotiating: Vive Les Differences!" *Sales & Marketing Management,* May 1992, p. 67. 10. See Paul B. Brown, "A Bird in the Hand," *Inc.,* August 1989, pp. 114–15. 11. Harvey B Mackay, "Humanize Your Selling Strategy," *Harvard Business Review,* March/April 1988, p. 47. 12. Norton Paley, "Seeing the Small Picture," *Sales & Marketing Management,* January 1995, pp. 22–23. 13. Andy Cohen, "No Deal," *Sales & Marketing Management,* August 1996, pp. 51–54. 14. Richard Kern, "A Follow-Up Program for Lost Sales," *Sales & Marketing Management,* November 1989, pp. 124–25. 15. Anne O'Kleefe, "Opportunity Calling," *Personal Selling Power,* November/December 1994, pp. 56–57. 16. Ted Pollock, "Service—More Important Than Ever," *American Salesman,* September 1990, p. 26. 17. Jay Finegan, "Stand and Deliver," *Inc.,* November 1992, p. 140.

Chapter 13

1. Weld Royal, "Keep Them Coming Back," *Sales & Marketing Management,* September 1995, pp. 50–52. 2. Christopher Power, Lisa Driscoll, and Earl Bohn, "Smart Selling," *Business Week,* August 3, 1992, pp. 46–48; Frederick F. Reichheld and Earl Sasser, "Zero Defections: Quality Comes to Services," *Harvard Business Review,* September/October 1990, pp. 105–11. 3. William O'Connell and William Keenan, Jr., "The Shape of Things to Come," *Sales & Marketing Management,* January 1990, pp. 36–41. 4. Thomas Stewart, "After All You've Done for Your Customers, Why Are They Still Not Happy?" *Fortune,* December 11, 1995, pp. 178–82. 5. Tony Vavra, *Aftermarketing: How to Keep Customers for Life through Relationship Marketing,* Burr Ridge, IL: Business One-Irwin, 1992. 6. Jon M. Hawes, Kenneth E. Mast, and John E. Swan, "Trust Earning Perceptions of Sellers and Buyers," *Journal of Personal Selling and Sales Management,* Spring, 1989, pp. 1–8. 7. "Eastman Kodak Brings Training into Sharper Focus," *Sales & Marketing Management,*

September 1992, p. 62. 8. Nancy Arnott, "It's a Woman's World," *Sales & Marketing Management,* March 1995, pp. 54–59. 9. Philip Burger and Cynthia Cann, "Post-Purchase Strategy: A Key to Successful Industrial Marketing and Customer Satisfaction," *Industrial Marketing Management* 24 (1995), pp. 91–98. 10. Hawes, Mast, and Swan, "Trust Earning Perceptions," pp. 1–8. 11. "Salespeople's Selling Skills," *American Salesman,* April 1990, pp. 10–11. 12. Millind Lele and Jagdish Sheth, *The Customer Is Key* (New York: John Wiley & Sons, 1987). 13. "What Qualities Make Sales Representatives Valuable to Customers? Survey Shows That Being the Customer's Advocate Is Most Important," *Agency Sales Magazine,* June 1987, pp. 34–35. 14. James P. Morgan, "How the Top Ten Measure Up," *Purchasing,* June 4, 1992, pp. 62–63. 15. Sarah Mahoney, "Think Before You Thank," *Selling,* July/August 1996, pp. 68–70. 16. Andy Cohen, "No Deal," *Sales & Marketing Management,* August 1996, pp. 51–54. 17. John Graham, "Turn Added Value into Added Sales," *Personal Selling Power,* January/February 1995, pp. 62–63. 18. Morgan, "How the Top Ten Measure Up," pp. 62–63. 19. Dwight D. Davis, with Bill Sharp and Mark Schlack, "Can Digital Sustain Alpha's Edge?" *Datamation,* March 1, 1993, pp. 24–31. 20. Christopher Hoyt and Hunter Hastings, "Re-Connect with the Consumer," PROMO/Progressive Grocer Special Report, *PROMO: The International Magazine for Promotion Marketing,* December 1993, pp. 14–15. 21. William Keenan, Jr., "Direct Results," *Sales & Marketing Management,* January 1995, pp. 78–84. 22. "MasterCard Program to Teach Cross-Selling," *American Banker,* January 26, 1993, p. 2. 23. "Quality Is Key for Purchasing," *Purchasing,* January 17, 1991, p. 137. 24. James P. Morgan and Shirley Cayer, "Working with World-Class Suppliers: True Believers," *Purchasing,* August 13, 1992, pp. 50–52. 25. Ibid. 26. James P. Morgan, "Supply Strategy: Buyer-Supplier Alliances," *Purchasing,* July 23, 1996, pp. 34B13–34B16. 27. Jean Graham, "A Simple Idea Saves $8 Million a Year," *Purchasing,* May 21, 1992, pp. 47–49. 28. Lisa M. Ellram, "The Supplier Selection Decision in Strategic Partnerships," *Journal of Purchasing and Materials Management,* October 1990, pp. 8–14. 29. Rahul Jacob, "Why Some Customers Are More Equal Than Others," *Fortune,* September 19, 1994, pp. 215–24. 30. Gilbert A. Churchill, Neil M. Ford, and Orville C. Walker, Jr., Sales Force Management (Burr Ridge, IL: Richard D. Irwin, 1993). 31. Paul Kelly, *Situational Selling* (New York: AMACOM, 1988). 32. This section is based on Kelly, *Situational Selling;* see also John F. Tanner, Jr., and Stephen B. Castleberry, "The Participation Model: Factors Related to Buying Decision Participation," *Journal of Business to Business Marketing,* 1, no. 3, 1993, pp. 35–61. 33. Kelly, *Situational Selling.* 34. Ed Rigsbee, "Positioned as Partner," *Personal Selling Power,* October 1994, pp. 50–51. 35. Howard Scott, "Winning Back a Lost Account," *Nation's Business,* July 1996, p. 31R. 36. Robert Bly, *Keeping Clients Satisfied* (Englewood Cliffs, NJ: Prentice Hall, 1993). 37. Ron Willingham, *Integrity Selling* (New York: Doubleday, 1987).

Chapter 14

1. For a complete listing of potential issues to be negotiated, see William F Morrison, *The Prenegotiation Handbook* (New York: Wiley, 1985), pp. 113–74. 2. Joseph Conlin. "Negotiating Their Way to the Top," *Sales & Marketing Management,* April 1996, p. 57. 3. Gregg Crawford. "Let's Negotiate," *Sales & Marketing Management,* November 1995, pp. 28–29. 4. Sharon Nelton, "The

Womanly Art of the Deal," *Nation's Business,* January 1993, p. 60.
5. See Nancy J Adler, *International Dimensions of Organizational Behavior* (Boston: Kent Publishing Company, 1986), pp. 157–58.
6. People who already have some experience negotiating can test their skills using another instrument. See "Put Your Skills to the Test," *Sales & Marketing Management,* April 1994, pp. 90–93. 7. R J Lewicki and J A Litterer, *Negotiation* (Burr Ridge, IL: Irwin, 1985), p. 47. 8. See, for example, Peter J D Carnevale and Edward J. Lawler, "Time Pressure and the Development of Integrative Agreements in Bilateral Negotiations," *Journal of Conflict Resolution,* December 1986, pp. 636–59. 9. See, for example, William A Donohue and Robert Kolt, *Managing Interpersonal Conflict* (Newbury Park, CA: Sage Publications, 1992), pp. 99–111. 10. Todd Graf, personal correspondence, used with permission. 11. Fred Edmund Jandt and Paul Gillette, *Win-Win Negotiating: Turning Conflict into Agreement* (New York: Wiley, 1985). 12. See Michael E Roloff and Jerry M Jordan, "Achieving Negotiation Goals: The 'Fruits and Foibles' of Planning Ahead," in *Communication and Negotiation,* Linden L Putnan and Michael E Roloff, eds. (Newbury Park, CA: Sage Publications, 1992), p. 35. 13. Negotiator Pro, Beacon Expert Systems, Inc., Brookline, MA. 14. Adler, p. 175. 15. See Alvin L Goldman, *Settling For More: Negotiating Strategies and Techniques* (Washington, DC: BNA Books, 1991), pp. 218–27 for a complete description of bargaining teams. 16. The information in this section was developed from Kenneth Thomas, "Conflict and Conflict Management," in *The Handbook of Industrial and Organizational Psychology,* Marvin Dunnette, ed. (Skokie, IL: Rand McNally, 1976). 17. Joseph Conlin, p. 62. 18. See Jan Gelman. "10 Booby Traps: One False Step, and It's All Over," *Selling,* November 1994, pp. 58–65. 19. See William A Donohue and Closepet N Ramesh, "Negotiator-Opponent Relationships," in *Communication and Negotiation,* Linda L Putnan and Michael E Roloff, eds. (Newbury Park, CA: Sage Publications, 1992); and Naoko Oikawa and John F Tanner, Jr., "The Influence of Japanese Culture on Business Relationships and Negotiations," *The Journal of Services Marketing,* Summer 1992, pp. 67–74. 20. Cynthia E. Griffin. "10 Best Ways To . . ." *Entrepreneur,* March 1996, pp. 102–03. 21. For a more complete discussion of agenda content, agenda sequence, stating the issues, etc., see Goldman, pp. 160–96. 22. See Donohue and Kolt, p. 56; also see Roderick Macleod, *China Inc.: How to Do Business with the Chinese* (Toronto: Bantam Books, 1988), pp. 75–76. 23. This section was developed from a number of sources, including Homer B Smith, *Selling through Negotiation: The Handbook of Sales Negotiation* (Chevy Chase, MD: Marketing Education Associates, 1987); and Gerard I Nierenberg, *The Complete Negotiator* (New York: Nierenberg & Zeif Publishers, 1986). 24. See Roger Fisher and William Ury, *Getting to Yes: Negotiating Agreement without Giving In,* 2nd ed. (Boston: Houghton Mifflin, 1991). 25. See Smith, *Selling through Negotiation;* Nierenberg, *The Complete Negotiator,* and Conlin,* p. 62; Anne O'Kleefe and Malcolm Fleschner. "All-Star Negotiator," *Personal Selling Power,* September 1995, pp. 63–66. 26. Griffin, p. 103. 27. Adler, p. 176. 28. Donohue and Ramesh, "Negotiator-Opponent Relationships."

Chapter 15

1. Jaclyn Fierman, "The Death and Rebirth of the Salesman," *Fortune,* July 25, 1994, pp. 80–91. 2. Robert Sharoff, "Not Just Fun and Games," *Selling,* November 1994, 32–36 3. Tim

Triplett, "More US Grocers Turning to ECR to Cut Waste," *Marketing News,* September 12, 1994, p. 3. 4. Alice Maddox, "ECR in Action," *Sales and Marketing Strategies & News,* September 1996, p. 24. 5. Craig MacClaren, "Manufacturers Are Setting a Fast Pace for ECR," *PROMO: The International Magazine for Promotion Marketing,* March 1994, p. 42. 6. Michael Levy and Barton Weitz, *Retailing,* 2d ed., (Burr Ridge IL: Richard D. Irwin, 1995). 7. Michael Levy and Barton A. Weitz, *Retailing Management* (Burr Ridge IL: Richard D. Irwin, 1992), pp. 248–56. 8. Nancy McCann, "One Open Door Doesn't Lead to Another," *Selling,* November 1995, p. 23. 9. Janet Wagner, Richard Ettenson, and Jean Parrish, "Vendor Selection among Retail Buyers: An Analysis by Merchandise Division," *Journal of Retailing,* Spring 1989, pp. 58–79. 10. Scott Corriveau, "Mott's USA Empowers Brokers," *Sales and Marketing Strategies & News,* June/July 1996, p. 24. 11. Geoffrey Brewer, "Shout It Out," *Sales & Marketing Management,* February 1996, pp. 30–42. 12. "How Much Does It Cost to Close a Sale?" Research Report SM17, Center for Exhibition Industry Research, Bethesda, MD 1996. 13. Wendy Hatoum, "Selling Your Soles," *Sporting Goods Dealer,* April 1993, pp. 40–42. 14. Christopher Hoyt, "Retailers and Suppliers Still Miles Apart," *PROMO: The International Magazine for Promotion Marketing,* March 1996, p. 49. 15. Hatoum, "Selling Your Soles." 16. Michael Sansolo, "Partners vs. Profits," *PROMO: The International Magazine for Promotion Marketing,* December 1993, pp. 8–9 of a PROMO/Progressive Grocer Special Report insert. 17. Kerry E. Smith, "No Brand Too Small," *PROMO: The International Magazine for Promotion Marketing,* December 1993, pp. 4–5 of a PROMO/Progressive Grocer Special Report insert. 18. Craig MacClaren, "Brokers Are a Natural Link in the Category Management Chain," *PROMO: The International Magazine for Promotion Marketing,* October 1994, p. 22. 19. This example is based on data presented in Christopher Hoyt and Hunter Hastings, "Re-Connect with the Consumer," *PROMO: The International Magazine for Promotion Marketing,* December 1993, pp. 14–15 of a PROMO/Progressive Grocer Special Report insert.

Chapter 16

1. Betsy Wiesendanger, "Bigger Sales, Same Budget," *Sales & Marketing Management,* July 1993, pp. 46–53. 2. Lawrence Tuttle, "Are You Ready to Improve?" *Personal Selling Power,* October 1994, pp. 38–44. 3. Michael Treacy and Fred Wiersma, "How Market Leaders Keep Their Edge," *Fortune,* February 6, 1996, pp. 88–98. 4. Adel El-Ansary and Waleed A. El-Ansary, *Winning Customers, Building Accounts: Some Do It Better Than Others.* Jacksonville, FL: Paper and Plastics Education and Research Foundation, 1994. 5. Carla Messer, Michael Lyons, and James Alexander, "Classifying Your Customers," *Sales & Marketing Management,* July 1993, pp. 42–43. 6. "Northwestern National Speeds Quotes," *Sales and Marketing Strategies & News,* June/July 1996, p. 4. 7. Stephen Rush, "From Baseball to Business," *Nation's Business,* October 1996, pp. 48–52. 8. T. J. Becker, "How to Make the Most of Downtime," *Selling,* October 1995, pp. 54–56. 9. Doug Loewe, "Long-Distance Manager," *Sales & Marketing Management,* October 1994, p. 25. 10. Tony Seideman, "Who Needs Managers?" *Sales & Marketing Management,* June 1994, pp. 15–17. 11. Melissa Campanelli, "The King of Email," *Sales & Marketing Management,* December 1994, pp. 13–16.

Chapter 17

1. George Day, "The Capabilities of Market Driven Organizations," *Journal of Marketing*, October 1994, pp. 37–52. 2. The Mescon Group, Inc., *Strengthening Teamwork* (Cincinnati: Thompson Executive Press, 1995). 3. Andy Cohen, "Should Reps Collect the Bills?" *Sales & Marketing Management*, June 1996, pp. 53–54. 4. Lawrence B. Chonko, John F. Tanner, Jr., and Ellen Reid Smith, "The Sales Force's Role in International Marketing Research and Marketing Research Information Systems," *Journal of Personal Selling and Sales Management*, Winter 1991, pp. 69–80. 5. Michelle Marchetti, "Person to Person: How to Sell Your Boss," *Sales & Marketing Management*, May 1996, p. 43. 6. Shelby D. Hunt and Arturo Vasquez-Parraga, "Organizational Consequences, Marketing Ethics, and Salesforce Supervision," *Journal of Marketing Research*, February 1993, pp. 78–90. 7. Much of this section is based on Richard P. Nielsen, "What Can Managers Do about Unethical Management?" *Journal of Business Ethics*, 1987, pp. 309–20, and "Negotiating as an Ethics Action (Praxis) Strategy," Journal of Business Ethics, 1989, pp. 383–90 8. Andy Cohen, "Managing" *Sales & Marketing Management*, April 1996, pp. 77–80. 9. Henry Canady, "Team Selling Works!" *Personal Selling Power*, September 1994, pp. 52–58. 10. Michelle Marchetti, "Compensation Gamble," *Sales & Marketing Management*, July 1996, pp. 65–69. 11. William Moncrief, Shannon H. Shipp, Charles W. Lamb, Jr., and David W. Cravens, "Examining the Roles of Telemarketing in Sales Strategy," *Journal of Personal Selling and Sales Management*, Fall 1989, pp. 1–12. 12. Francy Blackwood, "Whose Customer Is It?" *Selling*, April 1996, pp. 76–77. 13. Craig MacClaren, "Companies Find Benefits in the Team Approach," *PROMO: The Magazine of Promotion Marketing*, April 1996, p. 80. 14. Nancy Arnott, "Selling a Relationship," *Sales & Marketing Management*, January 1995, p. 14. 15. Frank Jossi, "Pulling It All Together: Creating Presentations as a Team," *Presentations*, July 1996, pp. 18–26. 16. Melissa Campanelli, "Road Warrior: Yikes!" *Sales & Marketing Management*, March 1995, pp. 25–29.

Chapter 18

1. Darrel Wash, "A New Way to Classify Occupations by Education and Training," *Occupational Outlook Quarterly*, Winter 1995–95, pp. 29–40. 2. *Occupational Outlook Handbook* October 1996 (http://www.stats.bls.gov:80/ocohome.htm. 3. Cyndee Miller, "Job Picture for Marketing, Sales Brightest in Years," *Marketing News*, August 29, 1994, pp. 1–2. 4. Eugene Johnson, "How Do Sales Managers View College Preparation for Sales?" *Journal of Personal Selling and Sales Management*, Summer 1990, pp. 69–72. 5. Alan Farnham, "Are You Smart Enough?" *Fortune*, January 15, 1996, pp. 34–48. 6. Seymour Adler, "Personality Tests for Salesforce Selection: Worth a Fresh Look," *Review of Business*, Summer/Fall 1994, pp. 27–31. 7. John L. Munschauer, "The Resume: How to Speak to Employer's Needs," *CPC Annual*, 1992–1993, pp. 27–41. 8. Gene Garofalo and Gary Drummond, *Sales Professional's Survival Guide* (Englewood Cliffs, NJ: Prentice Hall, 1987). 9. Ramon Avila, Joseph Chapman, and Pamela Reigle, "A Business Perspective on the Student Portfolio," *Proceedings of the National Sales Conference*, 1994, pp. 54–57. 10. Ed Holton, "The Critical First Year on the Job," *CPC Annual*, 1992–1993, pp. 72–75. 11. Jan Gelman, "If You Had $3,000 to Spend on Self-Improvement, What Would You Do?" *Selling*, September 1995, pp. 59–72. 12. Donna Cornachio, "How Not to Lose Your Job," *Sales & Marketing Management*, August 1996, pp. 58–63. 13. Ellen Pullins, Leslie Fine, and Wendy Warren, "Identifying Peer Mentors in the Sales Force: An Exploratory Investigation of Willingness and Ability," *Journal of the Academy of Marketing Science* 24, no. 2, pp. 125–136. 14. Sandra Fisher, "Stress, Part 1: Warning Signs and Identifying Characteristics," *Sales & Marketing Management*, November 1992, pp. 93–94. 15. Caroline Bollinger, "All in a Day's Work," *Selling*, December 1994, pp. 45–53. 16. Susan M. Keaveney and James E. Nelson, "Coping with Organizational Role Stress: Intrinsic Motivational Orientation, Perceived Role Benefits, and Psychological Withdrawal," *Journal of the Academy of Marketing Science*, Spring 1993, pp. 113–15. 17. John F. Tanner, Jr., Mark G. Dunn, and Lawrence B. Chonko, "Vertical Exchange and Salesperson Stress," *Journal of Personal Selling and Sales Management*, Spring 1993, pp. 27–35. 18. Ibid. 19. Gilbert A. Churchill, Jr., Neil M. Ford, and Orville C. Walker, Jr., *Sales Force Management*, 4th ed. (Burr Ridge IL: Richard D. Irwin, 1993). 20. John F. Tanner, Jr. and Stephen B. Castleberry, "Vertical Exchange Quality and Performance: Studying the Role of the Sales Manager," *Journal of Personal Selling and Sales Management*, Spring 1990, pp. 17–27; Rosemary Lagace, "Leader-Member Exchange: Antecedents and Consequences of the Cadre and Hired Hand," *Journal of Personal Selling and Sales Management*, February 1990, pp. 11–19.

Glossary

ABC analysis Evaluating the importance of an account; the most important is an A account, the second most important is a B account, and the least important is a C account.

accommodating mode Resolving conflict by being unassertive and highly cooperative; when using this approach, people often neglect their own needs and desires to satisfy the concerns of the other party.

account opportunity Another term for the sales potential dimensions of the sales call allocation grid.

active listening Process in which the listener attempts to draw out as much information as possible by actively processing information received and stimulating the communication of additional information.

activity goals Behavioral objectives, such as the number of calls made in a day.

activity quota A type of quota that sets minimal behavioral expectations for a salesperson's activities. Used when sales cycle is long and sales are few. Controls activities of salespeople.

adaptive planning The development of alternative paths to the same goal in a negotiation session.

adaptive selling Approach to personal selling in which selling behaviors and approaches are altered during a sales interaction or across customer interactions, based on information about the nature of the selling situation.

administrative law Laws established by local, state, or federal regulatory agencies, such as the Federal Trade Commission or the Food and Drug Administration.

adoption process Step or steps that a person or an organization goes through when making an initial purchase and then using a new product or service.

after-tax cash flows Used to evaluate a purchase; ensures that the company has enough cash to pay for the purchase.

agenda Listing of what will and will not be discussed, and in what sequence, in a negotiation session.

agent Person who acts in place of his or her company. See also **manufacturers' agents.**

aggressive Sales style that controls the sales interaction but often does not gain commitment because it ignores the customer's needs and fails to probe for information.

ambush negotiating A win-lose tactic used by a buyer at the beginning of, or prior to, negotiations when the seller does not expect it.

amiable Category in the social style matrix describing people who like cooperation and close relationships. Amiables are low on assertiveness and high on responsiveness.

analytical Category in the social style matrix describing people who emphasize facts and logic. Analyticals are low on assertiveness and responsiveness.

application form Preprinted form completed by a job applicant.

approach Method designed to get the prospect's attention and interest quickly.

articulation The production of recognizable speech.

assertive Sales manner that stresses responding to customer needs while being self-confident and positive.

assertiveness Dimension of the social style matrix assessing the degree to which people have opinions on issues and make their positions clear to others publicly.

assessment center Central location for evaluating job candidates.

avoiding mode Resolving conflict in an unassertive and uncooperative manner. In this mode, people make no attempt to resolve their own needs or the needs of others.

awareness phase The first phase in the development of a buyer-seller relationship in which salespeople locate and qualify prospects and buyers consider various sources of supply.

back-door selling Actions by one salesperson that go behind the back of a purchaser to directly contact other members of the buying center.

balanced presentation Occurs when the salesperson shows all sides of the situation, that is, is totally honest.

balance sheet method Attempts to obtain commitment by asking the buyer to think of the pros and cons of the various alternatives, often referred to as the *Ben Franklin method*.

barriers   Buyer's subordinates who plan and schedule interviews for their superiors; also called *screens*.

benefit   How a particular feature will help a particular buyer.

benefit approach   Approach method in which the salesperson focuses on the prospect's needs by stating a benefit of the product or service.

benefit summary method   Obtaining commitment by simply reminding the prospect of the agreed-on benefits of the proposal.

bird dog   Individual who, for a fee, will provide the names of leads for the salesperson; also called a *spotter*.

blitz   Canvassing method in which a large group of salespeople attempt to make calls on all prospective businesses in a given geographic territory on a specified day.

body language   Nonverbal signals communicated through facial expressions, arms, hands, and legs.

bonus   Lump-sum incentive payment based on performance.

boomerang method   Responding to objections by turning the objection into a reason for acting now.

bottoms-up forecasting   Forecast compiled by adding each salesperson's forecast for total company sales.

bounceback card   Card returned from a lead that requests additional information.

brainstorming session   Meeting in which people are allowed to creatively explore different methods of achieving goals.

bribes   Payments made to buyers to influence their purchase decisions.

browbeating   Negotiation strategy in which buyers attempt to alter the selling team's enthusiasm and self-respect by making unflattering comments.

budget bogey   Negotiation strategy in which one side claims that the budget does not allow for the solution proposed; also called *budget limitation tactic*.

budget limitation tactic   See *budget bogey*.

business defamation   Making unfair or untrue statements to customers about a competitor, its products, or its salespeople.

buyback   A seller's guarantee to buy back unsold merchandise from the buyer.

buy forward   Purchasing an entire year's inventory at the low price.

buyer's remorse   The insecurity a buyer feels about whether the choice was a wise one; also called *postpurchase dissonance*.

buying center   Informal, cross-department group of people involved in a purchase decision.

buying community   Small, informal group of people in similar positions who communicate regularly, often both socially and professionally.

buying signals   Nonverbal cues given by the buyer that indicate the buyer may be ready to commit; also called *closing cues*.

canned presentation   See *standard memorized sales presentation*.

cap   A limit placed on a salesperson's earnings.

capital equipment   Major purchases made by business, such as computer systems, that are used by the business for several years in its operations or production.

cash discount   Price discount given for early payment in cash.

category management   In selling to retailers, a current trend in the area of full-line selling.

center-of-influence method   Prospecting method wherein the salesperson cultivates well-known, influential people in the territory who are willing to supply lead information.

champion   Person who works for the buying firm in the areas most affected by the proposed change and works with the salesperson for the success of the proposal; also called *advocate* or *internal salesperson*.

change agent   Person who is a cause of change in an organization.

circular routing   Method of scheduling sales calls that involves circular patterns.

closed-ended questions   See *closed questions*.

closed questions   Questions that require the prospect to simply answer yes or no or to offer a short, fill-in-the-blank type of response.

closing   Common term for obtaining commitment, which usually refers only to asking for the buyer's business.

closing cues   See *buying signals*.

cloverleaf routing   Method of scheduling sales calls that involves using loops to cover different portions of the territory on different days or weeks; on a map it should resemble a cloverleaf.

cold call   See *cold canvass method*.

cold canvass method   Prospecting method in which a sales representative tries to generate leads for new business by calling on totally unfamiliar organizations; also called *cold calls*.

collaborating mode   Resolving conflict by seeking to maximize the satisfaction of both parties and hence truly reach a win-win solution.

collusion   Agreement among competitors, made after contacting customers, concerning their relationships with customers.

combination plan   Compensation plan that provides salary and commission; offers the greatest flexibility for motivating and controlling the activities of salespeople.

Commerce Business Daily   Publication that contains all the invitations for bids issued by the federal government.

commission   Incentive pay paid for an individual sale; often a percentage of the sale price.

commission base   Unit of analysis used to determine commissions; for example, unit sales, dollar sales, or gross margin.

commission rate   Percentage of base paid or the amount per base unit paid in a commission compensation plan, for example, a percentage of dollar sales or an amount per unit sold.

commitment phase   The fourth stage in the development of a buyer-seller relationship in which the buyer and seller have implicitly or explicitly pledged to continue the relationship for an extended time period.

common law   Legal precedents that arise out of court decisions.

compensation method   Method used to respond helpfully to objections by agreeing that the objection is valid, but then proceeding to show any compensating advantages.

competence   The buyer's perception that the salesperson knows what he or she is talking about.

competing mode   Resolving conflict in an assertive and noncooperative manner.

complacency   Assuming the business is yours and will always be yours.

compliment approach   Approach in which the salesperson begins the sales call by complimenting the buyer in some fashion.

compromising mode   Resolving conflict by being somewhat cooperative and somewhat assertive. People using this approach attempt to find a quick, mutually acceptable solution that partially satisfies both parties.

concession   Occurs when one party in a negotiation meeting agrees to change his or her position in some fashion.

consequence questions   Questions that illustrate the consequences of a disadvantage in a competitor's product.

consignment   Method of payment for goods in which the retailer makes no payment until after the product is sold.

conspiracy   Agreement among competitors, made prior to contacting customers, concerning their relationships with customers.

consultative selling philosophy   Form of customized presentation in which salespeople identify the prospect's needs and then recommend the best solution, even when the best solution does not include the salesperson's own products or services.

contest   Trade promotion a firm uses to increase sales by rewarding top salespeople with trips, extra money, or merchandise.

contract to sell   Offer made by a salesperson that received an unqualified acceptance by a buyer.

conventional resumé   Form of life history organized by type of work experience.

conversion goals   Measures of salesperson efficiency.

conversion rate   Similar to a batting average, calculated by dividing performance results by activity results, for example, dividing the number of sales by the number of calls.

co-op advertising   Advertising paid for by both retailer and manufacturer, often with some assistance in preparing the ad from the manufacturer.

corporate culture   The values and beliefs held by a company and expressed by senior management.

coupon clippers   People who like to send off for product information even though they have no intention of ever buying the product or service.

credibility   The characteristic of being perceived by the buyer as believable and reliable.

credible commitments   Tangible investments in a relationship that indicate commitment to the relationship.

credulous person standard   Canadian law stating that a company is liable to pay damages if advertising and sale presentation claims and statements about comparisons with competitive products could be misunderstood by a reasonable person.

creeping commitment   Purchase decision process that arises when decisions made early in the process have significant influence on decisions made later in the process.

cross-selling   Similar to full-line selling, except that the additional products sold are not directly associated with the initial products.

cultural relativism   A view that no culture's ethics are superior to another culture's.

cumulative discount   Quantity discount for purchases over a period of time; the buyer is allowed to add up all the purchases to determine the total quantity and the total quantity discount.

curiosity approach   Arousing interest by making an unexpected comment that piques the prospect's curiosity.

customer intentions survey   Method of forecasting sales in which customers are asked how much they intend to buy over the forecasting period.

customer orientation   Selling approach based on keeping the customer's interests paramount.

customer service rep   In-bound salesperson who handles customer concerns.

customer share   The average percentage of business received from a company's accounts.

customized presentation   Presentation developed from a detailed and comprehensive analysis or survey of the prospect's needs that is not canned or memorized in any fashion.

deal   Promotional discount offered by a manufacturer to a retailer, often (but not always) in exchange for featuring a product in a newspaper ad and/or a special display.

deception   Unethical practice of withholding information or telling "white lies."

deciders   Buying center members who make the final selection of the product to purchase.

decoding   Communication activity undertaken by a receiver interpreting the meaning of the received message.

deferred dating   Scheduling payment of a bill at a later (deferred) date; often done by the manufacturer to allow a reseller time to sell the product in order to generate the cash needed to pay for it.

dependability   The buyer's perception that the salesperson will live up to promises made; is not something a salesperson can demonstrate immediately.

derived demand   Situation in which the demand for a producer's goods is based on what its customers sell.

diagnostic feedback   Information given to a salesperson indicating how he or she is performing.

direct denial   Method of answering objections in which the salesperson makes a relatively strong statement indicating the error the prospect has made.

direct request method   Attaining commitment by simply asking for one in a straightforward statement.

disadvantage questions   Questions that ask a customer to articulate a specific problem.

disguised interview   Discussion between an applicant and an interviewer in which the applicant is unaware that the interviewer is evaluating the applicant for the position.

distribution channel   Set of people and organizations responsible for the flow of products and services from the producer to the ultimate user.

dormant accounts   Accounts that have not purchased for a specified time.

draw   Advance from the company to a salesperson made against future commissions.

driver   Category in the social style matrix describing task-oriented people who are high on assertiveness and low on responsiveness.

efficient customer response (ECR) system   Distribution system that drives inventory to the lowest possible levels, increases the frequency of shipping, and automates ordering and inventory control processes without the problems of stockouts and higher costs.

ego-involved   Refers to the perception of an audience member that presented subject matter is important to his or her own well-being. For a contrast, see *issue-involved*.

elaboration questions   Questions that are positive requests for additional information rather than simply verbal encouragement.

electronic data interchange (EDI)   Computer-to-computer linkages between suppliers and buyers for information sharing about sales, production, shipment, and receipt of products.

electronic mail   Method of sending correspondence from one computer to another.

emotional intelligence   The ability to effectively understand and use your own emotions and those of people with whom you interact. Includes four (4) aspects: (1) knowing your own feelings and emotions as they are happening, (2) controlling your emotions so you do not act impulsively, (3) recognizing your customer's emotions (called *empathy*), and (4) using your emotions to interact effectively with customers.

emotional needs   Types of organizational and/or personal needs that are associated with some type of personal reward and gratification for the person buying the product.

emotional outburst tactic   Negotiation strategy in which one party attempts to gain concessions by resorting to a display of strong emotion.

encoding   Communication activity undertaken by a sender translating his or her thought into a message.

encouragement probes   Questions or nonverbal signals that encourage customers to reveal further information.

endless-chain method   Prospecting method whereby a sales representative attempts to get at least one additional lead from each person he or she interviews.

end users   Businesses that purchase goods and services to support their own production and operations.

ethical imperialism The view that the ethical standards that apply locally or in one's home country should be applied to everyone's behavior around the world.

ethics Principles governing the behavior of an individual or a group.

ethics review board May consist of experts inside and outside the company who are responsible for reviewing ethics policies, investigating allegations of unethical behavior, and acting as a sounding board for employees.

evaluative feedback Information to a salesperson indicating how he or she is performing.

exclusive sales territories Method that uses geographic location of a prospect to determine whether the salesperson can sell to him or her.

excuses Concerns expressed by the buyer that are intended to mask the buyer's true objections.

executive summary In a written proposal, a summary of one page or less that describes the total cost minus total savings, a brief description of the problem to be solved, and a brief description of the proposed solution.

expansion phase The third phase in the development of a relationship in which it takes a significant effort to share information and further investigate the potential relationship benefits.

expense budget Budget detailing expenses; may be expressed in dollars or as a percentage of sales volume.

expert opinions Method of forecasting sales that involves averaging the estimates of several experts.

expert system Computer program that mimics a human expert.

exploration phase The second phase in the development of a relationship in which both buyers and sellers explore the potential benefits and costs associated with the relationship.

expressed warranty Warranty specified through oral or written communications.

expressive Category in the social style matrix describing people who are both competitive and approachable. They are high on assertiveness and responsiveness.

extrinsic orientation Orientation of salespeople characterized by viewing their job as a way to achieve rewards such as compensation given to them by others.

face A person's desire for a positive identity or self-concept.

factual questions Questions that ask for factual information and usually start with *who, what, where, how,* or *why.*

fax Electronic document transfer device; short for *facsimile.*

feature (1) Quality or characteristic of the product or service. (2) Putting a product on sale with a special display and featuring the product in advertising.

FEB Stands for *feature, evidence, benefit;* technique useful in interviewing.

feedback See **diagnostic feedback** and **evaluative feedback.**

feel-felt-found method Method of helpfully responding to objections in which the salesperson shows how others held similar views before trying the product or service.

felt stress Persistent and enduring psychological distress brought about by job demands or constraints encountered in the work environment.

field sales manager First-level manager.

field salespeople Salespeople who spend considerable time in the customer's place of business, communicating with the customer face to face.

field support representative Telemarketer who works with field salespeople and does more than prospect for leads.

FOB (free on board) Term used to designate the point at which responsibility shifts from seller to buyer.

FOB (free on board) destination Terms of a contract indicating the seller has title until the goods are received at the destination.

FOB (free on board) factory Terms of a contract indicating the buyer has title when the goods leave the seller's facility.

focus of dissatisfaction The person in the organization who is most likely to perceive problems and dissatisfactions; leads to the **focus of power.**

focus of power The person in the organization who can approve, prevent, or influence action.

focus of receptivity The person in the organization who will listen receptively and provide a seller with valuable information; leads to the **focus of dissatisfaction.**

follow-up Activities a salesperson performs after commitment is achieved.

Foreign Corrupt Practices Act Law that governs the behavior of U.S. business in foreign countries, restricts the bribing of foreign officials.

forestall To resolve objections before buyers have a chance to raise them.

free on board See **FOB.**

free-standing insert (FSI) Advertisement that is printed separately, then inserted in a newspaper.

full-line selling Selling the entire line of associated products.

functional relationship   Series of market exchanges between a buyer and a seller, linked together over time. These relationships are characterized as win-lose relationships.

functional resumé   Life history that reverses the content and titles of a conventional resumé and is organized by what a candidate can do or has learned rather than by types of experience.

gatekeepers   Buying center members who influence the buying process by controlling the flow of information and/or limiting the alternatives considered.

geographic salesperson   Salesperson assigned a specific geographic territory in which to sell all the company's products and services.

global account manager (GAM)   Sales executive responsible for coordinating sales efforts for one account globally.

good guy–bad guy routine   Negotiation strategy in which one team member acts as the "good guy" while another team member acts as the "bad guy." The goal of the strategy is to have the opposing team accept the good guy's proposal to avoid the consequences of the bad guy's proposal.

goodwill   Value of the feelings or attitudes customers or prospects have toward a company and its products.

greeter   Interviewer who greets the applicant and may conduct a disguised interview.

gross margin quota   Minimum levels of acceptable profit or gross margin performance.

group interview   Similar to panel interview, but includes several candidates as well as several interviewers.

guaranteed price   Price guaranteed to be the lowest. If the price falls, the buyer is refunded the difference between the original and the new price for any inventory still in stock.

halo effect   How and what one does in one thing changes a person's perceptions about other things one does.

high-context culture   Culture in which the verbal part of communication carries less of the information in a message than the nonverbal parts. The sender's values, position, and background are conveyed by the way the message is expressed. Examples of high-context cultures include Japan, France, Spain, Asia, and Africa.

honesty   Combination of truthfulness and sincerity; highly related to dependability.

house accounts   Accounts assigned to a sales executive rather than the specific salesperson responsible for the territory containing the account.

implication questions   Questions that logically follow one or more problem questions (in SPIN); designed to help the prospect recognize the true ramifications of the problem.

implied warranty   Warranty that is not expressly stated through oral or written communication but is still an obligation defined by law.

impression management   Activities in which salespeople engage to affect and manage the buyer's impression of them.

in-bound   Salespeople or customer service reps who respond to calls placed to the firm by customers rather than placing calls out to customers.

inbound telemarketing   Use of the telephone, usually with an 800 number, that allows leads and/or customers to call for additional information or to place an order.

incentive pay   Compensation based on performance.

indirect denial   Method used to respond to objections in which the salesperson denies the objection but attempts to soften the response by first agreeing with the prospect that the objection is an important one.

inflection   Tone of voice.

influencers   Buying center members inside or outside an organization who directly or indirectly influence the buying process.

influential adversaries   Individuals in the buyer's organization who carry great influence and are opposed to the salesperson's product or service.

inside salespeople   Salespeople who work at their employer's location and interact with customers by telephone or letter.

integrated marketing communications   Coordinated communications programs that exploit the different strengths of different communications vehicles to maximize the total impact on customers.

internal partnerships   Partnering relationships between a salesperson and another member of the same company for the purpose of satisfying customer needs.

internal selling   A communication process by which salespeople influence other employees in their firms to support their sales efforts with customers.

interview   Personal interactions between candidates and job recruiters for the purpose of evaluating job candidates.

intrinsic motivation   Motivation stimulated by the rewards salespeople get from simply doing their job.

intrinsic orientation   An orientation of salespeople characterized by seeking rewards from simply doing their jobs well.

introduction approach   Approach method in which salespeople simply state their names and the names of their companies.

inventory turnover   Measure of how efficiently a retailer manages inventory; calculated by dividing net sales by inventory.

invitation to negotiate   The initiation of an interaction, usually a sales presentation, that results in an offer.

issue-involved   Refers to the perception by an audience member that a subject is important although it may not affect him or her personally. For a contrast, see *ego-involved.*

job descriptions   Formal, written descriptions of the duties and responsibilities of a job.

just-in-time (JIT) inventory control   Planning systems for reducing inventory by having frequent deliveries planned just in time for the delivered products to be assembled into the final product.

keiretsu   A group (more than two) or family of Japanese companies that form strategic partnerships to jointly develop plans to exploit market opportunities and share the risks and rewards of their investments.

key accounts   Large accounts, usually generating more than a specified amount in revenue per year, that receive special treatment.

kickbacks   Payments made to buyers based on the amount of orders they place for a salesperson's products or services.

lead   A potential prospect; a person or organization that may have the characteristics of a true prospect.

leapfrog routing   Method of scheduling calls that requires the identification of clusters of customers; visiting on these clusters and "leaping" over single, sparsely located accounts should minimize travel time from the sales office to customers.

learning organization   Type of firm that acquires information about its environment and remembers this information so that it can guide organizational decision making even if employees in the organization change.

letters of credit   Common method of international payment; similar to a personal check, except that the company can collect cash from a customer's letter of credit only when it can prove that the customer did not pay for the merchandise.

life-cycle costing   Method for determining the cost of equipment or supplies over their useful life.

likability   Behaving in a friendly manner and finding a common ground between the buyer and seller.

list price   Quoted or published price in a manufacturer's catalog or price list from which buyers may receive discounts.

lowballing   Negotiation strategy in which one party voices agreement and then raises the cost of that agreement in some way.

low-context culture   Culture in which the verbal part of communication carries more of the information in a message than the nonverbal parts. The sender's values, position, and background are conveyed by the content of the message. Examples of low-context cultures include the United States, Canada, Germany, and Switzerland.

lubrication   Small sums of money or gifts, typically paid to officials in foreign countries, to get the officials to do their job more rapidly.

major sale   Sale that involves a long selling cycle, a large customer commitment, an ongoing relationship, and large risks for the buyer if a bad decision is made.

manufacturers' agents   Independent businesspeople who are paid a commission by a manufacturer for all products and services they sell.

market   (1) Mall where manufacturers show and sell products to retailers. (2) A short period of time when manufacturers gather to sell products to retailers.

market analysis   Method of developing sales strategies by looking for patterns among customers in their needs and methods of purchasing.

market exchange   Relationship that involves a short-term transaction between a buyer and a seller who do not expect to be involved in future transactions with each other.

market share   Percentage of total market sales that is accounted for by one product or total product category sales divided by brand sales.

marketing concept   Business philosophy emphasizing that the key to business success is determining the needs and wants of customers and satisfying those needs and wants more effectively than competitors.

marketing era   A business era, from 1960 to 1990, in which firms focused on practicing the marketing concept. Salespeople were responsible for employing all of the firm's resources to uncover and satisfy their customers' needs.

marketing mix   Elements used by firms to market their offerings—product, price, place (distribution), and promotion. Personal selling is part of the promotion element.

marketing-oriented salespeople   Salespeople who adopted the concept that the key to business success is satisfying customer needs (*marketing concept*) and who emerged during the *marketing era.*

markup   The percentage of sales by which the price for the product is initially increased.

material requirements planning (MRP)   Planning system for reducing inventory levels by forecasting sales, developing a production schedule, and ordering parts and raw materials with specific delivery dates.

maturity   A quality important for salespeople, that is gained by learning from failure.

mind share   The degree to which a manufacturer's product receives attention from (occupies the mind of) the distributor.

mini-max strategy   Approach used to set negotiation objectives that help the sellers understand and prepare for the trade-offs that will occur in the negotiation session.

minimum call objective   Minimum that a salesperson hopes to accomplish in an upcoming sales call.

minimum position   Negotiation objective that states the absolute minimum level the team is willing to accept.

missionary salespeople   Salespeople who work for a manufacturer and promote the manufacturer's products to other firms. Those firms buy products from distributors or other manufacturers, not directly from the salesperson's firm.

modified rebuy   Purchase decision process associated with a customer who has purchased the product or service in the past but is interested in obtaining additional information.

MRO supplies   Minor purchases made by businesses for maintenance and repairs, such as towels and pencils.

multiattribute model   Model describing how information about a product's performance on various dimensions is used to make an overall evaluation of the product.

multilevel selling   Strategy that involves using multiple levels of company employees to call on similar levels in an account; for example, the VP of sales might call on the VP of purchasing.

multiple-sense appeals   Appealing to as many of the senses (hearing, sight, touch, taste, and smell) as possible.

national accounts   Prospects or customers that are covered by a single, national sales strategy; may be a house account.

national account manager (NAM)   Sales executive responsible for managing and coordinating sales efforts on a single account nationwide.

need payoff questions   Questions that ask about the usefulness of solving the problem.

needs satisfaction philosophy   Form of customized presentation in which the prospect's unique needs are identified and then the salesperson shows how his or her product or service can meet those needs.

negotiation   Decision-making process through which buyers and sellers resolve areas of conflict and arrive at agreements.

negotiation jujitsu   Negotiation response in which the attacked person or team steps away from the opponent's attack and then directs the opponent back to the issues being discussed.

net present value (NPV)   The investment minus the net value today of future cash inflows (i.e., discounted back to their present value today at the firm's cost of capital).

net price   The price the buyer pays after all discounts and allowances are subtracted.

net profit margin   The profit on the product, expressed as a percentage of sales.

net sales   Total sales minus returns.

networking   Establishment of connections to other people and then using those networks to generate leads, gather information, generate sales, etc.

new task   Purchase decision process associated with the initial purchase of a product or service.

nibbling   Negotiation strategy in which the buyer requests a small extra or add-on after the deal has been closed. Compared to lowballing, a nibble is a much smaller request.

noise   Sounds unrelated to the message being exchanged between a salesperson and a customer.

nonverbal communication   Nonspoken forms of expression—body language, space, and appearance—that communicate thoughts and emotions.

objection   Concern or question raised by the buyer.

offer   Specific statement by a seller outlining what the seller will provide and what is expected from the buyer.

office scanning   Activity in which the salesperson looks around the prospect's environment for relevant topics to talk about.

open-door policy   General management technique that allows subordinates to bypass immediate managers and take concerns straight to upper management when the subordinates feel a lack of support from the immediate manager.

open-ended questions   Questions that require the prospect to go beyond a simple *yes/no* response.

opening position   The initial proposal of a negotiating session.

opinion questions   Questions that ask for a customer's feelings on a subject.

opportunity cost   The return a buyer would have earned from a different use of the same investment capital.

order   Written orders that become contracts when they are signed by an authorized representative in a salesperson's company.

original equipment manufacturer (OEM)   Business that purchases goods (components, subassemblies, raw and processed materials) to incorporate into products it manufactures.

out-bound   Salespeople, customer service reps, prospectors, account managers, and field support telemarketers who place phone calls out to customers.

outbound telemarketing   Using the telephone to generate and qualify leads to determine whether they are truly prospects or not; also used to secure orders and provide customer contact.

outlined presentation   Systematically arranged presentation that outlines the most important sales points. Often includes the necessary steps for determining the prospect's needs and for building goodwill at the close of the sale.

outsourcing   The purchase of goods and services from outside the firm that were previously produced inside the firm.

panel interview   Job interview conducted by more than one person.

partnering era   A business era, beginning in 1990, in which firms focus on developing long-term, mutually beneficial relationships with their customers. The role of salespeople in this era is to work with customers and their firms to develop solutions to problems that benefit both companies.

partnering-oriented salesperson   Value-creating salesperson who works with customers and their companies to develop solutions that enhance profits for both firms.

partnership   Ongoing, mutually beneficial relationship between a buyer and a seller.

participative leadership   Style of leadership that allows followers to make a contribution to decision making.

pass-up method   Responding to an objection by letting the buyer talk, acknowledging that you heard the concern, and then moving on to another topic without trying to resolve the concern.

payback period   Length of time it takes for the investment cash outflows to be returned in the form of cash inflows or savings.

performance goals   Goals relating to outcomes, such as revenue.

personal selling   Interpersonal communication process in which a seller uncovers and satisfies the needs of a buyer to the mutual, long-term benefit of both parties.

pioneer selling   Selling a new and different product, service, or idea. In these situations, it is usually more difficult for the salesperson to establish a need in the buyer's mind.

portfolio   Collection of visual aids that can be used to enhance communication during a sales call.

postcard pack   Cards that provide targeted information from a number of firms; this pack is mailed to prospective buyers.

postpone method   Objection-response technique in which the salesperson asks permission to answer the question at a later time.

postpurchase dissonance   See *buyer's remorse.*

preferred supplier   Supplier that is assured a large percentage of the buyer's business and will get the first opportunity to earn new business.

price discrimination   Situation in which a seller gives unjustified special prices, discounts, or special services to some customers and not to others.

primary call objective   Actual goal the salesperson hopes to achieve in an upcoming sales call.

prime selling time   Time of day at which a salesperson is most likely to be able to see a customer.

probing method   Method to obtain commitment in which the salesperson initially uses the direct-request method and, if unsuccessful, uses a series of probing questions designed to discover the reason for the hesitation.

problem questions   Questions about specific difficulties, problems, or dissatisfactions that the prospect has.

Procurement Automated Source System (PASS)   A Small Business Administration database that contains information on federal purchasing agents working on federal contracts.

producer   Firm that buys goods and services to manufacture and sells other goods and services to its customers.

product approach   Approach in which the salesperson actually demonstrates the product features and benefits as soon as he or she walks up to the prospect.

production era   A business era, prior to 1930, in which firms focused on making products with little concern for buyers' needs and developing products to satisfy those needs. The role of salespeople in this era was taking orders.

production-oriented salespeople   Salespeople prior to 1930 who had a production orientation and perceived their role as taking orders.

productivity goals   Objective concerning how efficiently a salesperson works, such as sales per call. Efficiency measures indicate an output divided by an input.

professional   Someone who engages in an occupation requiring great skill or knowledge and whose capabilities are respected by co-workers.

profit quota   Minimum levels of acceptable profit or gross margin performance.

prospect   A lead that is a good candidate for making a sale.

prospecting   The process of locating potential customers for a product or service.

puffery   Exaggerated statements about the performance of products or services.

pull   Marketing strategy designed to stimulate demand among consumers.

push   Marketing strategy designed to stimulate sales efforts by the manufacturer's salespeople and/or the resellers.

push money (PM)   Money paid directly to the retailer's salespeople by the manufacturer for selling the manufacturer's product. See also *spiffs*.

qualifying a lead   The process of determining if a lead is in fact a prospect.

quantifying the solution   Showing the prospect that the cost of the proposal is offset by added value.

question approach   Beginning the conversation with a question or stating an interesting fact in the form of a question.

quick-response system   Minimizing order quantities to the lowest level possible while increasing the speed of delivery to drive inventory turnover; accomplished by prepackaging certain combinations of products.

quota   Quantitative level of performance for a specific time period.

rapport   Close, harmonious relationship founded on mutual trust.

rate of change   A critical element to consider about change, refers to how fast change is occurring.

rational needs   Types of organizational and/or personal needs that are directly related to product performance.

reciprocity   Special relationship in which two companies agree to buy products from each other.

references   People who know an applicant for a position and can provide information about that applicant to the hiring company.

referral approach   Approach in which the name of a satisfied customer or friend of the prospect is used at the beginning of a sales call.

referred lead   Name of a lead provided by either a customer or a prospect of the salesperson.

reflective probes   Neutral statements that reaffirm or repeat a customer's comment or emotion, allowing the salesperson to dig deeper and stimulate customers to continue their thoughts in a logical manner.

relational partnership   Long-term business relationship in which the buyer and seller have a close, trusting relationship but have not made significant investments in the relationship. These relationships are characterized as win-win relationships.

relationship behaviors   Actions taken by a manager to deal with a subordinate's feelings and welfare, develop support, or build the salesperson's self-confidence or commitment to the job or organization.

relationship manager   The role of salespeople in the partnering era to manage their firms' resources to develop win-win relationships with customers.

Request for proposals (RFP)   Issued by a potential buyer desiring bids from several potential vendors for a product. RFPs often include specifications for the product, desired payment terms, and other information helpful to the bidder. Also called *request for bids* or *request for quotes*.

requirements   Conditions that must be satisfied before a purchase can take place.

resale price maintenance   Contractual term in which a producer establishes a minimum price below which distributors or retailers cannot sell their products.

resellers   Businesses, typically distributors or retailers, that purchase products for resale.

responsiveness   The degree to which people react emotionally when they are in social situations. One of the two dimensions in the social style matrix.

retail salespeople   Salespeople who sell to customers who come into a store.

return on investment (ROI)   Net profits (or savings) expected from a given investment, expressed as a percentage of the investment.

revenue quota   The minimum amount of sales revenue necessary for acceptable performance.

role accuracy   The degree to which a salesperson's perceptions about the sales role are correct.

role ambiguity   The degree to which a salesperson is not sure about the actions required in the sales role.

role clarity   The degree to which a salesperson understands the job and what is required to perform it.

role conflict   The extent to which the salesperson faces incompatible demands from two or more constituencies that he or she serves.

role stress   The psychological distress that may be a consequence of a salesperson's lack of **role accuracy**.

routine call patterns   Method of scheduling calls used when the same customers are seen regularly.

routing Method of scheduling sales calls to minimize travel time.

salary Compensation paid periodically to an employee independently of performance.

sale The transfer of title to goods and services by the seller to the buyer in exchange for money.

sales call allocation grid Grid used to determine account strategy; the dimensions are the strength of the company's positions with the account and the account's sales potential.

sales era A business era, from 1930 to 1960, in which firms focused on increasing demand for the products they produced. The role of salespeople in this era was persuading customers to buy products using high-pressure selling techniques.

sales-oriented salespeople Prior to 1929, salespeople with a sales orientation who believed their role was to create demand for products using aggressive selling techniques.

sales quota The minimum number of sales in units.

scope of change A critical element to consider about change, refers to the extent or degree to which the change affects an organization.

screens See *barriers*.

secondary call objectives A level of goals a salesperson hopes to achieve during a sales call that have somewhat less priority than the *primary call objective*.

selective perception Occurs when we hear what we want to hear, not necessarily what the other person is saying.

self-image The ideas and feelings that one has about oneself.

selling See *personal selling*.

selling deeper Selling more to existing customers.

selling history How well a product or product line sold during the same season in the previous year.

sexual harassment Unwelcome sexual advances, requests for sexual favors, and other, similar verbal (e.g., jokes) and nonverbal (e. g., graffiti) behaviors.

simple cost-benefit analysis Simple listing of the costs and savings that a buyer can expect from an investment.

situation questions General data-gathering questions about background and current facts that are very broad in nature.

situational stress Short-term anxiety caused by a situational factor.

small talk Talk about current news, hobbies, and the like that usually breaks the ice for the actual presentation.

sneak attack See *ambush negotiating*.

social style matrix Method for classifying customers based on their preferred communication style. The two dimensions used to classify customers are assertiveness and responsiveness.

Socratic approach Variation of the *question approach* in which a customer is queried for his or her opinion concerning a crucial topic related to the seller's product and the customer's need.

soft savings The value of offset costs and productivity gains.

speaking-listening differential The difference between the 120-to-160-words-per-minute rate of speaking versus the 800-words-per-minute rate of listening.

spiffs Payments made by a producer to a reseller's salespeople to motivate the salespeople to sell the producer's products or services.

SPIN Logical sequence of questions in which the needs of a prospect are identified. The sequence is situation questions, problem questions, implication questions, and need payoff questions.

spotter See *bird dog*.

standard memorized sales presentation Carefully prepared sales story that includes all the key selling points arranged in the most effective order; often called a *canned sales presentation*.

statutory laws Laws based on legislation passed by either state legislatures or Congress.

straight commission Pays a certain amount per sale; plan includes a base and a rate but not a salary.

straight-line routing Method of scheduling sales calls involving straight-line patterns.

straight rebuy Purchase decision process involving a customer with considerable knowledge gained from having purchased the product or service a number of times.

straight salary Compensation method that pays salespeople a fixed amount of money for working a specified amount of time.

strategic partnership Long-term business relationship in which the buyer and seller have made significant investments to improve the profitability of both parties in the relationship. These relationships are characterized as win-win relationships.

strategic profit model (SPM) Mathematical formula used to examine the impact of strategic decisions on profit and return on investment.

strength of position Dimension of the sales call allocation grid that considers the seller's strength in landing sales at an account.

stress interview   Any interview that subjects an applicant to significant stress; the purpose is to determine how the applicant handles stress.

submissive   Selling style of salespeople who are often excellent socializers and like to spend a lot of time talking about nonbusiness activities. These people are usually reluctant to attempt to obtain commitment.

subordination   Payment of large sums of money to officials to get them to do something that is illegal.

suggested retail price   Price for which the manufacturer suggests the store retail the product.

superior benefit method   Type of **compensation method** of responding to an objection during a sales presentation that uses a high score on one attribute to compensate for a low score on another attribute.

supply chain management   Set of programs undertaken to increase the efficiency of the distribution system that moves products from the producer's facilities to the end user.

systems integrator   Outside vendor who has been delegated the responsibility for purchasing; has the authority to buy products and services from others.

target position   Negotiation objective that states what the team hopes to achieve by the time the session is completed.

task behaviors   Actions taken by a manager to enable a subordinate to complete a task.

team selling   Type of selling in which employees with varying areas of expertise within the firm work together to sell to the same account(s).

telemarketing   Systematic and continuous program of communicating with customers and prospects via telephone and/or other person-to-person electronic media.

testimonial   Statement, usually in the form of a letter, written by a satisfied customer about a product or service.

tests   Personality or skills assessments used in assessing the match between a position's requirements and an applicant's personality or skills.

third-party testimony method   Method of responding to an objection during a sales presentation that uses a testimonial letter from a third party to corroborate a salesperson's assertions.

tickler file   File or calendar used by salespeople to remind them when to call on specific accounts.

total quality management (TQM)   Set of programs and policies designed to meet customer needs by delivering defect-free products.

trade   All members of the channel of distribution that resell the product between the manufacturer and the user.

trade discount   Discount in which the price is quoted to reseller in terms of a percentage off the suggested retail price.

trade fair   The European term for trade shows.

trade promotion   Promotion aimed at securing retailer support for a product.

trade salespeople   Salespeople who sell to firms that resell the products rather than using them within their own firms.

trade show   Short exhibition of products by manufacturers and distributors.

trial close   Questions the salesperson asks to take the pulse of the situation throughout a presentation.

trust   Firm belief or confidence in the honesty, integrity, and reliability of another person.

turnaround   Amount of time taken to respond to a customer request or deliver a customer's order.

turnover (TO)   Occurs when an account is given to another salesperson because the buyer refuses to deal with the current salesperson.

turnover   How quickly a product sells; calculated by dividing net sales by average inventory.

two-way communication   Interpersonal communication in which both parties act as senders and receivers. Salespeople send messages to customers and receive feedback from them; customers send messages to salespeople and receive responses.

tying agreement   Agreement between a buyer and a seller in which the buyer is required to purchase one product to get another.

Uniform Commercial Code (UCC)   Legal guide to commercial practice in the United States.

upgrading   Convincing the customer to use a higher-quality product or a newer product.

users   Members of a buying center that ultimately will use the product purchased.

value analysis   Problem-solving approach for reducing the cost of a product while providing the same level of performance.

variable call patterns   Occur when the salesperson must call on different accounts.

variable routing   Method of scheduling sales calls used when customers are not visited on a cyclical or regular basis.

vendor   A supplier.

vendor loyalty   Develops when a buyer becomes committed to a specific supplier because of the supplier's superior performance.

verbal communication   Communication involving the transmission of words either in face-to-face communication, over the telephone, or through a written message.

versatility   A characteristic, associated with the social style matrix, of people who increase the productivity of social relationships by adjusting to the needs of the other party.

visionary call objective   The most optimistic goal the salesperson thinks would be possible to achieve in an upcoming sales call.

voice characteristics   The rate of speech, loudness, pitch, quality, and articulation of a person's voice.

warranty   Assurance by the seller that the goods will perform as represented.

willingness   Salesperson's desire and commitment to accomplish an objective or task.

win-lose negotiating   Negotiating philosophy in which the negotiator attempts to win all the important concessions and thus triumph over his or her opponent.

win-lose relationship   Type of relationship charactzerized by one or a series of market exchanges wherein each party is concerned only with his or her own profits with no concern for the welfare of the other party.

win-win negotiating   Negotiating philosophy in which the negotiator attempts to secure an agreement that completely satisfies both parties.

win-win relationship   Type of relationship in which firms make significant investments that can improve profitability for both partners because their partnership has given them some strategic advantage over their competitors.

word picture   Story or scenario designed to help the buyer visualize a point.

zoning   Method of scheduling calls that divides a territory into areas called *zones*. Calls are made in a zone for a specified length of time, then made in another zone for the same amount of time.

Indexes

COMPANY INDEX

NAME INDEX

SUBJECT INDEX